Management for Professionals

The Springer series *Management for Professionals* comprises high-level business and management books for executives. The authors are experienced business professionals and renowned professors who combine scientific background, best practice, and entrepreneurial vision to provide powerful insights into how to achieve business excellence.

Ralf T. Kreutzer

Toolbox Digital Business

Leadership, Business Models,
Technologies and Change

 Springer

Ralf T. Kreutzer
Berlin School of Economics and Law
Berlin, Germany

ISSN 2192-8096 ISSN 2192-810X (electronic)
Management for Professionals
ISBN 978-3-658-37016-9 ISBN 978-3-658-37017-6 (eBook)
https://doi.org/10.1007/978-3-658-37017-6

Translation from the German language edition: "Toolbox für Digital Business" by Ralf T. Kreutzer, © Springer Fachmedien Wiesbaden GmbH 2021. Published by Springer Fachmedien Wiesbaden. All Rights Reserved.

© Springer Fachmedien Wiesbaden GmbH, part of Springer Nature 2022
This work is subject to copyright. All rights are reserved by the Publisher, whether the whole or part of the material is concerned, specifically the rights of translation, reprinting, reuse of illustrations, recitation, broadcasting, reproduction on microfilms or in any other physical way, and transmission or information storage and retrieval, electronic adaptation, computer software, or by similar or dissimilar methodology now known or hereafter developed.
The use of general descriptive names, registered names, trademarks, service marks, etc. in this publication does not imply, even in the absence of a specific statement, that such names are exempt from the relevant protective laws and regulations and therefore free for general use.
The publisher, the authors and the editors are safe to assume that the advice and information in this book are believed to be true and accurate at the date of publication. Neither the publisher nor the authors or the editors give a warranty, expressed or implied, with respect to the material contained herein or for any errors or omissions that may have been made. The publisher remains neutral with regard to jurisdictional claims in published maps and institutional affiliations.

This Springer imprint is published by the registered company Springer Fachmedien Wiesbaden GmbH part of Springer Nature.
The registered company address is: Abraham-Lincoln-Str. 46, 65189 Wiesbaden, Germany

In my remarks I was guided by the following **recommendation of the author Jean Paul**: *"Indeed, the reader cannot be kept soft enough, and we must, as soon as the thing does not forfeit, carry him on our hands with our writing fingers."*
Whether I have succeeded with this is up to you!
Just *do it!*
*Just **do it**!*

Central Idea for Digital Transformation

You can't eat an elephant with a knife and a fork!

Preface

Dear reader,

The idea for this work comes from the **intense discussion** on how we as a company, as a nation, but also as Europe can survive successfully, sustainably, and enjoyably in a highly dynamic world. I have discussed the challenges and possible solutions intensively with my **students and colleagues** at the *Berlin School of Economics and Law*. I have also struggled with students and professors to find convincing solutions in many MBA courses—be it at the *Berlin Professional School*, at *Donau-University Krems*, or at the *University of Bern*.

These dialogues were flanked and substantiated by extensive **research and studies** conducted by me, which I initiated around the topics of digitalization, dematerialization, disruption, digital business models, and digital transformation. At the same time, my **consulting and coaching activities** in a large number of companies have not only allowed me to gain deep insights but have also offered me a variety of opportunities to subject the concepts and solutions, which are developed and presented here, to a comprehensive practical test. At selected points, I let these experiences flow into my explanations using the keyword "**storytelling**".

At this point, I would first like to thank all my valued dialogue partners: my students and professor-colleagues, the board members and managing directors, as well as the executives and employees of the diverse functional areas. For me, it is always exciting to not only be active in the **boardroom**, but also to gladly work in the **engine room** with the key players located there. This sharpens the view for the challenges and for what is possible immensely! After all, the best ideas and the most convincing strategies will fail if their implementation is not successful.

I have incorporated this holistic view into this work. It is intended to be thought-provoking, inspiring, stimulating, pace-giving, toolbox, and guide in equal measure, so that **digital transformation** and the achievement of **digital excellence** can succeed.

Because *Michael Roth*, Minister of State for Europe at the Federal Foreign Office, formulated in a very appropriate way that (2020):

"**A strong, value oriented, confident and innovative Europe is our life insurance for the digital age.**"

At the same time, we should avoid today's Europe going down in history as the "**Silicon Valley of regulation**" (Berninger 2020, p. 19). Finally, companies and the key players active there need sufficient **creative space and scope of action** so that innovative ideas and concepts are not stifled by regulation.

My student assistant, *Maja Möller*, supported me in a dedicated way with the preparation of illustrations. Many thanks for this!

Reference

Berninger, M. (2020). Biotech darf nicht die nächste MP3-Geschichte werden. *Frankfurter Allgemeine Zeitung*, 15.12.2020, p. 19.

Berlin, Germany   Ralf T. Kreutzer
May 2021

Contents

1 **The World in Transition** 1
  1.1 VUCA World and Digital Darwinism 1
  1.2 Using a PESTEL Analysis to Identify Key Challenges
       in the Digital Age 8
       1.2.1   Challenges Arising Through the Political Circumstances .. 9
       1.2.2   Challenges Through the Economic Framework 12
              1.2.2.1   Challenge China 12
              1.2.2.2   Globalization: De-globalization—Glocalization .. 16
       1.2.3   Challenges Posed by the Social Framework 18
              1.2.3.1   Shifts in the Social Fabric 18
              1.2.3.2   Comprehensive Knowledge Building: Fiction
                           or Truth? 20
              1.2.3.3   Inflation of Expectations in Society and Among
                           Customers 28
              1.2.3.4   Future Distribution of Work and Income
                           in Society 31
       1.2.4   Challenges Posed by the Technological Framework
              Conditions 33
              1.2.4.1   Development of Industry 4.0 and
                           Economy 4.0 33
              1.2.4.2   Drivers of Industry 4.0 and Economy 4.0 35
              1.2.4.3   Dematerialization of Products and Services
                         as well as Processes 43
              1.2.4.4   From Time-to-Market to Time-to-Value 45
       1.2.5   Challenges Posed by the Ecological Framework
              Conditions 50
              1.2.5.1   Ecological Challenges 50
              1.2.5.2   Ecological Options and Constraints
                         for Action 51
       1.2.6   Challenges Posed by the Legal Framework 55
  Literature 59

2 Analysis and Design of a Digital Business Performance ... 61
2.1 Tools to Prepare the Analysis of Digital Business Performance ... 61
  - 2.1.1 Storytelling as an Attunement to the Digital Transformation ... 62
  - 2.1.2 Digital Gap Analysis ... 69
  - 2.1.3 Technology Impact Analysis ... 76
  - 2.1.4 SWOT Analysis: 5 Forces Analysis ... 77
    - 2.1.4.1 Basic Concept of the SWOT Analysis ... 77
    - 2.1.4.2 Identifying Relevant Competitors ... 79
    - 2.1.4.3 Implementation of the Strengths and Weaknesses Analysis ... 80
    - 2.1.4.4 Determination of Opportunities and Risks ... 82
    - 2.1.4.5 Synthesis to Conclude the SWOT Analysis ... 88
  - 2.1.5 Resilience Analysis ... 90
    - 2.1.5.1 Relevance of Resilience and Resilience Analysis ... 90
    - 2.1.5.2 Resilience of Companies and Business Models ... 91
    - 2.1.5.3 Resilience Analysis of the Business Model ... 94
2.2 Concept for the Analysis of the Digital Business Performance ... 107
2.3 Options to Develop a Digital Business Performance for Digital Excellence ... 116
Literature ... 119

3 Eight Fields of Action for Building Digital Excellence ... 121
3.1 Vision, Objectives, and Strategies for the Digital Age ... 121
  - 3.1.1 Digital Base Model as a Point of Orientation for Digital Transformation ... 121
  - 3.1.2 Requirements for a Vision in the Digital Age ... 124
  - 3.1.3 Developing a (Digital) Vision ... 128
    - 3.1.3.1 Ways to Develop a (Digital) Vision ... 128
    - 3.1.3.2 Powerful Visions and Ideas for Implementation ... 129
    - 3.1.3.3 Developing a (Digital) Vision ... 134
    - 3.1.3.4 Guidelines for Anchoring Values in Vision Work ... 140
  - 3.1.4 Developing a Strategy for the Digital Age ... 146
3.2 Developing Business Models for the Digital Age ... 148
  - 3.2.1 Labelling Business Models ... 148
    - 3.2.1.1 Business Models and Industry Logics ... 148
    - 3.2.1.2 Core Questions of a Strategic Business Model ... 151
  - 3.2.2 3 Horizons Model ... 153
  - 3.2.3 Prioritization and Focus on Macro Initiatives ... 158
    - 3.2.3.1 *Eisenhower* Principle as Guiding Concept ... 158
    - 3.2.3.2 Micro Initiatives vs. Macro Strategy ... 160
  - 3.2.4 Pitfalls of a Successful (Digital) Transformation ... 163

	3.2.5	Methods for Developing Business Model Innovations		172
		3.2.5.1	Process for Developing Business Model Innovations	172
		3.2.5.2	Strategy and Business Model Matrix	174
		3.2.5.3	Types of Business Model Innovations	176
		3.2.5.4	Business Model Canvas	180
		3.2.5.5	Platform Canvas	185
		3.2.5.6	Servitization as the Basis of Business Models	186
	3.2.6	Basic Types of Digital Business Models		189
	3.2.7	Methods for Evaluating Business Models		191
		3.2.7.1	Benefit and Growth Hypothesis	191
		3.2.7.2	Concepts for Increasing Benefit Delivery and Growth	193
		3.2.7.3	Testing Benefit and Growth Hypothesis Close to the Market	199
		3.2.7.4	Documentation of Business Model Innovations	205
	3.2.8	Process for Integrating New Business Models		208
	3.2.9	Examples of Consequent Business Model Innovations		212
		3.2.9.1	Business Development of *Amazon*	212
		3.2.9.2	Business Development of *Axel Springer*	217
		3.2.9.3	Business Development of the *Otto Group*	221
		3.2.9.4	Business Development of *Fuji*	224
		3.2.9.5	Business Development of the *Ant Financial Service Group*	224
3.3	Digitalization of the Value Chain			227
	3.3.1	Strategic Alignment of Value Chains		227
		3.3.1.1	From Value Chains to Systems of Value Chains	227
		3.3.1.2	Value Chain Analysis	230
		3.3.1.3	Predictive Maintenance and Predictive Servicing	232
	3.3.2	Ecosystems		236
		3.3.2.1	Analysis of Selected Ecosystems	236
		3.3.2.2	Analysis of the Effects of Ecosystems on Competition	244
	3.3.3	Platform Concepts		251
		3.3.3.1	Types of Platform Concepts	251
		3.3.3.2	Characterization of Platform Concepts	253
		3.3.3.3	Presentation and Analysis of Selected Platform Concepts	254
		3.3.3.4	Strategic Responses to the Advance of Platform Concepts	258
	3.3.4	Examples of the Digitalization of a Company		263

- 3.3.4.1 *Siemens* Electronics Plant in Amberg 263
- 3.3.4.2 *Körber*: Specialist in Mechanical Engineering .. 264
- 3.4 IT Infrastructure, Data Basis, and Artificial Intelligence 266
  - 3.4.1 IT as an Enabler 266
    - 3.4.1.1 Two-Speed IT 266
    - 3.4.1.2 Cloud Computing and Cyber Security 270
    - 3.4.1.3 Use of 5G and Trend Towards Softwarization .. 273
    - 3.4.1.4 Further Challenges in IT 278
  - 3.4.2 Basics of Data Management 281
    - 3.4.2.1 Big Data 281
    - 3.4.2.2 Business Analytics 286
  - 3.4.3 Artificial Intelligence 288
    - 3.4.3.1 Fundamentals of Artificial Intelligence 288
    - 3.4.3.2 Learning Methods of Artificial Intelligence ... 290
    - 3.4.3.3 Fields of Application for Artificial Intelligence .. 294
    - 3.4.3.4 Status of AI Use in Germany 297
    - 3.4.3.5 Explainable Artificial Intelligence 298
    - 3.4.3.6 AI Journey for the Own Company 301
- 3.5 Exploiting Digital Potential Through Marketing and Sales 304
  - 3.5.1 Digitization of the Customer Journey 304
    - 3.5.1.1 From Online and Offline to Noline 304
    - 3.5.1.2 The "Infinite" Customer Journey and the Flywheel 306
    - 3.5.1.3 Relevance of ZMOT 313
    - 3.5.1.4 Information Tsunami and Information Overload 315
    - 3.5.1.5 Trend Towards Individualization of Service Provision 317
    - 3.5.1.6 Customer Experience Management (CXM) ... 322
    - 3.5.1.7 Customer Relationship Management (CRM) .. 326
    - 3.5.1.8 From "Mobile First" to "Voice Only" 330
  - 3.5.2 Instruments for Exploiting Digitalization Potentials 333
    - 3.5.2.1 Persona Concept 333
    - 3.5.2.2 Conversion Funnel 336
    - 3.5.2.3 Customer Journey Map 338
    - 3.5.2.4 Empathy Map 342
    - 3.5.2.5 *Kano* Concept 343
    - 3.5.2.6 Net Promotor Score 346
  - 3.5.3 "Innovative Innovation Management" 349
    - 3.5.3.1 Customer Centricity: The Core of Innovation Management 349
    - 3.5.3.2 From Closed- to Open-Innovation-Concepts ... 351
    - 3.5.3.3 Design Thinking 354
    - 3.5.3.4 *Lego Serious Play* 361
    - 3.5.3.5 *Elon Musk's* DNA for Innovation Management 363

3.6	Human Resources Strategies for the Digital Age		365
	3.6.1	Qualification Campaign: Triggered by the HR Department	366
		3.6.1.1 Human Resources: Success Factors of the Digital Transformation	366
		3.6.1.2 Requirements for Human Resource Management	370
		3.6.1.3 Human Resource Management as a Driver of Personnel Development	371
		3.6.1.4 Readiness for Lifelong Learning in Different Countries	375
		3.6.1.5 Curiosity as the Fuel of the Learning Process	376
	3.6.2	Developing a (Digital) Training Agenda	377
	3.6.3	Analysis of Personal Competences of Employees and Managers	381
		3.6.3.1 Behavioral Preference Analysis	381
		3.6.3.2 *KODE* Concept	385
		3.6.3.3 Team Analytics	390
	3.6.4	Overcoming the Individual Comfort Zone	391
	3.6.5	Increasing the Employee Engagement	397
	3.6.6	Transactional and Transformational Leadership: Leadership at a Distance	403
		3.6.6.1 From Transactional to Transformational Leadership	404
		3.6.6.2 Leadership at a Distance	409
	3.6.7	Establishment of Network Structures	411
	3.6.8	Instruments to Increase Communication Efficiency	415
		3.6.8.1 *Sherpany*	415
		3.6.8.2 Slack and Microsoft Teams	416
		3.6.8.3 Tools for Video Conferencing	417
		3.6.8.4 Serendipity: Collaboration Tools for Creative Meetings	419
	3.6.9	Further Fields of Action in Human Resource Development	426
	3.6.10	From an Enabler Culture to Holacracy	431
		3.6.10.1 Enabler Culture	432
		3.6.10.2 The Concept of Holacracy	433
		3.6.10.3 Evaluative Analysis of the Holacracy Approach	437
3.7	Organizational Concepts for the Digital Age		438
	3.7.1	Requirements for Organizations in the Digital Age	438
	3.7.2	Social Media Listening Center: Newsroom	443
	3.7.3	Strategic Entrepreneurship	445
		3.7.3.1 Corporate Entrepreneurship	446
		3.7.3.2 Corporate Venturing	450

		3.7.4	Performance Engine and Innovation Engine as Concepts for Actions	459
		3.7.5	Installing a Chief Digital Officer	463
	3.8	Controlling for the Digital Age		468
		3.8.1	Controlling as an Enabler of Digital Transformation	469
			3.8.1.1 Self-Conception of Controlling in the Digital Age	469
			3.8.1.2 Reporting	472
			3.8.1.3 Analytics: Real Time Analytics	475
			3.8.1.4 Monitoring	476
			3.8.1.5 Predictions/Predictive Analytics and Prescription	478
			3.8.1.6 Balanced Scorecard for the Digital Transformation	479
		3.8.2	Digitalization of the Controlling Itself	483
	Literature			485
4	**Change Management: Shaping Change Processes Successfully**			**499**
	4.1	Guiding Principle of Change Management		499
	4.2	Stakeholder Analysis as a Starting Point for Change Managements		501
		4.2.1	Stakeholder of a Change Process	502
		4.2.2	Stakeholder Onion Model	504
	4.3	Tools for Identifying and Steering Change Management		507
		4.3.1	Information Needs to Start a Change Process	507
		4.3.2	Instruments to Manage Change Processes	513
		4.3.3	Flow of Change Processes	525
	Literature			530
Glossary				**533**
Index				**545**

About the Author

Ralf T. Kreutzer has been a professor of marketing at the *Berlin School of Economics and Law* since 2005, as well as a marketing and management consultant, trainer, and coach. Previously, he worked for 15 years in various management positions at *Bertelsmann, Volkswagen*, and *Deutsche Post*.

Through regular publications and lectures, Professor Kreutzer has provided significant impetus on various topics related to marketing, dialogue marketing, CRM/customer loyalty systems, database marketing, online marketing, social media marketing, digital Darwinism, artificial intelligence, voice marketing, digital branding, strategic and international marketing, and digital transformation and change management. He has also advised a large number of companies at home and abroad on these topics and trained and coached executives at middle and top management level. Professor Kreutzer is a sought-after keynote speaker at national and international conferences.

His most recent book publications are *Digitaler Darwinismus—der stille Angriff auf Ihr Geschäftsmodell und Ihre Marke* (2nd Ed., 2016, with Karl-Heinz Land), *Digital Business Leadership*: *Digital Transformation, Business Model Innovation,*

Agile Organization, Change Management (2017, with Tim Neugebauer and Annette Pattloch), *Führung und Organisation im digitalen Zeitalter—kompakt* (2018), *Digital Business Leadership, Digital Transformation, Business Model Innovation, Agile Organization, Change Management* (2018, with Tim Neugebauer und Annette Pattloch), *Toolbox für Marketing und Management* (2018), *Toolbox for Marketing and Management* (2019), *Künstliche Intelligenz verstehen* (2019, with Marie Sirrenberg), *Understanding Artificial Intelligence* (2019, with Marie Sirrenberg), *B2B-Online-Marketing und Social Media* (2nd Ed., 2020, with Andrea Rumler and Benjamin Wille-Baumkauff), *Voice-Marketing* (2020, with Darius Vousoghi), *Die digitale Verführung* (2020), *Kundendialog online und offline* (2021), *Praxisorientiertes Online Marketing* (4th Ed., 2021), *Toolbox für Digital Business* (2021), *Social-Media-Marketing kompakt* (2nd Ed. 2021), *E-Mail-Marketing kompakt* (2nd Ed. 2021), *Online-Marketing—Studienwissen kompakt* (3rd Ed., 2021), *Digitale Markenführung* (2022, with Karsten Kilian)

Abbreviations

AI	Artificial intelligence
AIOPS	Artificial intelligence IT operations
API	Application programming interface
APM	Application performance monitoring
AR	Augmented reality
BCG	Boston Consulting Group
BPA	Behavioural preference analysis
CBR	Cash burn rate
CCO	Chief Customer Officer
CDO	Chief Digital Officer
CEO	Chief Executive Officer
CFO	Chief Financial Officer
CHRO	Chief Human Resources Officer
CIO	Chief Information Officer
CMO	Chief Marketing Officer
COO	Chief Operating/Operation Officer
CPC	Cost per click
CPM	Cost per mille
CPU	Central processing unit
CRM	Customer relationship management
CSO	Chief Sales Officer
CT	Computer tomograph
CX	Customer experience
CXM	Customer experience management
DAX	*Deutscher Aktienindex*
DDOS	Distributed denial of service
DEM	Digital experience monitoring
DOS	Denial of service
EBIT	Earnings before interest and taxes
EBITDA	Earnings before interest, taxes, depreciation, and amortization
ECB	European Central Bank
ECTS	European Credit Transfer System

ERP	Enterprise resource planning
ESG	Environment, Social, Governance
EU	European Union
FED	Federal Reserve
FMOT	First moment of truth
FOMO	Fear of missing out
GAFA	*Google*, *Amazon*, *Facebook*, and *Apple*
GAFAM	*Google*, *Amazon*, *Facebook*, *Apple*, and *Microsoft*
GDPR	General Data Protection Regulation
GIGO	Garbage in garbage out
HIPPO	Highest paid person´s option
HR	Human resources
IA	Information architecture
IAAS	Infrastructure as a service
IIOT	Industrial IOT
IOE	Internet of Everything
IOMT	Internet of Military Things
IOT	Internet of Things
IPO	Initial public offering
LTE	Long-term evolution
MGM	Metro-Goldwyn-Mayer
MOOC	Massive open online course
MRI	Magnetic resonance imaging
MVP	Minimum viable product
n. a.	No author
NLP	Natural language processing
NOMS	National one-man sample
NPS	Net promotor score
OEE	Overall equipment efficiency
OFM	Other fools money
PAAS	Platform as a service
R&D	Research and development
ROCE	Return on capital employed
SAAS	Software as a service
SASE	Secure access service edge
SBF	Strategic business field
SBU	Strategic business unit
SLA	Service level agreements
SMOT	Second moment of truth
SSF	Swiss Smart Factory
TPI	Text performance index
V2V	Vehicle to vehicle
VEO	Voice engine optimization
VOC	Voice of the customer
VR	Virtual reality

VUCA	Volatility, uncertainty, complexity, ambiguity
VXLAN	Virtual extensible local area network
WTO	World Trade Organization
XAI	Explainable artificial intelligence
ZMOT	Zero moment of truth

The World in Transition   1

> *Never waste a crisis that offers an opportunity to change and improve things.*
>
> Winston Churchill

In order to be able to classify the **challenges for achieving digital excellence**, we first take a look at the big picture. How has our world developed into a **VUCA world**? What are the **challenges** that go hand in hand with this development? What impact does **digital Darwinism** have on our industry? How can the **opportunity and threat situation** be determined for your own company? For this purpose, a systematic analysis of the macro-environment is carried out using the **PESTEL-analysis**. The aspects that need to be taken into account in the development of digital excellence are systematically worked out.

1.1 VUCA World and Digital Darwinism

The unknown is the new normal.

Before we take a close look at our own company and its further development in a challenging environment, we should first take a look at the "**general weather situation.**" After all, this is what decisively determines where and how we can operate successfully as entrepreneurs today and tomorrow. We have to prove ourselves today—as individuals, as families, but especially as companies, as the economy, society, and the state—in the so-called **VUCA world**. By this acronym, the following contents are meant, which are united in Fig. 1.1 (cf. Braun, 2019, p. 6):

- **Volatility**
  Volatility describes the increasing **frequency**, the high speed and the extent of the (often unplanned) changes to which all market participants have to adjust over

© Springer Fachmedien Wiesbaden GmbH, part of Springer Nature 2022
R. T. Kreutzer, *Toolbox Digital Business*, Management for Professionals,
https://doi.org/10.1007/978-3-658-37017-6_1

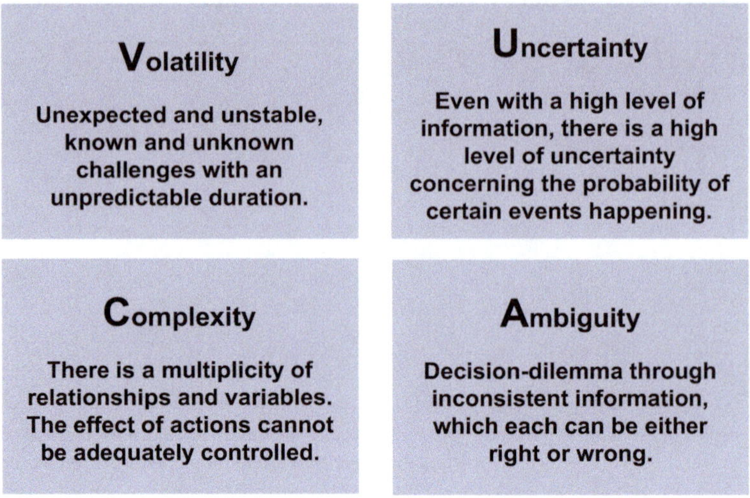

Volatility
Unexpected and unstable, known and unknown challenges with an unpredictable duration.

Uncertainty
Even with a high level of information, there is a high level of uncertainty concerning the probability of certain events happening.

Complexity
There is a multiplicity of relationships and variables. The effect of actions cannot be adequately controlled.

Ambiguity
Decision-dilemma through inconsistent information, which each can be either right or wrong.

Fig. 1.1 Explanation of the VUCA world

and over again. Volatility also means that certain phenomena require a great deal of attention in the short term, only to disappear again quickly.

Volatility is also evident in the **fluctuation** of oil and gold prices as well as in share prices. The *Dow Jones* stock index provides an example for this. The index, founded in 1884, took more than 100 years to exceed 10,000 points for the first time. In contrast to that, the journey from 20,000–30,000 points was completed in less than 4 years. The German stock index *DAX* rose by 15% in November 2020, showing a growth dynamic that was never seen before. Such developments contradict many previously held certainties. Such dynamics of change will not disappear in the future—quite the contrary!

- **Uncertainty**
  Uncertainty refers to the fact that it gets increasingly difficult to predict events and their effects in both private and professional life. Only a short time ago, the "specialists" were predicting Dollar-Euro parity and an end to the gold-price boom. Things have turned out quite differently. This also applies to **predictions** about the impact of the "checks and balances" (to be understood as the separation of power) in the USA to moderate even an erratic president.
- **Complexity**
  Complexity refers to the increasing **number of links and interdependencies** that make almost all areas of life and work more difficult to understand. The statement "everything goes" illustrates this phenomenon. At the same time, more and more things are being connected to more and more other things. The Internet of Everything and cross-border value chains come to mind here. Another example is the almost unmanageable number of tools that are available to a marketing manager today. Their relevance must be checked in each case.

1.1 VUCA World and Digital Darwinism

Paradigms of the pre-VUCA world	Paradigms of the VUCA world
The development of a company is controlled by precise, long-term defined targets.	The management of a company is more controlled by a "purpose" than precisely defined targets.
Long-term strategies are the fundament for the development of the company.	Continuous changes in the company and its environment question the use of long-term strategies and require flexibility.
Best-practice orientation and (cross-industry) benchmarking provide sustainable stimuli for the development of the company.	New (disruptive) business models undermine or destroy established business logics and make business models (in some cases) obsolete.
Once a business model has been developed, a company grows adding value off of it over many decades.	The continuous development of new business models goes well beyond industry boundaries and continuously challenges all players.
Competitors are considered enemies that have to be defeated.	Competitors are potential partners for corporations, because a lot of challenges cannot be overcome alone anymore.
Authoritarian, hierarchical management concepts are predominant. Employees are primarily considered a cost factor.	Network organisations with self organising teams use agile methods. Employees are considered an important factor for value creation.
Silos of information reinforce the power imbalance. Information as a resource is considered a scarce good.	An open, cross-departmental exchange of information and knowledge supports innovation and manufacturing processes.

Fig. 1.2 Establishment of new paradigms for existing in the VUCA world

- **Ambiguity**

    Ambiguity means that facts and situations can have **different meaning**, which makes a correct interpretation and decisions based on it increasingly difficult. This ambiguity is also the breeding ground for all kinds of conspiracy theories—as abstruse as they may look in a fact-based analysis. By ambiguity, however, we do not mean the euphemistically named "alternative facts," because these can be simply categorized into refutable lies!

This results in the following challenges for all companies: **paradigms of the pre-VUCA world** must increasingly be overcome and replaced by **paradigms of the VUCA world**. Figure 1.2 shows the exemplary steps that companies need to take here.

However, overcoming previously valid paradigms requires a **comprehensive analysis of the environment** in which your company operates. For this analysis, we can rely on proven methods to carry out the process in a structured way. To begin with, the PEST or PESTEL analysis is a good starting point, which is discussed in more detail in Sect. 1.2.

The following applies: Many changes are evolutionary. But their effects often have revolutionary dimensions. Companies that do not recognize these effects early enough will not survive! Figure 1.3 shows the dangers of **misjudging the impact of new technologies**. In the first period after the emergence of a new technology, there is often **disappointment** because the supposed silver bullet does not prove to be superior to everything else. If you are already working with it, your enthusiasm may suffer—or you may not even start because of perceived failures. Later on, **stress** can

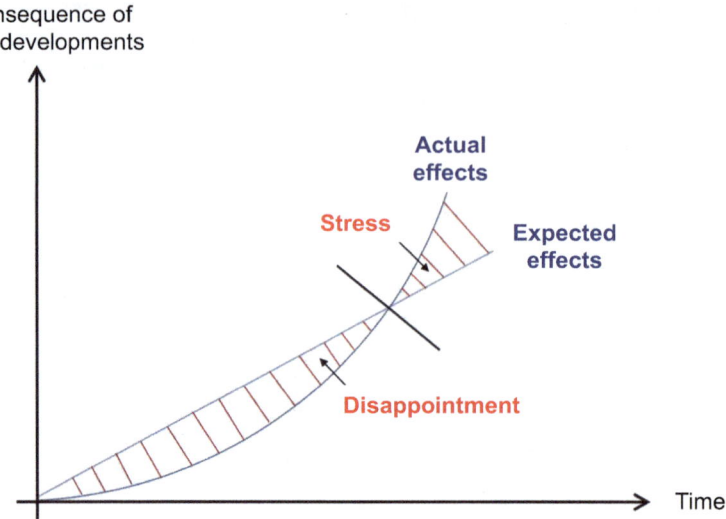

Fig. 1.3 Disappointment and stress caused by new developments

arise when the real potential becomes visible to the people involved, while you do not yet deal with such a technology yourself. This stress must be avoided through proactive behavior.

A sound analysis of the emerging changes is an important prerequisite for companies to not fall victim to digital Darwinism. What is meant by this—and why is *Charles Darwin* used in this context? **Darwinism** refers to the selection process that occurs quite automatically when—in this case—companies, but also industries and entire nations, do not adapt quickly enough to the changing framework and are therefore "sorted out" by the market. Since in the digital age it is primarily digital technologies that challenge the established companies, the concept of **digital Darwinism** arises (cf. basic Kreutzer & Land, 2016).

In digital Darwinism, there is no "**too big to fail**"—with the exception of the few systemically relevant companies, such as large banks and insurance companies. The merciless selection process caused by digitalization has killed companies like *Kodak, Toys "R" Us* and *Thomas Cook*. The publishers of lexica like *Brockhaus* and *Encyclopedia Britannica* and many others do not exist any longer. And the selection process of non-viable business models continues mercilessly!

The reference to **Charles Darwin** was made because he elaborated an important point in his central work *The Origin of Species* in early 1859:

> **Memory Box**
> It is neither the strongest of a species that survives, nor the most intelligent. Rather, it is those who can best adapt to change.

(continued)

1.1 VUCA World and Digital Darwinism

Digital Darwinism is forcing a struggle for survival on more and more companies and industries. Only those who accept the challenge early on have a chance of surviving this struggle. However, it can still be observed that a large number of companies have still not internalized the threat that is coming from the digital transformation.

As a reader of this book, however, you are not one of these people!

Memory Box
Digital Darwinism always sets in when technologies and society change faster than the ability of companies to adapt to these changes.

In sum, it can be said that very few companies are immune to the forces of **creative destruction** that take place here. Forecasts regarding the **longevity of S&P-500-companies** assume that the average period of time that a company belongs to this group will continue to shorten over the next decade. Based on the *Innosight* study, the average length of belonging to the group of *S&P-500*-companies has decreased significantly (cf. Anthony et al., 2018, p. 2).:

- The average length of belonging to the group of *S&P-500*-companies was **32 years** in 1965.
- By 2016, the "retention period" had already decreased to **24 years**.
- According to current forecasts, the retention period of a company in the group of *S&P-500*-companies will shrink to only **14 years** by 2030.

This is an **indicator of a comprehensive redistribution of power** in all industries. Taking into account the current **churn rate**, about 50% of the *S&P-500*-companies will be replaced by other companies in the next 10 years. Particularly threatened, besides the already struggling retailers, are the financial services, healthcare, energy, tourism, and real estate sectors. The automotive industry is also facing multiple challenges. Many turbulences indicate that companies have to undergo a **double transformation**. This is because in many cases it is not only the **technologies** that are changing, but also—triggered by them—the **customers' needs** to be satisfied (cf. Anthony et al., 2018, p. 1f.).

Memory Box
The *Fortune 500* and the *S&P 500* are concepts developed by two different providers to group US-companies. The *Fortune 500* is compiled annually and includes the 500 largest companies (based on revenue figures). It includes companies regardless of whether they are listed on the stock exchange or not. *S&P 500* is an index of 500 listed companies selected by the *S&P*-Index Committee.

A driving force behind the sorting out and replacing of previously market-dominant companies are the countless **start-ups** that are founded and released into the market as if on an assembly line. In Shenzhen in 2020, I learned that 1000 start-ups are founded in this region of China alone—per day. For every start-up, the first thing to remember is that there is no such thing as "**too small to succeed.**" Even if the vast majority of start-ups fail, individual companies always succeed in either founding new markets or disrupting existing markets. This **disruption** results in the destruction of existing industries, industry structures and the companies operating in them. Examples of disruptive companies include *Amazon, Airbnb, Delivery Hero, Klarna, N26, Revolut, Uber, Tesla,* and *Zalando*.

The aim of this book is to provide you with a **toolbox for digital business** in order to use the opportunities available in the market and in your company. Through the targeted use of these tools, you will not only be able to recognize the opportunities and risks of these developments at an early stage—especially those forced by new (digital) technologies—but also to actively use them. The challenges to be mastered here are particularly big for **established companies**, which must achieve a new dynamic in order not to succumb to digital Darwinism themselves.

▶ **Food for Thought**
The established companies have to master a **field of tension** here: On the one hand, these companies often (still) have financial resources, patents, customer relationships, know-how, processes, structures, technologies, etc. at their disposal. These resources have often accompanied the respective companies successfully for many years or even decades.

On the other hand, however, new technologies, new project management tools, new management models, new organizational concepts, etc. are available today, which are quite naturally used by start-ups from the very beginning. In established companies, the usage of such new concepts requires a comprehensive **change-management** in order to exploit the new possibilities. This slows down the change process massively and often leads to a competitive disadvantage!

In the face of these challenges, we must not retreat to the role of an observer, but must become an **active shaper of change**, also for the good of the economy and society. Only if we as a company are among the leading players in this environment can we also successfully defend our society with its values. The attackers are not asleep!

The current task of digital transformation can be characterized as follows: **digital transformation** describes a process of change—with no limits in perspective—of institutions with the aim of integrating digital technologies into their own value creation process, in order to make it more efficient, more effective and/or to create new business models. These institutions can include private households as well as companies, schools, universities, cities, communities, and entire nations. The potential opened up by digital technologies must be recognized and used in one's own area of responsibility as a manager, scientist, politician, teacher, etc. in order to optimize one's own service provision. The necessity for such optimizations often results from the **changed expectations of one's own stakeholders**—especially one's own customers.

Think Box: Questions You Should Ask Yourself
- Who in your company systematically analyses which challenges of the VUCA world are particularly relevant to you?
- Are you still holding on to the paradigms of the pre-VUCA world or are you already working with or on the new paradigms?
- Are PEST or PESTEL analyses carried out regularly in your company to systematically identify the opportunities and risks of the macro-environment?
- How great is the risk that the impact of new technologies is misjudged in your company?
- To what extent does digital Darwinism threaten your company?
- Which competitors are already victims to digital Darwinism?
- Which are currently under massive threat?
- Which are the supposed winners of the selection process described by digital Darwinism?
- Have you already analyzed how the "durability" of companies concerning the concept of *S&P 500* companies is represented in your industry?
- Are the companies in your sector more likely to be winners or losers?
- How comprehensively is change management installed in your company in order to take advantage of the new opportunities?

1.2 Using a PESTEL Analysis to Identify Key Challenges in the Digital Age

I'm more interested in the future than in the past, because the future is where I intend to live.
Albert Einstein

In the following, the biggest challenges that you should consider in the process of digital transformation are analyzed. The developments shown must be weighted and taken into account depending on your respective industry. The methodological tools for this are the PEST and PESTEL analyses. These acronyms stand for the areas to be analyzed by you. In the **PEST analysis**, you need to take a closer look at the following factors:

- **Political Factors**
  Here we analyze how the following criteria affect a target market, a potential production location, our suppliers and/or our entire business model: stability and reliability of the governmental system, changes in governmental responsibility, strength of right-wing/left-wing parties, economic policy orientation of those in power (including regulations on co-determination, collective bargaining autonomy, promotion of start-ups), economic promotion (including the granting of subsidies), private-sector fields of action, etc.
- **Economic Factors**
  The most important economic factors that we should include in our analysis include the level of economic growth, internal price stability (inflation/deflation), external currency stability (exchange rate development), the tax burden for companies, the interest rate level, the unemployment rate as well as purchasing power and its distribution in the population.
- **Social Factors**
  When analyzing societal developments, the following factors should be assessed concerning their relevance for our decisions: level of education (including literacy rate), population's age structure, extent of employment, cultural diversity, poverty risk, average family size, society's expectations of companies, the position of women in society, acceptance of nuclear energy or wind turbines, gene products and new technologies in general (like artificial intelligence). Ingoing and outgoing migration are also among these factors.
- **Technological Factors**
  The technical environment in which we operate entrepreneurially is highly influenced by the quality of the "hard" infrastructure (Internet, roads, railways, airports, ports, energy and water supply) as well as the "soft" infrastructure (education, health, and justice systems).

On top of these factors, the following factors are analyzed in the **PESTEL analysis**:

- **Ecological Factors**
  To shed light on the ecological environment, we can examine, among other things, the extent of environmental pollution (water, air, soil), resource consumption and recycling rates in the target countries.
- **Legal Factors**
  Legal factors have a lasting influence on the attractiveness of countries and regions and thus on our opportunities to actively create value there. To get an impression of the local situation, the following criteria should be included in the analysis: protection of private property (including intellectual property, such as patents, brand names), general legal security (legal institutions; possibility to enforce one's rights), form of laws and guidelines (codification of regulations through tax laws, law against unfair competition, price indication ordinance, trademark law, law against restraint of competition, environmental protection laws, customs regulations, minimum wages, workplace ordinance, approval procedures for new products and new technologies, etc.).

Depending on the goal of your analysis, you can focus on the defined four or six fields of the investigation.

> **Memory Box**
> The PEST or PESTEL analysis is a very helpful tool to systematically analyze the macro-environment of your company.

▶ **Food for Thought**
  Our newly discovered knowledge is leading to faster economic, social, and political change; with each attempt to understand what is happening, we accelerate the accumulation of knowledge, which in turn leads to even faster and greater upheaval. Consequently, we are less and less able to meaningfully interpret the present and predict the future! (Harari, 2018, p. 84f.).
  What is one answer to this challenge? **Agility**!

1.2.1 Challenges Arising Through the Political Circumstances

The weakness of democracy lies in its weak will to suppress the needs of the moment in favor of the future.
  Alexis de Tocqueville
  Do you feel the same way? When I hear, read or watch the news, I often think that there are more **irresponsible leaders in office** than ever before. You all know the officials who have neither their own country, nor friendly nations, nor even the world as a whole in mind when making decisions. Many of these people are concerned solely with their own retention of power and their own sinecures—gladly also for the whole family. Think of politicians who let themselves be appointed president for

life. Others change the constitution in 2020 in a way that they can act as president for many more terms—until they are 83 years old—and afterwards enjoy lifelong immunity with their family.

Others call the corona virus a "mild flu" and use the shifted focus of world's attention to destroy the rainforest even more vigorously than before. A former "leader" of the world's most powerful country is leaving the G20 summit with the presidents, prime ministers and chancellors of the leading industrial nations in 2020—to play golf. The country with the largest oil reserves in the world is running out of petrol. At the same time, there is national bankruptcy and hyperinflation, forcing millions of people to leave the country.

Another ruler has been waging a **war against his own people** for 10 years. More than 400,000 people have already lost their lives through this. In addition, more than six million people have left the country. A similar number of people are fleeing within the borders of this country. Other rulers beat up peaceful demonstrators after a lost and subsequently rigged election, arrest them and hold them as prisoner for months—with no prospect of a fair trial.

In parallel, **critical journalism is often eliminated**—either also through arrests or through the murder of courageous journalists. Accompanying this, critical publishing houses, TV and radio stations are closed down, taken over by the rulers or brought into line. In addition, the Internet is cut off at the whim of the rulers so that critical citizens cannot congregate to protest. Other rulers consistently weaken their own judicial system and align it with the prevailing party's course.

Other "leaders" question **multilateralism** and their institutions that have contributed to political stability and the economic prosperity of billions of people and peace for many decades. Now, in many countries, a strong **nationalism** is being shaped, and attempts are being made to protect one's own (weak) economy from exports through the use of import tariffs. At the same time, valid international treaties are being broken, for example, by simply ignoring the regulations of the WTO (World Trade Organization) if they run counter to national interests. In addition, power interests are again increasingly enforced through **military operations**.

Against this background, should we rather wish for more **intensive cooperation** between the **economic superpowers the USA and China**? Or does **fierce competition on the world markets** promise more convincing solutions? After all, a saying attributed to *Lee Kuan Yew* (former prime minister of Singapore) says very vividly:

When elephants fight, the grass suffers. But when they make love, the grass suffers, too.

Parallel to this—even more massively than ever before—**lies** are sold as "alternative facts." Since this process is also extremely important for your entrepreneurial activities, the underlying mechanisms are to be briefly described here. **False** or at least **misleading content** finds a **global spread** very easily and free of charge via the Internet—especially through "social" media and *Google*. Increasing radicalization—first in language, then in thought and action—is consistently promoted by the **use of algorithms** in social media.

These **algorithms** all pursue one goal: to provide users with more and more "relevant" data. These algorithms force **more of the same**! The logic of "more of the same" leads users being shown more content that is similar to what they have already clicked on. Anyone who repeatedly clicks on radical right-wing or left-wing content on *Google, Facebook, Twitter* & Co. or likes, comments on or forwards such content will soon receive more and more content of that kind. The colors in between extreme positions will be shown less or eventually not at all because, according to the platforms' algorithms, they are less likely to lead to engagement (clicks, likes, shares, comments). This creates so-called **echo chambers** and **filter bubbles**.

▶ **Food for Thought**
Algorithms do not know individuals, only data. And: algorithms are never neutral!

In addition, every bit of "**more data**" that users—often voluntarily—transmit to **data-sucking platforms** increases the risk of being manipulated even more comprehensively by these platforms. With every click, every like, every share and every comment, the puzzle of the user's personality becomes easier to read and consequently easier to manipulate. In this way, **filter bubbles** create **fake-news worlds**—in closed milieus, in relatively homogeneous groups.

A study impressively shows the effects of such a **formation of homogeneous groups** (cf. Seemann & Kreil, 2017). Its aim was to identify the **spread of fake-news**. At the same time, it should be determined whether **corrections** are a suitable way to fight fake news. For this purpose, the *Twitter* data of all accounts that had written something on a specific topic were used. The tweets with fake news were marked red and the tweets with corrections were marked blue. In addition, the accounts were arranged in a way so that the density of networks get visible. If accounts follow each other and/or the same people or are followed by the same people, they appear close together.

Instead of a large, intensively interwoven network, two almost **separate networks** resulted out of the study. On one side, a widely scattered **blue cloud** was identified. The relatively closely spaced large blue dots include German mass media such as *Spiegel Online, Zeit Online* and *Tagesschau*. The blue cloud contains the accounts that have published or retweeted a **correction**. On the other side, a concentrated and much smaller **red cloud** was detected. In this red cloud, the accounts are much closer together; it consists of the **fake-news spreaders**. These accounts are not only much more intensively interlinked, but almost completely separated from the "truth cloud."

Due to this **grouping**, there is virtually no exchange whatsoever between people with different opinions—**truth and lies coexist in separate worlds**. Thus, the negative and manipulative developments reinforce each other—and the **fake-news propagators** feel misunderstood and isolated from the rest of the world (cf. Kreutzer, 2020a).

▶ **Food for Thought**
Do the providers of social media platforms have an interest in preventing such developments? No! After all:

Angry people click more!

And social media thrives through this engagement—whatever it may cause to society—as long as it helps to earn more money.

We would not be good managers and decision-makers if we could not also ensure responsible action in this political world that has gone off the rails.

> **Think Box: Questions You Should Ask Yourself**
> - Which developments in the political area lead to the biggest opportunities for your company?
> - Which political developments threaten the marketing of your products and/or services?
> - Do political developments pose opportunities or threats for your business model?
> - What do the retreat of multilateralism and the advance of nationalism mean for your value chains?
> - What significance must you attach to demagogy pushed by algorithms?
> - Where does the responsibility for such regular analyses lie in your company?

1.2.2 Challenges Through the Economic Framework

The most dangerous worldview is the worldview of those who have not looked at the world.
  Alexander von Humboldt

1.2.2.1 Challenge China

The **economic balance of power** is shifting ever more clearly. The USA still leads the ranking of industrial nations—based on the gross domestic product. However, it is foreseeable that China, with a population of about 1.4 billion people and an unbroken striving for political, economic, and also military power, will replace the USA from the first place in the foreseeable future. The reason for this is not only the significantly smaller population of the USA of about 330 million. The loss of importance is also caused by the fact that the USA—like Europe and Germany, unfortunately—lacks a **master plan for the coming years**. Many countries do not even have an idea of a master plan!

▶ **Food for Thought**

The last time Europe—or more precisely, parts of it—agreed to **establish a European champion** was when *Airbus Industry* was founded. This took place in 1970! All Europeans know what we have in this globally active company:

technology, jobs requiring qualification, tax revenues—and the avoidance of a monopoly called *Boeing*!

In the **field of digital solutions**, Europe has not succeeded in creating **European champions**! Are there at least convincing plans for this? I tend not to see them!

What individual countries can achieve if there are convincing visions and goals is shown by the following example. It was only a little more than 40 years ago when *Deng Xiaoping* initiated a **policy of reform and open-doors** in 1978. This was aimed at **economic reforms** and opening up the **People's Republic of China** to the rest of the world. How did *Deng Xiaoping* describe his **economic reform strategy** so beautifully?

It is irrelevant, if a cat is black or white—the main thing is that it catches mice.

What has been achieved through the reforms that have been introduced can be seen every day, every hour, every minute in the specialized and popular media—online and offline. In addition, China, today, has something that neither Germany, nor Europe, nor the USA has: a **master plan for the development of the economy for the next years**. The Chinese government's master plan was already determined in 2015 by the Chinese leadership under **President *Xi Jinping*** under the title "**Made in China 2025.**" In it, the goals for China's own economy were precisely defined. China is no longer to be the world's extended workbench, playing only the "producing part" on behalf of internationally active and technological corporations.

The **focus of the Chinese master plan** is on its own **technological value creation** in order to **develop China into a high-tech producer** and to **replace technology imports with its own services**. In its goals, China is not satisfied with merely achieving parity with other countries by 2025. China is working towards the **position of world market leader** in key areas. This **leadership role** is being sought in the following ten economic fields:

- Aircraft industry/astronautics
- Machines for agriculture
- Power supply
- Energy saving and e-mobility
- CNC machines and robots (incl. artificial intelligence)
- Information and communication technology
- New materials/substances
- Rail transport
- Maritime equipment and high technology ships
- Medical technology

In all these sectors, China is also focusing on the **use of AI**—because this is where **strategic competitive advantages** can be achieved. The borderless access to the data stream generated by the 1.4 billion Chinese and the companies is precisely the resource that is necessary for the **rapid**

development of AI potential and will lead to offerings that will challenge us on the global market (cf. Bünte, 2020).

The effects that the implementation of the "**Made in China 2025**" master plan can have on the economy were highlighted by the Bertelsmann Foundation (2020) using the example of German mechanical engineering in various scenarios. We should take the warning that is given there seriously!

▶ **Food for Thought**

Such a **master plan for Germany or for Europe** has been missing for years! Instead of concentrating on the core tasks of Europe's economic orientation in the digital age, the political decision-makers here are splitting up over questions of migration and blocking important decisions that are indispensable for the sustainable well-being of the European community.

Instead of a **(digital) master plan for Germany 2025**, we get a **government grant scheme to support families building homes**, an (increased) **maternity pension**, a **basic pension** and other **patronage policies with no relevance to the future**. The situation is not much different in the political chaos of the USA, where the Republicans and Democrats are more irreconcilably opposed than ever, instead of working together to advance their own country through cooperating fruitfully with important partners.

Thus, China is going on the offensive in terms of industrial and power politics—and none of the leading economic powers is offering a rival.

We are at the beginning of the Asian decade!

In China, there is not only a master plan, but also the **billions of dollars of investment** needed to implement it! Funds in the billions are available for "intelligent manufacturing," the semiconductor industry and the further development of artificial intelligence. In Europe, one can only dream of such amounts!

Moreover, a high **stringency in implementation** can be observed in China, from which the western industrial nations are far removed. In the period of time in which "preliminary construction reviews" take place in Germany and Europe, airports are built and even opened in China! In 2019, the world's largest airport terminal with 700,000 square meters was opened in Beijing— right on schedule after 4 years of construction. In addition, China already has the longest high-speed rail network in the world, with over 20,000 km lengths.

Not all of the effects on the population and the environment that go hand in hand with this are welcomed by us. But China's strategic orientation has an impact on the global economy and the positions that Germany and Europe will have there in the future—whether we like it or not.

> **Memory Box**
> **Just standing on the sidelines and critically commenting on the game is not a strategy!**
>
> In addition, China is pushing ahead with comprehensive **infrastructure projects** along a route to Europe under the name **new silk road** (also known as **one belt, one road** or **belt and road initiative**). These include not only road and rail links, but also ports and power plants. In Pakistan, for example, a coal-fired power plant was built in a record time of only 22 months. To make such projects possible, Chinese banks have been encouraged by the government to provide loans for new silk road projects as easily as possible. In total, about **900 billion dollars** are to be invested in infrastructure projects in Eurasia to connect the Chinese city of Fuzhou with Rotterdam (cf. Chatzky & McBride, 2021).
>
> The beneficiaries of these large-scale projects are primarily Chinese construction, steel and transport companies that implement these infrastructure projects—often with their own workforce. This enables the participating companies to realize extensive experience curve effects in this area as well. So far, China has already involved more than 70 countries in its **silk road project**. China not only accepts, but also consciously strives for the state where concerned countries will become highly financially dependent on China as a result of the large-scale projects and thus will also come under Chinese political influence (cf. Chatzky & McBride, 2021 for more details). At the same time, investments in infrastructure projects in some EU countries are also intended to prevent or at least make it more difficult for the EU to take a uniform approach to Chinese activities!

▶ **Food for Thought**
Even if the "Made in China 2025" master plan is not perfect—China at least has one! If Europe—because one country alone cannot do much here—does not finally wake up (politically), competitiveness and thus prosperity here will decline massively.

The need to wake up is reinforced by a look at the **14th Five-Year Plan of the Chinese communist party**, which was adopted in 2020 (cf. China Embassy, 2020). In this plan, China relies on a so-called **double economic cycle**. **The first and all-important internal cycle** comprises the **domestic economy**. The Chinese leadership wants to make the country much more independent of foreign countries. Therefore, not only raw materials and important components and equipment, but also the know-how needed for further economic expansion are to come primarily from China itself. The US blockade on the supply of electronic components to China is having an effect here! The resulting reduced dependence on foreign countries should strengthen the **resilience of the Chinese economy** as a whole.

Foreign companies should merely support this internal cycle in the form of a second and **external cycle**, without building up major dependencies on external partners. At the same time, Chinese president *Xi Jinping* defines the goal: "to make the existential dependencies of international value chains on our country even tighter and thus build up the capacity for deterrence and countermeasures in view of deliberate supply stops by foreign countries" (Lang, 2020, p. 18).

▶ **Storytelling** During my visits to innovative companies in Shenzhen, Shanghai and Beijing, but also in Tokyo, Seoul and Silicon Valley, I learned one thing:
Seeing is believing!
It is one thing to read about things. It is another to feel them in their depth through all five senses and thus to grasp them holistically! Therefore:
Go east and west!

1.2.2.2 Globalization: De-globalization—Glocalization

In addition, the **Corona Pandemic 2020,** with its knock-on effects on almost all sectors challenged the existing economic structures (cf. Ziems et al., 2020). Here it very quickly became clear that the **globalization** that had been consistently pursued until then, with its value chains distributed across many countries and continents, would not be able to withstand a (regional) shutdown. However, critical **supply chains** did not only become apparent during the pandemic-induced demand for face masks, because such masks were no longer produced in Europe for cost reasons. Even in the years before, glaring **gaps in the supply** of indispensable medicines became apparent. Why? The raw material deliveries from China did not always take place as planned—and the production facilities primarily located in India no longer met the global demand.

The reasons for the consistent **relocation of production facilities** to the Asian region are not only the lower labor costs, but also—it has to be said so harshly—the more lax environmental and safety standards in other countries, which together lead to significantly lower production costs. Due to the price pressure exerted by end customers as well as by procurement managers in private and public organizations, we have visibly placed ourselves in **extreme dependencies**—and in times of the pandemic we are experiencing that the business models based on this do not have sufficient **resilience**.

The watchword now—often with nationalist or protectionist undertones—is **de-globalization**. As if the wheel of globalization could simply be turned back. At the same time, the critics of globalization also ignore the great macroeconomic and social achievements that have been made through globalization. The fact that globalization also has many problematic side effects should not be concealed here.

However, there are not only **fifty shades of grey** in literature, but at least as many varieties of the economic division of labor. The alternative is therefore not **globalization** or **de-globalization**. Differentiated solution concepts must be developed, oriented towards entrepreneurial and governmental objectives. Consequently, a consistent dismantling of transnational cooperation is not a realistic solution. However, there is a need for action to ensure a certain degree of **self-sufficiency** for individual countries—but better for communities like Europe.

This includes not only a more comprehensive **stockpiling** (keyword "national reserve," e.g., of material for health care) but also a **re-settlement of economically, politically, and/or socially relevant industries**. In addition to the pharmaceutical industry, which is already in the spotlight, this also includes the supply of energy. In addition, the self-sufficiency of defense systems—which many do not like to hear—is also part of this.

The necessary development can be called **glocalization**. This portmanteau word is formed from the terms globalization and localisation. It underlines that it is not a question of "either … or …," but rather of "both … and …." For example, important production stages can also be installed locally in order to reduce the dependence on global supply chains described above.

▶ **Food for Thought**
For our companies, this means above all that we must test our **business models** for **resilience.** After all, according to the predictions, we will not only face further pandemics, but also further environmental disasters, refugee flows, political upheavals and economic disasters, such as the insolvency of entire countries or the break-up of economic communities and other multilateral organizations.

All in all—also driven by the pandemic—a process of **slowbalisation** is to be expected in the future (cf. Economist, 2019). This refers to a **weakening of global growth dynamics** caused by a return to national and/or regional units. In addition, the aging of the population in many countries is leading to more saving and less consumption. Such developments must be taken into account, especially in the further development of our business models.

▶ **Food for Thought**
In the course of the Corona pandemic, "**capitalism**" as such was sometimes pilloried—as if this economic form had been the trigger of the pandemic. Even if we do not deny the dark sides that go hand in hand with uncontrolled capitalism, it is nevertheless worth noting: The pandemic has shown how quickly and flexibly companies—profit-oriented!—directed their resources towards overcoming supposed bottlenecks.

This applies not only to overcoming the apparent "toilet paper emergency" in Germany, but also to the hunger for certain products such as face masks and protective clothing. Even the development of a vaccine in record time is not the result of a 5-year plan, but the success of—profit-oriented—pharmaceutical companies that often operate with very heterogeneous teams within global research chains. These companies were financed by investors—will to take the risk of losing significant amounts of money!

The **strength of the market economy**, and thus also the **strength of capitalism**, does not lie in being prepared for every disaster. What system could possibly succeed in this? The strength of a market economy and capitalism lies in the fact that those who work here can adapt quickly and convincingly to new challenges. This is exactly what became clear during the Corona pandemic!

It is not only to overcome major challenges that I profess the **TINA principle** for capitalism—or more precisely—for the social market economy: **There is no alternative!**

> **Think Box: Questions You Should Ask Yourself**
> - In your position, can you help to develop a master plan for your country, for Europe or any region where you are active that addresses the real challenges?
> - Do you have the means to contribute to the establishment of new regional champions?
> - Can you help us find an answer to "Made in China 2025?"
> - Do you have ideas on how we can counter the dependencies and attempts at division associated with the New Silk Road?
> - What consequences are derived from the 14th Five-Year Plan of the Chinese Communist Party for your company, your business model and your value chains?
> - Will the (partial) relocation of production sites result in interesting business potential for your company?
> - Is there political support for the re-location of economically, politically and/or socially relevant industries?
> - Are your managers and employees aware of the strength of the market economy and thus also the strength of capitalism?
> - Who in your company is responsible to care about answers to these questions?

1.2.3 Challenges Posed by the Social Framework

Against a stupidity that is in fashion, no wisdom compensates.
  Theodor Fontane

1.2.3.1 Shifts in the Social Fabric

An important challenge for many companies is the political commitment that young people, previously described as largely uninterested in politics, are displaying under the motto *Fridays for Future*. A one-woman movement—started by *Greta Thunberg*—has become a worldwide network of activists who no longer want to leave the **management of the ecological survival of our planet** (alone) to the supposed professionals from politics. The articulated expectations will—sooner rather than later—also find their way into companies through the members of the generations involved here becoming employees. Corresponding expectations are attributed to Generation Z in particular. Their demands on companies will not stop at purely glossing **ethical marketing** (cf. Schlotter & Hubert, 2020; Wiesner, 2016). The accompanying challenges must be taken into account not only by human resources management, but also by the strategic orientation of the entire company.

At the same time, a significant **aging of society** can be observed in the leading industrial nations—and in China. This development brings various challenges with it. **Purchasing power** and thus **consumption** are shifting to more and more people who are over 60 years old. The offers of food, clothing, housing, travel, entertainment, etc. have to be geared to this. On the other hand, the increasing share of the older population increases their **political weight**. Finally, it is becoming increasingly difficult to win elections against their power. Social tensions are also to be expected here if a life in dignity is not guaranteed for larger parts of the population through the pension they earn—and the younger workers do not want to pay more and more of their remuneration into state pension systems without at the same time earning corresponding pension entitlements of their own.

The **aging of society** combined with the overall **shrinking population** in many industrialized nations and also in Germany is having an impact on the available (young) workforce, which will continue to be needed in large numbers despite increasing digitalization. After all, it is not only the baby boomers who are now increasingly retiring from working life who must be replaced—at least in part—by new forces. The population in Germany, for example, will fall from 83.5 million (2021) to 80.7 million as early as 2040 and to 74.4 million in 2060 (cf. Destatis, 2020). And for China is the saying that China may become old before it becomes rich! These developments must be taken into account in our business activities.

In addition—and we should also bear this inconvenient truth in mind—the **EU economic area** is becoming increasingly less important—at least in terms of pure population size. While the EU-28 still had a share of 13.4% of the world population in 1960, this will have fallen to 5.1% in 2060. The so-called "other countries" in Fig. 1.4 together will have a population 15 times larger than the EU-28 in 2060 (cf. BPB, 2019). Now we can say: **quantity is not everything**! This is true, but the EU-28 (excluding the UK: EU-27) will lose not only political power, but also economic relevance—both as a supplier and as a customer of products and services—and also of innovations.

▶   **Food for Thought**
One thing is becoming clear: if we can dominate less and less through quantity in the future, we must focus even more on quality for the good of our society.
And quality starts in the minds of the people living here!
The increasing **shift of jobs to the service sector** will—despite digitalization—lead to a further increase in employment. This applies not least to the health and care professions. A **shift to the service sector** has taken place in recent decades. The question may be asked: Where are the missing employees—especially in professions that are still poorly paid and

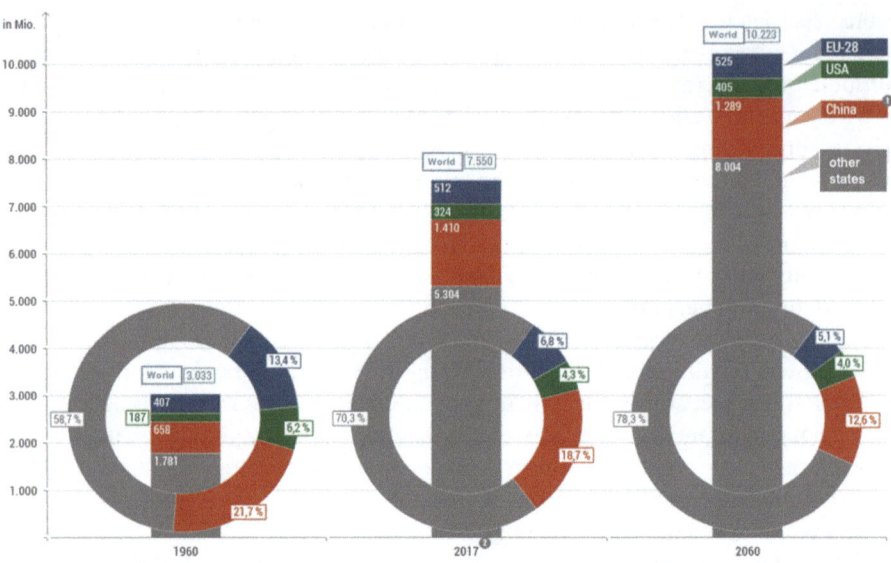

Fig. 1.4 Population development in EU—USA—China—1960, 2017 and 2060

unpopular—supposed to come from when the previous countries of origin of these workers are also prospering (e.g., Poland)? Who will take over these tasks if fewer and fewer people from the eastern countries of Europe make their way to Germany, France, Spain and Great Britain to work in care professions as well as in meat processing and agriculture?

1.2.3.2 Comprehensive Knowledge Building: Fiction or Truth?

We could now be hopeful if the **young people growing up in Europe** were not only highly motivated, but also resilient and highly qualified when they enter the labor market. But is this the case? The conditions for this are—at least apparently—excellent. **Digital natives** who are willing to learn and who have grown up with the media of the digital age have countless **reliable sources of information** (24/7) at their disposal today. Here, one could obtain well-founded and comprehensive information to acquire a great deal of one's own knowledge. In addition to a multitude of teaching materials (e.g., on *YouTube*), there are also a large number of so-called MOOCs (Massive Open Online Courses), offered, for example by *University*, *Stanford Lagunita* and *Udacity* (see Sect. 3.6.9).

However, this **multitude of information sources** has not led to the development of a sound knowledge base in broad sections of the population. Often the opposite has occurred! Online media are mostly not used to acquire comprehensive knowledge and achieve a deep understanding, but rather to be entertained and—as studies repeatedly show—simply to pass the time! Today, information must above all be "snackable" (consumable in a few seconds or minutes) and also "shareable" in order to share it on networks. *Snapchat* and especially *TikTok* pay exactly to this need—and even say so themselves!

Since all information is available at any place and at any time via various (mobile) devices, **building up one's own knowledge** is becoming less relevant for more and more people. Yet one's own knowledge is indispensable for one's own creativity, the classification of facts and for the development of one's own canon of values—especially for the **maintenance of a knowledge society** in Europe.

However, due to the predominant type of online usage, a **deep understanding of facts** often falls by the wayside. The result is **fragmentary knowledge**—even among the budding information-elite, to which I count our master's students. In order to ascertain the actual **level of knowledge of master's students**, I conducted a **study at the Berlin School of Economics and Law**. This was a **full survey in the following two master's programs**:

- **International Marketing Management**
- **Marketing Management**

The **survey to record the level of knowledge** took place on 2.10.2019, the first day of the master's program in the winter semester 2019/20. The 76 **master's students** surveyed had the following characteristics (cf. Kreutzer, 2020b, pp. 4–7):

- **Qualification**: Bachelor's degree in business administration with a marketing focus, documented through gaining at least 15 ECTS in marketing courses.
- **Grades**: 64 out of 76 students achieved an overall grade in their bachelor's degree between 1,2 and 2,0.
- **Origin**: Germany (84%), EU (without Germany; 9%), non-EU (7%).
- **Age**: Focus on 23 and 24 years (youngest participant 22, oldest participant 32 years).
- **Gender mix**: 89% female students, 11% male students

Two questionnaire versions with 63 and 62 open questions (no multiple choice!) were used. The respondents were asked to explain the questioned contents in their own words. The questionnaires contained questions on the **following topics**:
- **Business Administration Basics**
  ROI, ROS, EBITDA, cash flow, benchmarking, balanced scorecard, SWOT analysis, digital transformation, difference between nominal and real growth rate, organic growth, agile management, business model canvas, silo mentality, scenario analysis, inventory turnover rate, scalability, GIGO effect, difference between correlation and causation, etc.
- **General Education**
  VUCA world, Silk-and-Road-Initiative, Made in China 2025, exchange rate Dollar/Euro, unemployment rate Germany/Italy, inflation rate Germany, population figures Germany/USA/China/India, deflation, interest rate and inflation rate in the Euro zone, *LIBRA*, number of active *Facebook* users worldwide, rust belt,

current situation in Venezuela, *WeChat*, *BAT*, *GAFA*, *Cambridge Analytica*, Fracking, *Monsanto*, etc.
- **Marketing**
GDPR, opt-in, skimming/penetration/freemium pricing, CPI/CPO, A/B testing, NPS, marketing automation, sales promotion vs. PR, ZMOT, influencer marketing, relevant set, goals of CRM, greenwashing, customer experience, instruments of qualitative market research, dynamic pricing, CLV, quality criteria of market research, market segmentation, wholesale target groups, etc.
- **Online Marketing**
Retargeting, conversion funnel, ROPO effect, zero-click search, showrooming effect, retail media, conversational commerce, SEO vs. SEA, noline approach, bounce rate, *Google Analytics*, CTR, RTB, tag cloud, heat map, etc.
- **Special Knowledge**
Machine learning, additive manufacturing, gig economy, scrum, digital twin, basics of artificial intelligence, attention economy, augmented vs. virtual reality, platform business, VEO, etc.

The questioned **basics in business administration** should have been taught in the first semesters of the Bachelor's program and the **marketing and online marketing knowledge** should have been taught in the corresponding specializations. The questions on general education could have been answered by anyone who regularly watches or listens to serious TV and radio program and reads the relevant newspapers and magazines. That should not be too much to ask of the future information-elite. The questions on **special knowledge** should test whether there is already an "icing on the cake of knowledge."

The **results of the potential "information elite"** were equally disastrous in all five question categories and both questionnaire versions, as Figs. 1.5 and 1.6 show. Even for basics in business administration, only 8 and 18% respectively were able to answer the corresponding questions correctly. Even in the case of general education, more than 70% of the answers were wrong.

In only one questionnaire version and one question category ("marketing," Fig. 1.6) could just under 30% of the respondents give a correct answer. In all other areas, 70% and more were not able to answer the questions correctly.

The best knowledge of the master's students was in terms of **SWOT analysis**, the **situation in Venezuela**, the **content of digital transformation** and **agile management**. The students are also well informed about **influencer marketing**, the **difference between sales promotion and PR** and **customer touch points**. However, not a single business administration student could define the formulas to determine **ROS** and **cash flow**. The phenomenon of **fracking** was almost completely unknown, and the **size of India** was sometimes estimated at 200 million inhabitants, that of **China** at 400 million inhabitants.

At the same time, the **number of *Facebook* accounts** was occasionally estimated at 15 billion (with a world population of approx. 7.8 billion people!). The **unemployment rate in Germany** was estimated at 15% in some cases. Not a single marketing student could explain the **NPS** (net promotor score), let alone show how it

1.2 Using a PESTEL Analysis to Identify Key Challenges in the Digital Age

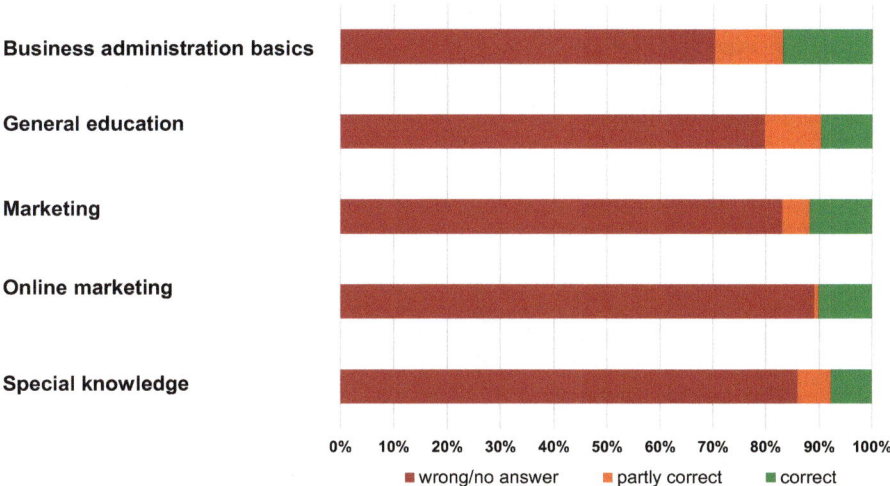

Fig. 1.5 Overview end results—questionnaire 1 ($n = 34$) (Source: Kreutzer, 2020b, p. 26)

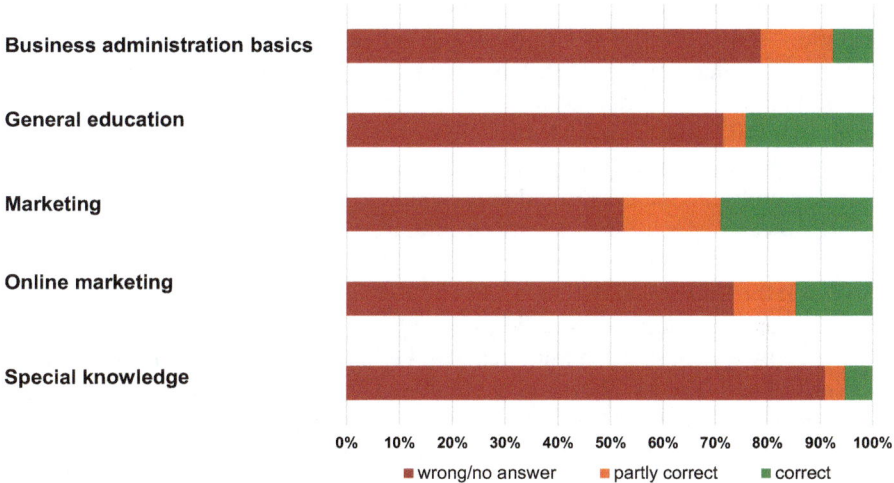

Fig. 1.6 Overview end results—questionnaire 2 ($n = 42$) (Source: Kreutzer, 2020b, p. 45)

is determined. And only two out of 42 students could correctly define the formula **ROI** and the content of **scalability**. None could correctly describe the method of **trend extrapolation**. Only three out of 42 students knew what to do with the term **algorithm**. Yet it is impossible to imagine our data-driven economy and society without algorithms, as we encounter them every day.

How could it come to such a dramatically poor result? Many lecturers find that so-called **bulimic learning** often dominates among students—and is also regularly confirmed by the students. This is understood as the short-term memorization of data and formulas in order to "throw up" this knowledge in an exam—and to forget everything learned immediately after an exam. Due to a lack of practice of what has been learned and a lack of exchange about it, not only in courses but also beyond, there is a lack of deep understanding and the ability to transfer what has been learned to other situations.

In addition, people generally do not read (much) anymore, and if they do, it is mostly online. In this regard, the **Stavanger Declaration** published in 2019 by 130 reading researchers from around the world shows that purely online reading is detrimental to deep understanding and longer-term memorization (cf. n. a. 22.1.2019).

Finally, all those **responsible for imparting knowledge** should ask themselves whether their form of teaching contributes more to bulimic learning or to deep understanding (cf. further Kreutzer, 2020a).

Incidentally, my students did not receive any grades or (frustrating) personal feedback on the basis of this test. Rather, I made the promise in my lecture that by the end of the winter semester, all students would know the content of the terms.

We all know it: **education** (also called **cultural capital**) is an important prerequisite for gaining and maintaining **economic capital**. An exception is the inheritance of larger fortunes. However, we see here that the heirs of the second and third generation—often due to a lack of motivation or education—often gamble away the inheritance (sometimes literally). On the one hand, a good education—as studies show time and again—enables people to take on more demanding tasks, which in turn go hand in hand with higher incomes. On the other hand, economic capital makes it possible to invest money in education and training, which can be accompanied by an increase in cultural capital. It is simply a matter of one thing: the **relevance of education, education, education!**

▶ **Food for Thought**
Genius needs a good breeding ground!
Why education is so important can be illustrated by the ***Dunning–Kruger effect*** (cf. Kruger & Dunning, 1999). This term is used to describe the systematically flawed tendency in which relatively incompetent people overestimate their own knowledge and skills while at the same time underestimating the competence of others. In several studies, the authors find that when comprehending texts, but also when playing chess or driving a car, unawareness often leads to more self-confidence than knowledge itself. In sum, the *Dunning–Kruger* effect can be described as follows:

- Less competent people tend to **overestimate their own abilities**.
- Less competent people **cannot recognize superior abilities in others**.
- Less competent people are **unable to recognize the extent of their own incompetence.**

But there is also some hope:

Less competent people can not only **increase their own competence through education or practice**, but also **learn to better assess themselves and others.**

This also shows that **weak performance** is accompanied by **greater self-overestimation** than stronger performance. Very simply, one could formulate: Those who are stupid cannot recognize that they are stupid. Those who are intelligent also know that they do not know everything and can be wrong with their partial knowledge.

Memory Box
Furthermore, according to Dunning (2010):
The skills and knowledge needed to find a good solution also correspond to the skills and knowledge needed to recognize that it is a good solution.

The *Dunning–Kruger* **effect** is likely to occur above all in those people who degenerate into veritable **headline-hunters** and no longer (want to) care about the depth of a message. However, this is no longer the case:
There's no cure for stupidity!
We can state against it—also in accordance with the findings of the *Dunning–Kruger* effect:
The antidote to stupidity—and thus also mental seductiveness—is education!
Therefore, one thing is important for a prosperous development of our societies: **building up one's own competence, one's own knowledge, one's own values.** After all, it has been stated (Kroeber-Riel & Gröppel-Klein, 2013, p. 432):
"Existing knowledge plays a key role in learning."
Therefore, it is important to have one's own knowledge, especially in the digital age, where any information is only a mouse click and a little research away. Only then can new findings be linked to existing knowledge, compared, evaluated, and creatively developed.

▶ **Food for Thought**
A personal **treasure trove of knowledge**—stored in a personal bio-computer—is still indispensable today. How else could one succeed in orienting oneself in these fast-moving times and in leading a planned and at the same time fulfilling life? Only one's own knowledge—as differentiated as possible and also familiar with opposing opinions and values—can help against algorithm-based demagogy!

That is why it frustrates me deeply when first-year students at university proudly tell us that they have never finished reading a book! I then ask myself how such a person could obtain the university entrance qualification! However, such behavior also explains the disillusioned report from a professor colleague who teaches mathematics: "When I ask students in the first semester what is 75% of 100, they all immediately call for a calculator."

Consequently, we should all—wherever we work—also and especially in a time with **instant access to the entire knowledge of mankind**, work towards as many people as possible acquiring knowledge themselves and, connected with this, developing their own values, their own opinions, their own views of the world. Because as the saying goes:

Who knows nothing must believe everything!

▶ **Storytelling** With this guiding principle in mind, I was very shocked when a representative of Generation Z told me during the lunch break of one of my seminars: "I don't read any more. I don't look at pictures any more either. It's too exhausting for me. I only watch videos now."

What education can such a person pass on to the next generation when their own cultural capital is diminishing?

I can also put it quite harshly: We cannot allow ourselves to act in such an **educationally distant way**, neither as individuals, nor as a team, nor as a company, nor as a society, nor even as a nation, if we want to help shape the future. Otherwise, others will do it for us—with all kinds of (undesirable) consequences.

When **analyzing the IQ development of humankind**, we have so far always been able to trust the so-called **Flynn effect** (cf. Flynn, 2012). This effect describes the observation that until the 1990s, IQ test scores in industrialized countries showed continuously higher results. This was interpreted as a **continuous increase in intelligence**. According to studies by *Flynn*, test results from 14 industrial nations showed that IQ scores increased by five to 25 points from generation to generation. From this it was concluded that intelligence as determined by IQ tests had increased in the first seven decades of the twentieth century. One explanation for this development was found in the improved environmental conditions, which were characterized by better nutrition and health care as well as higher educational efforts and access of many to mass media.

In the meantime, however, individual studies have shown a **negative Flynn effect**: this means that intelligence measured by IQ tests is now declining. Various explanations are offered for this (cf. Lynn & Harvey, 2008). For example, the question arises whether society is regressing not in spite of, but because of the extensive technological advances. Is a **deconstruction of civilization** already taking place or will such a deconstruction take place? Difficulties in reading maps, no longer memorizing important telephone numbers and addresses, the shift from comprehensive research to a simple *Google* search followed by copy-and-paste is on the rise. At the same time, **cultural techniques** that have been important and therefore learned over many decades are losing relevance (cf. Lobe 2019). And our brain remembers this—or not anymore!

Another explanatory factor for the decline in knowledge is the inability of more and more people to concentrate on a subject. We are already talking about the so-called **attention economy**, in which money or products are no longer the central

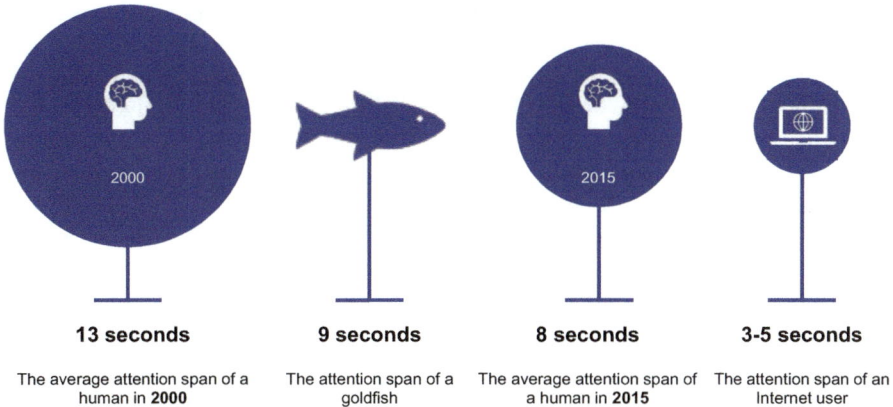

Fig. 1.7 Attention spans compared

bottleneck factor. Today, **people's attention** is increasingly becoming a scarce commodity (cf. Davenport & Beck, 2001; Bernardy, 2014).

Where does this development towards the attention economy come from? The **cost of accessing information and entertainmen**t is falling dramatically in the flat rate age. However, the use of *Facebook* and *Google*, for example, is only apparently free; after all, we pay for their use with our data. If you have a *Spotify* subscription for 9.95 € per month (ad-free), you can access (almost) all music and a large number of podcasts 24/7. Those who have a *Netflix* subscription from 7.99 € per month can access hundreds of thousands of hours of films anytime and anywhere. A similarly comprehensive offer is available to *Amazon Prime* customers. Online gamers also have an almost unimaginable offer to live out their passion for games. Consequently, it is no longer access to informative and/or entertaining content that is limited, but the **attention of the user**.

A study by *Microsoft*, which should be critically questioned, provides an interesting result that should give us all food for thought. As Fig. 1.7 shows, the **attention span** in 2000 was still 13 s on average. In 2015, it dropped to 8 s. Today, the **attention span of an Internet user** is even as short as 3–5 s. In comparison, the **goldfish**, with an attention span of—however, measured—9 s, virtually represents the epitome of the ability to concentrate (cf. Milano, 2019). As said: even if we do not trust the figures in detail, a **decline in attention** can be detected everywhere.

> **Memory Box**
> A goldfish has the ability today to concentrate itself longer than an Internet user.

▶ **Storytelling** All of us who look into the audience during lectures or sit in the audience ourselves notice again and again and more and more frequently: only a few of those physically present are also mentally present and concentrate on the respective lecture. Often between 30 and 50% of the apparent "listeners" use their devices. They usually do not do this to note down ideas or suggestions from the speaker, but to communicate with the world in other ways. They shop, chat, e-mail, like, share, and comment on *Instagram* photos and other posts, etc.

I always wonder why participants often invest not only time but also money to attend such events when they turn their attention to completely different activities during the lectures and discussions.

▶ **Food for Thought**
This development will intensify as more and more conferences and meetings take place online. Here, even the social control of the neighbors disappears when one switches off the microphone and camera and can devote oneself undisturbed to other topics while apparently listening to a lecture.

One **driver of the loss of attention** is the so-called **FOMO effect—the fear of missing out**. This effect describes people's fear that an interesting or exciting event is taking place somewhere that they could miss. This FOMO effect is mainly triggered by posts on social media. That is why millions of people are online all day long and scan the various news streams—often not to be informed about major world events, but to find out which A, B, or C celebrity has just had their dog or partner run away, who is having a crisis of purpose or creativity, or which taboos were broken during the weekend escapades by politicians or actors.

It is also important not to miss anything "important" from the circle of friends. Where did which party take place and where will one take place? Who bought what and where? Which events should not be missed, which series should be watched, which music should be listened to and—less frequently—which book should be read? The *Facebook* and *Instagram* stories as well as content on *Snapchat* & Co. are often only available for a few hours. If you do not want to miss anything, you have to be "always on." This FOMO effect leads to **pure stress**—and is not really conducive to profound knowledge building (cf. Kreutzer, 2020a).

▶ **Food for Thought**
I, personally, focus on the **JOMO effect**—the joy of missing out. JOMO is thus the opposite of FOMO. I am missing out on a whole lot and I am happy about it! Because this way I can concentrate on my own life—and not on that of other people!

1.2.3.3 Inflation of Expectations in Society and Among Customers
It is both exciting and challenging for companies that we have to cope with an **inflation of expectations in society and among customers** at the same time. This

1.2 Using a PESTEL Analysis to Identify Key Challenges in the Digital Age

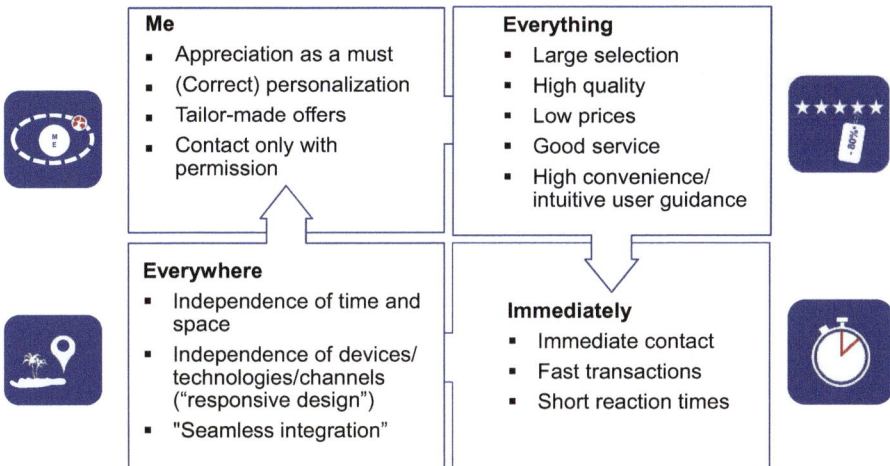

Fig. 1.8 Customer expectations become more concrete

can be described with the terms "**me, everything, immediately and everywhere**" (cf. Fig. 1.8; for further details, see Kreutzer, 2021, pp. 6-15).

Due to the high intensity of competition in almost all areas, the customer can afford to expect or demand a **high level of appreciation in the interaction** under "**me.**" If this is denied, there are usually many competitors waiting to win the customer over. "**Lived appreciation**" includes correct personalization, i.e., addressing the target person correctly by name.

At the same time, there is an increased expectation of being taken seriously as an individual with specific, possibly also individual wishes and consequently receiving individual addresses and offers. The self-centeredness of the customers documented in Fig. 1.8 is also is concretized in the **demands on the media**. Fewer and fewer—especially younger—people want to watch news, films, and documentaries when they are being broadcast on linear TV. Therefore, **on-demand and streaming services** are booming, making CD and DVD players superfluous in the long term in addition to linear TV. These developments challenge established business models, while other business models such as *Amazon Music/Video, Netflix, Spotify,* or *YouTube* are continuously gaining in importance.

The expectation of "**everything**" shows the high level of expectations that many people have in most industries today. Customers have learned that "everything is possible" often applies. Why does *Amazon* manage to provide me not only with the largest product selection, acceptable prices and almost always perfect customer service (with same-day or next-day delivery), while with other providers, I have to wait several days for delivery?

In addition, the expectation of "**immediate**" exists, forcing **acceleration effects** in a wide variety of areas. It is true that companies are being given less and less **time to react** by prospects and customers. If there is still no answer to an e-mail after 4 h, people often follow up. On *WhatsApp*, a response is even expected every minute.

And why should a customer often have to wait 2, 4, or even 6 weeks for a reply to an e-mail from a company when, for example, *Amazon* can ensure a callback in real time for product complaints?

▶ **Storytelling** I have already used this service at *Amazon* myself—and was simply thrilled. My contact person was not only available immediately but was also able to answer my technical questions competently and solve the problem through user guidance during the phone call. A real wow-experience!

In addition, companies are confronted with the expectation of "**everywhere/always.**" Mobile accessibility—not only via telephone, but also as access to service offers via the Internet—is now a matter of course in the developed industrial nations and increasingly also in many emerging countries. The expectation shows in particular in the **always-on-generation**—which itself is "always reachable"—and often expects this from companies as well. The expectation is often independent of whether an exchange takes place in a professional or private environment or whether it is stationary or mobile. This also increasingly blurs the boundaries between private and public or professional spheres. This is why prospective customers and clients often expect companies to provide access to the customer service center around the clock: every day, 7 days a week, 365 days a year—without thinking about the cost implications on the company side.

What challenge does this pose for you as a company? Access to company offers is increasingly shifting from "classic opening hours" at "specific locations" to a **customer-driven interaction process** that is **flexible in terms of time and space**. It is true that (prospective) customers can receive as well as send messages anywhere and around the clock, and in many cases, they want to do so. This challenge places high demands on companies. In this **instant society**, the motto is: "any channel, any device, anywhere, anytime." The streaming offers already mentioned are a perfect example of the fulfilment of this expectation.

The positive experiences made, for example, with *Amazon* and other companies are used as a **benchmark** (i.e., as a reference value) for the evaluation of the performance of other companies—even across sector boundaries. Whether this seems appropriate in the individual case from a provider's point of view is of little interest to the ego-driven prospect or customer. After all, by **channel hopping**, they can punish the slow companies with a mouse click at the competitors offers—and possibly be lost forever.

▶ **Food for Thought**
"With customers today being increasingly connected, informed, and ultimately empowered, their expectations only escalate. In short, they are more discerning and demanding than ever before."
Brian Solis (2012)

At the same time, it is also true that customers decide later and later due to the **variety of possible courses of action**—like an **orgy of options**. People want to keep as many options available as possible for as long as possible. That is why decisions (on purchases, invitations, but also on elections) are made later and later. Due to our constant accessibility and the omnipresence of countless options, we have become accustomed to being able to decide at the last moment. Here it becomes clear:

The zeitgeist has also become more volatile!

This makes it understandable why every company, in the (further) development of its business model, should deal with the demands of "me, everything, everywhere, immediately," which affects ever larger areas of society. This can be done with the objective of first comparing one's **own performance** with the expectations of the relevant target groups. At the same time, starting points can be identified in order to achieve **differentiation in the competitive environment** by convincingly fulfilling these expectations (see Sect. 3.5).

In order to meet the expectations outlined above, it is necessary to **design customer-oriented processes** with a consistent focus on efficiency and effectiveness. At the same time, it must be examined how valuable the customer relationships are in order to profitably serve the identified expectations (keyword "value-oriented customer management;" see further Kreutzer, 2021, pp. 30–43).

1.2.3.4 Future Distribution of Work and Income in Society

In connection with the technological changes, there is also the question of how work, which is foreseeably becoming less in some areas of the economy, is to be distributed in the future. The following concepts, among others, are being discussed for the **distribution of work and income in the future**:

- **Unconditional Basic Income**

    An unconditional basic income is a concept according to which every citizen, regardless of his or her respective economic situation, receives a **financial allowance from the state** that is fixed by law and equal for everyone—**without any service in return**. For me, the question of how such a basic income is to be financed remains unanswered. In addition, I would like to critically note that work not only serves to earn a wage, but also—ideally—serves many other human needs. These include recognition for the work done, personal growth and social integration into a larger whole—and perhaps also the pride of being able to finance one's life through one's own performance.

    In addition, the following questions remain completely unanswered for me:
    - What are people without work supposed to do at all with their time—which, after all, consists mainly of free time?
    - What happens when the work that gives many people an important structure for organizing their time is missing?
    - Do these people then do sport regularly?
    - Do they invest their time into their own personal and professional future?
    - If so, why should they, when no one is interested in their own performance potential?
    - Doing good for the world?
    - Contribute solidarity to the community?

- In my opinion: Dream on!
  The following questions also remain largely unanswered in the discussion so far:
  – Why is **the lack of meaningful employment** associated with health risks?
  – Why do the unemployed die earlier and are sick significantly more often than people in employment?
- Perhaps because for many people, money without work is not really the meaning of life. For many, but not for all!
- **Machine-Tax/Robot-Tax**
  The idea of a machine-tax is an additional **assessment basis for social security**. This is intended to compensate for the tax losses caused by a reduction in the "payroll" tax base when jobs disappear due to rationalization. The robot-tax is a specific manifestation of the machine tax. Both cases represent a form of **value added tax**.

  Those who say "yes" to the machine or robot tax also say "no" to any form of **productivity-enhancing innovation**. After all, such innovations are penalized by an additional tax!
  – Do we want to punish innovations in this way here, in Europe or worldwide?
  – Even those that perhaps lead to lower resource consumption?
  – Or not these, but all others?
- Who should make the binding decision—not only in one country, but worldwide, in order to avoid distortions of competition?
- **More Holidays for Everyone**
  A global rule could be adopted through the *United Nations* that all employees (including the self-employed?) work only 4 days a week. This global rule should avoid distortions of competition.

You mean all these ideas are not yet mature? I agree. Only we have to face these issues. The **efficiency potential of digitization** has just been demonstrated in the Corona pandemic. Many business trips will be eliminated by video conferencing—and with them all the jobs that were associated with it at airlines, railways, taxis, hotels, restaurants, etc. After many of us were forced to experience the benefits of digital exchange intensively, we will certainly not return to all the old habits!

> **Think Box: Questions You Should Ask Yourself**
> - What significance does the aging of society have for your business model?
> - What does it mean for your company that in many countries purchasing power and consumption are concentrated on people over 60?
> - What does the already existing and foreseeable shortage of labor in some areas mean for your business model?
> - What challenges do you face with an increasing shift to the service sector?
> - How will a potentially declining level of knowledge in society affect your company?

(continued)

- What consequences result from this?
- How can you ensure that your managers and employees are part of the "information elite"—and behave as such?
- Have you already dealt with the findings of the *Stavanger Declaration* and made deductions for the acquisition of knowledge in your company?
- Can you identify the *Dunning–Kruger* effect in your company?
- What is your response to the challenges of the attention economy—internally and externally?
- Do you notice a FOMO effect in yourself? If so, what can you do to counteract it?
- What about applying the JOMO effect?
- What does the inflation of expectations in society and also your customers mean for your company?
- What does the expectation "everything" mean for your company?
- What business opportunities result from the expectation "immediately?"
- Is the expectation "everywhere/always" associated with opportunities or risks for your company?
- What possible answers do you have to the question of the future distribution of work and income in society?
- What is your and your company's position on an unconditional basic income?
- Could a machine or robot tax be the solution?
- Who answers such questions in your company?

1.2.4 Challenges Posed by the Technological Framework Conditions

Clarity through reduction—insight through omission!

1.2.4.1 Development of Industry 4.0 and Economy 4.0

Today we are talking intensively about the need for a **digital transformation** of more or less all industries and companies. This is mainly due to the technological framework conditions, which have changed and will continue to change as quickly and comprehensively as never before. The relevant buzzwords here are artificial intelligence, platform economy, ecosystems, the Internet of Things and much more. A brief look at the **development of the industry** shows why the emerging changes are so relevant. Here it also becomes clear why we are talking about **industry 4.0** today (cf. Fig. 1.9):

- The **first industrial revolution** was caused by the invention and use of the steam engine in the middle or end of the eighteenth century. The steam engine was used

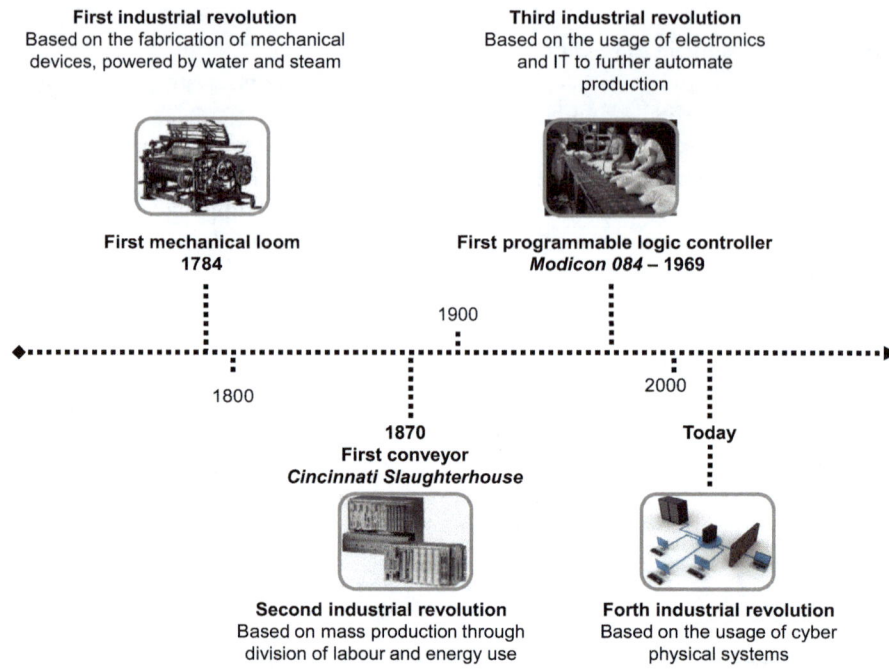

Fig. 1.9 From industry 1.0 to industry 4.0

to drive mechanical devices such as looms. The corresponding production facilities were located where the first steam engines were also found.
- The **second industrial revolution** was driven by the invention of electricity and the associated electrification at the end of the nineteenth and beginning of the twentieth century. This enabled mass production using assembly lines and the associated division of labor in production processes. Among other things, they were located where electricity was available (at low cost).
- The **third industrial revolution** began in the 1970s and was caused by ubiquitous computerization, which led to further automation of production through the use of electronics and IT. Industrial clusters emerged where qualified personnel, reliable framework conditions and the necessary further resources were available.
- We are now in the **fourth industrial revolution**. At its core, this is about cyber-physical systems that, among other things, enable value creation processes to be networked beyond the boundaries of individual companies. This is called industry 4.0! What location factors are relevant here? Above all, there must be powerful Internet access as well as well-trained and creative minds! By the way, China is placing artificial intelligence at the center of the 4th industrial revolution.

Today, there are practically no non-digital companies any more. All companies are—to varying degrees—digital! Even if it is only that invoices and contracts are no longer sent or received in paper form, but digitally. More and more frequently, appointments are now made online and no longer via a call centers. We do not even want to talk about the development towards cyber sex.

> **Food for Thought**
> As we can see, these diverse developments are not concentrated in the industrial sector alone. That is why we should speak more comprehensively of **economy 4.0** instead of only talking about **industry 4.0**. The term economy 4.0 makes it much clearer that the technological possibilities are not limited to the production sector, but can also contribute to shaping relationships with customers and other partners (such as suppliers, service providers, employees, etc.).

1.2.4.2 Drivers of Industry 4.0 and Economy 4.0

Which are the central **drivers of this development**? They can be characterized as follows (cf. Brynjolfsson & McAfee, 2018):

- We are experiencing an **exponential development in the performance** of available technologies and systems.
- **Digitization** is affecting more and more areas of value creation.
- The **combinatorics** of various objects, processes, and even living beings through the Internet of Things or the Internet of Everything is leading to real quantum leaps in solutions and concepts.

The linking of these drivers marks the **tipping point** in the sense of an important **acceleration of trends** that we are currently experiencing. Today, the developments described above intertwine intensively and reinforce each other, so that exponential developments can be seen in many areas.

To illustrate the **effects of exponential growth**, the following mental exercise helps: How many meters does a human being cover when one takes 30 analogous steps of one meter in length? Exactly 30 m. How many meters would one cover if one could complete 30 exponential steps, in which the step size doubles from time to time? When a human takes his/her 31st exponential step, he/she will have covered 1,073,741,824 m. With this number of steps, you could circle the earth 25 times at the equator. This is how **exponentiality** works—a dynamic that humans are often unable to visualize.

The effect of exponentiality is described by *Moore's* **Law** in the IT industry. According to this principle, which is based on empirical observations, *Moore* predicted as early as 1965 that there will be a **doubling of digital computing power** approximately every 2 years (cf. Moore, 1965, pp. 114–117). The impact of this doubling will become even more dramatic in the next few years because we are now on the **second half of the digital chessboard**, having already gone through more than 32 doubling cycles. A decisive driver of the digital revolution thus becomes abundantly clear: the ongoing **doubling of computing power**. However, this development is now gradually reaching its (physical) limits.

But what is it about the second half of the chessboard? Here we can fall back on an Indian legend that is told in various forms. In India, the king *Sher Khan* once lived. One of his subjects developed the **game of chess**. The king was so enthusiastic about this that he summoned the inventor to the royal court to thank him. He offered him a reward—freely according to the inventor's will. After all, the king was rich and powerful enough to fulfil any wish. After a moment's thought, the inventor shared his wish. He placed a grain of rice on the first square of the chessboard and asked the king to have two grains of rice placed on the second square, four on the third square, eight on the fourth square and sixteen on the fifth. This row was to continue until the 64th field.

The king was surprised at this uninspiring request—as perhaps we were too. After all, in addition to gold and precious stones, the king's daughter, lands and fancy palaces might have been on offer! The king was annoyed by this simple wish. Did the inventor perhaps think he was poor and stingy? Therefore he threw the inventor out of the palace and told him that the desired amount of rice would be delivered right to the palace gates. A few hours later, the king asked if the inventor had already received his reward. Then his advisors explained that all the rice available in the country would never be enough to deliver the promised amount. Not even in the whole world would there be enough rice available to pay the inventor.

The **court mathematician** provided the explanation: it was quite simple. All one had to do was to calculate "**2 to the 64th power**" to find the desired quantity of rice. The result:

18,446,744,073,709,551,616 (18 quintillion, 446 quadrillion, 744 trillion, 73 billion, 709 million, 551 thousand, 616 grains of rice) had been promised. With this amount of rice, one should be able to cover the whole of Germany with rice about 2000 m high!

We can choose the end of the **story about exponentiality** ourselves. Either the king had the clever inventor beheaded—or he appointed him as his advisor!

What does it mean that we are on the **second half of the digital chessboard**? We have already gone through more than 32 doubling cycles. This means that each doubling is now already taking place at a very high level of performance. To stay with the picture, we can already see gigantic differences between the rice mountains on the 32nd and 33rd squares! The greatest leaps in development are therefore still ahead of us. Here we can think of quantum computing and the still largely unexploited possibilities of artificial intelligence.

Memory Box

Therefore: **Let us enjoy the present time.**

Technological change in the future will not be as **slow** as it is today.

The acceleration has not even really begun!

If we add to the **effects of exponential growth** the **possibilities of digitization** described below and "multiply" these with the **implications of**

(continued)

combinatorics, the **dynamics of change** become clear, at the beginning of which we are now.

The **combinatorics** mentioned are initially promoted by the continuous growth of the **communication networks**. *Google/Alphabet, Facebook & Co.* are investing billions of US-$ to enable (low-cost) access to the Internet for all of humanity with drones, balloons, and satellites. At the same time, hardware manufacturers are trying to offer cheaper computers, tablets, and smartphones to give millions of people access to the Internet who could not afford the necessary devices because of their lack of purchasing power. This will make the Internet even more important in the coming years.

Finally, the developments discussed so far will lead to the **Internet of Everything** (IOE). The central service components can be seen in Fig. 1.10.

Which developments characterize the **Internet of Everything**?

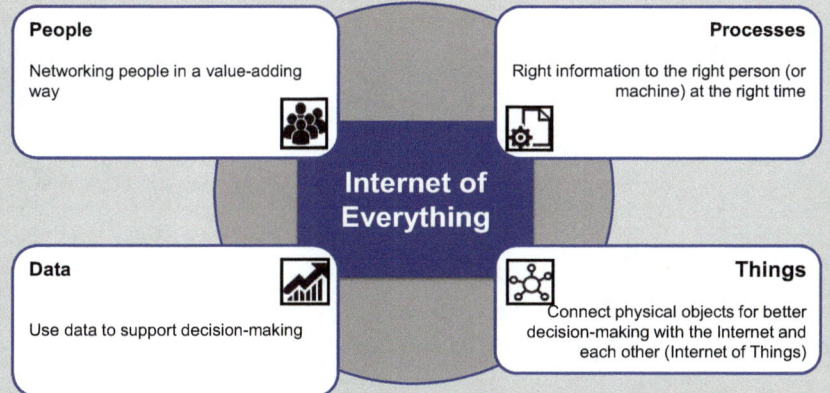

Fig. 1.10 Design of the internet of everything

- **Things**
  The starting point of the Internet of Everything was the Internet of Things (IOT; cf. Firouzi et al., 2020; Chui et al., 2010). The entry point for this development was created by the fact that more and more objects became "smart." This means that these objects are connected to the Internet. Today, many people can no longer imagine that there was once a time when mobile phones were not "smart" and consequently did not enable connection to the Internet. You could only make phone calls and send text messages with a phone! Today, we usually speak of smartphones because we naturally assume that there is a connection to the Internet. The same applies to computers, which we can hardly imagine without Internet access.

(continued)

Today, even dolls, toothbrushes, watches, refrigerators, washing machines, coffee machines, loudspeakers, radios, televisions, as well as shutters, heaters, air conditioners, escalators, lifts, cars, and many millions of machines and production plants have a connection to the Internet. A "smart condom" is also already offered today. I leave to your imagination what data is recorded here!

Today, "only" about 35 billion things are connected to the Internet (cf. Fig. 1.11). This number will more than double to over 75 billion within the next 4 years. The biggest **drivers of networking intensity** are the industrial applications already mentioned. But people will also use more and more "**connected devices**" and further increase the intensity of networking.

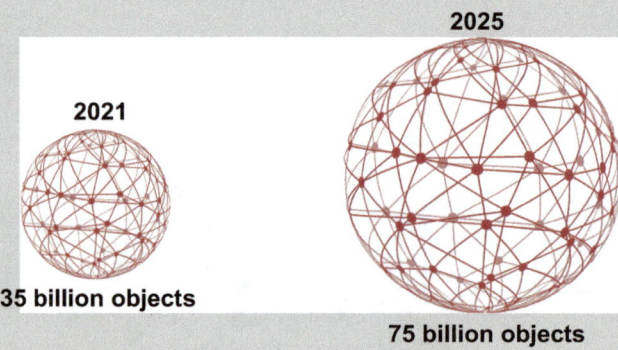

Fig. 1.11 Intensity of expected linkage through the Internet of Things

- **Processes and Services**
  Via the Internet, there is not only the possibility of **connecting one's own value chain with various supplier and production stages**. The Internet now also creates the possibility of establishing a comprehensive **connection to end customers** and linking them to the production process. Companies are now required to think and act upstream and downstream to a much greater extent than before!

  Upstream refers to the processual and informational penetration of upstream production stages. **Downstream** refers to this process in the direction of the end customer. In this way, ecosystems can be created in procurement, production, and marketing that deliver value added offers for the respective integrated partners—and do so with greater speed, accuracy and thus relevance.

(continued)

Examples of this are the **configurators** of car manufacturers. The data entered by potential buyers can—after a check by the manufacturer—flow directly into production planning. AI systems can take over such checks in the future. In addition, many companies already offer the possibility to configure consumer goods themselves. This ranges from muesli (at *mymuesli.com*), chocolate (at *chocri.de*), sports shoes (at *nike.com/en/nike-by-you*) to perfume (at *parfum-world.com*; see Sect. 3.5.1.5 for further details).

Drivers for new business models can be derived from the networking of further complex systems. One example is the monitoring of **urban water supply systems**. By using sensors, leaky pipes and dripping taps can be detected independently, reported via the Internet and switched off directly in order to reduce water consumption. Intelligent buildings ("smart buildings") can be fed relevant weather data via the Internet to use it for optimizing heating, cooling, electricity, and water supply.

The development of **smart grids** is also being discussed in this context. These are intelligent electricity grids that also represent an important prerequisite for the integration of renewable energy sources. The core areas of an energy system—specifically electricity generation and electricity consumption—are optimally coordinated via an intelligent grid. This is intended to predict generation highs and lows as well as consumption highs and lows (often AI-based) and thus balance them more easily. This should not only stabilize the grid, but also optimally utilize its capacity.

The fields of application relevant here also include **smart homes**. A smart home is a living environment that is comprehensively networked both internally and externally. For this purpose, the residents can connect all possible and impossible devices and processes to the Internet in order to control not only the washing machine and the coffee machine from outside, but also the room climate and the music.

Concepts such as "**If this than that**" (*ifttt.com*) are driving the linking of more and more things and processes. The motto here is: "Connect your apps and devices in new and remarkable ways. Make the things you love more powerful" (IFTTT, 2021). According to the company, more than 650 brands and services can already be connected with each other. These include *Alexa, Dropbox, Evernote, Google, Salesforce, Slack, Spotify, Twitch,* and *Uber*.

In addition, we can also think of the countless **video conferences** that we have completed in the meantime. Digital **collaboration tools** also promote the networking of processes across time, cultural, and spatial boundaries (see Sect. 3.6.8.4).

(continued)

- **Data**
  Through the use of **sensors** and other **measuring instruments** in all areas of human life and across all stages of the value chain, the quantity of data is increasing. At the same time also its quality and the speed of its provision are growing. Eventually, much of this data will be available in real time. For example, lift systems will be able to automatically call maintenance technicians when a part needs to be replaced or maintenance is due—even before a lift has to stop its services (cf. on predictive maintenance Sect. 3.3.1.3).

  Cows are monitored by sensors with regard to their health and fertility. Fields can be checked for moisture and possible pest infestation. These data streams, which are part of **smart farming** or **digital farming**, make it possible to take action at the best possible time.

  For this purpose, the companies involved must use **big data analytics** or **business analytics** in order not to get lost in the information tsunami. Only then can they succeed in gaining the insights that are indispensable for decision-making (see Sect. 3.4.2).

- **Humans**
  Today, people have the possibility to be permanently connected to the Internet via laptop, smartphone, tablet, smart glasses, smart watches and other so-called wearables (portable devices with Internet connection). In this way, many people are online 24/7—and in many cases can also be reached. This not only changes information, communication and learning behavior, but also accessibility during customer journeys (cf. on the critical effects of this development Kreutzer, 2020a).

  In addition, **fitness trackers** monitor central body functions (such as heart rate) and analyze the quality of our sleep. This **quantified self**—a kind of "self-measurement"—made possible by fitness trackers from *Amazon Halo, Fitbit, Garmin, Samsung, Xiaomi* & Co. generates a gigantic data stream that can become the basis for new business models. Various companies in the insurance industry are already using such health data to offer more attractive rates to the providers of such data. This is referred to as **vitality programs**. An example of this is the offer from insurance company *Generali*. The *Generali Vitality Health Program* is a bonus program that rewards measures for individual fitness (cf. Generali, 2021).

▶ **Food for Thought** Taking a critical look at this development. If healthy and fit policyholders are offered more favorable rates and/or gifts, this must be at the expense of the less healthy people in this insurance. In this way, the **principle of solidarity** that underlies social insurance is undermined. This principle means that a person is not solely responsible for himself, but that the members of a defined solidarity community provide each other with help and support. In the case of health insurance, this means that the person concerned does not pay for high medical costs alone, but that these costs are borne by everyone in solidarity.

If the **principle of solidarity** were to be **consistently undermined**, the consequence would be that insurance rates would have to rise again as health tends to decline over the decades. Instead of gift vouchers, there would then be rate increases. This could motivate one or the other policyholder to switch to an insurance provider who does not "punish" sicker people with higher tariffs and still feels committed to the solidarity principle. The question is, however, whether such a change without a health check is then still possible and should be possible!

A **continuous stream of personal data** also makes it possible not only for our cars to register themselves for **inspection**, but also for us to register ourselves for the next **fitness check**. Linked to our appointment calendar, **machine-to-machine communication** makes it possible to coordinate the best appointments to visit the doctor and automatically enter them into our online calendar. Expectant mothers will wear "smart tattoos" to monitor their babies' health and activities. In case of emergency, automatic messages will be sent to the doctor to request immediate help. These **wearable technologies** in particular will change our lives to an extent that was previously hardly imaginable (cf. for example, *Amazon Halo* Sect. 3.2.9.2).

Finally, people can also be directly integrated into the network. For this purpose, people can already be chipped themselves today and thus become **cyborgs** (cybernetic organisms).

Here, too, in addition to ethical considerations, it is always necessary to examine which new business models can be realized with such information flows.

Memory Box
Data is the new oil!
The Internet of Everything are the new pipelines pumping this data around the globe—24/7—in real time!

The **multitude of information** that can be generated by the Internet of Everything will further strengthen the trend towards **big data**. Data from different sources, generated mobile and stationary, are increasingly interlinked via uniform protocols (especially the Internet Protocol IP). This creates a variety of networks, including in these fields:

- **Cars** (smart cars)
- **Houses** (smart homes)
- **Administrations** (smart government or e-government)

(continued)

- **Production** (smart factories)
- **Payment** (smart cash)
- **Advertising** (smart advertising)

At the same time, data of a previously unknown quantity and quality is available for analysis (keyword "big data"). The data management required for this is discussed in more detail in Sect. 3.4.2.

▶ **Food for Thought**
We are about to enter the **age of digital by default**.
Everything—really everything—will be set to "digital" right from the start!
The **disruptive power** of these developments lies in the networking of the different areas of the Internet of Everything. The drivers behind new variants of value creation are therefore the connections between people, data, processes, and products (cf. Fig. 1.10). This means that a **new source of competitive advantage** is gaining relevance. This is because the **possibilities of the Internet of Everything** will be reflected both in the form of **savings** and in increasing **profits** for the companies that can best leverage the corresponding potentials. Particularly large **potential savings and profit increases** are expected in the following areas:

- Efficiency of plant utilization
- Staff productivity
- Supply chain improvements
- Optimisation of customer experience
- Increasing innovation

In the context of the **Internet of Things**, the following forms are discussed in particular:

- **Consumer IOT**
  The focus of consumer IOT is on developments around the smart home. This involves the networking of lighting, heating, home entertainment and other household appliances. Voice support and the "monitoring" of elderly people are also part of this area.
- **Commercial IOT-applications**
  This includes IOT systems in the health and transport sectors like intelligent pacemakers, monitoring systems and vehicle-to-vehicle (V2V) communication.

- **Industrial IOT (IIOT)**
  In the IIOT, digital monitoring and control systems as well as the management of production facilities are used. These are based on a comprehensive evaluation of a wide variety of data streams.
- **Infrastructure IOT**
  Infrastructure IOT enables the networking of smart cities through the use of infrastructure sensors, management systems and user-friendly user applications.
- **Internet of Military Things (IOMT)**
  IOMT includes the application of IOT technologies in the military sector. This covers sensors for recording biometric data of people in action. Combat robots also belong to this area of application.

The **implications of combinatorics** become visible when one considers the trend towards ever more and further simplified interfaces for controlling and accessing smart devices. These are the driving forces behind the fields of application described above. The increasing **use of sensors** contributes to this. Sensors connected via the **Internet of Everything**, coupled with powerful algorithms for pattern recognition, continue to drive the digitalization of processes, products, and services.

In addition, the **use of sensors** will increasingly extend to animals and humans (e.g., as patients). Computers are ideally suited for monitoring tasks because they never sleep, inertia is unknown to them, and the human bias in the evaluation is eliminated. We are therefore at the beginning of the **development of a sensor economy**, the effects of which are only just beginning to emerge. At the same time, these sensors generate billions of data that constitute the "fodder" for artificial intelligence algorithms (cf. Kreutzer & Sirrenberg, 2019).

1.2.4.3 Dematerialization of Products and Services as well as Processes

In addition, a **dematerialization of products and services** as well as a **dematerialization of processes** is taking place in a wide variety of areas. Data (e.g., about our customers) and processes (such as consulting, sales, payment processes, but also training, workshops, job interviews) are increasingly digitized and thus available online. In addition, products that were previously provided primarily physically are losing their physicality. At the same time, physical boundaries are being overcome, which used to be very important in many business models and often formed their basis.

Today, more and more activities are shifting to the smartphone or other smart devices, which are thus mutating into **smart service terminals**. Fig. 1.12 shows these developments. **Independent products** such as the landline phone, a stand-alone camera, the watch, the travel alarm clock, but also the water balance, the torch, the compass and the vanity mirror are being replaced by the smartphone or corresponding apps. This also applies to the voice recorder, which has gone out of fashion, and also—only partially—to stand-alone game consoles.

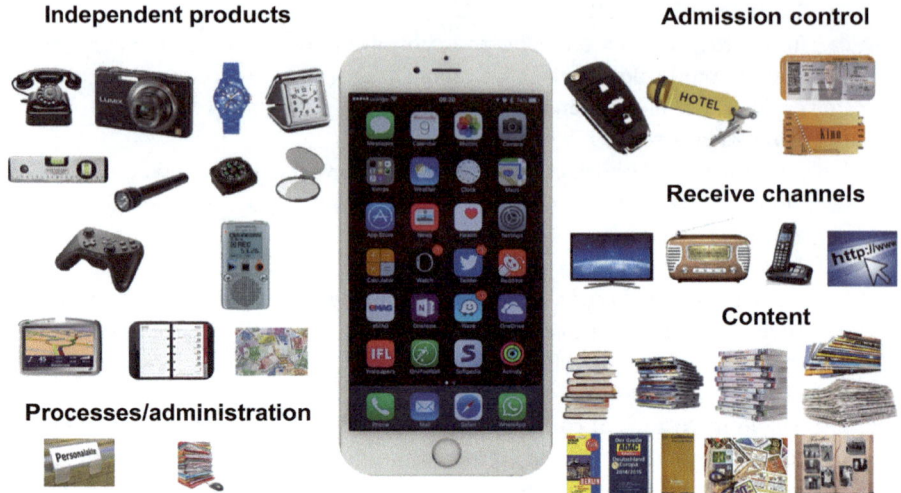

Fig. 1.12 Smartphones become smart service terminals

Navigation and appointment management are also increasingly digital. This also applies to payment processes, which are handled via the smartphone and which experienced a strong surge in demand as a result of the Corona pandemic. Here, the *Bitcoin* is the perfect dematerialization of money—a dematerialized scarcity, as it is!

Processes such as **access control** are becoming increasingly digitized. The spectrum here ranges from keyless drive to online check-in at hotels, airplanes, and cinemas. The smart service terminal also brings together the relevant **reception channels**: TV, radio, telephone, and Internet.

Finally, the smartphone becomes the central **content platform**: books, **newspapers**, **magazines**, **catalogs**, **CDs**, and **DVDs** used to be physically produced and transported to the customer lose their relevance. Today, a download or streaming of many contents is enough to be either entertained or informed. In addition, one can be active oneself at any moment—24/7—through search processes, shopping, or an engagement in social media.

Even **classic maps** (such as city maps or street maps) are increasingly dematerialized because navigation support is available online. Here, there is often even a real-time update with information on current traffic jams, traffic jam detours and delays in local public transport. Even the classic **flight schedules** (e.g., from *Lufthansa*) have not been available for years—and no one has missed them (except the printers, who lost many lucrative orders). **Coupons** are also increasingly transmitted online. And instead of a **photo album**, photos are quickly presented on tablet or smartphone (cf. Fig. 1.12).

There are no longer any limits to the further **combinatorics of different applications**. The digitized data available can be evaluated in real time if necessary, to optimize products, services, and processes—if necessary also in real time. An example of this is the linking of *Google Maps* with the navigation system, which receives—in real time—traffic radio data and enables dynamic traffic jam avoidance. Depending on the travel time already reached, the driver, who may be tracked via a wearable with regard to his bodily functions, can be recommended a restaurant on the alternative route at the same time. This restaurant is selected on the basis of customer ratings that match the driver's profile and are therefore considered relevant. In addition, restaurant preferences expressed by the driver on *Facebook* or *Yelp* can be taken into account. For some a horror vision—for others simply convenient and relevant!

▶ **Food for Thought**
In view of this unstoppable development, you should comprehensively address the question of how not only your own communication, but also the products and/or services offered as well as entire value chains could be made available on a mobile basis.

In addition—as already indicated—digital offers also eliminate the **digital transport to the buyer** to physically store content on an end device. This step is even omitted entirely if content is stored in the **cloud** and only made available via streaming at the moment of use. Decentralized data storage per user is replaced here by central data storage in the cloud. This trend towards shifting to the cloud is not limited to data but includes further processes and entire business processes (see Sect. 3.4.1.2).

An additional accelerator of digitalization is the increasingly **smart user interfaces** that accompany the **advance of digital assistants**. This development is fueled by AI-based natural language processing (NLP). These interfaces are making it increasingly easy for computers to respond to a whole range of human requests. Systems such as *Amazon Echo (Alexa), Apple Siri, Google Assistant* and *Samsung Bixby* recognize the spoken word, interpret its meaning and act accordingly. This development gives rise to further access to suppliers, business partners and customers and also promotes the development of new business models (cf. Kreutzer & Vousoghi, 2020; Kreutzer & Sirrenberg, 2019, pp. 24–39; Kahle, 2020).

1.2.4.4 From Time-to-Market to Time-to-Value

All in all, these developments are leading to an **acceleration in all areas of life and in all sectors**. The name **instant society** is already used:

Everything must take place now, if possible, even in real time!

This also brings a new challenge for you and your company: **increasing the speed of entrepreneurial action**.

Against this background, every company should examine whether its behavior is or should still be oriented towards the **time-to-market perspective** that has dominated up to now. Time-to-market is measured in days, weeks, months and/or years and characterizes the lead time between a product/service idea or a business model innovation and its introduction to the market. This period includes the development phases and any market tests that may have been carried out. Since no

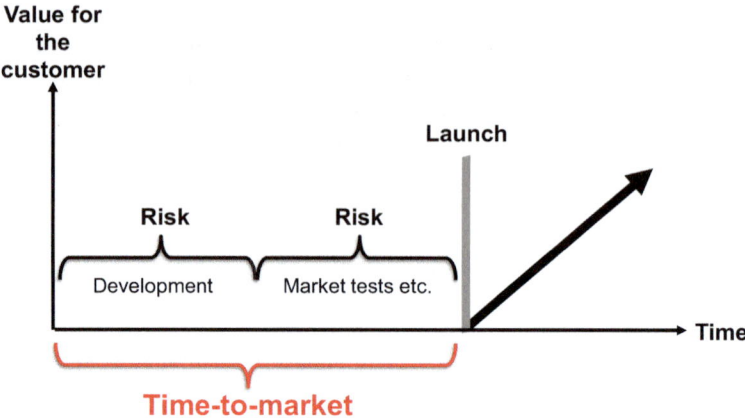

Fig. 1.13 Time-to-market

productive use takes place during this period, there are great risks associated with erroneous development. At the same time, costs for prototype construction, communication, market research, etc. are incurred. However, no turnover is generated. A value for the customer is also achieved by the innovation only after completion of the development and test phase and consequently after the launch of the product or service innovation (cf. Fig. 1.13).

However, every company is called upon to place product or service innovations as well as business model innovations on the market as quickly as possible in order to get ahead of competitive offers. In addition, it can then succeed in skimming off the higher willingness to pay of the so-called **innovators** and **early adopters**.

Many European and especially German companies still have a **too long time-to-market.** This means that a lot of time passes before a market-ready product or service innovation is available. A delayed market launch takes its toll especially on products and services with a very short life cycle. This is especially true if a lot of time has to be invested in development. The sooner an offering is replaced by a revised one, the more unsuccessful will the companies be that have not geared their development processes to speed.

> **Memory Box**
> **A time-to-market orientation is less and less in line with today's demands for speed in innovation processes.**
>
> To achieve speed, every company should focus more on **time-to-value** (cf. Fig. 1.14). I heard this term for the first time in Silicon Valley. Every company we visited talked about time-to-value—time-to-market was never an issue! Time-to-value is also measured in days, weeks, months and/or years and characterizes the **lead time** between a product/service idea or a business model
>
> (continued)

innovation and its **first benefit for customers**. Consequently, we do not wait until a perfect product or service innovation is available to introduce it to the market. An innovation is already presented on the market when it can create the first relevant value for users. The challenge today is: **focus on time-to-value**!

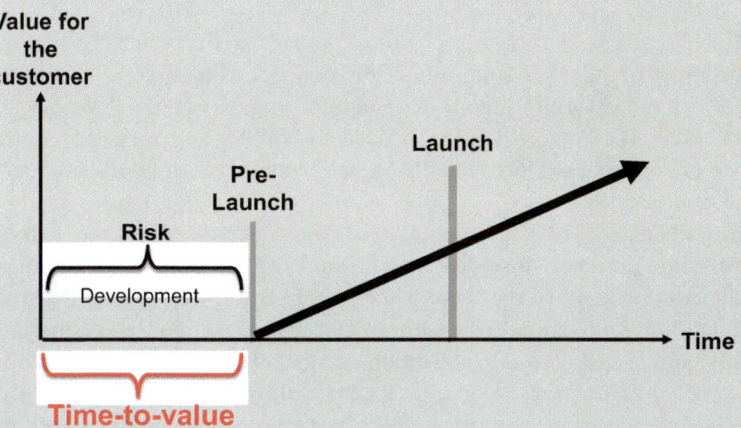

Fig. 1.14 Time-to-value

When implementing the time-to-value approach, a **pre-launch** takes place. This is characterized by a very early introduction into the market with a first functional product or a powerful service. Compared to the time-to-market approach, such a pre-launch enables the company to achieve a **benefit for the customer** much earlier. At the same time, the company learns in cooperation with real customers where there is a need for optimization and which further features need to be developed with particular urgency.

This continuous development goes hand in hand with the early **creation of value for the customer**. The launch of the "final" product or the "finalized" service takes place at a later point in time. Often, a smooth transition from the pre-launch phase to the launch phase is appropriate—accompanied by a continuous creation of value for the user (cf. Fig. 1.14).

By **focusing on time-to-value**, several goals can be achieved:

- On the one hand, a company can penetrate the market earlier with its own offers in order to at least make it more difficult for competitors to enter the market.

(continued)

- Secondly, the product or service can be fine-tuned in the real market environment, and undesirable developments can be recognized and stopped at an early stage.
- Thirdly, it may already be possible to generate initial revenues by offering a 70% or 80% solution. This means that costs incurred in the innovation process for market research, prototype construction, communication, etc. can be covered, at least in part.

▶ **Storytelling** Whenever I presented this concept to a circle of managers, I was faced with an almost **united front of rejection**. Statements like "We can't deliver a car with three wheels" or "We don't need to adopt every nonsense from Silicon Valley" were often heard. Or even: "Aha, the banana principle: the product matures with the customer!"

I always tried to make it clear in a nice but firm way that I was talking about "**time-to-value**" and not "**time-to-frustration.**" The key question is therefore: When has an innovation reached the stage where it is useful to customers? Then, and only then, should the innovation be brought to customers. But not later either!

At this point, I had gained the attention and usually the acceptance for the time-to-value approach! However, this requires a **rethinking of the innovation process**—especially in European and especially in German companies. Too often, an innovation has been tinkered with until it was not only 100%, but 120% perfect. All too often, however, an earlier market launch or even a market launch at all was missed and consequently also a convincing starting position in the competition. A **time-to-value focus** can make it much easier to consistently work out competitive disadvantages based on time.

> **Memory Box**
> To prevent misunderstandings: We do not want to offer our customers defective products or services through **time-to-value**, but solutions that already provide benefits for customers!
>
> The **time-to-value approach** does not propagate the **banana principle**, where the product (only) matures with the customer! With the banana principle, customers are presented with unfinished products or unripe services by the manufacturer without specifically pointing this out. In this case, the unfinished services are only gradually improved—based on user feedback. Customer frustration is pre-programmed—but no creation of customer value!
>
> A convincing example of an orientation towards the time-to-value concept is provided by *Amazon* with the **introduction of *Amazon Echo*** in the German market in 2016. Customers in Germany could apply to be the first to test the

(continued)

digital assistant *Alexa*. At the launch, it was made clear that this digital assistant had not yet reached its final stage of development. Rather, the aim was to gather experience with dialects in Germany and to identify which questions would be asked of such an assistant in Germany.

Due to this early form of market launch, *Amazon* was assured of a high level of media coverage. In addition, comprehensive results from daily use could be taken into account to optimize the assistants which were finally launched on the overall market in 2017. *Amazon's* aim was therefore to shorten the time-to-market by applying the time-to-value concept. If today *Amazon Echo* or *Alexa* is usually mentioned first when talking about voice assistants in Germany, this is related to this early market launch.

Memory Box
Time is the only resource we can't get back!

Think Box: Questions You Should Ask Yourself:
- What opportunities and risks does the exponential development of the performance of available technologies and systems bring for your company?
- What challenges does comprehensive digitization pose for your value creation?
- What options for action does the Internet of Things or the Internet of Everything bring for your company?
- What potential lies in the networking of things, processes, data and/or people?
- What are your starting points for upstream and downstream integration?
- What potential is offered by the integration of configurators into your value chain?
- Does the development of smart buildings, smart grids and/or smart homes offer you opportunities?
- How well are you already positioned in big data analytics or business analytics?
- What opportunities does the trend towards quantified-self offer you?
- What opportunities does the emergence of cyborgs reveal?
- What savings and profit improvement potentials does the Internet of Things offer you in terms of plant utilization efficiency, staff productivity, supply

(continued)

> chain improvements, customer experience optimization and/or increased innovation?
> - Which IOT manifestation is particularly exciting for you—the Consumer IOT, Commercial IOT applications, the Industrial IOT, the Infrastructure IOT and/or the Internet of Military Things?
> - What impact does the increasing dematerialization of products and services as well as processes have on your business model?
> - Where do opportunities and risks arise from dematerialization?
> - Does a time-to-market perspective still dominate in your company?
> - What is necessary to also adopt to a time-to-value perspective?
> - What mental blocks need to be avoided?
> - Who answers these questions in your company?

1.2.5 Challenges Posed by the Ecological Framework Conditions

The beginning is the most important part of the work.
  Plato

1.2.5.1 Ecological Challenges

In this section, it is not possible to show all the changes in the ecological framework that companies today also have to take into account in the course of the digital transformation. It is enough to hear the following buzzwords to send shockwaves through the bodies of not only the climate defenders:

- Climate change in all parts of the world
- Melting of the glaciers and the ice surfaces at the poles
- Thawing of permafrost (with corresponding release of methane gas and pathogens that seemed already defeated)
- Warming and littering of the oceans
- Further increase in species extinction
- Increase in days with heat in the temperate zones
- Flooding disasters, on the one hand, acute lack of rain on the other
- Increasing deforestation of the rainforest (our "green lung" to gain agricultural land or mine mineral resources)
- Increase in fire disasters (e.g., in California, but also in Australia)
- Scarcity of resources (e.g., rare earths, but also of clean water, clean air and uncontaminated soil)
- ...

These problems are exacerbated by the fact that humanity is reaching the so-called **Earth Overshoot Day** earlier and earlier in the year. This day indicates when humanity has used as many resources as the earth can renew in an entire year. In 1987, this was 19 December—almost perfect! Consumption and regeneration were in balance. In 2020, however, Earth Overshoot Day already fell on 22 August. This means that in 2020, humanity had already used up the resources that nature can regenerate in 1 year in just under 8 months. As a result, in 2020 we would all be living as if we had not just one, but 1.6 earths at our disposal. In a few years, we will need two or 2.5 earths to enable our use of resources without loss of substance.

However, we only have one Earth!

The calculation of Earth Overshoot Day is based on the so-called **ecological footprint**. This is an important indicator of resource consumption and documents the impact of human activity on the environment. Here are just a few examples: Today, more carbon dioxide is emitted—man-made—than forests and oceans together can absorb. More fish are caught than would be necessary to maintain stocks. In addition, livestock farming produces more manure than the soils can absorb. The still growing world population further accelerates these processes.

▶ **Food for Thought**
These few key words alone are enough to make one thing clear:
There will be no more "business as usual" for many business models and the products and services they produce in the coming years.

▶ **Food for Thought**
- Would you have thought that the physical process triggered by a single **e-mail** produces the equivalent of one gram of carbon dioxide?
- Did you know that **one hour of video streaming** is as "environmentally friendly" as one hour of driving a car?
- Have you guessed that the billions of **search queries** we generate every day, as well as our **likes, shares, and comments**, have an environmental impact equivalent to a multitude of transatlantic flights?
- Have you heard that **Bitcoin farms** consume as much electricity as Switzerland?

The **large data centers of Internet service providers** alone consume almost 3% of the electricity in Europe today (cf. Thiel, 2020, p. N4). The French think tank *The Shift Project* assumes that the **use of digital technologies** causes around 4% of total global emissions. Incidentally, that is twice as much as civil aviation produces! The annual growth rate of emissions caused by digital technologies is at remarkable 9% (cf. The Shift Project, 2019).

1.2.5.2 Ecological Options and Constraints for Action

It is not without reason that the calls for a much more **sustainable orientation of our economy** are becoming louder and louder. The keywords here are, among others, **CO2 neutrality** and **decarbonization**. Decarbonization is about the further development or conversion of processes to consume as little carbon as possible. The corresponding demands are not only aimed at the highest possible **efficiency in energy use**, but also at **energy production** away from fossil fuels towards renewable energies (such as water, air, and sun).

In view of the challenges described above, who has already sharpened their focus? The **investors**! They are increasingly looking at the so-called **ESG criteria**. This abbreviation stands for environment, social, and governance. It is used by investors to assess how a company behaves in environmental, social, and corporate governance matters. **Institutional investors**—and thus also those for whom they make their money available—are no longer only concerned with profit when investing money, but increasingly also with sustainability. For this reason, they are already increasingly examining what social or ecological consequences are associated with an investment. In addition, it is analyzed whether the decision-makers act according to the rules of good corporate governance.

Even if there are still investors who concentrate on lucrative arms deals and exploitative business models at the expense of other countries: a **rethinking process** has at least begun. This is already evident today in the exit from investments and the sale of companies that, for example, focus primarily on the extraction and processing of fossil fuels. **Greenwashing** by companies that try to cloak themselves in green words rather than deeds will not be enough to meet the challenges. Moreover, such strategies will be exposed more easily and more quickly by a critical public. We should therefore take the expectations of both stakeholders—investors and the public—into account in our considerations of the digital transformation.

But other institutions also have to rethink in view of the challenges described. **Decision-makers in cities and municipalities** also have to gear their building activities more strongly to the emerging changes. Here, for example, the relevant implications for building construction must be taken into account. Black facades and large sealed, heat-absorbing surfaces should no longer be built. Garden design in both public and private areas should also take the changes into account. The creation of "low-maintenance" rock gardens should be avoided because they store the heat of the sunlight for a particularly long time. Instead, more (heat-resistant) plants should be used in public areas, and vertical gardening should be used to increase oxygen production and reduce fine dust pollution.

Will there soon be a need for an ordinance requiring all new buildings—including those of private individuals—to be equipped with **air conditioning** as standard? Furthermore, urban decision-makers are called upon to consider what implications the irreversible **trend towards home office** has for urban development. At the same time, it is necessary to consider how the decline of retail space in cities and a balanced **triad of living, working, and shopping** can be compensated for. At this point, creative companies are also called upon to use the opportunities that arise here for completely new business models, for example in vertical gardening.

Finally, changes are also demanded or at least accepted by consumers due to a **change in values** that is reinforced by Corona. Today, customers ask themselves whether they really need 19 (!) different fashion collections from one supplier every year—or whether they prefer a few favorite pieces that can last a few years. Do you know how many garments are bought in different countries—per year (cf. Diemand, 2021, p. 22)?

- USA: 62.3
- Great Britain: 52.4
- Germany: 46.9
- Japan: 38.6
- Worldwide: 18.7
- China: 17.4
- India: 15.3

Now we see a partial **shift from fast fashion to slow fashion**. Instead of an **addiction to maximization**, comprehensive studies show a **longing for deceleration of lifestyle and consumption** (cf. Ziems et al., 2020). In addition, there are first tendencies that consumers are willing to pay more for sustainably produced food.

In addition, more and more consumers are realizing that they can contribute to improvement through their own behavior—even if in a small way. Saving energy, accessing regionally and seasonally available products, reducing the throwaway mentality and making more use of public transport (if available and reliable) are important steps.

And maybe it does not always have to be an SUV to drive to shopping in the city center with! The **inconsistency of human behavior** is hardly as visible in any other object as it is with an SUV. More and more people in Germany are buying an SUV to drive to the organic supermarket with!

For **B2C companies**, in addition to the consequences of such a change in values, it is also important to consider which fashion can still be worn at all in increasingly hot summers—and which foods make the heat more bearable. Which aspects need to be considered in innovative brand management (cf. Kilian & Kreutzer, 2022)? Here, too, diverse opportunities for new business models open up.

2B companies have the raw materials, the parts as well as the machinery and equipment to better cope with the foreseeable challenges posed by climate change. In **agriculture**, the question arises as to which products can still be grown if climate change progresses and which can be grown for the first time (e.g., wine in Scandinavia). What does forest management have to look like in order to increase the resilience of forests?

> **Memory Box**
> The challenges caused by the ecological crisis can be exciting triggers for the development of innovative business models.
>
> In the future, answers to the questions raised here will be taken into account even more than today when **choosing a career**. Already now, **Generation Y**, i.e., those born between 1980 and the late 1990s, is referred to as **Generation**

(continued)

Why. Even if generalizing statements about an entire generation are difficult to make, this generation in particular is attributed with asking more critical **questions about the meaning or purpose of an business activity**, especially when choosing a career. At the same time, they are said to question hierarchies more strongly and to demand more self-determination. In addition to striving for a **work-life balance**, the **question of the meaning** of one's own actions is raised again and again. This means that consideration of ecological factors is also important with regard to attracting qualified workers.

His trend will become even stronger with the advent of the **Generation Greta**. These young people, politicized by the *Fridays for Future* movement, will also bring their values to bear in future elections and also in decisions about fields of study and employers.

Finally, it should be noted that the following **vision** was already adopted for the European Union in 2018: A prosperous, modern, competitive and at the same time also **climate-neutral economy** should be achieved by 2050.

Memory Box
All these aspects of the ecological challenges must be considered in the course of the digital transformation and in the development of digital excellence!

▶ **Food for Thought**

Last, but not least, each of us, wherever we stand and bear responsibility—privately and professionally—should be interested in an environment worth living in for the long term. For us and for future generations!

The **Nimby principle** will be accepted by fewer and fewer people in the long run. This is the acronym for "Not in my backyard." Its meaning is literally and can be called the **Florian's Principle**: "O Holy St. Florian, please spare my house, set fire to another one." Companies that act according to this principle care about the working conditions in their own production facilities, but ignore the inhumane conditions in sweatshops at suppliers.

Waste disposal companies like to communicate the **recycling rates** they have achieved. However, this only refers to the input into the recycling system, as it is determined immediately after the waste is sorted—regardless of what is actually recycled, incinerated, or exported. The Nimby principle is particularly visible in the plastic waste exports that end up on African beaches or in Asian developing countries. The main thing is having it out of sight—and out of mind!

When we condemn corporate action according to the **Nimby principle**, we should also look at ourselves. How often do we put up resistance against

electricity pylons, wind turbines and solar parks that are indispensable for the implementation of the adopted energy transition. We often also oppose development plans and bypasses—as long as they are within our own sight and hearing range and disturb us. If not, then we do not really care.
Consequently, we all carry a Nimby potential within us!

▶   **Food for Thought**
Today, we do not have to and cannot play off the shareholder perspective against the stakeholder perspective. Sustainable, profit-oriented corporate governance integrates important stakeholder interests into the process.

Think Box: Questions You Should Ask Yourself
- Which environmental challenges affect your company the most?
- What is your company's "contribution" to reaching Earth Overload Day early or late?
- What does your company's ecological footprint look like?
- What consequences does the call for CO2 neutrality and decarbonization have on your business model?
- How strongly is your company already focused on managing the ecological survival of our planet?
- Do your investors also already focus on the ESG criteria?
- What consequences do you as decision-makers in cities and municipalities draw from the ecological challenges?
- Has a change in consumer values already reached you?
- What options do you have in light of this change in values?
- Do you offer solutions for a deceleration of lifestyle and consumption?
- What changes, if any, are necessary so that representatives of Generation Y would like to work for you and with you?
- What expectations does consumers and (possible) employees of the Generation Greta have on you?
- How strongly does your company follow the Nimby principle?
- Who answers these questions for you?

1.2.6 Challenges Posed by the Legal Framework

Give me the strength to change the things I can change, to accept the things I cannot change, and the wisdom to distinguish between these two.
   Reinhold Niebuhr

The **entrepreneurial scope** is also described and limited by the **legal framework**. The general aim of the legal framework is to enforce **fair and often also**

public welfare-oriented corporate action. It goes without saying that not all those affected agree with the regulations that are made.

In shaping the digital transformation, the **globally oriented legal systems** must first be taken into account. Of particular importance here is the ***WTO*** (*World Trade Organization*). The task of the WTO as an international organization is to dismantle trade barriers of all kinds in order to promote international trade.

In addition, all companies operating in Europe must take into account the **goals and values of the EU**, which define the **normative framework for action**. The **goals of the European Union** are (EU, 2020a):

- "Promoting peace, European values and the well-being of its citizens,
- freedom, security and the rule of law without internal frontiers,
- sustainable development based on balanced economic growth and price stability, a competitive market economy with full employment, social progress and protection of the environment,
- curbing social injustice and discrimination,
- promotion of scientific and technological progress,
- strengthening economic, social and territorial cohesion and solidarity between member countries,
- respect for their rich cultural and linguistic diversity,
- establishment of an economic and monetary union whose currency is the Euro."

In addition, the EU member states have committed themselves to defining common values and implementing them in their respective countries. Thus, the EU strives for a society "... in which inclusion, tolerance, the rule of law, solidarity and non-discrimination are self-evident" (EU, 2020a). The **common EU values** described below shape or should shape the European lifestyle (EU, 2020a):

- **"Human dignity**
  Human dignity is inviolable. It must be respected and protected. It forms the very foundation of fundamental rights.
- **Freedom**
  Freedom of movement allows citizens to travel and choose their place of residence within the EU. Personal freedoms such as respect for private life, freedom of thought, freedom of religion, freedom of assembly, freedom of expression and freedom of information are protected by the EU Charter of Fundamental Rights.
- **Democracy**
  The functioning of the Union is based on representative democracy. As a European citizen, you also enjoy certain political rights. Every adult EU citizen has the right to vote and to stand as a candidate in elections to the European Parliament. He or she can stand for election both in the country of residence and in the country of origin.
- **Equality**
  Equality is about equal rights before the law for all citizens. Gender equality is part of all EU policies and the basis of European integration. It applies to all areas.

The principle of equal pay for equal work was agreed by contract as early as 1957. While equality is not yet fully realized, the EU has made significant progress.
- **Rule of law**
  The EU is based on the rule of law. All its activities are based on treaties agreed voluntarily and democratically by its member countries. Law and justice are upheld by an independent judiciary. The member states have delegated the power of last resort to the European Court of Justice. Its judgements must be respected by all.
- **Human rights**
  Human rights are guaranteed by the Charter of Fundamental Rights of the European Union. These include the right to freedom from discrimination based on sex, racial or ethnic origin, religion or belief, disability, age or sexual orientation, and the right to the protection of personal data or access to justice."

These **common EU values**, which, however, do not shape political action in all EU countries, must also be taken into account in the course of the digital transformation and the development of new business models. However, the following also applies here (Günther, 2017, p. 12):

"Those who call for the digitization of the economy, schools and universities should also think about new instruments of regulatory policy in a digitized world. Rules that were once written to prevent monopolies and price-fixing by steel barons and paper manufacturers are worth as much in the Internet age as a slide rule and a steno pad."

At the EU level, attempts are now being made to put a stop to the dominance of the established players in digital services through the ***Digital Service Act***. In the digital markets, the ***Digital Market Act*** is supposed to define rules to curb the exploitation of a dominant position. It remains to be seen how these regulations will prove themselves in practice (cf. EU, 2020b).

In line with these overarching goals and values of the European Union, companies operating in Europe must take into account the specific **EU legislation**. This includes the EU treaties, regulations, and directives, which have varying degrees of impact on the design of business models. One set of regulations that is particularly important for all companies active in Europe is the **General Data Protection Regulation** (GDPR; cf. Moos et al., 2020). This is an EU regulation that uniformly defines rules for the processing of personal data by private and public institutions throughout the EU. The GDPR has formed the **common data protection framework** in the European Union since 25 May 2018. By restricting the use of data, it intervenes particularly intensively in the possible design of business models.

▶ **Food for Thought**
There are still many responsible parties—especially in politics—who consider the **GDPR** to be the best data protection law in the world. However, this piece of legislation does not prevent a massive outflow of personal data into foreign systems—especially in the USA and China—every day. At the same time, many attractive fields of use are prohibited for companies based in Europe!

In addition, the tendency to realize more and more company processes in **cloud solutions** leads to the fact that sensitive company data is also stored on servers of the software providers—often outside the EU. There, this data is subject to the legal system of the respective home countries and thus often also to the governments there and their access.

In this context, many overlook what was already described in 2009 as the **law of disproportionate information**: "The more information there is about a consumer or a decision-maker or a company, the more selectively offers can be placed. This means: we need more information about prospects and customers in order to provide them with less, but more relevant information" (Kreutzer, 2009, p. 69). Incidentally, the use of less and more relevant content—online and offline—also contributes to sustainability because less promotional material needs to be used to attract customers.

The **less data** that can be used as a basis for the development of business models, but also for the concrete development of offers and market-oriented communication, the fuzzier the corresponding content will be. As a result, more must be developed, more must be presented and more must be communicated in order to achieve the company's goals with lower marketing success and higher scattering losses in communication. This is the opposite of efficient, resource-saving action!

At the same time, we must ensure that **legal regulations** in other areas do not become a corset that makes agile, dynamic action impossible. How did *Werner Wenning*, former CEO and head of the supervisory board of *Bayer* put it so aptly (Wenning, 2020, p. 23)?

"While we are still filling out the approval documents, they have already built the factory in Silicon Valley."

The construction of the *Tesla* Gigafactory in Brandenburg in 2020/2021 shows that we in Germany can also do things differently—especially if the politicians want it!

▶ **Personal Reading Tip**
Yuval Noah Harari, Homo Deus: A Brief History of Tomorrow

Think Box: Questions You Should Ask Yourself
- What contribution can your company and your business model make in achieving the goals of the European Union?
- What are the implications of the *Digital Service Act* for your company?
- What are the implications of the *Digital Market Act*?
- What data-related leeway is still available as a result of the General Data Protection Regulation?

(continued)

- What are the implications of the law of disproportionate information for your business?
- Who is responsible when it comes to answering these questions?

Literature

Scott D. Anthony, Viguerie, S. P., Schwartz, E. I., & van Landeghem, J. (2018). *2018 corporate longevity forecast: Creative destruction is accelerating.* Accessed 14.8.2020, from https://www.innosight.com/insight/creative-destruction/

Bernardy, J. (2014). *Aufmerksamkeit als Kapital, Formen des mentalen Kapitalismus.* Tectum.

Bertelsmann Stiftung. (2020). *Was Chinas Industriepolitik für die deutsche Wirtschaft bedeutet, Szenarien für "Made in China 2025", am Beispiel des deutschen Maschinenbaus.* Accessed 4.1.2021, from https://www.bertelsmann-stiftung.de/de/publikationen/publikation/did/was-chinas-industriepolitik-fuer-die-deutsche-wirtschaft-bedeutet

BPB. (2019). *EU – USA – China: Bevölkerungsentwicklung.* Accessed 12.8.2020, from https://www.bpb.de/nachschlagen/zahlen-und-fakten/europa/135821/bevoelkerungsentwicklung

Braun, M. (2019). *VUCA – Ein neues Paradigma in der Arbeitsgestaltung?* Fraunhofer-Institut für Arbeitswirtschaft und Organisation.

Brynjolfsson, E., & McAfee, A. (2018). *The second machine age: Wie die nächste digitale Revolution unser aller Leben verändern wird.* Plassen Verlag.

Bünte, C. (2020). *Die chinesische KI-Revolution, Konsumverhalten, Marketing und Handel: Wie China mit Künstlicher Intelligenz die Wirtschaftswelt verändert.* Springer Gabler.

Chatzky, A., & McBride, J. (2021). *China's massive belt and road initiative.* Accessed 19.7.2021, from https://www.cfr.org/backgrounder/chinas-massive-belt-and-road-initiative

China Embassy. (2020). *China legt weiteren Entwicklungsverlauf fest.* Accessed 31.12.2020, from http://de.china-embassy.org/det/zgtphsz/t1827003.htm

Chui, M., Löffler, M., & Roberts, R. (2010). *The Internet of things. McKinsey Quarterly,* 2/2010. Accessed 1.10.2020, from https://www.mckinsey.com/industries/technology-media-and-telecommunications/our-insights/the-Internet of things

Davenport, T. H., & Beck, J. C. (2001). *The attention economy. Understanding the new currency of business.* Boston.

Destatis. (2020). *Bevölkerungsvorausberechnung für Deutschland.* Accessed 12.8.2020, from https://service.destatis.de/bevoelkerungspyramide/index.html

Diemand, S. (2021). Nicht Jacke wie Hose. *Frankfurter Allgemeine Zeitung,* 12.7.2021, p. 22.

Economist. (2019). *The steam has gone out of globalisation.* Accessed 13.8.2020, from https://www.economist.com/leaders/2019/01/24/the-steam-has-gone-out-of-globalisation

EU. (2020a). *Die EU – kurz gefasst.* Accessed 30.9.2020, from https://europa.eu/european-union/about-eu/eu-in-brief_de

EU. (2020b). *The Digital Services Act package.* Accessed 17.12.2020, from https://ec.europa.eu/digital-single-market/en/digital-services-act-package

Firouzi, F., Chakrabarty, K., & Nassif, S. (Eds.). (2020). *Intelligent Internet of things: From device to fog and cloud.* Springer.

Flynn, J. R. (2012). *Are we getting smarter?: Rising IQ in the twenty-first century,* Cambridge.

Generali. (2021). *Gesund leben und dafür belohnt werden.* Accessed 2.1.2021, from https://www.generalivitality.com/de/de

Günther, M. (2017). Die Politik muss Amazon bremsen. *Frankfurter Allgemeine Sonntagszeitung,* 15.10.2017, p. 12.

Harari, Y. N. (2018). *Homo Deus, Eine Geschichte von Morgen.* Beck.

IFTTT. (2021). *Do more with the things you love.* Accessed 3.1.2021, from https://ifttt.com/
Kahle, T. (2020). Voice-Marketing – Produkte und Services werden dialogfähig. In M. Stumpf (Ed.), *Die 10 wichtigsten Zukunftsthemen im Marketing* (2nd ed., pp. 107–129). Haufe.
Kilian, K., & Kreutzer, R. (2022). *Digitale Markenführung, Digital Branding in Zeiten divergierender Märkte.* Springer Gabler.
Kreutzer, R. (2009). *Praxisorientiertes Dialog-Marketing, Konzepte – Instrumente – Fallbeispiele.* Gabler.
Kreutzer, R. (2020a). *Die digitale Verführung, Warum wir uns auch mit den Schattenseiten moderner Entwicklungen beschäftigen sollten.* Springer Gabler.
Kreutzer, R. (2020b). *Studie zum Wissensstand von Master-Studenten zu Beginn des Master-Studiums an der Berlin School of Economics and Law/HWR im Wintersemester 2019/2020.* Berlin (unveröffentlichtes Manuskript).
Kreutzer, R. (2021). *Kundendialog online und offline, Das große 1x1 der Kundengewinnung, Kundenbindung und Kundenrückgewinnung.* Springer Gabler.
Kreutzer, R., & Land, K.-H. (2016). *Digitaler Darwinismus – Der stille Angriff auf Ihr Geschäftsmodell und Ihre Marke* (2nd ed.). Springer Gabler.
Kreutzer, R., & Sirrenberg, M. (2019). *Künstliche Intelligenz – Grundlagen, Use-cases, Methoden für die unternehmenseigene KI-Journey.* Springer Gabler.
Kreutzer, R., & Vousoghi, D. (2020). *Voice-marketing, Der Siegeszug der digitalen Assistenten.* Springer Gabler.
Kroeber-Riel, W., & Gröppel-Klein, A. (2013). *Konsumentenverhalten* (10th ed.). Vahlen.
Kruger, J., & Dunning, D. (1999). Unskilled and unaware of it: How difficulties in recognizing one's own incompetence lead to inflated self-assessments. *Journal of Personality and Social Psychologie, 77*(6), 1121–1134.
Lang, J. (2020). Chinas neue Wirtschaftsstrategie ist ein Warnsignal. *Frankfurter Allgemeine Zeitung,* 23.12.2020, p. 18.
Lobe, A. (2019). Gebaute Filterblasen. *Frankfurter Allgemeine Sonntagszeitung,* 3.2.2019, p. 39.
Lynn, R., & Harvey, J. (2008). The decline of the world's IQ. *Intelligence, 36*(2), 112–120.
Milano, D. (2019). *No, you don't have the attention span of a goldfish.* Accessed 11.8.2020, from https://www.ceros.com/originals/no-dont-attention-span-goldfish/
Moore, G. E. (1965). Cramming more components onto integrated circuits. *Electronics,* Vol. 38, Nr. 8, pp.114-117.
Moos, F., Schefzig, J., & Arning, M. A. (Eds.). (2020). *Praxishandbuch DSGVO.* Deutscher Fachverlag.
Schlotter, L., & Hubert, P. (2020). *Generation Z – Personalmanagement und Führung, 21 Tools für Entscheider.* Springer Gabler.
Seemann, M., & Kreil, M. (2017). *Digitaler Tribalismus und Fake News.* Von: Accessed 1.8.2020, from http://www.ctrl-verlust.net/digitaler-tribalismus-und-Fake News/
Solis, B. (2012). *The end of business as usual. Rewire the way you work to succeed in the consumer revolution.* Wiley.
The Shift Project. (2019). *"Climate crisis: the unsustainable use of online video": Our new report on the environmental impact of ICT.* Accessed 25.11.2020, from https://theshiftproject.org/en/article/unsustainable-use-online-video/
Thiel, T. (2020). Ein Katalysator für das Internet. *Frankfurter Allgemeine Zeitung,* 7.10.2020, p. N4.
Wenning, W. (2020). Kein Manager muss mehr als zehn Millionen verdienen. *Frankfurter Allgemeine Sonntagszeitung,* 26.4.2020, p. 23.
Wiesner, K. A. (2016). *Faires management und marketing.* De Gruyter/Oldenburg.
Ziems, D., Ebenfeld, T., & Winkler, R. (2020). *Global Viral Change, Auswirkungen von Corona auf Gesellschaft.* Konsum und Marketing in der globalen Kultur.

Analysis and Design of a Digital Business Performance

2

This chapter shows which **informational foundations** need to be gained in advance of the analysis of a digital business performance and which **tools** can be used for this purpose. In addition, the importance of **storytelling** in order to take the entire organization along on the journey of digital transformation is made clear. Finally, an innovative concept for **analyzing digital business performance** is presented and explained in detail so that every company can use this analysis independently.

2.1 Tools to Prepare the Analysis of Digital Business Performance

The best way to predict the future is to invent it.
Alan Curtis Kay

When gathering information, beware of **pseudo-empiricism**—where you take your partial view of the world for the whole truth. Above all, avoid the **NOMS method**. NOMS stands for **National One Man Sample**. Here, one person, preferably the son or daughter (especially in the case of online offers, with regard to influencers and social media), alternatively also the spouse of the gods, or also the boss or the boss's wife, has said something, which is then regarded as irrefutable knowledge and on which decisions are based. In the case of bosses, we also speak of the **HIPPO syndrome**. HIPPO is an acronym for "Highest Paid Person's Option."

Every individual who goes about things in this way is convinced that the world is exactly like this or like that! Do not believe it! I know you never do! Then you will be happy to watch out for others, so that they too refrain from the NOMS method, avoid the HIPPO syndrome and do not pull you up on the slippery slope!

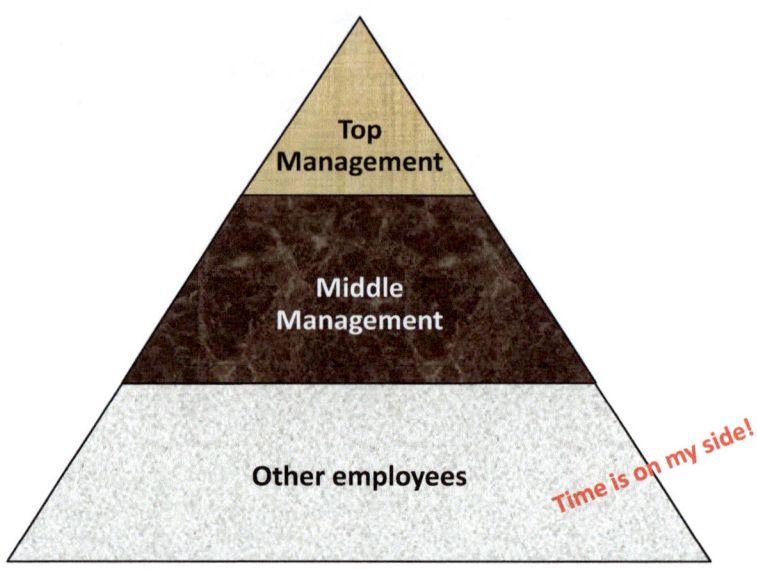

Fig. 2.1 Challenge: empowerment of employees

2.1.1 Storytelling as an Attunement to the Digital Transformation

There's always room for a story that can transport people to another place.
  J.K. Rowling

The orientation of a company and a business model to the digital age requires a **massive rethink** and **change of direction** in established companies. Massive **resistance** can often be observed here, which can be localized above all in **middle management**. Why is it middle management that most stubbornly opposes the necessary changes? The managers working there often have the most to lose: status, income, personal assistance, large team, influence, company car, etc. Often, however, these people—compared to younger employees—do not have the necessary qualifications (at first!) to actively shape the change themselves.

This is often referred to as the **strategic clay layer**, which interrupts the flow of information from "top down" as well as from "bottom up" (cf. Fig. 2.1). Thus, many ideas and suggestions from the bottom of the corporate pyramid are lost because such suggestions are not passed on from middle management to top management. The information disappears in entrenched hierarchical structures. Similarly, impulses from top management can seep into the hierarchy because they are ignored, boycotted, or even delayed by middle management. This is why we also speak of the **strategic paralysis layer**.

Top management is often much more open to change, or simply has to be. After all, that is what top management is paid for! On the one hand, members of top management have often already reached the zenith of their professional development. On the other hand, even failure and leaving the organization is literally "gold-plated" for them through "golden handshakes" and other things. From such a position, it is much easier to be courageous. Courage, a willingness to innovate and creative power are required at the top of the company in particular—but are nevertheless not always sufficiently present.

The **other employees** in the organization often have less status, income etc. to lose. Or they are only at the beginning of their own career, which is why many professional opportunities still open up to them—provided they have the appropriate qualifications. Especially for motivated and committed employees, changes in the company offer interesting opportunities to emphatically demonstrate their own ability and willingness to perform. Within the framework of change processes, new positions are created and positions previously occupied by other people become vacant! This gives courage for "attacks"—and for committed work in the course of the change process. After all, many young or young-at-heart people say to themselves:

"If it doesn't work out in this company, I'll look for a new employer or start my own company. I am young and have the courage to take risks! Time is on my side!"

▶ **Storytelling** In view of this initial situation, it is indispensable that not only the C-level or the top management, but also the middle management first understands and then internalizes the **necessity of a digital transformation**. For this—according to my own experience—the relevant decision-makers first have to be "softened up" a bit. In a consulting project I supervised, it was always said so nicely:

"We have to massage that into the board of directors!"

A nice image, because a certain **"loving forcefulness"** is necessary in the **persuasion work** that has to be done here. Motto: **never give up!**

To win the good arguments (to avoid the term "ammunition") necessary for the tough process of convincing a digital transformation, you can and should use the tools described below. The flanking methods to be used for the change management required here on the psychological side will be discussed in Chap. 4.

At this point, we are primarily concerned with **facts and figures** as the basis for a convincing **narrative for your storytelling**. These two terms are used regularly in the context of digital transformation—and rightly so. But what exactly do they mean? **Narrative** refers to a **meaningful story** that simultaneously conveys certain values and emotions. It is intended to influence the way the listeners of this narrative perceive the world—in this case, above all, the corporate context (cf. Etzold, 2018, pp. 101–165).

Particularly well-known **narratives** are the "myth from rags to riches" as well as "from the garage to the leading IT corporation" (*Bill Hewlett* and *Dave Packard* started in *Packard's* garage). There are also such narratives from the digital age, such as "from a moderately successful English teacher to the founder of one of the world's most successful corporations" (*Jack Ma* with *Alibaba* in China).

A nice narrative and at the same time a **founding myth** is provided by *Airbnb*. According to this, in October 2007, *Brian Chesky, Joe Gebbia* and *Nathan Blecharczyk* had an idea to earn the money to rent their three-bedroom flat in San Francisco. During a design conference, when the hotels in the city were already fully booked, they offered three air mattresses as places to sleep: the idea for *Airbnb* was born—and the company name right along with it, consisting of the combination of "Airbed" for air mattress and "BNB" for "Bed and Breakfast."

> **Memory Box**
> If you want to "touch" people with your stories, you must not stop at facts figures. These are indispensable as a foundation for your story. However, you need to use them in **pictorial narratives** that start movies in your listeners heads and trigger positive emotions. You will only succeed in the rarest cases with an Excel sheet projected on the wall!

▶ **Food for Thought**
"Humans are not ideally set up to understand logic. They are ideally set up to understand stories" (Shank, 2021).

What can, what should such narratives achieve? First of all, narratives can **encourage** people to believe in their own abilities and possibilities (motto: **the sky is the limit!**). An important aspect in this context is the so-called **self-efficacy**. This refers to a person's expectation that he or she can successfully carry out desired actions on the basis of his or her own abilities and competencies. People who believe that they can make a difference and achieve ambitious goals have a high **self-efficacy expectation**.

Self-efficacy expectations must be systematically promoted through narratives. In their development, people and the organizations in which they work are no longer victims of their environment, but the result of their own actions. It is not circumstances, luck, coincidence, and fate that determine one's career, but one's own powerful actions. In addition, **narratives**—well told—can also provide a certain **orientation in stormy times**, which have already dawned for most companies in the VUCA world (cf. Chap. 1).

▶ **Food for Thought**
You are today what you thought yesterday.
What you think today, you will be tomorrow.
Buddha

Narratives represent the core of so-called storytelling (cf. also Storr, 2019; Pyczak, 2018). **Storytelling** means nothing other than telling stories. It is about conveying explicit knowledge and implicit knowledge through narratives by means of certain leitmotifs, symbols, metaphors, etc. Both forms of knowledge are indispensable for a transformation process. **Explicit knowledge** is easily communicated through language. Here we also speak of methodical or specific knowledge, of mind knowledge or embrained knowledge. This is about facts and figures. Words and numbers are sufficient for its transmission. Because of its formalization, explicit knowledge can be easily stored, processed in a variety of ways and passed on in a variety of media.

This possibility of simple storage, processing and transmission does not exist with implicit knowledge. **Implicit knowledge**—also tacit knowledge, experiential knowledge, or embodied knowledge—arises through routines and a skill set that is gained through diverse experiences. It is reflected in memories, beliefs, and values. This implicit knowledge refers to the abilities of a person or a company of which the bearers of this tacit knowledge are often not aware and which is also difficult to express in language. As a result, tacit knowledge eludes formal linguistic expression. Implicit knowledge is usually considered to be action-bound. This means that it primarily becomes visible and tangible in action. Simple examples of tacit knowledge are running, cycling, and swimming. It is extremely easy if you can do it—but difficult to explain it to someone who would like to learn it. Here it is a case of "being able to do it without being able to say exactly how!"

Perhaps the following image will help with your own **personal persuasion**. On a three-lane motorway, we find on the left—in the fast lane—the **start-ups**. They use the latest vehicles, like to flash their lights and overtake on the right when others hinder their speedy progress. Mottos: "Done is better than perfect!" "Move fast and break things!" "The riskiest thing is to take no risks!" "Act, don't talk!" In the middle of the motorway are the **incumbents**. They are also making progress, but at a much slower speed. After all, they do not always drive the latest models, but they have already covered several 100,000 km and gained a lot of experience in mastering marathon runs. Motto: "There's power in rest!" And who is on the right lane—sometimes even on the hard shoulder? The **state** and far too many of its **institutions**, which unfortunately have still not recognized the signs of the times. Motto: "It used to work that way!"

Which lane do we want to drive in?

Memory Box

A particular **challenge of storytelling** is not only to make explicit knowledge easy to understand and remember. Rather, it is also the implicit knowledge that has to be conveyed through corresponding stories—and ideally to be penetrated through daily action and offered as a model for imitation learning! It is not least against this backdrop that **top executives** play such an important role as **role models**, especially in the change process (cf. Chap. 4).

Motto: **Walk the talk!** Words must be followed by deeds.

The necessary words can be conveyed through **townhall meetings** in which managers address all employees. In addition, narratives about the central projects and the results already achieved belong as a **standard item on the agenda** of all relevant meetings ... and then it is also important to act accordingly!

(continued)

Why are these narratives so important in today's world? We are all in a phase of **information overload**: we receive dozens of newsletters with relevant content every day. *Google* searches often offer not only thousands, but even hundreds of thousands of hits. Social media fires many hundreds or thousands of posts, status updates and stories into our field of vision every day that we "must not" miss (keyword "FOMO effect," see Sect. 1.2.3.2).

Every day we could attend several webinars and listen to podcasts for 90 hours a day. *Amazon Prime, Maxdome, Netflix, Spotify* & Co. additionally offer us an inexhaustible number of music and videos, all of which want to be consumed by us. Finally, we often even do not have to pay more for a more intensive use of them due to their flat rate payment model. Then there are also the classical media to keep us informed comprehensively and seriously through competently prepared content. Can we manage that? No.

Nevertheless, as a sender, we want to get through to the recipient with our information. This is where storytelling comes into play. We have to tell a story in a lively, vivid, and comprehensible way in order to get the **attention** and **concentration** of other people. In addition, what we say should **stick in the memory** for as long as possible in order to influence thinking and action. The story used for this can be based on facts and/or contain fictional elements. It is exciting that even complex knowledge can be passed on via stories—as has been proven over thousands of years.

For this purpose, storytelling can create a **meta-level** in order to convey an **overarching message**. This should certainly evoke stronger emotions such as fear, anger, joy, desire, etc. in the listeners. After all, such emotions contribute to better memorization of the content. If you are particularly courageous as a storyteller, you can also incorporate fables and anecdotes into your story and let the quintessence of an overriding wisdom or a pithy punchline flow into it. This is the way to be remembered. A **convincing performance** in the presentation of the story is part of it.

▶ **Storytelling** Here is an example from the **opening ceremony of an innovation center** of a health insurance company, where I was allowed to give a keynote speech. Before me, the CEO spoke to his executives. He stood in front of his team and first took off his jacket and then his tie. When he also took off his shirt, the team, most of whom were dressed in dark clothes and tie, became a little quiet. A T-shirt in the colors of the company was revealed under the shirt.

This "strip" was accompanied by the following words: "Ladies and gentlemen, when you go to our innovation center, you take off all insignia of your power and status! It's no longer about them. Rather, it is about who comes here with the best ideas and the boldest proposals—regardless of where he or she stands in the corporate hierarchy. That's the only way we can innovate in these turbulent times."

Although this ceremony took place several years ago, it has remained in my fondest memory—and I am sure in the memory of the participating executives as well. In this way—through words and deeds—not only role expectations can be defined. Life experiences can also be conveyed, important knowledge can be passed on and ideas for problem solving can be pointed out. Finally, certain traditions, norms, and values can be conveyed subliminally—and ideally also courage and the willingness to become active oneself (trusting in one's own self-efficacy).

What can an **anecdote** look like in order to motivate as many people as possible to perform at their best even in the phase of a crisis? An anecdote can take the form of a short, witty and/or funny description of a remarkable effort. For example, one could think of the commitment of the IT department, which, during the first Corona-related shutdown in March 2020, made it possible for 500 employees to become completely productive in the home office after 48 h by working two all-nighters with 123 cups of coffee, 27 pizzas and 10 *Aspirin*. Also nice are reports of how dedicated procurement staff at an airport in Shanghai secured important materials early to avoid a shutdown of the production process . . .

▶ **Storytelling** In an **international consulting project** I accompanied, the project team showed its commitment to concept development by visualizing to the board of directors that they had conducted workshops with clients on two continents, in eight countries, 17 cities with 65 clients and experts. This involved 174 h on planes and 312 h in meetings, consuming 1176 cups of coffee!

Great visions and inspiring stories that capture our attention usually start with "Just suppose . . ." or "Imagine . . ." This sets up an exciting **context** for the audience. In this way, we can create powerful images in the mind. An exciting story also needs turning points—and heroes!

Let your leaders and staff become heroes who successfully master turning points! To do this, it is important that your stories link **causes and effects**—to make clear what is possible when . . . By doing this, you increase the **belief in self-efficacy**. Then, in your story, you tell what results your company achieves after it has built up a profound AI competence and mastered the digital transformation. You tell how, for example, the use of chatbots and digital voice assistants like *Alexa* led more customers to your website and to order. As a result, you were able to . . .

> **Memory Box**
> **If you want to blow to the attack, then rely on timpani, tuba, and trumpet—and not on the flute or harp. Otherwise one will not hear the signal to set off—and it is easier to overhear this signal—consciously.**
>
> **After all, if you bang on the timpani, no one can say they did not hear it.**
>
> In everything we communicate on the **way to achieving digital excellence**, it is important that our messages are not only understood by the recipients, but also internalized. You can use the **10 × 10 × 10 rule** for this:

(continued)

> **Say something 10 times in 10 different ways so that your teams remember 10%!**
> If you provide relevant background information—over and over again—and at the same time convey clear ideas of where the journey should go, as a good communicator, you will avoid panic or hype in equal measure. In addition, your primary task is not only to motivate but also to empower your staff at the different levels for implementation (cf. Chaps. 3 and 4).
>
> The tools described below will primarily provide you with the explicit knowledge you need to back up your **digital transformation stories** with information. You will receive further impulses for conveying implicit knowledge in Chap. 4.

▶ **Food for Thought**
When it comes to storytelling, there is one thing you should avoid: Dishonesty and lack of sincerity. That would be disrespectful to your audience! That is why storytelling also includes clearly pointing out the expected frictions and painful cuts. **Clarity** is required here! After all, everyone in your team expects that these will also occur.

I use the term **growing-pain** for this—unpleasant, but indispensable if you want to grow—as a human being and as a company!

▶ **Personal Reading Tip**
Bitkom *(2020): Last Call: Germany!—The Bitkom Digital Strategy 2025*.
Here you will find wonderful visions—how these visions could become reality if we take action now!

> **Think Box: Questions You Should Ask Yourself**
> - How often do you use the NOMS method yourself—or have you noticed it being used by others?
> - Does your company use the HIPPO method?
> - How pronounced is the strategic clay layer in your company?
> - Where can this clay layer be localized, who are the central protagonists?
> - Is such behavior accepted, tolerated and/or even encouraged in your company?
> - Are there ideas and concepts on how to break through the strategic clay layer?
> - Do you use townhall meetings on a regular basis?

(continued)

- Do you have a storyteller on board who can tell a powerful vision in a motivating way?
- Is this person perhaps even at the top management level—or is at least involved by them in the storytelling process?
- What measures can help to increase self-efficacy?
- What narratives can your company use?
- Which anecdotes can help to identify implicit knowledge as well?
- Do you use the 10 × 10 × 10 rule to get through with your content?
- Is there clarity in your communication—even with uncomfortable truths?
- Who is responsible for storytelling in your company?

2.1.2 Digital Gap Analysis

Good hockey players go where the puck will be—not where it is now!

A first indispensable method to identify the urgency of a digital transformation for your own company is the **digital gap analysis**. This analysis helps you to identify the **threat potential in your industry**. To do this, you can first of all—as shown in Fig. 2.2—draw the potential for change into a frame. This potential is growing exponentially in your industry due to increasing digitalization. The frame is spanned by the time axis and the scope of the expected changes. Now we have to bear in mind that most companies only use a small part of the available (new) **possibilities**.

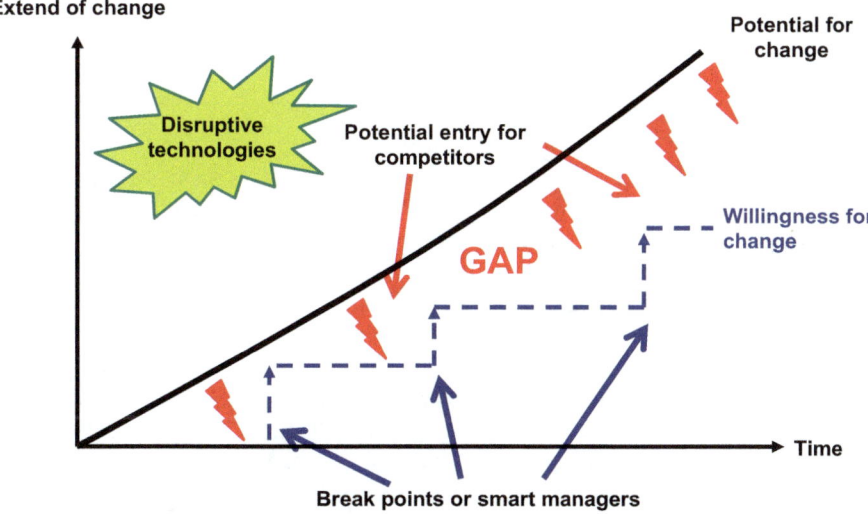

Fig. 2.2 Digital gap analysis

Perhaps in your company, too, the existing possibilities are not or only partially exhausted. At least you know corresponding companies where the managers are often only prepared to make changes when crises have already occurred. These are marked by the **break points** in Fig. 2.2. Or there are clever managers like you in charge who proactively initiate change processes even before crisis symptoms become dominant! But even in this case, those responsible usually only partially utilize the existing potential for change in the course of their strategic realignment of the company. This is made visible by the gap in Fig. 2.2!

What is the consequence if the space of possibilities is not or only partially exploited? The remaining **gap** between the readiness for change in the respective company and the actual possibilities for action is the **flight path for (new) competitors**. This means that only by doing nothing or not doing enough do companies invite the competition to attack!

> **Memory Box**
> **By doing nothing or not doing enough, the established companies invite competitors to attack!**
>
> Established competitors are threatened by companies that optimally align their own business model with the new opportunities for action. These are mainly **start-ups** that set out to attack completely unencumbered by their own history and often also unaware of the customs of an industry—often also in (conscious) disregard of legal regulations. After all, most start-ups do not come from the industry they are attacking. Start-ups can also make full use of all (new) technological possibilities because they do not have to take **legacy systems** into account. Finally, new applications—e.g., voice control, mobile data access or AI—cannot simply be connected to an "old" IT system in establish companies (see Sect. 3.4.1).

> **Memory Box**
> **Legacy systems** is a term for old systems in IT applications that have been in use in a company for many years or decades. Legacy means inheritance, bequest, estate, and also old burden in this context.
>
> A particular danger for established companies comes from so-called **disruptive technologies**. Such technologies destroy previously known development processes and business logics. As a result, they can make established business concepts partially redundant or even smash them. Here we can think of parts of the stationary retail trade, travel agencies, CD/DVD production and many print media. For example, the last *IKEA* catalogue was printed in 2020—in the 70th year of its publication. At its peak, the *IKEA* catalogue had a print run of around 200 million copies. It was published in 69 versions and
>
> (continued)

32 languages in over 50 countries. The print run is said to have been higher than that of the Bible and the Koran.

In start-ups, the use of innovative technologies is not hindered by **hierarchical organizational structures, rigid processes** (e.g., approval procedures) or innovative and, above all, rapid market development (keyword "time-to-value"). Often there is not even a lack of **financial strength**!

The aspects underlying Fig. 2.2 are described by **MarTec's law**. "MarTec" here stands for "Marketing Technology" (cf. Brinker, 2013). This "law" describes the connection between the speed of technological change and the willingness of companies to change. However, many companies are not able to keep up with the exponential growth of opportunities caused by technological change. The speed of change management tends to run logarithmically and thus much slower in established companies. The resulting gap is shown in Fig. 2.2.

One risk of this gap has already been described: competitors use new technologies faster and/or more comprehensively. However, there is a second risk. In many areas, it can be observed that end customers—especially consumers—pick up new technologies faster than companies. This can change customer expectations in a direction that established companies can no longer fulfil. The consequence: **digital Darwinism** (see Sect. 1.1)!

▶ **Food for Thought**

I recommend that every company assemble a **team of innovative, committed, and creative employees** (not necessarily a question of age!) who have one task to fulfil:

Develop a business model that could disrupt its own existing business model.

You say: "Too dangerous?" Then I retort:

If you don't create the thing that kills you, somebody else will!

By setting such a task, you would identify within your company—ideally before others—which areas of your business model would be particularly easy to attack.

We have to be clear about one thing. Competitors will first pounce on the so-called "low hanging fruits" that can be harvested from "our" garden without much effort. Only if we recognize these potential weak points ourselves at an early stage can we launch an appropriate digitalization—before we are decisively and perhaps even devastatingly attacked!

The example of the application of **digital gap analysis for the retail sector** shows the opportunities and risks at the same time (cf. Fig. 2.3). Due to the **hesitant or lack of willingness** to change on the part of established companies, many classic mail-order companies and traditional retailers have already disappeared from the market in the meantime—or they are in a

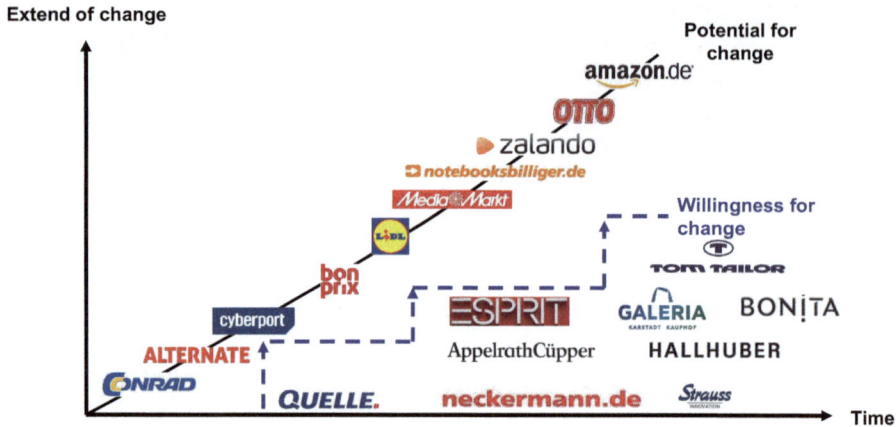

Fig. 2.3 Digital gap analysis—example retailer

difficult transformation process. The German mail-order companies *Neckermann* and *Quelle* have disappeared from the market. *Quelle*—almost forgotten—was once Europe's largest mail-order company! Retail companies like *Appelrath Cüpper, Bonita, Esprit, Galeria Karstadt Kaufhof, Hallhuber, Tom Tailor* and many more are in a thorough transformation process and/or in insolvency proceedings—the outcome is uncertain!

How did that happen? Too many **retailers** defined their business model too narrowly and focused primarily on the catalogue or the stationary shop. Those who operated in this way did not have to worry about online opportunities—and thus missed important information and/or sales channels to the customer (Internet). In addition, the companies operating in this way could not offer certain customer benefits. These include lower prices, but above all speed, flexibility, and consequently convenience. Due to the variety of offers, customers have the power to mercilessly punish this inability.

Here, too, the following applies: by consistently not doing enough or not doing anything at all, the established companies have created the gap that **newcomers** like *Alternate, Amazon, Cyperport, notebooksbillger,* and *Zalando* have filled with innovative, digital business ideas. At the same time, Fig. 2.3 also shows, in ascending order, the companies that have successfully undergone a transformation process and are now among the **top-ten online retailers** in Germany (cf. Statista, 2019, p. 2). These are *Conrad, BonPrix, Lidl, MediaMarkt,* and *Otto*.

> **Memory Box**
> In much of the turmoil we have seen in the retail sector, the Corona 2020 pandemic was only the **fire accelerant** and not the core of the problem!
> A **digital gap analysis** should be carried out regularly for your own company. This involves answering the question of which players in your industry are challenging your business model in the short, medium, or long term. Today, there is practically no industry that start-ups cannot successfully penetrate. Even in the highly regulated industry of financial service providers and in the legal sector, more and more new companies are establishing themselves. This is where the so-called **FinTechs** are operating; the term combines the words financial service provider and technology. Such start-ups build offerings based on the latest technologies and thereby achieve decisive competitive advantages. Examples in the financial sector are companies such as *Deposit Solutions*, *Klarna*, *Monzo*, *N26*, *Revolut*, *Trade Republic*, and *Wealthsimple*. In the insurance industry, start-ups are referred to as **InsurTechs** (e.g., *Hypoport*).

▶ **Storytelling** In recent years, I have often given **talks on digital Darwinism** to board members and managing directors of financial service providers. Here I have often succeeded in triggering **thoughtfulness** and **consternation** about what is coming—regardless of whether we want it or not.

But I have also experienced the following reactions: "That doesn't affect us!" "Our industry is so heavily regulated that it will not be possible for newcomers to penetrate our markets." I also heard, "We have always acquired our business through sales representatives—we will continue to do that unchanged in the future."

One thing we have learned:

Today, even comprehensive regulations do not protect against an attack by innovative start-ups!

A similar development can be seen in the legal industry with the emergence of **LegalTechs**. In the initial phase, lawyers were only supported by technological solutions for standard processes, such as document management, research, and billing. This was followed by the use of systems for automation, for example in document review and contract drafting. In the meantime, more and more AI applications are also being used in the legal industry for case processing and further technological offerings are on the rise.

The US company *LegalZoom.com* supports its customers in the **creation of legal documents** without the need to involve a lawyer. The Canadian company *clio.com* facilitates the administration of law firms. The Israeli company *lawgeex.com* relies on artificial intelligence for **automated contract review**.

Based on *IBM's Watson* AI solution, *rossintelligence.com* is a **legal research software** that helps lawyers search for legal texts and judgements. With *ROSS*, the

Fig. 2.4 Gartner Magic Quadrant

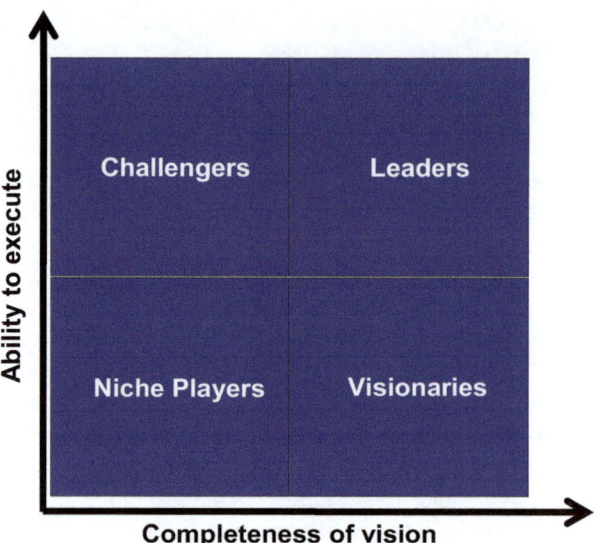

lawyer can communicate via **spoken language**. A different concept underlies *donotpay.com*. This is a **robot lawyer**. Behind it is a social network that users can consult for simple legal concerns. Selected legal questions can be dealt with using prepared question and answer sequences.

▶ **Food for Thought**
There are virtually no industries today where (digital) technologies cannot dramatically shift business logics!

You should regularly conduct a **digital gap analysis** for your company. This will allow you to document which of your competitors have already dropped out of the race, which are ticked off and which, if any, are engaged in a (successful) transformation process. Then you can position yourself in this environment. In addition, it is important to identify relevant, **disruptive technologies** as well as **disruptive business models** at an early stage, which could perhaps attack and/or destroy your business model in 1 or 2 years. The information and insights gained in the course of this analysis must be integrated into the **entrepreneurial storytelling for the digital transformation.**

To complement this, you can use a modified version of the *Gartner Magic Quadrant* concept. Originally, the *Gartner Magic Quadrant* is used to **rank vendors in key technology markets** (cf. Gartner, 2020a). It visualizes the relative positions of competitors in a specific market (cf. Fig. 2.4). The following characteristics are distinguished in this analysis:

- **Leaders**
  The leading companies to be positioned here have a comprehensive vision of their business model and are well positioned for the challenges of the future.
- **Visionaries**
  Visionaries have a comprehensive understanding of where the market is heading. Their corporate vision is aligned with this. However, the corresponding strategic and organizational implementation is still missing.
- **Niche Players**
  Niche players either focus successfully on one segment of the market. They can also be companies that have not yet had a clear focus and have not achieved major market significance. However, practically all success stories of companies initially start in a niche.
- **Challengers**
  The challengers are already achieving convincing results in a sub-market. Based on the expertise they have developed there, they have the potential to also operate successfully in a larger market.

You can use this concept for a **self-critical analysis** of your own company and your current and future competitors. Here you can check where you would position your own company (**determining the self-image**). In addition, it is indispensable to also ask the relevant stakeholders—and here especially the actual or desired customers—for their assessment (**determining the external image**). This is the only way to find out what your image in the market actually looks like and to what extent and in which dimensions it differs from the desired image or self-image. In this analysis, you can also rely on the support of consultancies—such as *Gartner*—which have a very comprehensive information base in many areas.

> **Memory Box**
> **The following still applies: Self-awareness is the first step to improvement!**

> **Think Box: Questions You Should Ask Yourself**
> - Have you ever conducted a digital gap analysis?
> - What key insights were you able to gain?
> - What threat potential exists in your industry?
> - How great is the willingness in your company to exploit the existing potential for change?
> - What gap do you offer your competitors as an attractive entry point?

(continued)

- Does your company also have legacy systems—and how do you deal with them?
- Which disruptive technologies particularly challenge your company and your industry?
- How strong is MarTec's law in your company?
- What do you think about the idea of one of your teams developing a business model for your company that could disrupt your own existing business model?
- Have you ever used the concept of the *Gartner Magic Quadrant* to position your company in the competitive environment—oriented towards the groups leaders, visionaries, niche players and challengers?
- Who answers these questions in your company?

2.1.3 Technology Impact Analysis

To gain further important insights for mobilizing your own workforce, make use of the **technology impact analysis**. Through this method, you systematically check how big the impact of different technologies will be on your company. Figure 2.5 shows an example of this analysis. Which technologies you should examine can be found in the *Gartner* Emerging Technology Roadmap 2020 to 2022 presented in Sect. 3.4.1.4.

The **assessments of different technologies** should be as neutral as possible. To this end, it is useful to involve external specialists in the assessment process. If you

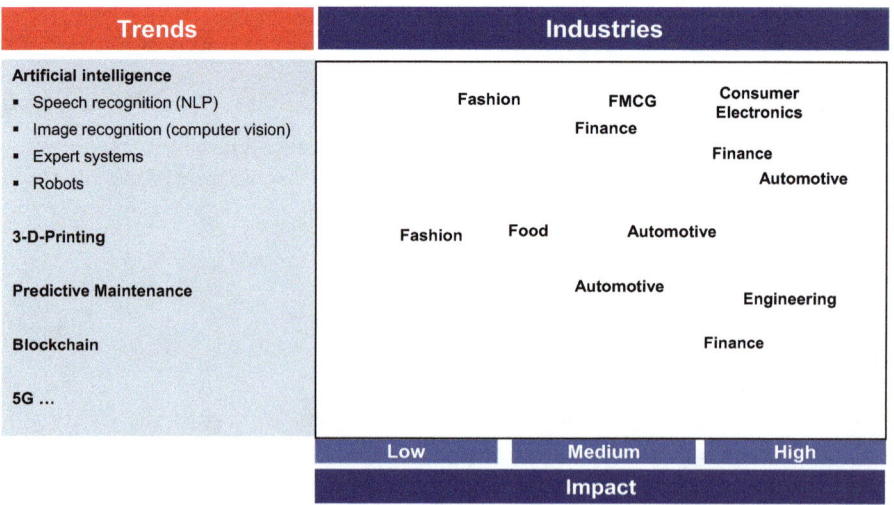

Fig. 2.5 Technology impact analysis

only carry out this assessment internally, there will be many—technology-phobic—people who give supposedly very good reasons why one should not deal with certain technologies.

The topic of **data protection** is always a popular deathblow argument when using new technologies (especially when using artificial intelligence applications)—and not only on the part of the legal department. Avoid that every argument about new technologies fails because of the General Data Protection Regulation (GDPR). That must not be the consequence of this piece of legislation, of which many politicians are surprisingly still proud.

▶ **Food for Thought**
When evaluating technologies, we should always start with the goals and the customer expectations, not with the technology!

Here, it is important to bear in mind that, in addition to external customers, we must also include very important internal customers when evaluating technologies.

Think Box: Questions You Should Ask Yourself
- Have you ever conducted a technology impact analysis?
- What insights can you gain from the technology impact analysis?
- Do you always start the evaluation of technologies with the goals or the intended customer benefits?
- Do you regularly consider internal customers in addition to external customers—and do you include them in the evaluation process?
- What measures do you derive from the insights gained?
- Does data protection serve as a central obstacle to the use of new technologies in your company?
- Where is the responsibility for a technology impact analysis located in your company?

2.1.4 SWOT Analysis: 5 Forces Analysis

2.1.4.1 Basic Concept of the SWOT Analysis

The insights gained through the use of the aforementioned methods can be incorporated into another important analysis that is indispensable for preparing the analysis of digital business performance: the **SWOT analysis**. Its aim is to make an assessment of your own performance in the light of relevant competitors while evaluating future market conditions (cf. Kreutzer, 2019, pp. 99–114).

In SWOT analysis, **SW** stands for strengths and weaknesses in the sense of comparative advantages or disadvantages of the company in direct comparison with competitors. This covers the **internal perspective** of the analysis and serves

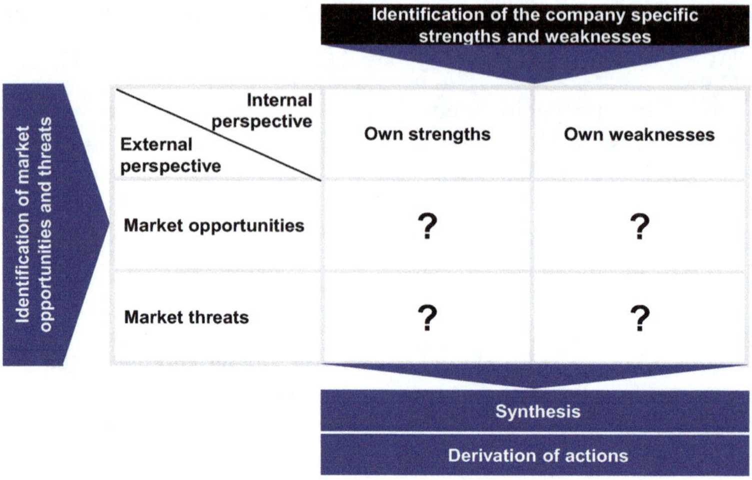

Fig. 2.6 Basic concept of the SWOT analysis

to determine the status quo of the company. **OT** stands for opportunities and threats and integrates the **external perspective** into the analysis. This perspective is future-oriented: What challenges and opportunities will arise in our industry?

Only from the **synthesis of external and internal perspectives** can you make strategic deductions for the further development of your company and your business model (cf. Fig. 2.6). In the case of a one-product company, you can use this analysis for the entire company. If your company is active on the market in different sectors and/or with completely different offers, you should carry out a corresponding analysis for each part of the company separately. This can be done on the basis of strategic business units (SBUs) or strategic business fields (SBFs).

There is one thing you should pay particular attention to when using the SWOT analysis, because this is often done incorrectly: a determination of corporate strengths and weaknesses can only be made in **comparison with relevant competitors**. Only in direct comparison with these, for example, does it become visible whether a market share of 12% is a strength or a weakness of the company. If all competitors have market shares between 1 and 3%, the market share mentioned is a strength (relative market share of 4). If the market is dominated by three companies with market shares of approx. 25% each, the market share is a weakness (relative market share of 0.48).

> **Memory Box**
> A company's **strengths and weaknesses** can only be **determined in direct comparison with the relevant competitors**. Therefore, the statement

(continued)

> "strength: we have a large product range" is meaningless for a SWOT analysis! Finally, a large product offering alone says nothing about market success.
> A relevant analysis result can be: "strength: we have a 20 % larger product range than our most important competitor; and—very important—all products enjoy a consistently high and profitable demand."

2.1.4.2 Identifying Relevant Competitors

Before you can come to precise conclusions about your own competitive strengths and weaknesses, you must first answer another question: How can the **identification of relevant competitors** be done? Only by answering this question, you can **define the relevant market**. You have two different options for identifying the relevant competitors:

- Customer-oriented approach to define the relevant set
- Supplier-oriented approach to identify the strategic group

In the **customer-oriented approach**, you determine the **relevant set** from the customer's perspective. The relevant set comprises the different offers that a customer considers to be of equal value and between which he/she decides in the purchase situation. To do this, you ask customers to find out with which other companies or offers your own offer is in direct competition. To determine this relevant set, you can ask customers the following questions:

- Which providers do you see as interchangeable?
- Which products/services do you switch between from time to time?
- Which products/services do you see as similar?

Such an approach can make it visible, that for a customer in the fashion segment not only *H&M, Zalando* and *Zara* compete with each other, but that small boutiques or second-hand shops are also taken into account in the buying process. These types of offers would therefore have to be taken into account in a corresponding competition analysis.

In the **supplier-oriented approach**, you identify the **strategic group** to which your company belongs. This is the mental grouping of those companies that use a comparable strategic concept in a particular industry (cf. Porter, 1999, p. 177). It is possible that different strategic groups exist in parallel in one industry. To identify the strategic group, you need to answer the following questions:

- Which companies pursue a comparable strategy?
- Which companies have a similar value proposition to end customers?

A few examples should clarify what exactly is meant by the term strategic group. In the pharmaceutical market there is the strategic group of **generics suppliers**, such as *Hexal, Ratiopharm,* and *Stada*. The **researching pharmaceutical companies** are to be distinguished from this. This group includes *Bayer, Merck, Novartis,* and *Sanofi-Aventis*.

With regard to the development of a **Corona vaccine**, the research-based pharmaceutical companies *AstraZeneca, Biontech/Pfizer, CanSino, Gamaleya, Moderna,* and *Sinovac* have become particularly important. Depending on the analysis question, a further distinction could be made within this group as to which approach was chosen for the development of the vaccine. The strategic groups defined in this way could then be analyzed in more detail with regard to their research success, the resources required for this and the underlying success factors.

Among the airlines, the **low-cost carriers** *easyJet, Eurowings, Jet2, Ryanair* and *WizzAir* form such a strategic group due to their similar business model. They are distinguished from **premium carriers** such as *Cathay Pacific, Emirates, Lufthansa, Quantas,* and *Singapore Airlines,* which form another strategic group. In the retail sector, two large strategic groups can be distinguished. On the one hand, there are the **classic food retailers** (*Edeka* and *Rewe*), on the other the **discounters** (including *Aldi, Lidl, Netto, Penny*).

> **Memory Box**
> The strategic group combines the companies that offer a comparable range of products and/or services.

2.1.4.3 Implementation of the Strengths and Weaknesses Analysis

To conduct a **strengths and weaknesses analysis** for your company, you can use the **critical success factors** of the respective business field as a guide. In determining these critical success factors, it can help to ask which factors significantly influence the success of a company, SBU (strategic business unit) or SGF (strategic business field). Such business units or business fields each comprise a section of the entrepreneurial areas of activity. When forming them, an attempt is made to find product-market combinations that are as homogeneous as possible and that encompass an independent, customer-related market task. In this way, the strategic business units determine how the market is seen—also and especially for analysis.

By **focusing on strategic success factors**, you can direct the information gathering and condensation to the really important facts. Often, the **identification of entrepreneurial strengths and weaknesses** is oriented towards the following **critical success factors**, whose relevance has been confirmed by research findings on success factors:

- Type, image, market position, degree of innovation and quality of products/services

- Degree of digitalization of the company
- Operational and organizational structure of the company
- Degree of digitization of the individual service offerings
- Degree of innovation and resilience of the business model
- Performance of production or service provision
- Sales strength (organization, size, efficiency, qualification)
- Intensity of networking of different sales channels (multi- vs. omni-channel concepts)
- Productivity of the overall organization and the sub-areas
- Cost situation (R&D, procurement, production, marketing, sales, logistics, HR)
- Financial strength (e.g., dependence on external financiers)
- R&D strength (e.g., qualification of the relevant employees, available budget)
- Extent of intangible investments (e.g., for software, patents, trademark rights, professional development, investments in organizational development)
- Access to key decision-makers in politics and society
- Qualification, loyalty and motivation of staff
- Market presence (regional, international, global) in terms of procurement and distribution
- Organizational structure (flexibility, customer orientation, speed, agility)
- Strategic alliances (in the sense of connections that the company has entered into with regard to purchasing, research, production, marketing, sales, logistics, etc., e.g., for the development or use of platform concepts)

When making indispensable comparisons with other companies, you should put certain criteria into perspective. It is not useful to compare advertising or R&D budgets in absolute figures—for example between a medium-sized retail company and *Amazon*. Here it makes sense and is necessary to state the amount of the advertising and R&D budget as a percentage of turnover and only then compare them. The situation is similar when the number of registered patents is used to evaluate R&D performance. In this case, a division by the total number of employees or, better, by the number of employees working in the R&D department is suitable to determine an important productivity indicator. This is the only way to determine relevant findings for competitive comparison.

> **Memory Box**
> You should work out a strengths and weaknesses analysis in teams. This has the "side effect" that all persons involved have the same level of information and can come to comparable assessments on this basis. At the same time, a cooperative approach promotes openness for an honest assessment and a transformation of the business model that may become necessary.
>
> You should prepare the results of the strengths and weaknesses analysis as shown in Fig. 2.7. Your own company is shown here in comparison to the two most important competitors A and B.

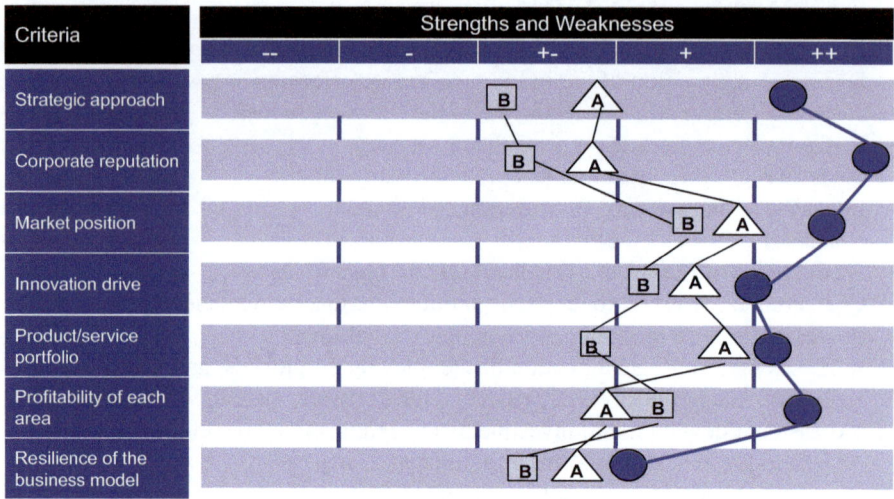

Fig. 2.7 Results of the analysis of strengths and weaknesses

2.1.4.4 Determination of Opportunities and Risks

The next step of the SWOT analysis is to analyze and evaluate the **opportunities and risks of the sector** in terms of expected future developments. In doing so, you can partly draw on information gained from the analysis tools already presented in Sect. 1.2, especially the PEST or PESTEL analysis. What is important here is that you identify the opportunities and risks for the sector as a whole. It is therefore not about the opportunities and risks of your own company at this point! Unfortunately, this is too often done incorrectly. Then at this point, we are already talking about opportunities and risks for our own company—and the logic of the analysis is destroyed.

> **Memory Box**
> The **analysis of opportunities and risks** in the SWOT analysis must necessarily refer to the entire sector! An industry focus is required here—not a company focus! Otherwise, a clean synthesis of the internal and external perspectives can no longer take place.
>
> To **determine the opportunities and risks** of the sector as a whole, the following areas can be analyzed:
>
> - Market development (growth, stagnation, shrinkage)
> - Changes in information and purchasing behavior (e.g., due to changing values, demographic developments, online use)
> - Customer expectations of products, services and/or companies

(continued)

- Access to new and/or old distribution channels
- Entry of new competitors and/or the exit of established competitors
- Market maturity of alternative technologies and alternative products and/or services
- Forward or backward integration of other companies
- Advance of new (disruptive) technologies
- Extent of dematerialization of products and services
- Price development and procurement opportunities for key raw materials and other materials
- Availability of skilled and motivated labor
- Openness of strategic partners to cooperation
- Availability or expiry of subsidy programs
- Legislative requirements and/or relief (e.g., with regard to emissions)
- Expectations from investors (e.g., with regard to ESG criteria)

These criteria address fields of analysis that are also discussed in the classic **5-forces analysis** by Porter (2004), which you can usefully integrate here. *Porter's* 5-forces analysis is an **industry structure analysis** that focuses on five drivers of industry competition. Within the framework of the SWOT analysis, you can—supported by this concept—carry out an in-depth analysis to determine the opportunities and risks for your industry. The basis for this is the idea that the attractiveness of an industry is significantly influenced by the market forces found in an industry. These in turn have a direct impact on the strategic behavior of the companies operating in the sector and, above all, on the profitability that can be achieved there.

Porter's **analytical concept** is based on the idea that the attractiveness of an industry is primarily shaped by the five **competitive forces** shown in Fig. 2.8. The stronger the five competitive forces are, the less attractive the respective industry is. After all, it will then be particularly difficult for you to achieve lasting competitive advantages and to operate profitably.

A strategic consequence of low industry attractiveness can show that you do not engage in the respective industry or stop your own commitment there. You can also think about business model innovations to break out of the intense industry competition. In this way, you can start an attempt to change the rules of the game in the industry or to leave well-trodden paths of market cultivation through innovations. The individual drivers of industry competition that influence these decisions are discussed below.

A key driver of industry competition that you should analyze first is determined by the **rivalry of the companies** themselves that are already active in the industry. This rivalry is particularly intensiv, among other things, when

- Many and large competitors are active in the market, offering fierce competition.
- There is only low or negative market growth, so that own growth is primarily to be achieved through competitive crowding out or price wars.

(continued)

- Companies have a high fixed cost burden and therefore accept orders that are not very attractive in terms of price, which increases the pressure on sales prices.
- Significant cost differences prevail between suppliers, which intensify price competition.
- The products and services are largely standardized and thus interchangeable for customers; this reduces the switching costs for customers when they change providers.
- There are high barriers to market exit, so that marginal providers (who make no profits or even losses) remain in the market because existing plants etc. cannot be sold lucratively.

It is necessary to check which **competitive position** your company has achieved within your own industry. The following questions help you analyse your position:

- Does your company occupy a dominant market position?
- Is your company more in the middle of the pack?
- Does your company have a competitive position that is difficult to defend, or even impossible to survive?
- Which established companies and/or start-ups in the market are planning to significantly expand their market position?
- Which are focusing on "holding" or "harvesting?"
- Which are preparing to exit the market?

If you examine the position determined here and the strategic thrust of your company in the light of the other drivers of sector competition, strategic decisions can be derived in a very well-founded manner.

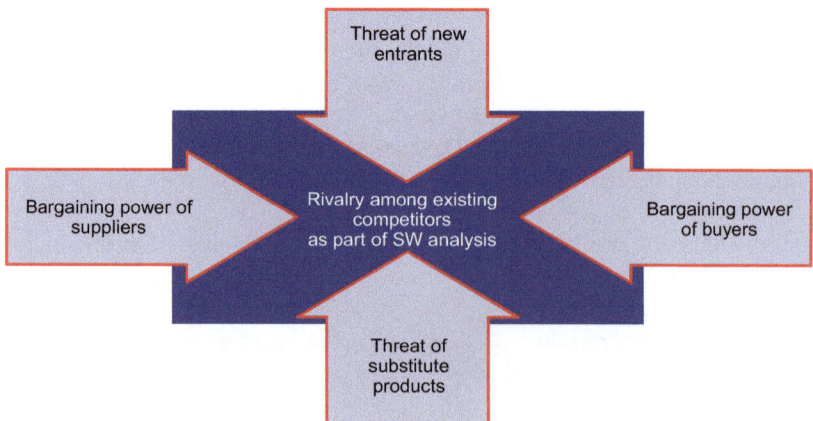

Fig. 2.8 Basic concept of the 5-forces analysis by *Porter*

Memory Box

You can integrate the results of the "rivalry of companies" analysis into the strengths/weaknesses part of the SWOT analysis. All further analysis stages of the 5-forces approach provide insights for the elaboration of opportunities and risks.

In the course of the 5-forces analysis, we speak of a **threat from new entrants** when new companies enter the market with a comparable offer (cf. Fig. 2.8). The probability of this is particularly high when

- Only low economies of scale can be achieved and therefore even small enterprises can quickly become competitive.
- There are few experience curve effects to be tapped, so that companies that have already been operating in the market for a long time do not have any clear cost advantages.
- Due to low switching costs, only low customer loyalty prevails and thus the acceptance of new providers is high.
- There are only weak brand personalities in the market, making it easier for products and services to be interchangeable in the eyes of customers.
- Only a small amount of capital is needed to start a new business (e.g., a publishing house compared to a car manufacturer).
- Easy access is given to the relevant distribution channels (e.g., online distribution platforms).
- There is a low degree of regulation (by laws, etc.), so that newcomers can also enter the market without large upfront investments.
- Only low costs are to be expected if one has to leave the market again (low exit costs).

If the suppliers of the analyzed companies have great **bargaining power**, this in turn reduces the attractiveness of this industry (cf. Fig. 2.8). The **bargaining power of suppliers** is high when

- One or a few suppliers are faced with a heterogeneous clientele (supply monopoly or oligopoly); in this case, the suppliers can easily influence the supply conditions in their favor.
- The suppliers are relatively independent of their customers because there is a sufficient number of potential buyers.
- There is only a low intensity of competition between different suppliers because their supply programs differ significantly.
- There is a lack of adequate substitute products.
- There are high switching costs for the buyers in the event of a change of supplier (e.g., when replacing ERP software from *SAP*).

(continued)

- The products supplied have a high degree of customization for the individual customers, so that the latter can only change the source of supply with difficulty.
- The current suppliers can easily become competitors of the current customers through forward integration.

Industry attractiveness also suffers when existing firms face a threat from **substitute products** (cf. Fig. 2.8). Substitute products distinguish themselves from new entrants in that substitute products offer a different solution concept for a specific customer problem.

For the classic book publishers, for example, the e-book in the sense of an electronic presentation of book content represents a major threat, as long as the established publishers do not include this variant in their own offerings. A lot of online information (such as *Wikipedia*), which is often offered free of charge, also represents an alternative to buying a textbook.

In the hotel and taxi industry, the new services of the so-called "sharing economy"—such as *Airbnb* and *Uber*—are considered a major threat. The established banks with an extensive branch network (with corresponding costs) are challenged by online banks (e.g., *N26*), which enter the market without a cost-intensive branch structure with the latest technologies (keyword "FinTechs").

Overall, a major threat-scenario based on substitute products can be assumed if

- Alternative offers are readily available.
- Substitutes have major price, performance and/or convenience advantages over the "original."
- Existing products and service offerings are completely or partially devalued by new technologies.
- The target persons show a willingness to switch and it is easy to make such a switch (low switching costs).

Bargaining power of buyers represents another field of the 5-forces analysis (cf. Fig. 2.8). High bargaining power of buyers means that the customers are in the dominant market position and can, for example, exert a significant influence on the conditions of the existing suppliers. This situation can be found in particular when

- Demand is concentrated on a few buyers (e.g., in the food industry on a few large retail chains or in the case of milk on a few large dairies); this is called a demand oligopoly.

(continued)

- The state is the only buyer of certain military equipment (demand monopoly).
- Customers are offered a large number of alternatives (e.g., many car models from different manufacturers).
- There is a high price elasticity of demand because, for example, substitutes are readily available, and buyers therefore respond to price increases with a significant drop in demand from the corresponding supplier.
- Standardized products are marketed for which the supplier can be easily switched due to low switching costs.
- A poor economic situation prevails in which the buyers are under high pressure to reduce costs and therefore have to depress prices.
- Buyers can become competitors of their previous suppliers through backward integration.
- Supply alternatives are transparent and easily available to buyers (e.g., through online price comparison sites).

This **analysis concept by *Porter*** is very powerful, but also requires precise application. You must always define exactly which company is the focus of the analysis. If such an analysis is carried out for the *Volkswagen* Group, the first thing to analyze is the intense rivalry between the **manufacturers active in the market** (e.g., between *Volkswagen* on the one hand and *Ford, Hyundai, Opel, Toyota* on the other). In addition, *Volkswagen* is challenged by **new suppliers** in the shape of the Chinese automotive industry—especially in the Chinese market itself. *Volkswagen's* **suppliers** (e.g., *Bosch, Continental, Recaro*) often have limited negotiating power when they are heavily dependent on *Volkswagen*.

Electric and hybrid vehicles (e.g., from *Tesla*) are still **substitutes** for *Volkswagen's* classic drive systems as long as *Volkswagen* itself does not offer a wide range of products on the market. In the future, self-driving cars will also be a substitute. Mobility concepts that use car sharing and other services to provide users with mobility when they need it (e.g., *Flinkster, Share Now*, but also *BlaBlaCar* and *Flixbus*) are also substitutes for the traditional sale of cars.

The direct **buyers** for *Volkswagen* are first and foremost, the authorized dealers and the customers they serve. However, these customer groups also include major customers such as *DHL* and *Sixt rent-a-car*. The indirect customers are private customers who purchase their vehicles from the dealer or online.

If, on the other hand, such an analysis is carried out for the *Bosch* company, the power constellations are quite different. Here, *Volkswagen* (alongside *Daimler* and *BMW*) becomes a customer of *Bosch*. Substitutes for *Bosch's* own offers are, for example, solar drives, as long as these are not offered by

(continued)

> *Bosch* itself. An analysis for the *Sixt* car-rental company, on the other hand, makes *Volkswagen* a supplier. Substitutes can be seen in private car-sharing concepts. The customers of car-rental service providers are companies, their employees and private individuals.
>
> The insights gained from this sector analysis can be incorporated into the **analysis of opportunities and risks**. It is crucial that this determination is carried out with an industry focus, but independently of the strengths and weaknesses of the respective company itself. Colloquially we often speak of opportunities and risks of a company. However, as already emphasized several times, in the SWOT analysis with regard to the opportunities and risks, you must carry out a consideration independent of the respective company.

2.1.4.5 Synthesis to Conclude the SWOT Analysis

If the above conditions are met, the **synthesis of internal and external perspectives** can be carried out logically and consistently. If company specifics were already included in the external perspective, the analysis would be distorted in the synthesis, or it would no longer be possible to present it consistently. Figure 2.9 shows which questions have to be answered within the synthesis.

The **example of such a synthesis** can be found for the **consumer goods market** in Fig. 2.10. Here it becomes clear once again that opportunities in the market or in the industry cannot be used by all companies. An optimal situation is given when opportunities or threats of the industry meet own strengths, whereby competitive advantages can be achieved. Companies are particularly at risk when threats meet their own weaknesses or opportunities in the market cannot be exploited because of their own weaknesses. This will cause a loss of competitive strength.

Based on such an analysis, you can gain important insights for (the survival of) your company, for the strategic orientation and thus for the digital transformation of your business model, but also for the orientation of innovation and acquisition processes.

External perspective \ Internal perspective	Own strengths	Own weaknesses
Market opportunities	Which market opportunities can be used thanks to our strengths?	Which are the market opportunities we cannot profit from due to our weaknesses?
Market threats	Which market threats can we profit from thanks to out strengths?	Which market threats are particularly severe due to our weaknesses?

Fig. 2.9 Synthesis of internal and external perspectives during SWOT analysis

2.1 Tools to Prepare the Analysis of Digital Business Performance

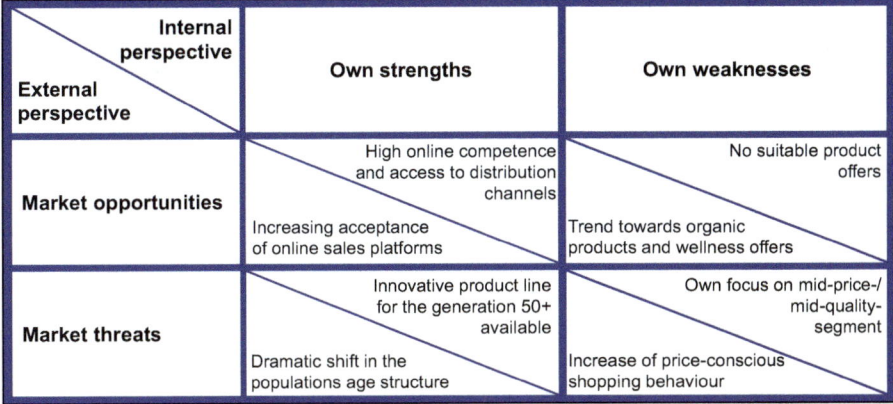

Fig. 2.10 SWOT analysis for the consumer goods market

There is a need for action for the company analyzed in Fig. 2.10 in the area of organic and wellness offerings, in which no adequate solutions are available today. In addition, it should be examined whether a second brand should be developed in order to meet the trend towards increasingly price-conscious shopping. Through such an analysis, important customer expectations regarding the services of companies can be incorporated into their strategic orientation. Here it becomes clear that these expectations are still very generic and that further marketing research tools should be used to clarify the exact requirements as well as their revenue potential.

You should include the **SWOT analysis** in your **digital transformation toolbox** and use it regularly once a year to identify relevant developments and changes at an early stage. It is advisable to carry out this analysis in a team in order to build up a deep industry and company understanding together. At the same time, you will gain many comrades-in-arms who, as multipliers, will carry the insights gained into the company and in this way, support the necessary transformation process.

> **Think Box: Questions You Should Ask Yourself**
> - How regularly is the SWOT analysis carried out in your company?
> - Do you involve a wide variety of company departments in this analysis?
> - Do you increase the probability of an "objective" picture by engaging external specialists for the analysis?
> - When identifying opportunities and risks, do you make sure to identify them for the entire sector and not already in relation to your company?
> - Do you determine the strengths and weaknesses of your company in terms of comparative advantages or disadvantages—i.e., in comparison to the relevant competitors?

(continued)

- How do you identify your competitors? Do you identify them through a customer-oriented approach by defining the relevant set or through a supplier-oriented approach by identifying strategic groups?
- Do you concentrate on the critical success factors of the respective business field in the strengths and weaknesses analysis?
- Do you use the 5-forces analysis to develop relevant content for the SWOT analysis?
- Do you carry out a consistent synthesis of internal and external perspectives to conclude the SWOT analysis?
- Are strategic deductions made based on the findings?
- Who is the initiator for such analyses?

2.1.5 Resilience Analysis

Information is fast. Truth needs time.
  Peter Glaser

2.1.5.1 Relevance of Resilience and Resilience Analysis

We can regularly read reports that once again **stress tests of banks** have been carried out. Such tests can be initiated as **macro stress tests** by external bodies, such as the *German Bundesbank* or the US *Federal Reserve (FED)*. **Micro stress tests** can be carried out by the credit institutions on their own responsibility or ordered by regulators. This is done, for example, by the *Federal Financial Supervisory Authority* or by the *European Central Bank (ECB)*.

The background to these stress tests is the **global financial crisis**. Collapsing financial services providers—starting with the New York-based US investment bank *Lehman Brothers*—caused gigantic shock waves that led to a global economic crisis starting in **2008**. In order to avoid the imminent collapse of the banking system, governments around the world had to invest billions to save especially the so-called **system-critical banks** (motto: "too big to fail").

The instrument of the **bank stress test** was developed to prevent these banks in particular, but also many other financial institutions, from getting into such difficulties. Above all, externally supervised bank stress tests are there to ensure that the institutions cannot give themselves good certificates, although there are actually serious risks. For this reason, **minimum standards** have been defined for financial institutions that must be met.

We are also familiar with corresponding **stress tests from the medical field.** Here, **people** have to be put through their paces in order to test their **resilience**. Not only astronauts have to undergo such tests, but also prospective managers and—in a weakened form—applicants who want to become civil servants. Here, the candidates are exposed to physical and often also mental stress. These mental challenges in the form of assessment centers include preparing a presentation under time pressure, speaking in front of an audience or representing extreme positions in discussions. In each case, how the persons deal with stressful situations is recorded in order to recognize their resilience in the run-up to a commitment.

A comparable situation exists with **business models**. Before the Corona pandemic, the following **criteria** were primarily used to **evaluate business models** (see Sect. 3.2.7):

- Profitability
- Scalability
- Possibility to create lock-in effects and/or build up switching costs for customers
- Use of a platform concept
- Use of a blue ocean strategy
- Establishment of a just-to-be-done concept

During the Corona pandemic, another criterion became the focus of analysis: the **resilience of business models**. Similar to banks and people, the question here is how well a business model can handle stress. In this type of stress test, the potentially serious effects of certain scenarios on one's own business model must be recognized at an early stage so that appropriate preventive measures can be developed.

The term **resilience** stands for **resistance** and **stability**. Resilience therefore refers to the ability to cope with stress due to **inner strength**.

People with resilience are able to react flexibly and appropriately to changing life situations and different demands. People with resilience can cope with stressful, frustrating, difficult and burdensome situations without suffering psychological consequences (cf. Hoffmann, 2016, pp. 3–11; Welter-Enderlin & Hildenbrand, 2012, p. 15; Oerter & Montada, 2002, p. 991; see Sect. 3.6.4).

Serious **resilience deficits** became apparent in many European states in the course of the 2020 pandemic in the important **education system**. The digitization of the education landscape revealed serious weaknesses in both hardware and software, as well as in their users. In many schools, WIFI was already missing, not to mention digital learning platforms and digitally skilled and/or motivated teachers. At some schools and many universities, there was a veritable **leapfrog digitization**. Within a few days and weeks, teaching had to be converted from "analogue" to "digital." Often this was achieved with surprisingly good results.

2.1.5.2 Resilience of Companies and Business Models

In the economic context, the **resilience of companies** or the **resilience of business models** is increasingly being discussed today. This refers to the ability to demonstrate **inner resilience in the face of crises and stress**. Such resilience enables behavioral patterns—especially in times of (digital) change—that go hand in hand with adaptability and the ability to integrate new opportunities while largely maintaining the entrepreneurial goal orientation.

Employees and managers make an important contribution to the resilience of companies and business models. If they have a high level of resilience themselves, this also has positive effects on the resilience of the company. Then neither the health of the staff nor productivity suffers—even in a very stressful environment. Teams or entire organizations that have resilience can also accept challenging realities more easily and act appropriately.

> **Memory Box**
> As the saying goes:
> **Only when the tide goes out do you discover who's been swimming naked.**
>
> In **corporate resilience**, the entire company is the focus of the analysis. Alternatively, it is primarily the company's own business model that can be subjected to a corresponding review. In order to strengthen the resilience of companies, the leadership is required to ensure optimism, satisfaction, self-confidence, self-efficacy, well-being and relaxation in the team through a **powerful vision** and a **relevant purpose**—communicated through **convincing storytelling** (see Sect. 2.1.1). Such alignment can be fostered through a **transformational leadership style** that promotes shared leadership within the team, shared learning and the development of a common social identity (see Sect. 3.6.6).

> **Memory Box**
> When **examining the resilience of our company**, we should keep in mind that a **resilient company** requires, above all, **resilient leaders and employees**.
>
> A company must additionally embed **resilience in every sub-area of the organization**: from procurement to production and logistics to sales and customer engagement—and also in the underlying business model. Any single weakness in a sub-area can affect the resilience of the company and thus its ability to survive and grow profitably.
>
> Because here, too, the following applies: **every chain is only as strong as its weakest link!**
>
> In the course of the Corona pandemic, it became apparent that many companies' business models were not sufficiently tested for resilience. Supply chains broke in the **automotive industry**, because important components were only supplied by one supplier and/or from one country. This meant that important parts for production were no longer available from one day to the next. Just-in-time supply chains also meant that there were hardly any stocks left to compensate for the resulting supply bottlenecks, at least temporarily.
>
> In the **pharmaceutical industry**, it became apparent that important raw materials for medicines were only produced in China and processed into medicines in India alone. Already glaring supply bottlenecks in European

(continued)

> pharmacies intensified dramatically. It also became apparent that there was a lack of companies in Europe that could produce protective clothing and mouth-nose masks of various qualities. Again, no stocks were kept, as is the case with the strategic oil reserve as well as the civil emergency food reserve, to ensure the supply of the population for at least several weeks even in crisis situations.

▶ **Food for Thought**

Important: this is not meant to be a condemnation of decision-makers who have taken advantage of **just-in-time manufacturing** as well as **globalization** to develop their own business model. Globalization has lifted millions of people out of poverty and unemployment (cf. on the growth effects of globalization Prognos, 2020).

The fact that globalization is also associated with environmental problems and the exploitation of people is also not negated. Against the background of the clear advantages of globalization, the demand for **de-globalization** does not fit the facts (see Sect. 1.2.2.2). In contrast, it is indispensable to strengthen the **resilience of business models** through various measures.

Neither German managers nor politicians are accused of not having read pages 5f. and 55–88 in the ***Report on Risk Analysis in Civil Protection 2012*** in printed matter 17/12051 intensively enough. There, under the heading "Pandemic due to virus *'Modi-SARS'*," it is almost perfectly described how the Corona pandemic will develop and which measures for prophylaxis are to be initiated (cf. Deutscher Bundestag, 2013).

To the "excuse" of all those in positions of responsibility, it should be noted: In our VUCA world, there are many possible scenarios at any point in time for which one could prepare. And: **we cannot take out fully comprehensive insurance for every eventuality in (economic) life!** That would simply not be affordable.

Companies that had diversified their processes found it easier to cope with the challenges posed by the Corona pandemic. These were, for example, **retailers** who—in addition to a brick-and-mortar shop—had either already established an **online shop** or at least had a **convincing online presence** to enable a pick-up service. For this, not only a website but ideally also a permission-based e-mail database with customer addresses was available. In contrast, companies with **extensive online abstinence** were hardly able to communicate with their customers during a phase of lockdown (curfew) and/or shutdown (closure of shops).

▶ **Food for Thought**

However, my recommendation remains: not every stationary retailer should set up its own online shop. Otherwise, we would soon have many retailers running an unsuccessful online shop and endangering their traditional business by the investments to be made there.

However, every stationary retailer must have one thing: a first-class online presence through a high-performance website and, if necessary, target group-oriented activities in social media. In parallel, an engagement on the existing online sales platforms should also be examined. This will sustainably secure the own business model and strengthen resilience.

2.1.5.3 Resilience Analysis of the Business Model

The **resilience analysis of the business model** examines how resilient the company's own business model is. It determines how stable the supply chains are, how comprehensive the stockpiling is, how sustainable the digital systems are and, last but not least, how resilient the own workforce is. The challenge is to make one's own business model as resilient to external disruptions as the rest of the company. In addition to (digital) technologies and processes, it is above all the employees and managers who influence the resilience of business models. Therefore, the key questions are:

- **How resilient is our business model?**
- **How resilient are our managers and employees?**

Findings from the *Boston Consulting Group* show that companies deal with crises in very different ways. According to them, in the past four downturns since 1985, about one in seven companies increased both sales growth and profit margins: the successful companies increased sales by 14 percentage points and improved margins by 7 percentage points. In contrast, 44% of the analyzed companies recorded declines in both parameters (cf. Close et al., 2020, p. 1).

This shows that profitable growth is also achievable in or after times of crisis. However, this is only possible if the necessary resilience is in place. The **core of this resilience** is not to scale back one's own activities in such a phase, but to immediately and powerfully adapt to a new reality. This seems all the more necessary because a return to **pre-Corona-normality** probably cannot (or should not?) be achieved. Rather, a **new normal** is to be expected, which will go hand in hand with changed demands of customers, partners and also society on companies and their business models (cf. Ziems et al., 2020).

A **convincing example of resilience** is provided by the family-owned German company **Reifenhäuser**—world market leader in mechanical engineering for nonwovens production. Around 75% of the world's medical nonwovens are produced on *Reifenhäuser* machines. The company realized early on in the Corona pandemic that Europe needed millions of protective masks, but that about 90% of them were manufactured in China. China had initially banned the export of protective clothing, but later these products were mostly exported at very high prices because many countries wanted to secure their supplies. To overcome this shortage, *Reifenhäuser* manufactures the fleece required for masks itself on the demonstration lines in its own research and development center in Troisdorf—24/7 and made the material available to further processors.

Heino Claussen-Markefka, Managing Director of *Reifenhäuser*, explains: "With this project, we want to make a further contribution to strengthening the internationally depleted production capacities in order to provide a sufficient quantity of high-quality protective clothing during the Corona crisis. We are happy to use our test facilities for this purpose" (Reifenhäuser, 2020).

To avoid short-time work, the automotive supplier **Zender** from Osnabrück, Germany changed its range of services. Instead of carbon parts and interior trim, during the Corona pandemic, the company manufactured the particularly high-performance FFP2 protective masks, which are approved for use in hospitals and for nursing staff. Here, the company recalled its core competencies: the processing of industrial fabrics as well as the cutting, sewing and welding of textiles. These are all necessary steps for mask production. The result: at *Zender Germany* it was now "mask production instead of short-time work." This was made possible by a quick action of the company management as well as the flexibility of the employees (cf. Müller, 2020).

German textile company **van Laack** showed a similar flexibility regarding the production of masks instead of "exclusive clothing for him and her." The fact that the impulse for the production of masks came from the Vietnamese plant manager in Hanoi—and that already in January 2020—speaks for the culture of this company. At first, the managing director hesitated, but was finally convinced by the initiative of the plant manager. As early as February 2020, the first 10,000 masks arrived in Germany. Quickly, a million pieces were produced at the peak—per day (cf. Wiebking, 2020, p. 12). The masks were not sold in luxury shops, but at German discounters. But of course, the masks were also available in *van Laack's* online shop.

> **Memory Box**
> **Resilience is also reflected in the flexibility of the business model, management and employees!**
> The Corona pandemic in the **airline-industry** showed how difficult it is for companies if their business models do not demonstrate such flexibility. Airlines without a cargo division could not even profit from the increased airfreight volume. This increased volume was caused not least by the fact that so-called belly freight was eliminated on a large scale. Belly freight is the term used to describe the transport of goods that is carried as additional cargo in passenger aircraft and accounts for about half of the volume of goods transported. **Travel agencies, cultural event organizers** and **artists** were also unable or hardly able to switch to other value-added activities to compensate for the loss of demand.

Memory Box

The **resilience analysis** should lead to **productive uncertainty or unrest** in your company. People, systems and processes should first be mentally led out of their state of stability or their comfort zone in order to subsequently realign people, systems and processes.

Through the **resilience analysis**, you can not only identify the **need for action**, but also develop **options for action**—ideally accompanied by the conviction that you have the necessary **power for productive change** in your own company.

A multi-stage concept is suitable for the **resilience analysis**, which comprises the following stages (cf. Gartner, 2020b; Close et al., 2020):

Stage 1: Structured Analysis of Own Business Model

The **business model canvas** is certainly part of your standard repertoire. As will be shown in Sect. 3.2.5, this tool is very suitable for **developing new business models**. However, you can also use it to **analyze the resilience of your own, existing business model**. In Fig. 2.11, the relevant fields of analysis are clustered according to "value proposition," "customers," "value architecture," and "financial aspects." Your task in this first stage of the resilience analysis is to succinctly describe your own business model within these fields. This step thus represents the **description of the status quo**.

Stage 2: Identify weak Points in Your Business Model

This stage is about identifying **weak points or points of attack** in your business model. Which areas of your business model would potential competitors choose to attack? Under which stresses and strains would your business model "go down" first and at what point? Where is the system's inherent resilience lacking? In order to achieve an as "objective" view of reality as possible, you should carry out this analysis in a heterogeneous team, preferably with the involvement of external consultants. These external partners should not only have a profound knowledge of your own sector, but should also ensure that you look beyond the end of your nose.

In this analysis, the following **aspects of resilience** in particular can be critically examined:

- Does the **company's "why"** go beyond day-to-day business and motivates its own workforce—and also entice (future) customers, business partners, managers, employees and investors to enter into and/or continue business relationships?
- Can disruptions and changing requirements in the **value chain** (R&D, procurement, inbound logistics, production, outbound logistics, sales) be

(continued)

flexibly implemented? How stable and resilient are the own **supply chains**—how resilient are the **integrated partners** and their **business models** themselves? Are indispensable suppliers active in different countries of the world (**global sourcing**)? Are core services sourced from more than one supplier (**multiple sourcing**)? Can supply fluctuations be bridged by warehousing—at least for a period of time deemed relevant? Which resources are indispensable for the provision of services? Are alternative sources of supply available?

An important indicator for the resilience of your business model is the **depth of value added** or the **vertical range of manufacture**. This indicates how much a company contributes to the production of a product itself. This shows how high the share of the total value added is that was provided by third parties. This reveals the extent of dependence on external service providers. Whether these dependencies are an advantage or a disadvantage in times of crisis depends on the resilience of these partners. The **depth of value added** is determined as follows:

$$\text{Depth of value added} = \frac{\text{Own production costs (own value added)}}{\text{Total production costs (total value added)}} \times 100$$

The depth of value creation depends on the extent of **vertical integration** undertaken by the own company. Here again the classic trade-offs occur. If a company uses the cost advantages that can be achieved through the integration of specialized suppliers in the manufacturing process, the dependencies on third parties also increase. This increases the risk that their problems will affect the company's own value chain. On the other hand, flexible and efficient partners can also help to cushion fluctuations in times of crisis. This needs to be analyzed here.

The **bandwidth of the depth of value added** is enormous today. While the depth of value creation at *Adidas* is about 5%, it is 85% at the manufacturer of agricultural equipment, *Grimme* (cf. Jung, 2020, pp. 72, 74).

- What events can particularly disrupt the **delivery of your value proposition**? Can you no longer deliver your value proposition if more than 30% or 50% of your employees work from home? What events cause your value proposition to become less relevant to customers? When are your services considered "dispensable?" Are changes (keyword "new normal") in **customer expectations** recognized early and comprehensively through consistent customer orientation and communicated within the company?

(continued)

- How resilient are the existing **customer relationships**? Do customers feel more **attached**—and are happy to break out of existing relationships? Or do your customers feel more connected to you—and ask, for example, whether they can contribute to the security of your company through advance payments, etc.? How do fewer face-to-face customer contacts, e.g., due to the cancellation of trade fairs and international conferences, affect your business? What restrictions on face-to-face customer acquisition can your business model withstand?
- Are your own **managers and staff** motivated and able to maintain work processes even under changed or more difficult conditions (e.g., home office)? How well are your staff prepared for these challenges—mentally, methodically and IT-wise?
- Are the **core IT processes** (incl. Cyber security) and the **IT infrastructure** used stable and scalable to allow for increased and, if necessary, decentralized access to business processes and information systems? How resilient is the IT technology to react to new requirements? This can mean that, for example, 100% of the team has to move to working from home office overnight and conferences and meetings have to be conducted completely digitally. The flexibility required for this can often be achieved more easily via **cloud-based IT solutions** than if these are operated on-premise, i.e., on the company's own computers. However, shifting IT processes to third parties also increases the company's own dependence on them.
- An indispensable prerequisite for resilience is the **profitability of your business model**. The resilience of the company depends on it. What is the saying? **Liquidity follows profitability!** When analyzing your profitability, you should not be satisfied with EBIT or EBITDA, which have been defined for reasons of international comparability. You should measure profitability here in the classical way by the key figure "profit after tax." Only this will enable you to build up sufficient **financial resources** (e.g., in the form of quickly available reserves) to cope with payment defaults by customers and possible advance payments in parallel with current payment obligations.

With regard to the **financial aspects**, the question also arises as to which losses in the revenue model are to be expected in the short and medium term if service chains are interrupted. In addition, it should be examined how quickly the largest cost blocks can be reduced. However, you should not only think about the training budgets and the marketing budget first!

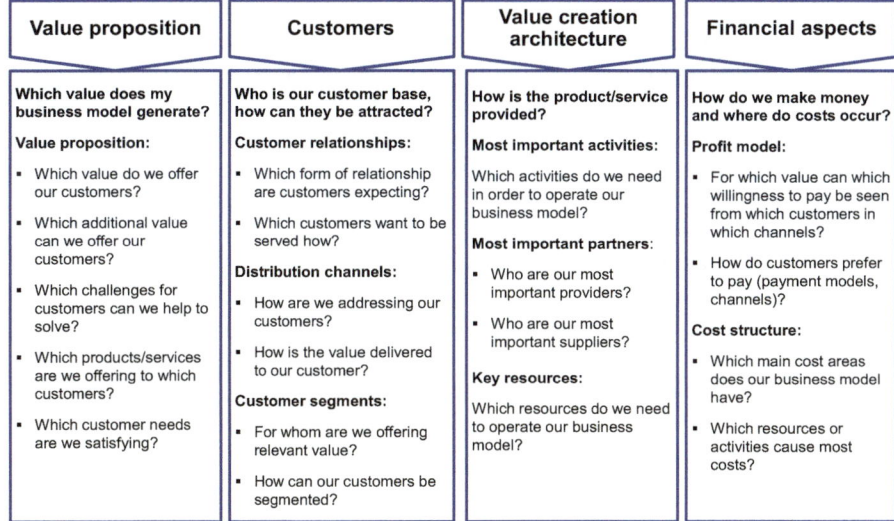

Fig. 2.11 Resilience analysis of a business model using the business model canvas

▶ **Food for Thought**
Your managers, but also all your employees, should be powerfully committed to the **goal of profit-making** in free-market enterprises. No company can survive in the long run without making profits. Companies that make losses cannot offer qualified and well-paid jobs. Nor can they invest in environmental protection and pay taxes. Neither a focus on EBIT or EBITDA nor on market share and turnover targets will meet this requirement.

▶ **Storytelling** In my marketing and management trainings, I often find that company leaders almost always only define turnover targets—especially in marketing! I then always say: "Turnover doesn't fill me up! Neither does market share!"

The harshest statement I have heard in response to my question "And what about profit?" from the owner of a smaller company was, "Profit? That's the tax accountant's job!"

A development that creates value for the company and its customers (including investment in future tasks) only succeeds through **profit-oriented corporate management**. We can also consciously commit to this—integrated into a **stakeholder orientation** in which we do not play individual stakeholders off against each other or pull the wool over their eyes.

A study by Simon (2020, p. 18) analyzed the **corporate profitability in Germany**. On average over the years 2003——2016, German companies achieved an **after-tax return on sales** of only 3.3%. This puts Germany in second-to-last place among the 23 OECD countries. Only in Japan is the value even lower, at 2.4%. The average after-tax return on sales in all countries is 5.7%—2.4% higher than in

Germany. There is still a lot of room for improvement in many countries—also to make companies much more resilient in this way.

Stage 3: Assessing the Impact on Business Operations

After identifying possible **points of vulnerability or attack**, you should determine what impact each could have on your business operations. Where is the risk of exposure most pronounced? Identify the particularly critical areas—after all, no company can be prepared for all possible hazards at the same time ("no fully comprehensive insurance"). To identify the particularly high-risk areas, you can use a **business impact analysis** to answer the following questions:

- What effects of attacks and/or supply bottlenecks are to be expected in which business areas?
- How pervasive and/or threatening will these impacts be?
- In what time frames will these developments occur?
- What possible interactions exist between different business areas?

At this stage, too, it makes sense to be accompanied and supported by external advisors. They can provide an unbiased view of the company and its business model. At the same time, they can also contribute experience and knowledge from other sectors and countries to the evaluation process.

Stage 4: Development of Options for Action

Based on the **major areas of risk** identified in stage 3, you now develop **alternative options for action** to avoid or reduce negative impacts. For example, you can use agile management methods to quickly come up with feasible solutions (see Sects. 3.6 and 3.7 for more information).

In a **resilience analysis**, the following **fields of action** have often turned out to be particularly critical for success:

- **Establishing or expanding digital channels** in procurement, research, production, sales and customer service to replace or complement traditional channels
- **Stabilization of production** to prevent supply bottlenecks, e.g., through increased digitalization or automation of production
- **Establishment or expansion of home office and digital communication** to ensure goal-oriented collaboration even at a distance (adaptation of skill sets and work models)
- **Provision of the necessary IT resources** (personnel and budget)
- **Strengthening the financial basis** (cost cutting, reducing fixed costs, ensuring greater variability of costs, building up financial reserves)

A central component of this phase is also the **creation of a priority list**. As usual, the **priority fields of action** are to be defined in this list. However, this step must also include the **allocation of human and financial resources**. Too often this is forgotten in times of crisis. In addition, **responsibilities** should be located as "close to action" as possible to ensure "proximity to the problem" as well as short decision-making paths. Agile action and centralized, strongly hierarchical decision-making structures are mutually exclusive. In order to ensure **orientation towards the vision and values of the company** even in decentralized action, the "start with the why," which is to be dealt with in more detail in Sect. 3.1, is of central importance.

> **Memory Box**
> When drawing up a list of priorities, **trade-offs** inevitably occur. Many decisions are in trade-off relationships, i.e., they are interdependent. If one project is given higher priority, this is at the expense of another project. Trade-offs describe the need to find a compromise. It is a matter of resolving conflicting goals. 15 Projects with an A1 priority must not and cannot exist!
> As Michael Porter (1996, p. 70) so aptly put it:
> **"Strategy is making trade-offs in competing. The essence of strategy is choosing what *not* to do."**
> Skilled leaders are aware of this need to compromise and set priorities—even painful ones if necessary. The wisdom also applies here:
> **"Doing right by all people is an art that no one can master."**
> The result is clear prioritization, which has to be "sold" internally and externally with good arguments.
> This **process of setting priorities** and making trade-offs also includes **drawing up a not-to-do list**. However, I have never seen such a list in use in any company as hard as it is presented here. Prioritization is also about consciously saying goodbye to projects that have become dear to one's heart. Saying "no" to projects that should have been successfully completed years ago ... should have. Time and again, a stop was postponed "for good and understandable reasons," old projects were reprioritized—often without convincing results.

▶ **Storytelling** At one company, I was allowed to accompany the process of digital transformation. The CEO proudly told me that 18 strategic projects had now been defined, which he would present at a management meeting next week.

I recommended not to "add" such a number of projects to the existing day-to-day business without buying additional resources, also not with the remark: "We can do it!"

> **Memory Box**
> **Space must first be created for the new. This can be achieved—even if it is painful—by keeping an open not-to-do list!**
>
> In this phase of the resilience analysis, an end must now be put to always defining new projects and new tasks without freeing oneself from previous tasks. If new projects are defined in the face of crisis developments or—much better—for the proactive orientation of the company, "old projects" must be given way. This is the only way to avoid a **burnout of managers and employees** and thus a **burnout of the entire company**.
>
> By stopping overdue projects that may only be dragged along, **resources** are freed up to turn to **new challenges**. Even if filling the **not-to-do list** is usually accompanied by tears, a "finally stopped" can usually be achieved afterwards with regard to sorting out unloved and/or unsuccessful projects. In the necessary weighing, however, a **binary decision-making** approach that only allows "stop" or "continue" should be avoided.
>
> Creative decision-makers are called upon to work out a variety of **possible courses of action**. Between 100% stop and 100% continue, there are often **fifty shades of options** that need to be evaluated in terms of the company's goals and contribution to the community. However, there is also a risk here that "lazy compromises" are reached in order to avoid making tough decisions.
>
> The general options for action are shown in Fig. 2.12. **Disinvestment** involves returning the investments that were made to a project previously. This shows the downgrading of priority through the reduced budget. With **shutdown**, a project is terminated if no profitable **divestment** (sale) can be achieved.

Fig. 2.12 Development of a not-to-do list

2.1 Tools to Prepare the Analysis of Digital Business Performance

> **Memory Box**
> In order to be able to use budget, management and staff for new projects, some existing projects have to be stopped!
> However, the following applies: processes, structures, projects, products or services are never as defensible—concerning those affected—as at the moment when they are to be abolished!

▶ **Storytelling** At *NetCologne*, the corresponding project was called **"fight the flab"** (in German "Speck weg," cf. NetCologne, 2021). The advantage of such a label is that it first of all puts a smile on the faces of the people involved and is even more figurative than a **fitness program** initiated by many companies!

After this step, each company needs to rethink its **strategy** and **roadmap** for the next 12–18 months and revise its **investment portfolio** accordingly. Projects that were at the forefront just a short time ago may have lost relevance. These should then be terminated quickly or given a significantly lower priority. Continuing to work on such projects unchanged until the next "normal" planning-cycle is certainly more of a **looser strategy**.

> **Memory Box**
> If you have reached a dead end, there is only one solution: turn around and run back in the opposite direction.

Stage 5: Implementing Changes

Again, implementing change starts with **storytelling** (see Sect. 2.1.1). To accompany the implementation process, a clear, honest, empathetic and also **simple communication approach** is essential. An **offensive communication** is necessary because we live in a time of rapid dissemination even of information with questionable quality. The central **decision-makers in the company** must be the **trustworthy source** from which the flow of information is fed.

> **Memory Box**
> If in the **process of implementation** an **accompanying flow of relevant information**—starting from top management—is missing, the resulting information gap is filled by rumors. The people involved here, whom sociologists like to call **proclaimers**, can be found in every company. These are people who not only have decisive views but also like to share them, especially in an informal setting, e.g., in the coffee kitchen. They do not need their own

(continued)

competencies or a comprehensive information base in order to correctly assess the facts.

Therefore, in the course of the development and implementation of a digital transformation, we do not allow ourselves any informational gaps that the proclaimers like to fill with their own opinions, which are not necessarily accurate, in order to raise their profile!

When **building up resilience**, it is important to note—as already indicated—that the **resilience of a business model** cannot succeed without the **resilience of the managers and employees** (cf. Sects. 3.6.3 and 3.6.4). In the new normal this means for board members and managing directors, that they must already set the course for the future at a time when important information may still be missing in some cases.

This requires a great deal of **self-confidence** in order to make decisions nevertheless. After all, decisions in the VUCA world are associated with a significantly higher risk of failure. This is why **"driving on sight,"** which was often criticized in the past, is now also increasingly—albeit forcibly—accepted in strategic projects. This also includes the ability and, above all, the willingness to repeatedly adjust one's own course based on new findings. The need for this must also be widely communicated so that the decision-makers cannot be accused of being lazy and fickle in their decisions.

Memory Box
Even those who do not decide have already decided!

Perhaps we can return to a strategy that I learned with great interest during my studies at the *University of Mannheim*: **"the strategy of muddling through."** We all know how important a strategy is for business direction. However, it can also stifle creativity if it is rigidly enforced. Above all, a certain **flexibility in action** seems to become more important than a fine-tuned strategic compass in the face of the challenges of the VUCA world (cf. Fig. 1.2 on the paradigm shift).

Today, in many cases, a mindset is necessary that allows flexibly approaching higher-level goals—whereby a certain "muddling through" is almost inevitable. Lindblom (1959) contrasted the so-called **"root"-method** with the **"branch"-method**. The root-method is based on a comprehensive assessment of the available options against the background of the defined objectives. The branch-method is about moving forward step by step and in small increments from the current situation. It is simply a matter of successfully muddling through even in the most adverse conditions—and also of saying goodbye to well-formulated strategies when they no longer prove effective. The **process of muddling through** is described transparently here (Bizshifts, 2010):

(continued)

"Successful muddlers know you must get into the problem to see what it's all about. And the best way to do that is to stick your nose in and go for it. It may be that things become more confusing before they become clearer. But every act results in increased knowledge."

A muddling through technique means—surprisingly:
"Ready—Fire—Aim!"

Planning and setting goals are important and remain to stay important components on the path to success. But the first step into the unknown, the courage to take that step, are equally indispensable. Here we speak of a "just-do-it" personality and recall statements by *Mark Zuckerberg***:**
"Done is better than perfect!"

Today, it is often a matter of solving a sub-problem (choosing a good first move) and then seeing what new tasks and follow-up problems arise that need to be addressed. Increasingly, the complexity of decision-making problems leads to such a step-by-step approach. Cheeky, you might say:

In the past one spoke of muddling through—today, we speak of agile management.

The type of crisis management and thus the presence of resilience is also a cultural issue (cf. Fig. **2.13; cf.** Sapriel, 2019). **The higher the resilience and the greater the vigilance in the company, the more proactive and creative a company will be able to act.**

This is where you are called upon to check what crisis management looks like in your company and what the underlying maxims for action are in each case.

A study by the *Boston Consulting Group* shows us in which industries the **development of digital resilience** seems particularly urgent. The following aspects were taken into account in the analysis (cf. Close et al., 2020, p. 6):

- **Digitization potentials of processes and services** to address important pain points of customers
- **Scalability of digital offers**
- **Level of risk capital for digital technology**
- **Threat to incumbents** from new market entrants

The basis of this study is the companies' self-assessments of the **challenges posed by digital disruption** and the **extent of necessary transformation processes**. The proportion of companies under stress in the sectors analyzed was determined on the basis of the proportion of companies with a probability of failure of more than 15% (cf. Close et al., 2020, p. 6).

According to this, **building digital resilience** is particularly necessary in the **wholesale and retail, automotive** and **logistics sectors** (cf. Fig. 2.14; cf. Close et al., 2020, p. 6f.). By contrast, there is a significantly lower degree

(continued)

of urgency in the **public sector** and in the **energy and utilities sector**. The majority of sectors are located between these two extreme positions.

Using Fig. **2.14, you can work out for your company and your industry how necessary it is to build digital resilience.**

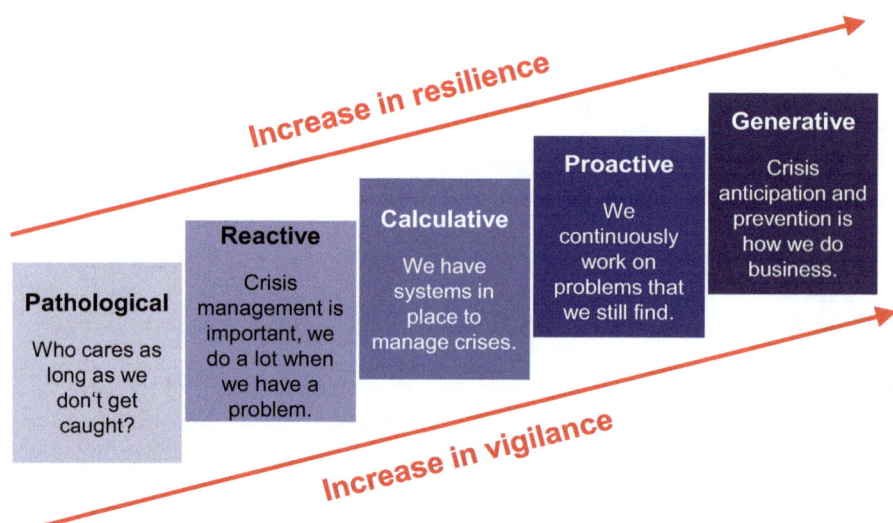

Fig. 2.13 Crisis management—a question of culture

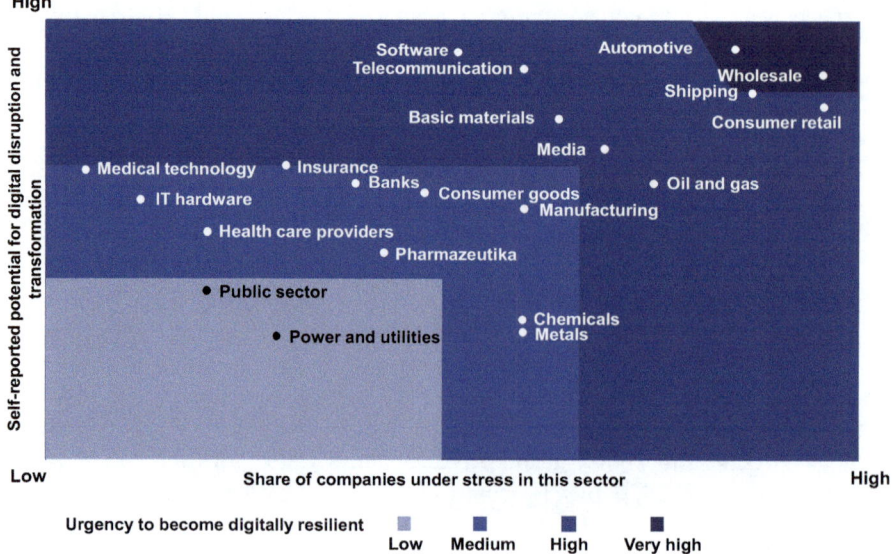

Fig. 2.14 Self-reported potential for digital disruption and transformation

> **Think Box: Questions You Should Ask Yourself**
> - Have you ever conducted a resilience analysis for your company, your business model and/or your core processes?
> - Has a resilience analysis ever been carried out for your managers and your employees?
> - Do you base your resilience analysis on the business model canvas?
> - Have you already identified the key weaknesses in your business model?
> - How does your company's profitability compare to Simon's study results on after-tax return on sales?
> - Have you already conducted a business impact analysis to run through the effects of different threat scenarios on your business model?
> - Have you already developed options for action for different scenarios?
> - Do you already have a not-to-do list that is continuously updated?
> - Have you revised your strategy, your roadmap and the investment portfolio—based on the contents of the not-to-do list?
> - Have measures to strengthen your resilience already been implemented in your company?
> - What do you think of the muddling-through technique "Ready—Fire—Aim?"
> - What does your crisis management look like as a characteristic of your corporate culture?
> - How does your industry perform in the *Boston Consulting Group* study on building digital resilience?
> - Where are you driving the development of corporate resilience?
> - How often do you hear the statement or excuse "everything is different here?"

2.2 Concept for the Analysis of the Digital Business Performance

Challenges do not disappear by ignoring them.

The tools presented in Sects. 1.2 and 2.1 provide the relevant information basis to carry out the **analysis of digital business performance**, which is indispensable in the context of digital transformation. This analysis determines how "fit" or how "mature" your company is to survive in the face of the challenges of digitalization. The literature provides a wide range of models for this analysis. These include the concepts of the Boston Consulting Group (cf. Close et al., 2020, p. 8), Fujitsu Limited (2018), Böhm et al. (2018, p. 76f.) and Peyman et al. (2014, p. 39).

Inspired by these concepts, the following **criteria** were selected to **determine the digital business performance of an organization**:

- Vision, goals and strategies for the digital age
- Sustainability of the business model
- Digitization of the value chain
- IT infrastructure, data basis and technologies
- Exploitation of digital potential through marketing and sales
- Human resources strategies for the digital age
- Organizational concepts for the digital age
- Controlling as an enabler of digital transformation

> **Memory Box**
> **For the analysis of digital business performance, eight dimensions of the company that are crucial to success are used.**
>
> By **analyzing the digital business performance** of your own company, you can identify the most important fields of action and concrete potential for optimization in the various performance areas. You start—ideally supported by a competent external moderator—a **process of self-analysis.** For this purpose, the following people are integrated into the analysis team: the managers from the corresponding areas, important top performers, innovative lateral thinkers of different ages and employees who have only been with the company for a short time. The latter usually have a lower degree of operational blindness.
>
> In a **step-by-step process**, the participants in small, hierarchically and professionally mixed teams evaluate the **perceived degree of maturity of the various dimensions**. Diversity in the results should be made conscious and visible to all, because this is where **exciting fields of action** usually open up. The model presented here has already been used many times in consulting and transformation processes to analyze the digital business performance and has proven its worth there.
>
> The findings of the analysis of digital business performance provide you with the informational basis for the next step: the **development of concepts for the digital age.** If necessary, certain analyses need to be refined again or new sources of information are required to support this process. In Chap. 3, you will find further important basics, tools and impulses for action for all the dimensions addressed here, in order to design these dimensions for your company in a goal-oriented manner.
>
> Figure 2.15 shows the basic concept of the **analysis of digital business performance**. Using the **criteria** defined above, you analyze your company in the eight dimensions with regard to their "digital" design. Five **levels of maturity** are distinguished for each of these dimensions:
>
> - **Not Defined**
>   There is no preparatory work in the direction of digitization

(continued)

2.2 Concept for the Analysis of the Digital Business Performance

- **Defined, But Not Yet Implemented**
  Conceptual considerations have already been made. Targets as well as measures have already been developed, but nothing has been implemented yet.
- **Defined, Partially Implemented**
  The implementation has already started, and the first goals have been achieved. However, the implementation level is still below 50%.
- **Defined, Mainly Implemented**
  Implementation is already well advanced, and major goals have been achieved. The implementation level is already above 50% but has not yet reached 100%.
- **Transformed Extensively**
  The defined target state has been fully achieved. The necessary changes are already holistically anchored in the operational and organizational structure of the company. Work on the digital transformation is ongoing—after all, it is never over.

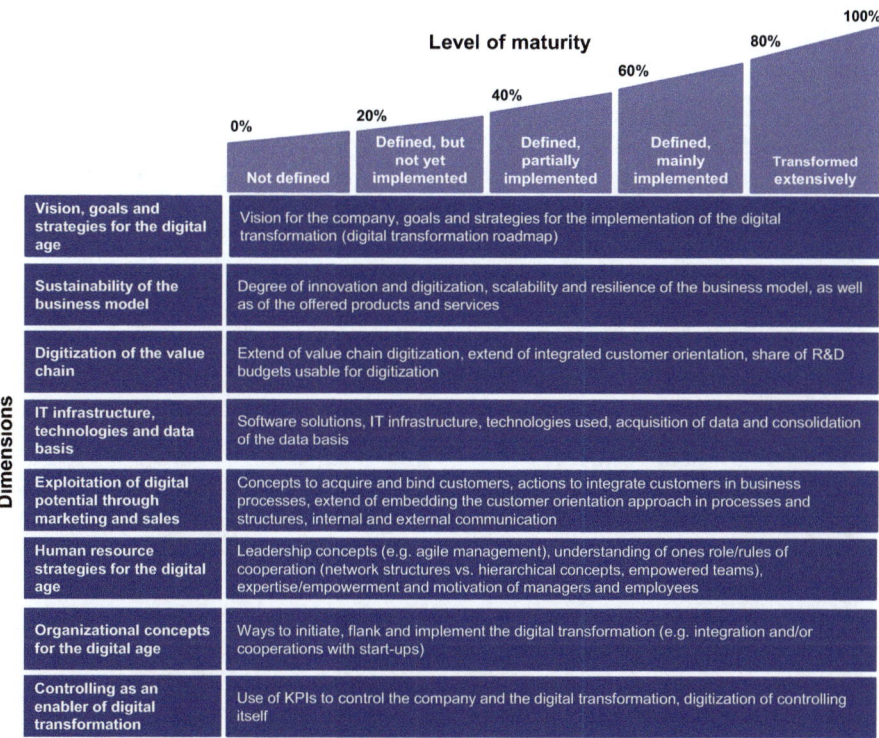

Fig. 2.15 Analysis of the digital business performance

> **Memory Box**
> **Five different maturity levels are distinguished in the analysis of digital business performance.**
> The interplay of the eight dimensions and the five maturity levels of the digital business performance analysis is shown in Fig. 2.15.
>
> You can use the following **eight dimensions** of the **analysis of digital business performance** for your company:
>
> - **Vision, Goals and Strategies for the Digital Age**
>   This is where the maturity of the corporate vision and the defined goals and strategies are determined. It is a core task of corporate management to first develop a **vision for the digital age** (keyword "start with the why") in order to subsequently concretize it in **goals** and **strategies** (cf. Sinek, 2011). Here it is important to evaluate the relevance of changing customer expectations, advances by new competitors and new technological possibilities for the company and to integrate them into the company's thoughts for a sustainable orientation.
>
>   In doing so, you should also work out whether your company is currently only concentrating on **micro-initiatives** to cope with the upcoming challenges or whether powerful **macro-strategies** have been developed (see Sect. 3.2.3). A **transformation-roadmap** is needed for implementation.
>
>   In the course of this dimension, you check to what extent the requirements described have already been thought about and/or been implemented. The maturity levels presented above are used for assessment.
>
> - **Sustainability of the Business Model**
>   With regard to the business model, it is first necessary to check on which **horizon level** your company has been operating so far (see Sect. 3.2.2). Does digitalization primarily focus on **cost and efficiency goals**, or is your company already striving to develop **business model innovations**. Here we also question how regularly and how systematically new business models are worked on.
>
>   How should your existing business model be evaluated in terms of **scalability** and **resilience**? A central component of this analysis is also the review of the **future viability of the company's own products and services.** Their relevance must be assessed against the background of changed customer expectations, new competitors and/or new technologies.
>
> - **Digitization of the Value Chain**
>   This dimension draws attention to the degree of digitization of the company's own value chain. One of the questions here is to what extent relative competitive advantages could be achieved through the already achieved **level of digitization** of the value creation processes. These can
>
> (continued)

be based on the cost or benefit superiority of one's own offerings compared to competitors. For this purpose, the entire value chain must be examined to see whether (further) digitization can lead to customer advantages and/or cost superiority. In addition, existing "digital offers" in the product and service range should be assessed for their further digitization potential.

In addition, you can determine here whether the **digitization of your value chain** is—wrongly—still interpreted as a pure "efficiency project" to reduce costs and not as an opportunity to develop innovative product and service concepts as well as completely new business models.

In addition, the **flexibility of the business processes** to cope with new challenges must be examined. The extent to which digital channels are already used internally and/or externally to network value chains is also recorded. **Networking within the industry** is often of great importance. The extent to which (own) **ecosystems** and/or **platforms** are established and/or concepts developed by third parties are used must be examined.

It should also be analyzed how comprehensively **customer orientation** is integrated into the value chain. In order to create seamless customer experiences ("seamless integration," "noline concept"), the digitization of core processes must be advanced in many areas. To this end, it is also necessary to determine to what extent **data and process silos**—but above all **silos in people's own minds**—have already been overcome or still need to be overcome. This all flows into the maturity of this dimension.

The level of **R&D budgets for digitization** also occupies an important position here. How high is their share compared to the R&D activities that focus on classic, non-digital areas?

- **IT Infrastructure, Technologies and Data Basis**
  In this area, the question is how comprehensively the IT infrastructure (e.g., cloud solutions) and the technologies used are already exploiting the potential of digitization. These fields of action are important "enablers" and thus "supporters" of the digital transformation. The extent to which innovative technologies can be used as the basis for new business models (e.g., for platform concepts or service offerings around predictive maintenance, etc.), for process automation and for the development of ecosystems must be examined. Top and middle management have the task of recognizing the relevance of new technologies and creating an awareness of the need for (digital) change throughout the company.

  A great deal of attention must also be paid to the **acquisition of first party data** and **access to second- and third-party data** (keyword "big data") as well as to the **consolidation of the company's own data bases**. These data resources are becoming increasingly important for creating competitive advantages. The technologies used should therefore also contribute to comprehensive **data analysis**.

(continued)

The requirements for this further development will be driven in particular by market, customer and thus sales/marketing and require a flexible design of the supporting systems. In order to be successful here, new **technological possibilities** must be continuously examined with regard to their contribution to value creation for the own company—and in the case of positive contributions—integrated into the own processes. In addition, the extent to which the **resources** required for implementation (especially budgets and personnel) are made available must be recorded in this area.

- **Exploitation digital potential through marketing and sales**

  This area of analysis focuses on **concepts for the acquisition and retention of value adding customers**. At the same time, the question arises to what extent customers should be integrated into business processes. A possible higher **customer proximity** (keyword "open innovation") can lead to more relevant offers (reduction of the flop rate) on the one hand, and on the other hand, increase customer loyalty and thus one's own value creation.

  In this context, **internal communication** (marketing to the inside or internal marketing) is also very important. An essential prerequisite for the implementation of a digital vision is not only to document it, but to communicate the vision across all company hierarchies. Only when this vision and the goals and strategies based on it are understood in their entirety by all members of the organization it can unfold its transformational effect. The task of "marketing inwards" is to create **awareness of the need for a digital transformation** of the entire organization.

- **Human Resources Strategies for the Digital Age**

  An indispensable prerequisite for successful digital transformation is the development of corresponding human resources strategies. After all, all transformation measures are initiated and implemented by people—or prevented by them. Therefore, within the framework of this dimension, it must be examined to what extent the established **leadership concepts** (keyword "leadership culture"), the existing **understanding of roles** by the participants, the **rules of cooperation**, established **work concepts** (e.g., network structures vs. hierarchical concepts, empowered teams, leadership at a distance) support the process of a digital transformation.

  In this context, the **expertise and empowerment of the staff** and, above all, their **motivation to participate** in shaping the digital transformation are of great importance. Therefore, it should be examined to what extent **digital expertise** has already been built up in the company's own workforce and/or corresponding learning processes have already been anchored within the company through **training-programs with digital content**. Finally, **new qualifications** are required in the digital (working) world. For the

(continued)

transformation process, **people with "digital know-how"** must be anchored at central points in the company.

A **commitment** to the necessary change not only from management but also from as many employees as possible is an important prerequisite for success. After all, all members of a company have to make a multitude of decisions in the course of a working day. Not all of these decision-making processes can be regulated by clear guidelines. For example, there is the question of which customer or which project should be given a higher priority. In these cases, employees often refer to the **vision** and **culture**, which is based on a specific **set of values of the company.** Consequently, the corporate culture has a direct impact on the daily work process. For this, it is important that this culture already contains "**digital DNA**" and an **openness to innovation**.

The **corporate culture** can either become a **brake on innovation** or an **accelerator of innovation**. This is why we also look at how the corporate culture is structured in terms of transparency, dynamism, communication intensity and willingness to change. The question of culture also includes how to deal with "failure." Therefore, the fault tolerance of one's own corporate culture must be determined. Are managers and employees whose projects were not successful sent to desert? Or is the effort acknowledged and there an attempt to learn from the failures for the future? The aspects addressed here should be taken into account when defining the maturity level for this dimension.

- **Organizational Concepts for the Digital Age**
  In this dimension, you analyze which forms of organization are already used or could be used to initiate, accompany and implement the digital transformation. Among other things, you should examine how innovation thinking can be anchored in the whole organization.

  It should also be determined whether your company has anchored **strategic entrepreneurship**. Does an **innovation engine** exist in which innovations are systematically and continuously worked on? Has a **Chief Digital Officer** already been installed to drive the process of digital transformation forward? To what extent did a **linking with innovation hotspots** took place in order to tap into inspiring sources of information? This can include the **involvement of or cooperation with start-ups**.

- **Controlling as an Enabler of Digital Transformation**
  In the context of controlling, it must be examined which concepts can be used by controlling to act as an **enabler of the digital transformation**. Various **KPIs** (key performance indicators) can be defined in the concept of a balanced scorecard. These should be used to monitor and control not only the entire company, but also the **process of digital transformation**.

(continued)

It is important to check whether strategic controlling is able to detect the relevant changes in the company's environment and in the company itself at an early stage. Can risks and opportunities, but also strengths and weaknesses, be recognized at an early stage in order to derive recommendations for action? Classical controlling concepts that do not sufficiently differentiate between digital and non-digital activities must be identified here and the need to overcome them must be worked out.

In addition, there is the question of the **digitalization of controlling** itself. Where can controlling tasks be simplified and/or automated by new technologies (e.g., artificial intelligence)? The answers found to these questions are taken into account when defining the maturity level.

Memory Box

The **benchmark**, i.e., the standard of comparison for your company, is defined by the organizations that show the **best performance** in the designated dimensions. Here you **ignore sector boundaries**—after all, today's and tomorrow's competitors usually no longer come from your own industry.

An introduction to what has already been achieved in the various dimensions today can be provided by short **impulse presentations**—ideally by external specialists with a broad view of the bigger picture. These lectures can contribute significantly to the—sometimes painful—**broadening of one's own knowledge horizon**. An external presenter can also convey the big picture of digital transformation to show what is possible in your industry. This often makes it clear to the participants how far or how little progress a company has already made on the path of a comprehensive digital transformation.

How well your company is positioned overall from an internal perspective can be summarized in the **analysis grid for digital business performance**, which can be found in Fig. 2.16.

It is exciting when the participants or the different company divisions make such an assessment independently of each other and the respective results are then made visible in Fig. 2.16 by markings. Often there is not only a **great deal of agreement**, but also serious **deviations in the assessments**.

The greater the **range of maturity-levels identified**, the more serious the internal communication deficits. Either those involved lack information about the level reached in each of the other areas—or too little information is available about what digitalization can achieve for the company as a whole or for individual areas. In both cases, you should promptly initiate measures to overcome the identified information deficits.

2.2 Concept for the Analysis of the Digital Business Performance

> **Memory Box**
> The **analysis of digital business performance** can be carried out as a **self-analysis** by managers and employees of one's own company. The moderation of an external consultant will make the assessment more independent if the consultant also has a profound knowledge of the possibilities of digitalization in different areas of the company.
>
> **You should carry out the analysis of digital business performance once a year—in each case against the background of new technologies and changed expectations of your stakeholders and new technological options!**
>
> The review of your own digital business performance is an indispensable—albeit often painful—examination of the status quo. However, only such an analysis can ensure that a necessary digital transformation takes into account the "true" starting situation and is not based on (wrong) assumptions. The next step is to systematically work on the individual fields analyzed in order to tap into existing **potential for managing the digital transformation**. You will receive valuable information on this in Chap. 3. In addition, powerful tools are again presented there.

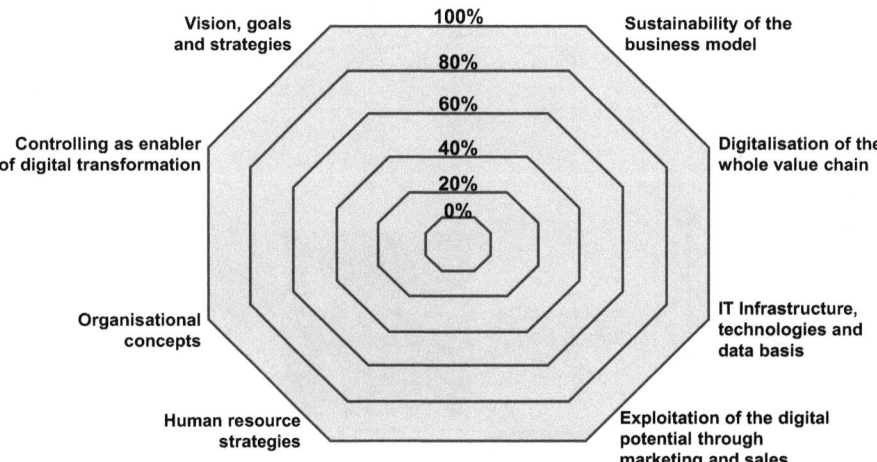

Fig. 2.16 Analysis grid for digital business performance

Think Box: Questions You Should Ask Yourself
- Have you ever conducted an analysis of the digital business performance in your company? If not, then you should do so as soon as possible. If yes, then the question arises as to what consequences you have derived from the information gained.
- Will an analysis of digital business performance be carried out once a year in the future?
- Who could provide external support for such an analysis process?
- Who in your company is responsible for regularly carrying out the analysis?

2.3 Options to Develop a Digital Business Performance for Digital Excellence

The options to be discussed in Chap. 3 are always about the question of how you want to react to the emerging developments. Your various options for action can be taken from the **strategic game board** (cf. Fig. 2.17). This first poses the question of whether your company is active or wants to become active in a market with **new rules** or **familiar rules**. The new rules are the phenomena increasingly referred to today as disruptive developments.

In addition, you can answer the question in the strategic game board whether you want to serve the **entire market** or a **niche**. Disruptive developments—often by

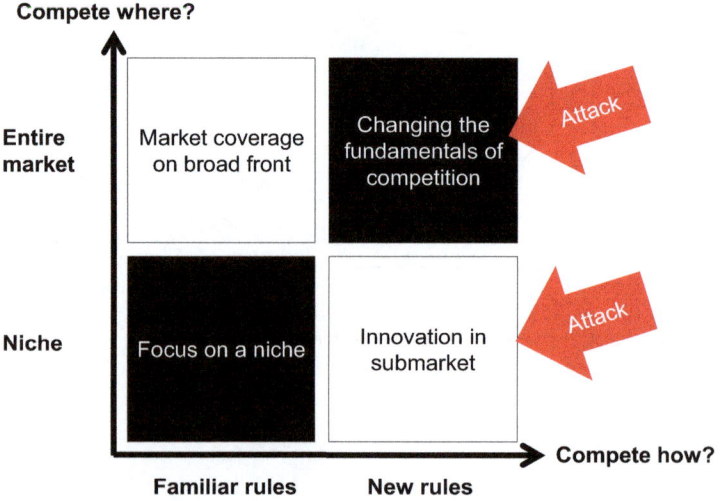

Fig. 2.17 Strategic game board

start-ups from outside the sector—initially start in a niche and are therefore often hardly noticed at the beginning.

Using the **strategic game board**, you can and should continuously monitor which players—perhaps hardly noticed so far—appear that can challenge your business models with new or modified concepts or even destroy them in the long run.

In this analysis, you should take into account that the entire **entrepreneurial playing field** is currently undergoing serious changes:

- The **playing field is getting bigger** because physical boundaries in product and service creation, communication and service demand are becoming less important. A key driver for this is the increasing digitalization and networking of products, services and processes, which is driving business model innovations.
- At the same time, **new rules for the game** are becoming valid because barriers to market entry are lowering and start-ups are coming off the assembly line. In Shenzhen, China alone, as already mentioned, 1000 start-ups are founded—every day! The established competitors are thus exposed to a continuous attack by new challengers. At the same time, many financiers are willing to provide start-ups with venture capital. Founders and investors are driven by the hope of finding the next unicorn (in the sense of the "next big thing"). The term "unicorn" is used to describe new companies that reach a market capitalization of more than 1 billion US-$.

  In addition, **new game devices** are constantly being introduced on the playing field. These are in social media such as *Snapchat* and *TikTok* or the streaming offerings of *Spotify*, *Netflix* and *Twitch*. Communication and collaboration platforms such as *Slack*, *TriCat*, *Miro*, *Mural*, *WhatsApp* and *Zoom* are also changing communication behavior. The new game changers also include platforms such as *blablacar*, *Share Now*, *Uber*, *wimdu* or *Zilok*, which are entering into direct competition with established business models.
- In addition, **millions of additional players** are pushing their way onto the playing field because more and more people are gaining access to the Internet. They can participate in any form of communication with questions or their own content and naturally also represent an important sales market.
- At the same time, the playing field is being expanded into the **third dimension** because the way information is provided—based on big data—allows a three-dimensional customer approach. This makes it possible for many providers to consider location, time and preferences simultaneously when addressing customers and to provide offers not only just-in-time and just-in-place, but also according-to-references. Here, the development towards context marketing is becoming apparent.
- In addition, "trust" is becoming increasingly important when entering into business relationships and especially when providing data. If we introduce "trust" as a further action-relevant component, the **playing field expands into the fourth dimension**. Trust as the new currency is above all!
- In addition, the **speed of the game** increases dramatically because information is not only available in an unprecedented density, but its changes are often available

in real time. Therefore, customers will become increasingly impatient to wait for reactions from their companies, forcing them to significantly increase their reaction speed as well (keyword "instant society"). In addition, process chains, even across national borders, can be networked and controlled in real time.

The dynamics of this change must not lead to a **state of shock**. After all, this is not really a strategy for success in mastering digital change! In the past, the belief still applied:
"If you move, you lose!"
Now it is:
"Whoever does not move today, has already lost today, or tomorrow at the latest!"

> **Think Box: Questions You Should Ask Yourself**
> - How do you position your company in the strategic game board?
> - Do you tend to play by new or familiar rules?
> - Do you focus on the market as a whole, or do you rather focus on a niche?
> - Use the strategic game board also to identify players who have hardly been noticed so far and who can challenge your business models with new or modified concepts or even destroy them in the long run.
> - Is your playing-field currently getting bigger or is it getting smaller?
> - Are new rules of the game—in the form of innovative business logics—being introduced into the market by existing or new competitors?
> - Are new game devices available to you that you should examine for relevance to your own business model?
> - How is the number of players in your market changing?
> - Is there—through access to relevant information streams—an expansion of the playing field into the third dimension (keyword "big data"), which allows a customer approach oriented equally to place, time and preferences?
> - What significance does the expansion of the playing field into the fourth dimension have for your industry—based on trust as the new currency?
> - How is the speed of the game changing in your sector—and are your structures and processes already geared to this (e.g., real time analytics)?
> - Does your company—also in the image of others—tend to be among the first or fast movers because you pick up on trends early and actively?
> - Or does your company rather fall into the group of late movers who like to let others go first? Here, however, there is a risk that the late movers become first losers because attractive market positions are occupied and platform concepts and ecosystems become established there.

Literature

Bitkom. (2020). *Last Call: Germany! - Die Bitkom-Digitalstrategie 2025*. Accessed 26.11.2020, from https://www.bitkom.org/Bitkom/Bitkom-Digitalstrategie2025

Bizshifts. (2010). *Muddling through business strategy: Strategic shifts....* Accessed 20.10.2020, from https://bizshifts-trends.com/%E2%80%9Cmuddling-through%E2%80%9D-strategic-shifts/

Böhm, M., Müller, S., Krcmar, H., & Welpe, I. (2018). Digitale transformation in ausgewählten Ländern im Vergleich. In: Oswald, G., Krcmar, H. (Hrsg.) *Digitale transformation*. Wiesbaden: Springer Gabler.

Brinker, S. (2013). *Martec's law: Technology changes exponentially, organizations change logarithmically*. Accessed 23.11.2020, from https://chiefmartec.com/2013/06/martecs-law-technology-changes-exponentially-organizations-change-logarithmically/

Close, K., Grebe, M., Andersen, P., Khurana, V., Franke, M. R., & Kalthof, R. (2020). *The digital path to business resilience*. Boston Consulting Group.

Deutscher Bundestag. (2013). *Bericht zur Risikoanalyse im Bevölkerungsschutz 2012*, Drucksache 17/12051, 17. Wahlperiode, Berlin, dipbt.bundestag.de, Accessed 10.9.2020.

Etzold, V. (2018). *Strategie, Planen – Erklären – Umsetzen*. Gabal.

Fujitsu Limited. (2018). *Global digital transformation survey report 2018*. Accessed 17.9.2020, from https://www.fujitsu.com/downloads/GLOBAL/vision/2018/download-center/FTSV2018_Survey_EN-1.pdf

Gartner. (2020a). *Gartner magic quadrant*. Accessed 13.10.2020, from https://www.gartner.com/en/research/methodologies/magic-quadrants-research

Gartner. (2020b). Create a resilient business model in the Face of COVID-19. Accessed 10.9.2020, from https://www.gartner.com/smarterwithgartner/create-a-resilient-business-model-in-the-face-of-covid-19/

Hoffmann, G. P. (2016). *Organisationale Resilienz, Grundlagen und Handlungsempfehlungen für Entscheidungsträger und Führungskräfte*. Springer.

Jung, A. (2020). Welt auf Abstand. *Der Spiegel, 19*(2020), 72.

Kreutzer, R. (2019). *Toolbox for marketing und management, creative concepts, forecasting methods, and analytical instruments*. Springer Gabler.

Lindblom, C. E. (1959). The science of "muddling through". *Public Administration Review, 19*(2), 79–88.

Müller, A. (2020). *Diese Unternehmen wollen dabei helfen, den Shutdown zu beenden*. Accessed 15.9.2020, from https://www.handelsblatt.com/unternehmen/mittelstand/familienunternehmer/schutzmaskenhersteller-diese-unternehmen-wollen-dabei-helfen-den-shutdown-zu-beenden/25733898.html?ticket=ST-3152934-Y2F5nr00tsY0mwjpQl0h-ap5

NetCologne. (2021). *PE-Entwicklungskonzepte bei NetCologne*, Köln.

Oerter, R., & Montada, L. (2002). *Entwicklungspsychologie*. Beltz.

Peyman, A. K., Faraby, N., Rossmann, A., Steimel, B., & Wichmann, K. S. (2014). *Digital transformation report 2014*, neuland und WirtschaftsWoche (Hrsg.), Köln.

Porter, M. (1996). What is strategy? *Harvard Business Review*, November–December, pp. 61–78.

Porter, M. E. (1999). *Wettbewerbsstrategie*. Campus.

Porter, M. E. (2004). *Wettbewerbsvorteile*. Campus.

Prognos. (2020). *Globalisierungsreport 2020, Wer profitiert am stärksten von der Globalisierung?* Accessed 15.9.2020, from www.prognos.com

Pyczak, T. (2018). *Tell me!: Wie Sie mit Storytelling überzeugen. Inkl. Praxisbeispiele. Für alle, die erfolgreich sein wollen in Beruf, PR und Online-Marketing*. Rheinwerk Verlag.

Reifenhäuser. (2020). *Hoher Bedarf an medizinischer Schutzkleidung: Reifenhäuser stellt weitere Versuchsanlage auf Produktion um*. Accessed 5.1.2021, from https://www.reifenhauser.com/de/news/hoher_bedarf_an_medizinischer_schutzkleidung_reifenhaeuser_stellt_weitere_versuchsanlage_auf_produktion_um

Sapriel, C. (2019). *How to continually build your crisis resilience: A checklist*. Accessed 20.10.2020, from https://www.iabc.com/crisis-resilience-checklist/

Shank, R. C. (2021). *Effective storytelling techniques for social media*. Accessed 5.1.2021, from https://masterclasses.marketing-interactive.com/virtual-masterclasses/effective-storytelling-techniques-for-social-media/

Simon, H. (2020). Es gibt nur einen richtigen Gewinn. *Frankfurter Allgemeine Zeitung*, 21.9.2020, p. 18.

Sinek, S. (2011). *Start with why: How great leaders inspire everyone to take action*. Penguin Group.

Statista. (2019). *ecommerceDB - Top Online-Shops in Deutschland*. Accessed 17.8.2020, from https://de-statista-com.ezproxy.hwr-berlin.de/statistik/studie/id/55068/dokument/ecommercedb-top-online-shops-in-deutschland/

Storr, W. (2019). *Science of storytelling (Englisch)*. William Collins.

Welter-Enderlin, R., & Hildenbrand, B. (Eds.). (2012). *Resilienz – Gedeihen trotz widriger Umstände* (4th ed.). Carl-Auer Verlag.

Wiebking, J. (2020). Ein Land trägt Van Laack. *Frankfurter Allgemeine Zeitung*, 20.9.2020, p. 12.

Ziems, D., Ebenfeld, T., & Winkler, R. (2020). *Global Viral Change, Auswirkungen von Corona auf Gesellschaft*. Konsum und Marketing in der globalen Kultur.

Eight Fields of Action for Building Digital Excellence

3

Per aspera ad astra!

The following eight chapters show in detail the steps a company can take to achieve digital excellence. This process starts with the development of **visions, objectives, and strategies for the digital age**. **Concepts for the development and evaluation of business models** are then presented. This is followed by ideas for **digitizing the value chain**. Subsequently, it is explained how the **IT infrastructure** and the **data basis** must be designed and which **fields of application artificial intelligence** offers.

In a further chapter, **concepts for exploiting digitalization opportunities in marketing and sales** are presented. This is followed by considerations on the design of **human resources strategy** and **organizational concepts** for the digital age. Finally, it is shown which **design of controlling** can support the transformation process.

3.1 Vision, Objectives, and Strategies for the Digital Age

If you don't know the harbor you want to sail into, no wind is right for you.
   Seneca.

3.1.1 Digital Base Model as a Point of Orientation for Digital Transformation

If you always follow in someone else's footsteps, you will never overtake them.

The **digital base model** was presented by Kofler (2018). At the center of this concept is the company's business model. A **business model** describes how a company develops, communicates, and captures values (cf. Osterwalder & Pigneur, 2011, p. 18). This business model is concretized in the **creation of specific products**

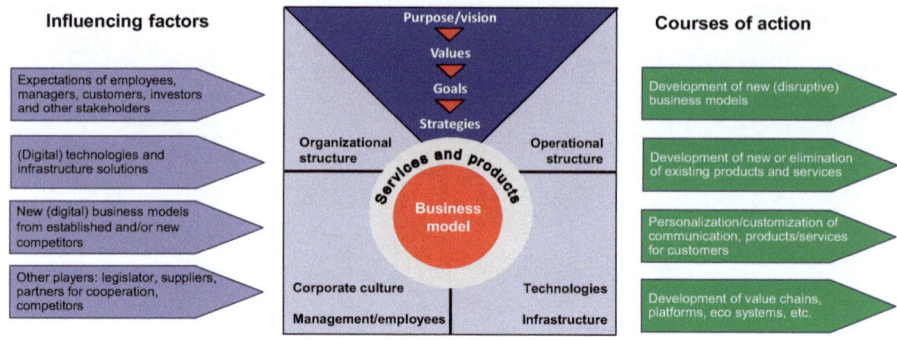

Fig. 3.1 Digital base model

and/or services for different target groups. The direction in which a company moves is significantly influenced by its **purpose, vision,** and **values**—task: "start with the why!" (cf. also Alter, 2019, pp. 27–31). These in turn are concretized in **corporate goals**, which are to be achieved through a **corporate strategy** (cf. Fig. 3.1; cf. Kofler, 2018, p. 52).

In order to achieve the goals and implement the strategy, both the organizational structure and the operational structure must be designed accordingly. The **organizational structure** describes the hierarchical structure of a company and is visualized by an organizational chart. The **operational structure** defines the company's internal processes. These can relate to planning, purchasing, production, human resources development, controlling or the development of innovations.

These structural and process-related specifications are filled in by people. In this context, the corporate culture is of great importance. With its values, the **corporate culture** not only shapes the **management** or **management styles** of a company, but also the behavior of each individual **employee**. The culture is, as it were, a compass for the behavior accepted or demanded by the company (cf. von Rosenstiel & Nerdinger, 2011, pp. 375–381).

In addition, **technologies** and **infrastructure** are required to enable the company to develop value-creating offers. In addition to classic ERP systems (Enterprise Resource Planning) for controlling the entire company, CRM software (Customer Relationship Management) for value-oriented customer management should also be considered here. Finally, all IT systems, production facilities, and other infrastructure areas are also included.

The illustration in Fig. 3.1 makes it clear that a business model can be successfully implemented especially if it is supported by all the facets of the company mentioned above. Therefore, **digital organizational development** must not be limited to sub-areas of the company. Therefore, it must be avoided that, for example, an artificial intelligence (AI) team is set up in the field of technologies and infrastructure that has no connection to other areas of the company. Even the installation of a Chief Digital Officer (CDO) at the top management level alone does not help if he or she cannot influence the entire company through a personnel substructure and by being responsible for certain processes—and also has the necessary financial and personnel resources (see Sect. 3.7.4).

Various **influencing factors** have an impact on this overall structure, which are listed in Fig. 3.1 on the left and have already been comprehensively examined in Chaps. 1 and 2. First and foremost are the **expectations of the stakeholders,** which are brought to the company directly or indirectly. In addition to the company's own staff, customers are of particular importance as stakeholders. After all, their acceptance of the company's offer is crucial to the development of the entire company. At the same time, in the digital age, companies have a multitude of **new (digital) technologies** and new **infrastructure solutions** at their disposal, which need to be examined for their relevance to the existing business model.

Furthermore, new technologies and infrastructure solutions also enable the development of **new (digital) business models** with which established and/or new competitors enter the market. These can also be disruptive business models. The term "disruptive" stands for approaches that can replace existing solutions or even completely displace them from the market. In addition, other actors have an impact on the company. These include **legislators, suppliers, cooperation partners,** and **competitors**. Some can restrict the company's scope of business (e.g., through legislation), others can expand it through innovative solutions.

The totality of these influencing factors continuously challenges the existing business model and the individual company divisions—in the digital age, however, more than ever before. Therefore, sooner or later, every company must react to these challenges in a more or less comprehensive manner. The **options for action** available to your company are shown in Fig. 3.1 on the right-hand side. First of all, you yourself can develop **new (disruptive) business models** as well as **new products and/or services** for the digital age or further develop existing offers. At the same time, check which **offers need to be eliminated** because they no longer fit the times (keyword "not-to-do list"; see Sect. 2.1.5). This can be the discontinuation of the offer of package tours, the stop of a production of CDs and DVDs—or the closure of distribution channels such as video stores, travel agencies, or stationary retail shops. This also includes the phasing out of the production of combustion engines and fewer and fewer printed books and catalogues.

> **Memory Box**
> **The digital base model provides a powerful framework for entering the process of digital transformation and achieving digital excellence.**

▶ **Food for Thought**
The biggest risk of digital transformation for companies is not wanting to take risks in the course of this transformation process.

> **Think Box: Questions You Should Ask Yourself**
> - Do you already use the digital base concept or a similar system to describe the challenges of a digital transformation and the relevant levers?
> - Are the defined purpose, vision, and values of your company sufficiently future-oriented?
> - Do your goals and strategies carry the company into a profitable future?
> - Does your organizational structure and operational structure support the implementation of the defined strategies?
> - Does your corporate culture promote or rather slow down the digital transformation?
> - How well does your company know the expectations of its stakeholders?
> - Is there comprehensive transparency in your company regarding the multitude of new (digital) technologies as well as new infrastructure solutions?
> - Do you follow the development of new (digital) business models by established and/or new competitors?
> - What influences can be expected from legislators, suppliers, cooperation partners, and competitors in the future?
> - Are you already actively developing new (disruptive) business models yourself?
> - Are new products and/or services in development?
> - Do you maintain a not-to-do list?
> - Whose responsibility is it to work with the digital base concept or a similar system?

3.1.2 Requirements for a Vision in the Digital Age

Only those who lead the way determine the direction.

When you initiate change processes in your company, you must be aware of encountering a **high level of resistance to any kind of change**. This resistance can only be overcome if the management at the top leadership level has a **powerful vision.** However, this vision should not be developed in an ivory tower. Rather, in order to have a company-wide impact, it should be developed with the participation of managers and staff from all levels of the hierarchy and from all functional areas.

In addition, it must be ensured that comprehensive **knowledge about the opportunities and risks of digitalization** influences the development of the vision. Therefore, an extensive analysis of the entrepreneurial environment must be carried out in advance of the development of a vision. For this, you can use the tools presented in Chaps. 1 and 2 and incorporate the information presented there. The entirety of the insights gained are to be fed into the process of developing a vision.

The **vision** to be created should function as the **guiding idea of the entrepreneurial activity**. It forms the background for action, which should describe the

3.1 Vision, Objectives, and Strategies for the Digital Age

future development of the company in a pictorial, credible, and attractive way. Only through this is it possible for a vision to fulfill the following **functions** (cf. Hungenberg, 2014, p. 26):

- **Identity function of a vision**
  The vision should contain directional goals to which especially the own staff can orientate themselves over a longer period of time. Ideally, the contents of the vision should become part of the identity of the staff, so that they virtually embody the desired target state. For this, it is important that the vision describes an image of the future, which ideally makes the company unique and unmistakable.
- **Identification function of a vision**
  The vision should show managers and employees of a company the deeper meaning and purpose of their own actions and thereby strengthen the feeling of belonging to the company. If the members of the company can identify themselves with the vision, they can also overcome resistance that is to be expected on the way to implementing the vision much more powerfully.
- **Mobilization function of a vision**
  The vision is intended to stimulate the joint pursuit of the company's desired image of the future as a goal. In this way, entrepreneurial power reserves can be activated and made usable for the change process.

Memory Box

What should be the orientation of executives, employees, investors, cooperation partners, and other stakeholders in an environment with high change dynamics? It is perfect if this orientation is provided by a comprehensibly described target image. Ideally, this is a vision that describes the (digital) future of the company in powerful words.

It is particularly important that your company also provides convincing answers to the question of **"Why?"** In essence, this is about the **purpose** of the company and the question: Why do we exist as a company? The **outcomes** to be achieved, i.e. the core offers of the company are derived from this purpose. These must always be checked to see whether they serve the company's purpose. The strategic and operational **work** to be done in the company is derived from the desired outcomes. It is crucial for an effective vision that purpose, outcomes, and work are intensively linked and form a consistent unit. This interdependency is an indispensable prerequisite for the vision to actually achieve the described identity, identification, and mobilization functions (cf. Fig. 3.2; cf. BCG, 2019a, p. 2).

It is crucial that this **vision** is not just a **wall decoration** on the executive floors, but becomes the **guiding image** for all managers and employees of the company. For this it is indispensable that the top management works towards

(continued)

Organizations should establish an unbroken chain of „Why?"

Therefore: start with the „Why"!

Fig. 3.2 Start with the "Why"!

the implementation of the vision—in a way that everyone can experience—and that the entire **incentive structure** of the company is also derived from the defined vision. This means that the company's monetary and non-monetary incentives are linked to results that are helpful and necessary on the way to implementing the vision.

▶ **Food for Thought**

The following example shows how powerful such a vision can be. During a visit to the *NASA*-Space-Center in 1962, President *John F. Kennedy* noticed a janitor with a broom. *Kennedy* interrupted his tour, walked over to the man and said, "Hi, I'm Jack Kennedy. What are you doing?" And the janitor replied, "Well, Mr. President, I'm helping put a man on the moon."

How many people limit the function of a janitor to the maintenance and upkeep of a building? How many janitors—or accountants, data typists, caretakers, secretaries, and workers on the assembly line—reduce their daily work to a few hand movements without seeing to what greater whole in their own company or in the economy, politics, and society they contribute through their daily work? All of us—wherever we stand professionally or privately—make it possible for bigger or smaller stories to be written; regardless of how big or small our role may be in each case.

3.1 Vision, Objectives, and Strategies for the Digital Age

In the pre-digital age	Level	In the digital age
Cost factor	Employee	Partner in the value chain
Sell	Customer	Delight
Exploit	Partner	Mutual support
Seduce	Market	Convince
Hide	Knowledge	Share
Win or lose	Business	Win – win

Fig. 3.3 Necessary changes in the mindset for the digital age

▶ **Food for Thought**
Frank Appel (Apple, 2020, p. 22), CEO of *Deutsche Post DHL Group*, a German multinational logistics service provider, made an exciting statement about this during the Corona pandemic:

"Our colleagues around the world realized very quickly how important they are in maintaining supply chains. Despite the challenging situation, employee satisfaction has increased significantly this year, more than in any previous year since we started measuring it. This is mainly because employees feel protected and see the purpose of their work."

Memory Box
The task—especially of managers—is to see and communicate this bigger picture.
As John C. Maxwell (2007, p. 169) so aptly put it:
People buy into the leader, then the vision.
Against this background, it becomes clear why the central elements of the **management mindset** need to be further developed for the digital age. Figure 3.3 shows what the goal can and should look like.
Every employee, but above all every manager, must work towards ensuring that the changes described in Fig. 3.3 flow into everyday life and into everyday management.

▶ **Food for Thought**
The sense of entrepreneurial activity can become the indispensable force that leads to a goal-oriented order of all activities in the company.

> **Think Box: Questions You Should Ask Yourself**
> - Does your company have a powerful vision?
> - Was this vision developed in an internal process or rather bought in from outside?
> - Is your vision lived out in the company and does it have a guiding function in terms of identity, identification, and mobilization?
> - Or is your vision primarily wall decoration, without relevance for managers and employees?
> - How is the "why" defined in your company, if it is explicitly defined?
> - Is the "why" linked to the "outcomes" and the "work" in a convincing way?
> - Who has overall responsibility for the "why" in your company?

3.1.3 Developing a (Digital) Vision

Perseverance is the secret of successful people—or also: genius is diligence!

3.1.3.1 Ways to Develop a (Digital) Vision

Developing a (digital) vision for a company can be done in two different ways:

- In the case of **company foundations** (today mostly start-ups) as well as in **family businesses**, it is often a **charismatic leader** who significantly shapes the vision and thus the development of a company with his or her ideas and conceptions.
- In established companies, it is the **top management** or the **executive board** that provides the company with long-term orientation by deciding on the vision.

It is important that in today's world a **digital vision** should not stand in isolation next to an **analogue vision**. Both contents should not only be merged together, but ideally developed as a unit. Otherwise, there is a danger that the company will disintegrate into a digital unit and an analogue unit. Unfortunately, such processes can be observed again and again today. In order to avoid this mistake, the adjective "digital" is often placed in brackets here.

> **Memory Box**
> **But: Visions alone do not generate profits!**
>   In order to not only survive in the digital age, but to comprehensively develop the existing opportunities for your own company and to skillfully master existing risks, your company's vision must not be limited to an **incremental optimization of the status quo**. This is still the case in—too many—companies today. Then, when it comes to digitizing the company, one

(continued)

focuses only on **reducing costs** and **increasing efficiency**. A vision with such content falls far short and endangers the survival of the entire company in the long term.

In contrast to this tunnel vision, a **powerful (digital) vision** must virtually provoke the following **triple jump** (see Sect. 3.2):

- **Questioning one's own business model** in the light of digital possibilities
- **Identification of complementary business areas**
- **Development of business model innovations**

The **Think Big** required for this is an indispensable part of developing a (digital) vision.

3.1.3.2 Powerful Visions and Ideas for Implementation

The dimensions that the realignment of a vision in the digital age can entail are shown by the example of the **automotive industry**. Today, all automotive companies propagate being or wanting to become a **mobility service provider** (alternative motto: "the end of the sheet metal benders"). The car manufacturers' sphere of action now goes far beyond the production and distribution of vehicles.

The CEO of the *Volkswagen Group, Herbert Diess*, has defined the necessary reorientation of *Volkswagen* in pithy terms (cf. Severlein & Bromberger, 2020):

- The car must learn to better understand its users and their needs through the data it collects.
- *Volkswagen* must be able to offer not only the transport shell, but also the brain that safely controls the vehicle with artificial intelligence.
- *Volkswagen* wants to bring together car, brain, and services and offer a unique mobility experience of the new age.
- To do that, the group needs capabilities that don't exist in our industry, even in our economic ecosystem in Europe today.
- *Volkswagen* must transform itself from a collection of valuable brands with products powered by combustion engines to a digital company. It should operate millions of mobility devices worldwide reliably, stay in contact with customers at all times and improve services, comfort and safety of the cars on a weekly basis, better on a daily basis.
- In order to not only take up the fight with *Tesla*, but to win, 27 billion euros will be invested in digitalization over the next 5 years. An investment volume of 35 billion euros is planned for electromobility. In addition, 11 billion euros will be used for the hybridization of the model portfolio (cf. Germis, 2020, p. 21).

The tasks to be mastered here have also led to **new cooperation agreements** in the automotive industry. The premium manufacturers *BMW* and *Daimler*, which have been in friendly competition with each other for decades, work together now. They have merged their—to a limited extent successful—involvement in car-sharing services *DriveNow* and *Car2go* in Europe to form *Share Now*. Taxis, ride-sharing services and support in finding parking spaces and charging stations are also to be provided in future via the jointly managed *Share Now* app. This platform is to become the core of a **new mobility provider** that will in future supply entire cities with various services and—looking far into the future—also with self-driving cars (cf. Fasse, 2019; cf. Weber, 2020).

> **Memory Box**
> **The automotive future will be EASCY: electrified, autonomous, shared, connected, and updated yearly** (cf. PWC, 2017, p. 7).
>
> In order to be better equipped in the future against competitors such as *Uber*, *Lyft* (US company for new mobility concepts and direct competitor of *Uber*), and *Waymo* (name of the *Google* driverless car project), as well as against Chinese providers, *BMW* and *Daimler* are also merging their multi-billion **developments in the field of autonomous driving.** The vision is to **establish a common industry standard**. This step was driven by the insight that it would become too costly even for today's global market leaders in the premium sector to tackle the issue of self-driving vehicles on their own. Compared to *Uber* and *Tesla*, however, *Daimler* and *BMW* initially only plan to jointly develop the next generation of technology for driver assistance systems, automated parking functions, and automated driving on motorways.

> **Memory Box**
> **In the digital age, you need allies to succeed!**
>
> These developments show the diversity and, at the same time, the power of change that established corporations such as *BMW* and *Daimler* must muster in order to successfully shape the digital transformation. Without a **reorientation** or at least a comprehensive further **development of the corporate DNA**, the companies will not succeed. The automotive industry is by no means the only sector that is facing considerable upheaval. Trade, finance, the printing industry, publishing houses—all these industries are in a merciless selection process that can rightly be described with the term **digital Darwinism** (see Sect. 1.1; for further details, see Kreutzer & Land, 2016).

Fig. 3.4 Hierarchy of leading principles

> **Memory Box**
> In **digital Darwinism**, the catchphrase is: **adapt or die!**
> The necessary adaptation of companies and business models must be driven by a powerful vision.
> However, differences in the visions of the companies are also becoming visible. *Uber* is striving to do without drivers altogether in the future in order to offer taxi rides in cities up to 70% cheaper. The power of this vision was witnessed when *Uber* went public on the 13th of June 2019: *Uber's* **market capitalization** on that day was US-$ 82 billion. This company value is comparable to that of one of the world's largest car manufacturers, *Volkswagen*.
> The basis of all change is a deep **examination of the individual opportunities and risks of digitalization** as well as the accompanying **changes in the company's purpose**. Digitally launched companies often see themselves as challengers to their industry and to society as a whole. Their corporate purposes—at least in public relations—go far beyond purely business aspects. As far as start-ups are concerned, they often deliberately ignore economic and often also legal aspects in the early phase (e.g., in the case of *Airbnb* and *Uber*) in order to first make an idea big. Compared to established companies, the following **advantages of start-ups** should be taken into account:
>
> - **Founders of start-ups** are often—literally—present day and night in these newly founded companies and can reach all team members equally directly and unfiltered with their ideas, their enthusiasm, their power, and their vision. As *Ralph Waldo Emerson* so aptly said:
>   ***Nothing great has ever been created without enthusiasm.***

(continued)

- **Short decision-making channels** due to the frequent **absence of hierarchy** increase **flexibility in entrepreneurial action**; new challenges can thus be responded to quickly and thoroughly.
- Start-ups—at least in the first years—do not struggle with **silo thinking**, which is common in many established companies. Since managers and employees share many tasks and open-plan offices with meeting points promote a continuous exchange of information, such silos can hardly arise, at least in the initial phase.
- Start-ups do not have **established structures, processes, and systems** (e.g., in the IT sector). There are no legacy systems. These young companies can use **agile management methods** (such as design thinking, scrum, lean start-up) from the beginning without encountering resistance from "veteran" colleagues.
- Developing a **business distribution plan** is not really a priority in start-ups—unlike in many established companies! You do and learn and do and learn. Therefore start-ups are much faster than other companies.
- Start-ups can use the **latest technologies** (e.g., cloud computing, platforms, apps) right from the start.
- Start-ups can hire exactly the **employees** with the **skills** they need. Since many well-qualified employees appreciate the working environment of start-ups, they often win the "war for talents."
- In the start-up phase, there is initially no need to take **existing customers** into consideration. If a realignment of the company's performance appears to be purposeful, this can take place.
- **Open-space solutions** allow start-ups to rent only as much office space as is currently needed. This keeps the corresponding costs manageable.

Based on these criteria, it becomes clear why the **vision in established companies** must be more powerful in order to compensate for the disadvantages compared to start-ups that have been pointed out. However, established companies also have resources that are very important when venturing into new business areas. The **advantages of established companies** include, to varying degrees, experience, capital resources, brand strength, access to distribution channels, customer base, process know-how, access to political decision-makers (political networks).

The development of an **entrepreneurial vision** must provide a powerful answer to the question "Why?". Then the vision is able to permeate the entire company starting from the top of the strategic goal hierarchy (cf. Fig. 3.4). Ideally, the vision should be broken down into a **mission** or **mission statements** in order to make it more tangible for the company's own staff and thus easier to implement. This **transfer task** must be supported by top management. Therefore, leaders—in start-ups as well as in established

(continued)

companies—must not only formulate a powerful, sustainable, and easily understandable (digital) vision. Their task is also to communicate this continuously—even and especially in the face of resistance—both internally and externally. Then and only then will it be possible for the vision and mission to shape the company's goals and be reflected in the business and functional area goals.

There are many **powerful visions** that have given companies decisive direction over years or even decades. Selected visions of particularly successful companies are presented below.

- **Bill Gates** formulated the vision for the company he founded, *Microsoft*, around 1980:
  "A computer on every desk and in every home."
- On the occasion of *Microsoft's* 40th birthday, *Bill Gates* stated in an e-mail to his employees: "Early on, Paul Allen and I set the goal of having a computer on every desk and in every home. It was a bold idea, and many people thought we were crazy because we couldn't imagine it. It's amazing to think how far computing has come since then, and we can all be proud of the role Microsoft played in that revolution" (Bae, 2015).
  Meanwhile, *Microsoft's* mission is as follows: "Our mission is to empower every person and every company on the planet to achieve more" (Microsoft, 2021a). One is inclined to add: the show goes on!
- *Jeff Bezos,* the founder of *Amazon*, formulated his vision in 1995 "to be Earth's most customer centric company, where customers can find and discover anything they might want to buy online, and endeavours to offer its customers the lowest possible prices" (Amazon, 2020).
  This powerful vision has provided the company with decisive orientation for decades—and continues to do so (see Sect. 3.2.9.1).
- *Jimmy Wales* and *Larry Sanger*, the founders of *Wikipedia*, have formulated their vision as follows (Wikipedia, 2021):
  "The goal is to make all of humanity's knowledge freely available to any person."
  Even today, the website simply states: "*Wikipedia*—The Free Encyclopedia." And it works—financed by donations!
- *Elon Musk,* the founder of *Tesla*, formulated the following vision for the company *SpaceX*, which was founded in 2002 (SpaceX, 2020):
  "SpaceX designs, manufactures and launches advanced rockets and spacecraft. The company was founded in 2002 to revolutionize space technology, with the ultimate goal of enabling people to live on other planets."
  In 2020, *SpaceX* enabled the USA to use its own rockets to transport astronauts to the ISS for the first time in 9 years.

(continued)

- ***Zappos***, a US-American e-commerce company, formulated its vision as follows (Zappos, 2021a):
"At Zappos.com, our purpose is simple: to live and deliver WOW. Twenty years ago, we began as a small online retailer that only sold shoes. Today, we still sell shoes—as well as clothing, handbags, accessories, and more. That 'more' is providing the very best customer service, customer experience, and company culture. We aim to inspire the world by showing it's possible to simultaneously deliver happiness to customers, employees, vendors, shareholders, and the community in a long-term, sustainable way. We hope that in the future people won't even realize we started selling shoes online. Instead, they'll know *Zappos* as a service company that just happens to sell."
In July 2009, *Amazon* acquired online shoe store *Zappos* for about US-$ 850 million.
- **Waymo** (2021) was the result of the *Google* project for self-driving cars and defined its company destination as follows:
"Waymo's mission is to make it safe and easy for people and things to get where they're going. The Waymo Driver can improve the world's access to mobility while saving thousands of lives now lost to traffic crashes."
The term "*Waymo Driver,*" by the way, refers to the robot that will steer the cars in the future. Like *Android* in the smartphone market, *Waymo* software aims to one day become the global operating system of the auto industry (cf. Fasse, 2019).

All of these companies have succeeded in achieving market-dominating positions, motivated by a **convincing vision**, but also by **powerful leadership** and a **persistence in implementation**.

3.1.3.3 Developing a (Digital) Vision

For the **development of a (digital) vision** for your company you can use the so-called **hedgehog concept** (cf. Collins, 2020a, b). You will receive central impulses for your strategy work if you answer the following three questions for your company:

- **What can you be the best in the world at?**
To answer this question, it is not only necessary to recognize what one can be the best at. The truth also includes recognizing in which fields you cannot do this and would rather fail there with an own offer. The answer to this question goes far beyond the mere definition of one's own **core competencies**. After all, the existence of a core competence does not mean that you belong to the world

Fig. 3.5 Hedgehog concept

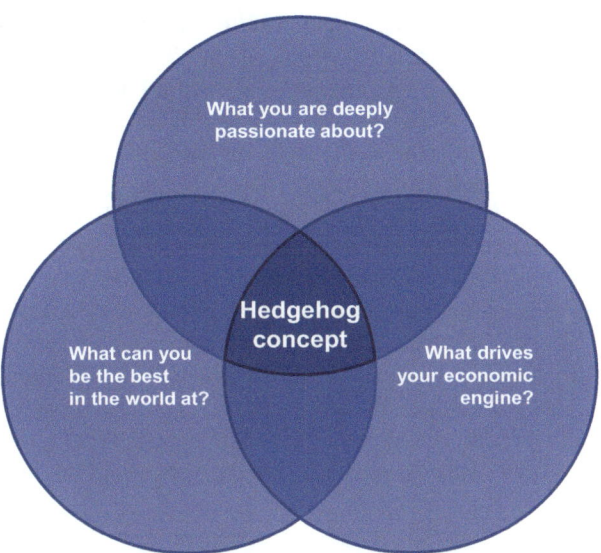

class! It may also be that you can achieve **top performance** in an area that you are not yet involved with—but for which you are particularly qualified.
- **What drives your economic engine?**
  This is about a deep understanding of how your business achieves consistent positive cash flow and sustainable profitability. In a nutshell, what is the most sustainable way to generate profit?
- **What you are deeply passionate about?**
  The answer to this question is about identifying what you, your managers, and your employees are passionate about. What activities spark a great passion throughout the company to help make it happen?

To bring this concept to life, Collins (2020a) recommends the following **thinking exercise**. Imagine that you could formulate a **professional challenge** for yourself based on the answers to the three questions above. First, think of a job for which you are mentally and physically well qualified. Secondly, you will be well paid for this work. Thirdly, you love doing this job and can therefore bring a lot of passion to it. At the intersection of these three circles you will find the **professional challenge** that is perfectly tailored to you (cf. Fig. 3.5; cf. Collins, 2020a).

▶ **Food for Thought**
Choose a job you love, and you will never have to work a day in your life.
Why is the term "hedgehog" used here? And why is this concept significant for vision work? Quite simply, the methodical approach shown here enables you to recognize the fields in which you are particularly good, act passionately, and are also well paid. There you are particularly difficult to attack because of a **perfect fit between ability, desire, and profitability**.

This is where the **metaphor of the hedgehog** comes into play. A hedgehog cannot attack its opponents itself. The hedgehog also cannot fly away, it cannot run away quickly, it cannot burrow or otherwise remove itself. What is its strategy? In case of danger, it simply curls up—and all classical predators see and, above all, feel only one thing—a very spiky something that they cannot harm.

This is the image that underlies the **hedgehog concept**. A vision that answers the three questions raised becomes a strategy for success when the answers to the aforementioned questions overlap in the intersection. If your company can make a lot of money with something without being the best provider of it in the market, you manage to become a successful company, but far from a great one. If, for example, your company uses superior technology but lacks passion among managers and employees, sooner or later you will be overtaken by competitors. And finally: What is the use of a superior offer and a passionate team if you cannot work profitably in the market on the long run?

Memory Box

The core of the hedgehog concept lies in recognizing in which fields you can become the best company.

If your company already has a vision or would like to develop one, you can orientate yourself on the following **criteria of a convincing company vision**:

- The vision is credible and comprehensively defined.
- The vision is long-term oriented.
- The vision is easy to understand.
- The vision describes the positioning which the company aspires.
- The vision outlines the future development of the company.
- The vision focuses on the customer experience.
- The vision includes forward-looking goals.
- The vision motivates the company's own managers and employees.

Memory Box

In order for your vision to have the desired effect, several criteria must be met.

In the course of **vision work**, it is very helpful to become aware of the **values** that underlie one's own (entrepreneurial) actions. These values are usually not conscious to the persons acting. However, they shape—also often unconsciously—the vision and the business purpose of the company. These values also influence the selection of personnel and the structure of business

(continued)

3.1 Vision, Objectives, and Strategies for the Digital Age

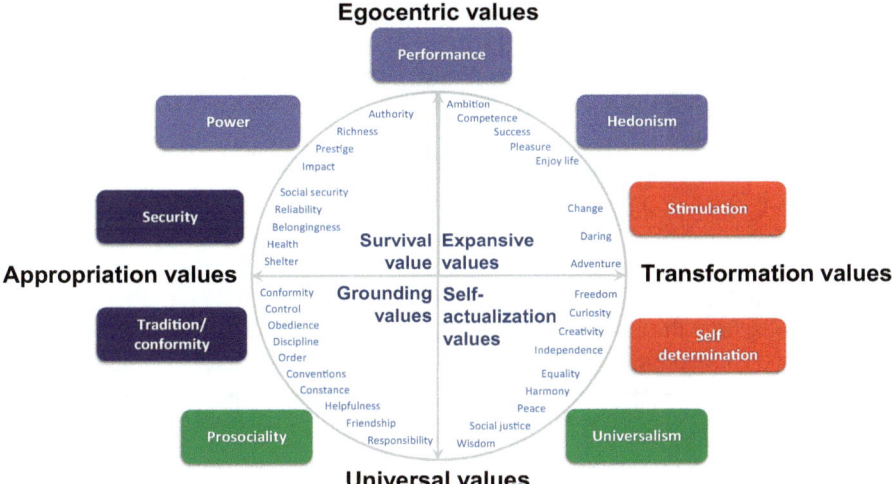

Fig. 3.6 Value circle—values are the triggers behind business models

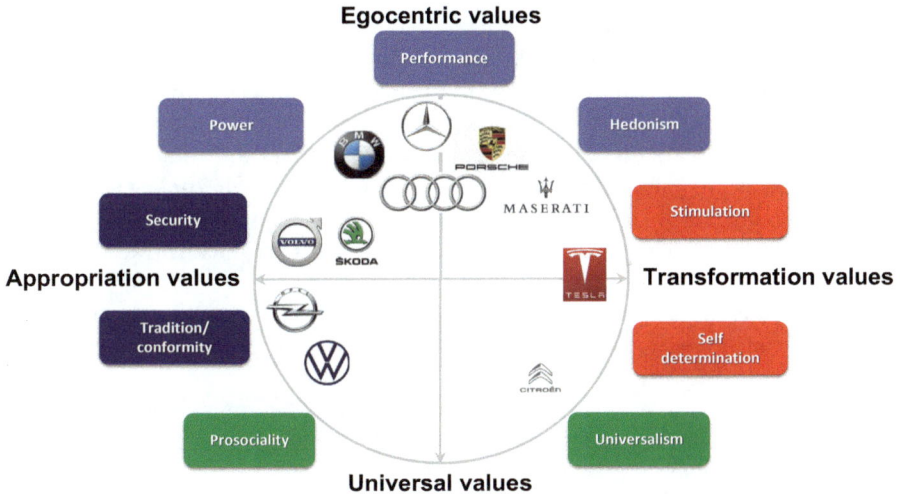

Fig. 3.7 Analysis of companies—based on the value circle

relationships. You can use *Schwartz's* **value circle** to make yourself aware of these values that shape your actions.

The **development of this value circle** was guided by the question of whether global values exist that are shared by all people. Such values are

(continued)

relevant because they represent guidelines that underlie the actions of people and thus also of companies. Schwartz (Schwartz, 1992; cf. Strack et al., 2008) developed a **model of values**, which can be seen in Fig. 3.6 (cf. Schwartz, 1992, p. 25).

The **circle of values** is made up of **superordinate values** that can be grouped into the following pairs of opposites:

- **Openness to change**, influenced by values of change (self-determination, stimulation, and hedonism) vs. **preservation of the existing**, influenced by values of stability (security, tradition/conformity)
- **Self-strengthening**, based on egocentric values (achievement, power) vs. **self-overcoming**, based on universalistic values (universalism, humanism)

The value circle also visualizes the **compatibility** or **incompatibility of values.** The closer the individual values in the circle are to each other, the more compatible they are. Opposite values, on the other hand, represent different extreme positions that are hardly compatible with each other. By concentrating on a limited number of relevant value types, the **value network** becomes manageable. The **superordinate values** (e.g., tradition/conformity or self-determination) can in turn be assigned to **specific values** (e.g., discipline and order vs. creativity and curiosity).

By conducting a survey in your company, you can determine which of these values are particularly relevant—for managers and/or employees—and thus steer the corporate agenda. Here you will find a few examples of these values and possible implementations in a **questionnaire to determine values**:

- **Self-determination** promotes one's own creative thinking and continuously questions existing products and services in order to independently arrive at new, better solutions.
  Statements: "It is important for me to form my own opinion and to have unusual ideas." "It is important to me to do as much as possible independently and autonomously."
- **Stimulation** is to be understood as an encouragement to keep looking for new things and challenges.
  Statements: "It is important to me to have all kinds of new experiences." "It is important to me to always meet new challenges."
- **Hedonism** or **striving for pleasure** describes the pursuit of pleasure and sensual enjoyment.
  Statements: "It is important to me to enjoy the pleasures of life." "It is important to me to have fun again and again."
- **Achievement** characterizes the dominant striving for success.

(continued)

Statements: "It is important to me to be very successful." "It is important to me to achieve something through my own efforts."
- **Power** strives for a position of supremacy in order to control others with it—also through access to material and financial resources.
Statements: "It is important to me to be the one who tells others what to do." "It is important to me to exercise power through my means."
- **Security** refers to the immediate environment as well as to society.
Statements: "It is important to me to live in a safe environment." "It is important to me that my country protects itself against all threats."

  At the same time, people often strive to be a reliable and trustworthy member of a certain group (such as their circle of friends).

  Statements: "It is important to me to be honest with those who are close to me." "It is important to me to be involved in a community."
- **Tradition** refers to the willingness to follow rules, laws, and duties. At the same time, cultural, family, and religious traditions are upheld.
Statements: "It is important to me to follow rules even when no one notices." "It is important to me to maintain family or religious customs."
- **Conformity** reflects adaptability to others. Here it is important to avoid annoying or harming someone.
Statements: "It is important to me that I do not upset others." "It is important to me to live together with others in harmony."
- **Prosociality** describes, among other things, one's own modesty and the knowledge that one is relatively insignificant in the overall structure.
Statements: "It is important for me to be content with what I have." "It is important to me not to always ask for more."

  At the same time, it describes caring in the sense of making an effort to look after the well-being of members of a group (e.g., the family).

  Statements: "It is important to me to care for the well-being of those close to me." "It is important to me that I care for others."
- **Universalism** characterizes social concerns, e.g., working for equality, justice, and the protection of all people as well as nature, and preserving the natural environment.
Statements: "It is important to me to support those in society who are weak and vulnerable." "It is important to me to protect nature."

  At the same time, universalism describes the recognition of otherness.
- Statements: "It is important to me to listen to people who are different from myself." "It is important to me to meet all people equally."

You can use Schwartz's value circle to capture the value structure of your company. At the same time, you can get to the bottom of an important aspect that is of great significance in the course of change management: the culture. The culture of any company is shaped to a great extent by the values of the

(continued)

people who work there—especially the managers. The cultural imprint of the various top performers is documented every day in words and deeds (or misdeeds). In the process of digital transformation, it is important to get to the bottom of these values in order to identify possible – value driven—brakes and accelerators of the transformation process at an early stage (cf. Chap. 4 for further details).

In Fig. 3.7 you can see how convincingly different car brands can be positioned in the value circle. The value structures visible here have an effect on all corporate activities—motivating and braking in equal measure.

Memory Box
With the value circle, you have an important tool at hand to make visible the values that exist in your company among managers and employees. In the value structures that become visible through this analysis, you can recognize those who promote and those who slow down a digital transformation. You can use this knowledge in the change management process.

▶ **Storytelling** In a consulting project, the customers of an international B2B company were segmented according to their respective value structures. In this way, the different driving forces of the acting persons in the key customer companies were recognized, which also significantly shaped the respective business model. The knowledge of the value structures of one's own customers was then used as a basis not only for communication, but also for the design of one's own range of products and services.

3.1.3.4 Guidelines for Anchoring Values in Vision Work

For the development and implementation of visions, goals, and strategies, the aforementioned values can often be transformed into powerful guidelines that provide important points of orientation for all managers and employees. How these can be shaped is illustrated here by the example of Amazon's 14 Leadership Principles by Jeff Bezos (cf. Rossmann, 2014). Here, central values of the company are translated into concrete leadership principles that are intended to address everyone in the company personally:

1. **Customer Obsession**
   The starting point of all activities of a manager is the customer: *start with the customer and work backwards*. Starting from the customer, the processes necessary for inspiring customer care are built up. In essence, it is about gaining and maintaining the trust of the customer. Managers also focus their attention on

competitors. Their heart and soul, however, is with the customers: *keep obsessing over customers.*

2. **Ownership**
   The managers act like owners in the company. They think long-term and do not sacrifice long-term values and success for short-term results. Leaders act on behalf of the whole company, not just their own teams. They never say: "That's not my job."

3. **Invent and simplify**
   Leaders expect and demand innovation and ingenuity from their teams. At the same time, they always find ways to simplify processes. Leaders are simultaneously outward-looking and look for new ideas everywhere. They do not let a "not invented here" limit their creativity. When leaders do new things, they accept that they can be misunderstood over a long period of time.

4. **Leaders are right—a lot**
   Leaders have strong judgment and good instincts. They seek diverse perspectives and work to constantly work to disconfirm their beliefs.

5. **Learn and be curious**
   Leaders never stop learning and are always trying to get better. They are interested in new opportunities and act to explore them.

6. **Hire and develop the best**
   Leaders raise the bar for performance with every hire and promotion. They recognize exceptional talent and are happy to make it available to the whole organization. Leaders develop leaders and take their own role in coaching others seriously.

7. **Insist on the highest standards**
   Leaders have relentlessly high standards. Others may think these standards are unreasonably high. Yet leaders constantly raise the bar and drive their teams to deliver high quality products, services, and processes. Leaders ensure that defect rectification is not put on the back burner. Problems are fixed so that they stay fixed.

8. **Bias for action**
   In business, speed matters. Many decisions and actions are reversible and do not require extensive investigation. Managers appreciate calculated risk-taking.

9. **Frugality**
   Leaders dare to do more with less. Constraints breed resourcefulness, self-sufficiency, and invention. There are no extra points for leaders for growing headcount, increasing budget size or higher fixed expenses.

10. **Deep dive**
    Leaders act at all levels, but always remain connected to the details. They check frequently and are skeptical when metrics and anecdotes differ. No task is beneath them.

11. **Have backbone, disagree and commit**
    Leaders have an obligation to respectfully challenge decisions when they disagree. This is allowed to be uncomfortable or exhausting. Leaders have the power of persuasion and are persistent. They do not compromise for the sake of

social cohesion. Once a decision has been made, they are fully committed to its implementation.

12. **Deliver results**

    Leaders focus on the most important performance contributions to their company. They deliver results in the right quality and on time. Even in the face of setbacks, they rise to the occasion and never settle for what has already been achieved.

13. **Think big**

    Thinking small is a self-fulfilling prophecy. Leaders therefore create and communicate a bold direction that inspires ambitious results. They think big and differently and are always looking around corners for new ways to delight customers.

14. **Earn trust**

    Leaders listen attentively. They speak candidly and treat others respectfully. They express self-criticism, even when it may be uncomfortable or embarrassing. Leaders measure themselves and their teams against the best.

If you let these guiding ideas have an effect on you, you will very quickly notice the power they contain. Let yourself be inspired by these principles to develop them for your own company. Here you can also use "copy & paste" if certain ideas are particularly appealing to you. In addition, you can identify the values in the value system that underlie these *Amazon* **Leadership Principles**.

If your workforce has these **points of orientation** constantly in mind, then they will also shape the company's actions in the long term. After all, these principles should be taken into account when making decisions in the company, when solving problems, in daily communication, and even when hiring new staff.

In addition, *Amazon* relies on another principle to implement the vision of customer obsession: **working backwards from the customer**. Here, the customer is placed in front of every innovation process in order to know his pain points, his expectations, his needs, his wishes and to take his perspective (cf. information on the pain points in Sect. 3.5.2.3).

In working backwards, a **fictitious press-release** is written at the beginning of an innovation process. In this, the fictitious product launch is communicated to the outside. In addition, the question is answered as to which articles in newspapers or trade journals and which resonance in the social media could be expected. For this purpose, the press releases must be formulated concisely and in simple language—regardless of how complex the new offer is. This document is also the basis for winning over the relevant decision-makers for the project—internally and externally (cf. Alsamawi, 2018).

Memory Box
Working backwards or **reverse product development** is an exciting method for consistently designing innovation processes in a customer-oriented way.

The convincing successes *Amazon* has achieved—also, but not only—due to its leadership principles are discussed in more detail in Sect. 3.2.9.1.

A look at ***Google's* 9 *Principles of Innovation*** is also very instructive. Here, too, you can gain valuable impulses. These principles can be described as follows (cf. Brands, 2017):

1. **Innovation comes from everywhere**
   Innovation is not included in any job title, but is everyone's responsibility. Moreover, ideas can come from anyone in the organization. This is independent of whether they are top-level managers or employees from departments not typically associated with innovation. Employees at the "lower end" of the hierarchy can and should also contribute their creative impulses.
2. **Focus on the user**
   Encourage staff to develop products with the user in mind, not the bottom line.
3. **Think 10 x, not 10%**
   Strive to improve something tenfold rather than optimizing it by only 10%. Aim for revolutionary change, not just evolutionary change.
4. **Bet on technical insights**
   Every company has unique insights. Using them can lead to great innovations. Therefore, the existing information in the company must be made widely accessible so that it can be used as fuel for innovation everywhere.
5. **Ship and iterate**
   "Innovation, not immediate perfection" is the challenge. That's why the first solutions have to be developed quickly as prototypes, which are then tested on the market. The feedback flows directly into further development, a new prototype is created, tested on the market, etc.
6. **20% of time for innovation**
   Employees are encouraged to spend 20% of their working time on projects they are passionate about. This applies even if these projects are outside their remit or the core mission of the company.
7. **Default to open**
   Innovation is promoted through an intensive exchange of information on the Intranet. In addition, cooperation between employees is promoted. New ideas are also to be gained from the public. Therefore, the basic attitude is: openness for innovations.

(continued)

8. **Fail well**
   Failure in innovation should not lead to stigma. Rather, it should apply: those who fail have learned something!
9. **Have a mission that matters**
   Every employee should have a very strong sense of the mission and purpose of the company.

▶ **Food for Thought**
You should check which of these **guiding ideas for innovation** can be anchored for your own company—after all, these guidelines are very convincing. They have made *Google* one of the highest-rated and most profitable companies in the world. The fact that the first self-driving car was developed by *Google* in 2014 and not by the world's leading automotive companies becomes understandable with these guiding ideas: for one thing, this was not about 10% better, but 10 x as good. Moreover, a self-driving car still has little to do with the core performance of *Google* or *Alphabet*!

The same applies to the project to beat the world champion in the Go-game with *Google's **AlphaGo**-computer* in 2016. Proven specialists had previously claimed that a computer could never do this! Why? The 19 × 19 Go-board has 361 positions. Each position can be either not occupied at all or occupied by a white or black piece. Therefore, the number of all possible positions is 3 to the power of 361. The result of this calculation is 10 to the power of 172.241. Connoisseurs claim that this number exceeds the number of atoms in the universe. That is because their number is "only" about 10 to the power of 80—in comparison with the possible Go-positions, therefore, almost a vanishingly small number.

However, I have not yet counted! But I know one thing for sure: If you are looking for examples of Think Big—here they are!

Memory Box
To ensure that such **powerful leadership principles** do not remain mere wall decorations, workshops must be held—across all hierarchical levels. In these workshops, managers and their teams work out ways to implement the individual principles in their respective areas of responsibility.

▶ **Storytelling** In many **workshops on the transfer of values and leadership principles into daily activities** that I have had the privilege of facilitating, there was usually a great deal of skepticism at the beginning. This was expressed in statements like: "this is so general, it doesn't fit for me and my team!" After

60 min of group work, the world suddenly looked very different. Then it was said: "that also works in my team!"

Incidentally, such an assessment was independent of whether managers and staff from the legal department, controlling, procurement, marketing, or sales took part.

Only one thing is important:

You have to take the time to discuss the possibilities for implementation. My experience is: it is worth it in any case!

> **Think Box: Questions You Should Ask Yourself**
> - Does a (digital) vision exist in your company due to a charismatic leader, or is this vision the responsibility of top management or the executive board?
> - Have you already done the triple jump to develop a powerful (digital) vision? This involves questioning your own business model in the light of (digital) opportunities, identifying complementary business areas, and developing business model innovations.
> - Is there a willingness to "think big" in your company?
> - How great is the will in your company to also cooperate with strategic competitors?
> - How can you compensate for the systemic advantages of start-ups by further developing your company's processes and structures?
> - Have you broken down your company's vision into mission statements to ensure easier implementation?
> - Have you used the hedgehog concept before?
> - Do you use the hedgehog concept for your vision work? Find out what—if any—other challenges lie in the overlapping area of the three questions that you can address as a company.
> - Does the need for action arise when you review your corporate vision against the defined requirement criteria?
> - Have you ever determined the value structure in your company using the value circle?
> - Do you know which values dominate—e.g., at which hierarchical levels and in which departments?
> - What can you borrow from *Amazon's* Leadership Principles?
> - What can be transferred to your company?
> - Have you ever used the working backwards approach?
> - What ideas can you take from *Google's 9 Principles of Innovation*—and implement?
> - Who is responsible for vision work overall in your company?
> - How often do people in your company deal with the vision—and above all with its implementation in everyday operations?
> - Who is responsible for answering these questions?

3.1.4 Developing a Strategy for the Digital Age

Hope is often a useful narcotic. However, it is not yet a strategy!

The next big challenge for you is to develop a strategy for the digital age derived from the vision work. For this you can use the **five-step concept of strategy development** (cf. Fig. 3.8).

Step 1: **Analysis of the digital business performance**

The first step in strategy development has already been taken with the **analysis of digital business performance** described in Sect. 2.2 (cf. Fig. 2.15). It is important that this analysis takes place throughout the entire company and across all hierarchical levels so that a realistic (internal) picture can be determined. A supplement and thus rounding off with an external picture from a neutral perspective is valuable in order to obtain an overall picture in view of new challenges and opportunities.

Step 2: **Definition of the desired (digital) position**

The second step involves defining the desired (digital) position. This is based on the (digital) vision of the company. Derived from this, **(new) business models** are to be developed. How far the company wants to move away from the existing business can be determined using the **3 horizons model** (cf. Fig. 3.10). The definition of the desired position also includes a comprehensive determination of the KPIs for

1 — **Analysis of digital business performance**
- Dimensions: vision/goals/strategies, sustainability of the business model, digitalization of the value chain, IT infrastructure/technologies/data basis, exploitation of digital potentials in marketing/sales, human resource strategies, organizational concepts, controlling
- Level of maturity: from „not defined" to „fully transformed"

2 — **Definition of aspired (digital) position**
- (Digital) vision of the company
- Development of (new) business models – orientated on the horizons that can be filled (base: 3-horizons model)
- Determination of KPIs to measure success

3 — **Derivation of the strategic areas of activity**
- Identification of the areas of activity in value chain, IT infrastructure/technologies/data basis, marketing/sales, human resources, organization, controlling
- Analysis of the required actions' practicability
- Definition of the required resources (employees, budget, access to certain technologies, etc.)

4 — **Development of a digitalisation roadmap for the implementation**
- Prioritization of the required steps
- Specification of the degree of achieved goals for each milestone
- Assuring agility in the implementation for achieving convincing results

5 — **Controlling of the overall process**
- Definition of the entities responsible for controlling
- Development of a KPI dashboard
- Determination of the type of methodical and procedural implementation support

Fig. 3.8 Five-step concept of strategy development

measuring success. Only then can it be precisely determined whether the targeted position has actually been achieved.

Step 3: **Derivation of the strategic fields of action**

The third step involves deriving the strategic fields of action. These concern **all areas of the company**: value chain, IT infrastructure/technologies/data basis, marketing/sales, human resources, organization, controlling. In this context, it must also be clarified, whether an **innovation engine** needs to be installed for the implementation of the strategy and what **human resources** are required. It must also be analyzed whether the planned measures can be implemented and whether the necessary resources can be made available. Here, not only the necessary **human performers**, but also **budgets** and access to certain **technologies** should be considered (see Sects. 3.2–3.8).

Step 4: Developing a digitalization roadmap for the implementation

The fourth step is to develop a **digitalization roadmap** for implementation. Here, above all, the priorities for the steps to be taken must be defined. In addition, the degree of **target achievement for each milestone** must be specified. In view of the dynamics in the business environment, sufficient agility in implementation must be ensured despite all the care taken in planning, not only to fulfill plans, but also to achieve convincing results.

Step 5: **Controlling of the overall process**

Step 5 is dedicated to the controlling of the overall process. The first step is to determine who is responsible for controlling. Based on the KPIs defined in step 2, a corresponding **KPI dashboard** or **balanced scorecard** must be developed, which brings together information flows on relevant criteria. In addition, it must be determined how the methodological and procedural support of the implementation is to be carried out by controlling. Such a controlling system should also ensure that the digitization initiatives are comprehensively integrated into the corporate strategy (see Sect. 3.8).

However, even with a convincing strategy, the most important **strategic bottleneck** remains: the implementation mentioned in step 4. How is it possible to turn "**strategy into action**"? Many brilliant concepts and strategies have failed to make the leap from paper (or the digital equivalent) into action and never saw the light of day. Strategic concepts also petered out on the way to implementation because managers and staff were unwilling or unable to consistently drive implementation. Therefore, in the next sections you will receive valuable tips for a successful implementation. In addition, powerful tools are presented that will help you get your horsepower on the road!

> **Think Box: Questions You Should Ask Yourself**
> - Check whether you get additional impulses from the five-step concept for strategy development.
> - In whose hands is the engagement with the issues raised here?

(continued)

> • Are the people and departments dealing with these issues allowed to present results that neither top management nor other managers and employees will like?

3.2 Developing Business Models for the Digital Age

3.2.1 Labelling Business Models

Many right notes do not make music!
Mark Mast, Principal Conductor of the Bavarian Philharmonic Orchestra

3.2.1.1 Business Models and Industry Logics

The **digital base model** in Fig. 3.1 shows: the **business model** is at the center of the company's activities and forms the basis for building digital excellence. When discussing business models, we need to distinguish between three different **types of business models** (based on Wirtz, 2018, pp. 24–26):

- **Process and system models**
  Process and system models are used to document, analyze, and design business processes, e.g., in information technology.
- **Organizational models**
  Organizational models represent the structures of a company in an abstract way (in the sense of an enterprise architecture). This is usually done in the form of organization charts.
- **Strategic business models**
  The core of a strategic business model is the holistic description of the entrepreneurial activity in aggregated form. It describes the way in which a company wants to create value for customers and for itself.

In the context of digital business, the **strategic business model** is of particular importance. It describes the **basic logic of a company** and shows which benefits are to be generated in which way for customers as well as for partners. In addition, the strategic business model specifies the form in which the benefit provided for third parties is to flow back to the company through sales as a source of profit. Strategic business models can be presented both at the level of the company as a whole and at the level of business units.

In large, highly diversified companies, **cascading business models** is a good idea. In this process, an overarching business model is broken down level by level, oriented towards the hierarchical organization of the company. In this procedure, too, the entrepreneurial vision can represent the central orientation framework for all business models.

A core task in the discussion of business models is to identify commonalities and differences between individual business models and to work out recurring structures. Osterwalder and Pigneur (2011) refer to these similarities as **business model patterns**. By working out such structures from a multitude of company concepts, different **groups of business models** can be found. This approach makes visible when companies break out of previous business logics with their approach and pursue new business models. Relevant **business model patterns** develop in a two-stage approach (cf. Hoffmeister, 2013, p. 17f.):

- **Stage 1: Individual rules become standardized sets of rules**
  In the first stage, companies develop **rules**—initially mostly unconsciously—through their activities and the associated experiences via a trial-and-error process, which are indispensable for profitable corporate development. These rules gradually become more and more visible. Through this, they become **recognizable success factors** for a company in an industry. Step by step, these insights can be incorporated into **standardized sets of rules** that will guide your staff's actions to ensure long-term business success.
- **Stage 2: Rules and regulations establish themselves as business model logic in an industry**
  In a second stage, such sets of rules developed by individual companies can establish themselves as **business model logic in an industry**. In this case, existing and new companies copy the processes that have emerged from other providers as relevant and conducive to success. Here we can speak of benchmarking, in which one or more particularly successful companies "exemplify" how a business model is to be designed in a particular industry (cf. on benchmarking Kreutzer, 2019, pp. 123–127). Through this process, more and more companies establish themselves that use comparable business models. As a result, a **dominant business model logic** develops from an individual business model architecture and establishes itself as the **industry logic**—valid for the companies working in one industry.

> **Memory Box**
> Only those companies will be successful in the long term that continuously develop their business models on several levels. This requires a fundamental understanding of the business model used by one's own company as well as the mechanisms, patterns, and content associated with it.
> Dominant **industry logics** can be found in virtually every industry. In the past, **book publishers** tried to fill relevant topics with competent authors in order to market the books produced in this way through classic sales channels. This business model has worked very well for years and has made it possible for large international publishers and small niche providers to coexist. In the pre-online age, authors were hardly able to sell their works without a publisher.

(continued)

For many decades, the **music industry** worked according to a similar industry logic: artists were signed to music labels that were responsible for the production of the music and its distribution via the stationary trade. The artists looked for the so-called major labels in particular in order to become known quickly and internationally. In many cases, the labels also dictated what kind of music an artist should concentrate on and how he should position himself in the public eye in order to achieve the greatest possible added value. In some cases, the type of music was also specified for the artists in order to increase recognition through specific branding.

Taxi companies also functioned very similarly worldwide for a long time. The owner of a local taxi concession was usually dependent on the central (but only regionally active) marketing as part of a network, as well as on its mediation of taxi rides.

Memory Box

Business models are manifested principles of success that have crystallized in one or more sectors as relevant for success. If these success principles are used in entire sectors, they are referred to as **sector logics**.

A **business model innovation** breaks with these established industry logics and relies on new rules and/or rules previously used in other industries.

Many of these rules that were the basis of the industry logics have lost their significance in the digital age. In the **publishing industry**, printed books are increasingly being replaced or at least accompanied by e-books. Print-on-demand and self-publishing offers (for example, from *lulu.com*) make it possible for practically anyone to publish their own texts—even without traditional publishing houses. Those who are less concerned with making a profit and more with publishing their own content can communicate this content via blogs, podcasts, posts in social media, and many other channels.

We see similar changes in the **music industry**. Here, too, the "delivery form" of music has changed: from the shellac record to the music cassette and the vinyl record to the CD, from mp3 formats to the streaming of music that dominates many target groups today. The diverse online platforms also allow newcomers—without a music label in the background—to build up a large fan base. The music labels themselves also earn their money less with CDs and DVDs today, but via the streaming service providers. The dominant source of income for music labels are—in the online age!—mainly live events by the stars, flanked by promotional products.

The online channels enable a **trickle-up effect** in these industries—against gravity, so to speak! Here, selected offers succeed in becoming visible to the

(continued)

world public via the most diverse online channels. These can be songs or lyrics by previously unknown artists whose popularity increases significantly within a short time due to viral effects on the Internet. This was the case with *Justin Bieber* and *E. L. James' Shades of Grey*, which has since mutated into a global bestseller.

In the **taxi industry**, too, the industry logics and with them the weights have shifted significantly. Taxi apps, ride-sharing services, *Uber, Didi & Co.* together with sharing services for cars, e-scooters, and bicycles are increasingly challenging the established providers as well as the car manufacturers.

3.2.1.2 Core Questions of a Strategic Business Model

When developing business models, the following **core questions of a strategic business model** need to be answered (cf. Schallmo & Rusnjak, 2017; cf. Fig. 3.9; cf. Gassmann et al., 2017, p. 8):

- **Value proposition: What do we offer our customers?**
  This dimension defines the services to be provided and the benefits they convey to customers.
- **Value chain: How do we produce our products and services?**
  Here it is determined which partners and which products and services are required from them. The type of relationships to be established with the partners is described in order to elaborate the value chain.

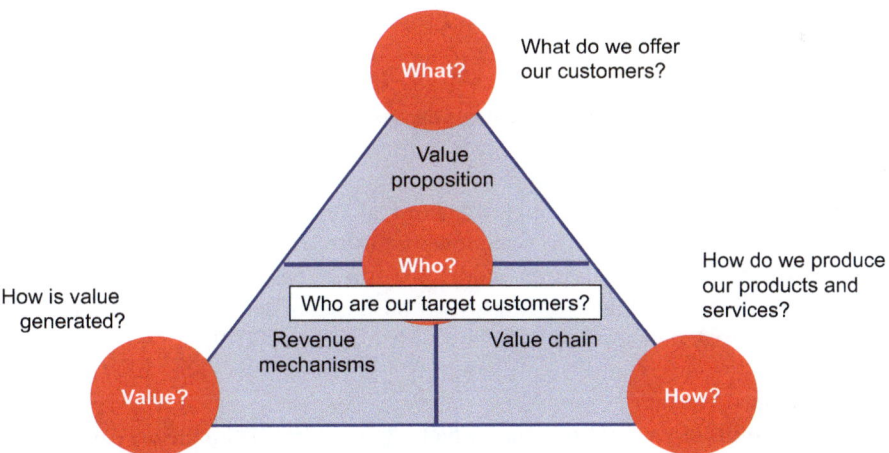

Fig. 3.9 Key questions during business model development

- **Revenue mechanics: How is value generated?**
  The cost and revenue streams generated by product and service delivery and marketing/sales are mapped here.
- **Customers: Who are our target customers?**
  The customer segments considered relevant, the main channels to reach them and the targeted customer relationships are described here.

The **great challenge in developing a strategic business model** is to design and interlink these different dimensions in such a way that they mutually reinforce each other in their positive effects. This is an important prerequisite for surviving in the market and achieving (sustainable) growth. After all, with such an approach, it is much more difficult for competitors to simply copy your own business model!

In the course of the **further digital development of an existing business model**, the following questions must be answered above all:

- Which elements of the business model can be digitally transformed?
- What are the effects of a digital transformation in terms of customer accessibility?
- In what way can relationships with customers be designed to create more sustainable value in digital form?
- How does digital transformation change the possibilities of generating benefits for customers?
- Does the digital transformation lead to the need for additional (other) partners to provide services?
- Can additional and/or other partners be integrated through digitalization in order to create additional benefits and/or reduce costs?
- Can fewer (existing) partners be used to provide services?
- What impact does digital transformation have on cost causation?
- How does digitalization affect the generation of revenues?
- Can (new) competitors be fended off through a digital transformation of the business model?

The **challenge for established companies** is to deal with the **digital transformation of their own business model** in a timely manner. The 3 horizons model described in the following section provides an important orientation framework for this. Ideally, dealing with the digital transformation should already take place at a time when the dominant logic of one's own industry has not yet been significantly changed by new digital business model patterns. Therefore, it is important to question the traditional logics of one's own business model early and comprehensively and to break new ground (cf. Meinhardt & Pflaum, 2019).

▶ **Food for Thought**
When **building a start-up**, cherry picking is possible from the very beginning compared to established companies. The founders of start-ups can focus equally on the "best fruits" in terms of the products and services offered, the customers to be approached, the technologies to be used, and the management methods.

Here, start-ups can test and try out which (digital) competences of a business model lead to success the fastest. Comprehensive change processes are not necessary in start-ups at the beginning, as fixed structures and processes have not yet developed. However, in many cases the financial resources of start-ups are less stable than those of established companies.

> **Think Box: Questions You Should Ask Yourself**
> - Has the business logic in your sector already changed?
> - What challenges do you see for your industry logic?
> - Have you already answered the key questions about the digital evolution of your existing business model in depth?
> - Who in your company regularly deals with these questions?

3.2.2 3 Horizons Model

First do what is necessary, then what is possible, and suddenly you will achieve the impossible.
Francis of Assisi

In order to determine the strategic pressure to act with regard to the **further or new development of the business model** in an established company, you should use the **3 horizons model** (cf. Fig. 3.10; Baghai et al., 2000, pp. 5–17; Blank, 2015). Through the 3 horizons model you can, on the one hand, determine where you are today in the process of the digital transformation of your business model. On the other hand, impulses can be gained for how thoroughly your own business model should be questioned and, if necessary, revised or even replaced. You can gain important informational foundations for this concept through the analysis tools already presented in Chap. 2.

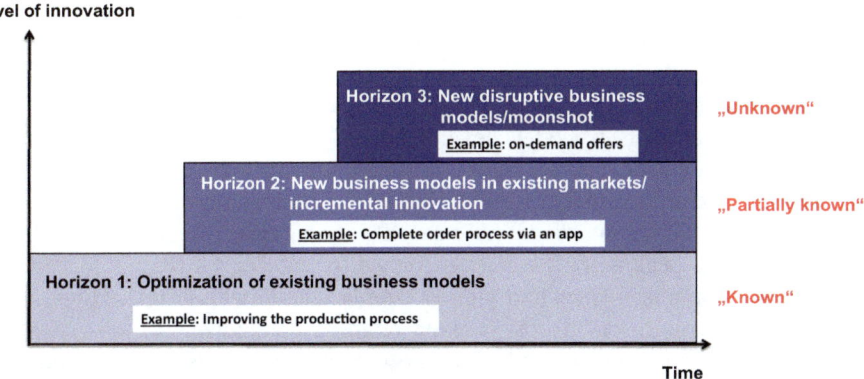

Fig. 3.10 3 horizons model

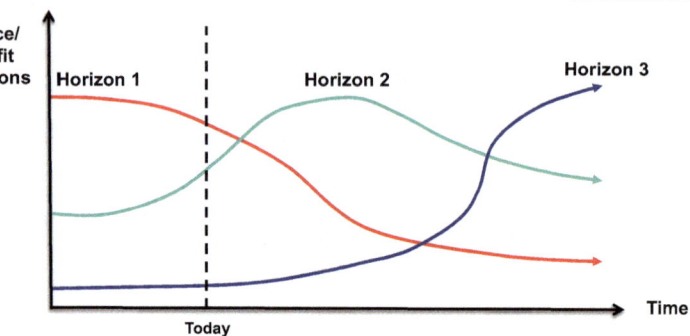

Fig. 3.11 3 horizons model for strategic analysis

The relevant contents of the business model located on the different horizons are as follows (cf. Fig. 3.11):

- **Horizon 1 business models—"Known"**
  The horizon 1 business models describe the **current status of a company**—the easily surveyed horizon 1. The business model that exists today is depicted and executed. The resulting earnings and cash flows are at the center of the analysis. They are not least a prerequisite for financing innovation activities. If necessary, this core business should be expanded and/or defended. In these **mature business models**, it is important to maintain growth and ensure profitability through **incremental improvements** to structures, processes, products, and/or services.
  At the level of the current horizon, a **managerial view** dominates with a clear focus on the current strategy. This works well until changes in the environment lead to decline. This is always just a matter of time—and it is happening faster and faster in the digital age!
- **Horizon 2 business models—"Partially known"**
  The horizon 2 business models develop options for business model innovation in relation to relevant markets of the existing horizon 1 business models. New, resulting **business model initiatives** are often built through significant investments. These business models can already generate initial returns, although their business peak will often not be reached for another 4–5 years. Successes of companies on this horizon partly result from integrating existing products and/or services into digital platforms or even building comprehensive ecosystems. A step in this direction can also be the development of various services around the existing product range.

On this second horizon, an **entrepreneurial view** is required. The decision-makers here must be aware that an economic decline of horizon 1 activities is usually only a question of time. Therefore—parallel to the activities on the first horizon—efficient concepts must be developed that can replace horizon 1 activities in the long term. The second horizon is already more difficult to keep track of than the first horizon.

- **Horizon 3 business models—"Unknown"**
The horizon 3 business models are highly innovative (often also disruptive) and represent **approaches for completely new business logics**. In order to develop such business model innovations, an in-depth analysis of individual company capabilities or customer groups is required—which goes far beyond the previous day-to-day business. In addition, it must be examined which completely new activities could be lucrative for the company. Here, **strategic options for disruptive change** are explored and ideas are translated into concrete models.

On the third horizon, a **visionary view** is required, as the third horizon cannot yet be grasped. Here, new paradigms can be applied in the industry, replacing previously effective business logics. Often horizon 3 activities appear too ambitious and innovative for a long time—before they become "mainstream" and thus the dominant industry logic. Horizon 2 innovations can partly act as enablers for these activities.

The 3 horizons model shows the different scopes of **business models innovation**. Horizon 1 business models are based on known business logics whose execution is the focus of the existing organization. The focus here is on **incremental (digital) optimization**. This can be the improvement of customer service by strengthening the service team. Or a customer relationship management system is introduced to improve the customer service of an e-commerce company. Incremental improvements to the production process also take place here. The level of innovation is low—the horizon is manageable (keyword "known"). On this horizon, you only improve parts of the existing business models. In this way, you can secure and/or expand existing competitive advantages.

It is important to note that in the context of digital transformation, it is not always just about **new business models**. The content of this transformation can also represent **optimization on the horizon 1** level or **further developments on the horizon 2** level. Then, for example, it is about technical innovations or new opportunities that go hand in hand with digitalization along the existing value chain. **Hybrid business models** are often found here: some business processes are already digitized, others are still stuck in an analogue state.

To describe the content of a digital transformation, the following **types of innovation** can be distinguished:

- **Product and service innovations**
- **Process innovations**
- **Business model innovations**

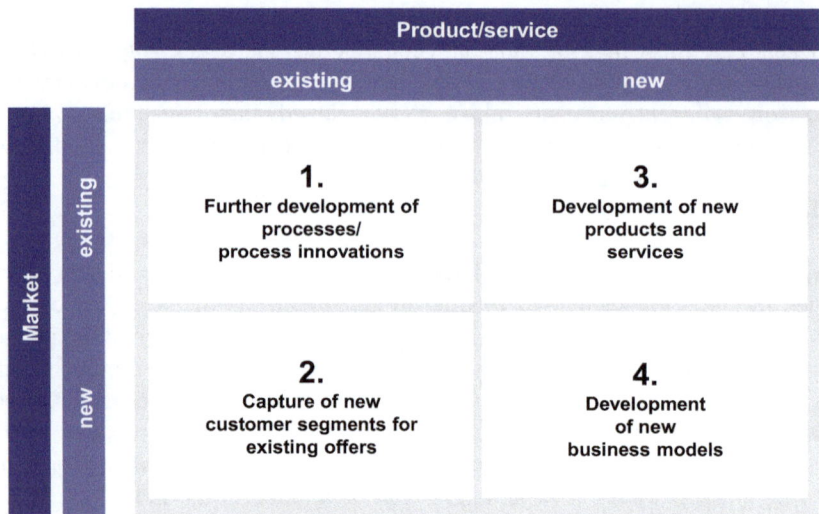

Fig. 3.12 Matrix of strategic thrusts

The **matrix of strategic thrusts** in Fig. 3.12 shows how these different types of innovation are to be located. This matrix defines the different strategic options based on the characteristics of products/services (old and new) and markets (old and new). The focus of activities at the first horizon level is in field 1. Here, it is primarily about further developed processes and process innovations without changing the offers themselves. These optimizations can serve to conquer new customer segments in field 2. This can be done by reducing prices due to more cost-effective production. Or sales processes are established that open up new customer segments. Product and service innovations are found in field 3 and comprehensive business models innovations in field 4.

You can use this **concept to analyze the innovation thrusts** in your company. To do this, position the current activities in this matrix and note which budgets are planned for the individual areas—as of today. Often, it is only through such a **self-critical stocktaking** that the necessary pressure to suffer for a digital transformation can be built up.

The 3 horizons model draws your attention to a particular strategic challenge. While day-to-day business is dealt with on the horizon 1 level, your company must be active in parallel on horizon levels 2 and 3 in order to be able to successfully shape the future. The term **ambidexterity** has become established in management language for this. It is simply a matter of mastering day-to-day business today ("with one hand") as well as shaping the future on horizons 2 and 3 ("with the other hand"). After all, the digital age is leading to the ever-faster emergence and demise of business models.

▶ **Food for Thought**
The 3 horizons model makes one thing clear: today it is no longer enough to deal with product and service innovations as well as process innovations primarily at the horizon 1 level. Due to the dynamics of the markets, you must additionally analyze whether your company is also working—or should be working—on horizon 2 and horizon 3 business models—simultaneously.
The emphasis here is on the word simultaneously!

Therefore, you should use the **3 horizons model** to analyze whether new business models are already being used or developed in your company on horizons 2 and 3 as well. The success relevance of business logics can still be recorded on the first horizon level through classic business-relevant metrics (KPIs). For example, it is sufficient to look at the development of profit, turnover, market share, customer satisfaction, and the number of new and returning customers.

These KPIs cannot be used for the evaluations on horizon levels 2 and 3, not alone or not immediately. Here, it is often first a matter of generating general **learning effects** that arise through iterative testing and the incremental development of new offerings. Classic business plans often do not help here because the prospects of **success of business model innovations** are difficult to grasp at the beginning. An important indicator of whether your company is on the right track here is a completely different KPI: the **stock market value**! It is well known that the future is traded on the stock exchange. Through the stock market value, well-informed market participants signal to you—at least with institutional investors—whether you are focusing on the right future fields with your activities!

Memory Box
If you make use of the 3 horizons model, you should be clear about one thing: in the course of a digital transformation, there can be no uniform organizational structure that optimally serves both the smooth handling of the core business and the generation of (radical) digital innovations. New structures are needed for this (see Sect. 3.7).

Think Box: Questions You Should Ask Yourself
- Analyze your existing business model using the 3 horizons model. Where do you currently stand in the (digital) transformation?
- Does your company currently only focus on cost reduction and efficiency increase on the first horizon?

(continued)

- Does your company have ideas for the further development of the business model on the second horizon?
- How innovative are you on the third horizon?
- Do you use the 3 horizons model to talk about the necessary further development of your business model?
- Are you already managing to be active on all three horizons?
- In whose area of responsibility do these topics belong?

3.2.3 Prioritization and Focus on Macro Initiatives

3.2.3.1 *Eisenhower* Principle as Guiding Concept

In order to meet the complex requirements outlined above—especially with regard to the necessary ambidexterity—most companies also require far-reaching **organizational changes** as well as a **further development** or even a **realignment of the human resources strategy**. However, the need for this—especially in established, often still successful companies—is all too often hindered by the "tiresome" day-to-day business. The underlying dilemma can be illustrated using the *Eisenhower* **principle** in the *Eisenhower* **matrix** (cf. Fig. 3.13). When applying the *Eisenhower* **matrix**, pending tasks must be classified according to the criteria of **urgency** and **importance**.

- **Category "not important and not urgent"**
  Tasks in this category are irrelevant for the achievement of entrepreneurial goals. They should be recognized as such without being processed. These tasks are real energy guzzlers without contributing to entrepreneurial value creation. Here we can also speak of **T-tasks**—with T for "trash"!

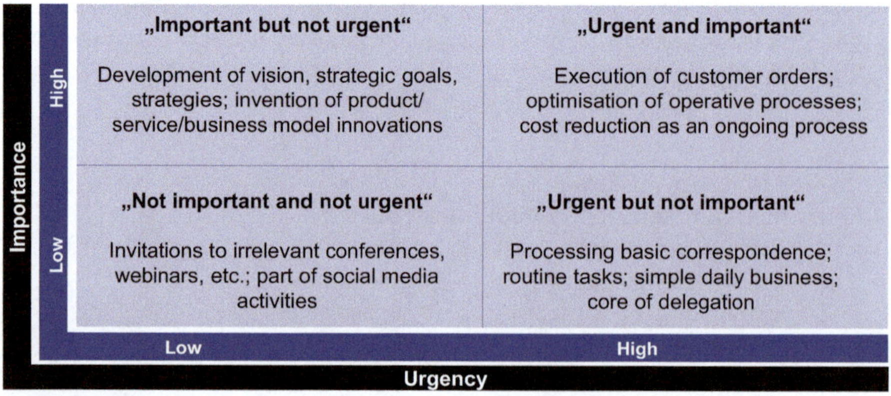

Importance	„Important but not urgent" Development of vision, strategic goals, strategies; invention of product/service/business model innovations	„Urgent and important" Execution of customer orders; optimisation of operative processes; cost reduction as an ongoing process
	„Not important and not urgent" Invitations to irrelevant conferences, webinars, etc.; part of social media activities	„Urgent but not important" Processing basic correspondence; routine tasks; simple daily business; core of delegation
	Low	High
	Urgency	

Fig. 3.13 *Eisenhower* matrix

Examples are invitations to conferences, webinars, or other events that have nothing to do with the company's goals, even in the broadest sense. This also includes newsletters that one actually wanted to discontinue long ago. The too intensive use of social media without company-related goals is also such an energy guzzler (cf. Kreutzer, 2020).

- **Category "urgent, but not important"**
Tasks in this category should be completed promptly. However, they can be subordinated to urgent and important tasks. Ideally, the company has departments in which these tasks, which can be classified as **part of daily business**, are competently handled.

   This includes, among other things, the processing of standard correspondence, travel expense accounting, applying for subsidies, etc. Managers should consistently delegate these tasks in order to have their heads free for the important tasks! Here we can speak of **D-tasks**—with D for "delegation"!

- **Category "urgent and important"**
Tasks classified in this way are of the highest value for the—often short-term—achievement of goals. Their processing as **operational business** must take place immediately.

   These include critical time targets in production that must be met in order to serve customer orders on time. The optimization of operational processes as well as measures to increase efficiency and reduce costs also fall into this category. Often, the core tasks that need to be worked on to achieve the current business goals are found in this category. Here we can speak of **OB-tasks**—with OB for "operational business"!

- **Category "important, but not urgent"**
These tasks are also of great importance for the general achievement of the company's goals. However, their completion is not urgent, so that they can be postponed again and again. After all, the consequences of this **non-processing**—also known as **procrastination**—do not arise so quickly. In essence, this is about **SB-tasks**—with SB for "strategic business"!

   The development of a powerful vision as well as more far-reaching goals and strategies belongs to this category. The development of business model innovations also belongs to this. Such projects are important for survival in the long term—but not yet urgent! This is true at least as long as the company's existence is not yet threatened. But every business model at horizon 1 level approaches the end of its life cycle—sooner or later!

   Consequently, you should not devote yourself to these tasks only when it is almost too late! That is why it is indispensable to schedule such tasks firmly—and not to postpone once defined deadlines because something more urgent and important has intervened.

Eisenhower **prioritization** is one of the basics of time management and also makes an indispensable contribution to strategic corporate management in setting the right priorities. Because **thinking in terms of future developments** is at least temporarily overshadowed by today and not infrequently completely slowed down. It is not only the dominating day-to-day business that makes it difficult to set the right priorities. Complex decision-making processes, multi-level hierarchies, and the fear of making mistakes also act as brake blocks. Digitalization initiatives in particular have to wrestle with these organizational-strategic challenges. In essence, it is always about the **organizational dilemma** of setting the right priorities between the **operational today** and the **strategically important tomorrow** (cf. Hauschildt et al., 2016).

> **Memory Box**
> The *Eisenhower* **matrix** provides you with a valuable tool for **setting priorities correctly**—both professionally and privately. Whether you can use it successfully for yourself depends on only one thing: your **self-discipline.**

▶ **Storytelling** Here is an example of a priority setting I did very early in my professional life. I learned that every day there is another good reason to forgo lunch. So, I decided never to give up my lunch and thus a creative break.

3.2.3.2 Micro Initiatives vs. Macro Strategy

The digital base model in Fig. 3.1 shows the **multitude of dimensions** to be considered in the (further) development of business models. This cannot and must not be about a "small-scale" approach to the steps to be taken. Rather, a **holistic approach to the further development of the company** is indispensable.

The *Boeing 737 Max* example tragically shows the risks associated with an approach that focuses on **micro initiatives** rather than tackling a **macro strategy** (cf. Mahrenholz, 2019, p. 25). What happened? The *Boeing 737* entered service back in 1967 and had been providing reliable service in aviation for decades, becoming a cash cow for *Boeing*. During this time, **incremental improvements** were made again and again to take advantage of new technologies to increase efficiency and thus reduce costs.

In 2011, to meet the increased expectations of the airlines, it was necessary to use the latest and much more fuel-efficient engines. Initially, a new development of the aircraft was planned, but only a revision was decided upon. However, the new engines no longer fit under the previous wings due to their size. Therefore, they were simply mounted further forward on the wings of the *Boeing 737 Max* model. However, this changed the lift behavior in flight considerably. Special software was developed to counteract the instabilities to be expected in flight. Its malfunction in combination with the actions of the insufficiently informed and inadequately trained pilots led to two crashes of this aircraft. A widespread flight ban for this aircraft type was the consequence—for 20 months!

In 2021, *Boeing* was additionally sentenced to pay a fine of US-$ 2.5 billion. One reason for this penalty was that safety-relevant information on the software used had been withheld from the *US Federal Aviation Administration*. The ministry's lawyer stated: "*Boeing* employees subordinated honesty to profit."

What would have been necessary at *Boeing* was not a **micro initiative** to attach the new engines to an old model of aircraft. Rather, it would have required a **macro strategy** to develop an entirely new model that would have made a convincing unit with the new engines. Of course, this would have required a lot of time and would have entailed significant development costs. To avoid these, a very risky path was taken with the micro initiative launched, which cost 346 lives. In addition, *Boeing's* reputation and earnings were massively damaged by the largest quarterly loss in its history. Contributing to this was the 2020 document published by *Boeing* itself, in which a company-owned pilot wrote to a colleague back in 2016 (Johnsson & Beene, 2020):

"**This airplane is designed by clowns, who in turn are supervised by monkeys.**"

The German *Commerzbank* also missed the opportunity to derive a **macro strategy** for the entire company based on the experience gained from the *Comdirect Bank* **micro initiative**, which was launched well and early in 1996. *Comdirect Bank* became one of the largest direct banks in Germany with 2.75 million private customers in the 2020 financial year. Instead of using the *Comdirect Bank* as a nucleus for successful online banking, *Comdirect* was integrated into *Commerzbank* in 2020 to breathe some digital expertise into the bank. It remains to be seen how successful this move will be. In addition, *Commerzbank's* business model was doomed by holding on to the branch business for far too long (keyword "not-to-do list").

After all, it has long been said:

Customers need banking—not (stationary) banks!

This is why *Commerzbank* was overtaken left and right by the FinTechs already mentioned—and its stock market value (keyword "future") fell from 55 billion euros in 2000 to around 6.5 billion euros at the beginning of 2021. This development also led to *Commerzbank* being kicked out of the *DAX*—in favor of *Wirecard*. *Wirecard* itself had to make way for *Delivery Hero* in August 2020—for well-known reasons!

An example of a convincing **macro strategy** is provided by *Elon Musk* with *Tesla*. With a clear **focus on e-mobility without compromising on previous concepts**, *Tesla*—as a newcomer to the automotive industry—has achieved one thing: the engineering knowledge of the global car manufacturers, built up cost-intensively over decades, and the competitive advantage based on it were almost marginalized within a few years. As a consequence, the world's leading companies went from being hunters to being hunted. Investors rewarded this with a market capitalization of *Tesla* that is always higher than that of the current automotive world market leaders—added together!

The established companies such as *Audi, BMW, Daimler,* and *Volkswagen* must now achieve the investment funds that are essential for the **development of digitized e-mobility** through large-scale savings programs and profitable sales. In doing so, they must manage the feat of earning these development budgets by marketing the combustion engines that many consider obsolete. It is exciting to note that *BMW* presented an e-vehicle as early as 2013 with the *BMW* i3, as did *Volkswagen* in the same year with the *e-Up* (cf. Schwarzer, 2013). However, in both companies the prevailing culture as well as the high costs of the vehicles stood in the way of further development of these models. The **strategic window of opportunity** at the time to become a pioneer in e-mobility was not used. The opportunity to develop a macro strategy from a **micro initiative** was not seized by the company leaders. Exclusively, one could say: the time was not yet ripe for e-mobility!

The agricultural machinery manufacturer *John Deere* reacted early and consistently with a **macro strategy** to **ward off digital entrants** in its industry. These entrants sought to increase agricultural productivity beyond what was previously imaginable through the use of sensors, data analytics, and artificial intelligence. This has put the sale and use of *John Deere* tractors and harvesting equipment at risk. *John Deere* is reducing this threat by building a **data driven service business**. This has involved collecting soil samples and analyzing weather conditions to help farmers optimize their work. Sensors in tractors and other machines provide the data needed for **predictive maintenance** (see Sect. 3.3.1.3). A **platform** developed by *John Deere* enables third parties to develop new service applications for agriculture. *John Deere* made an early commitment to **data driven agriculture** by enriching its existing product portfolio with a variety of innovative services (cf. Bughin et al., 2018, p. 5).

▶ **Food for Thought**
Check in your company which **micro initiatives**—and which **macro strategy** for the digital age exist. Are the right decisions already being made here—from a company-wide perspective?

> **Think Box: Questions You Should Ask Yourself**
> - What additional options for action can you identify for your company based on the matrix of innovation thrusts?
> - Which fields of action have perhaps not been illuminated or not illuminated comprehensively enough so far?
> - What do your KPIs say about the future viability of the existing business model?
> - Are there already first "weak signals" that the successes of the past can no longer be extrapolated to the future?
> - Use the *Eisenhower* matrix to analyze which priorities are set in your company.
> - You can also use the *Eisenhower* matrix to critically analyze your private activities to see whether you are setting the right priorities here too.

(continued)

- Check for your company which micro initiatives exist—and which macro strategies exist for the digital age.
- Who in your company regularly deals with these questions?

3.2.4 Pitfalls of a Successful (Digital) Transformation

What are the most common **causes of a missing or only half-hearted digital transformation**? Often the strategies or business models do not or not sufficiently reflect how the (digital) economy is changing. An analysis by *McKinsey* has identified the following five **pitfalls of a successful (digital) transformation** (cf. Bughin et al., 2018).

First pitfall: Fuzzy definition of "digital"

There is often no uniform picture among managers and employees of what could be meant by "digital," by a "digital business development" or by a "digital transformation." For some, "digital" equals "IT," for others, digital developments only seem relevant for marketing and sales. In many cases, there is a lack of a comprehensive, holistic view of the **opportunities and challenges** associated with **digitalization for the company as a whole**.

This includes developments via the Internet of Things or—more comprehensively—the Internet of Everything. The data brought together here can not only optimize entire value chains, but also enable new business models. Therefore, managers in particular should internalize that the **perspective of digitalization** cannot be reduced to efficiency increases and cost reductions alone. This would limit the view to first horizon level activities (see Sect. 3.2.2). Such a wrong focus leaves the comprehensive potentials of digitalization unconsidered. Nevertheless, such a focus still dominates the (digital) agenda in many companies today.

A survey by *Accenture* of the **500 largest German corporations** addressed this issue. The companies were asked to answer the following question: "Which of the following aspects do you use to measure the success of innovation projects in your company?" In essence, the aim was to determine which aspects the companies use to quantify the value contribution of an innovation project through concrete KPIs. Here, the following results emerged (cf. Accenture, 2020, p. 7):

- 91% of entrepreneurs measure the success of innovation processes in terms of **cost savings**.
- 87% of the respondents named **increases in turnover through new products and services**.
- 64% focused on **higher customer satisfaction and loyalty**.
- 53% targeted external **reputation** (i.e., the company's standing).
- 48% focus on **time-to-market** (not time-to-value; see Sect. 1.2.4.4).

▶ **Food for Thought** Digitization still means "increasing efficiency" for too many companies. Here one can speak of a veritable bottom-line trap. Companies see themselves as being on the right track here due to good financial returns, but at the same time are carelessly gambling away their future (cf. Accenture, 2020, p. 7).

Second Pitfall: Lack of understanding for the economics of digitalization

The saying **"technology changes, economic laws don't!"** has long been true. In essence, this statement is still correct, but in the digital age, many new phenomena are emerging that complement the existing economic laws. One such new phenomenon is **"zero marginal costs"** (cf. Rifkin, 2015). In the case of digital products—be it the digital counterparts of analogue books, newspapers, magazines, but also videos, photos, and music—no additional costs are incurred after the initial production during reproduction. Even "delivery" via the Internet in the flat-rate age is accompanied by no marginal costs (apart from electricity costs).

This is also referred to as the **first-copy-cost effect**, because many of these products are dominated by fixed costs. This means that the majority of the costs have already been incurred when the "first copy" is available—for films and music recordings, for example. There are hardly any further costs depending on the number of users. This development endangers entire industries that specialize in the production of books, newspapers, magazines, but also in the reproduction of videos, photos (think of *Kodak*), and music.

The frightening thing about this is that "zero marginal costs" also means **"no additional value added"** through the use of labor and money in the production of further products. After all, all the other stages of output that have been needed up to now are eliminated. In the book market, for example, these are paper and ink production, the development, production and maintenance of the printing presses, the printing of the book itself, and the subsequent stages of packaging and dispatch. The classic function of the bookseller is also eliminated when an e-book is downloaded via the Internet.

These **changes in competition** by breaking through the **dominant industry logics** have already siphoned off 40% of the revenue growth of the established companies worldwide and 25% of their growth in earnings before interest and taxes (EBIT), as a study by *McKinsey* shows (cf. Bughin et al., 2018, p. 3). One reason is that many companies have lowered prices in order to defend their market position of a business model in a downturn (horizon 1). Others have invested more in innovations (e.g., on horizons 2 and 3), which initially also has a negative impact on EBIT.

In addition, digitalization in many areas goes hand in hand with a far greater **transparency of offers**, but above all with comprehensive **price transparency**. This did not exist in the pre-digital age. This, too, is changing the industry's logic permanently! Today, customers have the opportunity to unbundle offers that companies have bundled to achieve higher profitability.

For example, package holidays are becoming less and less attractive for many customers because they prefer to put together an individual trip from the modules available online.

This **unbundling of offers** is detrimental to the profitability of the respective providers. This trend was one of the factors that led to the demise of the *Thomas Cook Group* in 2019. Another reason was the weak British pound, which suffered from the ongoing Brexit discussion. This made foreign travel increasingly expensive for the British. Price comparison sites such as *idealo.com* (with a price alert function) or *Google's* shopping offers systematically increase **price transparency** and thus support bargain hunters. Qualitative services lose importance with a pure price focus—and the margins of the providers sink.

In addition, a **"I-don't-pay" mentality** still prevails in many areas of the Internet. Why should a customer pay for content on a site when similar content is freely available elsewhere on the Internet? This is the case with recipes, newspaper articles, white papers, templates for strategy development, and even instructions for a wide variety of products.

In the **IT sector**, a **dematerialization of services** is also taking place. While companies have invested in server and storage capacities as well as in software themselves in the past, corresponding IT services are increasingly being moved to the cloud. In the so-called **cloud computing**, formerly stationary hardware and software systems (so-called on-premise solutions) are outsourced to external service providers. The necessary connections to these are usually established via the Internet. The corresponding service models are called infrastructure as a service (IAAS), platform as a service (PAAS), and software as a service (SAAS).

Third pitfall: Neglection of platforms and ecosystems

In addition, **platforms** are establishing themselves in more and more markets, inserting themselves between suppliers and customers. In many cases, this destroys established customer supplier relationships. At the same time, these platforms put suppliers in an unprecedented position of dependency. With this business model, the platform operators often demand a larger **margin share** from the supplier and at the same time cut them off from the customers and thus also from important information about them. At the same time, these platforms have a high **scalability** that enables rapid expansion. New industry logics dominate here, which endanger existing business models (see Sect. 3.3.3).

In more and more sectors, companies are building comprehensive **ecosystems**—often starting from platforms. The challenge here is called: **seamless integration**. This means the seamless integration of different applications of a provider, the joint use of which by the customer could previously only be achieved by overcoming interfaces of varying complexity. Ideally—from the perspective of the provider of such a solution—this results in ecosystems. These are self-contained systems that the user does not have to leave even if he wants to start different applications (see Sect. 3.3.2).

According to forecasts by *McKinsey*, digital ecosystems could generate more than US-$ 60 trillion in revenue by 2025. This would correspond to more than 30% of global group sales (cf. Bughin et al., 2018, p. 10).

Memory Box
Ecosystems do not stop at industry boundaries! Rather, they tear down industry boundaries—driven by data, value propositions, customers, suppliers and, above all, the profit that can be achieved via ecosystems.

This is why you have to align your business radar much more broadly than is often the case today with competitive analyses. If you align your business analysis to industry boundaries, you have already lost! After all, new (digital) competitors cannot be recognized in this way—because most of them do not come from your own sector! However, you should not underestimate the developments in your own sector!

Fourth pitfall: Overestimation of the "usual suspects"

Many companies worry about the effects **start-ups** can have on their own business model. In contrast to established companies, **start-ups** usually only pick **one part of the value chain** to attack established companies at the beginning. After initial successes, other parts of the value chain are then integrated. A lot of attention is—hopefully—paid to these developments. With this focus, however, there is a danger of overlooking the fact that established competitors are also working on their existing business models and developing them into the digital age. It is precisely the **digitalization of established companies** that can pose a great danger.

Today's **established companies** often still dominate many markets. At the same time, they often have high brand recognition and a loyal customer base. So, if large, established competitors act with offensive and innovative strategies on horizons 2 and 3—possibly even with **cannibalizing concepts**—this can have serious effects on the other established market participants. These effects are particularly great when the innovative "top dogs" realign **several areas of the value chain** at once. It then becomes difficult for the slow movers and late movers to regain the competitive advantage they have gained.

Analyses by *McKinsey* show that **courageously acting established companies** achieve an average share of 20% of a digitized market. Start-ups, on the other hand, achieve an average of only 5%. Against this background, it becomes understandable why slow movers and late movers in particular are exposed to particularly great risks of being left behind, especially by innovative established competitors, but also by start-ups (cf. Bughin et al., 2018, p. 12).

3.2 Developing Business Models for the Digital Age

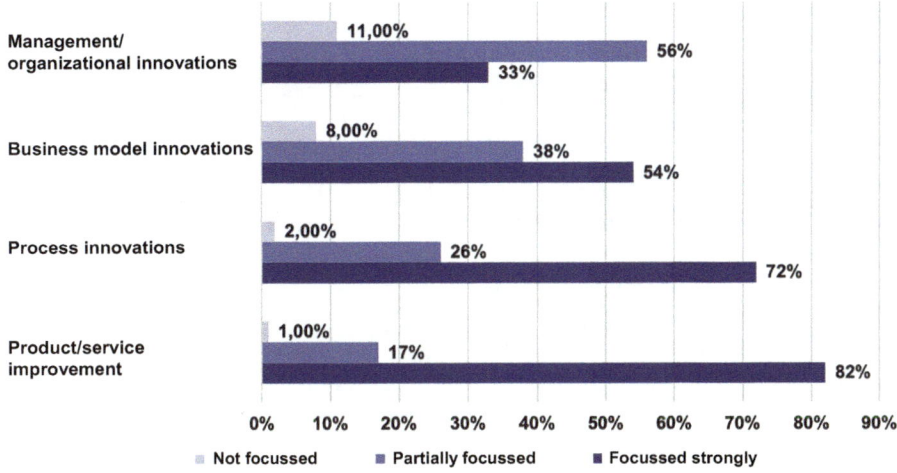

Fig. 3.14 Prioritization of German companies on future growth areas

Memory Box

Speed is of particular importance in the digital age. Often, the **first movers** and the **very fast followers** are rewarded by customers here. Consequently, it is time to act powerfully. As the saying goes:

The best time to act was 5 years ago, the second best time is now!

Fifth pitfall: The duality of the digital challenge is not mastered

The big challenge for many companies, which is often difficult to master, is to make the **day-to-day business** profitable, on the one hand, and to digitize it step by step. On the other hand, at the same time it is necessary to develop new ideas for the **existing business** and additionally think about business model innovations. This necessity was illustrated using the 3 horizons model and described with **ambidexterity**. The vast majority of companies still struggle to master the necessary **duality of digital challenges** (cf. Bughin et al., 2018).

A study by *Accenture* (2020, p. 8) analyzed **258 large companies** in Germany. Here, the following question was asked: "When it comes to innovation, which of the following areas does your company currently focus on strongly, partially or not at all?" Fig. 3.14 shows the focus areas. The results shown there only partially do justice to the **challenge of ambidexterity**.

The vast majority of 82% of companies focus on **product and service improvements** (horizon 1), followed by **process and procedure innovations** with 72% (horizon 1 and partly horizon 2). **Business model innovations**, on the other hand, are only strongly focused on by slightly more than half of the companies at 52%. Only one third of the companies are working extensively

(continued)

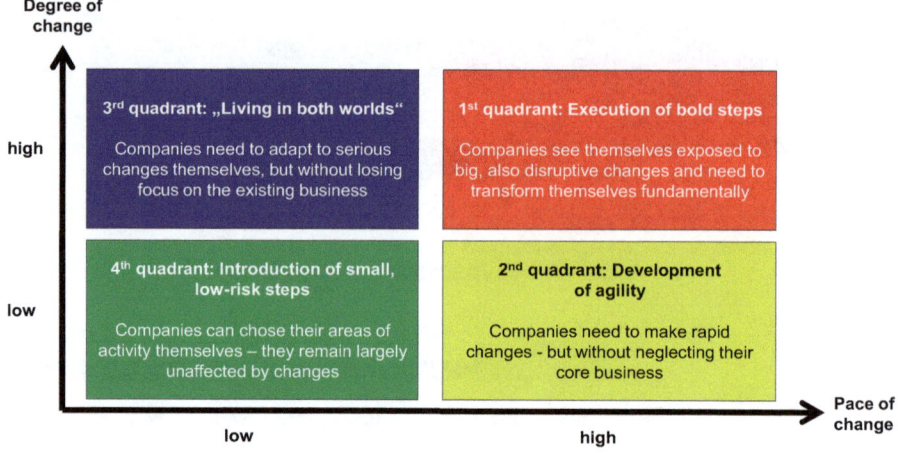

Fig. 3.15 Challenge matrix

Fig. 3.16 Tensions between daily business and innovation business—I

> on **management and organizational innovations** (see Sects. 3.6 and 3.7), without which a digital transformation cannot succeed.
>
> The **analysis of large companies** shows one thing clearly: companies that have consistently used digitalization for business model innovations and in some cases even generate sales on their own platforms can escape the general weakness in growth (cf. Accenture, 2020, p. 8).

(continued)

3.2 Developing Business Models for the Digital Age

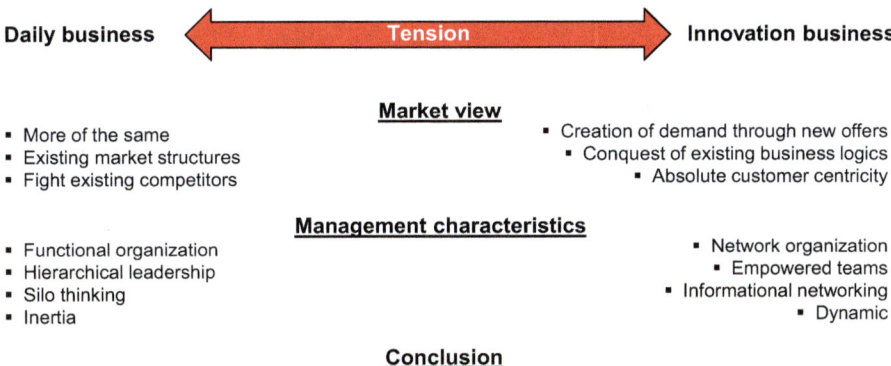

Fig. 3.17 Tensions between daily business and innovation business—II

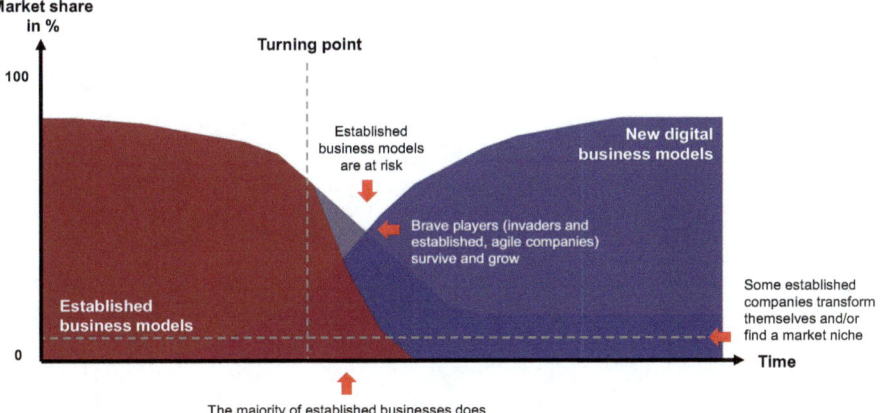

Fig. 3.18 Challenges that traditional business models face through digital business models

> You can use Fig. 3.15 to determine which challenges exist for you and your company (cf. Bughin et al., 2018, p. 13). The **challenge matrix** shown there is defined by the **extent** and **speed of the (digital) changes** that need to be mastered within the company. The further priorities for your digital transformation are to be derived from the positioning of your company in this challenge matrix.

(continued)

Companies in the first quadrant face massive and rapidly occurring disruptions (cf. Fig. 3.15). They have to take bold steps across the board to survive. The industries of stationary retail, music labels as well as publishing houses are located here. **Companies in the second quadrant** have to master fast but less radical changes. The speed of change within the company can be increased through concepts of agile management. Many financial service providers can be found in this field.

Companies in the third quadrant must master "living in both worlds" (cf. Fig. 3.15). This includes, for example, car manufacturers. They still have to operate profitably on the market today with the vehicles of yesterday and today in order to earn the funds for the transformation into providers of e-mobility and autonomous driving. Energy suppliers must also succeed in the feat of simultaneously phasing out "dirty" energy sources and making money from them—in order to generate "green" energy. The **companies in the fourth quadrant** face only minor changes. Many niche providers can be found here, who may even act according to the motto: "analogue is the new organic"! These include the modest renaissance of instant cameras, vinyl records, etc.

The challenges discussed as well as the accompanying **tensions** are brought together in Figs. 3.16 and 3.17.

You are welcome to determine the intensity of this tension for your own sphere of influence. Here it quickly becomes visible in which areas the greatest contrasts occur in order to derive appropriate actions based on them. These can be reflected in the **realignment of teams** as well as in the **required competences of managers and employees**, which can lead to the development of a digital training agenda (cf. Sects. 3.6 and 3.7). There may also be a need to improve internal storytelling (see Sect. 2.1.1).

What **challenges traditional business models** face from **digital business models** is shown in Fig. 3.18 (cf. Bughin et al., 2018, p. 6). Many classic business models have worked convincingly for years, for decades, and perhaps even a century. Nevertheless, in the digital age there is no guarantee that such a winning streak will continue for even the next 2–3 years. That is why it is important to employ **trend scouts** in every company who—depending on the size of the company—are assigned part-time or full-time to make corresponding observations in the markets. The focus in the identification of new business models should be equally on established companies and start-ups. The concepts found here and their possible implications are to be discussed with the management and employees.

The task to be mastered is to recognize the **threat to one's own business model** even before the turning point in Fig. 3.18 is reached. Only those who act in good time before such turning points have the opportunity to finance the

(continued)

development and establishment of a further developed or a new business model as a **hybrid strategy** with the proceeds of the "old" business model.

Parallel to the established companies acting in this way, **new digital business models** are being established—especially, but not only, by start-ups. Some of the established companies may also succeed in surviving in a niche with a more or less adapted business model. If companies do not react or do not react in time and therefore the decline of the classic business coincides with a high need for investment in new business model, the failure of the business model is certain. This is shown by the developments at *Toys "R" Us*, *Thomas Cook* and many other failed companies.

Memory Box
Only those who act in time have many options available for them!

Think Box: Questions You Should Ask Yourself
- How are "digital," "digitalization," and "digital transformation" translated in your company?
- Do the goals of increasing efficiency and reducing costs dominate the "translation," or are you also thinking about a further development of your business model that exploits digitalization potential?
- Does your company have a deep understanding of the economic effects of digitalization (keywords "zero marginal costs" and "first-copy-cost effect")?
- What importance does your company attach to platforms and ecosystems?
- Does your market analysis focus primarily on developments in the start-up sector?
- Or do you also try to systematically work out which measures your established competitors are taking to advance the digitalization of their products and services as well as their business models?
- Are you one of the first movers in digitalization—or rather one of the late or slow movers?
- How strongly do you remind yourself—especially at top management level—that you may have to master a duality of the digital challenge?
- How do you prioritize tomorrow's growth areas in your company?
- Where do you position yourself in the challenge matrix?

(continued)

> - What consequences do you derive from your position in the challenge matrix?
> - Determine the tensions between day-to-day business and innovation business for your company.
> - Are there trend scouts in your company who are tasked with exploring changes in the business models of established competitors as well as in the start-up landscape?
> - Where is the responsibility for these tasks located in your company?

3.2.5 Methods for Developing Business Model Innovations

Don't wait—innovate!

3.2.5.1 Process for Developing Business Model Innovations

The steps in the **process for developing business model innovations** on the way to digital excellence are shown in Fig. 3.19 (cf. Wirtz & Thomas, 2014, p. 45). Some of the steps required for this have already been discussed or will be discussed in more detail below. This figure already shows that agile management methods can be used very effectively in various process stages. This can reduce or avoid a high time requirement and the risk of failure when using the waterfall concept (keyword "time-to-value"; see Sect. 1.2.4.4).

Unfortunately, a procedure that can still be observed in many cases is to digitize companies from the bottom up. Products, services, and/or processes are digitized hoping that a convincing business model will emerge. That is far from the truth!

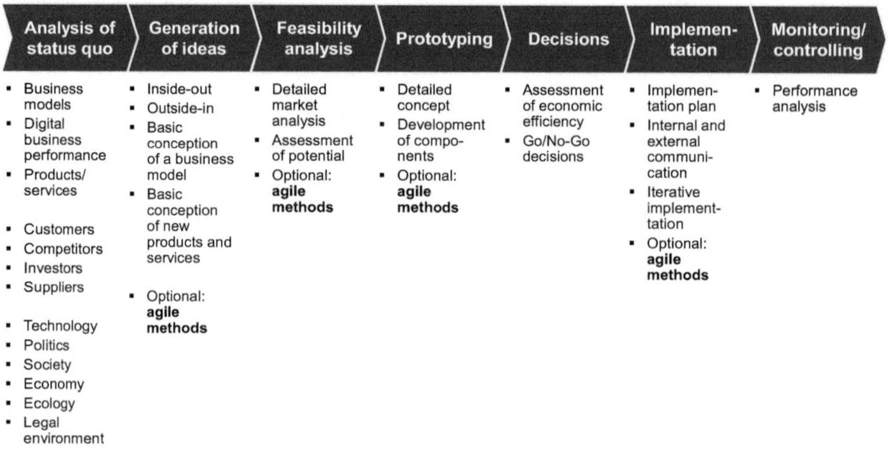

Analysis of status quo	Generation of ideas	Feasibility analysis	Prototyping	Decisions	Implementation	Monitoring/ controlling
• Business models • Digital business performance • Products/ services • Customers • Competitors • Investors • Suppliers • Technology • Politics • Society • Economy • Ecology • Legal environment	• Inside-out • Outside-in • Basic conception of a business model • Basic conception of new products and services • Optional: agile methods	• Detailed market analysis • Assessment of potential • Optional: agile methods	• Detailed concept • Development of components • Optional: agile methods	• Assessment of economic efficiency • Go/No-Go decisions	• Implementation plan • Internal and external communication • Iterative implementation • Optional: agile methods	• Performance analysis

Fig. 3.19 Process of business model development

3.2 Developing Business Models for the Digital Age

You can also put it more drastically:

If you digitize a shitty process, you will get a digitized shitty process!

If you only digitize the already existing offers and processes without transforming them at the same time, you cement the status quo. The challenge, however, is to critically and constructively question the existing business model and develop it further. To this end, it is necessary to examine in what way digitalization can support the implementation of a further developed or a new business model.

The following must therefore be taken into account here:

The **development of new digital business model** must not (any longer) be about the mere **transfer of existing business models into an online version**. We have to further develop our entire way of thinking—preferably directly from the customer. Only the linking of current and future customer needs with new (digital) possibilities opens our creative horizon for the development of business model innovations.

> **Memory Box**
> Before business model innovations can be generated, one's own business model must be critically analyzed and understood in its depth. This kind of **meta-analysis of one's own business model**—in light of current and potential competitors—is imperative. Only those who have understood their entrepreneurial roots and own DNA in depth and recognize what of it still carries into the future are capable of a successful transformation.

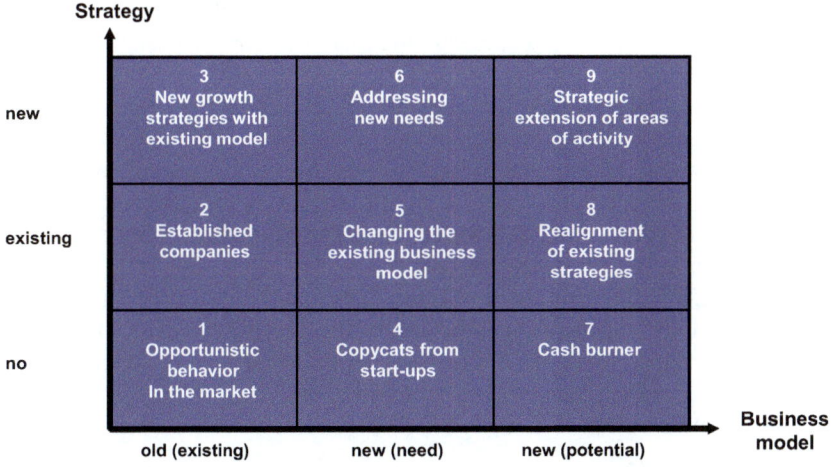

Fig. 3.20 Strategy and business model matrix to identify fields of action

3.2.5.2 Strategy and Business Model Matrix

Figure 3.20 shows which paths you can take in the concrete development of business model—oriented towards the **strategy and business model matrix**. Here nine different thrust directions are described (cf. Halecker & Hartmann, 2014, p. 226f.).

Focus on the existing business model (activities on the horizon 1 level):

1. Opportunistic behavior
   In the first field, the status quo enables the company to survive because there is no need to further develop the business model that can be derived from the current situation. The business model used enables the company to survive. Here one can speak of a **muddling through**. A clearly formulated and communicated corporate strategy is missing. Some start-ups are located here—you just try something out!
2. Established companies
   In the second field, all companies are to be positioned that work according to an established strategy with an established business model and do not focus on innovation. The strategy is: **concentration on the core business—with the existing strategy.**
3. New growth strategies for existing business models
   For the companies located in field 3, the growth strategy is based on the existing business model. Motto: **concentration on the core business—with a new strategy**. Here, an attempt is made to tap further growth potential of the existing business model.

   Focus on a new business model and existing needs (activities on the second and third horizon level):
4. Copycats at start-ups
   Some start-ups copy—without much strategic work of their own—the existing business model of another company (field 4). The copied business model has already been introduced in another country and/or for other products or services. This is called a **copy strategy**. A convincing example of this is *Zalando*, whose founders were more than inspired by *Zappos'* business model! *Wimbu* is the copycat of *Airbnb*. Many other examples in the field of car sharing, bike sharing, food delivery services, etc. could be mentioned. Many of these companies have now arrived in the second field—or are focusing on fields 3, 5 or 6.
5. Change of an existing business model
   In order to take account of changed framework conditions, the business model is further developed in the fifth field within the company's own strategy. This includes the conversion of the business model at *Heidelberger Printing Machines* or *Rolls-Royce* aircraft turbines to a subscription model (see Sect. 3.2.5.5). This is an **adaptation strategy** to cover new or changed needs with appropriate offers.
6. Addressing new needs
   In order to satisfy new needs in the market, new strategies and new business models are used by the companies to be located in field 6. Here, for the first time, **comprehensive innovation strategies** are being developed to give the company a new direction. As already reported, the *Reifenhäuser* company, a manufacturer of machines for nonwoven production, started its own production of face masks

in the Corona period (see Sect. 2.1.5.3). This development becomes a strategy if it complements the existing business model in the longer term.

Focus on new potentials through a new business model (activities on the second and third horizon level):

7. Cash burner
   Many start-ups still start with a potential-driven business model in the seventh field, but without a strategy. In most cases, failure is a foregone conclusion. This is why we can speak of a **cash burner strategy**.
8. Rounding of an existing strategy
   In order to meet changes in the market, a new business model is added to the strategic approach in field 8. This is a **horizontal diversification strategy**. In essence, the company remains true to its previous business model and the economic level it has covered up to now. However, the business model is supplemented by a new strategic orientation. An example of this is the founding of *Orphoz* by *McKinsey*. While *McKinsey* offers strategy consulting, the subsidiary *Orphoz* focuses on implementation. In this way, both business model can support and complement each other. Another example is *Amazon's* entry into the distribution of prescription drugs (see Sect. 3.2.9.1).
9. Strategic expansion of the field of action
   In the ninth field, a company opens up a further field of action through a new strategy and a new business model. This can be based on a vertical or a lateral diversification strategy. In the case of **vertical diversification**, a company moves into upstream and/or downstream economic stages. It thus now produces raw materials, supplier parts, or finished products itself (backward integration—upstream), as is the case with *Amazon's* own products (see Sect. 3.2.9.1). A company can also enter further processing stages in the value chain and/or take over the distribution of its own services (forward integration—downstream). This was the case with the opening of the *Nivea* stores by *Beiersdorf*.

   In the case of a **lateral diversification**, the company becomes active in areas that no longer have any connections with the existing business. This includes *Amazon's* entry into cloud solutions with *Amazon Web Services* (see Sect. 3.2.9.1).

However, the **copycat strategy** is not the only way to arrive at new business models without major innovation processes of your own. The further development or diversification of your own business model can also be achieved by **acquiring a business model from a third party**. The so-called **GAFA or GAFAM companies** (*Google, Amazon, Facebook, Apple, Microsoft*) in particular, but also German publisher *Axel Springer Verlag*, have been able to dynamically expand their business areas in recent years because they have acquired many new business ideas. These were either integrated into the existing business models or established in parallel. The financial strength of these companies opens up many attractive fields of action for them (see Sect. 3.2.9).

In 2012, *Facebook* acquired *Instagram* for US-$ 1 billion. At the time, *Instagram* had 30 million users but was neither generating revenue nor profit. In 2014,

Facebook bought a company that was only 5 years old for US-$ 19 billion. Not a bad price for an unprofitable company with only 50 employees! Its name? *WhatsApp*. However, in both cases, *Facebook* recognized the emerging competition here early on and acquired these companies. This is an exciting approach to keeping the number of competitors small—if you have the necessary investment budgets.

The list of acquisitions completed in recent years could be extended almost indefinitely. However, not all acquisitions are made public. The so-called **killer acquisitions** take place time and again. Here, the acquiring company has no real interest in a new technology, a product, a business idea, or the minds behind it. The driver of the acquisition is rather the **elimination of unloved competitors**, who are taken out of the market before they endanger the company's own business (cf. Cunningham et al., 2020).

> **Memory Box**
> The strategy is often: **copy, buy, kill**—especially when the company's money pots are well filled.
> The question is: **be lunch or have lunch!**

3.2.5.3 Types of Business Model Innovations

When designing the innovation process, you should consider what **type of business model innovation** you are aiming for. Figure 3.21 shows which areas can be the focus of the innovation process (cf. Schallmo, 2014, p. 8). We often focus primarily on **innovations of the offers**. This is about renewing or improving existing products and services. **Market innovations** involve the further development of existing markets or the identification of entirely new markets.

Process innovations can also change business models in part or in their entirety. An example of this is the partial or complete substitution of classic sales channels by digital concepts. Finally, the so-called **social innovations** can also be used in the

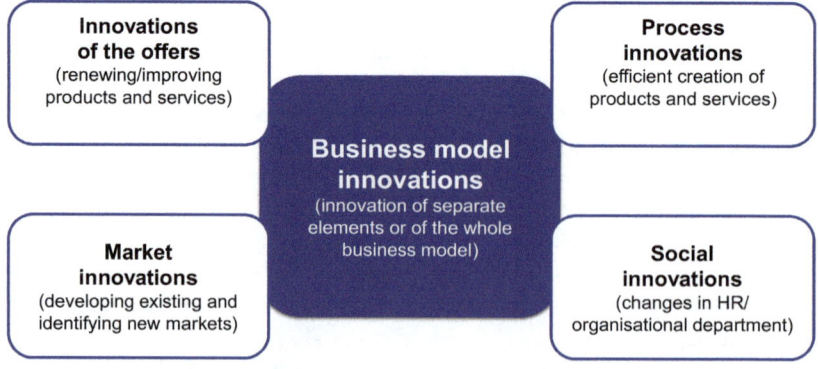

Fig. 3.21 Areas of business model innovations

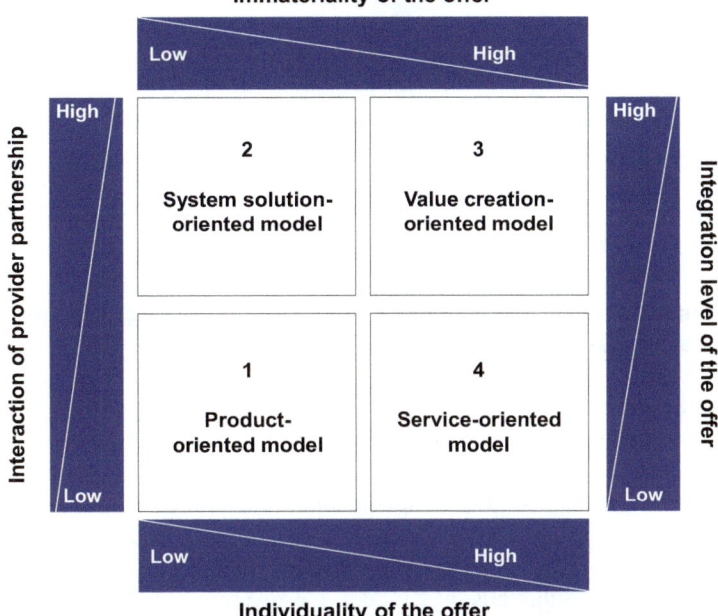

Fig. 3.22 Service transformation: from product manufacturer to service provider

context of business model innovations, which are accompanied by serious changes in the personnel and/or organizational area (cf. Sects. 3.6 and 3.7). A comprehensive business model innovation is based on two or more of these fields of action.

To develop such business model innovations, you have two tasks. The first is to **analyze the existing business model** in order to develop it further, if necessary. This applies to companies already active in the market. In addition, **new business models should be developed**—not only by start-ups, but also in established companies.

A concept developed by Bruhn et al. (2015, p. 139f.) can be used to support the development process of business model innovations. This showed interesting **fields of action for business field innovations** (cf. Fig. 3.22).

The creative process here is oriented towards the following dimensions:

- **Individuality of the offer**
  The spectrum ranges from standard offers to highly individualized offers.
- **Immateriality of the offer**
  This ranges from "low" for operational processes (such as maintenance work) to "high" for the immateriality of entire business processes (such as cloud services).
- **Interaction of the provider partnership**
  Provider partnerships are often the prerequisite for system solution- and value creation-oriented business models. Cooperation with different partners makes it

possible to offer a complete product/service bundle from a single source. This is therefore about the degree of cooperation between different solution providers.
- **Integration level of the offer**
From the customer's point of view, the degree of integration describes whether the company's offer is perceived as an additional service or as an integrated overall solution. Thus, in the product-oriented as well as in the service-oriented business model, additional services are offered that can be used optionally. In contrast, the system solution-oriented as well as the value creation-oriented model offers a holistic solution that can no longer be decomposed.

The **characteristics of the business models** described in Fig. 3.22 are as follows (cf. Bruhn et al., 2015, pp. 141–144):

1. Product-oriented business model
   Here, only **product-accompanying services** are marketed, if at all. This segment includes pure product manufacturers, product manufacturers with obligatory service (e.g., legally required documentation), product manufacturers with product-accompanying service (e.g., for maintenance and repair) as well as product manufacturers with product-service bundles (e.g., in the form of maintenance contracts). In this business model, the revenue generated depends on the intensity of use—for example, through replacement purchases and repairs when the products are heavily used.
2. System solution-oriented business model
   This business model aims at the **marketing of bundles**. System solution providers place the primary focus on either the product or the service. A bundle is offered that merges products and services into **fully integrated solutions**. For example, a manufacturer of milking machines can provide farmers with additional support in milk production, barn equipment, slurry processing, etc. This business model generates revenue not only from the sale of milking machines. In this business model, the revenue generated depends on the intensity of use of the whole bundle.
3. Value-added business model
   This is the marketing of the so-called **operator models** that combine the product-, system solution-, and service-oriented business model. A supplier of machine tools can use them to manufacture tools for third-party partners. The company, which was originally active as a manufacturer of machines, thus becomes a supplier of the products that can be manufactured with its machines. In this way, this company becomes an even more important partner within the value chain of the supplied company. In this business model, the turnover achieved depends on the intensity of use.
4. Service-oriented business model
   The services marketed here are aimed directly at the customers' business processes—for example, through consulting services or software offers. Here again, a distinction can be made between different forms of the business model. **Service providers** can integrate themselves into the customer's value creation processes.

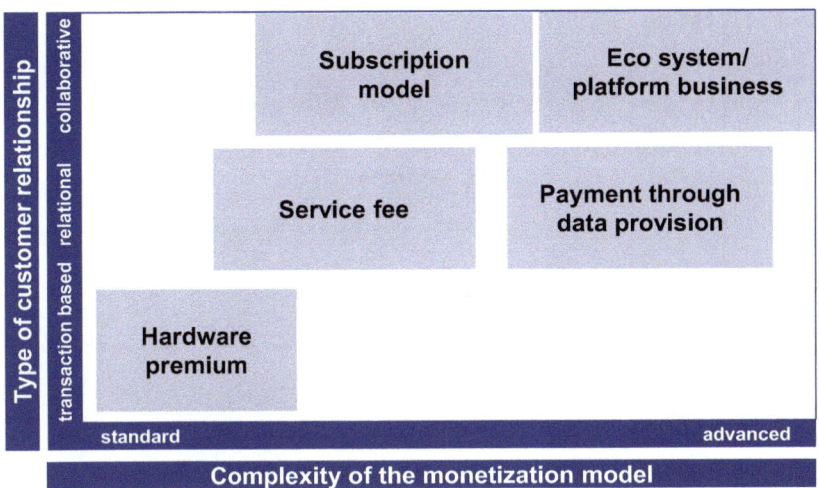

Fig. 3.23 Monetization models

An example of this is a truck provider who also offers software for fleet management. This can be standard solutions or individually developed solutions. Alternatively, providers can also enable industrial networking of customers, for example via platform models. In this business model, the revenue generated is often primarily based on a service and is consequently less dependent on the intensity of use.

The business models shown here go hand in hand with different **monetization models** (cf. Fig. 3.23; cf. Capgemini, 2014, p. 4). The classic is the attempt to achieve a **hardware premium** in comparison with competitors through a convincing product offer. Accompanying services are compensated by **service fees**. Optionally, a (partial) **remuneration** can be made by **providing data** that is used by the provider for the further development of its own offer. Much more intensive customer relationships exist in the **subscription model** and in the **development of a platform or an ecosystem**, because here the partners involved often aim for long-term cooperation.

The monetization models described in Fig. 3.23 go hand in hand with various advantages and disadvantages for the providers (cf. Bruhn et al., 2015, p. 142). First of all, it is important that the addition of services to the core offer leads to a **differentiation in competition**. At the same time, there is a **reduction in the comparability of prices**, as services are more difficult to compare due to their heterogeneity. There is a tendency towards **sustainable high value creation** because **customer relationships are intensified** and **additional barriers to market entry are built up**. In addition—particularly important here—**new business areas are opened up**.

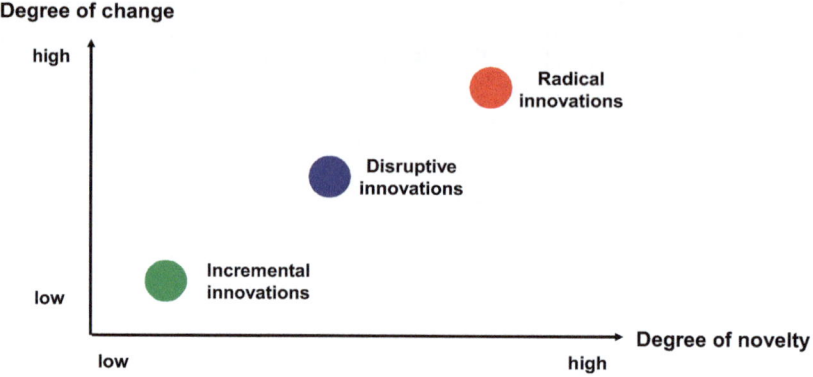

Fig. 3.24 Types of business model innovations

However, this service-based business model innovation is also accompanied by **higher risks**. This is because the companies are moving into new service areas that were previously not part of their own core business. This step is also accompanied by significantly higher **financing and investment requirements**. The stronger integration into customer relationships also increases the **dependence on customers**. Finally, the development of such innovations also requires an **organizational and cultural change** in the offering company. Exemplary implementations for these servitization concepts can be found in Sect. 3.2.5.5.

> **Memory Box**
> For a convincing **innovation process in established companies**, it is crucial that you open up the creative space as broadly as possible at an early stage. This means that there are **no prohibitions** on thinking far outside the box of the existing business model. The rule here is unrestricted:
> **Think big!**
> In order to send this important signal, especially internally, but also externally, you can make it clear that the creative process can encompass all the forms shown in Fig. 3.24. In addition to the often predominant **incremental innovations**, these are above all **disruptive and radical innovations**, through which a company moves far away from its traditional activities. Only in this way will you also succeed in developing innovations for the third horizon! Examples of this can be found in Sect. 3.2.9.

3.2.5.4 Business Model Canvas

To support processes for **analyzing and developing business models**, you can use different **canvas concepts**. The term canvas also stands for work surface and underlines an important aspect of these tools: **visualization**. Complex strategic

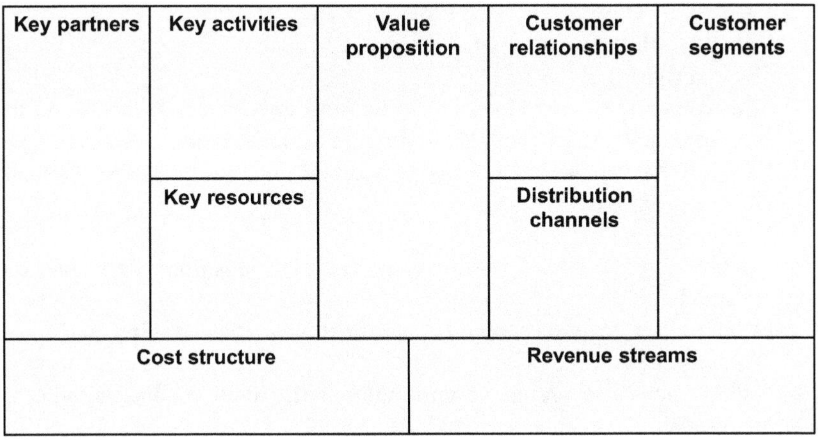

3.2 Developing Business Models for the Digital Age

Key partners	Key activities	Value proposition	Customer relationships	Customer segments
	Key resources		Distribution channels	
Cost structure			Revenue streams	

Fig. 3.25 Basic concept of the business model canvas

issues that arise in any discussion of business models can be visualized and are easier to discuss.

▶ **Food for Thought**
Without business model innovations, there is a danger of being degraded over time from lead provider to interchangeable supplier.

In the context of the business model discussion, the **business model canvas** is of the greatest importance (cf. Osterwalder & Pigneur, 2011). This model can be used as a conceptual template for the documentation and further development of existing as well as for the development of new business models and positioning. For this purpose, a **visual map** is developed that includes the different strategic elements of a business model. Figure 3.25 shows nine elements that need to be filled with content in the course of strategy development (cf. Osterwalder & Pigneur, 2011, p. 47). These elements are also called building blocks.

The different **building blocks of the business model canvas** in Fig. 3.25 are meant as follows:

- **Important partners**
  Companies create relationships between suppliers and other service providers in order to optimize their own processes and/or to reduce risks of the business model. This also includes entering into strategic alliances as well as establishing joint ventures—also with strategic competitors. Here the question arises with which (strategic) partners a company would like to cooperate with (in the future).
  The key questions here are:
  - Which are our most important partners?
  - What key resources do we draw from them?

- What key activities do partners engage in?
- What are the motivations for the partnerships?
- **Key activities**
  This component determines which the most important activities along the entrepreneurial value chain are in order to achieve competitive advantages. A value chain analysis can provide important impulses for this (cf. Kreutzer, 2019, pp. 68–72).
  The key questions here are:
- Which key activities require our value propositions and distribution channels?
- Which key activities require our customer relationships and revenue streams?
- Which activities are most important in distribution channels, customer relationships, revenue streams . . .?
- **Key resources**
  Key entrepreneurial resources include everything that is essentially necessary to create value for customers. The relevant resources include employees, financial resources, patents, production facilities, technologies. Here we examine which are the most important resources for creating, enriching, and/or further developing one's own business model.
  The key questions here are:
- What key resources do our value propositions and distribution channels require?
- What resources do our customer relationships and revenue streams require?
- Which of these resources are most important for production, distribution channels, customer relationships, revenue streams...?
- **Value proposition**
  The value proposition describes the products and services that make up the company's portfolio. It is important that the value proposition to be defined here ideally differs clearly from the competitor offers in terms of novelty, performance, customer orientation, price-quality ratio, and convenience. The central question here is what (further) expectations customers have of a provider or how additional added value could be created for customers.
  The key questions here are:
- What value do we convey to our clients?
- What is the core of our value proposition?
- What product and service packages do we offer to each customer segment?
- What customer needs do we satisfy?
- **Customer segments**
  Every company must precisely define which customer segments the offer should be aimed at. A clean market and customer segmentation are an important prerequisite for success here. Persona concepts should be used for this (see Sect. 3.5.2.1).
  The key questions here are:

- Who are we creating value for?
- Who are our most important customers?
- Which customers would we like to win over?

- **Customer relationship**

  The survival and thus the success of every company depend to a decisive degree on the ability to build long-lasting and profitable customer relationships. Here, the determination of customer value is of central importance.

  The key questions here are:

- What kind of relationships does each client segment expect?
- What intensity of client relationships have we been able to build?
- How are these client relationships integrated into our business model?

- **Distribution channels**

  Companies can communicate a value proposition to their customers through different channels. Different distribution channels can also be used to provide the company's offers. It is important to decide in which form this can best be achieved (e.g., online and/or offline)—ideally combined with additional added value for the customers (cf. Kreutzer, 2021a, b).

  The key questions here are:

- Through which channels do our customer segments want to be addressed?
- How do our offers reach the different customer segments?
- Which channels work best or are most cost-efficient?
- How are our channels integrated into the business model and with each other?
- How can our channels best be integrated into our customers' processes?

- **Cost structure**

  The cost structure of a company reflects all the factors described above. The cost structure also has a clear influence on which strategies a company can use in the market.

  The key questions here are:

- What are the main costs associated with our model?
- Which key activities and key resources are the most expensive?

- **Revenue streams**

  The success or failure of the business model and thus of the company as a whole is documented in the income stream. Here, for example, it is necessary to continuously check which profits and losses can be achieved with which customer segments and offers.

  The key questions here are:

- Which profits or losses are achieved with which customer segments?
- Which profits or losses are achieved with which offers?
- What values are our customers willing to pay for?
- How much does each revenue stream contribute to our total revenue?
- What are the drivers of revenue flow?
- Which areas (activities, processes, structures, etc.) hinder the revenue flow?

The **business model canvas** is a simple and highly effective tool to analyze your existing business model. Using the business model canvas, you can also systematically generate new ideas for the strategy process as well as for new business models. You provide the corresponding worksheet for internal workshops. Various online tools are also offered to support such an analysis and creative process. However, "physical presence" proves its worth immensely, especially in creative processes.

After a short briefing, different teams can work on a business model. It is important that employees and managers from different company divisions and hierarchy levels work together in the teams. The motto here is: **"diversity is key!"**

In this **analytical creative process**, the managers higher up in the hierarchy have to hold back a little so that they do not disrupt the creative process with their actions or (unintentionally) steer it in a certain direction. The results developed in the team can then be presented and discussed in a larger circle. This is particularly easy due to the canvas method, because in this process **no strategy manuals** are written, but an easy-to-follow **visualization of a business model** takes place. In this way, you can quickly and easily identify new strategic approaches or gain confirmation for concepts that have already been implemented.

> **Memory Box**
> The **business model canvas** allows you to understand your own business model in depth. Building on this understanding, you can make **further developments to the existing business model**. At the same time, you can also use the **concept to develop new business models** as well as to **analyze the business models of competitors** (such as start-ups). Only this deep understanding enables you to work comprehensively on your own business model—at all levels of the 3 horizons model.
>
> You can also use the business model canvas—especially in the B2B environment—to **analyze the business models of your important customers**. This will give you not only important ideas for the further development of products and services, but also impulses for your own business model innovations.

▶ **Storytelling** In several **B2B consulting projects**, we used the **business model canvas** to understand the business models of direct customers in all relevant facets. However, we did not perform these analyses at the green table. Rather, we organized workshops with the managing directors and other executives of our clients, usually even on their premises. When selecting partners, we made sure to visit not only the largest companies, but also those that seemed to have different business models.

Through this cooperation, we were able to achieve several goals. On the one hand, we understood our **clients' business models** much better—and were therefore able to consistently develop our products and services in a client-oriented way. On the other hand, our customers themselves also understood their **own business model** much better. After all, they are not often invited by a supplier to spend a whole day thinking about their own business model. Many of our clients had never done this before in a competently moderated form!

This last point led to a phenomenon that we had not envisaged before: the **intensive and trusting cooperation with our clients** in these workshops promoted mutual understanding and directly paid off in the **depth and stability of the client relationship**.

3.2.5.5 Platform Canvas

In the digital age, **platform concepts**, such as those used by *Uber, Airbnb,* but also *Amazon, Check 24, Flixbus,* and others, are becoming increasingly important (see Sect. 3.3.3). Therefore, a special **platform canvas** is presented below (cf. Fig. 3.26).

The first step in using this platform canvas is to work out the possible goals and ideas of a platform strategy. One difference to the business model canvas mentioned before is that you use this canvas to **identify already existing external platform operators** that could jeopardize your business model. In addition, you need to check which **partners** could be considered for the development of your own or a joint platform. The decisive factor here is also what added value you can offer platform users and potential platform partners.

With the platform canvas, you can focus your analysis on possible **threats from platforms** that are already established or being built. At the same time, you start a creative process to work out possible **goals and ideas for your own platform** or one to be developed with partners. In addition, you can check which **potential partners**

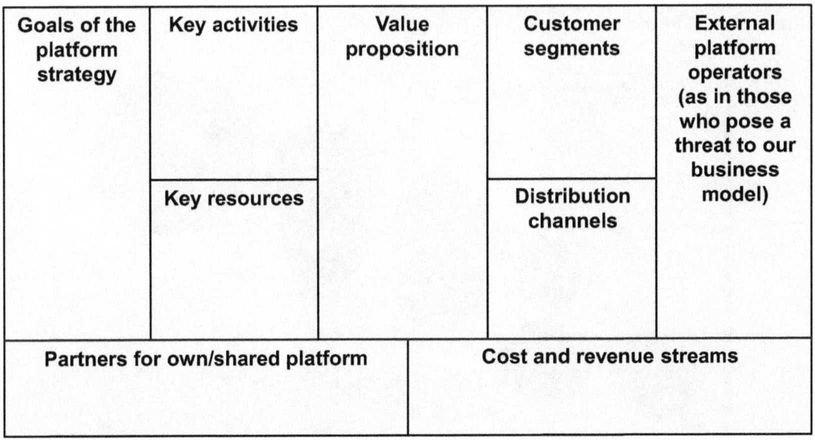

Goals of the platform strategy	Key activities	Value proposition	Customer segments	External platform operators (as in those who pose a threat to our business model)
	Key resources		Distribution channels	
Partners for own/shared platform		Cost and revenue streams		

Fig. 3.26 Concept of the platform canvas

would be of interest for a corresponding solution. By using the platform canvas, you also keep the reins of action in the event of **threats from platforms**.

▶ **Food for Thought**
In the future, the platform may become more important than the product or service itself. Then the platform itself will become the most important product or service.

3.2.5.6 Servitization as the Basis of Business Models

In the economy as a whole—across countries—a continuous **increase in the importance of services** can be observed. The general development is shown in Fig. 3.27. The trend here is called **servitization**. We speak of servitization when manufacturing companies shift their service portfolio away from physical products towards services and/or a combination of tangible goods and services. You should take this development into account in the further development of your business models.

Today, products are increasingly sold together with other services. One example is the purchase of a **mobile phone** for which **insurance** is offered at the same time. For the **purchase of a car**, there is already a wide range of **insurance and financing services** attached as a standard. **Hardware offers** are accompanied by contracts for **maintenance, training, and insurance**.

For industrial goods, too, **training and maintenance contracts**, but also **financing packages** are increasingly being offered in addition to **machines** and entire **plants**. With flight bookings—and thus with classic service offers—we are offered further services during the booking process, e.g., insurance, rental cars, hotel. Here, additional services are added to those already purchased (cf. Fig. 3.27).

In other areas, digitalization is **blurring the boundaries between physical products and immaterial services**. Instead of CDs and DVDs, people stream. Instead of buying printed books, newspapers, and magazines, their contents are

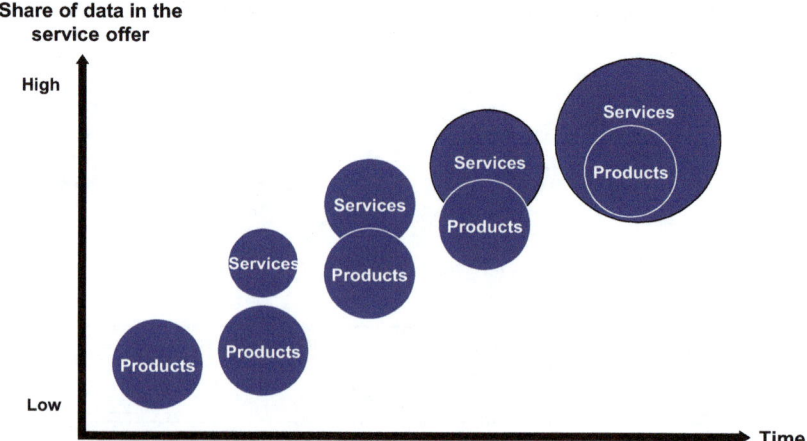

Fig. 3.27 From product to service—from service to service

accessed online when needed—often for a fee. Examples of developments in the consumer market are **fashion as a service, mobility as a service, food as a service, renting as a service**.

For private and business users alike, *grover.com*, for example, offers **electrical products on rent**. The advantages are highlighted here as follows (cf. Grover, 2021):

- Offer of more than 2000 technical products from ten categories.
- Assumption of 90% of the costs in the event of a claim.
- Provision from minimum terms of 1 month with flexible term extension.
- No deposit.

A particularly exciting **concept of servitization** are the so-called **subscription models**. Here, it is no longer individual products that are sold, but entire **service packages**. Such offers are available for the following products:

- **Aircraft turbines** from *Rolls-Royce*; **motto: power-by-the-hour**
- **Printing presses** from *Heidelberg;* **motto: pay-per-use**
- **Machine tools** from *Trumpf*; **motto: pay-per-part**
- **Lamps/Luminaires** from *Philips*; **motto: pay-per-lux**
- **Cars** from *Volkswagen/Audi*; **motto: pay-per-month**

In these cases, no product is purchased, but use is enabled and paid for. The product that was originally at the center of the business model is here completely embedded in a **service offer**. The provider makes its products available, often including consumables, insurance, financing, etc.—and the user only pays for the services that he has actually used.

> **Memory Box**
> Without any prohibitions on thinking, we should examine where we can use such service ideas in order to exploit the trend towards servitization for our own business model.

▶ **Food for Thought**
The guiding principle for all steps towards servitization is a consistent **focus on the achievable customer benefit**. In doing so, it is important to overcome the **dichotomy of product and service** that still exists—especially in thinking:
Products are to be thought of as services!
Car manufacturers are becoming **mobility service providers** (e.g., with the *Audi* car subscription). What is exciting here is that the customer can select and subscribe to the functionalities he wants from a physically very well-equipped car. This leads to an **individualization of the range of functions** used. Payment is here made via *AudiPay*.

Providers of health insurance become **health managers**. Sellers of CDs become **entertainment providers**, providers of lights offer light as a service (e.g., *Philips*) ... and manufacturers of drills will no longer sell drills in the future, but holes!
The trend is from product to service!

Think Box: Questions You Should Ask Yourself
- What process do you use in your company to develop business model innovations?
- To what extent do you already use agile methods to accelerate the process and reduce the risk of wrong decisions?
- Where do you position your company's approach in the strategy and business model matrix?
- Which options described there are also relevant for your company?
- Can you further develop your business model by acquiring a business model from a third party?
- Can this be done by acquiring the key players behind a business model?
- Should you think about the so-called killer acquisitions?
- Do you use the fields of action for business innovations to systematically check in your company in which direction you would like to further develop your company?
- Do you have the whole creative space in mind when designing business model innovations—innovations of products and services, market innovations, process innovations, and social innovations?
- How important is the concept of service transformation for your company—to develop your company from a product manufacturer to service provider?
- Have you ever thought about further options in the monetization models you use?
- Do you rely on a canvas model to develop new business models?
- Do you also use canvas concepts to analyze your existing business models?
- Have you ever analyzed the business models of your main competitors using a business model canvas to understand them in depth?
- Have you ever thought of using the business model canvas for or with your customers—primarily in the B2B environment—to gain ideas from them for the further development of your business model?
- Has the platform canvas ever been used in your company to work out possible goals and ideas for a platform strategy?
- What is the significance of the servitization trend "from product to service—from service to service" for your business model?

(continued)

- What are the consequences for your company if the trend is: from product to service?
- Who in your company has a critical creative view of your business model and continuously drives the process of business model innovation?

3.2.6 Basic Types of Digital Business Models

In order to promote the creative process in the development of new business models, it is worth your while to take a look at the **business models of the digital age**. For the innovation process, it is important that all stakeholders have a clear idea of which online business models to distinguish. Some of the models presented below are also used in combination by companies to achieve digital excellence.

- **Advertising-based model**
  Many online companies started with the business model of financing their content and/or services solely through **advertising revenue**. The classic billing concepts for this are CPM (cost per mille) and CPC (cost per click). Either payment is made for the placement of the advertisement (CPM) or only when the user clicks on an advertising banner (CPC; for further models see Kreutzer, 2021b).

  However, only a few companies have convincingly succeeded in making this model profitable. These include *Google* and *Facebook*. Many companies that started with an advertising-based business model have switched over time to other models described below or have supplemented the advertising-based model with other concepts. In many cases, subscription variants are also offered in parallel to an advertising-based model.

- **Membership model or subscription model**
  A membership or subscription model provides for regular payment of **membership fees** from users or to attract them to a **subscription**. This model is used, for example, in the premium versions of dating website *Elitepartner*, *LinkedIn*, *Xing* and *Spotify*, which complement advertising-based models (keyword "freemium strategy"; see Sect. 3.2.7).

  Comparable models are also used for many online services. For example, companies are offered simple social media services free of charge. Those who want to use a professional solution are asked to pay. *Google Analytics* is (apparently) free of charge, while the premium version *Google Analytics 360* has to be paid for.

- **Content payment model**
  Many publishers and other content providers supplement their originally free (advertising-based) offers with additional content, for whose access the user has to overcome **paywalls**. Those who want access to such content have to pay for it

per retrieval or download (as in the case of the magazine *Harvard Business Review*).

Other publishers offer the subscription model already described. This is the case with the offerings of *BILDplus, Spiegel+, Wall Street Journal,* and the *New York Times*. Therefore, there is an overlap here with the subscription models described.

- **Transaction-based model**

In the transaction-based online business model, the user has to pay when he carries out a **transaction**. This is the direction in which *eBay's* original purely advertising-based business model developed, as advertising revenues were not sufficient to finance the business model. This model also applies to *Amazon's* marketing platform for third parties (*Amazon Seller Central*). Here, the providers of products pay for the successful execution of purchase transactions and thus for the services provided by *Amazon*.

Airbnb, Uber, and many other **booking platforms** also pay for the services they provide based on the transactions they carry out. The transaction-oriented model is also used in the *Apple App Store*. Here, the app operators have to pay *Apple* a fee of up to 30%—often referred to as *Apple* tax. A corresponding business model is used by many platforms.

- **E-commerce model**

The e-commerce model transfers a proven offline business model to the Internet. Remuneration is made here through the **margins** that come with the **sale of products or services** themselves. This is the decisive difference to the transaction-oriented model. In the e-commerce model, remuneration is made through the margin of the goods sold, not as payment for the transaction that took place.

The e-commerce model is used by *Amazon's* main business, *AboutYou, Outfittery, Zalando,* and an almost infinite number of online retailers.

- **Donation model**

Some online business models rely on user donations to survive. This model is used by *Wikipedia*. When accessing this information platform, users are regularly asked to make a donation at the end of the year.

- **Data-based model**

A specific online business model represents the **provision of data** in return for access to content and/or services. The following applies to these approaches: the seemingly free online service is not free. Because whoever uses it is not the customer, but becomes the product himself!

Motto: **If you're not paying for it, you become the product!**

You should always remember this when using *Facebook, Google, Google Analytics, Instagram, YouTube,* and much more. In the case of *Google Analytics,* there is—as described above—the additional chargeable offer *Google Analytics 360,* which can be attributed to the subscriber model.

When using *Facebook* as a source of information, always remember the following: *Facebook's* business model is focused on generating advertising revenue—not on providing quality journalism! You must take this into account when evaluating the reports presented there.

Many companies require **users to opt-in to data use**, contact by e-mail or phone before being allowed to use "free" services, before access to further content, such as studies or white papers, is granted. This also applies to access to content from consultancies and from online service providers. Here, payment is visibly made in the currency "data."

All relevant online business models can currently be traced back to these basic principles. Often, several of the described concepts are combined. A suggestion for classifying business models is also provided by the **business model navigator** of the *University of St. Gallen*, which lists a total of 55 model types (cf. Gassmann et al., 2017; Becker et al., 2019).

> **Think Box: Questions You Should Ask Yourself**
> - How important have these different online business models already become in your industry?
> - Which of the described options for the design of business models represent an interesting addition or an alternative to your existing business model?
> - In which direction could your business model be further developed?
> - Who in your company is dealing with these questions?

3.2.7 Methods for Evaluating Business Models

You can't discover new oceans without the courage to lose sight of your own shore.
André Gide

3.2.7.1 Benefit and Growth Hypothesis

A major challenge for you is to evaluate the business models that have been developed. Only then can a decision be made on which business model innovation to invest in. In order to **evaluate business model innovations**, the assumptions developed in the creative process must be transformed into a **set of hypotheses**. These must then be subjected to **iterative testing close to the market**. For the profitable growth of a business model, the benefit hypothesis and the growth hypothesis in particular must be tested (cf. Ries, 2017, pp. 72–74):

Definition of the benefit hypothesis

For the **relevant design of a business model**, the focus must first be placed on the core area of every business model: the **value proposition.** This aspect is deliberately positioned in the center of the business model canvas (cf. Fig. 3.25). The following two questions can be derived from this value proposition:

What **value** is created for the customers?

How is the **value proposition** to be built up in concrete terms?
We can also define this **value proposition** by the following formula:
We help X do Y by doing Z.

This addresses the overarching question of which business models are particularly relevant for **consumers**. A look at the **usage patterns** shows that the following fields are particularly promising for **business model innovations** in the **B2C market**:

"Survival" (e.g., *Delivery Hero, Lieferando*)
Entertainment (e.g., *Instagram, TikTok, YouTube*)
Communication (e.g., *Facebook, WhatsApp*)
Self-realization/self-expression (e.g., *Facebook, Instagram, TikTok, YouTube*)
Shopping (e.g., *AboutYou, Amazon, Etsy, Zalando*)
Mobility (e.g., *BlaBlaCar, Flixbus, ShareNow* and the e-scooter providers *Bird, Circ, Jump, Lime, Tier, Uber, Voi*)
Learning offers (e.g., *Inversity, openSAP, Udacity*)

In the **B2B market**, successful business model innovations can be found in all areas of the value chain. Many of these are based on application fields of artificial intelligence. In the B2C market, but also in the B2B market, a central **benefit enhancer** must be taken into account:

Convenience!

Convenience for users represents one of the most important drivers of customer value. Most customers today do not want to make an effort to do or achieve something. It is imperative that you take this into account as you continue to develop business models.

In addition, you should check to what extent your business model pays into the trend towards **sustainability** (see Sect. 1.2.5). Even if today the topic of sustainability is more present in the minds than in the wallets of customers, the importance of sustainable trade by companies will continuously increase.

Memory Box

The **relevance of an offer to customers** says nothing about the potential **profitability of a business model**. This profitability must be determined via the **growth hypothesis**.

Definition of the growth hypothesis

For the **profitable design of a business model**, it is crucial that the fastest possible and also profitable growth can be ensured. To achieve this, the following questions must be answered:

Which **target groups** should the offer be aimed at in order to achieve rapid growth?

What **type of communication** can achieve particularly high growth?

Which **channels** should be used to communicate and through which channels should the service be distributed in order to grow quickly?

(continued)

> How can **customer relationships** be designed to create value?
> How quickly and sustainably can **profitable growth** be achieved?
> It is a consistent expression of **customer orientation** to first look for the target groups that can benefit most from a business model.
> **Relevance to the target group is an indispensable growth driver!**
> At the same time, it must be examined how these target groups can be addressed cost-effectively and reached with one's own offers. The following applies here:
> **Fish were the fish are!**

3.2.7.2 Concepts for Increasing Benefit Delivery and Growth

Various **strategic concepts** can be used to **increase the provision of benefits** and to **accelerate growth**. Important approaches are presented below and should be used to **assess the attractiveness of business models**.

- **Freemium strategy**
  In order to gain as many customers as quickly and cost-effectively as possible for one's own range of services, the so-called **freemium strategy** can be used in business models. The term freemium is made up of the terms "free" and "premium." With this pricing strategy, a basic service is offered free of charge. This is intended to avoid a price-related inhibition threshold to the use of a new offer. In this way, many test users can be attracted. If the service is convincing, users are more willing to pay for a larger scope of services (the "premium offer"). Many online providers have driven their growth quickly by using the freemium strategy (e.g., *LinkedIn, N26, Parship, Spotify, Skype, Xing*).

  Often, the premium version is integrated into a **subscription model**, where users pay a certain amount per month, for example. For companies, such subscribers have an invaluable advantage:
  Subscribers provide recurring, usually well-calculable income.
- **Setting up switching costs—lock-in concepts**
  In order to ensure the success of a business model, companies can set up a few hurdles for the termination, so that a change of provider is accompanied by **switching costs**. For example, it is important to remember that a playlist built up on *Spotify* cannot be transferred to *Amazon Music*. In addition, the new provider has to get to know me first before he can also make me customized offers. In contrast, the company that used to serve me was able to develop an important information advantage in the course of the customer relationship life cycle.

  This can be referred to as a **learning relationship** (cf. Peppers & Rogers, 2017, p. 23). You learn more and more about your prospects and customers through a dialogue with them—and can therefore make your customer related

activities more and more individual. In this way, you can carve out an important competitive advantage. After all, none of your competitors have exactly the same first-hand data at their disposal—apart from hacker attacks.

When **designing customer relationships**, various concepts can be used to retain customers for as long as possible once they have been acquired. Deliberately created **lock-in effects** can contribute to this. Here, the offering company tries to bring a customer into an (artificially created) dependency relationship. Such a dependency is achieved, when the transition of a customer to another provider is uneconomical due to high **switching costs**. This challenge is faced by all companies that have once opted for ERP software from *SAP*. Switching to another enterprise resource planning software is virtually impossible here.

A **lock-in effect** is also created by the fact that the use of a provider's service forces another product or service from the same provider. This is also referred to as the **razor blade concept**, because only specific blades fit a razor. This is often also the case with printers that only work with the cartridges of the same manufacturer. Analogous concepts exist with coffee machines that require certain capsules or coffee pads.

Many companies use the concept called **companion pricing**. The durable product (printer, coffee machine, shaver, electric toothbrush) is relatively inexpensive, while the consumables are comparatively expensive. This pricing concept initially attracts many customers who only look at the hardware price when buying. It is only when they buy the cartridges, coffee pads/coffee capsules, razor blades, brushes, etc. that they realize how expensive the overall offer is. Replacing the provider is only possible with high switching costs because the hardware would no longer be usable and would have to be disposed of. In addition, the customer may only be changing from one dependency relationship to a new one! All in all, this results in profitable and **long-lasting customer relationships** for the company because a replacement of the provider is associated with **high switching costs**.

- **Scalability of the business model**
  The growth potential is largely determined by the **scalability of the business model**. Scalability is the ability of a business model to significantly increase turnover without having to continuously invest the same amount in production, marketing, sales, personnel, and/or infrastructure. The fixed costs and also the variable costs increase far more slowly here than the turnover. Online business models often have a high scalability, so that turnover can be significantly increased even without major investments.

  A convincing example of a perfectly scalable business model is provided by *Zoom*, a company that offers **software for video conferencing**. Before the Corona pandemic, *Zoom* was known to only a few people and was limited to corporate use. During the pandemic, however, it was not only home office use that increased. Many private individuals also tapped into *Zoom's* capabilities to organize digital sports classes, church services, discussions, birthday parties, and much more via *Zoom*. In April 2020 around 300 million video conference participants were recorded—every day. In December 2019, this number was still around ten million. Even though *Zoom* had to make additional investments for this growth, they were miles away from a 30-fold increase!

In parallel, the **company's stock price** has increased fivefold in one year! Why? **Investors love the scalability of business models**!

> **Memory Box**
> **Scalability is one of the most important profit drivers in digital business models.**
>
> - **Platform concepts**
>   A highly interesting basis for your business models and consequently also an important evaluation criterion is the possibility to establish **platform concepts** (see Sect. 3.3.3). Platforms **bring together two-sided markets**. On the one side, there are (ideally) many suppliers, on the other side (ideally) many customers. The special attraction of the platform for the operator is that he does not have to offer any products or services of his own that go beyond the mediation of contacts and the processing of transactions between suppliers and customers. This keeps the necessary investment—even with dynamic growth—within limits. Platforms therefore have very good scalability.

> **Memory Box**
> **Platform models are often easily scalable and therefore highly lucrative because the platform operator "only" acts as an intermediary and therefore does not have to make large investments that go beyond the processing of online transactions.**
>
> - **Jobs to be done concept**
>   A **jobs to be done concept** could lead to an attractive business model. Here, solutions are offered for tasks that, from the customer's point of view, can simply be done—without having to or wanting to put a lot of heart and soul into it. Customers buy a product or request a service only to complete a specific task (a job)—again as conveniently as possible. This can be a low cost international money transfer, with which the British FinTech *wise.com* has achieved a fascinating growth story in recent years. It can also be the splitting of a restaurant bill if you were a guest there with several friends and one paid for all. A simple solution for this is offered by *splitwise.com*. This also makes it possible to simplify monthly billing in shared apartments.
>
> (continued)

> Another example is the FinTech *klarna.com*. This company offers customers who have made purchases in affiliated shops various payment methods (e.g., also hire purchase)—even for smaller amounts. The *switchup.de* offer is also an exciting jobs to be done concept. It helps with the unloved tariff change for electricity and gas. This company positions itself as a very effective "tariff watchdog." For this purpose, it regularly compares all available electricity and gas tariffs in order to help customers achieve price advantages by switching. The company carries out monitoring free of charge for the user and always reports when cheaper offers are available. It works very well, as I have experienced myself!

Memory Box
When developing the value proposition of a company, the jobs to be done concept simply looks at the question of which "jobs" can be done on the customer side with one's own offer.

- **Blue ocean strategy**
  If you succeed in developing a **blue ocean strategy** (cf. Kim & Mauborgne, 2016), this represents an important valuation aspect for your business model. With a blue ocean strategy, you try to find new market segments away from highly competitive markets (so-called **red oceans** with many sharks that color the ocean red) that have no competition, at least for a certain period of time (so-called **blue oceans**). However, you should be aware of one risk: the fact that there are no suppliers in certain market segments today could also be due to the fact that there are no customers (fish) there that could be hunted by the competitors (sharks).
- **Long tail concept**
  It is also interesting for you to ask whether you can use the concept described as the **long tail** as the basis of your business model (cf. Anderson, 2018). The emergence of the term "long tail" can be understood by looking at Fig. 3.28. To draw this curve, the relevant objects of investigation (e.g., products, services) must be entered on the X-axis in descending order according to the number of sales achieved (number of units or value). The corresponding sales figures of the respective products are plotted on the Y-axis.

  For example, on the far left of this X-axis are the very readable books by *Michelle* and *Barack Obama*. These works have topped the bestseller lists for many months and for good reason. This first part of the curve is called the **shoulder**: this is where the bestsellers or also called blockbusters are

(continued)

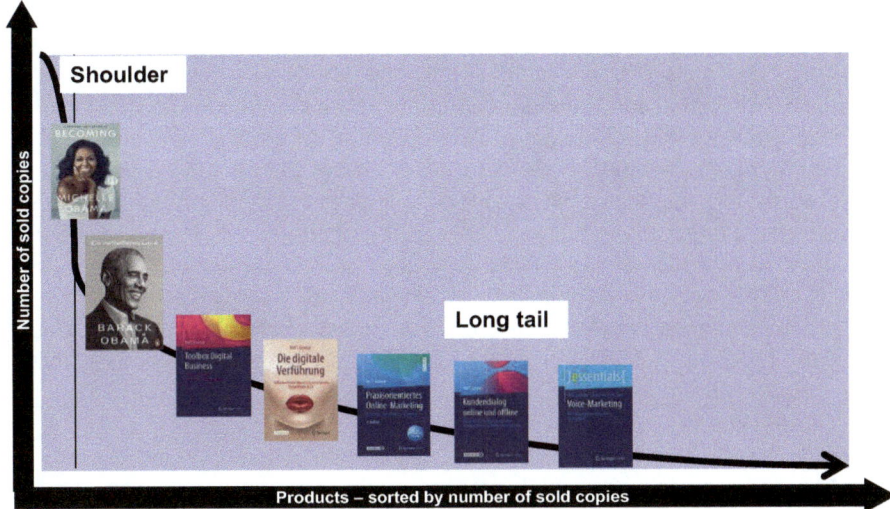

Fig. 3.28 Long tail concept

found. These can be products (such as books, clothes, music titles, or films), but also services.

The second part of the curve is called the **long tail**. Here one finds all other offers that enjoy a "somewhat" lower demand. For example, *Ralf T. Kreutzer's* marketing non-fiction and technical books are found in the middle section of the curve. Possible works on the "love life of bees in the Middle Ages" are probably rather at the very end of the long tail with buyer numbers between 1 and 10!

A growth-oriented business model consists of profitably serving small segments and market niches as a highly specialized provider. The following **mechanisms of the long tail concept** should be considered here (cf. Anderson, 2018, pp. 9–30):

- **Democratization of the means of production**
  The **widespread distribution of important means of production** (e.g., desktop PCs, tablet PCs, digital cameras, smartphones, 3D printers) as well as **do-it-yourself products** of all kinds makes it possible today for many millions of people to create their own creations. As a result, many new texts, music titles, photos, and videos as well as other products and services are created every day. Due to these offers, the curve in Fig. 3.28 extends to the right because the long tail is growing.
- **Democratization of sales**

(continued)

Anyone with access to the Internet can post information online about their own offers or access information about the offers presented there and, if necessary, order them immediately. This applies equally to products and services available offline and online. Distribution costs drop rapidly as a result, because the **online presentation** of offers can be achieved easily and cheaply, or even free of charge. Finally, no physical shelf space is required to serve a target group that may only be found regionally. So, the long tail thickens because more transactions can be done economically.

The drivers for such offers are, for example, *eBay* and *Amazon* as well as other relevant online platforms such as *etsy.com*, where anyone can present their products. Setting up one's own website to market products and services is no longer a major hurdle, even for semi-professional users.

- **Connection of supply and demand**
  The Internet also facilitates the bringing together of supply and demand. **Search engines** and **social networks**, but also **blogs, forums, and communities** are used for this purpose. The information that can be found and communicated here makes it increasingly easy to bring together niche suppliers and seekers of niche products. Customers who are not interested in standard products in the shoulder area will find countless alternatives in the long tail area that may better suit their own needs. This also makes the long tail thicker because the number of transactions is growing.

However, when developing a business model that uses this long tail approach, consider the following. Although online technologies facilitate the profitability of serving niche markets, the **Pareto principle** (also called the **80: 20 rule**) remains valid. This expresses the fact that there are **concentration effects** in all areas of private and professional life, including the purchase of products or the demand for services. This means that, for example, 80% of the turnover can be accounted for by 20% of the products offered (hence the 80: 20 rule).

It may be true that the sum of sales in niche markets exceeds that of blockbusters. However, it must be pointed out that behind a blockbuster like "Becoming" by *Michelle Obama* there is exactly one author and one publisher, while behind the offerings of the long tail there is a multitude of providers. It is therefore not very useful to simply summarize their sales without also adding up the distribution costs across all providers.

- **Future viability and the resilience of the business model**
  In order to evaluate the growth hypothesis, two further criteria must be taken into account: the future viability and the resilience of the business model. Both aspects are to be evaluated equally from the point of view of

(continued)

your company and your customers. We should also have the expectations of investors in mind when making this assessment. With regard to the **future viability of a business model,** a critically constructive look into the future should be taken in order to assess the longer-term relevance of your own offers. A look at the business models of travel agencies, video shops, and department stores as well as companies involved in the processing of coal illustrates the relevance of this aspect.

In contrast, almost all companies that claim "digitalization" as their slogan are given a positive future. Educational institutions with study programs such as SWM and SWD also have future potential. After all, these abbreviations express what many students want today: SWM stands for "something with media" and SWD for "something with digitization"!

In addition, you should check the **resilience of a business model**. This is about the **vulnerability** or **resilience** in the face of possible future challenges. Central aspects for checking resilience have already been presented in Sect. 2.1.5.

- **Existence of a convincing narrative**
One criterion for the evaluation of a business model that seems somewhat surprising at first is the **existence of a convincing narrative**. This is a story about the business model that everyone can relate to and believes (see Sect. 2.1.1). Think of the story of *Elon Musk* and *Tesla*. Then it becomes clear what power such a narrative can generate. The story about the supposed solution to future (emission-free?) mobility, combined with a storyteller who is both fascinating and irritating, has not only ignited investors and thus driven the stock price to unimagined heights. These narratives were also very appealing to employees and cooperation partners.

The narrative that underpins *Delivery Hero*, reflected in the slogan "Always delivering an amazing experience," particularly ignited and drove the company's growth during the Corona pandemic. This development has led to the inclusion in the German stock index *DAX* in August 2020 for the first time of a company that has never made a profit. At the same time, critics of this business model claim that such can also never be generated if the working conditions for the delivery staff, which are often described as exploitation, were to be overcome.

3.2.7.3 Testing Benefit and Growth Hypothesis Close to the Market

The **need to test business model innovations** very close to the market results from the content of the **analytical grid for business model innovations**. Figure 3.29 shows you what kind of innovations can be expected to be taken up by the market. If a business model is changed very extensively or is completely new, it tends to have a higher potential for success. However, the behavioral changes to be made on the part

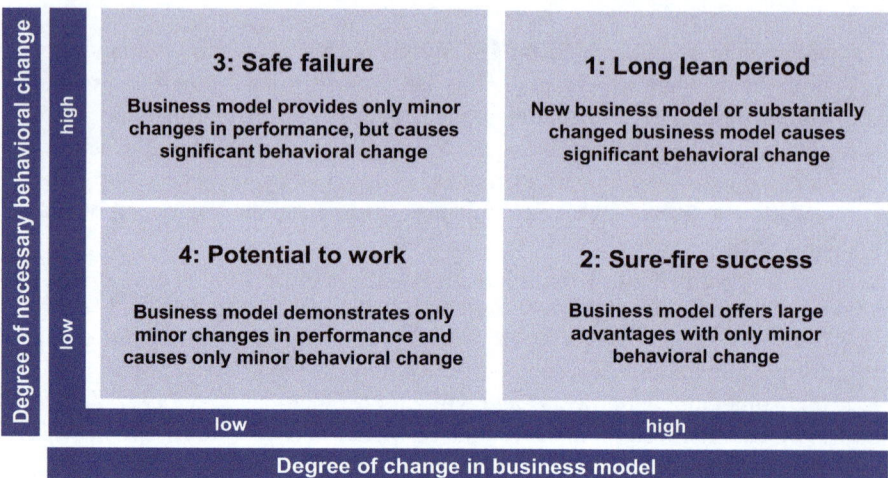

Fig. 3.29 Analysis grid for business model innovations

of the customers and thus also the resistance to the innovation are significantly greater. Consequently, the establishment of a new business model here will be accompanied by a long dry spell (field 1). Examples of this are the acceptance of e-mobility and car-sharing services, the majority of which are not yet convenient and/or profitable.

The business models involving streaming offers quickly became **big sellers** because they had decisive convenience advantages and were easy for users to manage (field 2). Home-sharing offers by *Airbnb* & Co. as well as many online banking and e-commerce offers experienced a similar triumph. Delivery services for food, such as *Delivery Hero, Foodora, Lieferando* and others, also create convenience without having to make major changes to one's own behavior. These services simply simplify classic purchasing processes and quickly become a **sure-fire success**.

Business models that only have minor changes to established offers, but mean a considerable change in behavior, will **certainly fail** (field 3). An **easy sell**, on the other hand, can go hand in hand with business model innovations that result in only minimal behavioral changes (field 4). However, from the customer's point of view, it is questionable why a change to a new provider should be made at all if not much changes!

After these considerations, a decisive question now arises for you:

What is the best way to check your benefit hypotheses and the growth hypotheses of your business model?

After all, what use are the most beautiful hypotheses if they run aground on the cliffs of reality?

It is indispensable that the assumptions underlying your business models are tested for their relevance as early as possible and close to the customer. The more concretely you have already worked out your business model innovation, the easier it is to test central elements of the **value creation structure of your business model**. Testing the hypotheses can be done according to the **lean start-up method**.

At the same time, another important goal of the lean start-up method is to also significantly shorten the **time span between development and market launch** of an innovation. The relevance of the time-to-value approach has already been discussed in Sect. 1.2.4.4. The **lean start-up method** builds on these considerations and offers a **market-oriented process model** in the three stages of building, measuring, and learning (cf. Ries, 2017).

The goal of this procedure—based on the idea of **time-to-value**—is to bring a product, a service or a complete business model to the market as quickly as possible. In order to achieve a high level of relevance for the target group, comprehensive feedback should be obtained from them as early as possible. This should provide impulses and ideas for further development and, if necessary, for a reorientation of the innovation work. This consistent **market orientation** can save both time and costs that would be associated with undesirable developments or complete flops. A convincing **supply-demand fit** should be ensured through a **customer-oriented test approach** (cf. on product-market fit also Gassner, 2021; Lennarz, 2017, pp. 63–72).

> **Memory Box**
> The **core idea of the lean start-up method** is as simple as it is obvious—and yet in many cases not consistently implemented. It is about developing a business model or a product or a service very close to the market and continuously incorporating feedback from potential customers already in the course of the development process. You leave the ivory tower here and face the criticism of your target persons early on and relatively unprotected.
>
> But it is far better to face the critical eyes of potential customers early and also relatively unprotected. If this is done only after the development work has been completed, when all the budgets for development and market launch have already been used, failure is much more painful!
>
> The **lean start-up method** uses a **three-step process** to iteratively test key performance features of a product, service, or business model. This also allows you to "test" pricing, distribution and communication concepts, positioning ideas and elements of brand management on the market while the development process is still ongoing. As this process is constantly repeated, it results in the **build-measure-learn cycle** shown in Fig. 3.30. By continuously obtaining feedback and incorporating it into your innovation, you consistently align your services with the requirements of the market and thus the expectations of your target customers. You repeat this cycle in the lean start-up method until the solution is accepted by the market.
>
> The concrete contents that characterize the individual **phases of the build-measure-learn cycle** are presented below.
>
> (continued)

Fig. 3.30 Lean start-up model

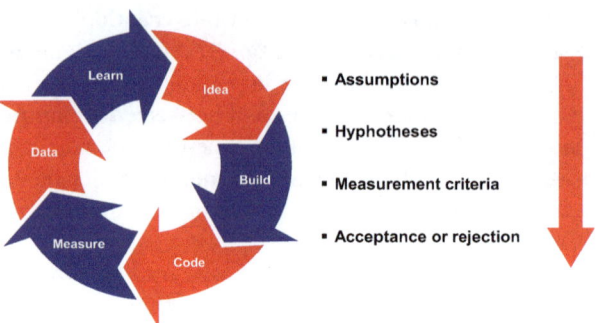

Fig. 3.31 Minimum viable product (MVP)

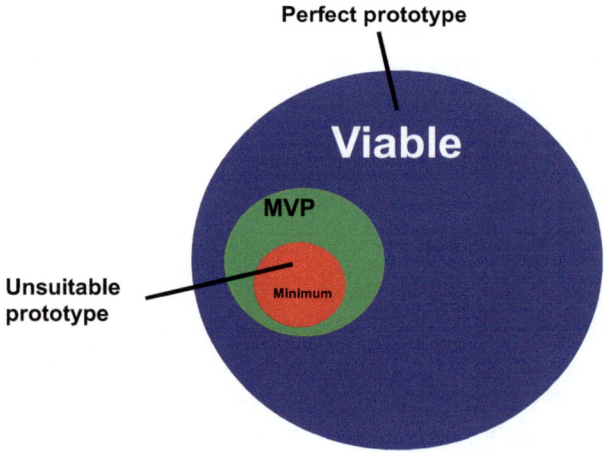

> **Phase 1: Building—lean business model development based on an initial hypothesis**
>
> The starting point of the build-measure-learn cycle is an **idea** in the form of a market problem that is to be solved. The start of the product, service, and/or business model development is based on various benefits and growth hypotheses that have to be tested on the market in the course of the process and adapted or will be sorted out if necessary.
>
> For **building** and thus for the process of developing a new solution, the concept of the business model canvas introduced in Sect. 3.2.5.4 can be used. A comprehensive business plan is not yet necessary at this early stage, as the solution idea can still change several times—sometimes dramatically—in the course of the iterative approach.
>
> Based on the results of the canvas, a first **prototype** of the solution can be created—if necessary using design thinking (see Sect. 3.5.3.3). This prototype should initially only contain the central functions and/or features of the

(continued)

envisaged solution in order to reduce complexity. Particularly important features of a business model can be depicted in the prototype with their core services—foregoing beauty and design. Even in the case of services, the process steps in a prototype can be limited to the central features.

For example, less emphasis can be placed on the appearance and unnecessary additional features can be dispensed with for the time being. In the case of services, the individual process steps are simplified as much as possible in order to be able to depict them easily. This "miniature version" of the final offer is called a **minimum viable product** (MVP). The product or service presented here must meet certain minimum requirements in order to be used by customers. Figure 3.31 shows the area of tension that needs to be covered.

The **minimum variant of a prototype** visualized in Fig. 3.31 cannot be tested meaningfully. Here, the user cannot recognize the core of the performance and consequently cannot evaluate it. The **perfect prototype** is too expensive; moreover, it can take too long to produce. Consequently, the **minimum viable product** is a real compromise solution.

In essence, **rapid prototyping** aims to shorten development time. From a product/service/business model idea, "tangible" products and services are to be generated as quickly as possible in order to test them with regard to their suitability by potential users. After all, the users decide on the success of the company by buying or not buying!

What is the saying?

The proof of the pudding is the eating!

With the MVP, the "eating" can begin at a very early stage!

Phase 2: Measuring—gaining comprehensive feedback from potential customers

When the activity called **code** in Fig. 3.30 has led to a minimum viable product, it comes to the phase of **measuring**. The aim is to test the found solution in the market for relevance and functionality. For this purpose, the prototype or the minimum viable product is presented to the target customers and feedback is obtained. In addition to focus groups and surveys, workshops can also be held with the target persons.

Memory Box

We should not use the results of market research like a drunkard uses a lamppost—namely to hold on to it. Rather, we should use the results to enlighten ourselves.

After all, market research should not take decisions away from us, but rather lead to better decisions through additional insights.

(continued)

The special thing about this research is that the prototype—be it a product or a service as a manifestation of a business model—is communicated to potential customers in a tangible way. Only in this way is it possible to obtain resilient insights from "real customers" and use them for further development. Through several **repetitions** of **the build-measure-learn cycle**, different forms of designing the offer, but also different price and communication concepts can be tested. In addition, different distribution models for marketing the innovation can also be checked.

Step by step, important feedback is gained from the target group, which immediately flows back into the next cycle. Such an approach combines the **iterative procedure** of a multiple run through of the build-measure-learn cycle with an **incremental approach** in which the solution is improved step by step. The **measurement phases** should also be kept as lean as possible in order to save time and money.

Phase 3: Learning—analyzing the feedback and developing new hypotheses

Based on the **data** obtained in the measurement phase, the necessary **learning** now takes place. For this purpose, the knowledge gained must be comprehensively evaluated in order to test the validity of the original hypotheses of the build-measure-learn cycle that has just been completed. After the initial run of this cycle, the following questions can be answered:

- Does the problem on which the first cycle was based exist and/or are there already (alternative) solutions for it?
- Are people interested in (further) problem solving at all?
- Does the solution have the relevant features expected by customers?
- Is the way of using the product or service accepted by the customers?
- Is there a willingness to pay a "reasonable" (from your point of view "profitable") price for the envisaged problem solution?
- Was the development based on the right target group?
- Can the defined target group be reached via the intended communication channels?
- Would the customers accept targeted loyalty concepts?
- Is the intended distribution channel suitable for the target group?
- Is the intended positioning understood?
- Does the brand concept convey the core idea of the service?

By going through the **build-measure-learn cycle** several times, you will certainly realize that some of the initial hypotheses were incorrect. Be glad that this became clear early on in the process!

> **Memory Box**
> **If you fail, fail fast, fail cheap, and fail early!**
> Based on the insights gained, you can formulate **new hypotheses for the next build-measure-learn cycle**. Then start the next cycle. In all measuring and learning phases, it is important that you base your findings on sufficiently large amounts of data. Otherwise, you may be led in the wrong direction by a small amount of data. This is why it can be very important, for example, not to use only online tools in the cycles, because otherwise you will only get feedback from online-affine people—and neglect offline-oriented target customers.
> After learning comes the next idea, the next building, the next coding, measuring, learning! Based on the knowledge you gain from this, you can not only align your hypotheses, but also the solutions more and more comprehensively to the market.
> The **build-measure-learn cycle** comes to a stop when you have the impression that the market is quite "hot" for your new business model and the associated products and services. Then, after a comprehensive profitability analysis, the go/no-go decision and a possible market launch follows (cf. Fig. 3.19). By going through the cycle several times, your risk of failure—with little time and resources invested—has been significantly reduced.

> **Memory Box**
> Companies such as *Airbnb, Amazon, Dropbox,* and *Zappos* have significantly driven their original business ideas through the lean start-up approach.

3.2.7.4 Documentation of Business Model Innovations

For the **documentation of business model innovations**, you can use Figs. 3.32, 3.33, and 3.34 as a guide. Here you will find a summary of all relevant decision criteria.

If you have several business model innovations in development at the same time, you can visualize the results in an **evaluation matrix for business model innovations** (cf. Fig. 3.35). Ideal business models are those that have a high benefit for the customers—but only a low implementation effort for you as a company.

Based on the knowledge and decisions gained here, the implementation process follows.

Criteria for evaluating business model innovation:	Description
Scope of the business model innovation (new element of an existing business model, additional business model, completely new business model)	
Type and extend of the business model innovations' benefits for the company (e.g. gain in image perception, sales/profit, accessing new markets)	
Reactions from the wide public and politics concerning the business model innovation	
Opportunities for differentiation against competitors – sustainability of this differentiation (innovations' imitability)	
Reactions from competitors concerning the business model innovation	
Reactions from own employees concerning the business model innovation	
Extend of internal (infrastructural/procedural) resistance against the realisation of the business model innovation	

Fig. 3.32 Description of a business model innovation—part 1

Criteria for evaluating business model innovation:	Description
Time-to-value of the business model innovation	
Sustainability of the business model innovation (financially)	
Sustainability of the business model innovation (environmentally)	
Staff needs for realizing the business model innovation	
Financial needs for realizing the business model innovation	
Customer loyalty elements to secure profitable customer relationships in the long term (lock-in effects, contractual solutions)	
Possibilities for customer acquisition (freemium strategy, jobs to be done concept)	

Fig. 3.33 Description of a business model innovation—part 2

> **Think Box: Questions You Should Ask Yourself**
> - Have you formulated a convincing benefit hypothesis for your business growth?

(continued)

3.2 Developing Business Models for the Digital Age

Criteria for evaluating business model innovation:	Description
Implementation of a blue ocean strategy	
Scalability of the business model innovation	
Implementation of a platform strategy	
Implementation of a long tail concept	
Resilience of the business model innovation	
Future orientation of the business model innovation	
Narrative of the business model innovation	

Fig. 3.34 Description of a business model innovation—part 3

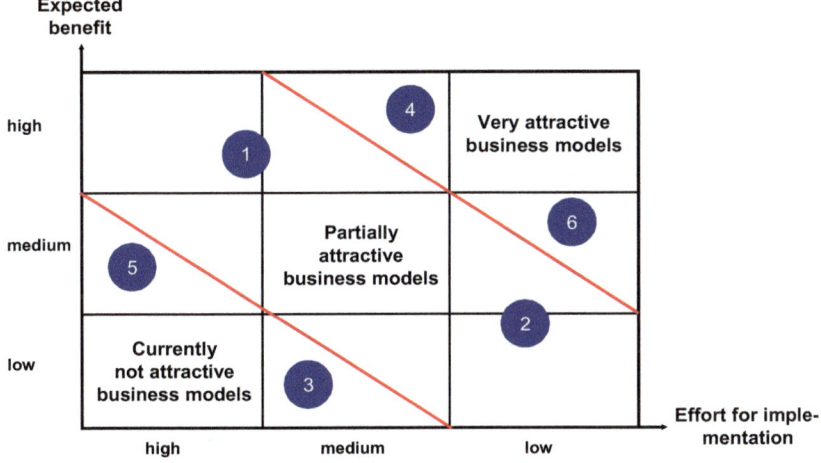

Fig. 3.35 Evaluation matrix for business model innovations

- What exactly is your value proposition?
- Formulate your value proposition once with the formula: we help X do Y by doing Z.
- How important is convenience in your business model?
- Can sustainability be an important benefit driver in your business model?
- How is your growth hypothesis formulated?
- Can you use a freemium strategy?
- Is there an opportunity to use a subscription model?
- Can you build "artificial" switching costs?

(continued)

- Does your business model offer the opportunity to create lock-in effects?
- Can you use companion pricing?
- What is the scalability of your business model?
- Can you use or build a platform model—alone or with partners?
- Can you use a jobs to be done concept?
- Is there an opportunity for a blue ocean strategy?
- Can you build on a long tail concept?
- How promising is the business model innovation you have developed?
- How would you rate the resilience of your business model?
- Do you have—in addition to a business model innovation—a convincing narrative that is almost indispensable for internal and external communication?
- Regularly use the analysis grid for business model innovations to check your ideas for their potential for success.
- Do you use the lean start-up approach for business model development?
- Who takes care of answering these questions in your company?

3.2.8 Process for Integrating New Business Models

Figure 3.36 shows how the **process of developing and integrating new business models in your company** is to be designed in order to achieve digital excellence (cf. Strategyzer, 2020). First of all, an **innovation engine** needs to be set up, which is presented in Sect. 3.7.4. The innovation engine should be your "greenhouse" for new

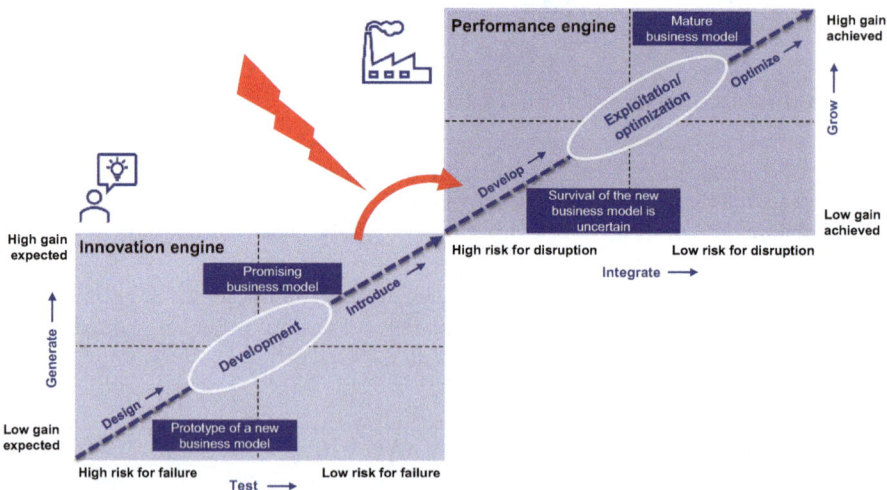

Fig. 3.36 Process of development and integration of business model innovations

business models. The task here is: explore! At the start of the development process, the expected return may be low, while the risk of failure is high. The business model must now be developed further and further until a high expected return and a low risk of failure can be expected. How to proceed here has already been discussed in more detail in Sect. 3.2.7. With these steps you are on horizons 2 and 3.

At the end of the development process, the big challenge for all companies is to transfer the business model innovation into the **performance engine** in order to integrate it there to generate profits (see Sect. 3.7.4). The task here is: **exploit**!

Depending on the respective business model innovation, there may be a great **risk of disruption for the existing business model**—especially on horizons 2 and 3. This must be reduced through a **transfer process to a new dominant business model** or through **parallel use of different business models**. For this, change management methods are indispensable, which are presented in Chap. 4. At the same time, the new business model must be brought to maturity in order to generate high returns. When business models at horizon 1 level are approaching the end of their life cycle, new business models must already be in use. Ideally, further business model innovations are already being worked on in parallel in the innovation engine (keyword "ambidexterity").

> **Memory Box**
> This **parallelism of processes** once again underlines the importance of the so-called **ambidexterity**—the ambidexterity of **profitably shaping day-to-day business** and **developing and implementing new business models**.
>
> When integrating business model innovations into the existing company, the question arises as to the **compatibility of business models**. To this end, you should intensively discuss the following questions:
>
> - Is the new business model complementary or substitutive to the existing business model?
> - Does the new business model access the same (scarce) resources (procurement, production, human resources, finance, marketing, sales, legal, controlling, etc.)?
> - Does the new business model address the same customer segments?
> - Does the new business model offer an alternative to the company's own previous offerings (cannibalization effect)?
> - Does the new business model use existing capacities for different offers?
> - Does the new business model reallocate unused capacities in procurement, R&D, production, logistics, marketing, and/or sales to new fields of application?
>
> Depending on the answers given here, the **integration of business model innovations** into the existing company may involve more or less pain. In sum,

(continued)

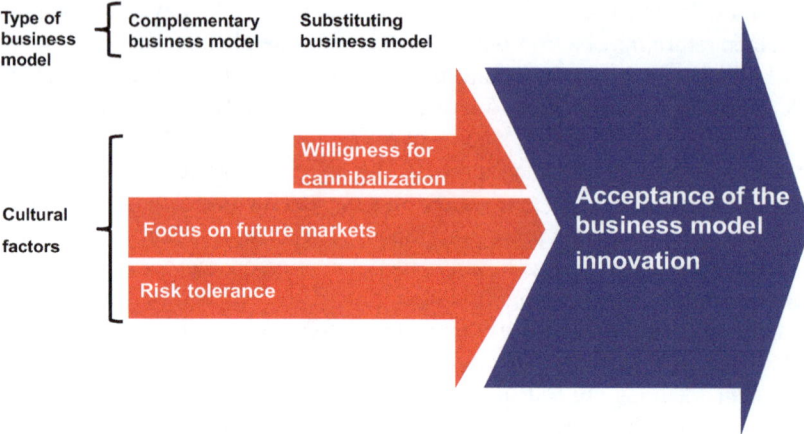

Fig. 3.37 Cultural factors as a condition for the acceptance of business model innovations

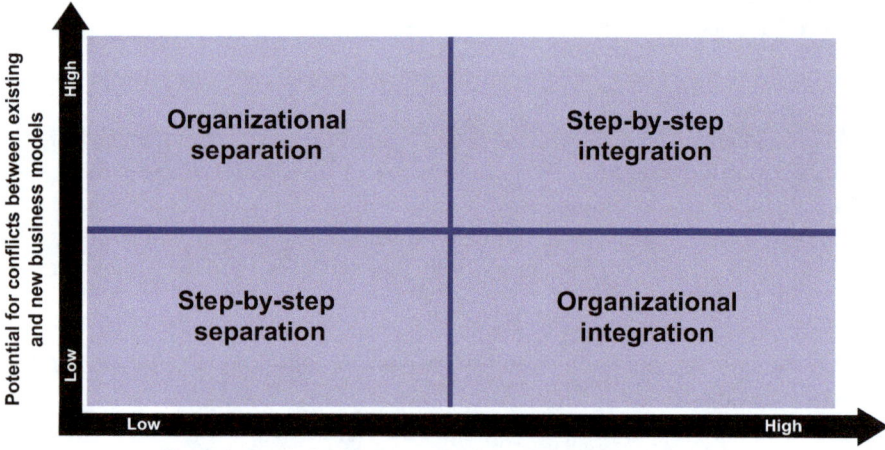

Fig. 3.38 Norm strategies for the integration of business model innovations in established companies

you should be aware that the **cultural acceptance factors** shown in Fig. 3.37 which are relevant for **business model innovations** (cf. Mezger & Bader, 2014, p. 253). Which factors prevail here depends on the type of innovation. Complementary business models can address **new markets** and thus trigger less cultural resistance. Here, acceptance depends primarily on the **willingness** of management and employees to **take risks**. The assessment is different for

(continued)

substituting business models that endanger or prospectively replace the existing business model. In this situation, acceptance depends on the **willingness to cannibalize**. In this case, however, significantly greater resistance is to be expected.

The factors outlined here must be taken into account in **change management** so that the integration of business model innovation does not lead to "rejection reactions" as we know them from medicine. In companies, such **rejection reactions** lead either to the failure of the innovation and/or the loss of the innovative minds behind it. Often, they are taken by more open-minded competitors or by innovation consultancies with a hand kiss. We should consistently avoid such an **exodus of top performers**!

Therefore, before a possible integration of new business models, you should intensively examine the options shown in Fig. 3.38 (cf. Zollenkop, 2014, p. 153). Rapid **organizational integration** is the order of the day if there is little potential for conflict between the business models, but rather a high degree of strategic proximity. **Step-by-step integration** is advisable if a higher conflict potential is to be expected. If the business models to be evaluated show little strategic proximity or if high conflict potential is to be expected, a **separation of the different business models** should rather be sought.

The GAFA/GAFAM companies, but also the German media group *Axel Springer*, have integrated many of their acquisitions and thus further developed the prevailing business model. Other acquisitions—such as *Instagram* and *WhatsApp*—have been positioned independently by *Facebook* in terms of their external impact. They operate as independent companies—and many users do not know that these two platforms also belong to *Facebook*. Internally, however, a comprehensive data integration was carried out, although *Mark Zuckerberg* had explicitly excluded this when he acquired *WhatsApp*!

An example of an extensive separation of two business models even after the acquisition is provided by *Siemens* with the software company *Mendix*, which was acquired in 2018. *Mendix* is a platform that enables low-code users as well as professional developers to create software applications. In order to ensure *Mendix's* business direction even after the acquisition, extensive entrepreneurial autonomy has been granted.

▶ **Food for Thought**
Take advantage of the various **options for integrating new business models** in your area of responsibility. It doesn't always have to be a full integration!

> **Think Box: Questions You Should Ask Yourself**
> - Have you developed a process for integrating a business model innovation into the existing company?
> - Do you systematically check the compatibility of a business model innovation with the existing business model?
> - What cannibalization effects are to be expected?
> - How can these be managed?
> - What is the importance of cultural acceptance factors for business model innovations in your company?
> - Do you use all norm strategies for integrating business model innovations into established companies?

3.2.9 Examples of Consequent Business Model Innovations

In the following, the business developments of selected companies are analyzed. The aim is to show how consistently and willingly these companies have developed their business models. You can derive ideas for the further development of your business model from the cases presented here. Moreover, it can and should also be a source to nourish the storytelling for your transformation process!

3.2.9.1 Business Development of *Amazon*

An **analysis of *Amazon's* business development** is fascinating and frightening at the same time. Here it becomes clear with what courageous steps *Jeff Bezos* has developed his company from an intensively ridiculed **cash burner** in the 1990s to a true **money printing machine**. It is exciting that the company has remained true to the core of online sales despite a wide variety of business model innovations. The development from 1995 to today consists of the following steps (cf. also Sect. 3.3.2.1 on *Amazon's* ecosystem).

In 1995, *Jess Bezos* started selling books over the Internet—with a starting capital of US-$ 10,000 from his own assets. The company **went public** as early as 1997. What was interesting at that time was that after each new report of losses by *Amazon*, the share prices rose almost by default. There was also talk of the **cash burn rate** (CBR). It describes how long it would take for a company to burn through the newly raised money in the face of a negative cash flow—talks about when the company would run out of money (again) if no more investors could be found.

$$\text{Cash burn rate} = \frac{\text{Cash and cash equivalents}}{\text{Negative operating cash flow per month}}$$

This cash burn rate (CBR) must be determined for start-ups and new business fields. Especially in the start-up phase of a company, the cash flow is usually negative and causes the financial resources to melt away. A **high cash burn rate** here serves as an indicator of **more stable corporate financing**, since it takes many months or years for the financial resources to be eaten up if the cash flow remains negative. A high CBR signals high liquidity, a low one indicates future liquidity difficulties. In addition to the cash burn rate, however, an analysis of the future viability of the business model must always be carried out using other KPIs.

Amazon needed 6 years to make its first profit. In many subsequent years, *Jeff Bezos* told his investors that no profits would be distributed. Instead, the funds generated were consistently invested in the further development of products, services, and the business model. The investors were put off until the future.

The first **expansion of the business model** took place with the **offer of music** in 1998. As early as 1999, the business model was expanded to include a **platform for third-party providers**. To improve its own logistics in the distribution centers, *Kiva*, a **manufacturer of warehouse robots**, was acquired. From an original peripheral competence of *Amazon*, a core competence was developed. Today, this company offers **mobile robot fulfillment systems** under the name *Amazon Robotics*.

In 2002, the **selling of clothing** via the *Amazon* platform began. As early as 2003, an additional business model was established with **webhosting**. This, too, emerged from an original peripheral competence, acquired through the company's own IT centers. In 2005, a **paid customer loyalty program** called *Amazon Prime* was launched to safeguard the classic business model. Today it is said that anyone who is a paying *Amazon Prime* member is considered lost to the rest of the retail trade.

In 2007 *Amazon* started marketing its **own hardware** with the *Kindle* E-reader. In 2008 *Amazon* acquired the **audiobook company** *Audible* and in 2009 *Zappos*, an **online shop for shoes**. This allowed *Amazon* to expand its online presence into other product ranges. The acquisition of the *Washington Post* newspaper for US-$ 250 million in 2013 is to be seen as a private pleasure of *Jeff Bezos* and not as a consolidation of the *Amazon* business model.

In 2014, the *Fire* smartphone was added to the **hardware offering**. In 2014, the foundations were also laid for *Amazon Prime Video*, *Amazon's* **streaming service**. Today, not only third-party productions are shown there. Rather, *Amazon* has become active in a new business field here—the **production of films**. In 2015, the first **stationary bookstore** was opened in Seattle. *Amazon* also launched sales of *Amazon Echo*—the **digital assistant** now known primarily as *Alexa*. In 2017, it again invested in **stationary retail**—by purchasing the organic supermarket chain *Whole Foods*. This chain had more than 400 shops at the time of purchase.

In 2018, *Amazon* acquired *PillPack*, a US **online pharmacy**. *Amazon* also entered into **healthcare delivery** together with *JPMorgan Chase* and *Berkshire Hathaway*. The goal of this joint venture, called *Haven Health*, was to manage healthcare for the three companies' combined workforce of more than 1.5 million employees. By pooling resources and using innovative technology, the aim was to reduce costs for the groups. However, this project was terminated in February 2021 without having achieved the intended goals. This is also a strength of *Amazon*: ending projects when they fail to meet their intended goals.

In 2018, the **webhosting services**, founded in 2003 under the name *Amazon Web Services*, generated revenues of US-$ 7.3 billion. That year, the first **shop without a cash register**—*Amazon Go*—opened in Seattle.

Today, *Amazon* sells over **500 million products** and employs about **700.000 people**. *Amazon* has become the **largest online retailer** and the **largest cloud service provider**. Over 50% of online shoppers use *Amazon*. Daily sales of more than $ 400 million are achieved—this corresponds to approx. **US-$ 17 million in sales per hour**—and the trend is still rising!

Amazon is currently working on a **mobile robot** codenamed *Vesta*. *Vesta* is based on the digital assistant *Alexa* and complements it with a camera-equipped robot body for use in the private sphere. In 2020, *Amazon* launched its own **Internet pharmacy**, *Amazon Pharmacy*, in the USA. Here, customers can now also order prescription drugs. This announcement leads to significant share price losses for US drugstore and pharmacy chains! A building block for the development of this Internet pharmacy was the 2018 acquisition of the online pharmacy *Pillpack* for approximately US-$ 750 million.

Amazon achieved an **online retail global market share** of 9.2% in 2020 (cf. Statista, 2021). In North America, the company has a 37.9% share of **e-commerce sales** in 2020. Measured against total US retail sales, this is around 7%. With its *Amazon Prime* offer, the company reaches 82% of US-households. In Germany, this figure is 41%, which corresponds to 17 million households (cf. Gnirke et al., 2020, pp. 68, 70).

At the end of 2020, *Amazon* introduced its own **fitness tracker**: *Amazon Halo*. The motto is: "Healthcare built around you." The wristband, which can be purchased via a membership, is intended to help users track their health more closely and optimize it in conjunction with the *Halo* app. This includes an analysis of the body fat percentage and monitoring of sleep and other activities. In addition, the *Halo* app offers, for example, at-home workouts and guided meditations.

An **AI-supported analysis** of one's own voice and an auditory emotion recognition should help the user to recognize his or her own emotional fluctuations via the *Halo* app—as well as their effects on others. Here, the term "halo" becomes comprehensible in the sense of the radiation on others. To make this possible, the sensor unit includes two microphones as well as a sensor for measuring the heart rate. However, the *Halo* app required for control does not allow the integration of one's own health data, for example, into the *Apple* Health app or the *Google* Fit app (keyword "ecosystem").

What does Amazon (2021a) promise regarding data use:

"Designed for your privacy—You can download or delete your data anytime. When it comes to your personally identifiable health data, no one will view it without your permission, and we'll never sell it."

The core idea of *Amazon Halo* represents **data-based support on the path to self-optimization** (cf. Maschewski & Nosthoff, 2021, p. 39).

Amazon plans to open 3000 *Amazon Go* stores in 2021! In addition, with *Amazon Braket*, the company offers interested researchers and developers a **quantum computing service** to accelerate research and discovery in this field (cf. Amazon,

2021b). Again, *Amazon* is putting itself at the forefront of the movement. Surely *Jeff Bezos* and his team will have many more—desired and unwanted—surprises in store for us.

Amazon's **market capitalization** was US-$ 1.68 trillion in August 2021. In the wake of the Corona pandemic, the business has grown massively. Therefore, from January to October 2020, 1400 employees were already hired—per day; in total, over 427.000 people (cf. Weise, 2020)!

The **thoughts** and **mindset** with which *Jeff Bezos* has led his company to success are underlined by the following quotes (eCom, 2019):

- "If you only do things of which you know in advance how they will go, your business will go down."
- "If you want to innovate, you have to be prepared to fail."
- "The only way we can compete is through better services provision and better customer service. The customers are gods."
- "I am a fan of all-you-can-eat concepts because they are easier for the customer."
- "What will not change in the next 5–10 years?"
- "We want to make money when our customers use our appliances. Not when they buy them."
- "Cannibalizing yourself is much better than being cannibalized by someone else."

In 1998, *Jeff Bezos* described his business model as **"I sell books."** In 2017, it became **"I sell whatever the fuck I want."**

I admit: *Amazon's* success story is inspiring. Again and again, **consistent further developments of the existing business model** were made. In addition, it was recognized that the company's **own competences**—for example, in warehouse robots and web hosting—can be the **basis for complementary business models**. The fact that a few projects were put on the backburner at this pace of expansion is inevitably part of the innovation process and does not diminish the success achieved!

What scares me, however, is *Amazon's* already **overpowering position**. Many stationary retailers have already had to give up their business or will do so in the near future. The retailers who sell via *Amazon* place themselves in a great **dependency on the *Amazon* platform**. Here, the suppliers are at the mercy of *Amazon's* decisions without being able to exert any relevant influence on these results. If, from *Amazon's* point of view, certain products from third-party suppliers are doing well, they can simply be added to the company's own range.

In addition, *Amazon* is increasingly getting involved in the **marketing of its own products**—and thus squeezing independent retailers out of the range. These additional offers go under the names *Amazon Essentials* (clothing) and *Amazon Basics*. These terms make it clear that *Amazon* is concentrating on the **fast-moving products** that guarantee high demand even in the absence of advertising and thus high added value.

The **analysis of the success story** naturally also includes a **look at the dark side of *Amazon's* success**. It is no secret that the **algorithms for displaying offers** on *Amazon* are primarily profit-driven and often do **not ensure fair competition**

Fig. 3.39 Entrance for employees at the *Amazon* logistics center in Hamburg

among the suppliers. Again and again, the offers are marked as *Amazon's Choice*. In my opinion, the profit motive associated with this is only acceptable if it does not cause any market distortions. With **retail media**, *Amazon* has secured another source of income. Suppliers who want to attract special attention on the *Amazon* platform have to pay separately for this.

It should also be mentioned that the **working conditions** at *Amazon* (including the monitoring of employees) are repeatedly criticized. Even the **lettering** above the **entrance to the Hamburg logistics center**, which so beautifully reads: "work hard. have fun. make history." does not change this (cf. Fig. 3.39). Moreover, *Amazon* does "orientate" itself in Germany to the regionally customary wages in the logistics industry. However, the question arises: is *Amazon* essentially a logistics company? In addition, *Amazon* uses all possibilities of tax avoidance!

All *Amazon* customers make this company richer and richer day by day. However, this **wealth** is not limited to **Euros and Dollars**. One source of wealth bubbles up even when we only search, but do not buy: the **data sources**. *Amazon* has stored gigantic amounts of data about all of us and is improving its competitive position more and more—which is already uncatchable today.

Anticipatory shipping is already being worked on. A product is already delivered to a warehouse near us when *Amazon* has calculated that we will buy it soon. This will make it possible to deliver within 30 min in the future. And maybe it will soon say: "Dear Ms. Paschen, you wanted to buy this book in the next few hours. We're delivering it to you now so you don't have to wait for delivery!"

Consequently, we should be aware of whom we are giving attention, trust, money and, above all, data to every time we buy from *Amazon*!

And: ***Amazon* can no longer be tamed by the forces of the market, but only by politics!**

> **Memory Box**
> The example of *Amazon* clearly shows how powerful and courageous a **continuous further development of one's own business model** can be—courageous also towards investors. **Newly acquired competencies** were consistently used in **combination with new technologies** to **further develop the existing business model** (horizon 2) as well as for **business model innovations** on horizon 3—even if these no longer had anything to do with the original business model.

▶ **Food for Thought**
Amazon's "**A-to-Z guarantee**," with which the company implements its customer obsession, is seen by many—including me—as **devil's stuff**. I, too, have made the experience that the customer is always believed, while the company selling through the platform is never believed. Claiming that the product is faulty 3 weeks after delivery is accepted by *Amazon* without complaint. If the trader points out that a fraudster is obviously at work here, this is ignored. This is even the case when *Amazon* customers order new *Tupperware*, return the old bowls and claim that the order was processed in an incorrect way. Bad for the retailer, whose rating gets worse—also and especially in the eyes of *Amazon*!

And the consequence? **Fraudsters** are systematically attracted who learn that they can get away with anything on *Amazon*. The "A-to-Z guarantee" in the back of their minds and the power of the trader rating in the fingertips of the customers do not bode well for the future!

3.2.9.2 Business Development of *Axel Springer*

For the German media company *Axel Springer*, the motto is **"innovation as a tradition."** Accordingly, entrepreneurial passion and innovative thinking, traditional values and a consistent attitude have never been opposites that first had to be overcome. Rather, this **DNA of the media company** was the prerequisite for the **cultural change** necessary for a digital transformation to take place. As early as 1978, *Axel Springer* himself formulated (Axel Springer, 2020a):

"In any case, I will not tire [...] of representing the publishers' claim to participate in the electronic media that have existed up to now and even more so in all the new information systems that are coming our way."

At that time, only a few media creators had already recognized the challenges posed by the slowly approaching online age to such an extent.

Spurred on by this, the *Axel Springer* company developed more and more in the 2000s from an originally German publishing house into an internationally active media company. Digitization is increasingly determining the company's business activities:

"Online first" as the corporate strategy.

To this end, new paths had to be taken, especially in classified advertising, since this profitable business has shifted almost completely to the Internet. In the tradition of the entrepreneur *Axel Springer*, the current CEO, *Mathias Döpfner*, formulated a clear goal at the annual press conference in 2013:

"We want to accelerate the digital transformation and make *Axel Springer* the leading digital media company."

This **visionary task** was the starting point for the **consistent development and expansion of digital offerings**. *Axel Springer* also entered into a large number of **strategic partnerships** and **international investments** to achieve this goal in the following figures. This thorough and consistent approach showed impressive results. Already in the first quarter of 2018, the digital offerings contributed 70% of the revenues and 80% of the company's results (cf. Axel Springer, 2020a).

Such a radical **(digital) reorientation** was not possible without an accompanying **cultural change**. The watchword here was that digital business ideas should not be kept away from the company or the core business. Rather, it was important to strive for a **dovetailing of the analogue and digital worlds**—also in the operational area—at an early stage. To achieve this, it was crucial not to separate the **responsibility for analogue and digital business**, but to consistently bring them together. In this way, the digital transformation could be driven forward with joint strength.

The digital transformation was supported by a **large number of acquisitions**. Through these, not only **digital business models**, but also **creative minds** were gained for the transformation process. In these acquisitions, the attempt was made to keep the **founders as entrepreneurs** in the company with operational responsibility. In innovative formats, this know-how was also spread widely throughout the company. This was intended to promote a "digital infection" to further **develop the print DNA into a digital DNA**. In addition, several **new companies were founded** and the **existing media offering was further developed** in a variety of ways. The most important steps are presented below (cf. Axel Springer, 2020a):

- 2010: *Axel Springer* presented the first offerings of its own media brands on the new **tablet computer** as early as the launch of the *iPad* in Germany.
- 2010: *Axel Springer AG* and the *Swiss Ringier AG* found the joint venture ***Ringier Axel Springer Media AG.***
- 2011: Acquisition of a majority stake in *SeLoger.com*, the leading **real estate portal** in France.
- 2011: Majority acquisition of *kaufDA*, the market leader for **online brochures** and **mobile couponing**; today *kaufDA* is part of *Bonial.com*, which addresses millions of shoppers every month with other platforms such as *MeinProspekt* (*meinprospekt.de*) and *Out of Milk* (*outofmilk.com*), pointing them to local shops.
- 2012: Founding of ***Axel Springer Digital Classifieds*** (together with *General Atlantic*) for the **classifieds market**.
- 2012: Acquisition of majority stake in Belgian **real estate portal** *Immoweb.be*.

- 2012: Acquisition of the majority in the **online portal** *Onet.pl*.
- 2012: Presentation of the **online database** *"The Archive—Rewind"* (includes more than 100,000 articles from over 1000 digitized issues of the music magazines *Rolling Stone, Musikexpress,* and *Metal Hammer*).
- 2012: Introduction of new **subscription models for digital offerings** of *Die Welt* (first paid model of a major German national news site to replace previously free online access to this content).
- 2013: Introduction of **paid online offers** by *Bildplus*.
- 2013: Launch of **24-hour online reporting** for *Bild* and *Die Welt*.
- 2013: Foundation of the *Axel Springer Plug and Play Accelerator* with the *Plug and Play Tech Center*, a leading start-up investor from Silicon Valley (support program for founders with digital and innovative business concepts).
- 2014: Majority shareholding in *Vertical Media GmbH*, which publishes the **online magazine for the start-up industry** *Gründerszene*.
- 2014: Foundation of a joint venture between *Axel Springer* and *Politico* for the development of a **digital media offering on European politics**.
- 2014: Acquisition of various **classified portals** by *Axel Springer Digital Classifieds* (including *Corall-Tell/yad2, Car & Boat Media/La Centrale*).
- 2015: Merger of the company-owned *N24 Media GmbH* with the *Welt Group* to build a **multimedia news company for quality journalism** (in 2018, the TV channel *N24* will become the provider *Welt TV*).
- 2015: Agreement on a strategic partnership between *Axel Springer* and *Samsung* to jointly develop new digital media formats for users in Europe; one result is *upday*, a **news aggregator platform** for smartphones (*upday.com*).
- 2015: Acquisition of a majority stake in *Business Insider* in New York, a leading **provider of digital offerings for business and financial news** in the USA (central building block for increasing the digital reach worldwide as well as for expanding the journalistic portfolio in the English-speaking world).
- 2016: Acquisition *of eMarketer Inc.*, New York, a renowned provider of high-quality **analyses and studies in the areas of digital marketing, digital sales, and digital trends** for companies and institutions.
- 2016: *Axel Springer* becomes the second-largest shareholder in *Group Nine Media*, a **digital-only offering** for the target group of 18- to 34-year-old users.
- 2017: *Bild* and *Ringier Axel Springer Media* present *NOIZZ*, a new **digital offering** for a young and urban audience, on the German market.
- 2017: *Axel Springer Plug and Play* cooperates with the affiliate marketing network *Awin* to jointly find and develop new **adtech companies.**
- 2018: *Axel Springer Digital Ventures* and *Porsche Digital* jointly establish the **start-up accelerator APX** in Berlin (offers financial support to promising start-ups as well as access to a network and qualification and further development opportunities).
- 2018: The *Axel Springer Media Impact* division bundles the **marketing of national media offerings** of the print and digital group of companies.
- 2019: *Axel Springer* presents a **refocused growth strategy**: the goal is to become the **world market leader in digital journalism and classified advertising** with

more dynamic growth (visualization through a further developed corporate design and a new logo; positioning: "*We empower free decisions*").
- 2019: Participation in *Media Pioneer Publishing GmbH* in Berlin as a strategic partner in the context of **digital journalism.**
- 2019: Entering into a strategic partnership between *Axel Springer* and *KKR* to **support the long-term growth strategy.**
- 2019: Acquisition of *MeilleursAgents*, the leading provider of **online real estate valuation** in France.
- 2020: *Bild* has gained 500,000 **Plus subscribers.**

Oriented to the guiding idea of also maintaining a **not-to-do list**, *Axel Springer* divested itself of various properties, some of which represented the nucleus for the publishing house. In 2014, for example, several regional newspapers, five TV guides and two women's magazines were sold to the *Funke Group* (including *Berliner Morgenpost, Hamburger Abendblatt,* and *Hörzu*).

Friede Springer said (Axel Springer, 2020a):
"The old has passed away. Really gone."

The vision, the most important values, the strategic focus, the central growth drivers, and the organizational setup for this comprehensive digital transformation of *Axel Springer* can be seen in the **House of Freedom**. There, the following aspects guiding action are brought together (cf. Axel Springer, 2020c).

Slogan: we empower free decisions.

Corporate values: integrity, creativity, entrepreneurship, sustainability, empathy.

Strategic focus: global market leadership, growth, content & classifieds

Growth driver: purpose, innovation, people, tech, speed, customer focus

Organizational setup: digital content, digital classifieds

To make the digital transformation clear in the analogue world as well, a new building was planned in Berlin and officially opened as the *Axel Springer New Building* on 6 October 2020. The new building complements the existing publishing tower at the headquarters of this media and technology company. It offers a total rental area of 52,000 m^2 with 3500 work opportunities on 13 floors. The spatial proximity is intended to promote even stronger networking and a more intensive exchange of knowledge. The chosen architecture impressively documents not only the future of work, but also stands as a tangible symbol for the digital transformation of *Axel Springer* (cf. Axel Springer, 2020b).

▶ **Food for Thought**
Looking at this success story, no one would say that there are no companies in Germany that have successfully managed a comprehensive digital transformation.

3.2.9.3 Business Development of the *Otto Group*

The *Otto Group* is a German trading and services company headquartered in Hamburg, which operates worldwide with around 52,000 employees and is active in the retail, financing and logistics, and mail order divisions. Its core business is retail. In order to remain successful in the market in the future and to meet the rapid pace of change brought about by digitalization, it is essential to break new ground. With the aim of permanently securing the future viability of the globally active group of companies in times of exponential digitalization, at the end of 2015 the *Otto Group* executive board and the shareholders *Michael Otto* and *Benjamin Otto* unanimously called for **Culture Change 4.0.** The idea: an open, participatory process and a radical questioning of existing structures with a maximum of creative freedom—beyond roles and hierarchies. Below, we present some of the measures taken in recent years that have driven the **transformation process** in the *Otto Group* and provide evidence of it. Here follows an excerpt:

- **May 2014: Setting up *AboutYou***
  AboutYou is a fashion and technology company based in Hamburg. The **online fashion shop** has digitized the classic city stroll for its customers. Through a high degree of personalization, a separate shop is created for all customers, which only displays relevant products, trends, and outfit suggestions—oriented towards the individual style of each customer. As a result, women and men between the ages of 20 and 49 can now find a range of more than 150,000 articles from over 1000 brands on *aboutyou.com* and in the *AboutYou* app, in addition to a wide variety of inspirations (cf. Otto Group, 2021g).
- **2016: Launch of the central culture change progam Team 4.0, the local culture change teams and the culture change platform 4.0.**
  Various **participation formats** were used to take all employees of the company on the "culture journey." These are designed to empower all individuals to live and drive change in their sphere of influence. This process is supported by a **collaborative digital platform** on the group-wide Intranet (cf. Otto Group, 2021a).

  Facets that make up **Cultural Change 4.0** at the *Otto Group* become visible there (in the so-called workhacks). The focus here is on **user-generated content.** The spectrum of topics ranges from workshop ideas to lateral leadership and mindfulness to virtual teamwork and feedback. Central guiding ideas are **more personal responsibility** through less coordination and approval to enable **easier information transfer**. In total, more than 600 "user generated workhacks" were carried out here—with exciting findings (cf. Otto Group, 2021a)!
- **May 2016—Start of *Agile Groupies Community***
  The *Agile Groupies Community* organizes **bar camps** for all *Otto Group* employees who want to learn or develop agility or new work. A **coaching circle** is intended to support the further perfecting of coaching skills within the *Otto Group*. This also includes promoting a **culture of experimentation** through coaching (cf. Otto, 2021b).

Product pioneers support the further development of product management within the group. An **#agileGroupie video channel** offers various lectures to make knowledge about agile methods accessible across the group. In parallel, **everyday heroes** offer individual learning formats, e.g., for kanban, story mapping, delegation poker. In addition, the **exchange of knowledge with external experts** is to be promoted. By **networking with external user groups**, the customer-oriented further development of the offers and the business model will be advanced (cf. Otto, 2021b).

- **Since 2017:** *"Digital Excellence"*
The *Digital Excellence* area focuses on digital topics and the digital aspects of transformation in the *Otto Group*. The **digital experts** support the *Otto Group* companies on their way to digital excellence (cf. Otto, 2021a).

- **January 2017—Setting up** *Otto Group Agile Center*
Through the *Agile Center* and the group-wide community of *Agile Groupies*, the use of **agile management methods** is being further promoted throughout the group. Agile-trained employees accompany the work of colleagues, work together to develop targeted proposals for changed ways of working, and provide support through workshops, presentations of agile methods and coaching for managers and teams. This is intended to further increase the reaction speed in the group (cf. Otto, 2021a).

- **November 2017:** *AboutYou* **enters the cloud business**
Building on its own core competencies, *AboutYou* offers its own **e-commerce infrastructure as a licensed product** with the *AboutYou cloud*: e-commerce technology as a service (cf. Otto, 2017).

- **February 2018:** *Otto* **shows augmented reality-app**
Otto introduces its own augmented reality (AR) app, which was developed in close cooperation with *Google*. This makes *Otto* one of the few companies to implement this AR core technology right from the start.

- **Since September 2018:** *Develop:her*
The *Develop:her* concept is about **female empowerment in tech and IT.** The core of *Develop:her* is a series of events that regularly offers women (and men) the opportunity to immerse themselves in the world of digital knowledge for 2 days in a protected space and to network with each other at the same time. Impulse lectures and panel talks round off the program—both online and offline (cf. Otto Group, 2021c).

- **Since 2018: Strengthening the culture of mistakes**
By holding **Fuck Up Nights** and **Courage Festivals** in the *Otto Group,* the aim is to achieve an **open, entertaining, and high-profile approach to mistakes**. This serves to strengthen courage and error culture within the company. This involves participation across the hierarchy—from the executive board to the trainee. The core message is: **mistakes are allowed** (cf. Otto Group, 2021d).

- **Since December 2018:** *Mindful@OTTO*
The *Mindful@OTTO* initiative focuses on the **health of employees and managers**. The need for this results from continuous change. At the same time, the entire staff is accompanied on the path of digital transformation. The initiative

is dedicated to the levels that burden the dimensions of health: the ego, the team, and the *Otto Group* as a whole (cf. Otto, 2021a).

- **Since 2019: Transformation of *otto.de* to a platform**
  To drive the company's growth, *Otto* is investing around 100 million euros in further development into a platform. This process is supported by the purchase of the IOT start-up *OrderThis*. In the course of the platform development, selected business areas will be completely reorganized. This also includes the possibility for external trading partners to automatically register on the *otto.de* platform and sell their products there. (cf. Otto, 2021e).
- **February 2019: *bonprix "fashion connect" store***
  The aim of the *bonprix "fashion connect"* store was to offer customers a new and unique shopping experience. This should minimize the classic weaknesses of stationary retail through digital support. An **assisted shopping tour** via the *bonprix* app serves this purpose. Using one's own smartphone, the products shown in the shop can be scanned, ordered for immediate fitting in the booth and immediately purchased via the easy checkout. The goal is to further **improve the customer journey**, including new features for the **displays in the fitting rooms** and the introduction of **endless aisle elements** to order additional products from the *bonprix* online shop via an "extended merchandise shelf" from the store. In 2020, this concept was awarded one of the *World Retail Awards* at the *World Retail Congress* (cf. Bonprix, 2020).
- **November 2019: Launch of the start-up *adsoul.com* for AI-based, automated search engine marketing**
  By using *adSoul's* **search engine advertising (SEA) automation software**, customers can implement their keyword-based forms of advertising in a fully automated way—with complete control and transparency (cf. Otto Group, 2021f).
- **December 2019: Starting point of *TechUcation***
  The *TechUcation* continuing education initiative is intended to create a common understanding and language for the topic of digitization across the group. Through *TechUcation*, learning and digital education are anchored in the *Otto Group's* everyday working life and corporate culture.
- **March 2020: Contactless delivery at *Hermes***
  In times of the Corona crisis, the parcel service provider *Hermes Germany* is taking additional precautionary measures to protect the health of its delivery staff and customers as best as possible. From now on, customers can receive their parcels contactless. For this purpose, the company has developed a solution that eliminates the need for a signature on the scanner (cf. Hermes, 2021).
- **September 2020: *Otto* established own payment provider**
  Otto becomes a payment provider—for its own retail group and for external stores on the *Otto* marketplace. In future, *Otto* will be able to process payments between sellers and customers from a single source. The official procedure for recognition as a payment service provider is underway, and the staff of the *Otto* payment company is growing.

- **July 2021: IPO of *AboutYou***
  The share of the online fashion portal *AboutYou* has made a successful start on the *Frankfurt Stock Exchange*. *AboutYou* is the third online fashion portal to venture an IPO in Frankfurt, following *Zalando* 7 years ago and *Global Fashion Group* 2 years ago. 842 million euros came in, bringing the **market capitalization** of *AboutYou* to around 3.9 billion euros.

These measures from the *Otto Group* are just a few examples of successful transformation and cultural change. The *Otto Group* will certainly present further exciting innovations.

3.2.9.4 Business Development of *Fuji*

An exciting development was also carried out by *Fuji* (cf. Fuji, 2021). In 1934, *Fuji* established itself as a **manufacturer of motion picture films**, which Japan had previously had to import from overseas. The company quickly established itself in Japan as the market leader for cinema films and photographic films. Here the company was very successful for many decades (horizon 1) until **demand for photographic film** collapsed. This was caused by the **spread of digital cameras** and peaked in 2000. Now *Fuji* was forced to **open up new business areas**.

In 2004, the **company was founded for a second time**, so to speak. *Fujifilm* ended its photo film-centered business model and started a business model innovation on the third horizon level. The skills acquired in the course of film production—including work with nanoparticles—were applied to the development of cosmetics as well as other new business areas.

In 2007, the development of a red ingredient for cosmetic products was achieved. This is the natural, reddish-violet coloring agent *astaxanthin*, which is produced by green algae. The **nanotechnology** used for processing promoted the stability of the ingredient and enabled its use in the red skin care range *Astalift*. The technology used was applied to the **development of many other cosmetic products** in the following years. In doing so, *Fuji* succeeded again and again in transferring its **technological superiority** into attractive cosmetic products.

> **Memory Box**
> The example of *Fuji* shows particularly clearly what is meant by **"think big."** Here, it was examined which interesting business models could be developed on the basis of the **core competences** acquired so far—regardless of how far these might be from the traditional business. The courage of the decision-makers is impressive.

3.2.9.5 Business Development of the *Ant Financial Service Group*

An example of an innovative further development of its own business model comes from China (cf. Ankenbrand, 2020, p. 25). Specifically, it analyzes how the *Ant Financial Service Group*, which emerged from *Alibaba*, has developed over the years to become the **most valuable FinTech in the world**. The meaning of the name *Ant Financial Services* vividly illustrates a business model that emphasizes the strength of a community and uses this to develop its own business model.

With *Alipay*, the company today operates the **dominant electronic payment service** in China. This was developed by *Alibaba* as early as 2004 to make it easier to process transactions on its own platform. Before *Alibaba's* IPO in 2014, *Alipay* was spun off from the group.

In 2010, the company piloted a solution for **microloans**—with a loan amount of no more than 150,000 €. Data obtained via the *Alibaba* platform was used to evaluate creditworthiness. Due to a very detailed evaluation of the borrowers, the default rate of unsecured loans could be reduced to about 1%. Worldwide, this default rate is around 4% (cf. FitchRatings, 2020).

The motto for applying for a loan is: "3-1-0."

The data required for the **credit application** are entered in 3 mi. The **analysis of the creditworthiness** takes one minute—with **"0" human interaction**. The consistent use of AI systems has made transactions faster, cheaper and also more secure (cf. Cornelius, 2019, p. 45).

In 2013, the **small change service** (*Yue Bao*) was introduced. With this function, *Alipay* users receive higher interest rates than with banks—and that already from a deposit of 0.1 Cents. Users can access the deposits at any time for payment. In 2014, the *Huabei* function was introduced. Users can get a **small loan** within three min. This is increasingly replacing credit cards. Every China traveler becomes aware—sometimes painfully—of the impact this has when they want to pay with a credit card. In many shops, the payment method credit card is no longer provided.

At an early stage, the company relied on an **AI-supported evaluation of the large databases** in order to identify particularly interesting target groups. Building on this experience, *Ant Financial Services* offered various **insurance companies** in 2017 to create risk profiles of drivers in order to calculate insurance premiums more accurately. More data about users makes it possible to **individualize risks** and thereby **also individualize premiums.**

Since 2018, the company has been insuring *Alipay* users against many diseases, malignant tumors, and rare conditions with the *Xianghu Bao* feature. This is a **dread disease health insurance policy**. With this business model, the insured do **not pay regular premiums**. Instead, the costs incurred are passed on to all customers. The **annual premium** is capped for the customers. Through the use of AI technologies to analyze big data and the integration of blockchain technology, the premiums incurred here are one tenth of those of traditional insurance companies (cf. Ankenbrand, 2020, p. 25).

The *Alibaba* trading platform already offers **additional insurance policies**, for example to compensate for financial losses due to damage to goods in transit or the return of goods.

The motto for damage claims is: "2-1-2".

A claim can be reported in 2 min, it is checked in one second and the payment is made to the customer's account after two hours (cf. Cornelius, 2019, p. 45f). Here, too, innovative AI systems enable such speed. A nice benchmark for the classic insurance companies!

All payments associated with *Ant Financial's* insurance policies are also processed via *Alipay*. *Alipay* is also directly linked to *Taobao*, an **e-commerce platform** belonging to *Alibaba*.

In 2020, a **platform** called *Trusple* was launched (cf. Trusple, 2020). This name stands for "trust made simple." This platform is intended to solve the problem that foreign buyers of Chinese goods do not know whether they will actually be delivered. At the same time, Chinese companies are pushing for payment. To solve this problem, the **payment methods and conditions** are recorded on the **blockchain**—traceable and forgery-proof. The banking partners operating on the platform offer additional services to improve the **security of transactions** and increase trust.

Because of this extensive and continuously growing ecosystem, *Ant Financial Service Group* currently represents the highest valued **FinTech company** in the world. It will be exciting to see how *Ant Financial Services* will continue to develop in light of the political environment in China. After all, with its innovative products it is attacking the traditional financial service providers, which are an important backbone for the Chinese economy today. This may also have been a reason why the company—2 days before its planned and world's largest IPO (planned volume US-$ 37 billion)—had to cancel its move to the Hong Kong and Shanghai stock exchanges in 2020 due to pressure from the Chinese state.

It can be assumed that the main reason for the stop of the IPO was some critical statements of *Jack Ma*, which he expressed at a summit in Shanghai on 24 October 2020. There *Jack Ma* has told that the regulatory system was stifling innovation and must be reformed to fuel growth. Chinese banks, he said, operated with a "pawn-shop" mentality (cf. Zhai et al., 2020).

> **Memory Box**
> The example of *Ant Financial* shows how a core competence—in this case data management—can be consistently used for business model innovations. In this case, the innovations developed are primarily located on the second horizon. It also shows the increasing influence of the Chinese government on successful companies in China.

> **Think Box: Questions You Should Ask Yourself**
> - What food for thought can you derive from *Amazon's* expansion strategy for your own company?
> - Which elements of *Jeff Bezos'* mindset would also fit your company?
> - What inspirations go hand in hand with the development at *Axel Springer* for you?

(continued)

- What inspiration could you gain from the *Otto Group* case study?
- What can *Fuji's* strategic business development motivate you to do?
- What core competencies—analogous to *Fuji* and *Ant Financial Service Group*—do you have that could be used for business model innovations on horizon levels 2 and 3?

3.3 Digitalization of the Value Chain

Many people don't get on in life because they think they are on an escalator that automatically takes them to the top.
  But that is not the case!

3.3.1 Strategic Alignment of Value Chains

3.3.1.1 From Value Chains to Systems of Value Chains

An important task area for achieving digital excellence is to examine the extent to which value creation can be increased by **digitizing one's own value chain**. However, digitization is not an end in itself in this area either. Rather, digitization should promote the resilience and future viability of the business model—and at the same time reduce costs and/or increase customer value.

The starting point of your approach can be based on the **classic value chain** developed by *Michael Porter* (cf. Porter, 2004, pp. 59–92). By using a value chain analysis you can achieve the following goals:

- **Identifying the courses of competitive advantages**—for both the own and other companies.
- **Identification of potentials for achieving competitive advantages for the own company** (focus: sources of additional customer benefits, starting points for improving the own cost situation and/or for the development of new business models).

The value chain analysis is about identifying **starting points for achieving competitive advantages** for your own company. You should focus the value chain analysis on the core of your business model to ensure manageability of the analysis process. The core elements of the value chain of your business model include those with a high customer specific differentiation potential and/or with a significant cost share. These activities can come from different business areas. You first assign each of these activities to one of the following types:

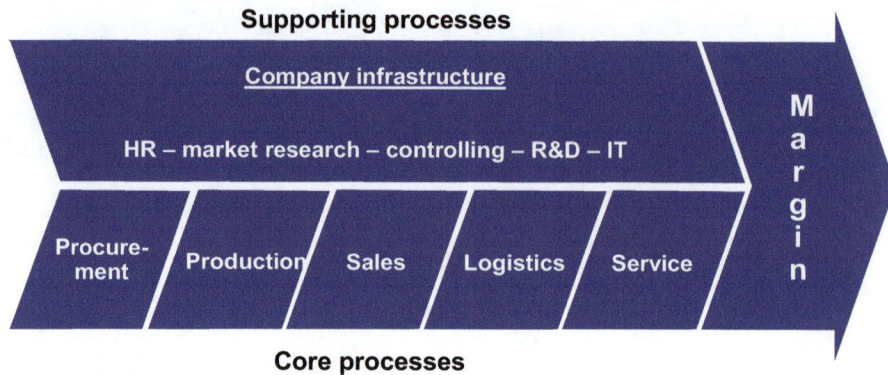

Fig. 3.40 Basic concept of a value chain

- **Core processes** (also called **direct activities**)
  The activities to be assigned to the core processes are directly involved in creating value for the customer.
- **Accompanying processes** (also called **indirect activities**)
  These include activities that only indirectly contribute to the creation of services. A classic example of this is the company infrastructure, which can include the HR, controlling or R&D.
- **Quality assurance**
  This category includes activities that contribute to ensuring a high level of quality in the most diverse areas of the company. These comprise quality tests and the ongoing monitoring of production as well as the continuous analysis of marketing and sales activities.

When assigning activities to one of these categories, you should take into account your specific company situation as well as the sector analyzed in each case. Therefore, the assignment shown in Fig. 3.40 is only an exemplary implementation (cf. Porter, 2004, p. 62).

In contrast to the classification shown in Fig. 3.40, **HR** is a core process in consulting companies, since the reputation and success of these companies stands and falls with the qualifications of their own personnel. In classic market research companies, **market research**—differentiated in various offerings—is one of the core processes. In research-based pharmaceutical companies, **R&D** is an essential part of the core processes, whereas this is not the case with a generic drug manufacturer. In view of the tasks associated with digitalization, the **IT infrastructure** is increasingly becoming a core process not only for IT service providers, but also for all companies.

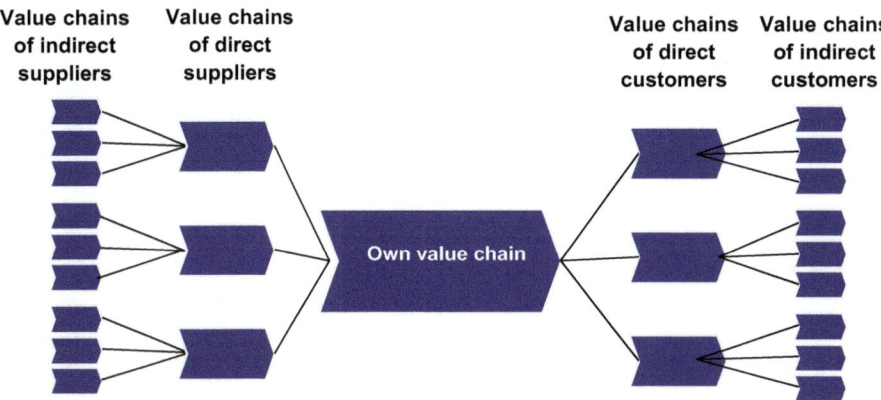

Fig. 3.41 Additional competitive advantages based on value chains

> **Memory Box**
> **You have to allocate supporting processes and core processes in your company according to the respective priorities.**
>
> The **value chain** is based on *Porter's* core idea that every company can be described as a **collection of activities** through which products or services are developed, produced, communicated, distributed, and delivered (cf. Porter, 2004, p. 63). The company-specific design of the value chain has a direct impact on the company's achievable **profit margin** (cf. Fig. 3.40).
>
> Every change in the design of the supporting processes or the core processes influences this profit margin, which results from the difference between the turnover achieved and the costs used to create value. The more efficient and effective the use of resources, the greater the **value added** for the company in terms of achievable profit. It thus becomes clear that every type of activity along the value chain can be a source of competitive advantage. Here, the leverage is particularly great in the core processes.
>
> In the course of digitalization and the **development of the Internet of Things** or the **Internet of Everything**, the value chain of a company is often no longer used in isolation. The value chains of companies are often linked in many ways with the upstream and downstream value chains of suppliers and customers. Together they form a **system of value chains** (also **value network**; cf. Fig. 3.41; Porter, 2004, pp. 59–61).
>
> How intensively such networks are already established or will be established in the future differs significantly from sector to sector. Your task is to analyze the optimization potential that can be achieved by linking with upstream and downstream value chains. This aspect of linking different value chains through the **computerization of manufacturing technologies**
>
> (continued)

represents the core of **industry 4.0** developments. The goal here is often the development of a **smart factory**. The **informational integration of suppliers and customers** is intended to enable or facilitate the company's own response to changes in supply and demand (see the example of *Siemens* in Sect. 3.3.4.1).

3.3.1.2 Value Chain Analysis

For larger companies, you can focus the **value chain analysis** on a product group, a service area, or on individual strategic business units. Only such a focus enables you to identify specific starting points for improving your own competitive position.

In the **first step of the analysis**, the following questions are dealt with in order to record the **status quo of your own company**:

- What are the particularly important activities in value creation?
- Which of these activities represent core processes, supporting processes or quality assurance processes?
- What costs are associated with the different activities?
- To what extent do these activities contribute to improving the competitive position?
  - What customer benefits are generated?
  - What cost advantages are achieved as a result?
- Are the activities customary in the industry? If not, do they generate visible customer benefits and/or cost benefits?
- Are the activities in your own value chain optimally coordinated and interlinked?
- Are there overlaps or avoidable dependencies?
- Are possible synergies left unused?
- Is your own value chain aligned with the value chain of your own suppliers?
- Does the value chain include those of the company's own customers?

The answers to these questions provide indications for **optimizing the cost structure** or **raising differentiation potential** to achieve competitive advantages in your company. The value chain analysis can—by comparing your own value chain with that of competitors—provide important clues for further development.

Answers to the following questions can contribute to this in the **second step of the analysis** in direct comparison to relevant competitors:

- What options are there for structuring the value chain within or outside your own industry?
- How does the same value chain process work for competitors?
- What links have competitors already made with upstream and/or downstream value chains?
- Which costs of a value creation stage are offset by which competitive advantages in one's own company?

3.3 Digitalization of the Value Chain

- Which costs of a value creation stage are offset by which customer advantages in the own company?
- Which stages of the value chain must be performed by the company itself and which can be outsourced (to suppliers, outsourcing partners, or customers)?

In the **third step of the analysis**, you can identify concrete fields of action to improve your own competitive position on the basis of the differences in the design of the value chains determined here. On the one hand, **clues for reducing costs** can be identified by, for example, identifying product features and/or service areas that generate costs but no relevant customer benefits. There may also be indications of how costs can be limited by reducing the number of variants, by reducing the depth of added value, by modular production, or by merging production volumes.

On the other hand, **fields of action** can be identified for **differentiating one's own services** from those of the competition. Finally, you can also identify **clues for optimizing the interfaces of value chains**—inside and outside your own company. This can reveal activities that should be delegated to suppliers or customers outside your own area of responsibility. In addition, activities that were previously outsourced may be identified and should be reintegrated to create value and/or reduce costs.

These **fields of action** make it clear that the value chain analysis is closely linked to the design of the business model (see Sect. 3.2). An important complementary contribution to the design of the options for action identified here can be provided by the insights gained through the use of the SWOT analysis and the resilience analysis (see Sects. 2.1.4 and 2.1.5).

> **Memory Box**
> The value chain analysis is a very important tool to identify cost differences and points of differentiation between companies. It allows you to compare your own business model in depth with that of competitors. In this way, you can gain ideas for the further development of your own value chain.
>
> Today, digitalization makes it equally possible—and in many cases necessary—to supplement the classic value chain with a **digital (informational) value chain**. Figure 3.42 shows you how the physical value chain is equally penetrated and enriched by a digital value chain. It promotes **informational networking** between the company's internal divisions and thus contributes to overcoming the silo mentality that still exists in many cases. At the same time, the digital value chain creates the (informational) prerequisites to enable the **development of value chain systems** described above. In many cases, it is precisely this networking that enables the further development of your current business model beyond your own company—right up to the development of new business models (e.g., in the form of predictive maintenance).

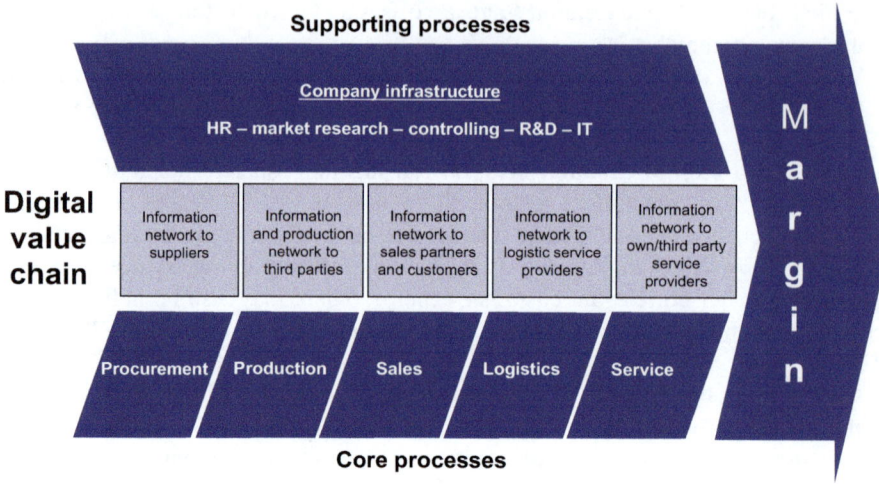

Fig. 3.42 Physical and digital value chains are interconnected

> **Memory Box**
> The **physical value chain** is increasingly being penetrated by a **digital value chain**. In this way, a variety of efficiency and effectiveness reserves can be realized in the value creation. In addition, indications for the further development or supplementation of the existing business model can be identified.

3.3.1.3 Predictive Maintenance and Predictive Servicing

Predictive maintenance is about **anticipatory maintenance**. The basic idea is that systems and machines should not be maintained only when they have failed or faults have occurred. The aim is to prevent failures as well as the occurrence of faults as far as possible in advance. For this purpose, measurement and production data of components, machines, and entire plants are recorded by a large number of sensors during the running process. From this information, **maintenance and replacement** needs can be derived—primarily through AI algorithms—and **possible malfunctions** can be predicted. Repairs or the replacement of wear parts can then already be carried out at a time when the units are still running correctly. This significantly reduces downtimes.

The following work **steps of predictive maintenance** must be mastered (cf. Kreutzer & Sirrenberg, 2019, p. 217f.):

- **Predictive maintenance** is based on the **collection, digitalization, and consolidation of data** from the various performance components of a machine, a production plant, etc. For this purpose, IOT sensors are used and maintenance

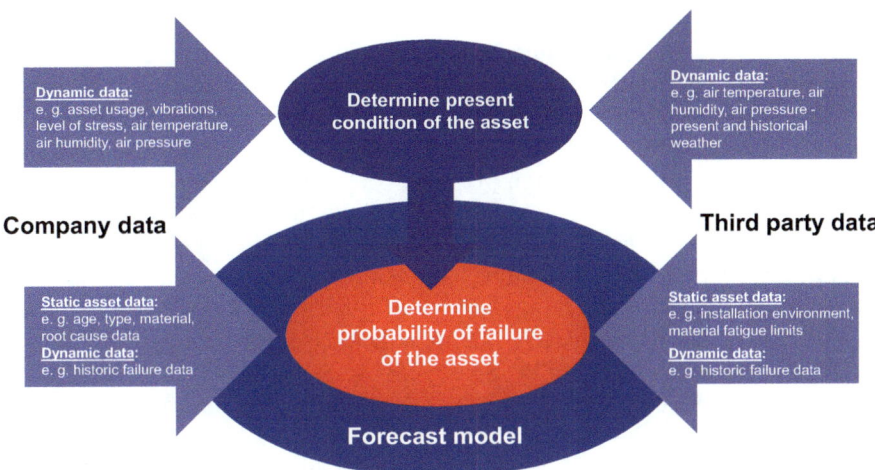

Fig. 3.43 Predictive maintenance model

logs are read out. In addition, reference data from external sources, e.g., on the performance and malfunctions of the same or similar systems, which may be in use worldwide, can be incorporated. Furthermore, environmental data can be taken into account. This includes room temperature, air pressure, and humidity in the area of use of the machines or systems, if these are important for maintenance.
- AI algorithms are used to **analyze and evaluate the collected data**.
- Based on patterns identified by AI, **probabilities of occurrence for malfunctions, maintenance requirements**, etc. are determined.
- The determined probabilities of occurrence are used to **initiate concrete processes** and to **derive recommendations for action**. Spare parts can be ordered and kept ready automatically. Maintenance and cleaning measures are triggered when the systems are still functioning smoothly.

Figure 3.43 shows the **interaction of different internal and external data sources** described above (cf. Hoong, 2013, p. 14).

> **Memory Box**
> The **core of predictive maintenance** is the **proactive recognition of the need for action for the maintenance, repair**, etc. of machines and systems—even before malfunctions occur. For this purpose, relevant data are evaluated in real time to determine the optimal time for "intervention." The necessary spare parts, etc. can be ordered in good time.
>   This can reduce downtimes and better control the deployment of service staff. In addition, stock-keeping for necessary spare parts, etc. can be

(continued)

improved. In the next step, impulses for the further development of machines and systems can be gained from the data obtained.

Predictive maintenance is already used in many areas today. These include the monitoring of engines, turbines, etc. (e.g., in aircrafts, ships, cars), wind turbines, production plants, lifts as well as pipelines, etc. There are few limits to the creativity of further fields of application. Predictive maintenance can systematically **reduce downtimes in production, increase plant productivity** (less downtime), **reduce maintenance costs,** and **lower monitoring costs**.

The **concept of predictive maintenance** also enables new business models, which have already been presented in Sect. 3.2.5.5 under the term subscription models. Instead of selling equipment or aggregates (such as printing machines, lifts, or turbines), customers are sold an "availability." The corresponding pricing concepts are **power-by-the-hour, pay-per-use, pay-per-part, pay-per-lux**—or simply: **pay-as-you-go**.

A comprehensive and continuous exchange of information between manufacturer and users often results in much more intensive customer relationships. The company's responsibility no longer ends with the delivery of a product, but only with its end of use. This delivery represents the **intersection between a product-oriented and a service-oriented sphere in the manufacturer-customer relationship** (cf. Fig. 3.22).

The basic idea of predictive maintenance can also be applied in the consumer market. Here we can speak of **predictive servicing**. The prerequisites are created by the **Internet of Things** and the ability of everyday objects to receive and send information online. These developments can not only meet consumer expectations for simplicity, but also meet the goals of businesses.

An example of predictive servicing is provided by the *Nespresso* **Prodigio Titan** machine. As it says here (cf. Nespresso, 2021): The *Prodigio* is the first *Nespresso* machine that can communicate directly with your smartphone or tablet via Bluetooth smart technology. Enjoy our coffee range in a whole new way with the benefits of the *Nespresso* App. Keep track of your capsule supply, plan the timing of your moments of enjoyment, start the brewing process remotely, and get reminders to service your machine.

Such a **comprehensive service** is possible because not only can the machine communicate, but customers have also "outed" themselves in terms of data via membership in the *Nespresso* **Club**. At the same time, the purchasing behavior of the different colored coffee capsules can be used to draw conclusions about enjoyment preferences, so that tailor-made offers can be made.

The *Nespresso* **system** already indicates when the capsule supply is running low via the app. To do this, the average future consumption, the time needed to make a decision (one press of a button is enough to reorder) as well

(continued)

as the time needed for shipping are taken into account. In the future, this can even be done in advance—based on predictive analytics. Because my provider knows that I drink more coffee in winter and prefer the stronger roasts, a supply package can be sent to me in advance—without any action on my part. The basis of this **anticipatory shipping** is the intelligent processing of all this data. Here it also becomes clear why the term **predictive servicing** (instead of predictive maintenance) is appropriate for this advanced service.

Memory Box

The concept of **predictive servicing** still offers largely untapped **growth potential for companies.** The following applies: If the customer is looked after competently and proactively in this service world, his willingness to switch to other providers decreases! In this way, you can increase the customer value for your company.

In many companies, the task of raising the comprehensive potential described here lies with a **COO**, a **Chief Operating Officer/Chief Operation Officer**. This person is not only responsible for the operational business, but also regularly participates in the further development of the operational processes in the conception and implementation phase.

Think Box: Questions You Should Ask Yourself
- How systematically do you examine your value chain to identify the causes of competitive advantages in your own company as well as in other companies?
- Do you analyze the value chain to identify additional potential for achieving competitive advantages for your own company?
- How intensively is your value chain already linked with the value chains of other upstream and/or downstream actors?
- What potential does your company have for building value chains?
- Is there a systematic review of how digitalization of your own value chain can be used to reduce costs, generate additional benefits, and/or develop new business models?
- What approaches do you see to complement your classic value chain with a digital (informational) value chain?
- Can you develop predictive maintenance concepts for your company?
- Are there any recognizable starting points for predictive servicing for your company?
- Who systematically analyzes such questions for you?

3.3.2 Ecosystems

The best way to predict the future is—to connect it!

In the digital age, **ecosystems** are becoming increasingly important in building digital excellence. A user no longer has to leave these closed systems, which are often built by a company, even if he or she wants to use completely different applications. The challenge here is called **seamless integration.** This means the "seamless integration" of different applications whose common use by the customer could previously only be achieved by overcoming interfaces of varying complexity. Ideally, an **ecosystem** is then created.

For **advertising companies**, an additional exciting effect occurs here: the user signals—documented in data—and the advertising approaches mutually reinforce each other in an **efficiency and effectiveness spiral**. More data from different sources lead to better ads, lead to more clicks and better deals, lead to higher revenues and provide further data for the optimization of the ads, which again lead to more clicks and better ads, which attract further advertising companies, which place further ads, which ...

In this context, algorithms play a key role. That is why they are explained here in detail. An **algorithm** is an **instruction to work**. More precisely, an algorithm can also be defined as a **formal rule for the sequence of operations** or as a **sequence of steps for the automatic execution of a certain task**. The task can be a calculation, solving a problem or making a decision. An **algorithm is valid** if the following **conditions** are met:

- **Finiteness of the calculation**
  Algorithms must produce results within a manageable time window.
- **Clarity of definition**
  Algorithms shall be written in clear and precise language.
- **Effectiveness of the work instruction**
  Algorithms should solve the problem for which they were developed.

The selection of content presented to us on *Amazon, Facebook, Google, Instagram, Parship, Tinder, Twitter, Zalando* & Co. is each based on an algorithm understood in this way. This algorithm decides what we see or do not see. A variety of algorithms are also used in autonomous driving (including route planning) and in determining creditworthiness.

> **Memory Box**
> Algorithms determine ever larger areas of our private and professional lives—often without us noticing!

3.3.2.1 Analysis of Selected Ecosystems
- The ecosystem of *Alphabet*

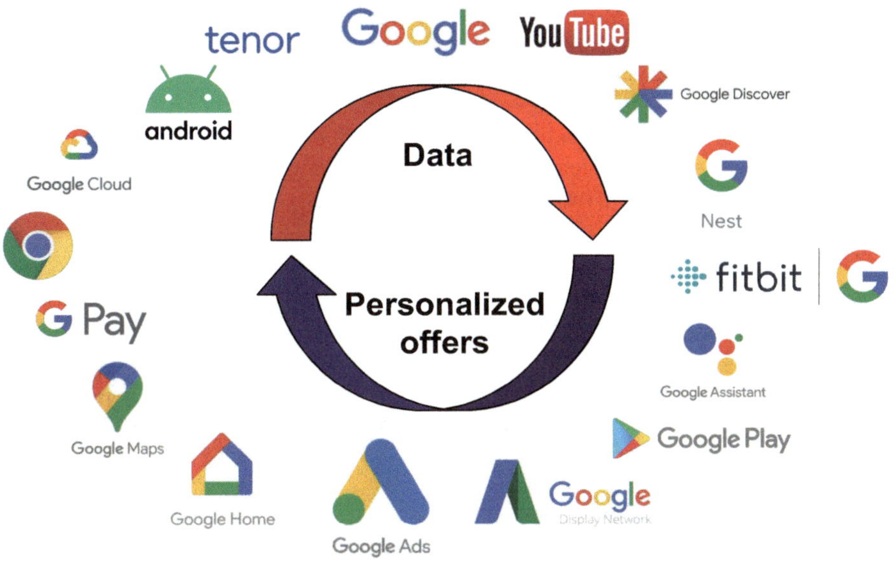

3.3 Digitalization of the Value Chain

Fig. 3.44 Ecosystem of *Alphabet*

Alphabet, the parent company of **Google**, provides an example of a comprehensive ecosystem (cf. Fig. 3.44). The central data source for this is first of all the approx. 100 billion **search queries** that are made worldwide—per month. In addition, exciting information about the acceptance of advertising offers is obtained through the *Google Ads* **advertising offers**—either on a person basis or at least on the basis of IP addresses. The appreciation of further content by users can be determined by evaluating the accesses to the video platform *YouTube*, which belongs to *Google*. In addition, about 75% of the smartphones in use worldwide use the *Google* operating system *Android*. There are also wristwatches on offer that also use *Android* and further feed the data stream.

This already lays the foundation for *Google's* own ecosystem. *Google* also offers its own hardware products. These are supplemented for the Internet infrastructure with its own satellites and access to private homes via the service provider *Nest*, which can monitor and control the home climate. This creates a ***Google*-owned platform** that gives rise to a **smart landscape** with a multitude of its own developments and comprehensive networking.

The **24/7 bubbling data sources** enable **smart advertising** on a scale tailored to individuals, which brings beads of sweat to the foreheads of competitors and data protectionists. Finally, *Google* can target its ad delivery on data that not only comes from search activity, but also includes viewing and usage behavior on *YouTube* as well as on the websites in the *Google Display Network*. Downloads from the *Google Play Store* also provide relevant data for the targeted playout of advertising. This data is also used by *Google Discover* as a push channel—as opposed to keyword ads.

The acquisition of fitness tracker *Fitbit* for US-$ 2.1 billion, approved in 2020, now also gives the group access to **health and wellness data**. We will see what business models can be developed based on this data base!

At the same time, *Google* is developing into a **one-stop shopping platform for information**—without a paywall for users. Through the cooperation with journalistic content providers agreed in 2020, *Google* is now also allowed to present content that was previously often found behind the paywalls of the content providers. Therefore, it can be said:

Google **is no longer reduced to finding answers.**
Google **itself becomes the answer!**

At the same time, *Google* as a **digital gatekeeper** can decide relatively autonomously which content fits its own value system and its own business model and is displayed algorithm-based—and which content is not displayed!

A commercially oriented private company becomes a **digital censor**—and almost all users allow this without complaint!

A little tip

Check once with https://myactivity.google.com/more-activity which data *Google* has stored about you. At this point you can also control the **traceability of your activities by *Google***. Under "other activities" you will find the settings for *Google* advertising that are tailored to your person. You'll also find some information about your *YouTube* feedback, your answers to *YouTube* surveys, your comments on *YouTube* videos, your comments on *YouTube* community posts, your "like" and "dislike" ratings on *YouTube*, your *YouTube* purchasing activity, your responses to locations, your suggested responses to location questions, your interests and notifications on *YouTube*, and call and message information.

If you use *Google* services such as **Google Fi** and **Google Voice** to call, receive calls, or send and receive messages from others, *Google* may store information about your call or message history. In addition, *Google* stores **Google Play library settings** (e.g., purchases of apps, movies, and books), your news settings, purchases and reservations made through **Google Search, Google Maps** and **Google Assistant.**

In addition, information about your podcast subscriptions in the **Google app**, your answers in **Google surveys** and your data archiving history are stored there. This shows what you have created, downloaded, and exported in your *Google* products. Through the "Download data from 'My Activities'" feature, you can export your data shown in "My Activities." If you participate in **Google research studies**, your answers may also be stored in your **Google Account**. Your ***Chrome* history** is also recorded here, as well as other information about bookmarks, passwords, and other synced data.

If you have **product price tracking** in use, the corresponding data can be found here. In addition, your ***Google* Shopping ordering activity**, ***Google* Assistant history,** and any registration for ***Voice Match*** and ***Face Match*** can be found here. Your feedback on ***Google* Play Books**, your choice of translation languages, and information about how you use "Dictionary" and "Pronunciation" in ***Google* Search** are also stored here. The ***Stadia* Store** allows you to view your ***Stadia* Store activity,** including purchases, subscriptions, code redemptions, and other requested content.

Fig. 3.45 Ecosystem of *Amazon*

Assistant Memory shows you the information that the *Google Assistant* should remember for you. Additionally, it contains information about your business that *Google* has collected from you.
That's all it is!

- **The ecosystem of *Amazon***
  Amazon is also striving to build up a highly developed ecosystem (cf. Fig. 3.45). *Amazon* is an unbeatable competitor for other providers primarily because it consistently uses its cost advantages—above all the **economies of scale**—to further expand its market position. In many cases, this destroys a previously **learned price level**. *Amazon Prime* customers and also frequent customers no longer pay shipping costs. This important competitive advantage also kills the **loyalty of customers** to previous suppliers, which has often been built up over years (see also Sect. 3.2.9.1 on *Amazon's* overall business development).
  Today, *Amazon* offers a **wide range of services**. These range from classic logistics tasks to payment functions and cloud services. At the same time, *Amazon* is developing more and more in the direction of a media company, because it not only distributes content, but is also increasingly getting involved in content production itself (for example, through films with *Amazon Prime*). In 2021 *Amazon* has acquired *Metro-Goldwyn-Mayer* (*MGM*) film studios. *Amazon* paid around US-$ 8.45 billion for *MGM*. That is the second-largest acquisition in the history of *Amazon*, following its purchase of the organic supermarket chain *Whole Foods* in 2017 for just under US-$ 14 billion.
  Amazon is also increasingly developing from an **online retailer** into a **hardware manufacturer**. The company not only offers the *kindle* e-book reader, but

has expanded its own range with products such as *Fire* tablets, *Fire* TV sticks, and *Fire* TV cubes. In addition, a whole range of products is offered under the name ***Amazon Basics***. This ranges from headphones and speakers to camera accessories, batteries, office supplies, shelves, bedding, kitchen and household appliances, bathroom products, travel accessories, products for sports, camping and gardening, and offers for pets. ***Amazon Essentials*** currently offers clothing items for women, men, and girls. However, this should only be the beginning!

At the same time, *Amazon* got into offering **cloud services** early on. In addition, *Amazon* is active as an advertising platform with retail media and thus competes with *Facebook* and *Google* in particular. **Retail media** refers to the possibility of placing ads within online shops and on marketplaces. In this way, paid hits are presented in addition to the organic search results. These are marked with the word "sponsored."

- **The ecosystem of *Facebook***

If you analyze ***Facebook's*** ecosystem, you can quickly see how consistently it has worked towards **merging different platforms**. *Facebook* started as a social network and added *Instagram* in 2012, *WhatsApp* and *Oculus* (producer of virtual reality headsets) in 2014, and *Giphy* in 2020. *Giphy* is an online database and search engine that allows users to search and share animated GIF files. Features such as the marketplace, groups, feed, and messenger were added over time.

Through *Facebook, Facebook Messenger,* and *WhatsApp*, the *Facebook* group dominates **online communication** today. Through *Instagram, Facebook* is also well positioned in the **video and image world** and ties millions of users here—every day. In addition to the feeds in the *Facebook* ecosystem, you can place ads in the story formats, in-stream videos, *Facebook* search, instant articles, and apps. The continuous information cycle also keeps this advertising machine running and—supported by our data—makes it better and better (cf. Fig. 3.46).

Due to the change of the algorithm, *Facebook* is reducing the **organic reach** more and more and today it is in the low single digits—at least when they have gained a larger fan base. This means that only 2 or 3% of your *Facebook* fans can still see your posts today—and the trend is still falling!

But *Facebook* has created a solution for this as well: you simply have to stick **social media stamps** on your posts and your posts will be comprehensively delivered again as **promoted posts**! *Facebook* can also change its algorithms overnight as it sees fit—and social media content is already played out significantly better or worse. And no one can do anything about it as long as they don't want to opt out (keyword "privatization of the right" in Sect. 3.3.3.4).

The important data streams do not only come from the various apps, the engagement in the news feeds and the likes, shares, and comments. They are also collected via websites that offer a **social log-in** by "logging in with *Facebook*." This data is also partially available to advertising partners. By using such data, competitors can of course also be fended off.

Facebook's ecosystem can be described as a **digital perpetual motion machine**—it continuously gains power from itself through further data and thus

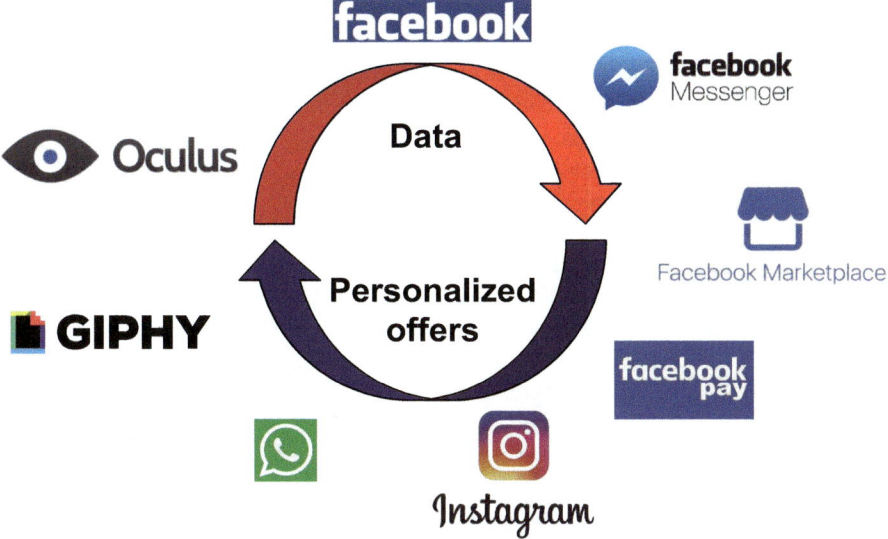

Fig. 3.46 Ecosystem of *Facebook*

becomes better and better in addressing customers (and its possibilities for manipulation) as well as in its advertising effect for companies!

> **Memory Box**
> **Ecosystems promote customer loyalty!** Finally—fed by countless data—more and more suitable offers can be made. As a result, the barriers to market entry for competitors are getting higher and higher!
> The—foreseeable—result: **the winner takes it all!**

▶ **Food for Thought**
A *Facebook* **study** commissioned by the company itself showed the insights this company can gain from the likes achieved alone. This study involved 86,220 volunteers with *Facebook* accounts. They had to fill out a comprehensive **questionnaire about their personality**. The challenge for *Facebook* was to use an algorithm to predict the answers of the study participants based solely on their *Facebook* likes (cf. Youyou et al., 2015). The results were astounding to the point of shocking!

In general, there was—unsurprisingly—an **increase in the quality of the prediction due to the number of likes**. The **predictions** achieved by the algorithm were compared with those of work colleagues, friends, family members, and partners. The following results were obtained:

- Ten *Facebook* **likes** are already enough to surpass a work colleague's assessment.
- With **70** *Facebook* **likes**, the algorithm does better than **friends**.
- By evaluating **150** *Facebook* **likes**, the statements become better than those of one's own **parents**.
- Based on **300** *Facebook* **likes**, the company knows more about you than your own **partner**.

The **depth of knowledg**e even goes beyond the knowledge of the person concerned. Here, the algorithm led to insights that were more precise than the **self-knowledge of the person** concerned. The authors of the study, YouYou et al. (2015) summarize their findings as follows:

"Furthermore, in the future, people might abandon their own psychological judgments and rely on computers when making important life decisions, such as choosing activities, career paths, or even romantic partners. It is possible that such data driven decisions will improve people's lives."

If you are an **active** *Facebook* **user**, *Facebook* also knows your secret wishes, opinions, dreams, expectations, fears, hopes, anxieties—and additionally has the possibilities to "take care" of you individually. Be it through the news in your newsfeed, through the display of advertisements—for whatever offers!

The rules and algorithms used by *Facebook* in this regard remain a **black box** for us as users!

Facebook has the power and the systems to manipulate us all—largely unnoticed. We know this—at least in part—and allow it to happen day after day.

The companies *Amazon, Facebook,* and *Google* originally started with a single platform. Step by step, they have developed or acquired further applications to build up their **ecosystem**. The data streams based on concrete behavior or behavioral intentions allow for **better and better advertising**, which leads to **higher revenues** and enables **expansion of the business model** at almost any price. A look at the market capitalization of these companies—i.e., their stock market value—underlines this assessment.

The next stage is called **ambient computing**: IT- and AI-enabled services should surround us wherever we are. One step in this direction is the *Amazon Halo* service presented by *Amazon* (see Sect. 3.2.9.1).

- **The ecosystem of** *Apple*
  Apple has built up an ecosystem that is **not dependent on advertising** (cf. Fig. 3.47). *Apple* initially started—almost forgotten—with the manufacture of computers. The foray into consumer electronics was completed in 2007 with a change of name from *Apple Computer Inc.* to *Apple Inc.* Finally, the company name was changed according to the products and services offered. Today, *Apple* is holistically about convenience, about **seamless integration** of the various *Apple* hardware and software offerings. Above

Fig. 3.47 Ecosystem of *Apple*

all, however, it is about the goal of ensuring the greatest possible added value for *Apple*. *Apple* has achieved a remarkable feat in the **compatibility of its offerings**: anyone who has ever wanted to connect *iPhone, iPad,* and other *Apple* devices knows that "plug and play" can actually work!

In order to serve users as comprehensively as possible, the original **hardware manufacturer has evolved into a portal provider**. With *iTunes, Apple* offers immediate user benefits through the integrated cloud applications. These include playing, converting, burning, organizing and buying music, audio books, podcasts, and films. The *Apple Music* and *Apple TV* offerings are also integrated into this cocoon.

The user—"captivated" by these offers—should stay as long as possible and undisturbed in the *Apple* world. This avoids touch points with other brands and companies. *Apple Pay* gives the user the opportunity to stay in the *Apple* world for many payment transactions. This generates not only additional revenue for *Apple*, but also further data on the previously unrecognizable purchasing behavior of users in a wide variety of life situations.

▶ **Food for Thought**
Such a constellation becomes problematic when—for example, in the *App Store*—*Apple's* own services come up against competing offers. The *Apple Music* app and *Spotify* come to mind here. Who will, who can only win or lose?

Apple **is the gatekeeper here—and gatekeepers have a lot of power!**

To **carve out further competitive advantages**, *Apple* has also been increasingly involved in **developing its own computer chips**. What began in 2010 with the first *Apple* chip now permeates the entire *Apple* product range. Now it also applies to the central computing and control components: chips designed by *Apple*.

3.3.2.2 Analysis of the Effects of Ecosystems on Competition

The developments just presented illustrate that **business models** that previously functioned undisturbed side by side are now increasingly competing with each other. *Amazon* and *Netflix*, along with *YouTube*, are becoming increasingly strong competitors of the **traditional TV broadcasters**. Hardware providers like *Apple* are becoming content providers through *Apple Music* and *Apple TV*. The TV program providers themselves are entering the domain of publishers and other content providers even more strongly through their apps and media library offerings. In addition, competition between existing competitors will become fiercer. An end to the **shift and overcoming of industry boundaries** is not yet in sight.

▶ **Food for Thought**

In many areas, a comprehensive **shift of industry boundaries** is taking place, which goes hand in hand with a **redefinition of business areas** across industries. This is creating more and more ecosystems that comprehensively integrate customers and make it more difficult for competitors to enter. The barriers to market entry are increasing!

The central question for you is:

How do I position my business model in this environment?

For customers, many of the emerging ecosystems offer a decisive advantage: **convenience**. This is because the services that the companies offer within their own ecosystems are highly interconnected and enable the seamless integration already mentioned. For the offering companies themselves, there are three decisive **advantages of ecosystems**:

- Each ecosystem dramatically increases the **barriers to switching** for users—that fosters **customer loyalty**.
- The longer a customer is on the road in his or her own ecosystem, the more extensive the **data sources** bubble up. The information gained here can be used to an even greater extent for individualized offers.
- At the same time, this creates high **market entry barriers for alternative providers**.

If the companies convince with their services in the long term, a new currency is created at the same time:

comprehensive trust!

The trust gained further reduces the barriers to market entry already erected for third parties.

Memory Box

Simple **user identification** becomes the central element of ecosystems. In future, I will no longer have to register—I will be recognized by my service partner: device-, channel-, place-, and time-independent! The resulting convenience can lead to users no longer being able to get out of this finely spun cocoon—or not wanting to!

Therefore, whoever is at the **forefront of identification** has direct contact with the user and is in the key position when it comes to acquiring further data and selling additional services!

The extent to which **concentration through ecosystems** has already reached is elaborated in the *Atlas of the Digital World* by Andree and Thomsen (2020). In the meantime, it is already the order of the day to critically question the **market power of GAFA companies**. Until now, however, it has been difficult to determine the **extent of digital concentration** more precisely. After all, these companies are good at keeping their market shares secret. An exciting approach to determining market power is the **type and intensity of use of different online offerings** in Germany. This was determined in the present study by five criteria:

- Which websites were visited?
- How long did the users stay there?
- How was the online time distributed among different offers, such as shopping, news, social media?
- From which pages did users switch to which pages?
- To which groups do the corresponding offers belong?

The underlying data collection period was the third quarter of 2019. The total German population over 14 years of age was taken into account. All end devices (desktop, smartphone, tablet) were combined. According to the results of this study, the **seven largest digital companies** managed to attract more than 50% of the total online usage to their sites. The **shares of online traffic of the top 10 sites and top 10 apps** by group affiliation look like this (cf. **Andree & Thomsen, 2020, p. 28**):

- *Alphabet*: 18.6%
  - *YouTube*: 13.2%
  - *Google*: 5.4%
- *Facebook group*: 15.6%
  - *Facebook*: 7.4%
  - *WhatsApp* 6.8%
  - *Instagram*: 1.4%
- *Apple*: 8%

(continued)

- *Amazon*: 3.9%
- *eBay*: 1.8%
- *Web.de*: 1.5%
- *Spotify*: 1.3%

The **quintessence of the analysis** is that the **concentration of online traffic** on only a very few corporations is still much greater than often assumed. The **usage shares of the other providers** are vanishingly small. Overall, 71.8% of the time spent on the Internet is concentrated on the 100 most frequently used Internet addresses. The users analyzed here accessed a total of 131,993 websites and apps in the 3-month survey period. They devoted 85.8% of their online time to the 500 strongest providers—although these 500 strongest providers only account for 0.38% of the online offering (cf. **Andree & Thomsen,** 2020**, p. 28**).

▶ **Food for Thought**
The **concentration effects** visible here once again support the criticism of the **long-tail approach** already expressed in Sect. 3.2.7.2. It is not the case that everyone has the same opportunity in the online sector! Mega and niche providers can exist side by side—but with serious differences in the achievable added value!

The study by Andree and Thomsen (2020) also shows the effects that **GAFA companies** in particular have been able to achieve by **building up ecosystems**. The underlying data for the analysis of the *Facebook* group is based on the November 2019 data collection period. Here, too, the total German population over the age of 14 was considered. The end devices required for online access (desktop, smartphone, tablet) were also combined here. According to this analysis, 36% of all users end up on another service of the *Facebook* group—i.e., *Instagram* or *WhatsApp*—after using *Facebook*. This is astonishing because *Facebook's* market share of total online traffic is only 7.4% (for more details cf. **Andree & Thomsen,** 2020**, S. 205**)

Staying in one's own ecosystem is sometimes deliberately induced. After all, *Instagram* prohibits links that lead away from *Instagram*. *Facebook* wants to keep users in its own ecosystem in order to suck data and generate advertising revenue. Therefore, external links cannot be posted in captions or in comments. External links can only be shared in one's own *Instagram* bio. In this way, *Instagram* systematically prevents users from migrating to other websites through external links!

Comparable results were found for *Alphabet*, the parent company of *Google* and *YouTube*. When users click on something on these platforms, 35% of them stay within the *Alphabet* family! Although this group "only" covers 19% of online traffic, users are kept within its own offerings to a large extent.

▶ **Food for Thought**
We should always bear in mind that the **digital corporations**, despite **harmless-sounding slogans** to the contrary such as:

- "*Facebook* helps you connect and share with people in your life."
- "Don't be evil." (*Google*)
- "Fast beautiful photo sharing." (*Instagram*)
- "Broadcast yourself." (*YouTube*)
- "Sweeten your day." (*TikTok*)
- "Simple. Personal. Real time messaging." (*WhatsApp*)

primarily pursue **commercial goals**. These companies systematically strive to make us dependent on these platforms so that we spend more and more time on them. In this way, they can suck data and generate advertising revenue. The more precisely the providers know us, the more specifically they can inform us and also manipulate us. After all, they know our pain points—because we make them visible through our actions. Their algorithms continuously generate **digital narcotics**—and we become addicted faster than we think! Only one thing helps against this: **building media literacy**!

▶ **Food for Thought**
In the 21st century, our personal data is probably the most valuable resource most people still have, and we hand it over to the tech giants in exchange for e-mail services and funny cat videos (Harari, 2018, p. 460).

Let's be aware of the **opportunities and risks of these ecosystems**—from a business and customer perspective alike. We also need to ask ourselves how we deal with these ecosystems as a company. After all, we can and could use much of the data generated there for our own business model. However, the ecosystems of the GAFA companies are a so-called **walled garden**.

These companies only make selected technology-, media-, and/or user-related information available to their business partners. They want to maintain an invisible **information monopoly** for themselves, on which the advertising companies are dependent. This is why the term "walled" is used. Here, too, dependencies are created quite deliberately—this time on the part of the advertising companies.

The GAFA companies are therefore also called **frenemies**—they are **friends** and **enemies** in equal measure! Such a false friend either falsely pretends to be a friend although he is an enemy. Or it is an enemy with whom you are compelled to maintain a friendly relationship because you depend on their support. Unfortunately, this is true for the majority of companies until the **information monopolies** are broken up. Whether and, if so, when this will happen is uncertain. Our business models must therefore make do with the (informationally) limited access to these walled gardens.

> **Memory Box**
> The **rise of digitalization** seems to be accompanied by a **retreat of competition**. Finally, we see more and more "**the-winner-takes-it-all**" situations. We are witnessing markets increasingly dominated by **overpowering players** (cf. Wambach & Müller, 2018).

▶ **Food for Thought**
The **ecosystems of GAFA companies** make them not only **gatekeepers**, but also **gatebouncers**. These decide which companies are granted what kind of access. Due to the still unchecked growth of these companies, they control **access to the digital world** to an ever greater extent—for companies and private users alike!

However, the following still applies to these companies today:
Too big to care!
This statement applies in two directions. On the one hand, the **GAFAM companies** can afford to impose **conditions on the extraction and use of data** on users at will because of their size and the dominance that comes with it. They do not really have to care about the customers' concerns (e.g., regarding data use). On the other hand, most users simply cannot afford to do without these services. In certain fields, customers simply have no other choice or alternatives are much more cumbersome to use. As a result, GAFAM & Co. hardly have to worry about the **(data protection) interests** of their customers.

Against this background, various possibilities are being discussed in the USA and Europe to break the **market power of these digital companies**. The range of considerations extends from breaking up the corporations to defining "blacklists" that reveal unauthorized business practices to banning platform operators from offering their own products and/or services on them. The future will show which side wins: the **regulators** or the **digital companies**.

In the **ecosystems** described above, one company sits in each case like the **spider in the web**—and all or the vast majority of the services are provided by the company itself. Such an approach is easy to demonstrate due to the profitability already achieved in at least some areas of these companies. If you do not work in one of these companies, **looking into setting up your own ecosystem** is an exciting challenge for you. Such a development can be tackled alone, but mostly together with partners.

Such concepts are being discussed in the **insurance industry**, for example. The question here is whether insurance will be marketed in the future as an integral part of "mobility services," as an integrated component in the area of "living" and/or woven into the overall complex of "health/fitness." After all, a person usually does not wake up in the morning and decide to take out a new insurance contract. The starting point of such a decision process is usually **changes in life circumstances**—e.g., buying or selling a car, moving house, getting married, or significant changes in one's state of health.

Integrated solutions are also being discussed in the **real estate sector**. These include not only the provision of living space, but also the provision of water, energy, Internet, and TV/radio as well as services that accompany the home (such as household insurance). A further step goes via the **smart home** in the direction of a comprehensive networking of all possible household appliances—possibly coupled with automated ordering processes (e.g., for detergent, coffee). In addition, insurance services can be integrated here.

In the context of **age-appropriate living**, AI-supported monitoring systems can be integrated for senior citizens in order to enable older people to live in their traditional homes for as long as possible. These include the areas of telemedicine, elderly care, and ambient assisted living (cf. Kreutzer & Sirrenberg, 2019, p. 205f.).

Such ecosystems are also being considered in the **automotive industry**. A comprehensive **mobility ecosystem for private individuals** would include the production and distribution of vehicles. In addition, such a system could provide a wide range of services for automobiles, as well as local and long-distance public transport, taxis, ride-sharing, car/bike/scooter sharing, traffic news, navigation, entertainment, shopping, restaurants, hotels, parking, etc. The fact that approaches of such systems are not always crowned with success becomes clear from the example of *Moovel*. The *Daimler AG* subsidiary was taken over by *Reach Now* in 2020—and not because *Moovel* was so successful!

Banks must overcome their **product thinking**. Banks still operate far too strongly in product worlds from C for call money, F for fixed-term deposit, H for home financing, I for installment loan to S for share purchase.

> **Memory Box**
> Therefore, other **focal points for ecosystems** include **entertainment, travel, living, cooking, education**, etc. Again, **"think big"**—to exploit the opportunities offered by the Internet of Everything!
> **Customers are looking for solutions to specific life tasks!**
> **Customers are looking for solutions to problems—not just products!**
> In all these cases, the challenge is to **partner with companies from outside the industry** to jointly offer products and services to customers in an ecosystem. **Building ecosystems**—besides the challenge of joint development—comes with the following **benefits**:
>
> (continued)

- **Cooperation with partners from outside the own industry** enlarges the creative pool and, through **sector diversity**, overcomes thinking and acting on well-worn tracks. This opens up **new perspectives for growth and value creation**.
- Ecosystems make it easier to obtain a **critical mass of customer, usage, and environment data**. This is necessary to develop **attractive offers** for customers and to market them profitably.
- Cooperation with several partners not only increases the **resources that can be used** for development. **Access to the partners' existing customer bases** and the **integrated use of sales power** also contribute to increasing the probability of success.

Should you embark on such a journey? The answer to this is clear. The turnover of the **500 largest German companies** increases continuously when they use **ecosystems** (cf. Accenture, 2020, p. 8). In this regard, this *Accenture* study (, 2020, p. 36) so aptly states:

"Top 500 corporations that want to pursue ambitious corporate strategies must master the transfer of innovations into business models and their subsequent scaling. One of the core competencies of scaling is building ecosystems in digital infrastructures. In these, more data can be generated and analyzed and used for deeper customer understanding."

▶ **Food for Thought**

Think big and examine the potential for your company to build an ecosystem with non-industry partners in which your own offers are woven in as an indispensable component. If you can become the **dominant partner**, you should give the go-ahead for the development yourself. Otherwise, it is still better to be a **service partner** of such a system—than to stand on the sidelines.

However, one thing is indispensable here:

Break the existing industry boundaries through your creativity!

We should also be aware of one thing: homogeneous or more homogeneous markets, such as those offered by the USA and China in terms of language, currency, distribution systems, etc. in comparison with Europe, facilitate scaling and thus promote profitable growth. That is why it is so important for many other countries to achieve **economies of scale through cooperation!**

The challenge is to scale fast!

> **Think Box: Questions You Should Ask Yourself**
> - Can your industry and thus also your company be threatened by ecosystems?
> - How important have ecosystems already become in your industry?
> - Who are the central drivers behind such developments?
> - What effects on your business model are associated with the shift in industry boundaries that can be observed in many cases?
> - In your market, does a cross-industry redefinition of business fields bring opportunities or risks for your company?
> - How can your business model be positioned in this environment?
> - What opportunities does your company have to win in the quest for ever more convenience for customers?
> - How can your business model help you to identify customers easily and quickly—without much effort for our customers?
> - Have you ever looked into setting up your own ecosystem—alone or with partners?
> - In whose area of responsibility do these questions fall?

3.3.3 Platform Concepts

3.3.3.1 Types of Platform Concepts

The terms **platform concepts** and **ecosystems** are often used synonymously. In my view, this is not purposeful. As was made clear in Sect. 3.3.2, **ecosystems** involve customers very comprehensively and try to offer a **variety of services from a single source**. The aim is to keep customers with one provider for as long as possible. As a result, the data streams continue to flow better and better, which makes it possible to continuously improve one's own performance—especially in the playout of advertising and other content.

In **ecosystems**, too, **platforms** are indeed used in most cases. This is the case with all the providers described in Sect. 3.3.2. These companies have either already started with platforms (such as *Amazon, Facebook,* and *Google*) or have added a platform at a later stage (such as *Apple*). However, not all existing platforms have succeeded so far, nor do all of these platforms have the potential to be further developed into ecosystems. *Airbnb, Lyft,* and *Uber* come to mind here. These platforms are used today for the temporary rental of living space or for the demand for transport services—and (so far) not for much else! Whether these platforms can be developed into ecosystems remains to be seen.

When discussing **platforms**, a distinction must be made between different forms. In this section, in addition to **communication platforms**, **transaction platforms** are of particular importance (cf. Haller & Wissing, 2018, pp. 174–176; Brynjolfsson &

McAfee, 2018; Müller & Wrobel, 2021, pp. 196–198). However, the different variants cannot always be neatly demarcated.

Communication platforms (also called **social platforms**) include *Facebook, Instagram, Twitter, WeChat, WhatsApp,* and *YouTube.* **Rating platforms** (such as *Yelp*) and **educational platforms** (such as *Udemy, Wikipedia*) can also be classified here. Furthermore, there are **innovation platforms** that bring together companies and creative people to jointly develop solutions to problems. **Workforce platforms** (such as *Angie's List, Bookatiger, Fiverr, Helpling, HomeStars, MyHammer, TaskRabbi*t) are used by people to offer their labor. Another category is **industry platforms**, which focus on IIOT applications.

The focus of **transaction platforms** is not only on classic **e-commerce**, but also covers the fields of **mobility, accommodation,** and **utilities.** The following providers, among others, come to mind here:

Platforms for shopping

- *AboutYou*
- *Amazon/Amazon Prime*
- *Alibaba*
- *Apple/Apple App Store*
- *autoscout24*
- *DeliveryHero*
- *eBay*
- *Google/Google Play Store*
- *immobilienscout24*
- *Zalando Zircle*

Platforms for accommodation

- *Airbnb*
- *booking.com*
- *HRS*
- *Tripadvisor*

Platforms for mobility

- *BlaBlaCar*
- *Jelbi*
- *Flixbus*
- *Free Now*
- *Uber*

Platforms for energy, telephone, and insurance contracts

- *Check24*
- *Idealo*
- *Verivox*

Many other platforms have already been established or are in the process of being established.

3.3.3.2 Characterization of Platform Concepts

Regardless of whether a platform can later be developed into an ecosystem or not, **platform models** are exciting for companies and demanders alike. Many platforms are **two-sided markets** that are connected via a platform. A platform should bring together as **many suppliers** as possible on one side and as **many demanders** as possible on the other. The attractiveness of the platforms is based on the resulting **positive network effects**. Many providers are interesting for the demanders. Consequently, demanders go where many suppliers are to be found because they expect a large selection and possibly high price pressure. Many demanders are also relevant for the suppliers. Therefore, suppliers (with their offers and their advertising) go where they can reach many demanders through one channel. Such an approach is simply efficient and effective!

The more hotels a platform like *booking*.com or *HRS* has as providers, the more attractive the platforms are for demanders. And the more demanders a platform attracts, the greater the attractiveness for the providers. Both sides are pushing each other up here. This also creates **lock-in effects**. People feel comfortable on a platform and stay there because switching would involve monetary or physical costs.

We speak of **negative network effects** when the benefit decreases as the number of people increases. This is the case, for example, on congested motorways or when intensive access to a website causes the IT system to crash.

> **Memory Box**
>
> The one who can tap into (positive) network effects first often achieves an uncatchable lead!
>
> The main thing here is: **platforms are great—especially for the operators!**
>
> This whole process is further "lubricated" by **data as the new oil**. This data keeps such business models running. At the same time, new business models can be developed—supported by data. The classic provider-demand relationships are thus abandoned here in favor of a **marketplace-like concept**.
>
> The attractiveness of the platforms for suppliers and demanders means that **the-winner-takes-it-all situations** often occur here. This means that one platform dominates certain business areas. Here you can think of *Google* for search, *Amazon* for online shopping, *Facebook* for social network communication, *YouTube* for access to video content, and *WhatsApp* for fast communication. Other companies find it very difficult to establish themselves against these top dogs with a similar business model.

> **Memory Box**
> The **acceptance of platforms** increases with their size—and with the ability to map powerful logistics and payment processes. Then the most important currency in the digital age emerges:
> **trust!**
> The more "trust" a platform gains, the greater the **risk for providers to lose the customer interface**. If this happens, one is dependent on the platform, its operator and its business practices, for better or worse. This must be consistently prevented!
> After all, the **platform operators** are in **pole position**: they have all the **transaction data** and often get **paid by both sides**. Since the platform operators (*Airbnb, Amazon Seller Central, eBay, Facebook, Google, Spotify, Uber* & Co. come to mind) in most cases do not create or hold any products or services themselves, the platform business models have a particularly high **scalability**. After all, the platform operators predominantly "only" have to offer convincing IT solutions without taking care of the core of the offers presented there. The majority of providers present on these platforms are largely deprived of opportunities for rapid scaling. After all, the providers have to take care of the—often—physical service delivery! At the same time, by collecting and evaluating data, the platform operators achieve an **information-based competitive advantage** that other companies can hardly catch up on.

3.3.3.3 Presentation and Analysis of Selected Platform Concepts

The **advantages of platform concepts** will be made visible here using selected examples. The **vehicle brokerage and logistics service provider** *Uber* does not own any vehicles itself. Although this company "only" offers a platform, it reached—as already mentioned—a **market capitalization** of US-$ 82 billion at the time of its IPO on 10 May 2019. At that time, this was roughly equivalent to the market capitalization of *Volkswagen*, the world's largest car manufacturer. However, at that time *Volkswagen* had decades of expertise, strong brands (including *Volkswagen, Audi, Skoda, Seat, Lamborghini, Porsche, Bentley, Bugatti*), a large number of production cities and a skilled workforce. Nevertheless, *Uber* was considered to have a more promising future than *Volkswagen*—measured by its stock market value. Further developments will show whether this was justified.

Airbnb practices a comparable business model as an **agent for private accommodation**. Here, too, the core of the business is not the company's own accommodation, but a platform and comprehensive provider and user data. The stock market value for this company was estimated at around US-$ 42 billion at the end of 2020—and this despite the fact that *Airbnb's* IPO prospectus stated (Heise, 2020): "We may never be able to achieve profitability." On 10 December 2020, the day of the IPO, the stock market value was initially US-$ 47 billion—then the price doubled and the stock market value exceeded the US-$ 100 billion mark on the evening of the same day.

▶ **Food for Thought**
However, the **high scalability** of the platform concepts on the one hand indicates that growth is accompanied by a far below-average need for investment. On the other hand, nothing is said about **profitability**. Even if little has to be invested in personnel and IT resources, expansion often requires considerable marketing expenditure. *Amazon*—as already shown—was not profitable for a long time (see Sect. 3.2.9.1). *Airbnb, Netflix, Spotify,* and *Uber* are also still struggling to generate sustainable profits in 2021.

Zalando—similar to *Amazon*—first took the path of building an **online sales platform**. In a second step, these platforms were opened up to third parties. At *Amazon*, this is called the ***Amazon Selling Center***—at *Zalando*, the ***Zalando Partner Program***. *Zalando's* own platform gives its partners access to 30 million customers in 17 European markets. According to the company, more than 450 brands and retailers are already integrated here (cf. Zalando, 2021a). The ***Zalando* fashion store** focuses on convenience for customers: they can access a very large assortment with a large number of brands—via one platform and one customer account (cf. Zalando, 2021b). The suppliers can benefit from *Zalando's* e-commerce expertise—but they pay for it with a great dependence on the platform. After all, the platform not only pays for the various services, but also pools all sales-related data. The direct contact to the end customer is taken over by *Zalando*.

In order to generate further sources of revenue, platform providers such as *Amazon Prime* and *Netflix* are also moving towards producing their own content. *Amazon* itself also offers its own products under *Amazon Basics* and *Amazon Essential*s as well as under labels that are not immediately recognizable as *Amazon* brands (e.g., clothing, food, furniture; see Sect. 3.2.9.1 for more details).

Memory Box
Once a platform is established, it can change the rules to its own liking. Not only the partners operating on the platform have to follow suit. Platforms can also set the pace for the entire industry.

We see a similar development with *Check 24* and *Verivox*. *Check 24* and *Verivox* have long ceased to be neutral **comparison portals**. They are increasingly becoming **marketing platforms** that receive lavish commissions for brokering contracts. In 2020, *Check 24* acquired a banking license and will prospectively offer various banking products under *C24*. The website says:

(continued)

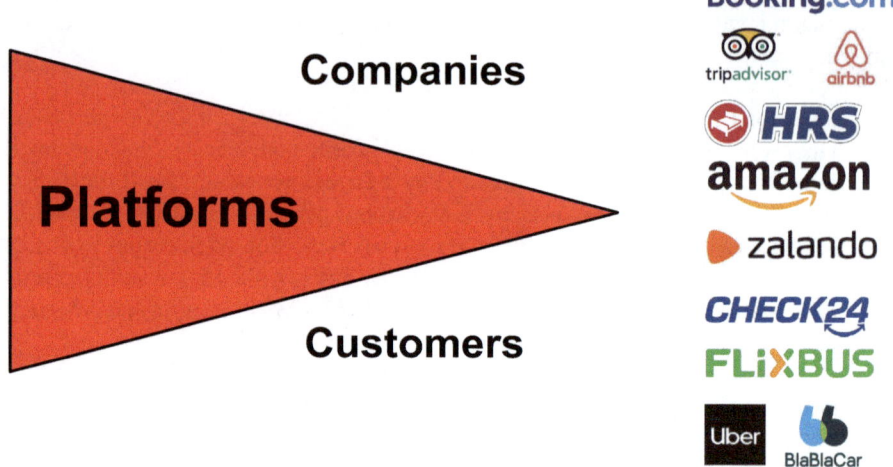

Fig. 3.48 Platforms destroy established customer supplier relationships

> "The open banking platform: experience a new dimension of mobile banking in 2020" (C24, 2020). In building up this additional business area, *Check 24* can build on the data and customer relationships that have been gained or established in the past. In today's world, this is a competitive advantage that should not be underestimated.

Memory Box

Through their **own offers**, **platform owners** become **competitors** of the providers previously represented there—nourished by the data (!) and revenues generated as platform operators. The multitude of data makes it easier for platform operators to expand their platforms into powerful **ecosystems**—and to degrade previous contractual partners into simple suppliers.

The risk is in name:

Platform beats product and platform beats pipeline!

In more and more markets, such **transactional platforms** are inserting themselves between suppliers and demanders, as Fig. 3.48 shows. This leads to a **destruction of the established customer supplier relationships**. With this business model, the platform operator not only extracts a considerable **margin share** from the suppliers—at the same time, it degrades them to mere suppliers who are punished by bad evaluations when not liked in the eyes of

(continued)

the customers and then often simply replaced. At the same time, these platforms continuously gain **information about the market** that the service partners themselves lack. In addition, these platforms have a high **scalability**. This means that 10,000, 100,000 or a million more customers can be served even without large additional investments.

▶ **Food for Thought**
We see a development towards a **platform economy**. The **platform operator** takes the **position of the spider in the web**. He has access to the customers—unfiltered, direct, data-based, and context-oriented. Classical sales channels lose importance if they are not also enriched with data technology. The platforms and the underlying networks transport the new oil: the data! In addition, platforms have a high scalability that facilitates fast and profitable growth.

At the same time, the boundaries between previously neatly separated industries are disappearing. A **convergence of markets and offerings** is taking place here. The competitors of the present and the future no longer come from the circle of "known" challengers in their own industry.

Consequently, all companies must sharpen their **monitoring radar for these developments**.

Although in many cases the focus is on B2C platforms, powerful **B2B platforms** have also been developed in recent years and you should check their relevance for your company:

- Alibaba (2021): Wholesales supply online
- CheMondis (2021): B2B online marketplace for chemicals
- Emarsys (2021): Cloud-based customer engagement platform to merge product, customer, interaction, and user-defined data (*SAP*)
- IBM (2021): Watson Anywhere
- Kaa (2021): Flexible open-source-IOT-platform
- Mercateo (2021): Procurement platform for business customers
- Microsoft Azure (2021): Development of cloud solutions
- MindSphere (2021): Industrial IOT as a service (*Siemens*)
- Oracle (2021): Intelligent applications cloud
- Predix (2021): *Predix* platform (*General Electric*)
- SAP (2021): Industry cloud as innovations platform of *SAP*, on which customers and partners can develop industry-specific cloud solutions and applications
- Scrappel (2021): B2B platform for the trade of scrap and metal
- Skywise (2021): The leading data platform for the aviation industry
- ThingWorx (2021): IIOT platform

- TOII (2021): IOT platform for networking machines from a wide range of manufacturers and generations
- Tontio (2021): Procurement platform for repair and maintenance
- Wucato (2021): The digital procurement platform for companies

If you are responsible for or in a B2B company, then you would be well advised to look for suitable platforms.

3.3.3.4 Strategic Responses to the Advance of Platform Concepts

To survive in the evolving **platform economy**, you have several options:

- Develop a platform alone!
- Develop a platform together with powerful partners (e.g., your biggest competitors)!
- Become a partner of an existing platform!
- Sell your products/services via a platform!
- After careful consideration, continue to work with your traditional business model.

There is only one thing you must not do: ignore platforms!

In your **evaluation of existing platform concepts** you should keep the following aspects in mind:

- The **quality of decisions** can increase if a multitude of relevant information flows together on one platform and is presented here in a processed form.
- A uniform platform for complex processes increases the **transparency of relevant processes**.
- Innovative platform operators provide secure **access to the latest technologies** (build-in updates on the platforms themselves).
- Platforms can support **resource-saving growth processes** of the using companies—especially in the use of capital and personnel.
- However, many platforms stand unconnected to each other and create a **lack of compatibility**.
- In many cases, platforms go hand in hand with a high degree of **complexity**, the mastery of which must first be learned.
- Encryption of data transmission can increase **data security**; at the same time, however, data security is jeopardized by complexity and dependence on external partners.
- Platforms also represent a popular **target for hacker attacks**.

If you want to work out a **business model for your company with its own platform** (possibly with partners), you can use the **platform canvas** already presented in Sect. 3.2.5 (cf. Fig. 3.27).

Fig. 3.49 Platform-centric norm strategies

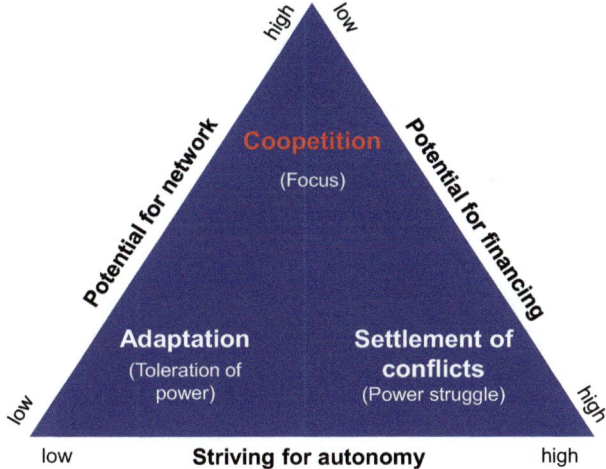

The major **challenge for companies** can be defined as follows (Bughin et al., 2018, p. 7):

"Companies need to change where and how they play—by creating their own network or by partnering with companies within and beyond industry borders."

Value-adding cooperation with competitors is called **coopetition** or **cooperative competition**. Coopetition describes the **overcoming of the duality of competition and cooperation**, which is particularly important in the development of platforms. Coopetition is a portmanteau of the terms cooperation and competition. For most companies, **coopetition** is the only strategy to be successful in building platforms (cf. the example of Körber in Sect. 3.3.4.2).

> **Memory Box**
> **As is true for countries, it is also true for companies:**
>   **companies have no friends, only interests!**
>   **Our task is to identify companies with the same interests!**
> **Tolerating the power of third parties**, expressed in mere submission and acceptance of the rules of the game, is not a sign of successful DNA. However, a **power struggle** to settle conflicts in the market is usually not a sign of cleverness either. If we opt for **coopetition**, we must—as Fig. 3.49 shows—give up part of our autonomy in order to work out solutions together with partners (cf. Haller & Wissing, 2018, p. 178). Only the partial surrender of autonomy allows us to become more involved in networks with partners. Through such a partnership, we can achieve our goals even with a lower funding potential.

▶ **Personal Reading Tip**
Sun Tzu: The Art of War.

▶ **Food for Thought**
For your platform to survive, you must also invite your competitors to your platform.

Otherwise someone else will do it—and your platform will lose relevance!

In the future, German and European companies run the risk of being ground down in a **sandwich position** between the already established US platforms and the globalizing Chinese platforms (by *Alibaba* and *Tencent*, among others). Therefore, the question of what German companies think about **platforms** is exciting. A study by *Bitkom* (2020, p. 6) surveyed a total of 502 companies with 20 or more employees. Here are the results concerning the **evaluation of platforms**:

- For 30% of the companies, the **risk** dominates.
- The **opportunity** is seen by 45%.
- 22% say "**no impact.**"

It is exciting that more than every fifth company assumes that platforms will have no impact on their own company. Yet ideas for platform solutions are emerging in almost all industries today!

In addition, the following results were obtained concerning the **intensity of use of platforms** (cf. Bitkom, 2020, S. 8):

- It was determined that 45% of the companies surveyed already offer **products/services on a platform**.
- 44% of the companies are **demanders for product/services on a platform**.
- 5% each **operate a digital platform with or without a partner**.
- However, 30% describe **digital platforms as not relevant** at the moment.
- It is also surprising that 9% confirm that they have **recognized the relevance of platforms** for their own company, but still **do not use any**. Can you understand that?

Two-thirds of non-users want to stay away from platforms in the future (cf. Bitkom, 2020, p. 10). The question arises as to whether these companies have sufficiently informed their decision.

It is not surprising that **large companies** in particular are concerned with platforms (cf. Bitkom, 2020, p. 9). However, platforms—in addition to all the risks described—offer smaller companies in particular the opportunity to increase their visibility and grow with relevant platform providers.

Also exciting in this study are the answers to the question about **responsibility for digital platforms** at the operational level (Bitkom, 2020, p. 16):

3.3 Digitalization of the Value Chain

- 37% of the companies say that **one employee** is responsible for the digital platforms—**in addition to other tasks.**
- In 20% of the companies, **one employee deals exclusively with digital platforms**.
- In 24% of the companies, **no one has an eye on it**.
- In 12% of the cases, **several employees deal with the topic**—in addition to other tasks.
- In 4% of the companies, **several employees deal exclusively with digital platforms**.

The result can therefore be summarized as follows (Bitkom, 2020, p. 16): **"In Germany, lone fighters dominate!"**

This raises the question of whether many companies are fully aware of the equally existing **opportunities and risks of the development towards a platform economy**. This knowledge is indispensable in view of the following developments (cf. Jodlbauer, 2018, p. 185):

- **Shifting the focus of performance from product to service and from hardware to software**
- **Shifting sales via a pipeline to a platform concept**
- **Development from lone wolves to network partners**

▶ **Food for Thought**

Platforms and ecosystems are the new gatekeepers!

We should reflect on the fact that due to the power of these new gatekeepers, there is a **privatization of law** (cf. von Westphalen, 2020, p. 15). This phenomenon dominates not only the major **social media platforms** (including *Facebook, Instagram, TikTok, WhatsApp*), but also the **transactional platforms** of *Amazon, Apple,* and *Google*.

Privatization of law comes about because the rules on how these platforms are to be used can be defined largely independently by the platform operators. For users on both sides of the platform, the rule here is:

take it or leave it!

Due to the great **contractual freedom** of the platform operators, they can design the business processes and the terms and conditions in the way that best suits their own profit-making. This applies, for example, to the use of our personal data (cf. von Westphalen, 2020, p. 15).

The **market power of the ecosystem and platform operators** forces us—sometimes daily or weekly—to accept the respective current **terms and conditions**. In most cases, we do so without having read them. Because the **TINA principle** also applies here: there is no alternative!

What is the cause? There are **asymmetrical power relations** between the platform operators and the users: after all, the operators simply have the **greater bargaining power**. We have to submit if we don't want to live without helpful, useful, value creating solutions.

If we as companies do not want to accept the **rules of the game of the platform operators**, we are not only threatened with termination of the contractual relationship (keyword "**delisting**"). However, this is not easy to enforce on the part of the operators. Much more "elegant"—at least from the platform operator's point of view—is the strategy of **dimming**. Here, the visibility of the offer of an "inconvenient partner" is systematically reduced. Then the provider is sidelined—and no potential customer will notice the offer. This is sometimes referred to as *Google* **prison** (cf. von Westphalen, 2020, p. 15).

Due to their market dominance, these companies also have the power to set **standards for business models** that other companies have to follow (see on the "devil's bargain" of *Amazon's* "A to Z guarantee" Sect. 3.2.9.1). What we learn here has been so aptly formulated by Boehme-Neßler (2017):

"The power of algorithms and the impotence of law."

▶ **Food for Thought**

Statement by Müller (2021, p. 1), after the accounts of the 45th president of the USA were blocked on *Facebook, Twitter* & Co. at the end of his term in office in January 2021:

"The blocking of the *Twitter* account apparently slows down the American president more effectively for the time being than the instruments of the constitution."

Think Box: Questions You Should Ask Yourself
- Which platform concepts already exist in your industry?
- Are transaction platforms and/or communication platforms more important for you?
- Which of these platforms have the potential to be further developed by the operators into an ecosystem?
- How important are positive network effects in your industry?
- How can you benefit from them?
- What possible negative network effects should be avoided?
- Which B2B platforms are important for you?
- What advantages can B2B platforms offer you (improved decision-making quality, higher transparency, data security, access to the latest technologies, opportunities for resource-efficient growth processes)?
- What risks do B2B platforms have to overcome (lack of compatibility, higher risk of cyberattacks)?
- Can you develop a platform yourself?
- Is there the possibility to develop a platform together with powerful partners (also with your competitors) to implement coopetition?

(continued)

- Can you become a partner of an existing platform?
- Can you sell your products/services via a platform?
- Is it promising to continue working—alone—with your traditional business model?
- To what extent are you—and your competitors—willing to engage in value adding cooperation with competitors (coopetition or cooperative competition)?
- Who in your company continuously analyzes the developments of the platform economy?

3.3.4 Examples of the Digitalization of a Company

3.3.4.1 *Siemens* Electronics Plant in Amberg

A convincing example of a consistent **transformation in manufacturing** is provided by Siemens (2021) with its **digital enterprise** at the *Siemens* electronics plant in Amberg. The challenges to be overcome here are impressive:

- 350 production changes daily
- Portfolio of around 1200 different products
- 17 million *Simatic* components per year

The components manufactured at the Amberg site are used for **automation and control technology** as well as at the **manufacturing execution level**. To ensure that production runs smoothly, around 50 million process and product data are continuously evaluated and used for ongoing optimization. Artificial intelligence applications, industrial edge computers, and cloud solutions are used for this purpose. These enable very flexible, efficient, and reliable processes.

Through the **use of edge computing**, data is processed where it is generated, directly at the plants and machines. The data generated by sensors is transferred to a cloud. **AI algorithms** are used to detect relevant patterns for quality assurance. An AI-controlled model develops reliable statements about the probability of product defects. The results obtained here are fed directly into production through **closed loop analytics**. This significantly increases the quality of the products.

In addition, a combination of edge computing and AI is also used for **predictive maintenance** (see Sect. 3.3.1.3). Based on production data, an algorithm determines correlations between abnormalities in the process data and downtimes in real time. These are fed back into production and lead to the necessary interventions there. A **performance insight app** makes the relevant results available to the users. The plant operators are thus informed between 12 and 36 h before a possible system failure and can act in time (cf. Siemens, 2021).

In addition, Siemens (2021) also works with the **concept of the digital twin** (cf. Armendia et al., 2019; Farsi et al., 2019). This is a **digital representation** of a tangible or intangible object. Processes can also be represented in the form of a digital twin. A digital twin consists of data and models of the represented object or process and further descriptive information. This makes the twin "computable." What is exciting here is that—contrary to the term "twin"—an object or a process does not (yet) have to exist in the analogue world in order to create a digital twin.

In **industrial applications**, digital twins are used for the development of products and services, but also for machines and systems. A **digital twin** of cruise ships can already exist before the birth of the analogue twin. Such digital models can be used to simulate various usage scenarios and determine their effects. Of particular importance here is the renunciation of physical prototypes—without losing the possibilities of usage simulations. A digital twin can take various forms. It can be a **behavioral model**, a **3D model**, or a **functional model** that represents the real properties as well as possible.

Several digital twins can also be linked with each other—as can be the case later with the analogue twins. This enables an analysis and **optimization based on this over several value added steps**. If an analogue twin is already alive, data from its use can be analyzed in the digital twin and used for optimization.

Institutions and companies such as the *Fraunhofer Gesellschaft*, the *Helmholtz Association of German Research Centers* as well as *Siemens Healthineers* and *Philips* are working on **digital twins of humans**. Today, it is not yet foreseeable when the corresponding breakthroughs will be achieved. The vision is to carry out an **integrated evaluation of all relevant patient data**, such as laboratory values and data from CT (computed tomography) and MRI (magnetic resonance imaging) examinations using this digital twin. In a digital twin, the entire **process from prevention to diagnosis and therapy to aftercare** should also be simulated—and based on this, optimal patient care should be established.

3.3.4.2 *Körber*: Specialist in Mechanical Engineering

The *Körber* company is a leading international **technology group** with around 10,000 employees. It operates at more than 100 locations worldwide (cf. Körber, 2021a). The group operates in five business areas: digital, pharma, supply chain, tissue, and tobacco. The *Körber Digital* business area consistently relies on artificial intelligence to increase efficiency in production. From the company's point of view, **artificial intelligence** is a central component of the so-called smart factories (see Sect. 3.4.3 for more details).

Successful **digitization of manufacturing** is based on the combination of digital technologies and expert knowledge from mechanical engineering. The development of digital products and services relies on data science and the Internet of Things. The primary goal is to **increase production efficiency**, which is measured by **overall equipment efficiency** (OEE)—an important domain of the COO (Chief Operating/Operation Officer). OEE can be achieved by increasing equipment availability (through less downtime), increasing energy efficiency, extending equipment life, and optimizing production output.

AI-driven manufacturing enables industrial companies to analyze large amounts of data. The insights gained from this increase the availability of production facilities. This is not only about **transforming industrial production facilities**, but also about **developing new digital business models**. Since this task can hardly be accomplished by individual companies alone, the company is striving to **build a digital European ecosystem for mechanical engineering**. In this regard, it states (Körber, 2021a):

"For us, technological progress is a joint effort. That is why solutions are always developed in interdisciplinary teams. *Körber Digital* develops products and services together with customers—and shares findings with other providers of digital solutions. One priority is to network machines from different manufacturers. This co-creation approach enables *Körber* not only to solve very specific problems, but also to increase the performance of the manufacturing industry as a whole. The future of industrial manufacturing lies in the optimized use of AI to increase production efficiency.

Körber Digital embodies the belief in a new European manufacturing ecosystem that can only be created through co-creation. As a technology leader, *Körber* drives innovation and creates the conditions for successfully and meaningfully connecting people, data, machines and processes."

To drive this process forward, *Körber* also relies on **acquisitions** and the **establishment of its own start-ups**. The *Körber Lab* also plays an important role in this process (cf. Körber, 2021b). This **innovation hub** sees itself as a **digital ecosystem** for the tissue industry in the region around Lucca in Italy. Design thinking and other agile methods are used in close cooperation and exchange with start-ups, universities, suppliers, and other institutions (see Sect. 3.5.3.2 on this open innovation approach).

The goal is to build a **network of interconnected production sites** to create networked production through intelligent hardware and software (cf. Körber, 2021b). The combination of smart machines, smart software applications, and smart services form the foundation for the creation of a **smart factory**. An innovative **monitoring system** supports the storage, analysis, and transfer of a multitude of machine data from the entire production process. The data collected here is made available to the technicians via a mobile terminal. This enables predictive maintenance, which makes a decisive contribution to increasing **overall equipment efficiency** (see Sect. 3.3.1.3).

The **vision of an industry 4.0** is paraphrased as follows (Körber, 2021b):

"The data obtained and evaluated across factories in a fully networked environment is an immeasurably valuable treasure. Their use can catapult production at our customers into a completely new dimension."

The **target direction** for the *Körber* company is also clearly defined (Marx, 2020, p. 23):

"In each of our business areas, one third of sales should come from the digital and software business."

> **Think Box: Questions You Should Ask Yourself**
> - What ideas did the *Siemens* case gave you?
> - What is the importance of digital twins in your industry?
> - Do digital twins represent an opportunity for you to accelerate the development process?
> - Can you engage yourself as a provider of digital twins?
> - Do you have the opportunity to build a digital ecosystem—together with strong and innovative partners—in your industry?
> - How can you manage to incorporate the relevant data streams into a unified monitoring system?
> - What areas of application do you have for predictive maintenance?
> - What goals have you defined for the digital share of turnover or profit?
> - Who in your company answers the questions raised here?

3.4 IT Infrastructure, Data Basis, and Artificial Intelligence

*Our future **is a** race between **the** growing power **of** our technology **and the** wisdom with which we use it.*
  *Let's make sure **that** wisdom **wins**.*
  Stephen Hawking

3.4.1 IT as an Enabler

The world belongs to the brave!

3.4.1.1 Two-Speed IT

The frequently heard slogans "**software eats the world**" or "**every company is becoming an IT company**" show the great importance of IT in the course of the digital transformation. However, today it is also said: "**AI eats the software!**"

Without **powerful IT**, a transformation process will not succeed. Start-ups can use the latest IT infrastructure. In established companies, such a step is usually opposed by IT landscapes that have already been installed and possibly developed over years or decades. This obstacle has a name: **legacy systems**. Many experts see the solution to this dilemma in **two-speed IT**.

With regard to the **existing business**, IT must above all pay attention to **reliability and security**. Here, it is important to ensure stable processes and to make changes only after comprehensive tests and based on release plans that have been worked out in detail. However, such stability, for which there are good reasons, prevents many innovations. IT is then branded as an **impediment to innovative** processes, which stands in the way of using innovative online services, new hardware and new software.

In order to resolve this tension, a **two-speed IT** or **bimodal IT** is often needed:

- **Traditional IT**
  This term traditional IT is used to describe the IT area that ensures **secure operations** as the **basis for day-to-day business**. The central requirements are efficiency, security, and process conformity. Here, IT works with known, proven, and also established techniques for infrastructure and applications. At the same time, it is important to work as cost-efficient as possible.
- **Agile IT**
  Agile IT should develop and offer **new services and applications** as quickly as possible, based on the ideas and requirements of the business units. Here, agile methods are increasingly used in order to quickly and efficiently develop new solutions that also work through a high degree of customer and user proximity. However, this also requires a different mindset. It is important to be more willing to take risks, to be allowed to fail once in a while—and not every investment has to be backed up by a comprehensive business plan. Such an approach can only be accepted in the IT sector if it does not have a disruptive influence on day-to-day business.

Your challenge is to manage the situation described by this **dualism** in intensive cooperation with the IT managers—another step on the way to digital excellence.

> **Memory Box**
> In established companies, the **two-speed IT** is the prerequisite for mastering a digital transformation within an acceptable timeframe.

▶ **Food for Thought**
Check in your company which **budgets are invested in advertising** and which **budgets in IT**! Then you should determine the respective **return-on-investment**—even if this will not earn you any additional popularity in the marketing sector!

It has already been pointed out several times how important IT is in shaping the digital transformation. As with the design of the organization (see Sect. 3.7.4), IT must master the **balancing act between error-free and stable processes,** on the one hand, and **participation in the development of new (digital) business models,** on the other.

This raises the question of responsibilities. Figure 3.50 shows a continuous **decrease in the responsibilities of the CFO and CIO** on the one hand, and an **increase in the responsibilities of the entire C-level** on the other. This development will become even stronger as the IT-based tasks of corporate development become more innovative on the path to digital excellence (cf. Direktgruppe, 2016).

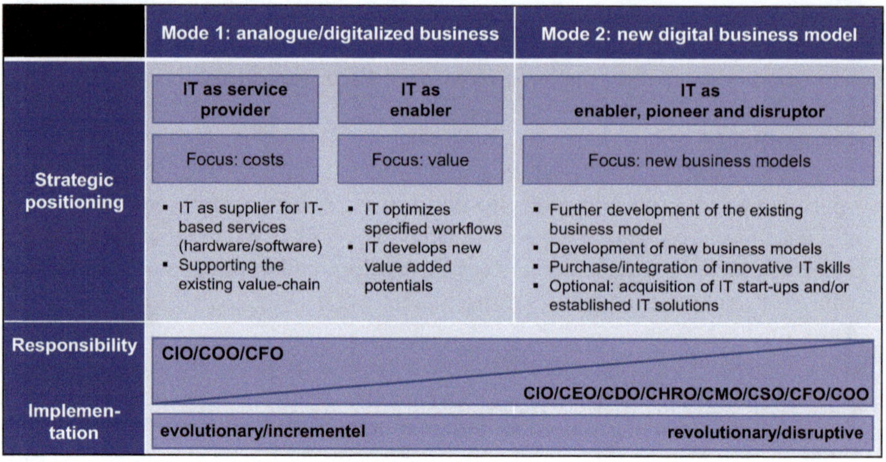

	Mode 1: analogue/digitalized business		Mode 2: new digital business model
Strategic positioning	IT as service provider	IT as enabler	IT as enabler, pioneer and disruptor
	Focus: costs	Focus: value	Focus: new business models
	• IT as supplier for IT-based services (hardware/software) • Supporting the existing value-chain	• IT optimizes specified workflows • IT develops new value added potentials	• Further development of the existing business model • Development of new business models • Purchase/integration of innovative IT skills • Optional: acquisition of IT start-ups and/or established IT solutions
Responsibility	CIO/COO/CFO		CIO/CEO/CDO/CHRO/CMO/CSO/CFO/COO
Implementation	evolutionary/incrementel		revolutionary/disruptive

Fig. 3.50 Responsibility focus of a two-speed IT

The **optimization of established business processes** is mainly the responsibility of the CFO, COO, and CIO (**mode 1**). In many companies, a visionary CEO is responsible for business model innovations—ideally in conjunction with a visionary CDO who is above all strong in implementation. However, the CHRO, CMO, and CSO must also be involved in this development—a team solution at the highest level is indispensable (**mode 2**).

A **goal-oriented and often joint responsibility** for the required processes is an indispensable success factor. When assigning tasks, competences, and responsibilities, avoid the **formation of information silos at the highest corporate level**. You will hardly be able to overcome such a silo in operational action. Why not start with **joint responsibility** right at the top? The responsibility is then broken down through the existing hierarchies or (at least partially) removed through network structure (see Sect. 3.6.7).

Three basic **alternatives for assigning responsibilities** are shown in Fig. 3.51 (cf. Direktgruppe, 2016). Each variant has advantages and disadvantages. The initial situation in many companies is a **divided responsibility between the different business units** (variant 1). Here, responsibility for (digital) strategy, budget, and operational resources lies with the different business units and IT. Time-consuming coordination routines and power struggles between those involved are often the result. This leads to a **silo solution**: information is not shared between the business units because of competition.

In the **centralization solution** in variant 2, responsibility for the (digital) strategy and budget lies with the holding company or the executive board (cf. Fig. 3.51). The danger here is that great strategic visions are developed, but without always having the necessary grounding (in the sense of being close to the market and problems).

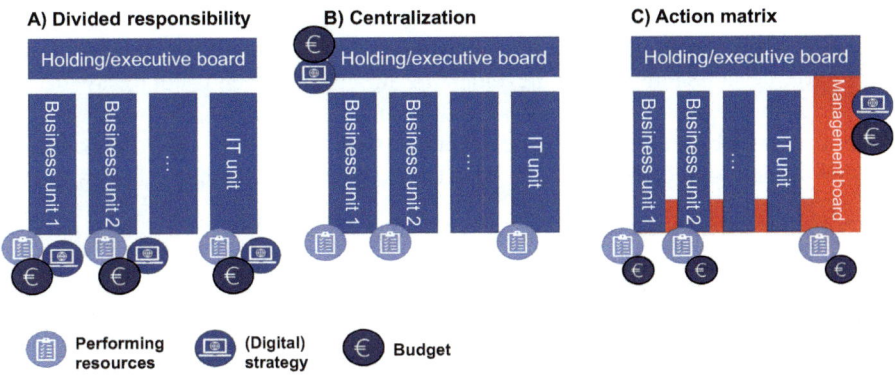

Fig. 3.51 Concepts for allocation of responsibilities

Variant 3 shows a **solution with a steering committee** (cf. Fig. 3.51). This committee is made up of delegates from the business units and IT. The jointly developed (digital) strategy and the necessary budgets are approved by the executive board. In this way, the strategic perspective of the executive board can be combined with the know-how about what is feasible and imaginable (company-specific). The shared responsibility of business units and IT inevitably leads to the fact that the top performers talk more to each other than about each other. After all, they have worked out the direction of travel together!

In many cases, the steering committee of variant 3, which comes close to a matrix structure, has proven its worth. Which solution is the right one for your company also depends on the digital business performance (see Sect. 2.2). For here, too, the following applies:

There is no **best-practice solution** for all companies in the various phases of the digital transformation on the path to digital excellence.

Memory Box
Wherever major **tensions exist between business units, swearing them to common goals**—and above all **incentivizing them on the basis of common goals**—can work wonders. You can also achieve the same thing when those responsible for different business units have to **report to the same body** all at once. This can help move mountain!

▶ **Storytelling** After my appointment as managing director in an international cooperation, I was asked for suggestions on how to structure the individual targets for the second managing director and me. I suggested that we should both have the same individual targets. The supervisor's response: "that's not our practice!"

Eventually we agreed to set identical targets for my colleague and me. The result? Each of us had clearly defined areas of responsibility—but in substance we always fought for the same thing: the achievement of our goals! Which is not to say that we always had to be of one mind.

In another subsidiary of the same group—on the floor below us—the managing directors (each with different goals) only communicated with each other by e-mail ...

3.4.1.2 Cloud Computing and Cyber Security

In order to achieve greater flexibility, more and more companies are using **cloud solutions**. In **cloud computing**, IT infrastructure and IT services are provided by third-party partners as a service via the Internet. These services include storage space, computing power, and application software. A great advantage of such cloud services is that these services can be called up as needed and thus dynamically. We can also speak of **breathing IT** here, because the necessary resources are available as needed. At the same time, a **usage-based billing model** is used, in which the costs are primarily oriented to the concrete use of these cloud services.

> **Memory Box**
>
> **Cloud computing** involves **outsourcing software and hardware solutions** to an external cloud computing provider. Cloud computing—quasi **data processing in a cloud**—is referred to because the services are not provided by a specific computer at a specific location. Rather, these services are provided by a **virtual computing cloud** consisting of several interconnected computers.
>
> **Cloud computing** thus represents the counterpart to the so-called **on-premise solutions**, where companies have to take care of the provision, installation, and support of their own computing systems themselves. Own solutions not only require IT managers to analyze all relevant **technological developments** with regard to their relevance for their own company. The IT resources must also be dimensioned so that they can handle the expected volume (incl. reserve capacity) as well as foreseeable growth. However, this is becoming increasingly difficult to determine in the VUCA world. Furthermore, necessary **software releases** must be carried out independently. In addition, **back-up systems** must be provided and **data back-ups** routinely carried out.

▶ **Food for Thought**
  Cloud services also make it easier for a company to cope with an extraordinary rush of customers, such as **Singles Day in China 2020**. On this day, *Alibaba* received **583,000 orders**—per second (cf. n. a. 11.11.2020). It is good when a company does not have to continuously maintain the resources for such performance peaks itself.

The **increasing demands on on-premise solutions** mean that more and more companies are turning to cloud computing to achieve **higher application availability** at more easily **predictable costs**. However, when **selecting a cloud service provider**, in addition to the **classic service level agreements** (SLA), you should carefully check where your data is physically located (e.g., within or outside the EU). In addition, you should intensively check which **security standards apply** and which **data protection measures** are taken.

▶ **Food for Thought**
If you use cloud services in Europe and the service providers involved are not located in the EU, then all your data processed in this way will leave the **legal area of the EU**. The data is then subject to the legal system at the respective locations of the cloud service providers—and consequently also to the access of the governments there!

Incidentally, this is also the case with **cloud-based office systems** such as *Google Docs* or *Microsoft Office 365*.

Last but not least, the increasingly frequent **cyberattacks** pose a great challenge to every IT manager—every day. The following **forms of cyberattacks** can be distinguished:

- **Theft of digital identities (ID theft)**
  The term **identity theft**, or more precisely **identity abuse**, refers to the misuse of personal data and thus the identity of a natural person by third parties. The aim of identity theft is to obtain a pecuniary advantage through fraud and/or to discredit the rightful owner of the identity (e.g., by publishing compromising content, for example in social media).
  Phishing e-mails (phishing stands for password fishing) are used to try to obtain not only the name of the target person but also their date of birth, address, bank account, and credit card numbers or access codes to online services. By using this data, the attacker appears as the authorized user and receives all the services and options for action to which this user is entitled.
- **Malware** (a portmanteau of "malicious" and "software")
  Malicious programs are computer programs that have been developed with the aim of executing functions that are undesirable and often harmful from the victim's point of view. The challenge for the developers of malware is to disguise the malicious functions as well as possible so that they are not so easily detected by the victims.
  Such **malicious functions** can manipulate the contents of files or delete them. These functions can also lead to the theft of data in order to gain access to company secrets. Malicious functions can involve the unauthorized harvesting of user data in order to track customers and target them more specifically (with advertising). The malware can also aim to disable security software (such as firewalls or anti-virus programs).
- **Ransomware** (digital extortion, digital blackmail)

Ransomware refers to malware with which an attacker prevents the legitimate user from accessing their data and/or using the IT infrastructure as a whole. For this purpose, private data on the foreign computer is either encrypted or access to it is blocked. A ransom is demanded by the attacker for decryption or release.

- **DDOS attacks (distributed denial of service)**
 The term **DOS** stands for "denial of service." This refers to the unavailability of an online service that is supposed to be available. A common reason for this is an **overload of the network**. If such an overload of the data network is deliberately caused by a large number of targeted requests by a many computers or servers (often connected in a botnet), this is called a distributed denial of service attack. Since the requests come from a variety of sources, it is usually not possible to block the attackers without completely stopping communication with the network.

The **magnitude of cybercrime** in Germany alone can be seen in the *Cybercrime Situation Report* of the *German Federal Criminal Police Office* (cf. BKA, 2020, p. 3, 46). Only the crimes that have become known after the conclusion of the police investigation are included in this so-called **police bright field**. In 2019, this number was exactly 100,514, an increase of 14.5% compared to the previous year! Especially in the area of cybercrime, however, an **above-average dark field** can be assumed.

The entire **development of cyberattacks** can be described by the following statements (cf. BKA, 2020, p. 6):

- The **professionalism of cyber criminals** continues to rise.
- Cybercrime generates and is based on **criminal value chains**.
- **Ransomware** remains the biggest threat to commercial enterprises.
- Both the number and intensity of **DDOS attacks** are increasing rapidly.
- The **perpetrators** are **globally networked**, operate internationally, with a division of labor and are very well organized.
- The **most important protective mechanisms** against cybercrime are above all **sensitive Internet users**.

Among the Internet users with a particularly large **area of responsibility** are the **IT managers**. In their hands lies not only the weal and woe of **day-to-day business operations**. They also have to be able to **deal with future challenges** and **defend against cyberattacks**—24/7.

▶ **Food for Thought**
Every **IT manager** must ensure that **not a single cyberattack succeeds** 24/7. For the **cyber-attackers** it is enough if **one out of 100 or 1000 or 10,000 attacks is successful** in order to seize company secrets or customer data.

Today's **digital burglars** no longer have thick arms and a big chisel. They are often very intelligent people who network with other intelligent people across countries to target specific companies. **CrimeTechs** are emerging here—and the **crime as a service** business model has already established itself on the Darknet!

> **Memory Box**
> **Home offices** increase the number of possible gateways for **cyberattacks**. All companies must ensure that their **home office infrastructure** also offers their own staff sufficient protection against cyberattacks.
> In this regard, the *German Federal Criminal Police Office* (cf. BKA, 2020, p. 3) wrote in a special evaluation on the Corona pandemic:
> "In the wake of the Corona crisis, society is increasingly shifting to the digital world—a perfect breeding ground for cyber criminals."
> However, it is also true:
> **The major challenges in cyber security should not be used as an excuse not to embrace digital transformation.**
> In addition, the question arises whether cyber security is seen as a pure cost factor in your company? Does the responsibility for this lie solely in the IT department—while the responsibility for digitization (hopefully) lies with the company's management?
> However, the **focus of top management** must be on both: **digitization and information security!**

3.4.1.3 Use of 5G and Trend Towards Softwarization

Particularly exciting solutions will be supported by **5G** in the future. 5G enables an **Internet of Everything in real time**. The "5" in the **mobile radio standard 5G** stands for the fifth generation. Here are the **characteristics of 5G** listed (cf. Deutsche Telekom, 2021):

- Significantly **faster data transmission** compared to 4G networks (transmission rates of up to 10 gigabits/second instead of 500 megabits/second; an increase of 20 times)
- Use of **higher frequency ranges**
- Increase in frequency capacity enables **higher data throughput**
- **Real time transmission** supports 100 billion mobile devices worldwide
- Extremely **short latency times** (in the sense of reaction, delay, or transmission time) of only one to three milliseconds, even over greater distances (humans need about ten times this time for transmission from the eye to the brain); the latency time in the LTE network is about 50 milliseconds (LTE or long-term evolution is a designation for the third-generation mobile radio standard)
- Significant **reduction in energy consumption** for data transmission compared to 4G

- 5G can connect one million devices per square kilometer; ten times more than the 4G standard

The **speed of 5G** is illustrated by the following example. If the **content of a DVD** (4.5 GB) is to be downloaded, the following time requirements result for the various mobile radio standards:

- **2G** (at 0.25 megabits/s): one day, 16 h
- **3G** (at 42.2 megabits/s): 14 min, 33 s
- **4G** (at 500 megabits/s): 1 min, 13 s
- **5G** (at 10,000 megabits/s): 3.7 s

The **introduction of 5G** will enable not only **real time machine-to-machine communication**, but also **real time human-to-machine communication**. 5G provides the foundations for the development of new business models. New forms of interaction will be supported, for example in the area of industry 4.0 and in medicine. In addition to the **network infrastructure**, an important prerequisite for this is the development of common **standards for data transmission**.

The low latencies described above are also of central importance for **self-driving cars**. Here, data transmission and response must take place in real time to enable safe navigation. Decisions have to be made in fractions of a second. In humans, the reaction time from recognizing a danger to braking is about one second. In this time, a vehicle at a speed of 100 km/h covers about 28 m. With a latency of one millisecond, an autonomous vehicle can react 1000 times faster than a human. Then, after less than one centimeter of travel, the braking process is triggered.

When **evaluating 5G solutions**, the following factors are important, which go hand in hand with the **concept of softwarization** (cf. Fitzek & Boche, 2020, p. 20):

- Compared to previous generations, 5G is no longer based on highly specialized hardware. 5G is primarily based on software solutions and generic hardware. This process is called **softwarization**. This means that **more cost-effective, flexibly interchangeable, and easily available products** can be used for 5G applications. These are a driver for a fast and sustainable implementation of 5G solutions.
- This softwarization enables the use of **mobile edge cloud solutions**. Here, cloud services are no longer placed at a great physical distance from the application, but close to the location of the operational application (cf. Grund et al., 2020, p. 19).
- Softwarization means that **communication networks** are not only used to transmit data. **Data** can now be **processed and stored** in the network itself. This means that AI applications can be made directly from the network—again, close to the action.
- Through softwarization, operators can gear their networks more quickly to future use cases and thereby **increase the pace of innovation**. In the past, this was only possible through the introduction of a new generation—at intervals of about 10 years. Consequently, the innovation dynamic will continue to increase.

Whether it is worthwhile for your company to enter the 5G future should be answered by looking at the study results of Nokia (2020). This study determined that **5G-enabled industries** have the potential to increase the **global gross domestic product** by **US-$ 8 trillion** by 2030. To evaluate this figure, a comparison helps: in 2018, Germany's gross domestic product was just under US-$ 4 trillion. An additional driver for 5G deployment is the Covid pandemic. It has already triggered a wide range of medium- and long-term digital investments. These will further accelerate the share of digital value creation.

The *5G Business Readiness Report* combines research from *Nokia Bell Labs* with the results of a survey of 1628 technology purchasing decision-makers across eight countries and six industries. These include energy and utilities, mining, manufacturing, public sector, healthcare, and transportation. In addition, this report incorporated the analysis and opinions of 5G experts from around the world. In sum, it was found that companies that use 5G technologies intensively grow significantly faster. The **technology leaders** were also the only group to record a **net increase in productivity** (here by 10%) despite the pandemic.

In addition, Nokia (2020) reported the **5G readiness of various countries**. 47% of companies in Saudi Arabia and 40% of companies in South Korea were certified as "5G-ready." In Germany, the figure was only 23% and in the UK 20%. However, even in a tense economic environment, 71% of the companies want to invest in 5G in the next 5 years. In Germany, 58% are planning to do so. Overall, a **global boom in 5G investments** is foreseeable.

However, there is a clear **discrepancy** between the **knowledge of the advantages of 5G** and the **current level of acceptance** in the companies surveyed. Specifically, the following **obstacles to the introduction of 5G technologies** need to be overcome (cf. Nokia, 2020):

- The **lack of a comprehensive ecosystem** (i.e., the necessary infrastructure), especially outside urban centers, was cited as an obstacle by 28% of decision-makers.
- 17% stated that there is a **lack of 5G know-how among decision-makers**.
- 14% diagnosed their own **lack of 5G know-how**.
- In addition, there is still a **lack of awareness of 5G relevance** in many cases. 22% of technology buyers stated that 5G implementation is not currently a priority for their company.
- Another barrier is the **cost and complexity of 5G technologies**. 15% said they were not confident they had the necessary technologies in-house to implement.
- Another barrier is the issue of security. More than a third (34%) said they are concerned about the **security of 5G**.

Based on these findings, the following **recommendations for action** are derived in order to achieve a better understanding, more trust and ultimately a higher acceptance of 5G technologies. The calls for action focus on improved regulation, more intensive cooperation between the companies involved and a greater willingness to innovate (cf. Nokia, 2020). A third of technology buyers said they would be encouraged to invest more in 5G by **government investment in infrastructure** or **subsidies to reduce costs**. Many companies will also only adopt 5G technologies if network operators offer **acceptable price-performance packages**. These are influenced by governments and/or regulators.

Creating widespread acceptance among **users and adopters of 5G** technologies will require a **flurry of information**. Businesses and consumers need to be much more fully informed about the technology and its fields of application. For this, it is important that many more people—especially in companies—deal with the **potential of 5G**. Wherever large amounts of data are generated and have to be evaluated—often in real time—the **increases in capacity and bandwidth** with a simultaneous **reduction in latency** will lead to a **race for innovation in products and services**.

The spectrum of innovative fields of application ranges from **virtual reality** and **augmented reality** in professional and private environments to **robotics**, which will connect production and AI even more comprehensively. **Autonomous driving** will also receive a further boost from 5G technology. **Tele-medicine** will change **healthcare**. Finally, new areas of application for **blockchain** will emerge (cf. Grinschuk, 2019).

Collaboration across national borders will allow businesses and consumers alike to use resources more intelligently. These technologies can also enable the relocation of jobs from low-wage to high-wage countries (keyword "reshoring"). **Exciting use cases** must be developed for all these areas in order to awaken knowledge, interest, and possibly also enthusiasm for the new possibilities.

A deeper **understanding of 5G technologies** not only makes it possible to **optimize existing business processes** by increasing efficiency and reducing costs (horizon 1 activities). It will be particularly exciting to use 5G technologies to **further develop existing business models** or **launch business model innovations** on horizons 2 and 3 (see Sect. 3.2.2).

> **Memory Box**
> The **success of a deployment of 5G technologies** requires an intensive knowledge of the possibilities of this technology—among companies and users alike.
> **Ignorance has never been a good navigator!**

▶ **Food for Thought**
IT must (no longer) be reduced to mapping predefined processes.
   IT can and must increasingly become a (co-)designer of digital business models.

   You should also avoid turning every single department into an IT start-up—with high risks of failure. An **agile master development plan for your IT**—with a cross-departmental steering team—is indispensable for the success of the IT transformation as the basis for the digital transformation of the entire company.

Think Box: Questions You Should Ask Yourself
- Is your company's digital transformation being held back by legacy systems?
- Could two-speed IT be a solution here?
- Who is responsible for taking a closer look at this scenario?
- If your company does not have sufficient budgets for IT projects, then ask for a report on which budgets are invested in marketing and advertising compared to IT and determine the respective return on investment.
- What is the division of labor in your company between CFO, COO, CMO, CSO, CHRM, CIO, CDO, and CEO? If you have no C-level, it is about the responsibilities in the management team or at the level of the division heads.
- How much joint or separate responsibility is there at the top management level?
- Do you have a silo solution or is centralization predominant in terms of IT use?
- Or has a solution with a steering committee already been installed?
- Which strategies does your company rely on—cloud services or on-premise solutions?
- Were and are the alternatives continuously examined with regard to their relevance for your company?
- Which concepts can not only optimally support day-to-day business, but also promote digital transformation?
- How well prepared is your company for the increasing number of cyberattacks?
- What does the advance of the 5G standard mean for your company and your industry?
- What new business models will be promoted or enabled by 5G?
- Will existing business models be threatened by 5G deployment?
- What are the possible 5G barriers in your company (including lack of a comprehensive ecosystem, lack of 5G know-how among decision-makers, lack of awareness of 5G relevance, cost and complexity of 5G technologies, risks of 5G deployment)?
- How can you ensure that a high level of information about the possibilities of 5G is achieved in your company?
- Who receives the "educational mandate" for this?
- Who in your company is responsible for developing possible use cases for 5G deployment?
- Does your company have an agile master development plan for your IT—as a basis for digital transformation?
- Who in your company deals with these topics and their implications?

3.4.1.4 Further Challenges in IT

Gartner (2020a) has drawn up an **Emerging Technology Roadmap 2020 to 2022** for large companies and SMEs. *Gartner* differentiates between large companies with more than US-$ 1 billion and companies with less than this turnover. The **deployment risk** is shown in a traffic light system and is based on an analysis of where the technology has potential risks with regard to the following criteria:

- Market/vendor maturity
- IT infrastructure adaptation/complexity
- Security
- Availability of necessary talent
- Implementation costs
- Potential disruption to existing processes and services due to new technologies
- Regulatory compliance challenges

The determined **value for the company (enterprise value)** is based on an evaluation of the areas in which a technology can achieve one or more of the goals:

- Potential to increase cost efficiency
- Increasing speed and agility
- Increasing staff productivity
- Increased revenue through improved products and services

To create the **Emerging Technology Roadmap for mid-sized companies**, IT professionals from 218 corresponding companies worked together. These professionals ranked 112 emerging technologies according to **phase of adoption, risk of adoption, and value to the business** (cf. Gartner, 2020b).

The most important findings for mid-sized companies are shown below (cf. Gartner, 2020a). These are divided into the areas of remote work, productivity, and operations. In the **remote work** field of action (home office and mobile working), a comprehensive **modernization of their networks** is emerging in medium-sized companies. This is intended to enable their own staff to work from home or on the move to a greater extent. To this end, investments are being made in secure access service edge (SASE), virtual extensible local area network (VXLAN), and container networking.

Containers are a virtualization technology in the IT environment. It separates applications including their runtime environments from each other, although they are executed on the same computer and operating system. Unlike virtual machines, containers do not contain their own operating system. Rather, they use the operating system of the system on which they are installed. All the files, configurations, dependencies, and libraries required for execution are present in a container. A container also represents a separate package with the runtime environment of the respective application.

In addition, **investments are made in edge computing**. In contrast to cloud computing, edge computing refers to decentralized data processing at the edge of a network. With this, companies want to prepare for the use of applications such as the Internet of Things (IOT), augmented reality (AR), and virtual reality (VR). Despite the expected risks, 49% of CIOs in these medium-sized companies are piloting corresponding projects.

In the field of **productivity**, many CIOs are striving for a **democratization of task processing**. This should help teams in development and analytics to become faster and more agile. 70% of CIOs plan to use the so-called **citizen integrator tools** by the end of 2020. A **citizen integrator** is an end user who can develop software without in-depth knowledge of programming languages. In contrast to the **citizen developer**, the focus of the citizen integrator is on front-end-back-end integration and various applications. This should enable more people to carry out simple tasks of application, data and process integration in compliance with corporate standards. The so-called **low-code tools** or **no-code tools** are to be used for this purpose by 2022 at the latest.

To further increase productivity, CIOs are investing in **IT automation** and **AI tools**. This should streamline product development and increase staff productivity. The use of bots and natural language processing (NLP) is often still in the planning phase. CIOs plan to deploy these tools by 2021 to achieve a balanced division of labor between humans and machines. This should increase the achievable productivity.

In addition, investments in **monitoring technologies** are planned in order to comprehensively determine the impact achieved. Accordingly, 50% of CIOs are piloting different platforms of digital experience monitoring (DEM), application performance monitoring (APM) and artificial intelligence IT operations (AIOPS). The goal is to identify relevant impacts on staff. In addition, 85% of the CIOs of medium-sized companies plan to use company-wide **workplace analytics** solutions by 2021. This will train machine learning algorithms to better understand employee experiences and diagnose the root causes of productivity issues.

In the **operations** field of action, CIOs are investing in technologies for **front-end operations** while modernizing the existing **back-end infrastructure**. Three out of four CIOs plan to deploy **serverless computing, operating system containers** (OS Containers) and **microservices** on a large scale by 2021. These are expected to support cloud infrastructure and improve application development processes. CIOs see serverless computing as a low-risk, high-value investment. After all, it allows administrators to spend less time managing infrastructure.

Increasing virtualization and investments in edge technology allow CIOs to rethink **security concepts**. CIOs have caught up with large companies in this respect. They are increasingly using virtualized firewalls and firewall as a service solution to simplify the provision of security services.

It is interesting to see how, in contrast to the medium-sized companies, the **Emerging Technology Roadmap for large companies** turns out (cf. Gartner, 2020b). To create this, IT professionals from 438 organizations analyzed and evaluated new infrastructure solutions and operating technologies, again according to **deployment phase, deployment risk, and value to the company**. The **risk of deployment** is also made visible here by a traffic light system.

Overall, the following insights were gained for large enterprises through this study (cf. Gartner, 2020b). Infrastructure and operations companies see a strong need to continue **investing in technologies** to support the accelerated **transformation to a new virtual work environment**. The number of technologies being piloted and deployed has increased despite delays in investment. Here, the importance of **resilience** and **reliability** has increased significantly. However, **increasing speed** and **agility** remains the main driver for technology adoption.

In parallel, the **testing of digital technologies for the workplace** is being accelerated. This is to ensure staff productivity after the shift to remote working. The number of relevant technologies in the pilot phase has almost doubled to 82% in 2020, compared to 44% in 2019, with many **automation IT technologies** moving from the evaluation to the production phase to support the digital transformation process.

In addition, the large companies studied here are looking to transform their **network infrastructure** in the medium to long term. This is necessary to effectively support the growing volume and diversity of traffic from the cloud, edge and IOT applications, and remote workers. 60% of all **network technologies** currently on the roadmap are expected to increase speed and agility. However, companies are cautious about deploying new network technologies. One reason is the increasing focus on ensuring resilience.

Large enterprises are actively investing in a **hybrid computing environment and containers** to support flexibility with multiple hosting options. This is to better align with business model requirements. In parallel, **investments in cloud technologies** continue. **Investments in storage and back-up** are focused on supporting a hybrid environment through cloud and modernized on-premise storage. The trend towards the adoption of cloud-based storage and database technologies continues unabated.

Investments in artificial intelligence, edge technology, and IOT platforms have also increased outside of IT due to growing interest from top management. Adoption of these technologies has accelerated by leaps and bounds compared to 2019, when most of these technologies were in the planning stages or had their adoption monitored.

> **Memory Box**
> **IT performance will largely determine how successful your company will be in mastering digital transformation.**

> **Think Box: Questions You Should Ask Yourself**
> - How well is your company positioned in remote work to support home office and mobile working (keyword "virtual working environment")?

(continued)

3.4 IT Infrastructure, Data Basis, and Artificial Intelligence

- How relevant is the development of edge computing for you?
- Are citizen integrator tools relevant to your company?
- How much can your company benefit from IT automation?
- How important are AI tools for you?
- Where can you use powerful monitoring technologies?
- Which areas in your company could benefit from workplace analytics?
- What potential can you leverage through serverless computing, operating system containers and/or microservices?
- What about the resilience of the security concepts in your company?
- Is cyber security seen as a mere cost factor?
- Does responsibility for cyber security lie solely with the IT department?
- Where does the overarching responsibility for these topics lie—with IT alone or also with the specialist departments?

3.4.2 Basics of Data Management

3.4.2.1 Big Data

As has already been mentioned, data sources are bubbling up as never before. Consequently, the term "**big data**" is used with good reason. This term describes large amounts of data that come from a wide variety of areas (including companies and the private sphere) and can hardly be handled with manual or classic methods of data processing (cf. Fig. 3.52).

The five **dimensions of big data** are:

- **Volume** (in the sense of data volume or data quantity)
  Volume describes the extent of the available amount of data. This volume is affected by the breadth and depth of the available data. User-generated content

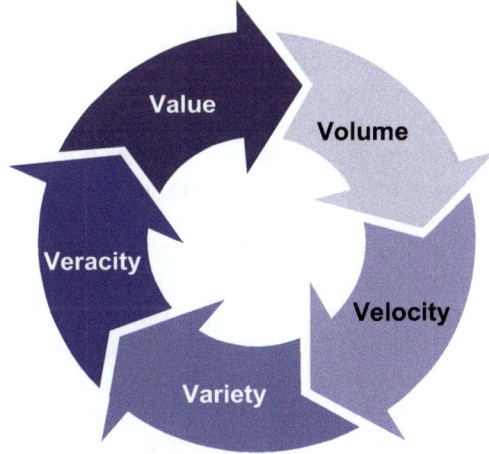

Fig. 3.52 The 5 Vs of big data

(e.g., in social media), the increasing use of sensors, and the progressive networking of objects are generating ever more extensive data streams.
- **Velocity** (in the sense of the speed of data generation)
  Velocity describes the speed at which data is either generated or existing data is updated, analyzed, processed, and/or deleted. Today, much data can be captured, documented, and evaluated in real time to immediately trigger further processes—some of them automated.
- **Variety** (in the sense of the variety of data sources and data formats)
  Variety refers, on the one hand, to the large number of internal and external data sources. On the other hand, variety also refers to the different data formats (such as structured, semi-structured, and unstructured data), which usually have to be evaluated in parallel.

  Structured data have a normalized data structure. They can be stored directly in a row- and column-oriented database. In contrast, **unstructured data** has an unidentifiable and non-normalized data structure. This includes texts in natural language, presentations, images as well as audio and video files. With unstructured data, only the file type is known. However, the content is not available in the form of interdependent data fields. Therefore, they must be prepared accordingly before processing.

  In contrast, **semi-structured data** has a certain basic structure. The e-mail is an example of semi-structured data. An e-mail has a constant structure—with sender, recipient, subject line. The actual content of the e-mail is in the form of text in natural language (possibly with emojis). This text is therefore unstructured data.
- **Veracity** (in the sense of the quality of the data and data sources)
  Veracity refers to the quality of the available data and data sources. In comparison with the downstream criterion of value, veracity is not concerned with the meaning of the data in the sense of semantics, but solely with its formal information content. The quality of the data in veracity focuses on the following dimensions:
  - **Correctness** (in the sense of freedom from errors)
  - **Completeness** (in the sense of coverage of all relevant fields)
  - **Consistency** (in the sense of freedom from contradictions)
  - **Timeliness** (in the sense of the validity of the data)
- This also raises the question of the **trustworthiness of the data**, i.e., the freedom from systematic distortions. Here it is especially important to critically evaluate the statements of **pro-domo sources**. "Pro-domo" literally means "for the house" and figuratively speaking means "in one's own cause" or "for one's own benefit." If, for example, the *Association of the Automotive Industry* or the *Association of Research-based Pharmaceutical Companies* presents or interprets statements or analysis results, it can be assumed that such presentations or interpretations tend to be favorable to the activities of the represented companies. Thus, a (partial) "distortion" of the data or their interpretation may be present. In principle, this applies to all associations as well as to the publications of companies that want to present their performance in a positive light.

If such effects are not taken into account, the **GIGO effect** can occur—even with highly developed algorithms: "garbage-in-garbage-out." The GIGO effect describes the phenomenon that only bad insights can be gained on the basis of bad data. Colloquially, this effect is also called "shit-in-shit-out."

- **Value** (in the sense of the data's worth)
  Value refers to the relevance of the data with regard to a specific application. Logically, this dimension is on a higher level and is influenced by the aforementioned 4 Vs.

> **Memory Box**
> **Managing the five Vs of big data** is a major challenge for companies. However, many companies today are already failing in the management of "small data"—in the evaluation of the data that already exists in their own company. Incidentally, this is particularly valuable **first party data**.
>
> It may sound paradoxical, but the **entry into the age of big data** should be made through a **comprehensive processing of small data**—a use of the data that is already available in the most diverse places in your company.
>
> Many companies have a **gigantic treasure trove of data** that has been gained through their own business operations (keyword "small data"). However, this is often neither seen nor exploited. Therefore, your **first challenge in data management** is to systematically collect the company's own data and data sources and to transfer them into a **single point of truth** (also called **single source of truth**). This single point of truth describes a data stock that can claim to be correct. The data available here can then also be used as a basis for the controlling tasks described in Sect. 3.8.
>
> The **second challenge in data management** is to examine for which processes this data can be used. These can be the activities for the development of business model innovations or for the elaboration of new offers. Customer communication can also often be designed much more successfully with data support, as long as this is permitted within the narrow legal framework of the GDPR. This regulation contains provisions on the **protection of natural persons** with regard to the **processing of personal data**. This means that the processing of data generated by devices, machines, and/or systems without a personal reference is subject to significantly fewer restrictions. You should use this leeway as intensively as possible to further develop your options for action.

▶ **Food for Thought**
What **type of data protection specialist** is active in your company? A **designer** who helps you to use the legal options creatively? Or an **obstructionist** who blocks all creative possibilities of use out of sheer fear?

There are different **categories of sources of small and big data**. We speak of **first party data** when you yourself are the "first party" to have collected this data (the core of small data). This data—collected by you yourself—is often the most important of all possible data. This includes, for example, all information about **prospects and customers** that you acquire in the course of acquisition, support/retention, and win-back. It also includes all reactions to your communication impulses, the transactions carried out, calls to the service center, and information about the visit to your website.

You can target your prospects and customers by using information about their previous purchases and product interests. This enables individual recommendations for further "suitable" product or service purchases. Think of the various recommendations from *Amazon*: not only for book purchases through an individualized newsletter, but also for *Amazon Music* and *Amazon Video* (analogously also for *Netflix, Spotify* and Co.).

Information from procurement, production, and distribution processes also belongs to first party data. They are not only necessary for monitoring, control, and optimization for ongoing processes, but can also provide impulses for the optimization as well as for the further development of your business model.

Memory Box

Apart from customer related information, all other data that you generate directly from your applications, machines, and systems also belong to first party data. Often, **first party data** is the most useful and valuable for developing your business.

After a comprehensive evaluation of your first party data, you should consider what second and third party data you should also access. Second and third party data is data from other parties. **Second party data** is not usually "traded." It can often only be accessed through an agreement with trusted partners. For example, if you set up a **production network with suppliers** and/or a **marketing network with distribution partners**, important information can be exchanged here (cf. Fig. 3.41 for these value chains). Your creativity is required to develop **value adding partnerships with other companies** to share relevant data sources. Companies that operate outside these networks cannot access this data.

Third party data is traded on markets and is available to all companies with access rights who are willing to pay for it. You can either acquire such data and integrate it into your systems. Or you can at least access such data for use. These **data providers** (also **data aggregators**) include providers of information on the weather, the traffic situation, commuter flows in city centers, fashion trends, price developments on the commodity and stock markets, etc. **Address publishers** and **data service providers** also have access to such data. Address publishers and data service providers, who can

(continued)

systematically support you in customer acquisition and customer development with comprehensive data pools and powerful analysis tools, are also among these important data sources (cf. Kreutzer, 2021a, pp. 101–103, 116f.).

The advantage of **third party data** lies in its large quantity. This is why it is right to speak of big data here in particular. However, you usually **do not acquire exclusivity** when accessing this data—unless you are willing to pay for it ("exclusive data use" or "competitor exclusion"). Customer related third party data is usually not 1:1 data on individual persons (due to data protection!), but information that describes a larger group of consumers, managers, or companies. Nevertheless, you should also check the relevance of such data for your company development.

> **Memory Box**
> A distinction must be made between **first party data** (obtained by the company itself), **second party data** (jointly generated and/or used in partnerships), and **third party data** (provided by third parties for use). First party data is of the greatest importance in many areas because no competitor also has exactly this data. Competitive advantages can be achieved through this.

> **Memory Box**
> **Who owns the data, owns the business, owns the industry!**

▶ **Food for Thought**
Against this background, it would be more than desirable if the European *GAIA-X* project were crowned with success. The aim of this project is to create an **own data infrastructure** for the states, companies, and people in Europe. Through this, **digital sovereignty** is to be established and at the same time **data-based innovations** are to be promoted.

The **infrastructure** to be built in the course of this project is to become the **nucleus of an ecosystem** in which data and services are brought together and made available in a trustworthy manner. Uniform standards for data protection and the exchange of data are also to be developed within this framework (cf. BMWI, 2021).

3.4.2.2 Business Analytics

The great challenge is to develop a basis for business decisions from the multitude of data. The term business analytics is used for this. **Business analytics** describes both the skills and technologies as well as the processes of examining corporate data in order to make business decisions on the basis of the insights gained. The objective of the analysis can have four different directions (cf. Fig. 3.53).

- **Descriptive analyses (description, reporting)**
  Descriptive analyses show what happened in the past. This includes classic reports on the **development of turnover and results** of the company as a whole or of individual business areas. The presentation of the development of customer value as well as **response analyses for online and offline activities** also belong to this category. In the **procurement sector**, reports are made on supplier relationships, and in the **production sector** on the utilization and susceptibility of machines, output quantities, overall equipment efficiency, etc. In the **logistics sector**, it can be shown which delivery reliability was achieved, how the utilization rate turned out, etc. The reports can also be used to show the development of the company as a whole or of individual business units.
- **Diagnostic analyses (inspection)**
  Diagnostic analyses look for the causes, effects, and possible **interactions of different circumstances**. Here, **correlations** and **causal relationships** are sought in order to understand an issue in depth. As with **descriptive analyses**, the focus here is on the past. One wants to understand why something happened. This could be a large number of terminations received in the last few weeks. Or it is to be determined what led to a significant increase in visitors to the e-commerce shop and a significant increase in the conversion rate. At the same time, it can be determined what has caused supply chains to break and what are the underlying

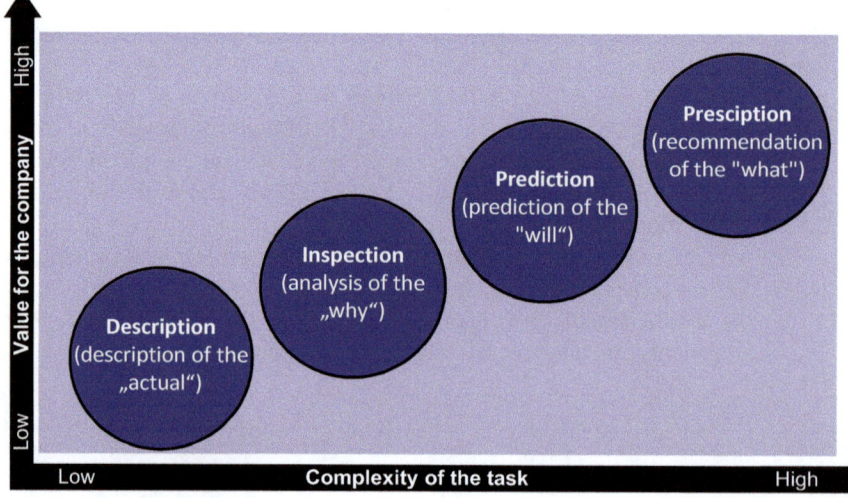

Fig. 3.53 Area of application for business analytics

causes of serious losses in product quality. Increased staff turnover can also be the subject of analysis.
- **Predictive analyses (prediction)**
Predictive analysis attempts to make predictions about future events. These predictions can relate to the **response behavior** of customers to various marketing campaigns, to the **prediction of payment defaults** and to the **failure of machines** (keyword "predictive maintenance"). Corresponding predictions are also important when determining the success of business model innovations as the basis for a business plan.
- **Prescriptive analyses (prescriptions, recommendations)**
Prescriptive analysis develops **recommendations** about how a company should act. Such recommendations can relate to **investments in financial assets**, to milestones in **establishing new business models** or—quite specifically—to the derivation of **customer acquisition and retention measures**. The selection of suppliers and the **design of production and logistics processes** can also be based on prescriptive analyses.

▶ Food for Thought
An exciting, invaluable, and at the same time quasi-free source of information can be your own managers and employees. Why don't you, as CEO or managing director, set up an **hour of truth**? This offers employees and managers at all levels the opportunity to directly address the management with their concerns, wishes, ideas, and problems.

Too dangerous? Doesn't fit the corporate culture? What might the others think?

Again:
Problems and tasks do not disappear by not wanting to see them!

Think Box: Questions You Should Ask Yourself
- How important is big data in your company?
- Who is dealing with the associated issues?
- How successful are you already with the processing of small data—the data that is already available in various places in your company?
- Are the company's own data and data sources systematically collected on a regular basis?
- Is it regularly determined for which processes this data can be used?
- Does your company ensure that it operates within the relevant legal framework (e.g., the GDPR)?
- As a data protection officer, do you have a designer in your company who helps you to creatively use the legal possibilities?

(continued)

- Or do you, as a data protector, have a preventer who blocks all creative possibilities of use out of sheer fear?
- What other data sources—beyond first party data—are already used by your company (second and third party data)?
- What optimization opportunities do you see here?
- Can you enter into value adding partnerships with other companies to share relevant data sources (second party data)?
- Which sources of third party data are relevant to your business model?
- Are the most important data providers known in your company?
- Do you use the relevant address publishers and data service providers—e.g., to acquire new customers?
- How important is business analytics in your company?
- To what extent do you already—regularly—use descriptive analyses in the various business areas?
- How regularly are diagnostic analyses used—and in which fields?
- What importance does your company attach to predictive analyses?
- Are prescriptive analyses already used?
- Have you ever thought about introducing an "hour of truth" in your company?
- Who is responsible for all these questions?

3.4.3 Artificial Intelligence

3.4.3.1 Fundamentals of Artificial Intelligence

Artificial intelligence is of great importance for data utilization (cf. Fink, 2020; Kreutzer & Sirrenberg, 2019; Gentsch, 2019; Wirtz & Weyerer, 2019a, 2019b; Bünte, 2018). In the case of artificial intelligence (AI), a distinction must be made between two areas. First of all, this includes research into how **"intelligent" behavior** leads to the solution of problems. Based on the insights gained in this way, systems are developed that (should) automatically generate **"intelligent" solutions**. However, the approach is not limited to developing solutions only as humans would do. Rather, the aim is to find **results that lie outside the solution and imagination space of humans**.

Artificial intelligence refers to the ability of a machine to perform cognitive tasks that we usually associate with the human mind. This includes possibilities for perception as well as the abilities to reason, to learn independently and thus to find solutions to problems on its own. This also includes the **types of evaluations** mentioned in Sect. 3.4.2.2, which can be used in combination or in isolation:

- **Description**
- **Inspection**

3.4 IT Infrastructure, Data Basis, and Artificial Intelligence

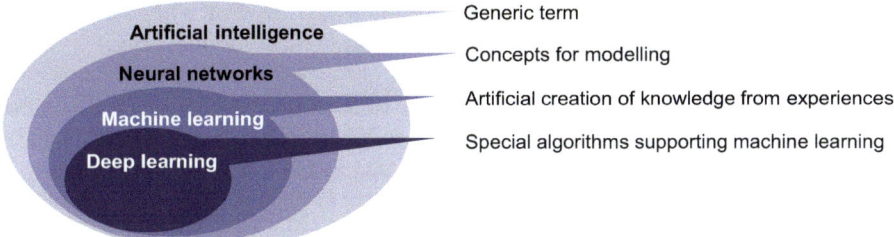

Fig. 3.54 Terms of artificial intelligence

- **Prediction**
- **Prescription**

The big **advantage of artificial intelligence** consists of three areas:

- AI applications make a **contribution to the processing of semi-structured and unstructured data** that should not be underestimated. Here we can think of speech and image recognition.
- AI systems are designed to **process large amounts of data**.
- AI programs make it possible to **develop new kinds of solutions** that were not previously thought of by humans. This is made possible by the so-called machine learning.

> **Memory Box**
> **Data is the new oil!**
> **The Internet of Everything are the new pipelines!**
> **And artificial intelligence is new refinery!**

The central contents of artificial intelligence are best approached via Fig. 3.54. The generic term **artificial intelligence** includes various elements. One of them is the so-called **neural networks**. This term originally comes from the neurosciences. There, a neural network refers to the connection between neurons that perform certain functions as part of the nervous system. Electronic neural networks based on these principles can also recognize very complex, non-linear dependencies of the original information. It is crucial that neural networks learn these dependencies independently (cf. Lackes, 2021).

In the course of its use, the "machine" increasingly emancipates itself from the original inputs (data and rules). In classical **rule-based systems**, the data is processed as defined in advance by algorithms. In contrast, **artificial intelligence** attempts to learn independently in order to further develop these algorithms. On the basis of these further developed algorithms, better results are to be achieved. Consequently, the algorithms used at the beginning only represent the initial breeding ground for the development of new algorithms. If new algorithms prove to be more meaningful in the course of the learning process, the "machine" continues to work with them independently. This process is called **machine learning**.

Deep learning is a special form of neural networks and a subset of machine learning (cf. Fig. 3.54). Deep learning is a type of machine learning that can process a wider range of data resources, requires less data pre-processing by humans, and can often deliver more accurate results than traditional machine learning approaches.

The core performance of artificial intelligence is to be able to recognize relevant patterns even in the largest volumes of data (keyword "**pattern recognition**"). We must take into account here: AI systems today cannot (yet) recognize the actual "meaning of objects." They do not have an overarching "picture of the world" and therefore cannot establish a "world reference" for individual steps—which a human being builds up quite naturally. In addition, today's AI systems are only good at one thing, for example playing chess. But such a system fails at playing Go and can also recognize neither language nor pictures. That is why it is not yet possible to foresee a time frame in which artificial intelligence will reach or even surpass the ability of human intelligence. This project is called **artificial general intelligence**.

> **Memory Box**
> Today's **AI systems** concentrate on **pattern recognition**. In this they exhibit an **insular talent**. This is why they are colloquially referred to as **specialist idiots**. This is also the reason why AI systems cannot recognize larger contexts that go beyond the current focus—today!

3.4.3.2 Learning Methods of Artificial Intelligence

In machine learning and thus in the development of increasingly powerful algorithms, different types of learning can be distinguished:

- **Supervised learning**
- **Unsupervised learning**
- **Reinforcement learning**

In **supervised learning**, the AI system already knows the correct answers and "only" has to adapt the algorithms so that the answers can be derived as precisely as possible from the existing data set. The goal or the tasks of the algorithm are already known here. In order to create a **training dataset**, humans have to label each element of the input data in this learning approach. In addition, the output variables have to be defined. The algorithm is trained on the input data to find the connection between the input variables and the output variables. Linear regression, linear discriminant analysis, and the decision tree method, among others, are used for this. Training is completed when the algorithm is sufficiently accurate. Then this algorithm is applied to new data.

3.4 IT Infrastructure, Data Basis, and Artificial Intelligence 291

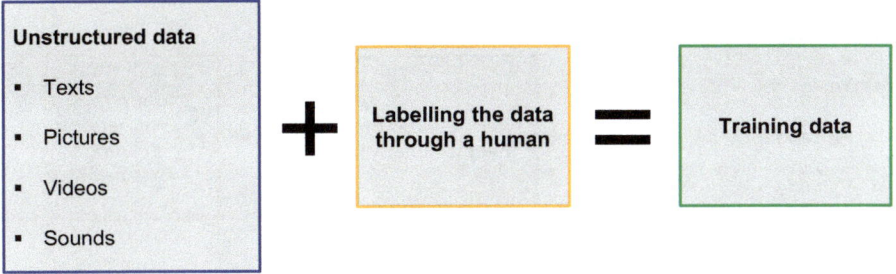

Fig. 3.55 Process of supervised learning—stage 1

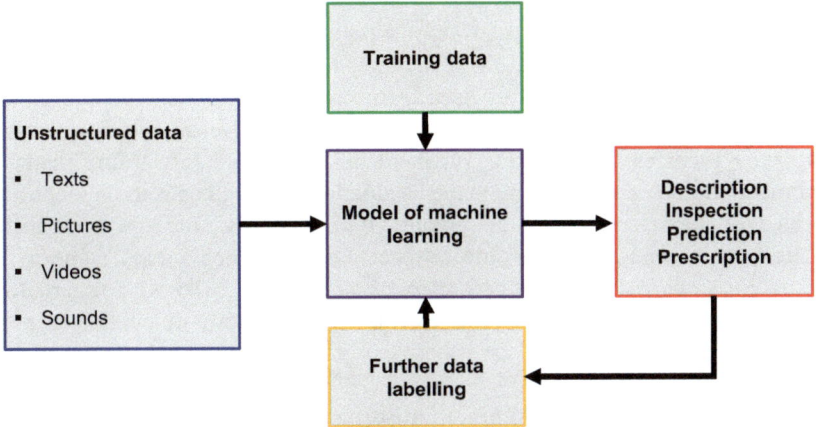

Fig. 3.56 Process of supervised learning—stage 2

The task of such an AI system can be, for example, to recognize faces of wanted persons in photos or video recordings. For this, corresponding **training data** must be created. For this purpose, the photos of the persons being searched for are labelled as human faces (keyword "labelling"; cf. Fig. 3.55).

Subsequently, this training data is used for the development of algorithms to recognize the photos of searched persons in a multitude of different files (cf. Fig. 3.56).

An AI system trained in this way was used as a **test for facial recognition** at a Berlin railway station. The task here was to recognize people who were in advance marked as "wanted" within the crowds of people who use the station every day. Regardless of whether a "wanted" person was wearing glasses or a scarf, the AI system was able to reliably identify the relevant faces in over 80% of cases.

The so-called **false hit rates** (system recognizes person A, but it is person B) were less than 0.1% on average. This means that out of 1000 matches in this test run, only one match was incorrectly recognized by the system. It is to be expected that this value can be further reduced through a combination of different systems (cf. BMI,

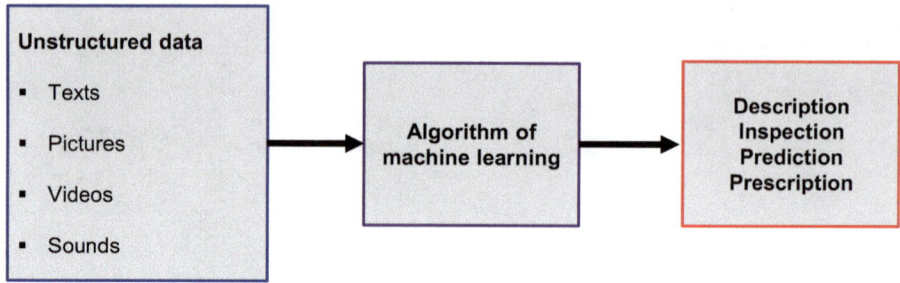

Fig. 3.57 Process of unsupervised learning

2018). The use of such systems can support police work if the legislator creates the necessary framework conditions for this.

Another exciting task for supervised learning is to identify the people in **social media** who are particularly susceptible to **believing false messages** or **trusting conspiracy theories**, commenting on them positively and forwarding them. The phenomenon to be explained here is the "seductibility" that needs to be identified—by whatever characteristics—in the gigantic data set of social media. Such insights may lie outside what people would suspect. One such application came to light through the *Cambridge Analytica/Facebook* scandal in 2016 with regard to the manipulation of the US presidential election. Again, the core of this is pattern recognition, on which manipulative messages are then based (cf. Kreutzer, 2020, pp. 82–84).

In contrast to supervised learning, in **unsupervised learning** the AI system does not have predefined target values and must recognize similarities and thus patterns in the data independently. Consequently, the user of the AI system is not necessarily aware of such patterns in advance. The insights gained by the system can therefore also lie outside of what was previously "humanly conceivable." The algorithm receives unlabeled data as input. It should independently recognize a structure in this data. To do this, the algorithm identifies data groups that show similar behavior or similar characteristics (cf. Fig. 3.57). Hierarchical and k-means clustering, among other methods, are used here.

To convey the basic principle of unsupervised learning, a very simple example is sufficient. Imagine that a large **shopping basket** contains all the products you have bought. These represent the **data input** here. The AI system now has the task of recognizing **patterns in the shopping basket**. To do this, one product after the other is taken out of the basket and is examined.

First of all, packaged and unpackaged products can be recognized and grouped. Among the packaged products, refrigerated products can be recognized and those that are at room temperature. Further, these products can be grouped according to weight, volume, color, packaging material, etc. Whenever something suitable is found, it is assigned to the appropriate group—for example, the tenth carton of milk. In the case of unpackaged products, long (e.g., bananas, leeks), round (lemons, oranges, grapefruits), flaky (pineapples), etc. products can be identified. If the

3.4 IT Infrastructure, Data Basis, and Artificial Intelligence

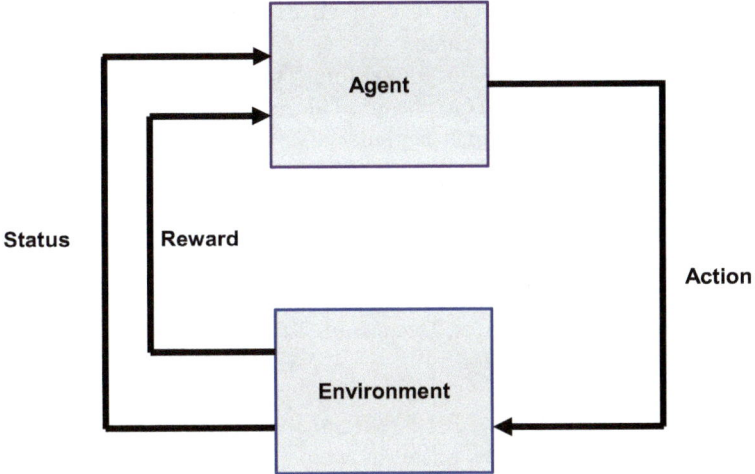

Fig. 3.58 Process of reinforcement learning

comparison process does not result in a pair, a new group is opened. This process is carried out until all products are matched. The result is different **groups** or **clusters**. A structure in the initial data becomes visible. Further processing steps can now follow.

In **reinforcement learning** (also **learning by reward**), there is no optimal solution path at the beginning of the learning phase. The system must iteratively try out solutions independently through a trial-and-error process in order to subsequently reject and/or further develop them. This iterative process is driven by "rewards" (for good solution ideas) as well as "punishments" (for bad approaches). This learning concept is often used when there is little training data or the ideal outcome is not clearly definable. It is also used when something can only be learned from interaction with the environment.

In the course of this learning process, the algorithm makes a decision and acts accordingly. If the action leads the machine to an approximation of the goal, the system receives a reward (e.g., a victory in a chess game or a successful investment decision). Alternatively, it experiences a punishment if one moves away from the goal. This can be the loss of a Go game or falling prices of a share that has just been bought, if the system has not bet on falling prices! The algorithm optimizes its actions independently by constantly correcting itself (cf. Fig. 3.58).

The neural network of *AlphaGo Zero* was trained with *TensorFlow*. This is a special framework for data stream-oriented programming. Remarkable is the fact that the neural network used here knew nothing about the game of Go on the start day—except for the rules to be followed (cf. DeepMind, 2017). Unlike the earlier versions of *AlphaGo, AlphaGo Zero* only perceived the stones of the board. Information about unusual Go board positions and other historical data were not communicated to the system. The AI system learned by reinforcement, playing against itself until it could anticipate its own moves and recognize how those moves would affect the outcome of the game.

The results were measured by the **Elo rating**. This is a rating number to describe the playing strength of chess and Go players. This measurement shows that *AlphaGo Zero* reached the level of a human beginner after only three hours. After 19 h, it behaved like an advanced player, and after 70 hours, like a true super-professional. Here it already crossed the competence level of *AlphaGo Lee*. In the first 3 days, *AlphaGo Zero* played a total of 4.9 million games against itself in rapid succession. The former *AlphaGo* needed several months of training to reach the same level. After 40 days, *AlphaGo Zero* achieved the world's best results—without human intervention and without historical data (cf. DeepMind, 2017).

3.4.3.3 Fields of Application for Artificial Intelligence

For you, the question naturally arises in which areas artificial intelligence can support your company. To answer this, the **fields of application of artificial intelligence** shown in Fig. 3.59 must be scrutinized for their entrepreneurial relevance.

An important field of application for artificial intelligence is initially **natural language processing (NLP)** or **speech processing**. This makes it possible for computer programs to understand human language—both spoken and written. In this case, it is a specific form of automated pattern recognition called "linguistic intelligence." The following forms of application of natural language processing can be distinguished:

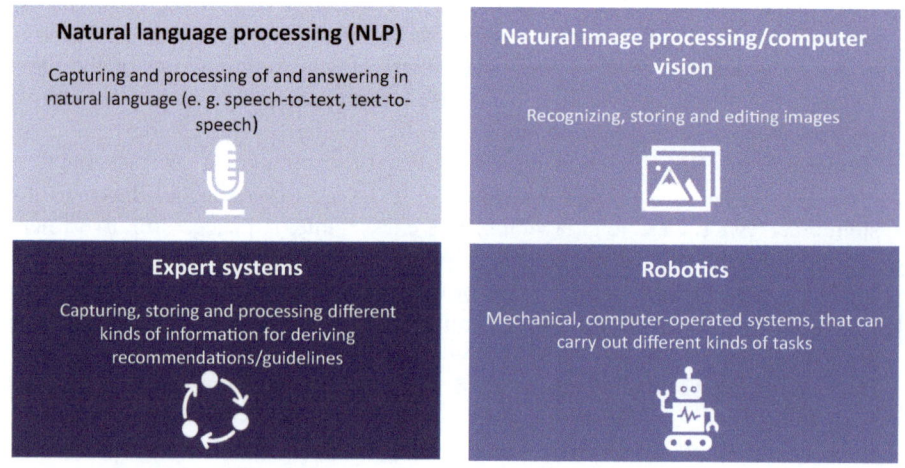

Fig. 3.59 Application areas of artificial intelligence

- **Speech-to-text (STT)**
  In this application, the spoken word is immediately converted into a digital text. This is the case with the *Siri* application (*Apple*), when e-mails or notes are dictated directly into the smartphone.
- **Speech-to-speech (STS)**
  Spoken language is answered here in spoken language. Such question-and-answer sequences are present in the use of digital personal assistants (such as *Alexa* or *Google Home*). STS is also used with *Google Translate*. Thus, a voice input can be made in German, while the voice output (after translation) is in Japanese or Chinese.

  However, it should correctly be: STT—processing—TTS. This is because before spoken language is processed, it is first converted into a digital text, interpreted and processed. Then a digital text is generated that is played out via speech.
- **Text-to-speech (TTS)**
  A spoken version of the text is generated on the basis of digital documents. E-mails, text messages, and other content can be "read aloud" in this way. An example is provided by *kindle*, the e-book reader from *Amazon* that can read books aloud.
- **Text-to-Text (TTT)**
  TTT applications convert an electronically available text into another electronically available text. Examples are translation programs such as *DeepL* or *Google Translate*.

Image processing (also called **natural image processing** or **computer vision**) is the processing of signals that represent images (cf. Fig. 3.59). This primarily includes photos and video content. The result of image processing can either be an image or a data set that represents the characteristics of the processed image. The latter is referred to as **image recognition** (also machine vision). This image recognition can refer to still images (photos) and moving images (videos). In a subsequent step, the image information is processed to initiate decisions or further process steps.

During **image processing**, there are always more or less surprising error detections. The explanation for this is quite simple: the algorithms used today are trained by hundreds of thousands of images that show different objects and are provided with corresponding descriptions. However, the AI systems do not (yet) understand the content-related meaning of the photo as such. As already mentioned, they lack a reference to the world. Today's AI systems cannot yet recognize the actual "meaning" of an object. They focus on pure pattern recognition. The human intellect can—with playful ease—distinguish a living being from a biscuit, a plush teddy bear from a real bear. After all, humans recognize more than just shadowy patterns in illustrations. This challenge is visible in Fig. 3.60.

The **limits of image recognition by AI systems** are therefore (still) determined by the fact that only visual patterns are compared with each other. The meaning behind the patterns (still) remains hidden from the systems. In contrast, we humans recognize the essence of a thing. Consequently, our perception goes beyond the superficial impression because we associate further content to the visual impression

Fig. 3.60 Limits of image recognition

that we have already learned and can thus establish a reference to the world (cf. Hofstadter, 2018, p. N 4).

> **Memory Box**
> Algorithms approach image recognition tasks differently than humans. Algorithms lack a "**model of the world**" as a generic wealth of experience (cf. Wolfangel, 2018, p. 33). This also leads to the fact that larger contexts—which humans intuitively infer—are often not recognizable to AI systems.
>
> Another field of application of AI are **expert systems** (cf. Fig. 3.59). These are computer programs that support people in solving complex problems—like a human expert. For this purpose, the programs derive concrete recommendations for action on the basis of a knowledge base available through the system. To do this, the systems must be supplied with a variety of information. The basis is initially provided by if-then relationships, for example, which make human knowledge comprehensible to computers.
>
> Through the use of artificial intelligence, the expert systems that have been in use for many decades could be decisively further developed. In the next few years, we will see very large leaps in development. In marketing, such expert systems can further perfect **programmatic advertising** (also called "real time bidding"). In the future, such expert systems will not only support media planning, but may even take over completely.
>
> The **robo-advisor** automatically prepares recommendations for investment and also implements them. This is also an expert system, even if the name "robo" rather refers to a robot. A robo-advisor also uses reinforcement learning in parallel to other learning methods. Here, it is quite simple: a successful

(continued)

investment decision corresponds to a reward, a wrong decision to a punishment.

With the **advance of robo-advisors**, the services of a classic investment advisor will become obsolete in the future. The advantage of a robo-advisor is that it is not subject to emotional fluctuations, can be used 24/7, and can analyze gigantic amounts of data in a short time—usually even in real time. For the client, this eliminates the traditional fees for a fund manager.

However, it has already been found out that robo-advisors can amplify **processes pro-cyclically**. It has also become apparent that robo-advisors were often not convincing in the Corona pandemic. Data sets that had to do with such a dramatic collapse of stock markets worldwide were not available when the robo-advisors were trained. Here, the systems first had to learn.

Robots represent the fourth field of application of artificial intelligence (cf. Fig. 3.59). Robots are technical devices that take over work or other tasks from humans—previously mostly mechanical. **Service robots** can completely take over the check-in process in hotels and at airports. **Mobile robots** already support a wide variety of **logistics processes** (e.g., in *Amazon's* warehousing). **Humanoid robots** are another exciting development. These look like humans and are becoming increasingly similar to humans in their behavior (cf. Kreutzer & Sirrenberg, 2019, pp. 44–51).

3.4.3.4 Status of AI Use in Germany

In view of these diverse fields of application, the question arises as to how extensively AI systems are already being used in Germany today. A representative company survey by TÜV (2020, p. 6) identified a large **backlog in AI applications in Germany**. In detail, the following findings were obtained, which should inspire intensive reflection:

- Only 11% of companies in Germany are already using AI applications.
- 19% are currently planning or discussing the use of AI.

Such a result is difficult to swallow for every **leading industrial nation** that would like to maintain this position over the next 10 years and perhaps even beyond. This is especially difficult in view of the other results (cf. TÜV, 2020, p. 6):

- 77% expect AI to fundamentally **change the world of work**.
- 45% believe that very many **new jobs** will be created through the use of AI.
- 52% expect the use of AI to lead to the **loss of many jobs**.
- 83% are in favor of **state support for artificial intelligence**.
- 42% fear **legal problems** with the use of AI.

These figures document what I consider to be the dramatic state of AI deployment in Germany—as of 2020!

Only slightly more than every tenth company is already using AI applications today, while 19% are planning or discussing their use. At the same time, 77% expect a fundamental change in the working world through AI—however, very few companies act accordingly!

"Nice" is also the call for state support—instead of taking action themselves and quickly, as an entrepreneur should! The aforementioned GDPR has an impact on the fear of legal problems. Instead of encouraging, the legal framework conditions tend to slow down companies and make cautious companies hesitate further!

> **Memory Box**
> **AI needs data!**
> What is the saying?
> **No AI without IA!**
> IA stands for information architecture and is essentially generated by people.

▶ **Food for Thought**

At the **EU level**, there is a goal that companies should be forced to regularly disclose their AI algorithms and have them certified! This would require the most qualified AI specialists to work in the EU administration! And how long would companies then be allowed to wait for a release—weeks, months, or years?

Those who allow themselves to be guided by such ideas are visibly gambling away the chance to achieve AI-supported competitive advantages for Europe!

In 2020, the EU Commission presented a **white paper on artificial intelligence** (cf. EU, 2020a). This is intended to achieve two things. On the one hand, it is about **promoting the development and use of AI** in Europe. On the other hand, the **risks of AI are to be reduced**. In the *"Horizon Europe" program*, corresponding research activities are planned for the years 2021–2027 (cf. EU, 2020b). It is to be hoped that the activities promoted here will not be stifled by overregulation.

3.4.3.5 Explainable Artificial Intelligence

Before you do better and embark on your very concrete **AI journey** to integrate AI applications (even) more strongly into your business processes, you should deal with one topic intensively:

Explainable artificial intelligence (XAI).

The attempt of explainable artificial intelligence is to avoid a **black box "artificial intelligence"** and to create a **grey box "artificial intelligence."** This should

Fig. 3.61 Black box artificial intelligence

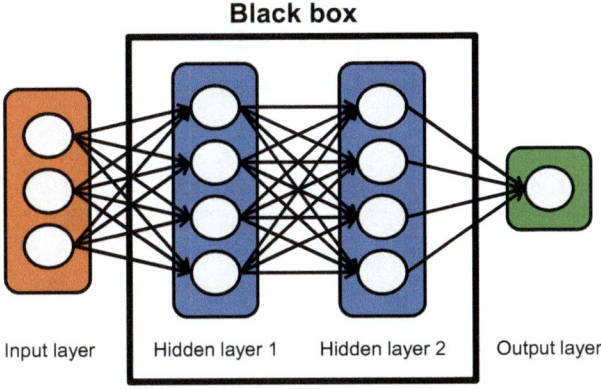

enable at least a partial comprehensibility of results and decisions—especially on the company side, in order to achieve competitive advantages!

The step towards **grey box AI** is important and necessary because the users of AI systems—at least today—do not want to rely unreflectively on the results of AI. After all, users would like to understand at least roughly how a result came about.

Artificial intelligence users often want to see the following questions answered:

- How did this result come about?
- Why was no other result presented?
- When is the AI system successful and when does it fail?
- When can I trust the system?
- How can I recognize errors in the results and correct them if necessary?

Machine learning and deep learning stand in the way of directly answering these questions. The reason is very obvious: the user of an AI system only sees the input and the output. The processes themselves remain invisible for the average use (cf. Fig. 3.61).

The content of the **black box AI** with its human-independent learning processes is intransparent, non-intuitive, and consequently difficult to understand. Nevertheless, the task of explainable artificial intelligence is to build at least a **grey box AI**. This should enable at least a partial comprehensibility of results and decisions. **Transparency must be built up** in three areas:

- **Transparency of data**
  Since the quality and "incorruptibility" of AI stands and falls with the available data basis, it should be possible for the interested user to check the **data basis of the AI application**. If distortions or irrelevant populations are detected in these data, the results of the AI system are not to be trusted (keyword "GIGO effect," see Sect. 3.4.2.1).

  It should be noted, however, that **expert knowledge** is often required to critically examine these data bases. This is usually not possible for laypersons.

Certification processes for data with corresponding seals of approval for the data used could help here if publicly available data pools can be accessed.

> **Memory Box**
> A major challenge for AI applications is to also defend against cyberattacks. Today, **data poisoning attacks** are increasingly being launched to mislead algorithms by manipulating data sets. In addition, AI systems are used by cyber criminals themselves to create **deep fakes**. These are authentic-looking photo, audio, and video contents that have been so "intelligently" faked that they can no longer be recognized as fakes. AI users must therefore also prepare their AI systems for possible cyberattacks right from the start.
> - **Transparency of algorithms**
>   In AI applications, it is particularly important to recognize which algorithms were used to achieve certain results. Since the machine learns independently, this process is not easy to understand. For the acceptance of AI results, however, it is indispensable to be able to know at least the **main factors influencing a decision**.
>
>   The user of an AI system for evaluating **customers' creditworthiness** must be able to understand which criteria had the greatest influence on a decision. In the case of an AI-based recommendation as to which applicant should be offered an **employment contract** and to whom not, the user must be able to comprehend the central criteria of the decision. If a **production process** is automatically stopped by AI, the reasons for this must be quickly comprehensible.
>
>   The willingness to entrust oneself to AI systems stands and falls with such transparency. After all, no one (today) wants to rely on systems and their decisions that are not at least roughly comprehensible.
> - **Transparency of the delivery of data**
>   Another important prerequisite for AI results to be accepted is the **preparation of the results**. The results must be prepared for the users and/or those affected in such a way that even a person with little mathematical and/or statistical training can understand and at least partially comprehend the findings.
>
>   This necessity does not apply if such results are automatically incorporated into further processes. This makes sense in production control and quality monitoring. Here, too, the user must be informed, at least afterwards, why a product was defined as a "reject."
>
>   Without **explainable artificial intelligence**, AI applications remain a black box. However, through the term **grey box AI**, it has already become clear that a comprehensive transparency will not succeed. Otherwise, the users of the AI system will not be able to focus on the "results of the AI process" because "dealing with the AI process itself" will take too much time.

> **Memory Box**
> The development of **explainable artificial intelligence** is an indispensable **prerequisite for the acceptance of AI**. In order to promote this acceptance, an—at least partial—transparency in the areas of data, algorithms, and delivery of data must be established for AI users.

3.4.3.6 AI Journey for the Own Company

A look at the short-, medium-, and long-term developments should provide information about where the **AI journey** can go in your company (cf. Fig. 3.62). This reveals how comprehensively AI can permeate your company, your business models, your processes, and your offerings.

In the **present**, the most important thing is to quickly recognize and utilize the already existing opportunities for AI use. These include standardized, repetitive, and scalable tasks. In addition, it will become increasingly possible to feed AI programs with a variety of semi-structured or unstructured data from a wide range of sources.

The improved results will make it possible to handle even more complex cases and develop ever more powerful systems. It is one of the most important tasks for you to comprehensively examine the use of AI for your company in the **future** and to start your first AI finger exercises—if you have not yet started your **AI journey**. In doing so, you are welcome to focus on the "low hanging fruits." You do not have to and should not start with the most challenging task!

Only if you start looking at the possibilities of AI now will you be ready for what AI has in store for us. The **Hype Cycle for Artificial Intelligence** from Gartner (cf. , 2020c) gives an impression of this. If you want to act here and not just react, it is important to build up the corresponding **AI know-how in your own company** now.

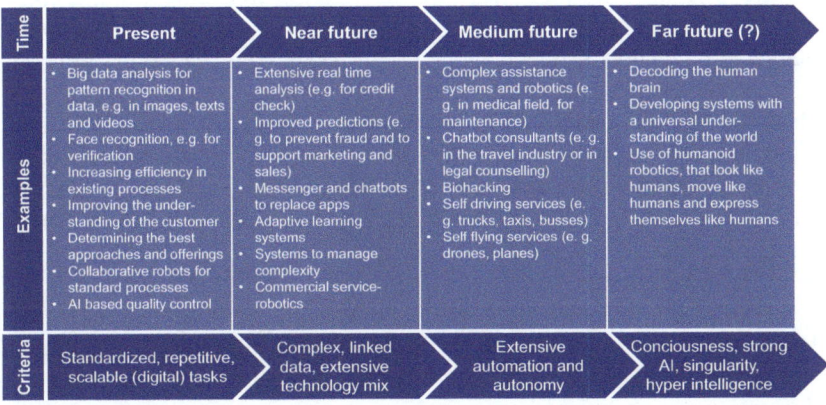

Fig. 3.62 Time horizons of possible AI developments

Already today, **AI specialists** are scarce and expensive. And if—after you—many more companies jump on the AI bandwagon, this scarcity will increase.

Therefore, **it is time to act!**

Which of the technologies mentioned in the **Hype Cycle for Artificial Intelligence** should you focus on today? And which technologies will take a long time to reach market maturity? This Hype Cycle, updated annually by *Gartner*, shows which **phase of the life cycle** various **AI concepts** are in across industries. These technological life phases are defined on the basis of the expectations placed in the various technologies. Here it becomes clear which technologies may still be overvalued and which have already become or are developing into established tools.

The Hype Cycle also shows how much time will pass before an AI application can be used productively on a broad front. For this purpose, Gartner (2020c) defines five different phases—based on the **expectations of AI**—that provide information about the status of market uptake.

- **Innovation trigger**

  In this phase, the **first success stories** of new technologies are published and readily picked up by the media. Whether these technologies will find sustainable use is not yet foreseeable at this early stage.

  An example of this is the development towards **artificial general intelligence**. This will only reach the productivity plateau in more than 10 years.

- **Peak of inflated expectations**

  During this period, **success stories** are published that further fuel expectations of a new technology. At the same time, however, the first failures in the use of the technology become visible, pushing expectations to their limits. Technological use remains limited to a few companies.

  An example of this is the already mentioned **edge AI** (see Sect. 3.4.1.4). **AI cloud services** have also already exceeded the peak of expectations.

- **Trough of disillusionment**

  This trough in the technological life cycle is based on the knowledge that many **expectations of new "wonder weapons" have not been fulfilled**. In this phase, only those technology providers survive who can sustainably convince early adopters and innovators of the benefits of their technology. The other providers drop out of the competition.

  Chatbots and **computer vision** are on their way to this nadir. With these technologies, the limits of what is feasible have become increasingly clear. **Autonomous vehicles** have arrived here at the very bottom. Finally, it has now become clear to almost every specialist that it will be more than 10 years before they are used productively.

- **Slope of enlightenment**

  Here it is becoming increasingly visible how **technologies can be used beneficially**. Technological developments of the second and third generation of initial technology are offered and increasingly taken up by innovation-open companies and integrated into the workflow.

Insight engines are an example of this. These are systems that rely on machine learning and deep learning to analyze, prepare, and link data (keyword "business analytics," see Sect. 3.4.2.2).
- **Plateau of productivity**
The technology is now being widely used because its benefits are not only visible but also comprehensively profitable. Its use as a mainstream technology is preordained. Its use in more and more companies and application areas is only a matter of time.

Solutions such as **CPU accelerators** are in this phase. These are components that make it possible to reduce the load on the central processing unit (CPU). For example, particularly computationally intensive tasks are delegated to systems that are specialized in such tasks.

How should you deal with the developments shown in *Gartner*'s **Hype Cycle for Artificial Intelligence**? First of all, it is important for you to look at the annual **update of this technological life cycle**. If you are an **innovation leader**, your focus is primarily on the first phases of the life cycle. If your company is more of a **late mover**, you should focus on the technologies that have already proven their efficiency in other companies in order to secure their use now at the latest.

> **Memory Box**
> There is only one thing you should not do: underestimate emerging technologies!
> However, managers tend to overestimate the short-term effects of new developments and underestimate the long-term effects. You can avoid this!

▶ **Food for Thought**
AI is a game changer. Therefore, the biggest risk of AI is not engaging with it. Moreover, here—and not only here—it is important to consider:
If a superior technology exists, it will take over the business!

> **Think Box: Questions You Should Ask Yourself**
> - How important is artificial intelligence in your company at the moment?
> - What AI know-how is currently available in your company?
> - Where should AI know-how be built up as quickly as possible?
> - In which fields would an AI application be particularly exciting for you (description, analytics, prediction, and/or prescription)?
> - Which functional area of your company could particularly benefit from the use of AI?

(continued)

- What areas of application do you see for natural language processing?
- In which fields could image processing be used—not only to reduce costs and/or increase efficiency, but also and especially to further develop the business model?
- How important is the use of expert systems in your company or in your industry?
- In which areas can expert systems simplify internal processes and/or create additional value for customers externally?
- Which fields of application are offered to the different robot variants in your company?
- Which (additional) tasks could a robot take over?
- Has your company already dealt with the demand of explainable AI or grey box AI?
- What results have you already achieved in transparency of data, algorithms as well as delivery of data?
- Have you already done your first AI finger exercises in your company and thus started your AI journey?
- Do you regularly follow the publication of the *Gartner* Hype Cycle to stay on top of emerging AI technologies?
- On whose to-do list is the topic of "artificial intelligence" in your company?

3.5 Exploiting Digital Potential Through Marketing and Sales

It often takes more courage to change your mind than to stay true to it.
Friedrich Hebbel

In the so-called customer front, there are a multitude of opportunities to exploit the potential offered by digitalization. Particularly exciting areas of application in marketing and sales are shown below. Digital excellence can only be achieved if these fields are worked on intensively!

3.5.1 Digitization of the Customer Journey

"Digital transformation" is when a user checks the weather on his mobile phone instead of looking out of the window!

3.5.1.1 From Online and Offline to Noline

The **customer journey**—i.e., the journey of a person to a company—starts with the receipt of the first information about a company or an offer, continues with the interest in it and also includes the phases of purchase, use and, if applicable, repurchase or the submission of a rating about the company and/or the offer. The

3.5 Exploiting Digital Potential Through Marketing and Sales

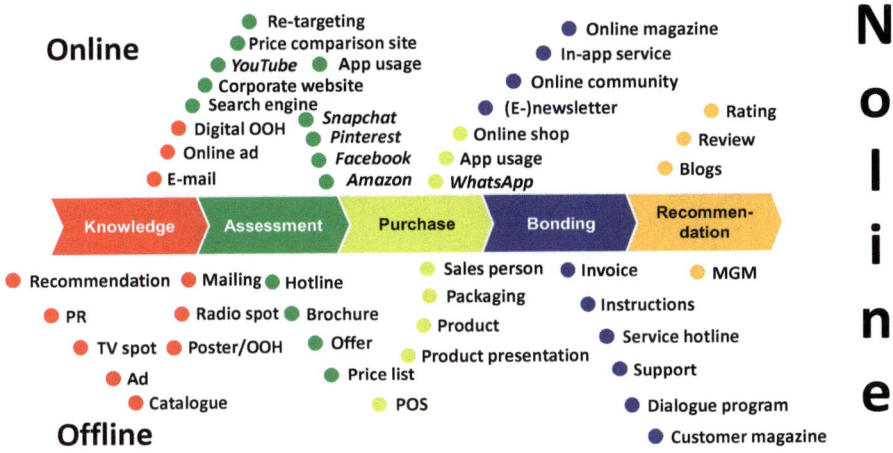

Fig. 3.63 Design of the customer journey today

customer journey thus describes the entire process along the various stages of decision-making that your customer goes through with regard to your company and/or your offers.

A look at a typical **customer journey** in Fig. 3.63 shows which tasks are connected with this for you. Here it becomes visible which **online and offline touch points** can be used. However, the touch points shown there (points of contact between companies and interested parties/customers) represent only a small selection of the possibilities.

At the same time, it becomes clear that the boundary between online and offline is becoming less important, because prospects and customers—also mobile—can continuously switch back and forth between the different worlds. That is why it is better to speak of **noline** today. Consequently, marketing and sales concepts in particular must be developed and implemented "noline." Then the recipients do not have to put together the individual communication morsels and process steps—only to discover that they do not fit together at all!

▷ **Food for Thought**

How a comprehensive **integration of a multitude of touch points** and a large number of functions can succeed in a single app is shown by the **all-in-application WeChat** of the Chinese provider *Tencent*. From online shopping, a general payment function (*WeChat Pay*), the management of travel tickets to *Tinder-*, *Twitter-*, *Facebook-*, and *eBay*-like functions to the organization of trade fair appearances, more or less all areas of life can be controlled via this app.

It is not for nothing that you can find smartphone chargers in many public places in China, because it is virtually impossible to survive there without a smartphone. The great relevance of this and other *Tencent* apps means that this company has over one billion monthly users—not hits! The fact that the state has direct access to this data is well known—and does not slow down its use!

A central aspect of the **digital customer journey** has changed. Whereas in the past in stationary sales the product selection usually took place after the supplier selection, in e-commerce the reverse order often dominates:

In many cases, the supplier selection comes after the product selection!

This must be taken into account in our online and offline—or better—in our noline communication.

To determine the customer journeys of your most important customer groups, you can use the **customer journey map** presented in Sect. 3.5.2.3.

In any case, the **customer journey** needs to be comprehensively considered. It develops in four important dimensions:

- **Noline usage** is becoming increasingly dominant among customers. Access to the various offline and online channels is increasingly merging.
- Customer behavior is shifting from stationary to more **mobile use**.
- Instead of device-specific use, there is increasingly **cross-device use**.
- In the future, control via keyboards will be replaced by **control via voice**.

Think Box: Questions You Should Ask Yourself
- Do you know the customer journey of your most important customer groups?
- To what extent has a fusion of offline and online channels already taken place among your prospects and customers?
- To what extent has the behavior of your prospects and customers already shifted towards mobile use?
- To what extent is cross-device use already taking place?
- To what extent has a corresponding noline approach already been implemented internally?
- Where is there still a need for optimization?
- Do you know the decision-making processes of your customers?
- In your offers, does product selection take place after provider selection or does provider selection dominate after product selection today?
- Who should answer these questions in your company?

3.5.1.2 The "Infinite" Customer Journey and the Flywheel

Ideally, you will succeed in involving your (valuable) customers in an **"infinite" customer journey**, as shown in Fig. 3.64 (cf. also Felten, 2018). The customer journey shown in Fig. 3.63 above ideally does not end with a possible recommendation, but continues to create value for your company over a long period of time.

3.5 Exploiting Digital Potential Through Marketing and Sales

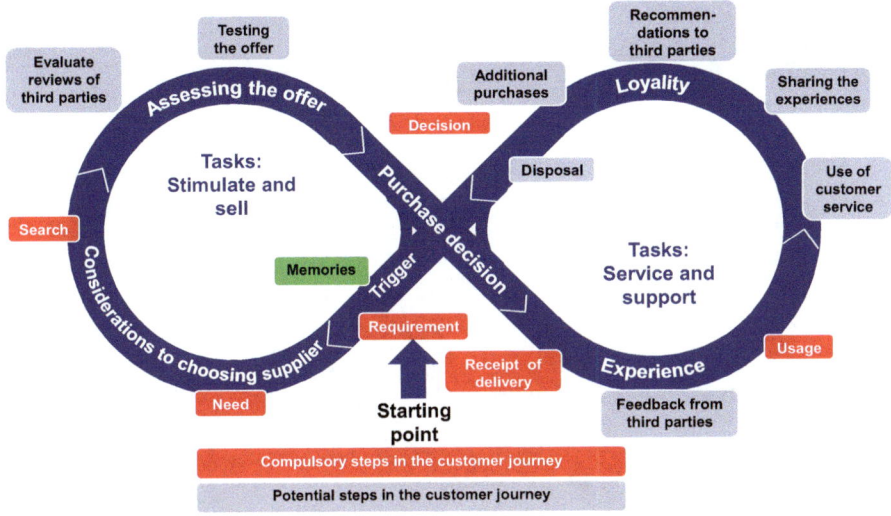

Fig. 3.64 Infinite customer journey

A customer can receive **feedback from his friends and acquaintances**. This information can have a positive or negative impact on the customer's own journey. Depending on prior knowledge and usage experience, **customer service** is taken up. In addition, customers can **share their own experiences with third parties**. In addition, **recommendations** can also be made themselves. **Follow-up purchases** and/or **disposal** may follow. Either a customer now ends the relationship with your company, or a new **trigger**—possibly based on positive **memories**—lets the customer journey start all over again—ideally with you!

> **Memory Box**
> The **average conversion rate in e-commerce** is about **3%**—in **stationary retail** it is about **30%**. These values illustrate the challenge for a convincing (digital) customer journey.
>
> The following applies to the customer journey, whether justified from your point of view or not. For more and more customers, the leading **digital companies** are becoming the **benchmark for other providers**. Here they ask themselves—from the customer perspective—the following questions:
>
> - If *Amazon* can deliver within 24 h, why can't company B?
> - If *Google* can offer a tablet-optimized website, why not concert organizer K?
> - If an order can be placed at *Zalando* with just a few clicks, why not at the ticket online shop M?

Memory Box
The digital key players dictate the standards that customers set for (online) services.
And one thing is certain:
The impatience of users is very great in the absence of convenience! Because the competitor is always just a click away!

To design the **journey in a customer-oriented way**, you need a lot of information to answer the following questions:

- What do the customer journeys of your most important customer groups look like?
- Which touch points are most important from your customer's point of view?
- Do you offer the appropriate content—from the customer's point of view—in the different phases of the customer journey?
- Which or how many of your touch points are real customer trust points—which build trust in your company and your offers?
- What needs do your prospects and customers have at the individual touch points of the customer journey?
- What pain points exist from the user's point of view?
- Do you succeed in presenting your services consistently across all phases of the customer journey?
- How easy is it for users to switch between different channels?
- How successful are you in using information to convert prospects into buyers?
- What are the most important triggers within the customer journey?
- Where do you lose customers in your conversion funnel?
- What measures can you take to further increase customer value?
- What information can be found about your company and your offers at touch points that you cannot control directly (e.g., rating platforms, blogs)?

Section 3.5.2 shows which tools you can use to answer these questions. There you will also see the importance of the **conversion funnel**. The challenge is to ensure a highly **individualized customer approach**. To achieve this, comprehensive data streams must be brought together and evaluated with intelligent evaluation tools—ideally in real time. The offers presented should not only fit a user's profile, but also their **context**. This requires a convincing **customer relationship management** (see Sect. 3.5.1.7).

HubSpot (2021) has taken up the idea of a cycle, which is already present in the infinite customer journey, and developed it further in the concept of the **flywheel** or a **cycle model**. This is based on the mechanical flywheel invented by *James Watt*. The **energy** available in the system of a flywheel depends on

(continued)

Fig. 3.65 Marketing flywheel

the rotational **speed**, the **size,** and the **friction** created when using the flywheel (cf. Fig. 3.65; cf. HubSpot, 2021).

All projects that promote customer orientation and lead to satisfied customers pay into the **rotational speed factor**. This includes the most diverse acquisition concepts, customer loyalty programs, a high-performance customer service center, etc. Low costs, low prices, high quality, and an overall convincing customer experience also increase the speed.

This should make it possible to win as many customers as possible for one's own company. The number of prospects and customers influence the **size factor**. In addition, the aim is to motivate and ideally inspire the acquired customers to interact in a variety of ways. This enthusiasm should spread from one's own customers to other people in order to supply the flywheel with further energy and keep it running. Appreciative customer relationships should become value adding customer relationships that also attract other people. This is to achieve economies of scale and increase profitability. As a result, further investments can be made in the system as a whole to add more energy to the marketing flywheel.

At the same time, it is important to avoid resistance in the system – which is call the **friction factor**. However, such resistance can still be found in many companies today. For example, online and offline activities are often not sufficiently interlinked (keyword "silo thinking" instead of a "noline approach"), websites are not optimized for mobile use, call center agents are not sufficiently trained, ordering and payment processes are not transparent and/or do not function smoothly—and no company representative responds to customer complaints.

(continued)

In contrast, platforms and ecosystems can significantly reduce the **friction** in the sense of acquisition costs because they are highly attractive to many suppliers and demanders and then also contribute to positive word-of-mouth effects. However, the question arises here as to which flywheel is supplied with additional energy—that of the provider or that of the platform operator!

In order to get the flywheel going and keep it going, it is necessary to check in the **conversion funnel** where and why potential customers are lost (cf. Fig. 3.73). In addition, it is important to direct the customer driven energy in the form of **data streams in the company** in such a way that improvements and innovations of products and services are developed from them, which can also lead to new business models. To this end, it is important to regularly motivate those responsible for the performance and innovation engine to exchange ideas (see Sects. 3.4.2 and 3.7.4).

Memory Box
The inefficiency of internal company processes still often slows down the marketing flywheel that was set in motion with a lot of money!

In the conversion funnel already briefly mentioned (cf. Fig. 3.73), the customer is seen as the result of a process geared to him. In contrast, in the flywheel the **customer** himself represents a **central and indispensable source of energy**—and is treated accordingly. The acquisition energy you have put into customer acquisition should not be seen as spent after a successful acquisition. Rather, this energy should continue to have an effect on the customer and motivate him to engage in various activities. For example, the customer should report on his experiences on online platforms, get involved in innovation processes, and/or actively recruit new customers. In this way, the energy that you have put into the acquisition should live on in the acquired customers and help your **marketing flywheel** to gain momentum (cf. Fig. 3.65):

- The **"attract" phase** covers the acquisition steps. This is less about push measures. It is more about wooing customers with exciting and relevant information and offers (pull measures)—and less about "coercing" them to buy with aggressive requests. This is where content marketing becomes very important.
- In the **"integrate" phase**, the challenge is to make the acquisition and purchase process as well as subsequent interactions as simple and—for the customer—as value adding as possible. Friction should be avoided as much as possible.

(continued)

- In order to reach the **"delight" phase**, it is important to provide the customer with the best possible support during the acquisition phase and also after a purchase has been made. In this way, the customer can become an advocate and brand ambassador for the company.

If you think in such **cycles**, then a customer acquired is not the final result of an acquisition process. Rather, winning a customer is the start of a new acquisition process—beyond the customer won in each case (keywords "friendship advertising," "rating and review management," "content marketing"; cf. Kreutzer, 2021a; Kilian & Kreutzer, 2022).

▶ **Food for Thought**
In this **circular model**, responsibility for prospects and customers in the company is not passed on from one party to another. There must be intensive cooperation—across departments and divisions. Otherwise, too much energy is lost through frictions. Continuous, value creating interaction within the company as well as with customers should add further energy to the marketing flywheel. Such an approach can become the dominant content of **customer experience management**.

In order for the marketing flywheel to run as smoothly as possible, marketing and sales in particular must work together more intensively than is still the case in most companies today. It is imperative to overcome the **classic line of conflict between marketing and sales**. The best way to do this is to agree on **common goals** for these two areas. It is also very helpful if the **reporting lines of marketing and sales converge** with a member of top management.

Alternatively, the overall responsibility for **marketing and sales could be in the hands of a top manager**. Then the managers responsible for marketing and sales talk less about each other and more with each other. After all, the customer does not care which department is responsible for which customer touch point.

Today, it is also necessary to involve another player at an early stage and not just declassify it as a "processor": IT. As discussed in more detail in Sect. 3.4, **IT** plays an indispensable **key role in the digitalization of the customer journey**. Therefore, the areas involved—oriented to the purpose of the company—must be committed to common goals and a common strategy. The **concept of the action matrix** presented in Fig. 3.51 can provide important support for this.

A study by Hensel-Börner et al. (2018) shows which mindset is still common today. Here, 55 explorative, semi-structured in-depth interviews were conducted with representatives from the areas of marketing, sales, and IT. The sample includes companies from B2B and B2C (incl. Service providers) in Germany. The following result shows how the **cooperation** between marketing, sales, and IT is perceived (cf. Hensel-Börner et al., 2018, p. 23):

- 30% experience a **three-way battle**, concretized by a pronounced silo mentality and tough and uncoordinated cooperation.
- 34% describe cooperation as a necessary evil, a **challenging partnership**.
- 36% see a **triad**—in the sense of "one team, one target." Here, cooperation is based on mutual appreciation.

Only when these areas come together to form a **value creating triad** can the challenges described below be mastered. If necessary, other corporate divisions can be integrated to put an end to the silo mentality once and for all (cf. Fig. 3.51).

▶ **Storytelling** I was recently involved as a consultant in the **introduction of a CRM system** by a large regional bank. In the kick-off meeting, the company's internal project manager from the marketing department announced: "we don't talk to IT. We are not working with IT on this project."

What was the first task in this project? Together with my team, the first task was to overcome the **deep divide between IT and marketing**. How could that possibly be achieved? In a multitude of conversations, the first task was **to build trust** and **to bridge the gap** step by step.

The great thing was: at the end of the project, the company not only had a **functioning CRM system**, but also a resilient **working relationship between marketing and IT**!

> **Think Box: Questions You Should Ask Yourself**
> - To what intensity have you already achieved an infinite customer journey?
> - How well do you know the journey of your customers—and how successful are you in influencing this journey?
> - Have you ever checked which marketing and sales activities have an impact on your marketing flywheel?
> - Do the different measures reinforce each other—or do they rather slow each other down?
> - How does your company's marketing flywheel perform in terms of speed, size, and friction?
> - Where does your company stand in terms of cooperation between marketing, sales, and IT: a three-way battle, a challenging partnership, or a triad?
> - Can you take a path towards a value creating triad, if this is not yet being followed?

3.5.1.3 Relevance of ZMOT

In the age of digitalization, the **customer journey** has changed dramatically in many areas, also in terms of content. Many purchase processes take place completely or partially digitally during the initiation, implementation, and follow-up (keyword "e-commerce"). In addition, private as well as professional users can inform themselves comprehensively—online—about potential partners and their performance in the run-up to and parallel to the purchase process. Therefore, the classic **purchase decision processes** that have dominated up to now need to be developed further.

Up to now, a distinction has only been made between the first and second moment of truth in the course of the purchase decision process. The **first moment of truth** (FMOT) refers to the time when a potential buyer can physically see a product or service for the first time—often directly in the shop or after delivery. This is where the expectations built up by your advertising, as well as by the promises of your sales staff, meet the "hard reality" of the advertised product or service—seen through the eyes of the customer.

The **second moment of truth** (SMOT) encompasses the time when the buyer actually uses a product or service. This is often where two worlds collide: on the one hand, there are the expectations built up through advertising, sales, and the first direct contact with the offer. On the other hand, there are the experiences gained with the actual performance and experiences of using the product or service.

We speak of the **"moment of truth"** here because these two "moments" show whether the expectations built up through advertising, the presentation of the offer and the consultation are actually fulfilled—always from the customer's perspective. The evaluation of these "truths" through the eyes of the customers decides whether the customer journey continues or ends abruptly!

The **zero moment of truth** (ZMOT) has now been added to the first and second moment of truth (cf. Fig. 3.66; cf. Lecinski, 2014, p. 17). This refers to the online access—preceding the other two "moments"—to an almost unmanageable amount

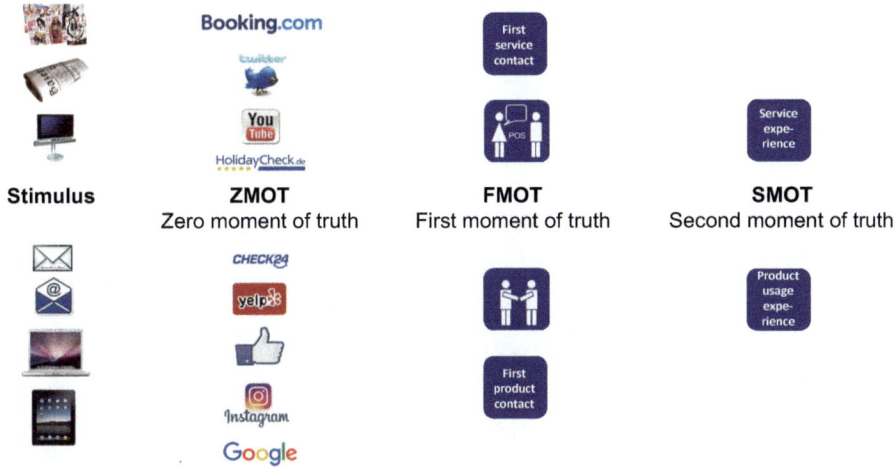

Fig. 3.66 Positioning and sources of ZMOT

of third-party information. Particularly relevant here are **customer ratings and reviews**, in which frequently unknown third parties report on their experiences before, during, and after acts of purchase and use. This means that users can communicate the content of their very personal first and second moments of truth on various platforms. In this way, these users enable third parties to have a zero moment of truth—without ever having come into direct contact with the provider and/or the offer.

> **Memory Box**
>
> The core of **ZMOT** is information from third parties in blogs, communities, and comments on *Facebook, Google, Instagram, Twitter,* or *YouTube*. In addition, reviews are also presented on various rating and booking platforms (e.g., *Yelp, Booking.com* or *Holidaycheck*). The content to be found there enables prospective buyers to **self-serve in someone else's experience**, so to speak.
>
> Even before a potential buyer engages intensively with your offers or your business (online as well as offline), a great deal of information can often be gained about the pre-sales, sales, post-sales, and usage phase of other people with regard to your offers. The **ZMOT** is fed by the experiences that other people have gained during their customer journey.

> **Memory Box**
>
> The important about this is: if your company and/or your offers have not convinced other users and this assessment is made public online, this can deter many potential users from entering into a business relationship with you. Therefore, you should attach great importance to a **rating and review management** in your company (cf. further Kreutzer, 2021a, pp. 86–90).

> **Think Box: Questions You Should Ask Yourself**
> - How well do you know your customers' first moment of truth (FMOT) and second moment of truth (SMOT)?
> - Do you also keep an eye on the zero moment of truth (ZMOT)?
> - How actively are you involved in a rating and review management?
> - Who deals with these topics at your company?

3.5.1.4 Information Tsunami and Information Overload

Due to the multitude of information channels and the content presented there, the majority of online users regularly experience **information overload**. The extent of information overload is illustrated by the following figures—showing the **use of communication channels** and **access to online services per minute** (cf. Smart Insights, 2021):

- 4000 people reading *Yelp* reviews
- 26,000 apps downloaded
- 210 million e-mails sent
- 694 million songs streamed in the USA
- 283,000 US-$ spent online shopping on *Amazon*
- 4.2 million *Google* searches
- 12,500 ride-shares taken at *Uber*
- 7000 actives users on *LinkedIn*
- 510,000 comments posted on *Facebook*
- 350,000 tweets sent via *Twitter*
- 4100 clicks on sponsored *Instagram* posts
- 1300 product-rich pins pinned at *Pinterest*
- 21 million snaps created at *Snapchat*
- 694,000 videos viewed on *TikTok*
- 97,200 h of content consumed on *Netflix*
- 3.47 million videos watched on *YouTube*.

These figures clearly show that e-mails still play a dominant role in online communication. The channels *Facebook, Google, Instagram, YouTube, Twitter, Instagram* & Co. also contribute to a veritable **information tsunami**. This has already led to a veritable **content shock** in many areas, because users are less and less able to defend themselves against the multitude and variety of content.

This leads to an important phenomenon that must also be consistently taken into account when designing corporate communication: **selective perception**. Of all the information that impacts on customers—be it via TV, radio, posters, newspapers, magazines, telephone, mailings, apps, social media (blogs, social networks), banners, etc.—only a small fraction is perceived today. You can assume that in view of the **information tsunami**, significantly less than 1% of the information accessible to a user is perceived. All other messages—well over 99%—already miss the first communicative goal: at least to be noticed (cf. Fig. 3.67; cf. Kilian & Kreutzer, 2022).

The reason for this is that all people have built up a **filter** to protect themselves from this flood of information. This protection is essential for survival! Otherwise, **burn-out** or—with regard to social media—**social media burn-out** is guaranteed. This can occur when people fail to master the variety of information that comes at them via social media (cf. Kreutzer, 2020). Figure 3.67 also makes one thing clear: the more data has not enlarged the information funnel, but only reduced its permeability!

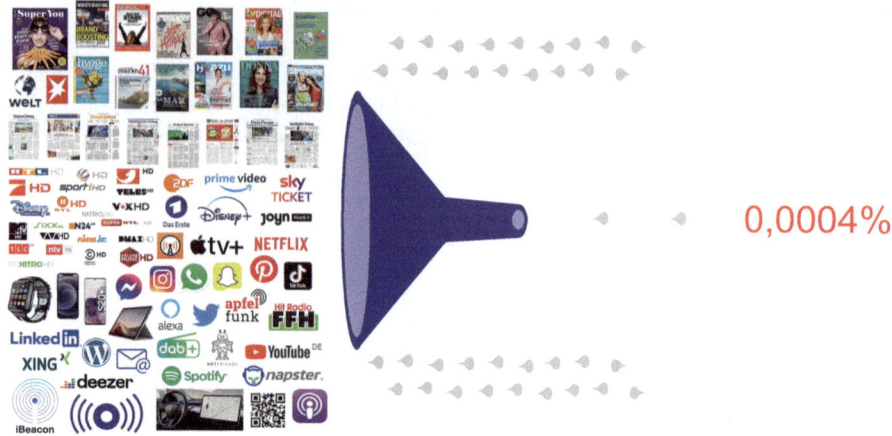

Fig. 3.67 Extent of information overload

> **Memory Box**
> You should use the **illustration of information overload** as a **humility slide** in your company. All those responsible for communication—both internally and externally—should remember when developing communication tools and messages that they must penetrate the increasingly impermeable information filter. What is the answer to this challenge?
> **Relevance, relevance, relevance!**
> Against this backdrop—as already mentioned in Sect. 1.2.3—there is talk of an **attention economy,** where people's **attention is the scarce commodity**. In the highly developed industrial nations, there is often no longer a shortage of product and service offerings. On the contrary, there is often a real **terror of diversity** or a **terror of options**. This applies equally to private individuals and companies.
> At the same time, the **costs for the exchange of information** are constantly decreasing due to the networking of people, and its intensity is increasing. **Private individuals** have to decide whether they want to be present in social networks, and if so, in which ones. In addition, it has to be decided which content should be shared there and, if applicable, via rating platforms, blogs, forums, and communities as well as on the social media platforms.
> For **companies**, the **variety of options** is no less great. Here, too, the question arises as to the necessary presence on the various media sharing platforms, involvement in the social networks, participation in or the establishment of one's own blog, or the use of messenger services for sales communication. Consequently, the limiting factor here is no longer access to or the provision of information and offers, but the attention paid to them.

Memory Box
Today, attention is the scarce resource that is decisive for success.
We live in an attention economy!
The variety of offers described here has led to a continuous **decline in customer loyalty** for several years (cf. Kreutzer, 2021a, p. 12f.). There is the group of **variety seekers**. These are customers who enjoy changing their provider again and again, even if they were satisfied with their offers. The importance of the ecosystems and platform concepts described in Sects. 3.3.2 and 3.3.3 becomes even easier to understand against this background. The **ecosystems** try to serve and retain customers more and more comprehensively in order to make it more difficult to switch to other providers. The **platform models** themselves lead to customers being loyal to the platform operator, but there they can try out other providers again and again.

Think Box: Questions You Should Ask Yourself
- How severe is the information overload already for your customers?
- Have you ever asked your customers about the state of content shock?
- How can you ensure that relevance of your communication—from the customer's point of view—can be achieved?
- What consequences does the attention economy have for your business model?
- How high is customer loyalty in your industry and in your company?
- Are variety seekers more of a curse or a blessing for you?
- Who answers these questions on a regular basis?

3.5.1.5 Trend Towards Individualization of Service Provision
In order to counteract customer churn and at the same time build relevance in the eyes of customers, many companies are focusing on **individualization of service provision**. The trend away from mass products to individualized offerings is facilitated by the **system of value chains** described in Fig. 3.41.

This involves the **interplay of online configurations with collaboration tools and digital sales channels**. In this way, customer requirements can be digitally recorded in a **closed information loop** and converted into instructions for production. With a high degree of automation—possibly supported by AI-based test routines—humans no longer need to intervene in this process. The flexibility required in production is being driven by the **trend towards the smart factory** and the increasingly widespread use of **3D technology**.

The linchpin for **entry into the customization of products and services** is often an **online configurator**. Using a configurator, thousands or tens of thousands of customers can select their wishes regarding color, size, shape, functions, equipment, and other technical details. The keyword here is **mass customization**. This describes the mass provision of individual offers, which, in addition to the advantages of mass production for the company, also tries to take into account customer wishes for individualization—and all this at acceptable costs. In this concept, the provider often provides the **space of possibilities**, which also analyzes plausibility checks and the compatibility of different wishes (keyword "feasibility check"). Companies like *mymuesli.com* and *outfittery.com* have built their business model on such a concept.

L'Oreal relies on **BeautyTech** to round off its own range by individualizing its products. *L'Oreal's* vision here is: "Building long-term one-to-one relationships with each of our consumers to better understand and meet their **individual needs**" (L'Oreal, 2021). To this end, consumers are not only offered the opportunity to experience product services virtually. By **cooperating with start-ups** and **acting as an incubator**, the company is also able to identify trends at an early stage.

This has made possible developments such as *Modiface*, which uses **augmented reality** for product tests. Anyone interested in a new lipstick can immediately see if it fits by looking at their mobile phone when using the app—and not just statically, but also in motion. With the *L'Oréal Perso* device, customized cosmetics can be produced through the **use of AI**.

Individualized products of the *SkinCeuticals* brand are marketed under the sub-brand *Custom D.O.S.E.* Based on the data and experience gained here, *L'Oreal* also plans to further improve **individual customer advice**—specifically through forecasts regarding the coherence of certain products for each individual customer (cf. L'Oreal, 2021).

Through the use of **collaboration tools**, individual visual ideas can also be incorporated into the production process. The **refrigerator manufacturer** Liebherr (2021) not only offers its customers a simple **configurator** with preset options. Here, customers can apply their **own lettering** and even **individual photos** to the appliances. They can also choose from almost 20 million colors. What an appropriately designed refrigerator might look like is immediately displayed in 3D.

The company *spreadshirt.com* not only enables its customers to **design T-shirts** on its own online platform, but also to sell their own creations there. Other providers make it possible to incorporate one's own photos into **wall decorations**, **photo books, calendars,** and other products.

The *Coca-Cola Freestyle* offer is also based on collaboration. Here, users are offered the opportunity to mix their own **personal soft drink**—in more than 100 different variations. Customers can use the **app** to create a drink, which may even remain unique. This mix has to be saved. At the *Freestyle* **vending machines**, the generated QR code is scanned—and the customer's own creation is dispensed. The topic of **sustainability** also finds its way into this if you bring your own cup. In addition, logistics are reduced because there is no need to transport full and empty bottles (cf. Coca-Cola, 2021). And every customer gets exactly the drink of their choice!

For *Coca-Cola's* partner companies, such a concept has the advantage that they can now offer a much greater variety of beverages without investing in storage

3.5 Exploiting Digital Potential Through Marketing and Sales

space. In addition to the stand space, only a power and water connection is required. The respective desired flavors come out of the various cartridges of the beverage vending machine.

In the meantime, *Nike* allows the buyers of its shoes not only to **apply individual lettering**, but also to **customize the color of many individual parts of the shoe**. For this purpose, the company provides the corresponding digital tools (cf. Nike, 2021).

To make the packaging of the *Nivea* **cream** even more individual, *Beiersdorf* allows users to enhance the tins with their own photos. An **online editor** playfully supports this process. There are no limits to creativity. However, users are asked to refrain from posting illegal or offensive content that would violate the rights and dignity of others. It is important to note that *Beiersdorf* reserves the right to reject images that violate this requirement.

Memory Box
Collaboration tools open up an almost unlimited potential for integrating consumers into the production process.

Augmented reality applications make it easier for customers to visualize the solution being developed. Carpets or pieces of furniture can be placed in a room using a smartphone camera. A **digital overlay** makes it possible to move the trying-on of clothes and shoes into the digital space. This is not only possible in the **smart fitting rooms** of the fashion houses themselves, but also at home. The photos created in this way can be shared immediately on social media to receive feedback from friends—in real time, even during the buying process. Thus, shopping is increasingly becoming **social shopping** (cf. Kreutzer, 2021b).

Several furniture retailers offer a **3D planning tool** for **kitchen planning**. Here, too, customers are actively involved in the creative process to ultimately receive a highly individualized product.

However, the use of mass customization is not limited to consumer goods. Corresponding concepts also lend themselves to the **B2B market**. The configurator of the construction machinery manufacturer *Zeppelin* enables you to individually configure even complex construction equipment of the *Caterpillar* brand, e.g., with regard to the cabin, paint, etc. (*zeppelin.com*).

You can use the following aspects to **evaluate the individualization potential of your own offers**. Here you should check which of the criteria are of particular importance to you:

- The **sales department is relieved** when the customer takes over many configuration tasks himself. The classic sales department is supported by a digital colleague, as it were. This can reduce sales costs.
- By using a configurator, **serious prospective buyers** can be identified more easily and distinguished from users who just want to look. This would also reduce acquisition costs.

(continued)

- Customers ideally **enjoy engaging with your offers**. A well-made configurator can increase customer loyalty. However, this can only be achieved with a configurator that is really convincing—from the customer's point of view—and intuitive to use.
- A product configurator leads to an **increase in price transparency**—for customers and competitors alike.
- Marketing, sales, product management, and R&D very quickly and easily recognize the current **preferences of customers for products and services—including the available budgets.**
- Companies that previously sold through intermediaries gain **immediate access to the customer interface** through these concepts—and first-hand customer information!
- The elimination of intermediary partners also eliminates the **information pollution** that occurs when information is passed from station to station (keyword "silent mail").
- The information gained here provides the **fuel for innovation**. This can succeed above all if customers can also express wishes that go beyond the status quo via a configurator.
- By definition, own creations increase the **relevance of the product in the eyes of the buyer**.
- In the case of customized products, **return or exchange of a product is usually excluded**. This is an important argument for the return rates in e-commerce. Today, these rates—depending on the product and delivery conditions—are often around 25%. In the case of clothing, they easily rise above 50%! This entails an enormous logistical and financial effort for retailers, which is avoided with individual products.

Digitization of the customer journey implemented in this way goes hand in hand with the **opportunity to obtain a large amount of profile and behavioral data from prospects and customers**. As long as this data is collected and processed in accordance with data protection regulations, it can be used for customized communication and the individualization of offers. However, not all companies make use of this possibility (see Sect. 3.4.2.1 on the keyword "small data"). The comprehensive use of these information sources should lead to a **closed loop of data acquisition and use** (cf. Fig. 3.68).

In such a **closed-loop approach**, many actions or interactions of prospects and customers can be tracked—especially online. This allows customer migration to be recognized, targeted measures for more-, cross-, and up-sell to be initiated, customer values to be determined and thus profitability analyses for the entirety of marketing and sales activities to be carried out. This lays the informational foundation for **value-oriented customer touch point management**.

(continued)

3.5 Exploiting Digital Potential Through Marketing and Sales

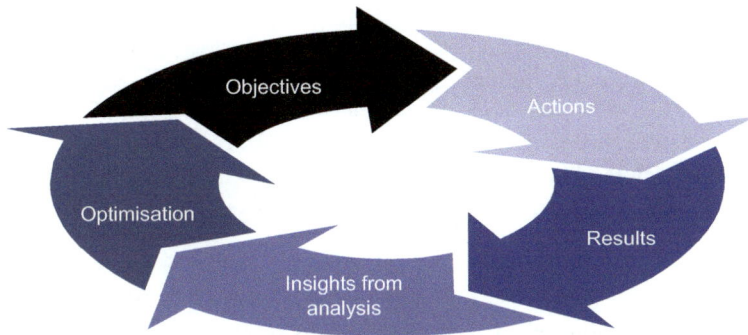

Fig. 3.68 Closed loop of data acquisition and use

For **value-oriented customer management**, the customer experience (CX) at the different touch points is becoming increasingly important. The experiences gained here will decide which provider a customer will give his loyalty to. Therefore, you need to increase your focus on **customer experience management** (CXM). The management of customer touch points is a sub-task of this.

Memory Box
Data is the "fodder" for compelling customer experiences!
  Our task is to create an inspiring "digital quality of stay"!

Think Box: Questions You Should Ask Yourself
- What possibilities for individualizing product and service provision already exist in your sector?
- Which approaches have you already exhausted and where do you still see potential?
- Can you establish closed information loops with your customers?
- What opportunities does the trend towards the smart factory offer you?
- Where can you use 3-D technology to individualize your products?
- Can you succeed in individualizing products and services through an online configurator?
- Can you achieve individualization of products and services through an online editor?

(continued)

- Does your business model offer the possibility for mass customization?
- Where can you use augmented reality in marketing and sales?
- Which aspects in your company speak for or against exploiting the individualization potential of your own offerings?
- Have you already installed a closed loop of data acquisition and use?
- Where does the responsibility for answering these questions lie with you?

3.5.1.6 Customer Experience Management (CXM)

Today and in the future, what matters most is the **customer's experience** with you as a provider. You do not necessarily have to offer the best product or the most convincing service—nor the lowest price. What is increasingly decisive is the overall experience a customer has with you at the various touch points. These experiences will influence further development more than the product or service you offer alone. Even the pricing, your advertising, your online presence will have a less lasting effect than the **perceived experiences**—always from the customer's perspective.

> **Memory Box**
> **Experience is the new product!**
>   **Therefore, the task is to establish a customer experience management.**
>   However, an **analysis of customer experience management** in Germany shows that so far only a few companies are on the way to establishing a qualified CXM. The *"Mind the Data Gap"* report from Adobe (2019) paints the following picture for Germany:
>
> - Only 19% of German companies put **data at the center of their customer experience management**.
> - Companies primarily blame an inappropriate **corporate culture** with a **dominant departmental mindset** and associated **data silos** (30%) for inadequate customer experiences.
> - An obstacle on the way to data-based CXM is seen by 26% of companies in **strict data protection regulations.**
> - **Fragmented technologies** and a **lack of skills for appropriate data management** are further obstacles to the development of CXM (24% each).
> - For example, only 12% of German companies see themselves in a position to use personal and non-personal data to **create cross-channel customer profiles** in real time.
> - Only 15% of the platforms used for CMX can manage an open and smooth **transition from behavior-based, transaction-based, and operational data.**

(continued)

3.5 Exploiting Digital Potential Through Marketing and Sales

- However, 43% of respondents also see great potential to achieve more compelling CXM results in the future through **the use of AI.**
- The focus of future AI use is the gain in knowledge that can be achieved through **AI-based access to previously hidden information** (33%).
- Additional AI fields of application are seen in **targeting** (28%), **personalization** (28%), and **target group segmentation** (28%).

Here it becomes apparent that **CXM development** is still in its **infancy** in many cases. This is due to the cultural, organizational, and process-related obstacles that have been identified. In some cases, a high-performance infrastructure is also lacking. Legal hurdles also impede the installation of a convincing customer experience management.

▶ **Food for Thought**

Determine how important customer experience management is in your country and in your company. What obstacles do you have to overcome here? What opportunities are seen for CXM?

If you want to know what you should consider when **setting up a powerful customer experience management**, it is worth taking a look at the CX study conducted by NTT (2020, p. 36). This presents the results of a survey of 1020 companies from 13 industries and 79 countries across the Americas, Asia Pacific, Australia and New Zealand, Europe, and the Middle East and Africa. The following **characteristics of the best CX-oriented companies** were identified:

- The top CX performers define the **value proposition of CX for the company's success** and understand why customer experience management is a crucial **part of the company's strategy**. By integrating CMX into the strategic direction, these companies get a significantly better NPS (net promoter score; see Sect. 3.5.2.6) score. Therefore, you should consistently identify the added value you can achieve through CX with regard to your business objectives (see Sect. 3.8).
- An important CX success factor is the **joint development of a CX design**. Based on the noline approach (see Sect. 3.5.1.1), CX processes link all relevant touch points, even across different business units. This significantly increases the speed of processing customer-oriented processes. This is an important driver of positive customer experiences. The challenge for you is to develop **company-wide CX solutions** to connect all customer touch points.
- Another CX success driver is systematic **VoC integration**. VoC stands for "voice of the customer." By comprehensively integrating the "voice of the

customer" into corporate processes, their needs and wishes can be taken into account much more easily. Such an approach has a lasting positive impact on customer loyalty and customer value as well as on the company's profit situation. Consequently, you should install feedback mechanisms and formalize regular customer dialogue. It is also important to integrate customers into innovation processes (see Sect. 3.5.3.2).
- Companies that operate a successful CXM systematically use **business analytics** to identify **factors influencing CX**. This can also identify important inhibitors of convincing customer experience management. A convincing CXM requires relevant customer insights (see Sect. 3.4.2.2)!

The **design of the customer experience** also includes the question of whether you should use the possibilities of **dynamic pricing** to increase the profitability of your company. *Amazon*, for example, permanently changes its prices throughout the day. This **dynamic price adjustment** is based on the knowledge that **price elasticity** varies depending on the **buyer** and the **time of purchase**. However, this has always been the case. The possibilities that exist today to evaluate a multitude of information about the buyer and the buying environment in real time now make one thing possible in the online sector:

Different customers are offered different prices for the identical offer at the same time.

In this way, the different price elasticity can be optimally exploited to increase corporate profitability. A **low price elasticity of demand** means that a price increase does not have a significant impact on sales—in extreme cases it can even lead to an increase in turnover. Therefore, companies look for **indicators of low price elasticity**. These include, for example, expensive devices (such as those from *Apple*), because they signal purchasing power. People who look for an online shop with an *Apple* product may therefore pay a higher price. Someone who searches a second or third time for certain shoes, polo shirts, flight or train connections from Cologne to Milan signals a high level of interest and thus in turn a lower price elasticity. This can also be assumed when a flight or train connection is searched for taking place within the next few days. What is the answer of dynamic pricing? We can offer higher prices to these customers—there already seems to be a certain pressure of suffering.

What is special about this **price differentiation** is that it is not offered in the same way to certain target groups (such as students, job seekers, pensioners) or to everyone in certain time periods. In this case, the price is set individually—quasi **one-to-one pricing**. It is obvious that customers are often not enthusiastic about such a procedure. Customers who feel they have been cheated can spread their displeasure widely via social media. In addition, one thing is also lost with dynamic pricing—**price reliability** and thus also **trust in providers from the customer's point of view**. We should therefore carefully analyze whether we want to take this risk. Dynamic pricing is again about a classic trade-off: higher profits vs. a possible loss of customer trust.

▶ **Food for Thought**
Given the relevance of customer experience, we should beware of one thing: **bad profit**. Bad profit refers to profits made by deceiving, misleading, and/or overreaching customers. These effects can be deliberately brought about by misleading messages, non-transparent pricing strategies (such as dynamic pricing), incomprehensible and unexpected general terms and conditions, non-transparent subscription conditions, excessive fees (popular for car rental as well as airline tickets), or falsified ratings.

Bad profits are consequently made at the expense of customer relations.

They can and will have a negative impact on business development in the long run. Finally, such experiences are now widely disseminated via social media and lead to a zero moment of truth for potential customers.

Therefore:

Refraining from bad profit today can be the basis for a long-term profitable customer relationship. After all, lost trust is difficult to regain.

The renunciation of bad profit is an expression of the return to the basic principles of fair cooperation!

After all, the saying goes:

Turnover is the applause for a company!

Think Box: Questions You Should Ask Yourself
- What is the significance of the statement "experience is the new product" for your company?
- What about the development of customer experience management in your company?
- Do you have a corporate culture that avoids dominant departmental thinking and the associated data silos?
- Do you have the necessary technologies for CXM in place?
- Does your data management support the development of a CXM?
- Do you consistently put data at the center of your customer experience management?
- Does your company succeed in creating cross-channel customer profiles in real time?
- Do you rely on the use of artificial intelligence in your CXM today?
- How can AI help you with targeting, personalization, and audience segmentation in the future?
- Are you systematically capturing the value proposition of CX for business success?
- Is customer experience management part of your corporate strategy?
- Do you develop a CX design across departments and divisions?
- How consistent is your voice of customer integration?

(continued)

- Do you systematically use business analytics to determine the success factors of the customer experience?
- Do you consistently avoid generating bad profit?
- Are all top performers in your company aware of what is meant by "bad profit"?
- Who is dealing with the questions raised here in your company?

3.5.1.7 Customer Relationship Management (CRM)

Customer relationship management is an indispensable building block for achieving convincing customer experience management. This applies at least to all companies that have customer data. CRM refers to customer relationship management geared towards long-term value creation. This includes the conception, implementation and, above all, the controlling of all customer-oriented measures to promote the initiation and expansion of **profitable customer relationships** (see also Sect. 3.5.2.2).

The many **data streams** available in the online age offer the opportunity to directly adapt the content to be communicated to the respective context of the user—in terms of time, space, and content. This requires a well-maintained **customer database** as well as various software tools to support data management, especially with large customer bases. This is the only way to achieve **customer acquisition** and **customer loyalty** that sustainably contribute to value creation. After all, even the best employees cannot retain all the information necessary for an individualized approach, so that a powerful CRM becomes indispensable (cf. Stadelmann et al., 2020; cf. Kreutzer, 2021a, pp. 15–59).

Up to now, **classic CRM** has attempted to address target groups or target persons on the basis of concretely collected or statistically determined preferences. Today, however, it is increasingly possible to significantly increase the relevance of advertising messages for the recipient by establishing a proximity of the advertising influence in terms of **time, place, and content**. This can significantly increase the relevance of the communication as well as the presented offers in the eyes of the prospects and customers.

This connection becomes visible in the **three-dimensional CRM** (cf. Fig. 3.69). The big challenge is to work out a **single point of truth** or a **single point of information** from the diverse analogue and digital footprints of the target persons (see Sect. 3.4.2). These create a **holistic data view** of the prospects and customers. To achieve this, however, many companies first have to bring together the data on prospects and customers that is available in various places—in compliance with data protection regulations.

Figure 3.69 shows that the **relevance of information** increases with the spatial, temporal, and content-related proximity of a message to the planned purchase. The

3.5 Exploiting Digital Potential Through Marketing and Sales

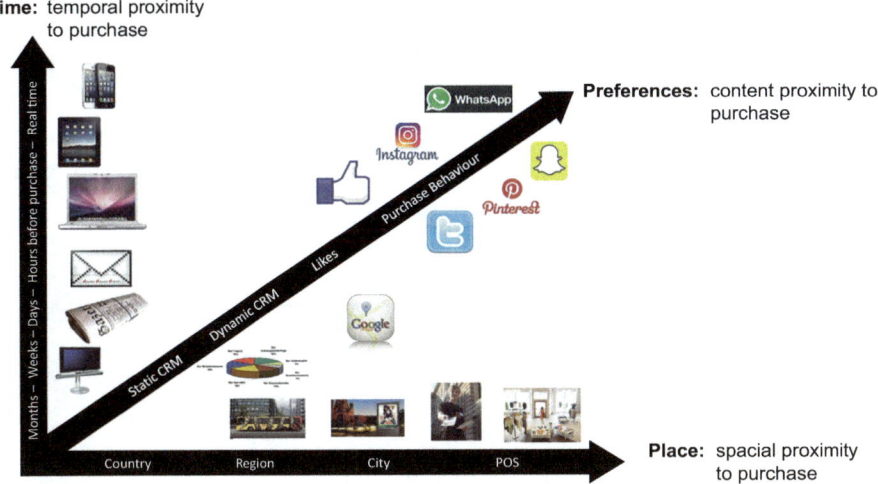

Fig. 3.69 Three-dimensional CRM: relevance of information based on the proximity in time, space and content

spatial proximity to the purchase can be increased by the display of advertising tailored to the respective location of the target person (**location**). By allowing the localization of users via GPS or through the use of beacons (technologies for the localization of users), the location of the user can be determined more and more precisely. This enables you to tailor your offers to the respective location (keyword "**location-based services**"). Then, for example, you can take the current weather forecast into account when playing out local content via e-mail or push notification!

Figure 3.70 shows you the possibilities that beacon technology already offers today. Users can be recognized with **beacon technology** in the spatial vicinity of your shop (all permission-based). For example, you can motivate people in the catchment area of your shop to visit by offering coupons. This is achieved through the so-called **geo-fencing**. This artificial word is made up of the terms "geographic" and "fence." You define such a (digital) fence around your stationary shop—or also around your competitor's shop (cf. Sultan & Banerjee, 2018). If a person who has given you permission to localize crosses the digital boundaries of the regions defined in this way, you can send predefined messages to such a person. This can be done through a prize coupon with the message "visit us—now."

In the shop itself, you can also address your prospects and customers with customized offers through beacon-based **in-store navigation**, which is based on the knowledge stored in the CRM database. Forecasting processes, which are increasingly based on artificial intelligence methods, can be used to informally prepare the next purchase (cf. Kreutzer & Sirrenberg, 2019, pp. 180–185).

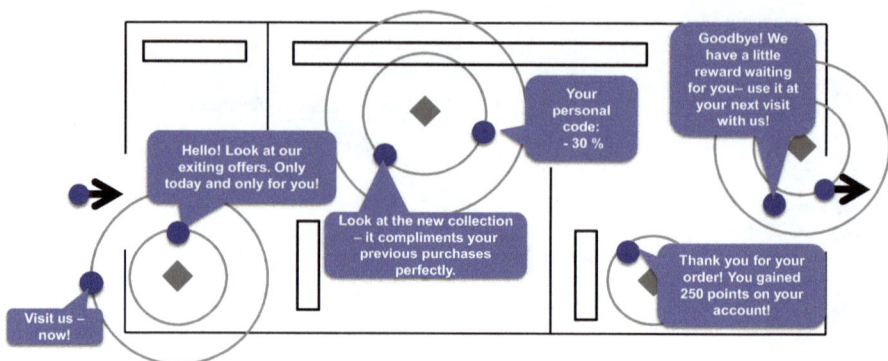

Fig. 3.70 Application areas of the beacon technology

In the case of TV and radio advertising, but also in the case of newspaper advertising and mailshots, a **temporal proximity to the purchase** is often not achievable or only achievable to a very limited extent (cf. Fig. 3.69). A stationary, but especially a mobile online presence can, however, have a much greater temporal proximity to the online and offline purchase (**timing**). This is achieved by sending the **push notifications** described above to the users' smartphones—for example, when they are on the move in the vicinity of my shop.

Online banners and retail media, which are gaining in importance, also enable this kind of temporal proximity to the purchase. **Retail media** refers to the possibility of placing ads within online shops and on marketplaces—exactly where the customer is in the mood to buy. This option is offered by companies such as *Alibaba, Amazon, eBay, Otto Group Media*, and *Zalando*.

Finally, the **content proximity to the purchase** is also of central importance (**preferences**, cf. Fig. 3.69). These can lead to recommendations based on previous search and purchase behavior. Such preferences can also be derived from the comments, shares, and reviews—the so-called social signal—on the social platforms.

> **Memory Box**
> Through a **three-dimensional CRM**, you try to achieve the greatest possible **proximity** to the purchase in terms of **time, space, and content**—to help your messages achieve greater relevance.
> All three dimensions together—in conjunction with other data—depict the respective context in which the target person is located. In the **static CRM systems** that still dominate, customer data is usually only updated at longer intervals, e.g., on the basis of customer surveys. In contrast, **dynamic CRM**

(continued)

systems strive to continuously record the activities of customers. Every time a new approach is made, the information that has just been obtained should also be taken into account. Especially on *Facebook, Instagram, Pinterest*, etc., but also in the online shops themselves (such as *Amazon* or *Zalando*), very current preference data is available, which is documented by "likes" or previous search and purchase behavior.

Companies that succeed in bringing together these three "proximity-generating poles" of **location, timing,** and **preferences** will be able to convey much more relevant information. The key here is to consistently work towards achieving a **single point of truth**, so that all customer-oriented information flows—permission-based—converge in one place.

Information changes its value with time and space—and consequently with the respective context. Against this background, a term is gaining in importance: **context marketing**. Here, the attempt is made to comprehensively determine the respective life and action environment of the customer and to take it into account when addressing the customer. The relevant sources of information include offline activities in addition to the analysis of online usage behavior and social media engagement. Here, even **real time (informational) marketing** is made possible that reacts immediately to the activities of prospects and customers and plays out "appropriate" information. Then we could speak of **real time context marketing**!

To support these processes, you can use, for example, tools from crossengage.io (cf. CrossEngage, 2021). This platform supports you in the task of combining all user data into comprehensive **360° customer profiles**. In addition to customer profile data, this data also includes information on customer history and current user behavior.

> **Memory Box**
> **Content is King, relationship is Queen, and context is God!**

▶ **Food for Thought**
The challenge for marketing and sales is to let their own offers become a **share of lifestyle for customers**—ubiquitous, value creating, and thus indispensable.

Intelligent use of data is the necessary **basis for building emotional relationships**.

> **Think Box: Questions You Should Ask Yourself**
> - How important is customer relationship management in your company?
> - Have you so far relied more on a classic or a dynamic CRM?
> - Have you already tried to set up a three-dimensional CRM in order to achieve a temporal, spatial, and content-related proximity of the advertising approach?
> - How well have you succeeded so far in developing a single point of truth or a single point of information where all customer relevant data flow together?
> - Can you increase the relevance of your offers through location-based services?
> - What application possibilities does your business model offer for the use of beacon technology?
> - Have you worked out what relevance you can achieve through geo-fencing?
> - Can you improve customer guidance through beacon-based in-store navigation?
> - Can you achieve greater proximity to purchase timing through push notifications, the use of online banners and/or retail media?
> - How well are you aware of your customers' preferences?
> - Can you install context marketing—or perhaps even real time context marketing?
> - Where does the responsibility of these questions lie?

3.5.1.8 From "Mobile First" to "Voice Only"

Not long ago, we were taught "**mobile first.**" This was associated with the requirement to develop websites for mobile devices first, because these dominate online use today. The requirement still applies. Now it is already called "**voice first**" in some cases and perhaps soon also "**voice only,**" because a **triumphant advance of digital assistants** is imminent.

The **voice marketing** required here represents a prime example of the combination of powerful AI algorithms and comprehensive databases (cf. also Kahle, 2020; Kahle & Meißner, 2020; Kreutzer & Vousoghi, 2020; Hundertmark, 2021). The pioneers of **digital assistants** in the western world are *Amazon Echo* (*Alexa*), *Google Home* (*Google Assistant*), and *Siri* (*HomePod*). Some of these digital assistants can already integrate other media, such as pictures and videos. What digital assistants will be able to do in the (near) future can be heard in the following (fictitious) dialogue:

Ralf: "*Alexa*, please order for me the *Nike* running shoes that I looked at in Bonn a fortnight ago. You already know where. But they should also have the two red stripes that I designed during the individual product configuration."

Alexa: "Hello *Ralf*. I have done that. For this, I redeemed the *payback* coupon for 20%, which was still valid until the end of the month. I also bought the red sweatshirt from *Tommy Hilfiger* for you, which you had already put in the shopping basket twice without buying it. Today it was 50% off."

The **drivers of user acceptance** of digital assistants—in the professional, but especially in the private environment—are **convenience** and **speed of use**. Here, written text is no longer needed for communication, no menu structures have to be worked through. Communication via speech alone is sufficient. With the **increasing performance of the algorithms** used as well as with an **increasing database**, the dialogues can tend to become more and more intelligent and consequently also more and more personal. The technical basis for this is provided by the so-called **conversational AI platforms**.

The **entirety of voice marketing tasks** can be seen in Fig. 3.71 (cf. Kilian & Kreutzer, 2022; cf. Reinsclassen, 2019, p. 21). The basis of voice marketing is the definition of the **corporate language** or the **brand language**, if not the company but a brand is at the center of voice marketing. Here it is defined in which language or tonality the company or brand wants to communicate. Is it rather a language that one also uses with one's best friend? Or should a certain distance be conveyed linguistically? In Germany or France in particular, this is about the use of "Du/Tu" which is equivalent to using the first name (for example at *IKEA*, where the form of address "Hej Ralf" is initially surprising) or "Sie/Vous," equivalent to addressing someone with their surname. The "Sie/Vous" still dominates communication at many banks (though not at *N26*) and several airlines (such as *Lufthansa*).

In this process, the positioning of companies or brands is transformed into a **linguistic positioning**. This also includes defining the keywords that should be used as often as possible in communication. In addition, dos and don'ts can be defined that need to be taken into account when using language.

This includes, for example, the question of **text comprehensibility** for the recipient. After all, it does not necessarily serve every sender to always present information in a "snackable" and "shareable" way (cf. Kreutzer, 2020).

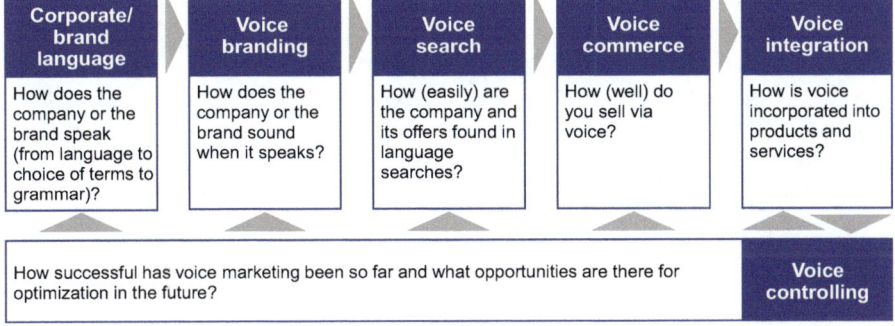

Fig. 3.71 Tasks of voice marketing

Sophisticated language, the understanding of which requires a certain intellectual potential, can be a deliberate part of linguistic positioning. This can be observed, for example, in the German newspapers *Frankfurter Allgemeine Zeitung, Handelsblatt* or *Die Zeit*, English newspapers like *New York Times, Wall Street Journal,* or *Washington Post*—in comparison with the *Daily Mirror* or *The Sun*.

This linguistic positioning can be rounded off by a **claim** or a **slogan**. For voice marketing, this can be combined with a special jingle that builds a bridge to **sound branding**. For example, the jingle of *Deutsche Telekom* or *Audi* comes to mind here. Sound branding defines how the company and/or a brand should sound in a very concrete and literal sense. For example, should a male or female voice be used? Various studies have shown that users tend to react more positively to female voices than to male voices. It is not a coincidence that *Alexa, Cortana,* and *Siri* have female voices. However, some devices also offer the option to choose from different voice offerings. Meanwhile, a **digital voice** called *Q* has even been developed that is genderless. It is in a frequency range where the human brain cannot distinguish between men and women (cf. Unckrich, 2019, p. 20).

> **Memory Box**
> By deciding on the type of voice, the emotional charge of the company or brand is significantly influenced.
>
> **Voice search** in Fig. 3.71 is about finding content in search processes in order to inform the user and possibly prepare upcoming purchases. **Voice commerce** focuses on the actual conclusion of a purchase. An additional field of activity is **voice integration**. This is the integration of voice into the products and services of a company itself. The integration of *Alexa* into the vehicles of automobile brands comes to mind here.
>
> Another indispensable area of work is called **voice search engine optimization (voice SEO)**. For this, the information provided by companies about their offer, location, etc. must be prepared in such a way that the probability of being played out as voice search results increases. A second important component of voice marketing is **voice search engine advertising (voice SEA)**. Through advertisements in the context of search engines, users should be made aware of voice offers (cf. further Kreutzer & Vousoghi, 2020).
>
> **Voice marketing** is not only aimed at **conveying content** in the sense of **voice communication.** In the future, the **sale of products and services** will also be increasingly driven by **voice commerce**. But distribution in the sense of "delivery" can also take place directly via digital assistants for digital products and services (**voice distribution**). This is already the case today with streaming content from *Spotify* & Co.

▶ **Food for Thought**
You would do well to intensively examine today which opportunities and risks are associated with the advance of digital assistants for your business model.

Due to these diverse tasks, the question arises whether a **CMO** (Chief Marketing Officer), a **CSO** (Chief Sales Officer), or a **CCO** (Chief Customer Officer) should be installed in your company—just please not all at once! Ideally, a package of tasks should be put together that places marketing and sales responsibility in one hand.

There is only one thing you should not do: let the responsibility for the complex tasks described here diffuse into the organization, because you will not achieve a convincing overall concept this way.

> **Think Box: Questions You Should Ask Yourself**
> - What is the importance of voice marketing in your industry?
> - Does a "voice first" or even a "voice only" approach already apply in your industry?
> - Can you make an initial use of chatbots?
> - Do you see fields of application for digital assistants?
> - Have you already familiarized yourself with conversational AI platforms?
> - What is the status of corporate language or brand language in your company?
> - Do you have sound branding—or should you?
> - Have you already dealt with voice search (voice SEO and voice SEA)?
> - How important is voice commerce in your industry?
> - Where do fields of application for voice integration arise?
> - Are there possibilities for voice distribution?
> - What are the implications for marketing, sales, and IT from all the above developments?
> - Who bears the responsibility for these questions?
> - Have you already installed a CMO (Chief Marketing Officer), a CSO (Chief Sales Officer), or a CCO (Chief Customer Officer) for this area?

3.5.2 Instruments for Exploiting Digitalization Potentials

In the following, particularly **powerful methods** are presented with which you can gain the information that is indispensable for the **digitalization of the customer journey**. The customer insights gained through these tools also provide an important informational basis for the general further development of products and services as well as the entire business model.

3.5.2.1 Persona Concept

An indispensable prerequisite for using the instruments presented below in a goal-oriented way is a **description of your target groups**. In order to enable your managers and employees to put themselves in the target persons' shoes even better, many companies today use the so-called **persona concepts**.

Personas are fictitious archetypes that represent the target group and give them—literally—"a face." They are described like real people. Personas have a life story, hobbies, a philosophy of life as well as a name and a photo. When working with personas, the **template for a persona development** shown in Fig. 3.72 can be used to gather the relevant information (cf. Pruitt & Adlin, 2006, pp. 230–234).

Criterion	Characteristic value
Identifying details	
Name	Typical name for the peer group (oriented to names that are typical for an age group)
Age	Typical age
Tag line	Slogan, life motto or a typical statement
Quote (regarding product/service)	Statement concerning product/service, that this persona was developed for, e. g. about expectations, quality, usage or special features of the offer
Family	Persona's family of origin: parents, siblings, possibly also other influentel people belonging to the "clan"
Marital status	Own family situation, e. g. in a relationship, married, divorced, single
Residence	Current geographical location (country/city, large/small city, etc.)
Roles and tasks	
Company	Naming employer or the self-employed fiel of work
Position	Role at work, e. g. hierachal ranking, area of responsibility
Typical activities	Activities and tasks that the persona executes on a regular basis and that can be relevant for the products/services
Important atypical activities	Activities and tasks that one would not believe he/she is capable of at first sight, e. g. odd hobbies, extreme sports, social/political commitments
Challenges, pain points	Requirements that the persona needs to fullfill on a daily basis at work/in private life
Responsibilities	Responsibilities at work/in private life
Interaction with other personas, systems and products/services	Contacts with other personas within the workplace or the daily life that have a special significance for the product/service offers; description of systems and products/services that are important for the role of the persona
Goals	
Life goals short/medium/long term	Goals; tangible and intangible, possibly ranked in temporal dimension
Goals regarding the product or service	Goals that are/should be reached with the product/service
Goals regarding work	Goals in the workplace
Fundamental goals, longings	Fundamental targets, wishes, hopes, expectations
Skills and knowledge	
Basic computer skills and online usage	Know-how and intensity of use of hardware and software
Specialized fields	Expertise in one or more specialized fields
Often used products/services	Used products or demanded services for work and daily life
Special know-how	Special know-how, e. g. concerning work or private life
Knowledge about competition	Knowledge about alternatives to the products/services
Context	
Equipment	Equipment, e. g. technology relevant for work or private life, materials, tools
„A day in the life"-description	Description of a typical day in the life of the persona; this does not need to be completely realistic, but includes the relevant, often recurring and therefor typical activities and contacts
Specific usage locations	Places at which the product/service can be used
Household and leisure activties	Typical activities in leisure time or on vacation
Relationships to other personas	Naming the personas, that do not belong to the workplace but to the personal daily life
Psychographical and personal details	
Character traits	Describing the personality using human characteristics (honesty, loyality, curiosity, spirit of adventure, etc.)
Values and attitudes	Beliefs concerning religion and politics
Fears, obstacles, disturbances	Emotional states, that influence the thinking and feeling of the persona
Personal artefacts (cars, gimmicks)	Description of belongings, that have a significance for the persona concerning the product/service

Fig. 3.72 Template for a persona development

The results developed on the basis of this template are then documented and provided with a **photo** depicting a typical representative of the target group. This person is also given a **name** typical for the age group. For customer-oriented measures, the following questions can be answered from now on with a view to the respective persona:
- Through which media would Sabine (47) inform herself about our offer?
- How much would she be willing to spend on our offer?
- What alternatives would Sabine consider in her decision-making process?
- Where would Sabine purchase the product or service?
- What uncertainties would have to be overcome in the purchasing process?
- Does our offer contribute to overcoming possible pain points?
- What would be the most important aspect of our offer for Sabine?
- How would she use the product?
- Which features bring Sabine the greatest benefit?
- Etc.

By orienting to a very **humanly described persona**, a consistent customer orientation can be achieved in the minds of the people involved.

Memory Box
Personas should not be filed in a folder. Ideally, the personas should be visualized on **posters** in a large format so that they are always in view in the marketing and sales rooms.
Motto: **Always keep the customers in sight!**
In addition, a **chair** can be placed in the meeting rooms for the persona—fictitious or real. Looking at this chair sharpens the view of the people for whom products and services are ultimately developed!
And yes: customers can also be the valued colleagues for whom solutions are being developed!

Think Box: Questions You Should Ask Yourself
- Do you already work with personas?
- Are marketing and sales activities consistently based on personas?
- Are these personas—especially for marketing and sales—always in view?
- Do you already work with a chair for the personas so as never to lose sight of them?
- Who maintains the personas—and also retires them once they no longer represent the most important target groups?

3.5.2.2 Conversion Funnel

The **conversion funnel** provides an important orientation for the use of different instruments to gather information. This funnel expresses the impulses through which a person can develop over various stages (conversions) from an interested party to a regular customer and possibly to a referrer (cf. Fig. 3.73).

When using the conversion funnel, ask yourself the question of what percentage of interested parties (prospects, leads) are lost from stage to stage on the way to purchase or customer retention. You can only achieve this analysis through comprehensive data collection across the various stages of the conversion funnel.

To control and monitor these processes, you should use **marketing automation software**. With a large number of differentiated prospects and customers, it is often only such software that makes it possible to **address them individually** without exponentially increasing the time and costs involved. Below you will find some particularly important **marketing and sales workflows** that you can support via **marketing automation tools**.

- Lead generation and lead nurturing

  Lead generation, i.e., the **systematic acquisition of potential buyers**, is a classic use case for marketing automation. By integrating calls-to-action in advertisements, banners, flyers or on a landing page as well as by issuing coupons and offering contact forms, you motivate potential buyers to take various actions.

  If the **address and profile data** made available offline or online are evaluated, the desired information can now be provided automatically for a further dialogue with the interested parties. Through coordinated measures, you try to systematically develop the lead (in the sense of a prospective buyer) into a buyer. For this purpose, **trigger chains with different contents** are defined in advance.

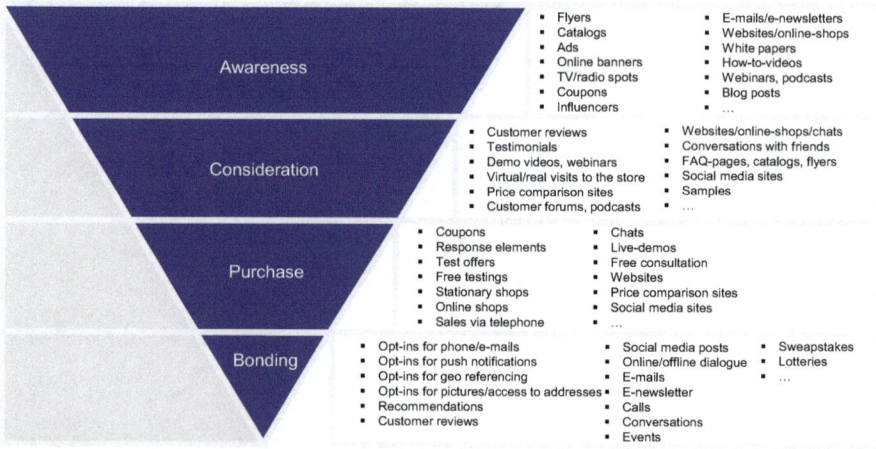

Fig. 3.73 Conversion funnel

This is called **lead nurturing** because not every prospective buyer becomes a buyer immediately. This process has to be accompanied by different impulses—until the prospect buys or is no longer interested in our offer. This lead nurturing is so important because on average only 20% of leads are already willing to buy during the first contact. Therefore, the challenge for you is to nurture leads until they are ready to buy. If you do your job well, according to analyses by Marketo (2021), you can achieve 50% more purchases through lead nurturing—and at the same time reduce the acquisition costs per lead by 33%. An exciting task for you is to determine the corresponding values for your company.

- The action and reaction data obtained in the course of these activities should in turn flow into your **CRM database** to identify particularly **successful conversion paths**. You can then define the most convincing measures as standard—until even better concepts are found.
- **Lead segmentation and customer segmentation**
  The leads acquired are continuously recorded in the CRM database. Automated segmentation processes can run here to form relevant **groups of leads**. These groups can be formed, for example, depending on the acquisition channel (online or offline) or based on the downloaded or clicked content. All leads that have subscribed to a newsletter for the first time within a week can also be combined into one lead segment.

  The marketing automation workflows also support **customer segmentation**. For example, your top customers, shopping basket abandoners, intensive returners of goods or also bad payers can also be combined into groups to be processed uniformly in order to process them in a differentiated manner depending on the behavior shown so far.
- **Lead scoring and customer scoring**
  In order to know even more precisely which leads are of particular importance to you and should therefore be given the highest attention, **lead scoring** can be used. You can classify the acquired leads according to their progress in the buying process and assign them point values. **Scoring concepts** form the basis for this (cf. Kreutzer, 2019, pp. 114–116). For this purpose, points can be assigned to each action of a lead. The number of points achieved serves as a trigger for certain address chains. In this way, the leads are to be further qualified step by step until they finally become a buyer—or are excluded from the further approach due to a lack of reactions.

  Customer value models can be used for customer scoring. Depending on the customer values determined in each case, different impulses can in turn take place—automatically. These can aim for more sell, cross sell, or up sell targets, request friendship referrals or ask for ratings of your services on various rating platforms (cf. Kreutzer, 2019, pp. 157–173).

> **Memory Box**
> **Marketing automation** can sustainably support you in achieving the following goal:
> **The right content should be made available to the right recipients at the right time via the right channel.**
> You should comprehensively check which of the possibilities of **marketing automation** could also be of interest for your company in order to successfully design the conversion funnel. It is precisely these tools that enable you to get closer to your customers with relevant communication impulses (cf. Hannig, 2017, 2020; Kreutzer, 2021a, pp. 136–148).

> **Think Box: Questions You Should Ask Yourself**
> - Do you consistently use the conversion funnel in your analyses?
> - Do you systematically check where prospects or leads are lost on the way to your goal?
> - How consistently do you rely on lead generation and lead nurturing?
> - Do you have different trigger chains in use?
> - Are these continuously tested for their performance?
> - How consistently does your company use lead and customer segmentation?
> - Do you use lead and customer scoring?
> - Do you use different customer value models to manage acquisition and support?
> - How consistently does the information gained here flow back into your marketing and sales activities?
> - Do you use marketing automation software to make the processes efficient?
> - Who takes care of these questions?

3.5.2.3 Customer Journey Map

The **customer journey map** is an important analysis tool for you. It visualizes the process that a person goes through from the first latent need to the act of purchase and the use of a product or service to a possible repurchase or feedback on your services (cf. Kaplan, 2016). The visualization of this customer journey helps you to identify the relevant customer needs as well as possible "pain points." Recognizing these helps you to make more convincing approaches and offers.

A **pain point** is an occurrence that customers typically want to avoid and/or overcome. We distinguish between two types of pain points. Pain points can initially be rooted in the **customer's everyday life**. This can be a specific customer problem that the customer would like to solve or avoid completely. For example, a customer has the feeling that he is paying more for a service than necessary (e.g., for electricity and gas). For certain processes, a higher time investment is necessary than a person is willing to make (e.g., when investing money). Other people may feel overwhelmed by certain information, but still want to understand the facts (keyword "easy language"). Others would like to achieve a goal, but are currently finding it difficult to do so (for example, further training). In essence, the pain points from the customers' everyday life are about **needs** that **are not yet (optimally) satisfied**. Here we can also think of the jobs to be done already mentioned (see Sect. 3.2.7.2).

However, **pain points** can also occur during the **customer journey**. This is the case, when the customer is disappointed on his "journey to the company" because expectations are not fulfilled to a great extent (keyword "moment of truth," see Sect. 3.5.1.3). The spectrum ranges from unfriendly staff to inadequate performance of the products purchased or services used. "Pain" can also be caused by cumbersome processes. For example, complex registrations in the online shop with complex passwords or long waiting times for phone calls or correspondence.

A **pain point analysis** is used to determine these special "events." This is a central element of the customer journey map. On the one hand, it is important to find convincing solutions for the paint points in everyday life. On the other hand, paint points caused by the company on the customer journey must be consistently avoided.

The starting point for creating a customer journey map are the **personas** defined in Sect. 3.5.2.1. A specific customer journey map must now be developed for each persona. To do this, first define on a rough timeline which scenario (e.g., which pain points) is to be assumed. Here it must be clarified with which goals the persona begins the customer journey and which actions come into play in this. It is important that you also include the thoughts and emotions of the users that prevail in the different phases in the map to be developed here.

The totality of these insights flow into the **design of the customer journey map**. For this purpose, two tools—**storytelling and visualization**—are combined. If you tell stories from the customer's point of view and illustrate them, you will succeed in presenting relevant information in a "user-friendly" way. Journey mapping also provides an **impressive and holistic view of the customer experience**. Figure 3.63 already shows how diverse the customer touch points are today.

In order to create a **customer journey map**, you should therefore put yourself completely in the role of the customer. Although journey maps differ according to the specific context, they often follow a general model as shown in Fig. 3.74. In the first part of the customer journey map, the "Who?" and the "What?" are defined. Here it must be determined with which concern, which goals, and with which expectations a persona starts the journey.

In the second part—the heart of the journey map—the different phases, the actions and channels as well as the thoughts and feelings of the user during the entire journey are supplemented with quotes and/or videos from market research. Here, it is important to check at which customer touch points the persona finds exactly what he or she is looking for. Where might genuine customer enthusiasm be achieved? At which touch points is the persona rather disappointed by the content

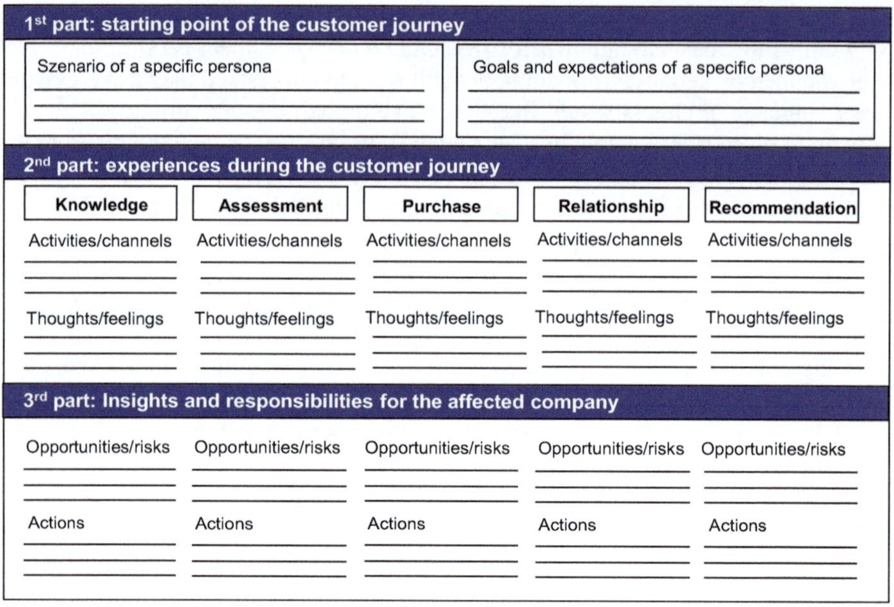

1st part: starting point of the customer journey	
Szenario of a specific persona	Goals and expectations of a specific persona

2nd part: experiences during the customer journey				
Knowledge	Assessment	Purchase	Relationship	Recommendation
Activities/channels	Activities/channels	Activities/channels	Activities/channels	Activities/channels
Thoughts/feelings	Thoughts/feelings	Thoughts/feelings	Thoughts/feelings	Thoughts/feelings

3rd part: Insights and responsibilities for the affected company				
Opportunities/risks	Opportunities/risks	Opportunities/risks	Opportunities/risks	Opportunities/risks
Actions	Actions	Actions	Actions	Actions

Fig. 3.74 Basic concept of a customer journey map

provided? And where are there serious pain points that need to be avoided or overcome?

> **Memory Box**
> The creation of a customer journey map is a good training of empathy. In addition, the results of relevant customer surveys should be included here in order to have as vivid a picture of the customer reality as possible!
>
> In order to find the **relevant content for the customer journey map**, the following questions need to be answered:
>
> - How does a need arise in the persona for the products and services offered (search for initial pain points)?
> - What are the particularly strong triggers for the start of the customer journey?
> - How and where does the persona obtain information in the "zero moment of truth" (e.g., on rating platforms, among friends, in forums) before visiting the company's own touch points?
> - What is the importance of the circle of friends and social media in obtaining information?
> - What other media does the persona use—online and offline?
>
> (continued)

- How credible does the persona think the various information offers are?
- What is the significance of the various touch points within and outside the company within the customer journey?
- Which competitive offers are analyzed, to what extent and via which media?
- With what expectations does the persona encounter the offers of their own company?

In addition to the actions themselves, the persona's thoughts and feelings must also be determined. These **emotions** can be depicted in the customer journey map in Fig. 3.74 with values ranging from ++ (very positive) to −− (very negative). You can round off the picture by briefly **outlining the underlying thoughts** (keyword "storytelling"). In addition, the **importance** of the **customer touch points** for the persona can be noted in the journey map. Values from 1 (low importance) to 5 (high importance) can be assigned.

If you determine at this point that phases on the customer journey with high importance for the customers are evaluated very negatively by them, there is an urgent need for action in the third part. Here, the **fields of action for the company** are derived, in which opportunities and risks are comprehensively described. From these, very concrete actions are to be derived and the managers responsible for them are to be named (cf. Fig. 3.74). To improve the **customer experience**, the first step is to identify and eliminate possible negative experiences. To do this, it is important that you know the expectations with which customers begin their customer journey. Only then can you satisfy these expectations (cf. Fig. 3.74).

Memory Box
The **customer journey map** is an indispensable element if you want to trace the customer's path to your offers. It reveals not only relevant customer paths, but also necessary fields of action for your marketing and sales activities.

In order to align your offers and your business model with customer expectations, you should develop **customer journey maps**. These offer an exciting and highly informative **framework for action**. You should involve people from the areas of communication, service, sales, and product management in order to obtain as holistic a picture as possible. Based on the insights gained, the customer experience management is to be designed—an approach that is to be developed across different departmental boundaries (see Sect. 3.5.1.6). In doing so, you should break down the information and activity silos already mentioned in your own company—because all experiences converge at the latest with the customer—regardless of whether they have been holistically preconceived by you or not!

> **Think Box: Questions You Should Ask Yourself**
> - Does your company regularly create customer journey maps for different personas?
> - Do you know the biggest pain points of your customers that cause the start of a customer journey?
> - Are your offers and your communication consistently geared towards overcoming these pain points?
> - Is the design of your customer journey itself—in the eyes of the customer—the cause of pain points?
> - Are you able to define fields of action and derive concrete actions on the basis of the results?
> - Where is the responsibility for such analyses?

3.5.2.4 Empathy Map

You can achieve an even deeper understanding if you enrich the insights gained with a customer journey map by using an **empathy map**. To do this, answer the questions posed in Fig. 3.75.

Empathy helps us to understand the expectations of different target groups. We learn something about the needs of other people. We put ourselves in their shoes. Only empathy enables us to enter into a genuine relationship with other people—especially with our customers. That is why real customer contacts should be replaced as rarely as possible by the **presentation of** *PowerPoint* **slides of market research**.

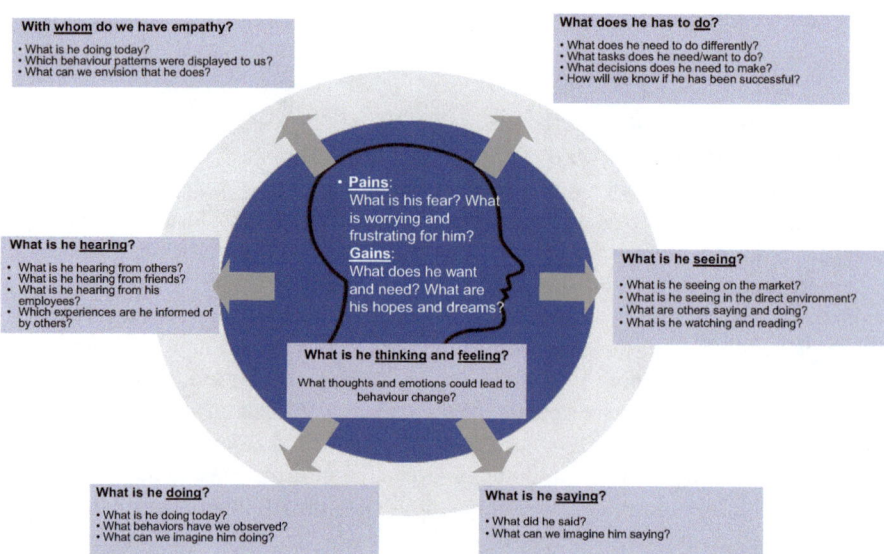

Fig. 3.75 Empathy map for a persona

The **empathy map** systematically supports you in identifying the relevant **customer wishes, pain and gain points** as well as the individual needs of the persona. With an empathy map, you focus particularly on the **emotional state of a persona** by tracing the individual sensory organs and their perceptions or sensations.

For this purpose, the persona is positioned in the center of the **empathy map** with the fields "pain" (for "pain points") and "gain" (for "achieved"). Around them, further sectors are defined and illuminated with questions. These six defined sectors are now to be filled with content—always consistently from the perspective of a concrete persona!

> **Think Box: Questions You Should Ask Yourself**
> - Do you already use an empathy map in your company?
> - Who could start such a process?
> - In which areas could the information gained through this be particularly value adding?

3.5.2.5 *Kano* Concept

To gain important ideas for business model innovations, but also for the further development of your own products and services, you can use the *Kano* concept. With this concept you can recognize the **importance of the different offers** of your company in **achieving customer satisfaction**.

In order to determine such correlations, *Kano* examined the relationship between the **fulfillment of different customer requirements** and the **achievement of customer satisfaction** (cf. Berger et al., 1993). It became clear that the fulfillment of customer requirements partly has no or only a minor influence on customer satisfaction.

The non-fulfillment of such requirements, which are called **basic requirements**, leads to dissatisfaction, but their fulfillment does not lead to satisfaction or enthusiasm (cf. the lower curve in Fig. 3.76). Customers simply assume that these basic requirements will be met. Their non-fulfillment leads to dissatisfaction, their fulfillment itself is taken for granted without making a lasting contribution to satisfaction. In the case of air travel, these basic requirements include the safety of the aircraft—and that one arrives at the booked destination. With books, it is expected that the pages do not come loose from the binding when working through a book several times. If this is the case, customer satisfaction does not increase – but non-fulfillment triggers dissatisfaction (cf. Berger et al., 1993, p. 26).

The customer evaluates **performance requirements** according to the principle "the more, the better." More fulfilled service requirements increase satisfaction (cf. the middle line in Fig. 3.76). In the case of air travel, this includes a higher-quality tasting even in economy class or the free selection of newspapers and

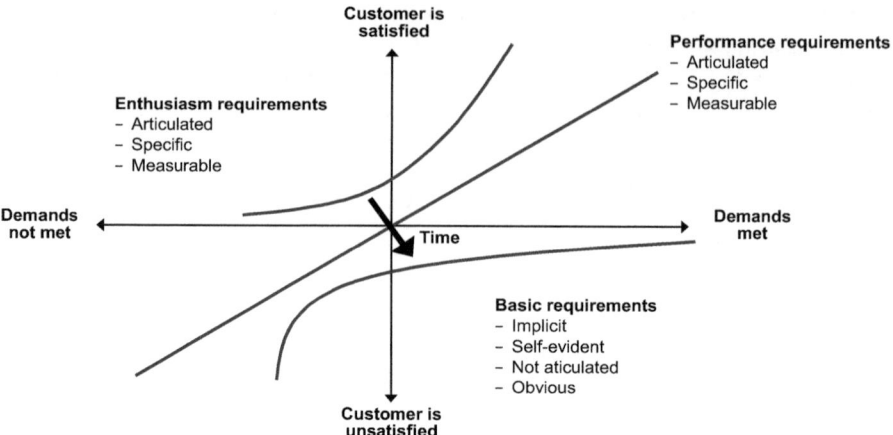

Fig. 3.76 *Kano* model of customer satisfaction

magazines. In the case of a textbook, this can be an online platform on which further important teaching content or questions are made available.

Only the third category in the form of **enthusiasm requirements** can trigger enthusiasm in the customer because services are provided here that were not expected. If such services are provided frequently, however, there is a danger that these mutate into performance requirements and are then also expected (cf. the upper curve in Fig. 3.76). In the case of a textbook, the daily provision of relevant articles, videos, case studies, etc. could lead to enthusiasm—until this too is taken for granted and has thus become a performance requirement.

In order to determine what counts as various requirements for your clients—not for yourself—you should conduct **workshops using the *Kano* concept**. For this purpose, you should ideally invite a cross-section of your customers or desired customers. In this context, you yourself—or better an external moderator—can ask the customers about their basic, performance, and enthusiasm requirements. Use a *Metaplan* **technique** to record and document the results for all to see. This is how you promote creative exchange.

It is helpful if employees and managers of the company (e.g., from marketing and sales) participate in these workshops—ideally by listening. They will often be surprised which (new) services could already trigger enthusiasm among the customers. In many cases, the customers develop ideas that are simply ingenious. At the same time, glaring gaps in the customers' knowledge about the company's existing services often become visible. This means that companies often already provide important services—but customers have not yet noticed this. Such customer insights and suggestions often provide material for many months of creative work.

Storytelling
I facilitated a workshop of this kind for a company that manufactures **heating and cooling systems**, among other things. The participants of the workshop were planners and architects who need corresponding products for their projects in building construction. When asked about "enthusiasm requirements," they said: "It would be great if you could provide us with your data in a *Word* file format. Then we can copy and paste them into our tenders." The marketing manager almost fell off his chair when he learned "how little" he could do to inspire his most important customers.

In a workshop for a **mail-order company for sporting goods**, the workshop participants mentioned as a request for enthusiasm that small videos be made available via *YouTube* in which, for example, new games are presented. The marketing manager pointed out that such information was already included in the present catalogue. The customer's answer: "I've never seen them before."

In a workshop for *Volkswagen*, we asked the participants which offers we should include in the program of the *Volkswagen Club* to trigger enthusiasm. The answer from a 22-year-old participant was: "I'd like to visit the birthplace of my Bulli one day!" The wish for factory tours could not be more emotional.

There would be dozens more exciting incidents to report from such workshops. It was also interesting to see how easy it is to motivate customers to participate and how creative the participants are. And no, hardly ever was it said, I'm only excited when you give away your services!

Memory Box
You should use the *Kano* concept regularly to get to the bottom of what customers really want!

Think Box: Questions You Should Ask Yourself
- Have you ever used the *Kano* concept before?
- Do you know the basic requirements of your customers?
- Do you know what your customers consider to be performance requirements and evaluate according to the principle "the more, the better"?
- Do you know the enthusiasm requirements of your customers?
- Who could initiate such a workshop?

3.5.2.6 Net Promotor Score

An indispensable tool for measuring the results of your customer facing activities is the **net promoter score** (**NPS**). It is both a powerful and easy-to-use concept to measure the extent of customers' emotional connection and trust in your company. The NPS is a measure of how many of your customers would (net) recommend your company or its offerings to others. The **basic concept of the NPS** is described in Fig. 3.77.

To determine the **net promoter score**, the question is asked: "How likely are you to recommend this company, service, product, brand to a friend or colleague?" Answers can be given on a scale from "0" ("very unlikely") to "10" ("very likely").

Promoters (supporters) of a company or brand in this concept are only those who give a value of "9" or "10". **Detractors** (critics) are those who only give values between "0" and "6" with regard to recommendation. **Indifferents** are those who give the value "7" or "8". When calculating the net value of recommenders, the percentage of detractors is subtracted from the percentage of promoters. The group of indifferents is not taken into account in the calculation. Consequently, the **calculation formula of the NPS** is:

NPS = Promoters (in %)—Detractors (in %).

In the best case, the **NPS values** can be "100%" if all customers have given the value "9" or "10". In the worst case, the result is "- 100%" if all customers have only given values between "0" and "6".

The **significance of the NPS** is always critically questioned. Nevertheless, its use in companies is recommended because the **net promoter score** is a quick-to-install

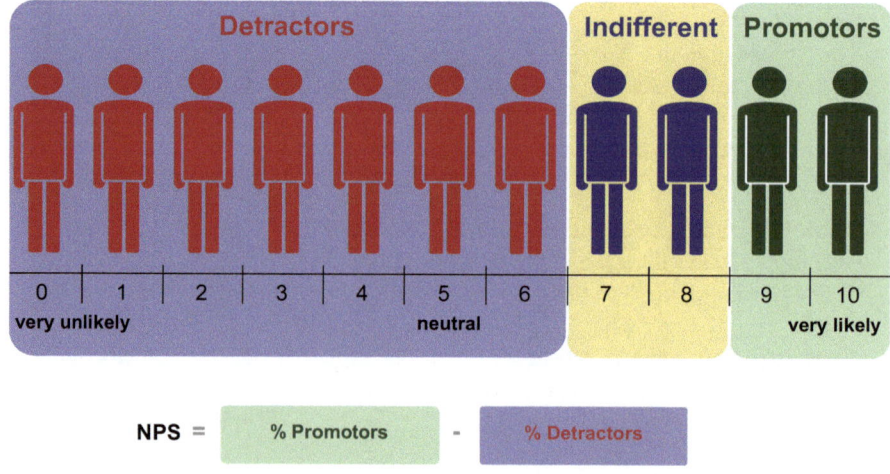

Fig. 3.77 Basic concept of the net promoter score

instrument to determine trust—measured by the degree of willingness to recommend.

The value determined for the first time as NPS documents the **zero measurement of your company**. By means of in-depth analyses, it is necessary to work out why this value in particular came about. In addition, it must be determined by which measures the NPS value can be improved. In order to receive initial suggestions for this, you should also ask for a short **explanation** after the question on the intention to recommend. In this way, you will receive immediate feedback and often also important suggestions directly from your customers!

Once the **results of the net promoter score** are available, two questions remain unanswered in many companies:
- How do you deal with the customers who have taken the time to write such a review (possibly even with comments)?
- And who is responsible for further communication with the customers?

Figure 3.78 shows how you could act if you really care about your customers and their satisfaction and long-term loyalty. Service staff can thank the **promoters**. The **indifferents** should be contacted by higher-ranking sales staff in order to pick up on possible bad experiences or disappointed expectations and to find a solution. Middle and top management are required to contact the **detractors**. The greater the dissatisfaction, the higher the management level should be when contacting them in order to find solutions. At the same time, such an approach offers members from top and middle management the perfect opportunity to regularly hear the customers' "O-tones."

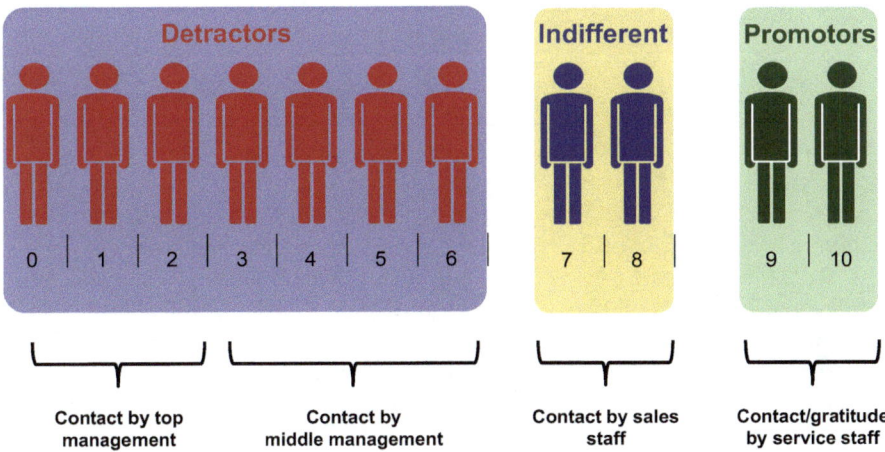

Fig. 3.78 How you should use the results of the net promoter scores

> **Memory Box**
> **Listening to O-tones**—especially in top and middle management—is tremendously grounding. It sharpens the view of the customer and helps to set the right priorities in entrepreneurial action—and is therefore indispensable.
>
> Regular **VoC** (voice of the customer) integration is a key success factor (see Sect. 3.5.1.6).
>
> It is interesting to take a look at **international NPS benchmarks**. You can use these as benchmarks when you determine NPS values for the first time. If you collect them continuously—and this is my recommendation—the comparison with your own results of the previous months or years is particularly exciting. The development of the NPS values ultimately reflects the evaluation of your performance in the eyes of the customers. Here are **international benchmarks for the net promoter score in different industries** (cf. Retently, 2020):
> - Education and training: 71%
> - Insurance: 70%
> - E-commerce: 62%
> - Digital marketing agency: 61%
> - Consulting: 51%
> - E-commerce agency: 48%
> - Enterprise software: 44%
> - Construction: 43%
> - Financial services: 34%
> - Software as a service: 30%
> - Logistics and transportation: 29%
> - Healthcare: 27%
>
> For several reasons, you should anchor the calculation of the **NPS as a standard process** in your company. The NPS methodology can be integrated quickly, cost-effectively, and easily into your business processes—online and offline. The NPS values provide you with an immediate impression of the perception of your overall performance from the customer's perspective.
>
> NPS scores are easy to understand and can—and should—be communicated throughout the organization. Good NPS scores and justifications encourage the whole team to keep doing the right thing. Poor NPS scores and especially their justifications provide a variety of impulses to optimize one's own processes and/or to better train, support, and/or motivate the staff.

Memory Box
You should make the NPS concept a **basic instrument for your company**. It is important here not to mistakenly plan the use of the net promoter score as a project. Rather, it is a process that, once started, never ends.

Think Box: Questions You Should Ask Yourself
- Do you already use the net promoter score (NPS) regularly?
- If you have NPS scores, do you know the reasons that led to these results?
- Have you compared your results with the scores of NPS studies?
- Who could initiate the required zero measurement of your company?
- What is the response in your company to the results obtained?
- Who is responsible for the follow-up—or is this not planned at all?
- Will your top management and middle management be integrated into the follow-up in order to also hear customers' O-tones?
- Who would be responsible for the use of the NPS in your company?

3.5.3 "Innovative Innovation Management"

If things don't fail, they are not innovative enough.
  Elon Musk

3.5.3.1 Customer Centricity: The Core of Innovation Management

An important **mind change** that you should achieve throughout the entire company is the consistent implementation of the following requirement:
  Customer centricity is key!

In times of consistently decreasing customer loyalty and previously unseen pressure to innovate, the **consistent orientation of the entire company towards the customer is the success factor** par excellence. The explanations in Sects. 3.5.1 and 3.5.2 already contribute to this. All managers and employees must therefore understand even more comprehensively that they can only survive in competition if they create sustainable **added value for their customers**.

Here we should bear in mind that the **customers** to be considered in this way are to be found **both inside and outside our company**. We should also consider the teams from the other departments and divisions of our own company as "customers" and look after them accordingly in an appreciative manner.

The implementation of **customer centricity** therefore includes first and foremost that especially the managers **get back in touch with the "normal" customers** on a regular basis. In many larger companies, a frightening phenomenon can be observed: the higher you climb in the company hierarchy, the less often you have customer contact. And when personal customer contact does occur at top management level, it is often only with key accounts, who usually enjoy comprehensive and personal support. However, this does not provide a representative picture of the overall satisfaction of one's own customers.

That is why **managers**—indeed, all managers—must be in regular contact with customers. This is the only way to gain—unfiltered and quite emotional—first-hand central messages from a company's most important stakeholders (keyword "VoC integration"; see Sect. 3.5.1.6). The importance results from the fact that customers are still the biggest winners of digitalization so far: more offers, more competition, better prices, more convincing services. Such a "spoiled" and "pampered" customer can only be (re)won through convincing offers if all important decision-makers in the innovation process are comprehensively informed about the sensitivities of their own customers in a timely manner.

In order to recognize how well your company is already prepared for this **customer-oriented innovation management**, the following questions for a **status quo analysis on innovation management** must be answered honestly:

- Which departments are involved in your innovation processes (e.g., R&D, procurement, production, logistics, controlling, HR, marketing, sales)?
- How and what is delegated to innovation teams in your company (tasks, competences, responsibilities)?
- How are suggestions for improvement dealt with in your company?
- How is learning done in your company—not least from the customer?
- How is information about key changes provided—formally or informally?
- What does your company focus on: time-to-market or time-to-value?
- Do the incentive systems you use break through or encourage silo thinking in the company?
- Are your managers rewarded or "punished" for "lending" their best employees to projects and network structures?
- How do you "deal" with project managers who have "bungled" an innovation project?
- Is the willingness to take risks more likely to be rewarded or punished in your company?
- What happens to employees and ideas that challenge the status quo?
- ...

Only a **critical stocktaking** offers you the chance to actually bring about groundbreaking changes in your company.

Think Box: Questions You Should Ask Yourself
- How important is the guiding principle "customer centricity is key" in your company?
- To what extent do your top managers and other executives have contacts with "normal" customers?
- How often and how regularly do such dialogues take place?
- Does your top and middle management know the customers primarily from *PowerPoint* slides of market research or from direct conversations?
- Do you regularly conduct a status quo analysis of innovation management in your company?
- Where in the hierarchy is the topic of "innovation management" anchored?

3.5.3.2 From Closed- to Open-Innovation-Concepts

Innovations are both **a curse and a blessing** for companies. On the one hand, innovations—in business models, processes, products, and services—are indispensable for the long-term survival of most companies. At the same time, **flop rates** of 70–90% are the order of the day for product and service innovations by established companies. This means that 70–90% of the innovations introduced on the market were not successful. "Unsuccessful" here means that the companies behind it could not achieve their goals. A look at start-ups even shows flop rates that are between 90 and 99%. Here, too, many founders do not achieve their original goals.

Often the **causes of unsuccessful market launches** lie in a lack of customer orientation. From the customer's point of view, this can be an insufficient degree of innovation. Or there is overpromising, where customers are promised more than is delivered. However, the reason for failure can also be the lack of a coherent price-performance ratio. The **analysis grid for business model innovations** shown in Fig. 3.29 can be used here analogously for the evaluation of new products and services.

To increase the **probability of success of innovations**—for business models, products, and services alike—you should carry out a comprehensive integration of those who decide on the success of your innovation: the customers. Such **customer integration in the innovation process** requires overcoming the still widely used **closed innovation model** or **inside-out process** (cf. Fig. 3.79). When using this model, companies primarily develop and market ideas generated within the company (especially in R&D or product management). In contrast, there is no interaction with the market or other partners outside the horizon of the own company.

In contrast, the **open innovation model** takes up external ideas and suggestions in addition to the impulses for innovations gained internally. External development partners (customers, but also suppliers, competitors, start-ups, or universities) are actively involved in the company's own innovation processes. This systematically expands the company's own innovation potential. The innovation processes are

Fig. 3.79 Closed innovation model

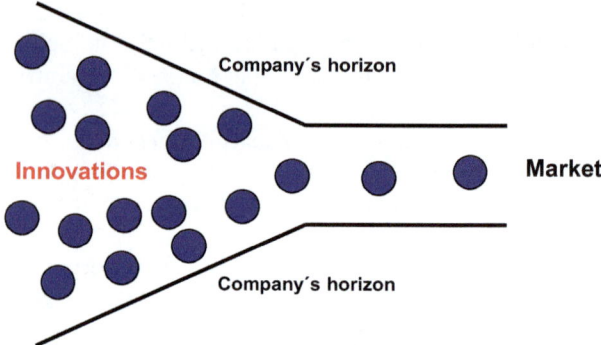

Fig. 3.80 Open innovation model

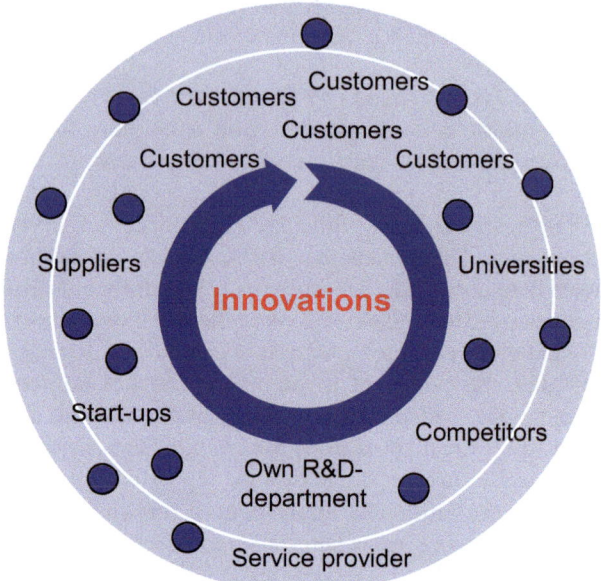

configured as an open and thus distributed system and promote intensive interaction with various entities (cf. Fig. 3.80; Piller et al., 2017, pp. 56–84). Such an **outside-in process** integrates external knowledge into the company's internal innovation process in order to accelerate and enrich it and—insofar as customers are involved—to align it consistently with (future) customer needs at an early stage.

In sum, it is important to establish **networks** with partners outside the company boundaries in order to integrate them into the open innovation model. The particularly **important integration of customers as development partners in the innovation process** can take different forms (cf. Fig. 3.81; cf. Dahan & Hauser, 2002):

3.5 Exploiting Digital Potential Through Marketing and Sales

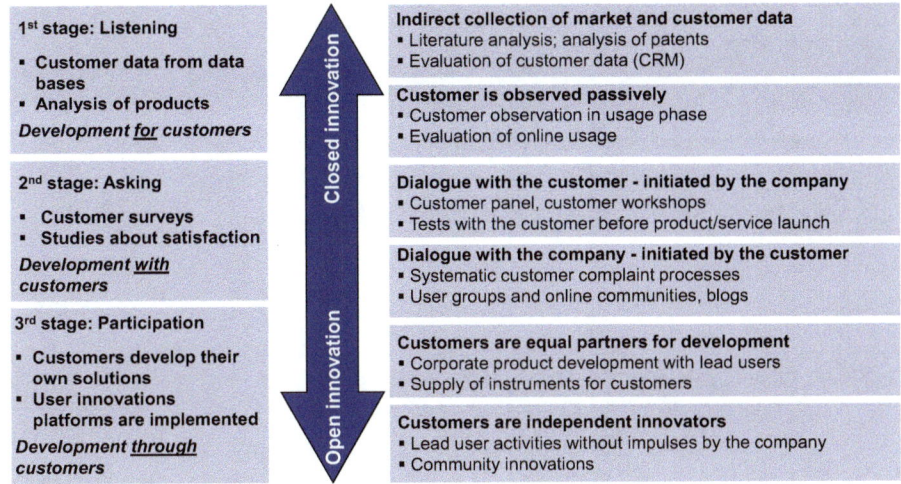

Fig. 3.81 Company customer interactions in innovation processes

- The **first stage "Listening"** gathers information about customers from different sources. These are used as the basis for a **development *for* customers**. This is the classic form of customer integration.
- The **second stage "Asking"** involves the customers much more comprehensively through different approaches—for example, through customer panels or customer workshops. This is how **development *with* customers** is achieved.
- In the **third stage "Participation,"** customers become real development partners. Here, **development *through* customers** takes place. This can be achieved in lead user workshops, online communities, and within social media.

These multi-layered **types of customer integration** trigger joint learning processes between customers and companies. Due to the different approaches, the different starting situations and backgrounds of experience of those involved, previous **patterns of thought and action can be broken** and **new paths can be taken**. At the same time, the results are more customer-oriented because the impulses, expectations, fears, and perhaps even desires of the customers flow into the process at an early stage.

In many cases, customers are happy to be involved in such development processes without expecting a monetary return. The **appreciation** expressed by the integration of customers alone is often a central **motive for cooperation**. Making the customer an "employee," as it were, is a target-oriented method for leaving the beaten track of innovation management and tapping into almost inexhaustible external sources of creativity.

> **Memory Box**
> Innovation only comes about when as many people as possible dare to break with the conventional, the familiar, the usual.
> Being stuck in one's own comfort zone, a pronounced sense of security and the preservation of possessions at all costs kills all creativity. The corresponding brakes on the innovation process must be countered consistently.

> **Think Box: Questions You Should Ask Yourself**
> - How "innovative" is your innovation management?
> - Does a closed innovation approach still dominate in your company?
> - Who is already or who could be integrated into an open innovation approach?
> - What opportunities exist to integrate customers more intensively into the innovation process?
> - What obstacles stand in the way of such integration—and how can they be overcome?
> - Where does the responsibility for this lie in your company?

3.5.3.3 Design Thinking

Design thinking is particularly popular in the context of innovation management. Design thinking is often used to **work on complex tasks** and is based on the approach of designers. In their work, designers follow the phases of observation, understanding, idea generation, prototype development, refinement, and execution in order to find convincing solutions. If necessary, they jump back and forth between the phases. In this way, not only can great learning effects be achieved, but they can also be used directly for the further process.

The core idea of design thinking is to replace a product-centric design with a **customer-centric design** in innovation processes. As can be seen in Fig. 3.82, the direction of development is reversed. In design thinking, the starting point is no longer a product, a service or a business idea, but the customer.

> **Memory Box**
> **In product-centric design, the motto is:**
>   "We build the best product!"
> **In customer-centric design, the motto is:**

(continued)

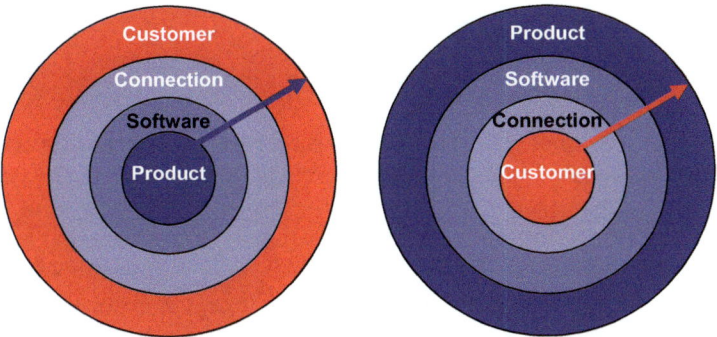

Fig. 3.82 From product- to customer-centric design

> "We solve a customer problem!"
> The **creative process of design thinking** makes use of these fundamental considerations through a special methodology and various tools. The focus here is also on **consistent customer orientation**. You can use this equally for the development of products, services, processes, and business models. You should take the following **characteristics and principles of design thinking** into account (cf. also Poguntke, 2018):
>
> - **Forming teams in design thinking**
>   In design thinking, **multidisciplinary teams** are formed that bring in different horizons of experience. **Diversity** here means male and female, young and older, as well as starters and "old hands." In addition, the most diverse corporate divisions should also be reflected in these teams. After all, no one has to be less creative just because they work in an area that does not have "creativity" in its job profile (cf. the first principle of *Google's 9 Principles of Innovation* in Sect. 3.1.3).
>   When putting together a team, you should look for the so-called **T-shape personalities**. These are people with a wide range of interests who at the same time have a high level of technical expertise. The vertical part of the letter "T" stands for a deep knowledge in a certain field. The horizontal part of the letter "T" expresses the necessary broad and overarching knowledge that the respective persons should bring to the table.
> - **Stages of the design thinking process**
>   Design thinking process often includes the following steps (cf. Fig. 3.106):
>   - **Emphasize**: building empathy for the target person.
>   - **Define**: defining the task to be addressed.
>   - **Ideate**: generating ideas for solutions.
>   - **Prototype**: developing prototypes.

(continued)

- **Test**: checking the solutions found.
- **Decide** (after several iterations in the sense of runs): decision for a solution idea.

- A special feature of design thinking is the **consistent target group orientation**, which is reflected in all process steps. In the course of the process, phases of divergence and convergence alternate. In the **phases of divergence**, the focus is on the quantity of solution ideas. The aim here is to develop the greatest possible variety of ideas. In the **phases of convergence**, the focus is on condensing and combining the insights gained and the ideas developed.

  The **visualization** of the developed ideas is of great importance in all phases. This already starts with the presentation of the **persona**, for whom a new service concept, an app or a new product or an entire business model is to be developed (see Sect. 3.5.2.1). The use of the **customer journey map** and the **empathy map** can promote the necessary empathy. The customer insights gained and possible solution ideas should be visualized in the form of sketches and storyboards. **Storytelling** is used to further promote understanding and thus empathy. For this purpose, concrete application situations, pain points, and expectations of the target customers can be packaged in small stories that further promote understanding. Important:

  The user stories should be formulated from the customers' point of view and in the customers' words—not as a technical requirements profile!

  An important component of design thinking is **rapid prototyping** (keyword "MVP," cf. Fig. 3.31). This process deliberately avoids the expensive development of prototypes that are as realistic as possible. Instead, the aim is to develop multiple (simple) prototypes quickly and at low cost in early phases and to have their functionality tested by the final users.

  This results in **iterative loops** (iterations). The same process steps are run through several times: new insights lead to new ideas, to new prototypes, to new test results. These results represent new insights that drive the creative and evaluation process again. Thus, the process of learning and thus a step-by-step approach to an ideal solution continues over several rounds. This is where the process shown in lean start-up comes into play (cf. Fig. 3.30).

- **Shaping space and time in the design thinking processes**

  The space and time concept must promote the flexibility and dynamics of the design thinking process. The room should therefore have a high degree of flexibility in terms of the media to be used. *Metaplan* walls, flipcharts, high tables, and game corners are part of the basic equipment. In addition,

(continued)

creative processes can be supported by *Metaplan* cards and Post-it notes of different colors and sizes. Different materials can be used for the development of prototypes. The spectrum here ranges from modelling clay to *Lego* bricks to other building materials.

To ensure that the participants in a design thinking process are not permanently caught up in day-to-day business, it is advisable to use premises that are detached from the usual workplace. This can still be in the same building—but visually separated and, if necessary, provided with large notices, such as "Please do not disturb creative processes!". It is not for nothing that many agencies offer their clients such premises so that they can work undisturbed.

Memory Box
Creativity needs time.

That is why a design thinking process should not be scheduled quickly between "soup and lunch" (unlike brainstorming). Rather, all participants should have their backs free to concentrate fully on the defined task. Therefore, the following applies here: simply turn off mobile phones, tablets, laptops for once. That is possible!

The **stages of the design thinking** described above are now explained in detail here so that you know exactly what should happen in which phase (cf. Fig. 3.83).

- **Empathize: building empathy for the target people.**
  The design thinking process starts with the **empathize phase**. For this, the various information and studies that create a good understanding of the initial situation are gathered. Insights gained through focus groups and/or in-depth interviews are particularly helpful. These often provide a particularly comprehensive insight into the state of mind of the target persons.

  To sharpen this perspective, the so-called **personas** are often used. These are fictitious people who represent specific target groups (see Sect. 3.5.2.1). They help to achieve a user-centered focus. The so-called **empathy maps** can be developed for these personas, which visualize central aspects of the previously researched state of mind and express other relevant aspects. An empathy map supports you in determining the relevant customer wishes, pain, and gain points as well as the individual needs of the persona (see Sect. 3.5.2.4). Further important customer insights are determined by using the **customer journey map** (see Sect. 3.5.2.3).

(continued)

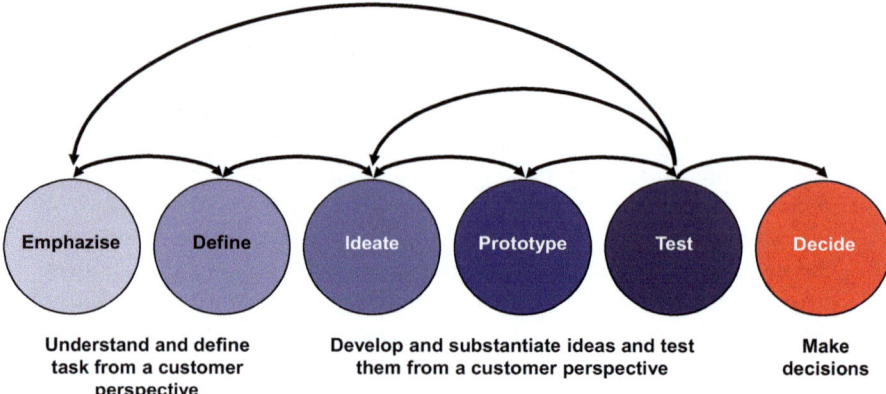

Fig. 3.83 Stages of a design thinking process

> **Define: definition of the task to be dealt with**
> Based on the above information, the **define phase** is about formulating a question that is as precise as possible. This is also referred to as a **design challenge**. Now, with a concrete persona in mind, a formulation of the initial question must be found. This is referred to as the **point of view** as the basis for idea generation:
> – What specifically does this persona need?
> – Why does she need it?
> – What does she want to achieve through it?
> – What resistance might stand in the way of its use?
> – What support does the persona expect from us?
> – Which side could provide additional support?
> – What would a solution, a service offer, a product has to look like that could meet these expectations?
> - **Ideate: generating ideas for solutions**
> In the **ideate phase**, ideas and initial solutions to problems are developed. Initially, this involves a large number of ideas for solutions (keyword "**phase of divergence**"). Various creative methods can be used (e.g., brainstorming, attribute listing). In order to promote the creative process, the "most absurd idea" can also be specifically sought. This frees the minds for new ideas! A **phase of convergence** follows, in which a selection of possible solution ideas is made, which are further processed in the next phase. After the creative expression, a higher rationality returns here!
>
> A central task in the development of product and service ideas, but also of business model innovations, is to convert the developed solution ideas into a **set of hypotheses**, which are also to be subjected to the **iterative**

(continued)

market-oriented testing described below. Here, two central aspects of the value proposition are to be tested with the highest priority: the **benefit hypothesis** and the **growth hypothesis**. How these are to be tested was already explained in Sect. 3.2.7 using the example of business model innovations (cf. also Fig. 3.30).

- **Prototype: development of prototypes**
  In the **prototype phase**, the so-called **rapid prototyping** is used (keyword "MVP," Fig. 3.31). Here, the simplest means are used to create initial prototypes for learning and testing purposes. Depending on the respective solution idea, sketches, wireframes, storyboards, or even 3D models can be used. Creativity is only limited by time and budget.

  When designing **processes** and **service concepts**, **role plays** can also be used to test the functionality of certain processes. It is important that the prototype is suitable for testing the benefit hypothesis defined above.

  In the case of complex innovations, aspects of the **value creation structure of the business model** must also be taken into account at this point in the prototype development. These must be examined in the subsequent test phase with regard to the benefits and the achievable growth potential.

- **Test: test the solutions found**
  The prototypes are shown to users in the **test phase** in order to verify the **benefit hypothesis**. The focus here is on the people who actually use a smartphone, software, vehicle, or industrial plant. An evaluation by the client—carried out in the ivory tower—is not meant with this type of test.

  Depending on the insights gained, various alternatives arise. If the prototype failed with the user (!), the ideate process can be started again—based on new findings. If the prototype was liked—but with rough edges—these can be worked on in a new ideate process. These possibilities are made visible in Fig. 3.83 by the jumps back and are intended as part of the process and thus also wanted.

Memory Box
Jumps back or iterations in the innovation process are not a sign of failure, but an expression of a continuous learning process.

And this is how they should be treated! Instead of a **failure culture** we should talk about a **learning culture**!

Parallel to this, the **growth hypothesis** must be examined. What can promote the rapid growth of an innovation? Is the business model scalable?

(continued)

What are the important communication and distribution channels for the persona?

If the prototype has been accepted by the target persons (after several iterations/runs, if necessary) and the benefit and growth hypotheses have been comprehensively tested and positively evaluated, the transition to the final stage takes place. This is where the great flexibility of design thinking becomes apparent: individual phases are simply run through as often as necessary until a convincing solution is found.

- **Decide: decide for a solution idea**
  After the "acceptance" of the prototype by the target persons, the design thinking process is completed. Now the developed concepts can be transferred to the "classic" organization (keyword "performance engine") to be developed to market maturity and introduced there. This step is illustrated in Fig. 3.19.

The following **guiding ideas of design thinking** underlie throughout all these phases:

- Fail often and as early as possible (and cheaply)!
- Failure is an inexhaustible source of learning!
- A large autonomy of the team is important!
- Constructive feedback is a must!
- Learn continuously!
- Make solutions tangible!
- Let the customers—here to be understood as users—decide what really succeeded!

There are (almost) no limits to the **use of design thinking**. Wherever you have a need for convincing innovative solution ideas for products, services, processes, and business models, you can use the concept.

Memory Box
The **success factors of design thinking** can be expressed with **3 Ps**:
People—Place—Process
It is about involving appropriately qualified people in a protected space in a well-designed process.

> **Think Box: Questions You Should Ask Yourself**
> - Which design dominates in your company—product-centric or customer-centric design?
> - Is design thinking already used in your company?
> - Do you pay attention to diversity in the design of the teams?
> - Do the people involved have a T-shape personality?
> - Do you use different forms of visualization in the design thinking process?
> - Do you align your innovations with concrete personas?
> - Do you incorporate the results of empathy maps and customer journey maps?
> - Do you consistently define the point of view from the customer's perspective?
> - Do you achieve speed through rapid prototyping?
> - Do you intensively test the benefit and growth hypotheses of your innovation?
> - Where is the competence for the use of this method located in your company?

3.5.3.4 *Lego Serious Play*

With *Lego Serious Play*, you have another tool at your disposal to arrive at new approaches to solutions through a **moderated process** (cf. Ematinger & Schulze, 2020). In workshops, the participants—again, preferably from different company divisions—can develop new business strategies, processes, products, and services. The facilitators of these workshops play a central role here because they have to align the playful component of this approach with concrete tasks of the company.

Lego Serious Play is a concept with which—even at a high level of abstraction—creative solutions can be developed in mixed teams in a playful and yet serious manner. The aim is for the participants to use various *Lego* building blocks to create models that are as detailed as possible, quasi as **metaphors for different aspects of the workshop topic**. In this way—initiated as a game—an intensive exchange between the participants on the defined topic areas succeeds. Several interesting effects can be achieved here:

- **Creativity and innovative strength** are promoted, as cognitive and manual processes are linked by working with the *Lego* building blocks.
- The basis for this is the so-called **hand-brain connection**. As the hands are particularly intensively connected with the brain cells due to their fine motor skills, thinking in conjunction with doing leads to a particularly deep and lasting understanding of the topic being dealt with.

- **Problems and tasks** that were previously only dimly visible to some participants suddenly become—in the truest sense of the word—"tangible" and thus "graspable."
- At the same time, things become easily changeable or "manipulable" by simply exchanging or changing a few stones. **Change becomes feasible and visible.**
- Through the ongoing **process of constructing, deconstructing, and reconstructing**, creative processes can be promoted and new ideas for solutions can be developed.
- **Constructing real things** makes important connections easier to grasp and at the same time promotes the development of new solutions.
- The use of a common "vocabulary"—here in the form of the *Lego* building blocks—breaks down **communication barriers** between specialized units and across hierarchical levels.
- At the same time, **problem areas** can be addressed more openly—because playfully—and ideally solved.
- At the same time, the playful approach leads to a **shift in attention** and a new **definition of roles**—detached from the classic tasks of the workshop participants. In this way, new creative sides of the participants can be expressed.
- The play approach leads to the participants themselves feeling spurred on to **high performance** and to go beyond classic—self-made or externally defined—creative boundaries. It is ideal if a real flow develops in such situations, which leads to the players becoming absorbed in their task.

For which questions can you use *Lego Serious Play*? There is the possibility to support the **entrepreneurial strategy development** as well as the **development of business model innovations** through this approach. For this purpose, the internal and external influences on the company are first visualized. In a second stage, possible scenarios can be run through and evaluated with regard to their long-term solution contribution to the company's development. However, concrete **challenges of the company** can also be visualized and made comprehensible through this approach in order to arrive at new approaches to solutions. The *Lego* building blocks provide the material to promote the analysis of the status quo and to develop innovations.

The use of *Lego Serious Play* requires **trained and experienced facilitators**. Only they can ensure the success of the approach. If thematic "laymen" try to moderate such a process, they can only fail. Therefore, you should only use this method with **external support** if you do not have appropriately trained moderators yourself. It is important that the participants of such a workshop understand the relevance of the concept at an early stage. However, a comprehensive introduction to the theoretical basics should be avoided so that the participants do not get too "cerebral" and block themselves (cf. on the gamification approach in management Sects. 3.6.4 and 3.6.9).

▶ **Food for Thought**
In a game you can get to know a person better in an hour than in a conversation in a year.
Platon

Think Box: Questions You Should Ask Yourself
- Have you ever used *Lego Serious Play* in your company as part of a strategy process?
- Where would an exciting first use be possible in your company?
- Where could you buy in the necessary expertise to make the deployment a success?
- Who would have to be convinced in advance so that the use of *Lego Serious Play* is not torpedoed from within?
- Who has the courage to take such a step?

3.5.3.5 *Elon Musk's* DNA for Innovation Management

The editors of *DUB* magazine have talked to experts to find out what **Elon Musk's innovation success** can be traced back to. The central findings can be found in the following 10 **success strategies for innovation management** (cf. DUB Unternehmer, 2020, pp. 8–14):

- **Work hard!**
  A statement by *Elon Musk* underlines this orientation: "No one with a 40-h week has ever changed the world." If you work twice as hard or twice as fast as the competition, you at least have the chance to carve out a competitive advantage. It is also important to concentrate your energy on a few projects so as not to get bogged down.
- **Focus is key!**
- **Put on a thick skin!**
  It is not only about developing visions and innovation, but also about realizing them in the face of resistance. After all, visionaries are often ridiculed for a long time and not taken seriously—before success is achieved. In *Tesla's* case, this took about 15 years—and the company also had to overcome major existential crises several times.

  In order to withstand the massive headwind, **solid stamina** is necessary.

- **Challenge the status quo!**
  An entrepreneur is not satisfied with the status quo. He is driven by the motivation to rethink things and take them to new shores. Electric cars, rockets, and tunnel boring machines existed before *Tesla*, *SpaceX*, and *The Boring Company*.

It is about the **courage to introduce new technologies and concepts into traditional industries** in order to decisively advance them.

- **Don't blindly follow every trend!**
Copying the success patterns of competitors is not an innovation strategy. Perhaps this will enable you to reach the same level a few years later that your competitors are already at today.

It is more promising to **venture into new territory**—even in established sectors.

- **Think of a product or service only from the customer's point of view!**
This idea is made very transparent by this statement by *Elon Musk*: "The path to the CEO's office should not lead through the CFO's office, and it should not lead through the marketing department. It has to go through the engineering and design department."

Only by having a "**direct line to the CEO**" can it be ensured that, in the case of innovations, discussions are also consistently customer-oriented at the C-level.

- **Take risks consciously!**
If you want to change the world—in large and small ways—you have to consciously take risks. The motto here is:

The only thing worse than losing is not trying at all.

- **Work towards a higher goal!**
Elon Musk also has this to say: "I am interested in things that **change the world for the better** or **influence the future**. And I'm interested in wondrous new technologies that make you wonder, 'Wow, how did that even happen? How is that possible?'" Here you can think of the *Neurolink* project—a chip for the brain—new company of *Elon Musk*.

- **Be attractive to skilled workers!**
Innovative solutions come about when the right people with the right mindset come together in the right place at the right time and are guided to peak performance by a suitable working environment. However, *Elon Musk* is not known for an empathetic leadership style—quite the opposite. Rather, extreme working hours, extreme micro-management, tough announcements, and also a hire & fire mentality can be observed.

Nevertheless, *Elon Musk* succeeds in attracting and often retaining highly qualified top performers because he offers them one thing:

The feeling of working on something really big.

At the same time, he employs the **transformational leadership** style. Leaders inspire and motivate their teams—and also work intensively with them at the operational level (see Sect. 3.6.6).

The recruitment of 12,000 employees for the *Tesla Giga Factory* near Berlin was kicked off by *Elon Musk* in September 2020—not quite in line with industry practice—with the following tweet:

"Please please please work at *Tesla Giga Berlin*! It will be super fun."

- **Get constant feedback!**
Elon Musk's idea on this is: "I think it's very important to have a **feedback loop** where you're constantly thinking about what you've done and how you could do

it better. And even if you don't agree with someone's criticism, you should at least listen very carefully to what they have to say."
   Listening is crucial!
- **Failure? That's part of it—but you're above that!**
   What does *Elon Musk* have to say about it? "**Failure is always an option**. If you don't fail, you're not innovative enough." During the financial crisis, both *Tesla* and *SpaceX* faced bankruptcy. *Elon Musk* used the last of his money to save both companies. The production of the *Tesla Model S* as well as the *Model 3* was temporarily in chaos—but *Elon Musk* just kept going. When presenting the "unbreakable" windows of the *Tesla* pick-up *Cybertruck*, they broke twice in November 2019. So what? Keep going.
   The trick is to **keep going despite setbacks**!
- What does *Elon Musk* say about this? "If something is important enough, you do it even when the odds of success are not favourable."

What else distinguishes *Elon Musk* from others? He is a very **active media influencer and power player**. Such personality structures often cause a lot of trouble in established companies. After all, these are people who are uncomfortable, annoying, think disruptively, question the status quo, and push others out of their comfort zone. In order not to give up here and make oneself comfortable in one's own comfort zone, **self-confidence**, a high **frustration tolerance,** and above all **resilience** are needed (see Sect. 3.6.4).
Modesty is not enough if you want to be at the top.

▶   **Food for Thought**
   Ambition is never modest. If being modest means having mediocre success, then all I can say is: I don't care!
   Emmanuel Macron, President of France

> **Think Box: Questions You Should Ask Yourself**
> - What food for thought can the *Elon Musk* DNA give you for your innovation management?
> - What obstacles would you have to overcome?
> - Who is working on these issues in your company?

3.6   Human Resources Strategies for the Digital Age

Success usually comes in the following order:
   People, process, product, profit!
   Employees and managers make decisions, develop (digitized) processes that lead to products and services. Whether these lead to profit depends on how customer-

oriented the company thinks and acts. Here one can formulate—in reference to a well-known saying from the election campaign of *Bill Clinton*:
It's the people, stupid!

3.6.1 Qualification Campaign: Triggered by the HR Department

I've learned that people will forget what you said, people will forget what you did, but people will never forget how you made them feel.
  Maya Angelou

3.6.1.1 Human Resources: Success Factors of the Digital Transformation

Together with the *Fraunhofer Institute for Industrial Engineering IAO* and with the participation of the *Otto Group*, the *Bertelsmann Foundation* attempted to identify the most important **success factors of the digital transformation** (cf. Bertelsmann Stiftung, 2020, p. 83). Twenty executives from 15 companies of different sizes and industries were involved in the study. The spectrum ranged from IT and software companies to banks and insurance companies to construction firms and producers of printing inks. The survey used a mix of methods including qualitative face-to-face interviews and a quantitative, online-based assessment center.

A **key finding** was that the following **human factors** in particular are especially important **prerequisites for a successful digital transformation** (cf. Bertelsmann Stiftung, 2020, p. 8f.):

- A high **willingness to try things out**
- A comprehensive **culture of innovation**
- **Open communication**
- A great **willingness to change at management level**

These findings apply irrespective of the size of a company, its industry affiliation, and the business areas it serves. It also became clear during the survey that a **technical changeover to digital applications and work tools** can only mark the **beginning of a change process**. Since a digital transformation encompasses and permeates the company as a whole, it is crucial, according to the respondents, that **representatives of top management** embrace the changes, exemplify them, and communicate them transparently. **Middle management** has a particularly important mediating role to play here. Overall, however, it is important to mobilize the **know-how and flexibility of all employees** in order to develop innovative solutions together. By **opening up to the outside world**, for example through cooperation with start-ups or scientific institutions, valuable impulses can be gained from outside (cf. Bertelsmann Stiftung, 2020, p. 8f.).

If the transformation process calls for **greater personal responsibility on the part of employees**, this often requires a **new understanding of leadership** and a **distinct culture of error**—or better—a **distinct culture of learning**. When using flexible organizational forms that replace classic hierarchies, the **manager is**

3.6 Human Resources Strategies for the Digital Age

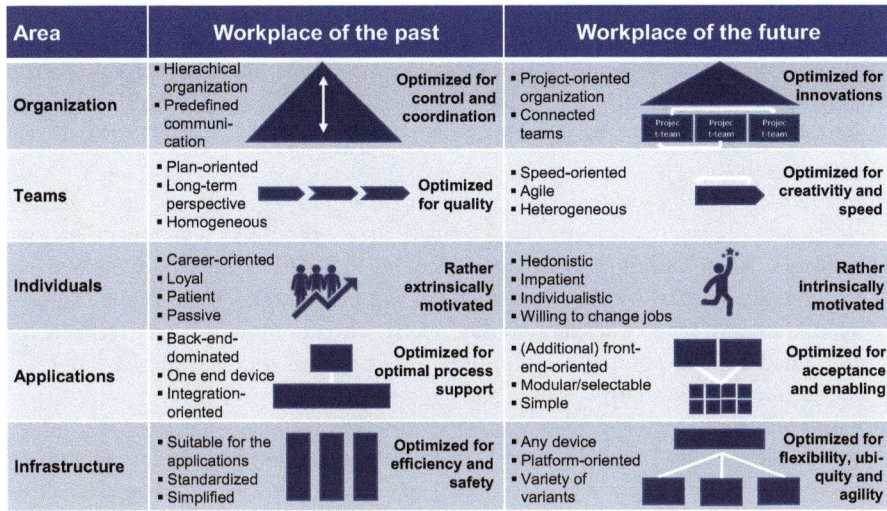

Fig. 3.84 Accompanying the changes in organizational and IT architecture through personnel development

required to act as a moderator and enabler. Such a process must be supported by a **comprehensive qualification campaign**. All these factors are analyzed in depth below and possible courses of action are identified.

Figure 3.84 brings together central **challenges for HR management** that are necessitated by the diverse changes already described (cf. Jäger, 2020, p. 25). Here, the focus is primarily on those measures that are caused by a further development of the organizational and IT architecture (see Sect. 3.4). The steps initiated or foreseeable there are to be supported by **human resources development**. Here it becomes clear once again how intensively the individual departments must work together to master the digital transformation and build digital excellence.

Figure 3.84 brings together the **central challenges for HR management** that are necessitated by the many changes in the company and its environment. The focus here is primarily on those measures that are caused by further development of the organizational and IT architecture

- **Organization**
  The process and organizational structure, which has been geared to management, control, and coordination up to now, must be supported with regard to the development and marketing of innovations. To this end, the players must be oriented towards more networked, project-oriented work—and to create the necessary conditions for this.

- **Teams**
  While in many companies the teams were focused on achieving high (error-free) quality, there now needs to be an orientation towards creativity and speed—in addition. To achieve this, managers and employees must be familiarized with the methods of agile management.
- **Individuals**
  In many companies—as the *Gallup* studies on employee engagement show anew every year—employees who have only a low emotional attachment to their company often dominate (see Sect. 3.6.5). In many cases, they tend to be motivated extrinsically. In order to meet the challenges of the digital age, on the other hand, employees are required today who are more strongly intrinsically motivated by the company's purpose. This purpose must be worked out and communicated internally.
- **Applications**
  The challenge for IT and HR alike is no longer just to provide employees with the best possible support for processes, but also to ensure further enabling. The aim is to ensure that managers and employees are supported more comprehensively by applications (e.g., from the areas of AI, VR, AR, business intelligence), especially with regard to the necessary innovations.
- **Infrastructure**
  "Infrastructure" is also not a pure process or technology issue. If the infrastructure was previously focused on efficiency and security and now flexibility, ubiquity and agility are gaining in importance, then this will only succeed if the workforce follows suit. A prerequisite for new technologies not primarily triggering fear but productive curiosity is comprehensive knowledge of the opportunities and risks associated with a technology.

Here it becomes apparent: HR must create a **(digital) training agenda** to support the transformation process with qualified and motivated employees and managers.

> **Memory Box**
> In the **center of the competition between established companies and new competitors** (often start-ups) is often not (alone) the **better idea** or **high-performance processes and methods**, but **well-trained, committed and creative employees and managers**!
>
> If you implement the measures described below in an integrated way, you can develop the flywheel borrowed from growth hacking (see Sect. 3.5.1.2) into a **flywheel of human resources**. The activities shown in Fig. 3.85 can constantly add new energy to this flywheel and motivate others to join in. Ideally, a **perpetual motion machine** will be created in your company.

(continued)

3.6 Human Resources Strategies for the Digital Age

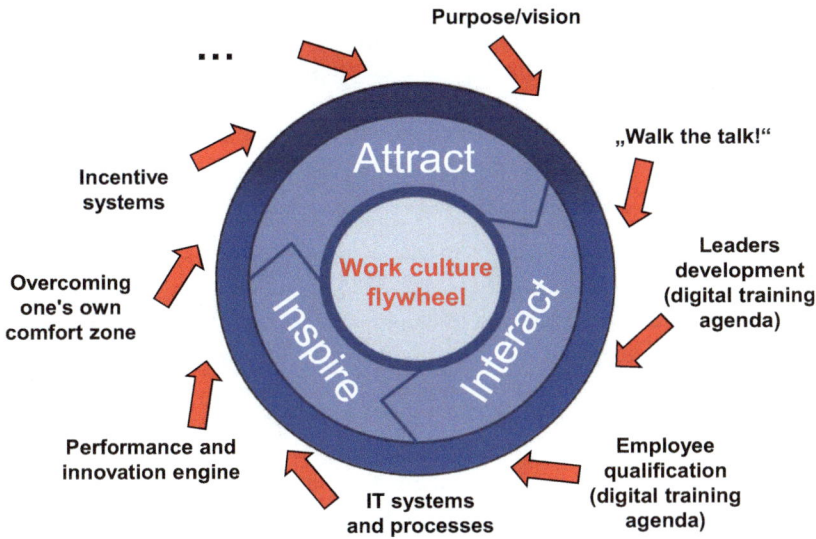

Fig. 3.85 Flywheel of human resources

> The individual elements of the **flywheel of human resources** work as follows:
>
> - The **purpose** or **vision** must provide a motivating direction for business development for all managers and employees. Purpose or vision can add a lot of energy to the flywheel.
> - It is important that the "saying" is followed by the "doing." The challenge here is: "**walk the talk**." This is the only way to continuously supply the flywheel with further energy—more about "doing" than just "talking."
> - In order for the flywheel to become larger and at the same time receive additional energy, **digital training agendas** must be developed for the executives and the employees – to achieve "walk the talk." If more people support the transformation process, the flywheel not only becomes larger, but also faster. Ideally, this will motivate more people to join and support the journey of change.
> - A transformation can only succeed if the **IT systems and other processes** also add further energy to the flywheel. IT and processes can also make a decisive contribution to ensuring that the flywheel runs as smoothly as possible. This is achieved when information for purchasing, production, marketing, and sales is provided in the desired form. Networking production processes across site boundaries is also part of this.
>
> (continued)

- In the course of organizational development, an **innovation engine** must be installed alongside the performance engine that dominates in established organizations. New products and services as well as business model innovations are to be developed in the innovation engine. The results achieved here feed further energy into the flywheel. At the same time, the organizational separation of "day-to-day business" and "innovations" prevents friction losses in the flywheel.
- Transformation forces people to move beyond their own **comfort zones**. If this succeeds, there are not only fewer brakemen in the process, who scatter sand here in order not to have to change themselves. Those who transform themselves from brakemen to actors in the process inject new energy into the flywheel.
- To ensure that as many managers and employees as possible are prepared to extend their personal comfort zones, the established **incentive systems** must be overcome. After all, what good is a convincing vision if the people acting on it are not rewarded for behavior aimed at achieving it? Then the rewards act as brake blocks because they prevent desired behavior. This drains important energy from the flywheel.

You will certainly find other aspects in your company that make this flywheel run—or slow it down. The **image of the flywheel** is a **metaphor** that you can also use for internal company storytelling. Finally, it becomes very clear which actions lead to energy build-up and which behaviors lead to energy reduction due to friction losses.

3.6.1.2 Requirements for Human Resource Management

As shown in Fig. 3.86, the process of digitizing your company brings with it significant demands on **human resource management** (cf. von Rosenstiel & Nerdinger, 2011, p. 12). It is necessary to determine how the individual, the group, and the organization are to be aligned with the tasks to be mastered.

Between task, individual, group, and organization, there are classic **tensions** that have to be shaped and moderated by managers and employees. The four areas of task, individual, group, and organization cannot be considered independently of each other. Through **training measures** (especially for the top performers), through the **structural and procedural organization** and, above all, through **leadership** and **communication**, care must be taken to ensure that individuals, groups, and the entire organization work together with as little friction and in a goal-oriented manner as possible in order to master the defined tasks (cf. von Rosenstiel & Nerdinger, 2011, pp. 12–16; further Nerdinger et al., 2014, pp. 30–45).

The change processes caused by the increasing digitalization of the corporate environment lead to new tasks and have an impact on all areas shown in Fig. 3.86.

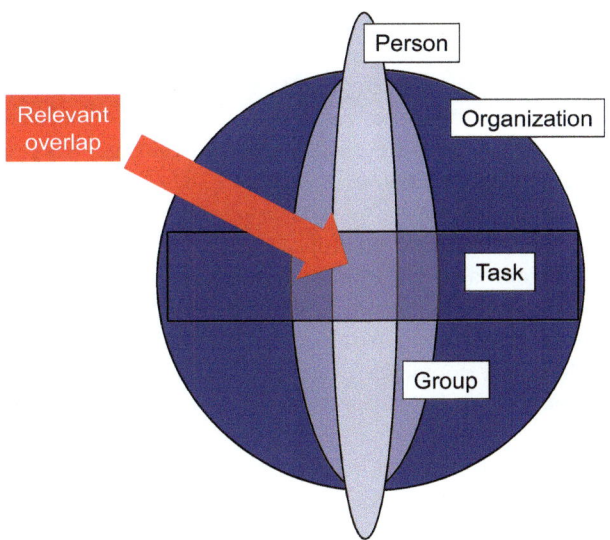

Fig. 3.86 Merging of task, individual, group, and organization

They are accompanied by changes at the level of the **person** (here specifically employees and managers), the **group** (in project teams, departments) as well as the **organization** (here companies). Particularly important fields of action are discussed below.

One of the **core tasks of human resource development** today is to continuously support its own staff in their professional development. Only then will they be able to meet the challenges of the new **working world 4.0** and the demands of the **VUCA world** (see Chap. 1). These developments are also constantly changing the **corporate competence goals** and thus also the required **competence profiles of employees and managers**.

In the digital age, a long-term **human resource development and planning** is becoming less and less viable. Therefore, a more **agile human resources development** is needed so that your company can continuously align itself to the new tasks that arise.

In spite of the agility demanded everywhere, it remains an important task of the HR department or the CHRO (Chief Human Resources Officer) to ensure a **structure of qualification** in **competence development** in the company, so that the necessary competence development takes place in a coordinated manner and individual measures build on each other. For this purpose, it can also be helpful to create a specific company-wide **toolbox of methods** that can be used across departments.

3.6.1.3 Human Resource Management as a Driver of Personnel Development

In many companies the pressure for change and consequently the need for learning is so great and time-critical that a **centralized management of human resources** cannot always meet the requirements. Consequently, it may be necessary, especially in larger companies, to install **personnel development officers** in the various company divisions. As **learning coaches** and **learning advisors**, they have the task of supporting employees and managers closely and continuously in their qualification measures. This can be done at the divisional, departmental, or team level. These learning coaches and learning advisors can also develop **individual qualification measures**.

HR development becomes a **service provider for competence development**—for managers and employees alike (cf. Kudernatsch, 2019). Parallel to this, **managers** also have an important task. It is and remains their non-delegable responsibility to systematically support and accompany the employees entrusted to them in developing and expanding their respective competences.

The developments described below illustrate the **dynamics of competence development** that will have to be mastered in the coming years:

- Hundreds of thousands of employees today perform functions that did not exist 20 years ago: 3D artists, app developers, big data analysts, CDOs (Chief Digital Officers), cloud architects, cloud service managers, community managers, content managers, data scientists, feel-good managers, AI programmers, mobile developers, scrum masters, SEO specialists (SEO stands for search engine optimization), social media managers, VEO specialists (VEO stands for voice engine optimization), UX designers (UX stands for user experience), etc.
- Accordingly, about 70% of today's students will be working in jobs that do not even exist at the moment.
- In 10 years, employees and managers will be working with technologies that are not yet operational today.
- Some of the teams will have to solve problems that are not yet known.

> **Memory Box**
> One thing is becoming clear:
> **The half-life period of knowledge is getting shorter and shorter!**
> Even today, many companies are desperately trying to find appropriately qualified personnel on the market because the in-house development of such skills was not or not sufficiently promoted in the past. Therefore, it is a **core task of human resource development** to identify the **strategic qualification gap** in your company shown in Fig. 3.87.
> Through the **development of a (digital) teaching and learning agenda**, it is important to systematically and regularly supplement **qualifying** with **requalifying** in order to close the **strategic qualification gap**. For this, offers for **reskilling** (refreshing existing skills) and **upskilling** (acquiring more advanced skills) must be developed.
>
> (continued)

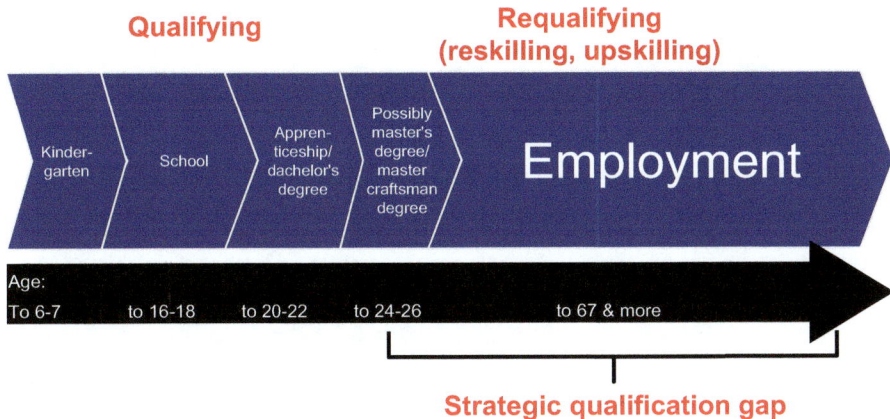

Fig. 3.87 Strategic qualification gap

Parallel to this, the **challenge for all employees and managers** is to empower themselves for further qualification. "**Lifelong learning**" has long been considered a guiding idea, but it has never been as important as it is today! Education and training in the industrial nations and in every company requires a strategic reorientation and further development in order to meet the demands associated with the digital transformation.

Memory Box
The upheavals to be mastered during a working life are so great that we need a second or even third vocational training.
  Learning—quasi in advance—no longer succeeds today!
  We have to integrate learning into our everyday life and at the same time build up self-learning competence!
  The **focus of today's (state) educational efforts** is on early childhood education, school education, vocational training when entering working life, and higher education (cf. Fig. 3.87). It remains largely unconsidered that people devote their longest time—often over 40 years—to professional activities whose requirements will change to an ever greater extent and at an ever faster pace in the future.
  Already the **baby boomer generation**, which will leave the labor market in the next few years, has to prove itself in a working environment for which neither schools, nor vocational training, nor universities could adequately prepare. The Internet, for example, with its many possibilities, was not part

(continued)

of the training content at the time because it did not yet exist. In addition, typewriters instead of computers were part of the standard equipment of a student, who also had to get by without a smartphone, without a tablet computer, and without the Internet!

It is indispensable that each individual in your company does not delegate the **responsibility for further qualification** to the HR department. It is and remains a **core task of every single employee and every manager** to keep refreshing his or her working capacity through lifelong learning. The great challenge for each individual is **employability**. For this, it is important that no one just waits for the company to do something for them!

> **Memory Box**
> Today, **each individual employee and manager must take the initiative to close the strategic qualification gap** if their own employer has not recognized the signs of the times or is not acting appropriately.
>
> Each and every one of us must take responsibility for our own development—companies and the state can support this.
>
> Each individual has a duty to contribute his or her own talents and to remain capable and willing to learn in order to maintain and develop his or her own employability.

▶ **Food for Thought**
He who plays with life never gets along. He who does not command himself always remains a servant.
Johann Wolfgang von Goethe

In order to support the required **lifelong learning**, it is a continuous task of the HR department to repeatedly address the need for this and also to make corresponding proposals for the content. To this end, a **(digital) learning agenda** must be developed for the entire company as well as for the individual functional areas and for managers and employees. At least some of the time required for **participation in qualification measures** should be granted. In addition, incentives can be given if people commit themselves (if necessary also in their free time) to their job-relevant continuing education.

> **Memory Box**
> **The time of the all-knowing manager is over!**
> **Is it already time to install a Chief Learning Officer?**

3.6.1.4 Readiness for Lifelong Learning in Different Countries

How does the **willingness to engage in lifelong learning** compare internationally? The international labor market study *Decoding Global Trends in Upskilling and Reskilling* provides exciting results. It was conducted jointly by the online job platform *StepStone*, the *Boston Consulting Group (BCG)*, and the global job exchange network *The Network*. A total of 366,000 people from 197 nations were surveyed, including more than 17,000 from Germany (cf. BCG, 2019b, p. 2).

Worldwide, 61% of respondents assume that the **megatrends** will have a lasting impact on their profession. In Germany, however, only 55% see this as the case with technological change (automation, artificial intelligence, robots) and 50% with globalization (cf. BCG, 2019b, p. 3f.).

The study grouped the countries according to the perceived **impact of the megatrends** and the **time required for their own further qualification**. Four clusters were formed through this **country segmentation** (cf. BCG, 2019b, pp. 3–5):

- **Intrinsic learners**
  Intrinsic learners engage in continuing education on their own, even though they expect only minor effects of the trends described. This attitude is found in **China** and **Russia**.
- **Proactive change agents**
  The proactive change-makers invest a lot of time in further training because they also expect major effects of the trends on their own professional lives. This group includes countries such as **South Korea, Japan,** and **Turkey**.
- **Spectators**
  The spectators currently invest little in continuing education because they expect only minor spill-over effects on their working environment. In **Belgium, France,** and **Austria**, less than 43% of people spend significant time learning each year. Other countries in "spectator" status are **Switzerland**, the **UK**, **Sweden**, **Canada**, and the **USA**.
- **Procrastinators**
  The procrastinators expect major effects from globalization and automation, but are hardly preparing for them. Many of the countries found here are from Western Europe—the **Netherlands**, **Italy**, and **Germany**. Germany occupies a particularly strong position. Major effects are expected in Germany. At the same time, very little time is invested in further qualification. With a value of 38%, Germany is the country in the group of the 30 largest countries with the lowest proportion of people who spend a few weeks or more per year on their training.

There is a relatively high degree of agreement on the question of which **skills** are required in the face of increasing globalization and the use of new technologies. For skilled workers, these include above all a strong **ability to communicate**. **Problem-solving skills, leadership skills,** and **analytical skills** are also crucial for future professional success (cf. BCG, 2019b, p. 7f.).

▶ **Food for Thought**
One thing becomes clear from the study: the **willingness to reskill and upskill** must be massively promoted by companies and politics in many countries. However, in my opinion, a greater willingness to embark on the **journey to further qualifications** should also be expected from every employee and every manager.

3.6.1.5 Curiosity as the Fuel of the Learning Process

How can we motivate our workforce to **continuously learn**? The key incentive for this lies in **curiosity**. When people are curious, structures in the brain are activated that predict the expectation of a reward. Pursuing curiosity and filling knowledge gaps is an **intrinsic reward** for the brain (cf. Chang, 2016):

- **Information from which we can learn affects the human brain like the expectation of good food, money, or sex!**
- **Curiosity makes us learn more easily and remember what we learn better!**
- **Curiosity is the fuel for lifelong learning!**

However, simply valuing curiosity is not enough to build a **culture of curiosity** in your organization. You should take concrete measures to foster a working culture and atmosphere that actively supports curiosity. To do this, you can give your employees and managers **creative freedom** (take a look at the *Google* example in Sect. 3.1.3).

The challenge is: "**time for curiosity.**"

In addition, you can teach different **methods** to (playfully) develop new ideas and acquire new knowledge (see Sect. 3.5.3). This needs to be accompanied by **regular and appreciative communication** about the successes, but also the failures, achieved through curiosity. Through a convincing **vision**, you can direct the curiosity of your teams into the fields that are particularly important for the company (cf. Merck Curiosity Studies 2016, 2018 for further details).

▶ **Food for Thought**
MarTec's law (see Sect. 2.1.2) can also be applied to each and every one of us. The **relevant learning potential** and the **theoretically available opportunities** increase exponentially.

Again, it is up to us how we deal with it. However, the **rules of digital Darwinism** also apply to us as employees and managers in a figurative sense: **Adapt or die!**

> **Think Box: Questions You Should Ask Yourself**
> - How regularly do you identify tensions that exist between task, individual, group, and organization in your company?
> - How are the tensions identified here dealt with?
> - Can you derive the qualification needs for your employees and managers from the vision of your company and the corporate competence goals required to achieve them?
> - How is human resources development organized in your company?
> - Are there personal development officers in the different divisions of the company?
> - What competences do learning coaches or learning advisors have?
> - Does your human resource department function as a service provider for competence development—for managers and employees alike?
> - Is there a strategic qualification gap in your company?
> - What requalifying (reskilling and upskilling) topics are on your digital teaching and learning agenda?
> - Do you regularly communicate that it is a core task of every single employee and every manager to keep refreshing his or her workforce through lifelong learning (maintaining employability)?
> - Have you ever tried to classify your employees and managers into the categories "intrinsic learners," "proactive change-makers," "spectators," and "procrastinators"—separately for employees and managers?
> - What consequences can be derived from such a classification?
> - Have you ever considered how you can systematically use and promote curiosity as the "fuel of learning"?

3.6.2 Developing a (Digital) Training Agenda

The limits are not yet set, which would call out to the talent and diligence: up to here and no further!
Ludwig van Beethoven

To **safeguard your qualification offensive**, you should focus your attention on developing a **(digital) training agenda**. Such an agenda should be developed departmentally, but above all employee-related. In order to create the **"right" training portfolio**, start by **asking managers and employees what they are interested in**. In order to avoid a **lottery mentality** when presenting a list of possible qualification measures, where everything possible is ticked off at random, the following procedure has proven successful.

When asking for the **priorities for qualification**, you should immediately ask for the respective **priorities A, B, and C**. This way you force the respondents to set relevant priorities. If necessary, you can also set an **individual budget** that is to be

Individual qualification passport
Joe Average (budget of points for 2022: 100 points)
✓ Leadership training (60 points)
✓ Online marketing essentials (15 points)
✓ Social media marketing essentials (15 points)
✓ Concepts and methods of change managements (30 points)
✓ Digital business models (20 points)
✓ Agile management (25 points)
✓ Digital controlling (20 points)
✓ Resilience training (20 points)
✓ Media competence (15 points)
✓ …

Fig. 3.88 Personal qualification passport

used to the best possible extent. You can also create a **personal qualification passport** for your staff. With this passport, everyone receives a certain number of **qualification points**—depending on their area of responsibility and hierarchical level—which can—and should—be invested in further training each year. An example of a **qualification passport** is shown in Fig. 3.88. In this qualification passport, the **qualification levels** to be achieved can be included in perspective.

Over time, you can use the **personal qualification passport** to determine which managers and employees are willing to continuously invest in their own further training. These findings can also be incorporated into **salary and wage discussions** as well as into considerations regarding the **promotion of team members**.

The crucial question in this context is how you can create the necessary **training and development culture** in your company. How can you optimally support the employees of your company in **building up their learning fitness** and thus enable them to **self-determined learning** and self-effective action? There are various starting points for this (cf. Jacobs et al., 2017, p. 32):

- **Address individual motives for "non-learning"**
  This can be achieved through individual coaching, time management offers, different learning options, and compensation for downtime.
- **Strengthening self-efficacy**
  You can strengthen self-efficacy by granting greater individual leeway in decision-making. Presenting convincing role models and setting up learning mentorships can also contribute to increasing self-efficacy. This also includes positive reinforcement as well as constructive feedback to promote experiential learning—including the crucial experiences of success.

- **Individual monitoring of the learning process**
  Ideally, the learning processes and learning opportunities are tailored to the personal needs and interests as well as with a view to the desired learning success of each individual. The individual qualification passport serves this purpose.
- **Various further education and learning opportunities** as well as **needs-based access**
  Ideally, a variety of further education and learning opportunities are used to support self-directed learning and to expand peer learning (keyword "cafeteria system," where employees can choose what fits best).
- **Always emphasize the benefits of lifelong learning**
  In order to promote motivation for lifelong learning, continuous reference to future employability must be made at the individual level as well as at the team and company level. In addition, a specific incentive/benefit argumentation must be formulated that targets intrinsic motivation and communicates it to as many people as possible: "learning can be fun!"
- **Establish a climate conducive to learning and favourable boundary conditions**
  In order to promote the joy of learning, a climate conducive to learning must be established. This starts with the attractiveness of the learning materials, the learning environment (e.g., an online platform) as well as the premises in which learning can take place together.

When shaping the (digital) training agenda, all managers responsible for HR development should be aware of the following **future trends towards lifelong learning** (cf. Jacobs et al., 2017, p. 33):

- **Flexible learning**
  Learning is increasingly taking place independent of time and place. Mobile learning sessions and **"just in time" learning** will increase.
  Principle: "I decide when and where I learn."
- **Participative learning**
  Due to an increasing orientation towards the **"we-qualities"** required today and tomorrow, learning will increasingly take place in cooperative processes, e.g., through co-creation and co-working.
  Principle: "I learn, teach, network and work with others."
- **Learning in networks**
  Parallel to this, learning takes place in networks, which can complement existing educational institutions or even replace them as preferred learning environments.
  Principle: "I decide how and what I learn, depending on the concrete needs at my workplace, and I am in close exchange with a "peer group" inside and outside the company."

Orientation towards these **future trends in lifelong learning** is another important building block for you to achieve digital excellence. The demands on HR development will continue to change in the future. Therefore, HR managers—for example, in the form of a CHRO—are called upon to be at the forefront of developments. Only in this way will it be possible to make the necessary **deductions for the company's own competence development** at an early stage.

One possibility to further qualify employees and managers—oriented towards the above-mentioned trends—is offered by the Swiss start-up Eggheads (2021) with the following objective:

"Our mission it to make knowledge easily accessible and shareable via conversational interfaces like chatbots."

With short and interactive chats, companies can convey the knowledge that their own employees need for success in the company. For this purpose, the company *eggheads.ai* has developed a **cloud-based platform** on which automated chats (chatbots) can be created, distributed via SMS or e-mail, and evaluated.

The company calls this form of digital communication and knowledge transfer: **conversational microlearning**. Through this innovative format, the simplicity and popularity of chat is tapped for training, internal communication, and knowledge management. The platform is used for onboarding new staff, for sales training and for creating awareness for IT security and sustainability (cf. Eggheads, 2021).

> **Think Box: Questions You Should Ask Yourself**
> - Does your company have a (digital) training agenda?
> - If "yes": is it regularly updated and backed up with corresponding training offers?
> - If "no": who could develop such a (digital) training agenda—in a timely manner—and use it as a basis for a qualification offensive?
> - Do you regularly survey the main areas of interest for qualification measures of managers and employees in order to create the "right" further education portfolio?
> - Does your company have a personal qualification passport for each employee and manager?
> - Are the qualification goals also defined in this qualification passport?
> - Do the contents of the personal qualification passport also flow into wage and salary discussions as well as into considerations regarding the promotion of team members?
> - What measures exist in your company to promote a culture of further training and development and to enable self-determined learning and self-effective action?
> - Have you already dealt with future trends in lifelong learning?
> - Have you checked possibilities of conversational microlearning?
> - What consequences can be derived from this for your qualification offensive?
> - In whose hands are these tasks?

3.6.3 Analysis of Personal Competences of Employees and Managers

A "blind spot" is no longer a "blind spot" when I have recognized it.

For every manager and especially for the HR department, the question arises as to which **qualification profiles are to be acquired by new employees** for the company. In addition, for every **promotion** and also for the **composition of teams**, it is necessary to examine which behavioral patterns the available candidates should exhibit in order to achieve the desired results. Here, of course, you do not focus solely on **professional competencies**. In addition, the teams—depending on the task—should also have a certain **diversity** in terms of **personal competences**. In order to recognize which characteristics the respective candidates have, you can use various concepts. A small selection is presented below.

3.6.3.1 Behavioral Preference Analysis

Behavioral preference analysis (BPA) is based on a wide range of findings from behavioral research. The **three basic types** on which BPA is based (red, green, blue) can occur in different forms (cf. MCG, 2021). Orientation to these **color sectors** provides a classification system. In this system, the typical behavior of a person, his or her individual characteristics, and important aspects of his or her personality are brought together under one color.

- **The red one**
  In its pure form, the red one is the **impatient and spontaneous doer**. He wants to determine the direction to a great extent, decides spontaneously, and wants to see results quickly. In return, he is more willing than others to take risks. In the negative version, he is the steam talker who always marches ahead—also argumentatively—and can dominate others. In this, the red one will make sure to communicate in an exciting way, with intense gestures and convincing dramaturgy, in order to always put himself in the limelight. However, he also likes to overturn decisions when other information is available that is now relevant. Deep file study is not his thing! He prefers to be already on the lookout for the next challenge, for the next kick!
  Through these behavioral patterns, the red one often becomes a playmaker. With his striving for dominance, power, and influence, he likes to go ahead and thereby shows leadership, decisiveness, and willingness to take risks. In this, tasks and results are often more important to him than the people and relationships he surrounds himself with. Reds don't like to beat around the bush, but will tackle hot issues head on—in order to reach a solution quickly. Their behavior is often very consistent and direct. They live in the "now and immediately."
- **The green one**
  The green one, unlike the red one, lives more in the past. He attaches much more importance to good **personal relationships**. He is very helpful and likes to take advice and recommendations from others. The green one cares about his listeners and their well-being—gladly also in **personal contact**. Since good relationships

are very important to him, he invests a lot of time in personal conversations and expects a corresponding willingness to do so from his partners. An appreciative scope is very important to him.

These characteristics make the green one an **integrator**—the **mother of the companionship**, as it were. His **sociability, human flexibility, ability to integrate and cooperate** as well as his **team orientation** contribute to this. The green one also loves **consistency** and **routine** with its **fixed procedures**. He is strongly oriented towards the past, the experiences gained there as well as the relationships built up so far. He is characterized by a sure feeling for people and situations. It is very easy for him to get into contact with other people. He can be motivated to make changes if they are based on sustainable personal relationships.

- **The blue one**

  The blue one is the very **cautious, thoughtful, and deeply analyzing thinker**. He wants as much information as possible in advance of decisions, which he also evaluates, compares, and questions in depth. He often cannot get enough data, carefully examines all available facts and arguments to arrive at a sound decision. In meetings, he is often silent for longer; however, not because he has nothing to say, but because he is looking for the best possible answer. A blue person is rather quiet, sometimes appears boring, but is much more profoundly oriented and better informed than the other two color types.

  The blue one is the **expert** without whom hardly any project will run successfully. He ensures **order, analysis, and systematics** in the team. He is very future-oriented in thought and action. This is due to the good **ability to abstract** and the talent to cope with a high degree of **complexity**. There is a certain reticence towards strangers. Personal relationships are not entered into easily. The blue often prefers to keep his distance. Every team leader is well advised to know his "blues" in order to motivate them to participate again and again with open questions. In many cases, the performance contributions of a blue person are of great value—even if you often have to wait longer for them. However, it is usually very worthwhile!

The characteristics shown can occur in different combinations in you and your employees and managers. Either the individual **color types are almost equally distributed**. Then there is a balanced personality structure. These people are very adaptable and can bring in their strengths according to the situation. **One color type can also be dominant**, in which case the personality structure is more one-sided. The greater the dominance of a color, the more pronounced are the associated personal characteristics—both positive and negative. In such persons, few behavioral patterns dominate. Their flexibility is rather limited.

By means of a **questionnaire**, you can easily identify for yourself and your team members the dominant color type, if any. This gives you the opportunity to look at the strengths and weaknesses associated with them as well as the dominant behavioral patterns—in yourself and in others—through an external image, as it were. In addition, it becomes clear to everyone why their own requirements for cooperation do not have to be the same as those of the other team members. For a **rough**

classification of people into color types, the following grid helps, which of course has to be somewhat woodcut-like:

- **Colortype "red"**
  People of this type often show a more extroverted behavior. They like to share their assessment frequently and also unasked and want to enforce it when making decisions. The body language is often very intense. They can hardly be overlooked or overheard.
  Their natural territory is the podium!
- **Colortype "green"**
  These people are often very open-minded, likeable, and are the perfect bridge builders. They love communicating with others and are also always very helpful.
  Their natural territory is the coffee kitchen!
- **Colortype "blue"**
  These people initially appear very distant and show little expression in body language, facial expressions, and voice. They are very interested in facts and ask specific questions. They are often the only ones who study instructions for use, manuals, and instruction leaflets intensively—and also work through the documents in the run-up to meetings. When they make a statement, it is well-considered and well thought out. That's why they present their assessments later than everyone else.
  Their natural territory is the study room!

With this information in mind, you can now assemble your teams. And what you need is diversity! Figure 3.89 shows which characteristics the different color types can bring to a team (cf. MCG, 2021). These must be taken into account when **putting together high-performance teams**.

▶ **Storytelling** I have been using behavioral preference analysis very successfully in my **management trainings** for many years. In this way, the participants not only get to know themselves better. This is an important **building block for self-management** and especially for **leadership work**. In many cases, they also understand why team members needed more time (for relationship building with the "greens") or more data (for sound analysis with the "blues") than they did. After all, many managers have a distinctly "red color" in the sense of this concept and are already on their way to new shores, while other team members are still looking for certainties ("green") or additional facts ("blue").

Based on the **color structure of the respective discussion partners** and team members, training is given on how to prepare **briefings and work meetings** in each case when the participants tend to be green, red, or blue. It is always exciting to see how different and also how successful appropriately prepared meetings look. In addition, these trainings also teach participants how to correctly interpret the behavior and reactions of interlocutors (question: "which color is dominant right now?") in order to react appropriately. Through **video analysis**, the actors themselves as well

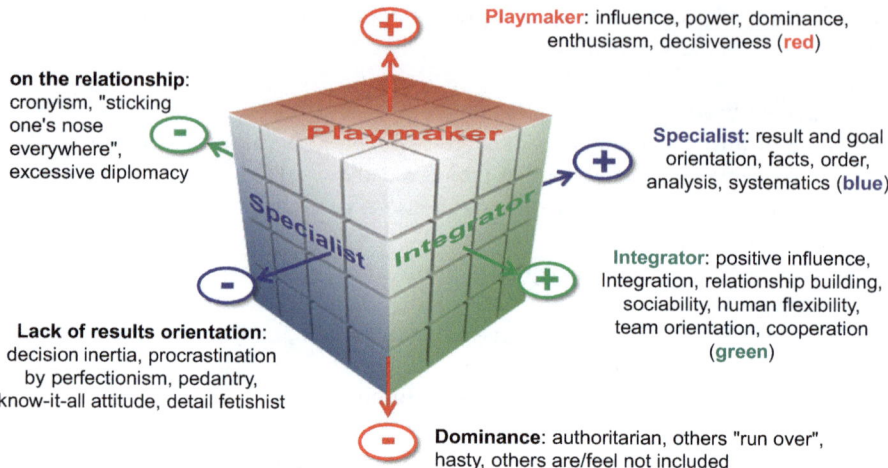

Fig. 3.89 *MCG* role model of work and team behavior – based on der behavioral preference analysis

as all other participants can gain groundbreaking insights that have a consistently positive effect on further leadership work.

Orientation towards the different color types should also be taken into account in **presentations** and **briefings**. It is obvious that we often design these in the way we ourselves would like to be addressed and briefed. However, this approach will only convince those listeners who have the same color type as we do. People with a different color type, on the other hand, will not be reached at all, or at least not as well. Your challenge is either to identify the color types of your audience in advance. This should be possible in a team environment. Or you can deliberately target your content to the different color types in order to bring everyone along. This can look like this:

- For the **"reds" in the auditorium**, you should deliver an exciting story, good entertainment, and quick results. Here you need to get to the point quickly so as not to bore these people. Often executives are "red" and drop out of presentations where a significant benefit or a pithy challenge is not quickly apparent. For the "reds," you can get right to the core without a long preamble.
  Leading question: "Where's the beef?"
- The **"greens" in the auditorium** will be grateful if you point out in your presentations that the results presented are based on very good teamwork. The statement that a new task can only be successfully mastered in a good team with appreciative interaction also falls on very fertile ground here and wins over the "greens" for you and your concern.
  Leading question: "Will I be sufficiently supported by others?"
- To pick up the **"blues" in the auditorium** well, your presentation or briefing must have a highly visible and convincing structure. A well thought-out agenda is

indispensable for a meeting. After all, the "blues" expect you to have taken as much time to prepare as he or she would have done in your place. This also applies to the facts. You cannot win a pot with "blues" by "boldly claiming is half proving" (a rather "red behavior pattern"). If the "blue" is brave, he asks questions when the facts are thin—but often he remains silent and unconvinced! The "blues" check the sources, which you should therefore also include in your documents right away. And these sources must support your argumentation. By the way: if you present a structure and an agenda, you should also stick to it (even as a "red")—anything else is not appreciated, especially by the "blues." And a "green" lacks the commitment that is indispensable for building relationships!
Leading question: "Have all relevant facts been sufficiently considered?"

▶   **Food for Thought** that such an approach contains a **manipulative element**. From my point of view—and based on my experience—it is rather an **expression of a lived appreciation**. After all, you are—very importantly—not telling the untruth. Instead, you emphasize certain aspects more or less—based on their importance in the eyes of your interlocutors. For me, this is the **recipient orientation** known from marketing.

You can convince a "red" with the following briefing: "Ms. X, I have a great challenge for you. A new task—that hasn't been done before. Are you in?" Here, an exciting story is often enough as a start. A "green" and a "blue" person will roll their eyes at such an announcement. For a "green" it is important to start with small talk and to be able to build on existing relationships, to get support from you and to always be able to turn to you if necessary. Extensive trust building is essential here. For the "blue" person, it is important to first familiarize himself with the subject. This requires time and documentation.

Perhaps this small example shows that we as "reds" like to work with "reds," as "greens" like to work with "greens," and as "blues" like to work with "blues." After all, they tick just like us. However, in every team we need the specialist, the integrator, and the playmaker. We can well imagine what a **team of playmakers** comes out with—thousands of ideas for immediate implementation, but lacking substance. A **team of integrators** creates the best atmosphere in the team—but without results. A **team of experts** can spend months getting to grips with the issue—again without tangible results, but with a great gain in knowledge!

This shows the positive power that comes with diversity!

3.6.3.2 *KODE* Concept

Another valuable **tool for self-analysis and team analysis** is the *KODE* concept. *KODE* is a German abbreviation that stands for competence diagnostics and development (cf. KODE, 2021). This analysis procedure enables a **direct measurement of individual abilities** to act. For this purpose, work is done exclusively with human strengths and potentials. The aim is to consistently develop existing competences.

Competences are used here to designate the **abilities for self-organization**. These include knowledge, qualifications, values, and norms (cf. Heyse, 2020). The following applies here (Erpenbeck, 2020):

"Competences are founded by knowledge, constituted by values, disposed as skills, consolidated by experience, realized on the basis of will."

In this sense, competences include **skills, knowledge, and qualifications**, but are not limited to these. For what use are skills, knowledge, and qualifications to a person if they are not integrated into a **value-based ability to act**?

> **Memory Box**
> **Skills, knowledge, and qualifications are a necessary condition for achieving something, but not sufficient for success.**

▶ **Storytelling** People who have achieved a high level of knowledge but do not put their horsepower on the road are what I call **silent geniuses**. These are people who have built up a profound knowledge and have the capacity for deep reflection. There is only one thing they do not manage to do, or hardly manage at all—to make these resources visible to the outside world.

I can identify such people at every exam at the university. Brilliant knowledge, perfectly written down, deeply thought out and competently applied. But I cannot remember the author of such an exam, despite the small group concept at my university. In the lecture or—as it is called at my university—in our "seminar-style teaching," this person never became visible. By the way, this is a typical expression of the color type "blue" of the behavioral preference analysis (see Sect. 3.6.3.1)!

My didactic goal at university and in other training situations is to use positive feedback to get these participants (if I can recognize them early enough) out of their protective position and to give them a **sense of achievement through participation**.

Competences are to be understood as **prerequisites for action**. They describe the basic abilities to prove oneself especially in unknown and unmanageable situations and to act actively here. The *KODE* approach is guided by the idea that **competences are learnable and expandable**. Competences become visible in different situations and can also be lost over time (cf. KODE, 2021).

The **key dimensions of competence** that are central to the *KODE* approach can be seen in Fig. 3.90. They are divided into four basic competencies.

Figure 3.91 shows which **leadership competencies** can be derived from this for everyday management (cf. Kersten & Dörries, 2019, S. 8). However, these competences and their characteristics are important for all employees and not only for managers—albeit with different weighting. After all, many project managers—without personnel responsibility—also have to prove themselves as managers. Every secretary and every assistant also has a major leadership task!

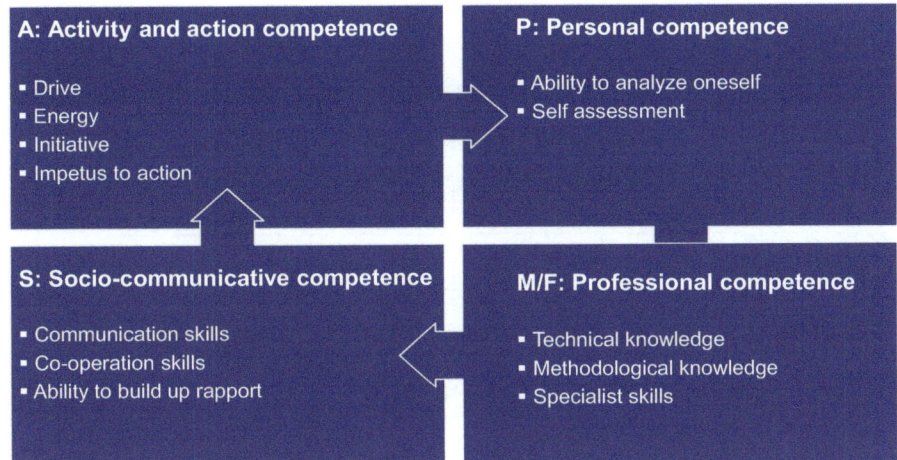

Fig. 3.90 Basic competencies and their dimensions

Fig. 3.91 Dimensions of leadership competence

In the *KODE* concept, the **determination of one's own competence map** is based on an online questionnaire. Derived from the answers given there, a **differentiated evaluation** of the level within the **individual competence fields** is carried out. These are recorded once under **normal conditions** and once under **stressful conditions**. This makes it possible to determine how one's own competences are used in different situations. This is an important **indicator of personal resilience**.

A **zero-sum game** is used as the **basis for the competencies**. This has the following consequence: If one field of competence is more pronounced, this must be at the expense of the other fields of competence shown in Fig. 3.92. The dominant

Competence profile	Personal competence	Action and activity competence	Professional competence	Socio-communicative competence
Under normal conditions	27	39	29	25
Under stressful conditions	33	33	27	27
Difference	6	-6	-2	2
Average	30	36	28	26

	>= 12 and <= 22	Low competence level
	>= 23 and <= 34	Middle competence level
	>= 35 and <= 40	High competence level
	>= 41 and <= 48	Very strong (tendency of exaggeration?)

Fig. 3.92 Competence profile base on the *KODE* concept

position of "activity and action competence" with 39 points necessarily leads to the other fields being less pronounced (cf. Kode 2020b). By the way, Fig. 3.92 is my own evaluation!

It is interesting to see in Fig. 3.92 whether people tend to accentuate an already strongly used competence even more under stress. Or whether they succeed in using a **different set of competencies** in **stressful situations**. By doing so, a person would show **mental flexibility**. This mental flexibility can be seen in my evaluation (fortunately). Under stress, I don't step on the gas even more, but reduce it from 39 to 33 points. Instead, I put more emphasis on my "personal competence" (increase from 27 to 33 points). In addition, I also increase the use of my "social-communicative competence" (increase from 25 to 27). This shows a flexibility that tends to contribute more to solutions through a differentiated use of competencies.

> **Memory Box**
> What is the saying?
> **The greatest weaknesses are the exaggerated strengths!**
> Memories of the law of diminishing marginal utility come to mind! Therefore, it is important that in stressful situations you do not make even greater use of the competencies on which you have already relied very heavily.

▶ **Storytelling** I have been using the *KODE* concept very successfully for years in my Master's program at university and in the corporate environment. Time and again, I often find that participants are initially astonished at the external image that becomes visible as a result of the analysis. In a self-critical stocktaking or after conversations with honest friends, it can often become apparent that a **blind spot** has been revealed: known to others, but not to myself!

If you get feedback on your blind spots, you can work on them specifically!

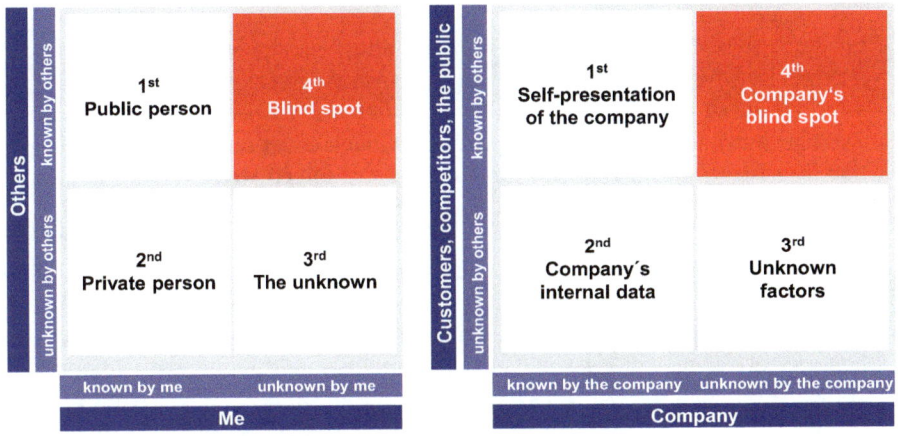

Fig. 3.93 Determining the own blind spots using the *Johari* window

After working with participants, a deep understanding of the results is usually achieved—and a desire and joy to work on one's own competence map!

We should systematically **avoid the presence of blind spots**. The "**blind spot**" is the **contrast between one's own image and that of others**. The relevance of this contrast can be illustrated by the *Johari* window. The name is derived from the authors *Joseph Luft* and *Harry Ingham* of this concept (cf. Rechtien, 2007, p. 55 f.). We can distinguish between four quadrants in self-perception and perception of others (cf. Fig. 3.93).

In the personal sphere, we speak of the **public person** in the first quadrant in Fig. 3.93 (left). Here we are dealing with the behaviors and motives that are known to myself and my environment or are perceptible to them. The **private person** of the second quadrant contains aspects that I know myself but keep hidden from others or do not want to make known to them. The third quadrant is reserved for the **unknown**, about which neither I am aware and which is also not known to others. This is often referred to as the unconscious. The **blind spot** in the fourth quadrant is particularly critical. It includes the behavioral patterns that others perceive in me but that I myself am not aware of. These include ingrained habits, such as always pressing a biro during presentations, and having linguistic quirks (such as the filler words "like," "well," "right," or "exactly").

> **Memory Box**
> **It is what it is. But it becomes what you make of it!**
> Transferred to the everyday life of a company, the first quadrant shows the planned and thus consciously staged **self-presentation of the company** externally and internally (cf. right-hand illustration in Fig. 3.93). The second

(continued)

quadrant contains the **company's internal data**, which are known internally and are used there, for example, for corporate management. The corresponding data can and should remain hidden from the outside. The **unknown factors** of the third quadrant include **unused strengths**, such as certain employee talents that flourish in secret. But they also include **unnoticed weaknesses**, such as deficits in the R&D area, which have not yet been noticed either in the company or in the market.

You should pay special attention to the fourth quadrant and thus the **blind spot of your own company**. What do others know about us as a company that we ourselves are unaware of? What do others see that we do not? This can be a convincing image with a specific customer group that is not known within the company. It can also be a "lousy" quality in the customer service center or in the online presence as well as a far below-average product quality that everyone talks about—but not the company in question.

The analysis presented in Fig. 3.93 is intended to help ensure that the fourth quadrant does not remain "**terra incognita**" (in the sense of an unknown country or an unexplored area of knowledge). Positive aspects can be developed in the direction of the first quadrant, while identified weaknesses need to be reduced.

Memory Box
We should be aware of our "**blind spots**"—as people and companies alike.
This is about identifying the "unknown unknowns."

3.6.3.3 Team Analytics

To align **team development** with the challenges ahead, you can also use the *Team Analytics* concept from monday.rocks (2021). This enables you to identify the **structures and dynamics in your teams**. Based on this knowledge, you can develop the **blueprint for an optimal team composition**.

For this purpose, *Team Analytics* offers you an app with which you can easily and quickly create the **individual team profiles** and derive a goal-oriented team architecture. It is important here that you first recognize your own personality and its importance for the team. You can then compare your characteristics and working style with those of your team colleagues. By developing a **team values map**, you can work out which values are shared in your team and which perspectives are particularly important. With such knowledge you can improve not only **internal communication** but also **cooperation** as a whole and increase the **willingness to find solutions to conflicts**.

The insights gained here help you to find the **right task for each team member**. In addition, it can become clear which **competences** are still **missing** in a team. If you succeed in assigning tasks, competences, and responsibilities—based on the respective value profile—you can achieve a high degree of intrinsic motivation (cf. monday.rocks, 2021).

▶ **Food for Thought**
A strong "we" is only created by many strong "Is" who have a high level of social competence!

Think Box: Questions You Should Ask Yourself
- Do you already use instruments to analyze the personal competences of employees and managers?
- What experience have you gained from this?
- Do you always make a clear distinction between professional and personal competences when recruiting employees and staffing teams?
- Do all your managers do the same?
- Do you know or use the behavioral preference analysis?
- Who could initiate a test application to determine its relevance for your company?
- Do you know or use the *KODE* concept for self and team analysis?
- Where could its application be particularly useful?
- Do you know your—previous—own blind spots?
- Do you regularly help other people to recognize their blind spots and, if necessary, to overcome them?
- Can you contribute to identifying your company's blind spots?
- Do you already use *Team Analytics* for self-analysis and/or team development?
- In which area could it be usefully applied?
- Who in your company deals with such tools?

3.6.4 Overcoming the Individual Comfort Zone

The main cause of stress is daily contact with idiots.
Albert Einstein

For a successful digital transformation, one thing is indispensable:
The company must leave its comfort zone.
The following applies here:
A company's comfort zone is often even more than the sum of its employees' comfort zones.

Therefore, the comfort zones found at all hierarchical levels must be consistently expanded. The **comfort zone** describes the area determined by established habits in which a person has settled comfortably and feels at ease (cf. Bardwick, 1995). In such a comfort zone we know our way around and know exactly what is expected of us. We also have the certainty that we are up to the tasks and challenges to be mastered here. Our learned habits and rituals contribute to this. Consequently, our own comfort zone ends where the familiar realm stops and overcoming or effort is required to master new challenges. The feeling of fear (for example, when taking on a new task) is a good indicator that we are about to leave our own comfort zone (cf. Fig. 3.94).

Each of us has an **individual comfort zone**. While one person gets sweaty when he has to present his concept in a team meeting with three colleagues, another says "Chakka, I can give a talk in front of 1000 people and five cameras for the *Swiss Post* in Bern!"

Mark Twain formulated a beautiful sentence on this:

The human brain is a great thing. It works right up to the point where you stand up to give a speech.

Leaving your comfort zone and entering the **fear zone** is not comfortable and comes with the so-called **growing pains**. Because in **terra incognita**—in unknown territory—you can make mistakes because you don't know exactly what to expect. Uncertainty, negative stress, the rejection of such challenging situations, more or less

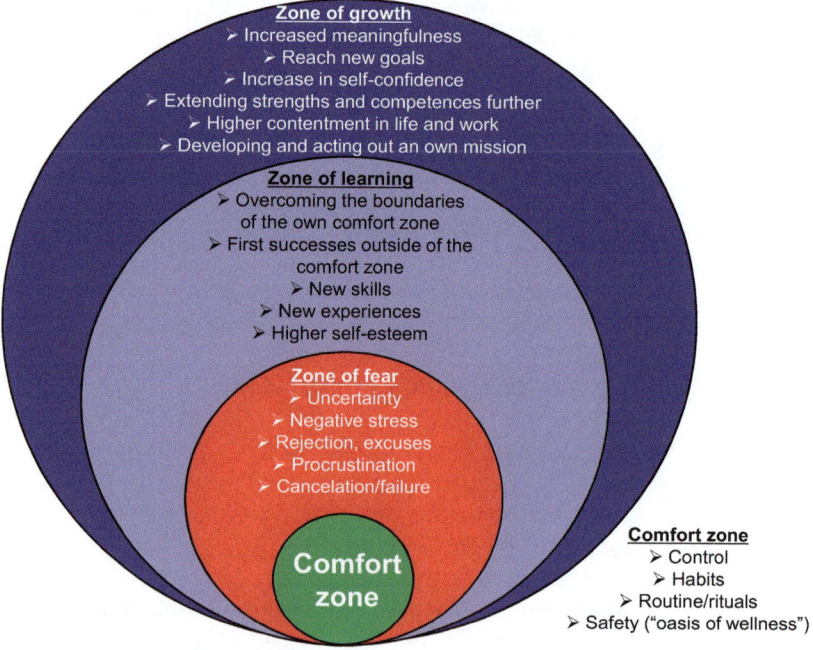

Fig. 3.94 Phases to extend the comfort zone—for individuals and companies

creative excuses to avoid them, as well as abandonment, procrastination, or failure can be the result (cf. Fig. 3.94).

> **Memory Box**
> However, it is also true that **growth begins behind the boundaries!**
>
> A manager who ticks like this will not ask for more employees, a bigger car, or a higher salary (alone) when being promoted, but for exciting and challenging new tasks.
>
> Therefore, every person who is interested in his or her personal growth should strive to **expand the own comfort zone**. This is the **core of personal development** (cf. Hoffmann, 2018, pp. 55–60). By passing through the fear zone, the comfort zone is overcome and one enters the **learning zone** (cf. Fig. 3.94). Here, new skills and experiences are gained. With a positive evaluation of the new experiences, self-confidence—based on the experienced self-efficacy—can increase.
>
> The **learning zone** has a smooth transition to the **growth zone**. Here, new fields of meaning for life can be closed because goals that previously seemed unattainable can be realized. This contributes to an increase in self-confidence. This can promote the ability, the willingness, and the will to further develop (new) strengths and competences. This can go hand in hand with higher job satisfaction and possibly also life satisfaction. Finally, there is now the chance to actually develop and live one's own mission.
>
> In order to accept the **growing pains** inevitably associated with this process and to advance into the growth zone, frustration tolerance and resilience are required. **Frustration tolerance** describes the individual ability of people to endure disappointments or frustrations even over a longer period of time and to deal with them constructively without glossing over the situation itself. **People with low frustration tolerance** break off very quickly when they try to expand their comfort zone if this is more arduous or happens less quickly than they expected or desired. Such people easily become upset. Often they also become angry or react discouraged or depressed. They often feel disadvantaged (important: not "are disadvantaged"!) because they have a hard time dealing with defeat. After each "defeat," the motivation to tackle new challenges decreases. People with low frustration tolerance therefore tend to avoid increased efforts as much as possible.

▶ **Food for Thought**

Experience is the sum of the mistakes you have made.

Arthur Wellesley, first Duke of Wellington
People with high frustration tolerance also accept critical situations. They patiently continue on their way until they have reached their goal.

Even small progress is seen as success—and setbacks are accepted as "part of the game." Empirical studies show that people who are good learners have a significantly higher frustration tolerance. They can engage with an object of learning for longer and more durably and also show more pronounced interests. Although frustration tolerance is a relatively stable personality trait, everyone can work on overcoming low frustration tolerance. Coaching programs make an important contribution to this.

A **playful approach** to **overcoming the comfort zone** is offered by the *Singleton* app (cf. Singleton, 2021). This app supports you in finding time for the things that are important to you but are nevertheless often neglected (cf. the *Eisenhower* matrix in Fig. 3.13). Instead of relying on classic concepts of time management with daily and weekly plans as well as to-do lists, a **playful approach** is used for this. For this purpose, the *Singleton* app records how the various processes run until the goal is achieved. The effect of various motivational factors in the game itself is also determined. By evaluating the generated data, typical dropout points, the effect of interventions as well as the duration of the game, etc. can be determined.

Singleton is a **mobile app**. It also enables you to support change processes. **Universal packs of cards** are used for this purpose. Alternatively, **individual playing cards** are developed by the *Singleton* team with the respective company partners. The **core aspects of Singleton** (2021) can be summarized as follows:

- *Singleton* is an **action-centered format**—don't talk, do!
- The app works like a **digital game** on a smartphone—with real impact!
- **Individuals** can (be) motivated through play!
- **Teams in competition** motivate each other!
- The **solution is scalable** and can be used by 10, but also by 20,000 people!
- **Changes become measurable**!

The concept can be used not only for self-management, but also for **anchoring management guidelines**. For this purpose, companies can develop a set of cards that transforms the leadership guidelines into concrete actions. The **playful approach** helps to integrate the targeted action patterns into everyday life. A gamification approach rewards commitment and can also be used for a competition between managers.

Resilience has already been discussed in Sect. 2.1.5. In the VUCA world, resilience is equally relevant for companies, managers, and employees. In order to strengthen the resilience of your company and within your company, so that your managers and employees remain mentally healthy even during and after very stressful phases, you should put resilience on your (digital) training agenda. Through this, you can make your teams more resistant to a hectic daily routine and the continuous demands of the working world. A high level of resilience helps to provide inner protection, as it were, and at the same time promotes your own flexibility.

Memory Box
Resilience strengthens the immune system of your teams and thus arms them for future challenges. This is indispensable in view of hyper-complexity and the increasing demand for maximum speed in thinking and doing.

It is important to realize that everyone is capable of strengthening their **inner resilience**. To support this process in your company, you can involve the so-called **resilience coaches**. Depending on the size of your company, such resources can be hired externally or provided internally. **Resilience training** focuses on learning how to **deal with stress** in a **constructive way**. The following exercises, among others, are used in such training (cf. Mauritz, 2020; Drath, 2018; Heller, 2019):

- **One-minute meditation**
  The aim of this meditation is to pause regularly, even in stressful phases, to give yourself peace and relax. To do this, it is sufficient to take just one minute, close your eyes and breathe calmly and naturally. Regular breathing promotes **relaxation**. You can enhance this effect if you imagine letting the existing tension flow out of your body with each exhalation.
- **Keeping a gratitude journal**
  Stress often leads to a narrowing of perspective and a one-sided **concentration on obstacles and problems**. Then the **progress and successes** that are always present are no longer seen. To avoid such a negative spiral of bad thoughts, direct your gaze once a day to the successes you have achieved even in the most stressful environment. To do this, you can ask yourself the following questions: What went well today? What do you feel grateful for?

  If you answer such questions daily, you will train a more **balanced view of reality** and also promote your own optimism. At the same time, your view is (re)sharpened to also see the **positive developments** that are otherwise not recognized in a pessimistic view of the world. Through this, you can overcome your **selective perception**. To achieve this, keep a small **gratitude journal** in the form of a diary.

  The goal is not to see the world as rosy now—it is not rosy. But it is not always jet black either.

  So that we do not overdo it with a re-focus on our successes, here is an excerpt from a **demotivation seminar for the over-motivated** (cf. Hauck & Bauer, 2020, p. 9):
  – Some problems are not "challenges."
  – Problems are not always "wake-up calls" or "opportunities in disguise."
  – Several problems are simply problems.
  – And sometimes problems remain unsolvable.

(continued)

- **Reframing**
  You can also strengthen your resilience through reframing. Reframing means "to put a circumstance into a new frame." By changing the frame, a **change of perspective** is to be achieved. It is about changing existing descriptions, relationships, and evaluations.

  The **labels** or **terms** we use to describe the world have a great influence on how we see our world. If we describe marketing managers as cash burners, IT specialists as nerds, controllers as bean counters, and our lawyers as angle advocates or shysters, we cannot encounter these people unencumbered. Those who permanently call their boss, colleagues, and/or employees idiots and themselves the only ones with the big picture will have a hard time achieving value creating cooperation. Those who paint the company headquarters as a bullshit castle will meet everything that comes from there with resistance.

  With such images in our heads, we systematically poison our working environment.

▶ **Storytelling** Against this background, I avoid the term "subordinates" because it creates an image that I do not value. I prefer to speak of "team members." I also never speak of my occupation as a "job," but rather as my "profession." In this way I make it clear to myself and others how seriously I take my professional tasks.

▶ **Food for Thought**
We should also avoid speaking of our staff in the way I heard a CEO do at a change management workshop I facilitated in Silicon Valley:

"The church calls its members little sheep. I call my employees sheep. I have to lead them out to pasture in the morning and peg them so that they don't do anything stupid. Then in the evening I take them back to the barn."

The audience waited for a signal to resolve this irony or sarcasm. But it did not come. The CEO meant exactly what he said.

Memory Box
My personal opinion is that every single word we use counts. Because words—as we all know—can cause lifelong injuries.
Words are important emotion triggers!
As the saying goes:
We cannot retrieve a careless word, a missed opportunity, or a shot arrow.

(continued)

> Consequently, we should be careful in small and large things—always—about the labels we put on the world. This also applies to the label we give to the phenomenon of stress. Do we see **stress as a burst of energy** that enables us to achieve new heights? Or do we see **stress as a killer** that robs us of all our energies and abilities?
>
> You think the exercises described above are too banal for you? Then perhaps you have just arrived in your own personal anxiety zone (cf. Fig. 3.94). Just try it out—but for at least 2 weeks. Then you will notice the first changes. It is not for nothing that such and similar exercises are part of the standard repertoire in yoga, Pilates, self-management/time management.
>
> Here too: **practice makes perfect!**
>
> That's why **strengthening your own resilience** is also a lifelong process!

▶ **Food for Thought**
Work in the fields of **"expanding the comfort zone," "reducing frustration tolerance,"** and **"strengthening resilience"** among your own employees and managers is an indispensable **prerequisite for mastering a digital transformation**. However, you should bear in mind that such processes take time and not all people will be willing to take on such an arduous journey.

> **Think Box: Questions You Should Ask Yourself**
> - Have you ever explored your company's comfort zone?
> - Do you systematically support your employees and managers in identifying and overcoming their individual comfort zones?
> - Are you helping your team increase frustration tolerance and resilience?
> - Have you ever considered using a mobile app like *Singleton* to support change processes systematically and playfully?
> - Does your company use resilience coaches and/or organize resilience trainings?
> - Who deals with these topics in your company?

3.6.5 Increasing the Employee Engagement

In addition, we have to address another important point—also in the digital age: **employee engagement**! This criterion—as *Gallup* studies repeatedly show—decisively determines the success or failure of companies. Gallup (2020a) defines **engaged employees** as those who are fully involved in their work, intensely committed to their jobs and enthusiastic about their work. Recording employee engagement helps you to see whether your employees are actively involved in the company's development or whether they are simply "doing their time." That's why you should also regularly focus on the indispensable **key performance indicator "employee engagement."** After all, what good are the most innovative technologies and allocated budgets if they are not used by employees and managers?

Every day, your employees and managers make decisions and take actions that impact not only your entire workforce, but also your company's overall business performance—for better or for worse! **Research on employee engagement** has shown for years that companies with a high level of engaged employees achieve significantly better business results than companies whose employees identify to a lesser degree with the company, its goals and tasks. Similar results are found in all industries, in different company sizes and nationalities, and—quite surprisingly—also in good and bad economic times (cf. Gallup, 2020a).

> **Memory Box**
> You should avoid the common mistake of **viewing employee engagement** as a kind of fun event that you only do once every few years—to make your employees and managers happy. The misunderstanding on the subject of employee engagement could not be greater!
>
> Today, employees and managers increasingly demand—quite apart from a **good salary check—a comprehensible meaning and purpose of their work** (keyword "purpose"; see Sect. 3.1). They also want to be seen and appreciated in their **uniqueness**. And they expect **sustainable relationships**—especially with their leaders. They want to be noticed for what makes them unique. These factors drive employee engagement to a great extent. Gallup (2020a) has found that managers or team leaders alone are responsible for 70% of the variance in engagement of the teams they manage!

> **Memory Box**
> **Managers have the greatest influence on employee engagement through their behavior—and thus also on the company's overall results!**
>
> Against this background, one of the biggest challenges for HR is to take into account the **paradigm shift in human resource management** shown in Fig. 3.95 (cf. Gallup, 2020a)
>
> Surprisingly, studies over decades still show that nearly 85% of employees worldwide are still not engaged or not actively engaged enough in their work, despite various efforts by companies. A **high level of employee engagement** is present in only **15% of employees** (cf. Gallup, 2020a). Consequently, one of the **most important starting points for increasing corporate performance** remains largely untapped. However, we should also tap into this
>
> (continued)

3.6 Human Resources Strategies for the Digital Age

Fig. 3.95 Paradigm shift in human resource management

In the past	In the present
My salary check	My meaning of my work
My contentment	My development
My boss	My coach
My annual performance review	My regular reviews
My weaknesses	My strengths
My job	My life

potential in order to be successful with our digital transformation. We will not achieve digital excellence without a high level of employee engagement.

It's actually quite simple: a look at the **statements used to determine employee engagement** by Gallup (2019, p. 3) shows what—and often how little—actually needs to be done to significantly increase employee motivation.

1. I know what is expected of me at work.
2. I have the materials and equipment to do my job right.
3. Every day at work I have the opportunity to do what I do best.
4. I have received recognition or praise for good work in the last 7 days.
5. My supervisor or someone else at work cares about me as a person.
6. There is someone at work who encourages me in my development.
7. At work, my opinions seem to count.
8. The mission/purpose of my company makes me feel that my work is important.
9. My associates/fellow employees are committed to doing quality work.
10. I have a very good friend at work.
11. In the last 6 months, someone in the company has spoken to me about my progress.
12. During the last year I have had opportunities to learn and grow at work.

Figure 3.96 shows which needs the contents of the above-mentioned statements pay attention to in a **needs pyramid**. Here, a distinction is made between **basic needs** and the **needs for support, teamwork, and growth** (cf. Gallup, 2019, p. 3).

You can take responsibility for the engagement of your employees by asking for and evaluating their assessment of these twelve statements. In this way, you can—supported by *Gallup*—determine the status quo for your company. Using the above questions in your company requires *Gallup's*

(continued)

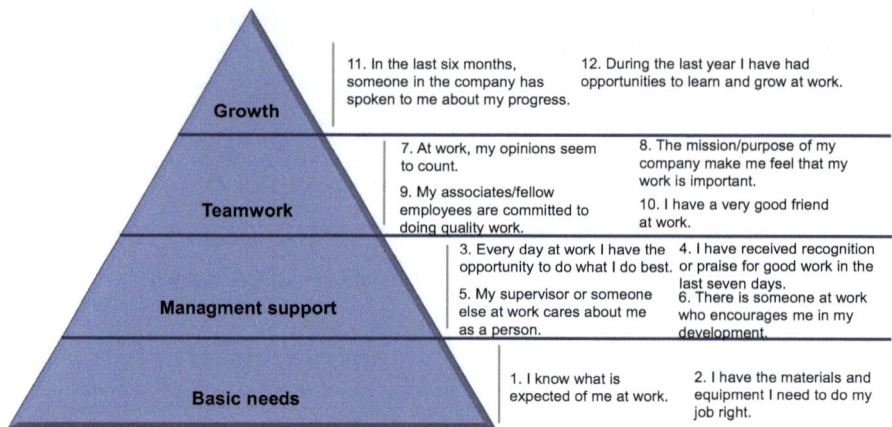

Fig. 3.96 Placement of the *Gallup*-questions in a hierarchy of needs

approval. Only the satisfaction of the needs behind these statements creates an environment of trust and support in your company. So you can and should—on a regular basis—be very committed to achieving the highest possible level of employee engagement!

Memory Box
Over time, your employees' expectations can also change. That's why you should conduct an **Employee Engagement Inventory** by Gallup at least every 2 years, but better still every year.

In order to capture the state of **employee engagement in Germany**, *Gallup* surveyed 1000 employees in 2019. The results below are representative of the German workforce aged 18 and over. You can use the values shown in Fig. 3.97 as benchmarks for the results of your own survey (cf. Gallup, 2019, p. 5). As in previous years, only 15% of employees in Germany show a **high emotional attachment**. 69% have a **low emotional attachment**—and 16% have **no emotional attachment**!

▶ **Food for Thought**
I always ask myself why these data have not triggered an **outcry in the management floors of companies** for decades and a variety of measures to raise the performance potential that lies dormant here. Gallup (2019, p. 7) estimates that the **economic costs due to internal resignation** in Germany alone amount to between 105 and 122 billion euros. It is interesting and frightening at the same time that these figures for Germany—in both good

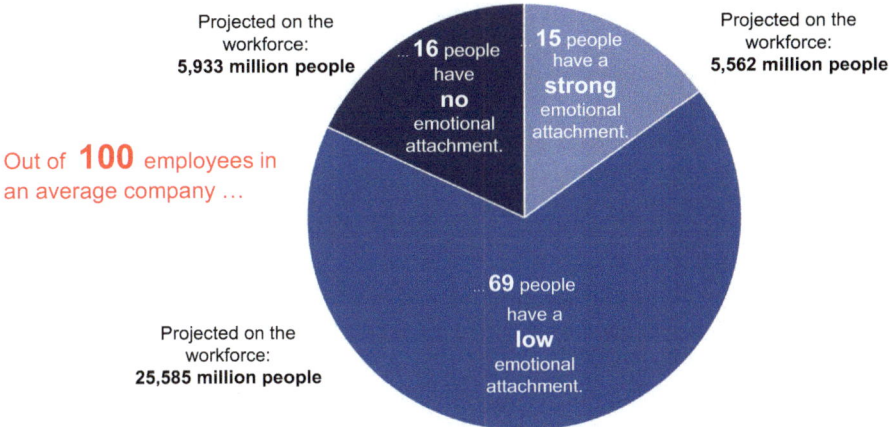

Fig. 3.97 Results concerning the employee engagement index in Germany

and bad phases of the economy—have not changed. As if the companies and their managers do not care about these results at all!

Do better! Check the status in your company together with *Gallup*—and take action! Because of the stability of these scores, you may be one of the few in your industry to finally take comprehensive action on this—and sustainably increase the opportunity to build digital excellence!

The **tenth meta-analysis of employee engagement** by Gallup (2020b) shows what other negative effects are associated with low engagement values among your own employees. For this purpose, a large number of *Gallup* studies from 54 industries, in 96 countries, at 276 organizations with a total of 112,312 business/work units and 2,708,538 employees were analyzed. When comparing employee engagement in the top quartile ("top 25%") of organizations with engagement in the bottom quartile ("worst 25%"), *Gallup* found that business units and teams at the median had the following differences in key KPIs. In contrast to the mean, the median is the central value, which is exactly "in the middle" when the measurements are sorted by size.

Reduction of negative events:

- 81% **less absence**
- 18% **less fluctuation** at companies with a fluctuation rate of more than 40%
- 43% **less fluctuation** at companies with a fluctuation rate of 40% and less
- 28% **less theft/shrinkage**
- 64% **less accidents**
- 41% **less quality defects**

Improvement through positive events:

- 10% **Increase in customer loyalty or customer engagement**
- 14% **Increase in productivity in the manufacturing**
- 18% **Increase in sales productivity**

Increasing of company success:

- 23% **higher profitability**
- 66% **higher well-being of employees**
- 13% **higher engagement in the society**

In sum, it can be said that in highly committed teams, significantly **fewer negative events** occur and significant **improvements take place in various functional areas as well as at the company level** as a whole.

> **Memory Box**
> Particularly in the course of a digital transformation, it is important to leverage the often very large **growth potential** that comes with an **increase in employee engagement** in your own company. For this, you do not need new technologies, no new IT system—but a **further development of the mindset of your managers**! The figures show that the investments to be made here can pay off to a high degree—for all sides!

▶ **Food for Thought**
Digital transformation is an exercise in mindset change.

An interesting tool with a comparable objective is offered by Great Place to Work (2021). With the help of the *Great Place to Work* **concept**, you can analyze where your company stands with regard to a **future-oriented workplace culture**. The topics of agility, ability to change, innovation, leadership, and health are also taken into account. It is useful to distinguish between **mental agility** ("agility in the mind") and **structural agility** ("agility in the structures of the organizational and operational structure")—and to become active in both areas.

In addition, you can review your **HR activities** with regard to their **effectiveness** and develop concrete **strategic fields of action**. A special motivation—especially for HR managers and the CHRO—is that every year awards are given for particularly successful developments in national and international employer competitions, with which the companies can "adorn" themselves. At the same time, dealing with these topics is accompanied by a variety of **inspirations** for one's own **HR work**, e.g., through the exchange with other successful employers.

Think Box: Questions You Should Ask Yourself
- Have you ever surveyed employee engagement in your company in cooperation with *Gallup*?
- Do you know which factors in your company particularly influence the strong or weak engagement of your employees and managers?
- What do you think of the paradigm shift in human resource management?
- How can you implement this paradigm shift in your company?
- Which aspects of the paradigm shift are particularly important for your company?
- Do your managers have the necessary mindset?
- How well does your company satisfy the basic needs identified in the pyramid of needs as well as the needs for support, teamwork, and growth?
- What conclusions can you draw from the results of *Gallup's* meta-analysis of employee engagement?
- What level of mental agility ("agility in the mind") have you already achieved?
- What is the status of structural agility ("agility in the structures of the structural and process organization) in your company?
- Are you familiar with the help of the *Great Place to Work* concept?
- Who is working on these questions?

3.6.6 Transactional and Transformational Leadership: Leadership at a Distance

Whereas the heroic manager of the past knew all, could do all, and could solve every problem, the post-heroic manager asks how every problem can be solved in a way that develops other people's capacity to handle it.
Charles Handy, Irish economic and social philosopher

Empowering staff is an important task for all managers. In order to achieve the necessary speed in internal processes, employees and teams must be able to work more autonomously. To achieve this, not only tasks, but also competencies and responsibilities must be consistently delegated. At the same time, managers must be prepared to "let go." This requires a new or further developed **leadership culture** in many companies!

Memory Box
The following applies:
Every type of leadership always begins with the leadership of one's own person.

3.6.6.1 From Transactional to Transformational Leadership

Human resource development must first start with the **leaders**, who set the style and direction in the company with their actions and inactions, with their communication and non-communication. This shapes the culture and values of your company more than wonderful glossy brochures and beautiful posters on the office walls. In order to make clear the changes that are often demanded today, a distinction is made here between two leadership styles (cf. Sprenger, 2017, pp. 3–16; Schütze-Kreilkamp, 2017, pp. 17–32; Rosenstiel and Nerdinger 2011, p. 257; Bass, 1990, pp. 19–31; Scholz, 2014, pp. 1077–1199):

- the **transactional** (i.e., exchange-oriented) **leadership style**
- the **transformational** (i.e., changing) **leadership style**

A **leadership style** encompasses all the actions and behaviors with which a superior confronts his or her employees and which he or she uses to achieve certain results. In the **transactional leadership style**, leadership takes place in the sense of an exchange process or trade between managers and employees (cf. Fig. 3.98; cf. Morhart et al., 2012, p. 398). Here the **focus** is on individual **transactions**. The underlying principle is: **do ut des** ("I give so that you give."). The supervisor defines the expectations and goals, while employees receive something in return in the form of a reward if they achieve them. The emphasis is on target agreements against which the performance of employees is measured at regular intervals. This **management by objectives** style is often complemented by **management by exception**, where the supervisor only intervenes in the case of serious deviations from targets.

Companies that rely on a **transactional leadership style** set standards for how employees are expected to behave. This makes it unmistakably clear to employees which tasks and behaviors are expected of them. Depending on performance, corresponding positive or negative consequences are to be expected (cf. the upper course in Fig. 3.98).

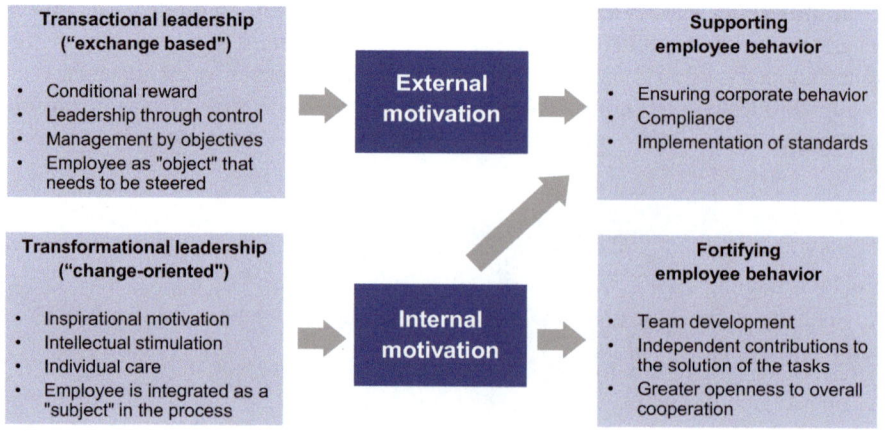

Fig. 3.98 Mechanisms of transactional leadership and transformational leadership

▶ **Food for Thought**
Extrinsic motivation is especially necessary when the sense for one's own actions has been lost!

Transformational leadership, on the other hand, focuses on transformation (cf. the lower course in Fig. 3.98). These are **processes of change**. The transformational leadership style focuses on the "soft" factors and uses the idea that employees can also be motivated by the prospect of self-fulfillment. The approach aims to transform employees' needs and goals so that they put their own interests behind the company's goals. Consequently, managers and employees do not face each other as opponents, but as **supporters** in the pursuit of the common goal derived from the overarching corporate vision.

This succeeds above all through managers who communicate an **attractive and meaningful vision**, act as **role models** themselves, and actively **support the intellectual and personal development of employees**. Experience has shown that if employees are placed at the center of the company's transformation process, a higher affective, i.e., emotion-based commitment to the company and its new direction can be achieved than with a management style that only focuses on the processing of narrowly defined tasks.

▶ **Food for Thought**
In the following introduction of a manager, one wonders if he understands his position as an **enabler of his team**:

"The management of some companies in the XY Group report to me, plus I am responsible for digital cross-cutting issues in the XY Group. I am also in charge of innovation and responsible for our venture capital activities and our own company builder, XYZ, with the aim of establishing the XY Group as a fully digitalized trading and services group."

Or is this a **one-man show**? If so, the workload is really considerable if he's doing it all on his own! If he also manages people, that sounds more like an **understanding of leadership 1.0** to me.

Other managers are already further ahead with the following insight when they formulate:

"We will not be successful with our hierarchical structure!"

In order to achieve efficient cooperation in the company, a **mixed form of the models** from Fig. 3.98 lends itself to combining the advantages from both approaches. Through components of transactional leadership, **behavior that conforms to the company** can be forced to a certain extent and thus desired **standards of behavior** can be ensured in all areas. However, guidelines and directives should only be emphasized to such an extent that the components of transformational leadership can have an additional effect. Managers should succeed in triggering **commitment, identification,** and **self-motivation** through the "soft" factors of transformational leadership. This creates important prerequisites for mastering the challenges of a digital transformation.

However, we must abandon the idea that all employees can be motivated by a convincing vision and demanding tasks. Also, not all employees are willing to continuously invest in their own professional and personal growth. For many employees—often even the majority—the main part of their life does not take place in the company, but outside. If all employees were only hot for the next career step—whether measured in salary, hierarchical level, number of employees and/or in the importance of projects—it would get pretty crowded at the top of the company. Every company also needs—to varying degrees—employees who simply want to do a certain job without putting too much heart and mind into it.

In view of the different motivational starting points of your employees and perhaps also of your managers, a **situational leadership style** is called for. This means that we should align our leadership style with the expectations of our employees—but oriented towards our own set of values and the goals we are striving for. Here it is important to pick up the employees where they are at the moment. With situational leadership, you adapt your style of leadership to the employee—not vice versa. The **self-knowledge** that you have gained about yourself and your team through the methods presented in Sect. 3.6.3 is indispensable here. The fact that you nevertheless always try to recognize and promote growth potential in your team is part of your leadership task. A situational leadership style incorporates the framework conditions, the situation of each individual employee and the relationship between manager and employee into the design of leadership.

In fact, new employees often need to be led much more closely than employees who have been with the company for a longer period of time. Regardless of the company affiliation, there are team members who demand the often spurned **micro-management** from their managers. Micro-management is a narrow transactional style of leadership in which the manager tells the employee exactly what to do and in which steps. Here, the employee avoids having to take responsibility himself—and not all employees want to take responsibility.

Memory Box

The **concept of situational leadership** is based on the idea that there is no general best leadership style that always fits and leads to success. There are only leadership styles that are more suitable than others in specific situations. Consequently, the leader must have the widest possible range and thus flexibility in his or her behavior in order to meet different circumstances.

The challenge for you is therefore: **situational leadership**!

▶ **Food for Thought**
To lead yourself, use your mind.
  To lead others, use your heart.
  Eleonor Roosevelt

The **levels of leadership** shown in Fig. 3.99 can serve as important guiding ideas for leadership in the digital age (cf. Maxwell, 2013). These ideas applied before, but now consideration is especially important for successful digital transformation.

At level 1, **power** rules. Here, employees follow you because they have to due to their hierarchical position. At level 2, employees follow you because they want to. The employees have quasi **permission** to choose a "follow." This is where relationships are built, usually because of a good personal connections between you and your employees. Level 3 is about the **results** you have already achieved in the past. Employees turn to you because they want to be part of a winning strategy. At level 4, you attract people by being committed to **employee development**. You gain the trust of your team members by being committed to their development and advancement. At level 5, **respect** dominates. People follow you for who you are and what you stand for.

With these levels—with the exception of level 1—it is not a question of either or. Level 2—a high degree of voluntariness—provides the **basis for successful cooperation**. A successful leader—together with his or her team—delivers good results, invests time and money in the development of employees, and ideally manages to be a fascinating leader. This does not mean being "everybody's darling"—because that will not succeed.

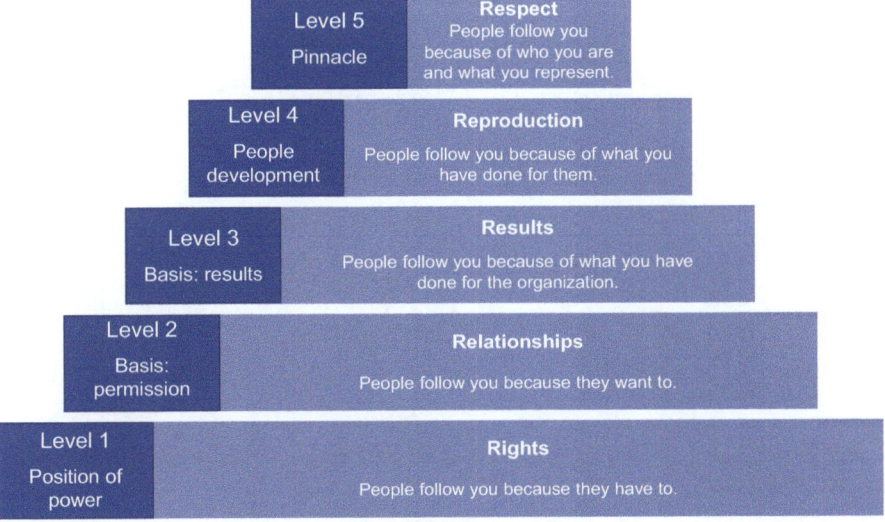

Fig. 3.99 Guiding principle for leadership—"levels of leadership"

Memory Box

One of my mottos is:

Better an edgy something than a round nothing.

As the saying goes.

If you're open on all sides, you can't be completely tight.

Follow your values even with rough edges if they are valuable for achieving the purpose in your company.

Every **leader** should be aware that he or she is **under constant observation**—with everything he or she does or does not do. If greetings are given or not given in the morning, if a depressed or cheery facial expression is shown, if appointments are kept or postponed—every single attention is registered by the employees.

Memory Box

Attention in companies is directed from the bottom up. An employee usually knows more about his superior than vice versa.

In a tense situation, this **attention** increases even more—and every gesture, every action or inaction is evaluated, interpreted, and passed on in many ways. If managers do not communicate clearly and honestly, but ambiguously, the **rumor mill** is virtually fueled. A high degree of **predictability on the part of the manager** is indispensable, especially in times of crisis.

Therefore:

If there is bad news to be announced, it should be announced.

The rumors about possible changes can do more damage than the bad news itself. Inform your staff precisely about what will happen and when. Explain what the impact will be on individual employees, on the team, and/or on the company as a whole. Then all those affected can adjust to it—and see themselves as participants rather than just those affected. Consequently, one thing is required in communication here: **clarity**!

Memory Box

In tense situations, the **manager as communicator** is challenged even more than usual. In these situations, managers must also plan much **more time for communication** than under "normal" conditions.

Communication spaces that you as a manager do not fill with clarity are deliberately filled with **rumors** by individual employees, but possibly also by other managers.

▶ **Storytelling** I once asked my boss at *Deutsche Post* to provide me with much more comprehensive information than before. The following answer made me think hard:

"Mr. Kreutzer, even if I try very hard, I will certainly not be able to meet your legitimate request for more information by more than 50%. The central question is therefore: How do you fill up the missing 50%—with trust or with mistrust?"

A brilliant statement!

3.6.6.2 Leadership at a Distance

Home office and **mobile working** will remain with us much more extensively in the future than was previously imaginable. However, this brings with it a new challenge: **leadership at a distance**. For this, **leadership qualities** are more important than ever. In order for leadership at a distance to work, the following questions need to be answered in the team to shape this leadership at a distance:

- Which **availability** is expected on which days and in which time windows?
- What **form of communication** is to be used primarily?
- What are the **desired response times** to e-mails, *WhatsApp* messages, and other forms of internal company communication that are to replace spontaneous conversations in the office?
- What are the **information needs of the manager** to be sure that projects are running and staff have all the necessary resources to achieve the defined project goals?
- What **information and support** do employees need in order to understand these measures as assistance and not to misunderstand them as harsh control, coercion, or surveillance?
- How is **individual performance progress documented**?
- What **time sovereignty** is desired and made possible?
- What **room sovereignty** is accepted for mobile working?

The development of **guidelines for leadership at a distance** is an indispensable investment to avoid feelings of surveillance, bullying, and mistrust and thus the impression of a **helicopter boss** in the first place. The HR department should develop specific recommendations for leadership at a distance. The manager can then concretize these recommendations in an intensive dialogue with the respective team (see Sect. 3.6.5.1 on "situational leadership").

> **Memory Box**
> One thing is indispensable in **leadership at a distance: trust between the leader and the staff**, but also **trust between the staff themselves.**
>   **Jointly developed and adopted rules create trust.**

(continued)

> Those who, as leaders, have not yet succeeded in building a trusting relationship with their team will now reap the "reward" of personal misconduct. **Home office** is a **fire accelerator for disturbed manager-employee relationships**. Differences, faulty processes, communication gaps and, above all, a lack of trust now become visible as if under a burning glass, although they may have existed for a long time.
>
> In addition, power-oriented managers in particular are **afraid of losing control**. Here the question dominates: Do my employees still work even if I cannot see them regularly? The challenge of leadership at a distance is therefore to replace **leadership by physical presence and supervision** by controlling the use of time with **leadership by results**. Depending on the task, daily, weekly, and/or monthly goals must be agreed upon. At the same time, these goals form the basis for regular **feedback discussions on performance progress**.

▶ **Food for Thought**
Feedback is like a gift. Whether you unwrap it is up to you!
In order to achieve the necessary performance even in home office, managers and team members have to apply a high degree of **self-discipline** for the indispensable **self-management**. If the manager—or even better: the team member himself—knows the corresponding strengths and weaknesses, very specific training on time management can be used. If you as a manager have these skills, you can support your employees as a coach.

Memory Box
The **self-discipline of leaders and project managers** also includes not immediately taking on all the work when problems arise.
One thing is important—and not only in leadership at a distance—and that is to **treat each other with respect**. That's why the—honestly meant—question at the beginning of a two-person video conference can be about the current state of the home office. After all, in addition to company matters, homeschooling, childcare, pets, laundry, shopping, etc. may also have to be managed there. The statements about situational leadership also apply here: some have more, others less need for this important form of **small talk**. However, as leaders we should be aware of these needs—or obtain the knowledge through the behavioral preference analysis in Sect. 3.6.3.1!

Storytelling
In my management training courses, which I have conducted for many years, I have repeatedly noticed that—especially male—managers were often not informed about the birthdays as well as the approximate ages of their employees. There was also a lack of at least rough information about the family environment—information that is indispensable for assessing observable behavior (for example, when ordering overtime or weekend work). These gaps in knowledge can easily be overcome by asking appreciative questions!

Think Box: Questions You Should Ask Yourself
- Which leadership style dominates in your company—the transactional or the transformational leadership style?
- Or have you already achieved an optimal mix of both leadership styles?
- Are all your managers able to use a situational leadership style?
- Have your managers been trained in this direction?
- Do you micro-manage your employees when explicitly requested?
- Which levels of leadership dominate in your company?
- How "appropriate" do you find them and what consequences would you like to derive?
- What is the importance of home office and mobile working in your company and consequently of "leadership at a distance"?
- Have company-wide and/or team-related guidelines for leadership at a distance been developed?
- Do you help your employees and managers to strengthen the self-management and self-discipline required for home office and mobile working—where necessary?
- Is it allowed to speak "plain language" in your company where "plain language" is required?
- Who keeps an eye on the issues described here?

3.6.7 Establishment of Network Structures

Trust reduces complexity.
Niklas Luhmann

A further development in leadership style is also necessary because digitalization is forcing many companies to provide their services more in a **cross-divisional cooperation** and often also a **cross-hierarchical cooperation**. This means that the previously so important divisional and departmental boundaries are losing importance and an **overarching network structure** is becoming more important. This is accompanied by another challenge for managers:

Not only their employees, but also you must think, plan, and work more in networked structures.

After all, customer wishes have never been oriented towards departmental boundaries—for example, between marketing, sales, and service. At the same time, it is necessary to break down the information and process silos that still prevail in many (large) companies, because these stand in the way of working in networks. However, this also requires a **high degree of willingness to change** on the part of the managers themselves.

▶ **Food for Thought**

We must overcome the mindset that "**knowledge is power.**"

The new slogan is: "**power to sharing knowledge!**"

For **thinking and acting in network structures**, employees, teams, managers, and the whole organization have to be aligned differently. Often, the organizational structure and processes of established companies are still from the pre-digital age. As a result, they are often not geared to the increasingly demanded speed or agility. Then the strictly hierarchical structures shown in Fig. 3.100 (left) often still dominate. However, you should examine whether network structures—for example, in the form of **virtual teams**—can contribute to accelerating internal company processes (cf. Ebers & Maurer, 2014, pp. 386–406; Klimmer, 2016, pp. 203–206; Laudon, 2017, p. 69f.).

The **network organization** represents a form of corporate organizational structure to define competences, responsibilities, and tasks more dynamically. The core idea is to connect relatively autonomous employees not through a fixed organization, but through common goals and tasks—for example, in projects (cf. Fig. 3.100, right). The aim of such networks is to build **productive working relationships** between employees—even across different hierarchical levels. It is possible—but only in particularly courageous

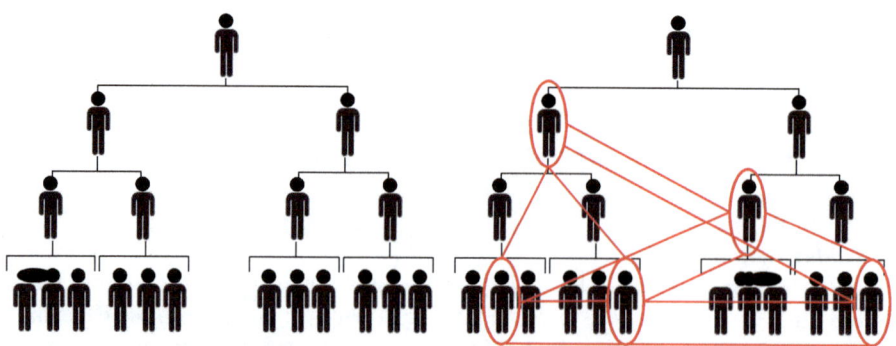

Fig. 3.100 Hierarchical vs. network-oriented organizational structure

companies—for such a network to be led by an employee from a lower hierarchical level, because this employee might have a special competence with regard to the task to be performed. The "supplying" employees from higher hierarchies have to adjust to this.

A successful integration of this kind would be a successful example of the frequently demanded **role flexibility of managers**. This is because networks function less through clearly defined reporting channels and other formal structures, but rather through personal contacts, collegial relationships, and cooperation based on partnership—geared towards achieving common goals—and above all on the basis of valuable and honest communication.

The core of such a **network organization** is a **multi-line system**—combined with a high degree of decentralization. The multi-line system arises from the fact that the individual positions and thus also the employees concerned are subordinate to several instances. On the one hand, the employees are still integrated into the classic organizational structure with the corresponding reporting lines. This is also referred to as **disciplinary subordination**. On the other hand, there are additional, often **project-related reporting lines** in the parallel network organization. Therefore, there is a **multiple subordination** of persons here.

The network structures have to be provided with the necessary **competences and responsibilities** in addition to taking over the tasks themselves. This is why the decentralization already mentioned occurs. An important prerequisite for networks to function is a precise definition of the goals to be achieved. These must be communicated transparently both in the company and in the network itself.

▶ **Storytelling** On the occasion of the **opening of an innovation center** of a large health insurance company, in which I was allowed to participate with a keynote, I experienced the following: the CEO stepped up to the lectern in front of his executives and first took off his jacket—and then his tie. When he also got rid of his dress shirt, there was some commotion in the hall. Then, however, a t-shirt in the company color became visible.

Only now did the CEO begin his speech: "ladies and gentlemen, when you go to our new innovation center, you take off all the insignia of your power and status, such as your jacket and tie. There, it is no longer about what position you hold. It's only about how committed you are to ongoing creative projects."

This **picture of the CEO in a branded t-shirt** and his words will surely be remembered by all involved. This is a fine example of "**walk the talk**"!

It should be emphasized that networks temporarily complement or overlay the existing organizational structure. This is why we also speak of a (temporary) **secondary organization**. This has the decisive advantage that once the goals have been achieved, the network can be dissolved and the employees can return to their previous tasks or be delegated to differently composed networks with new tasks. In this way, it is possible to react much more quickly and without an extensive reorganization to changing framework conditions and associated tasks.

However, the employees involved in a network organization often find themselves in a **sandwich position**. On the one hand, they are expected to contribute their resources to the **project work**. On the other hand, **day-to-day business** may be left undone and the disciplinary superior may complain and even sanction them. Such conflicts of objectives can only be avoided if all those involved support an appropriate network organization and this is also reflected in the incentive mechanisms for managers and staff.

When setting up such network structures, a higher **coordination and communication effort** is to be expected. After all, coordinated action is required within the network between employees who come from completely different areas of the company—and thus possibly also from different management cultures of the same company. If this coordination fails, **unwanted parallel work** or a **failure to handle processes critical to success** can occur. Goal-oriented, intensive communication is therefore of paramount importance, especially in network structures. This communication is also a necessary condition for building the indispensable trust within the networks.

> **Memory Box**
>
> When defining an optimal group size for project work, the **pizza rule** has proven its worth. Teams should not have more members than can be satisfied by two large pizzas at the same time.
>
> **External networks** can also be used (cf. Dillerup & Stoi, 2016, pp. 514–521). For this purpose, the network participants are recruited from various legally and economically independent organizations. The tasks to be tackled can be geared towards the development of innovative products and service concepts, the interlinking of procurement and/or production processes or the joint digitalization of sales processes. Initially, there are no limits to creativity. The dominant goal here is also the **acceleration of processes**. In addition, the **exploitation of synergy effects** through the pooling of complementary resources can also be targeted.

> **Think Box: Questions You Should Ask Yourself**
> - What experience does your company have with cross-departmental and/or cross-hierarchical cooperation?
> - Do you regularly work with or in network structures?
> - Is it still "knowledge is power" or already "power to sharing knowledge"?
> - Do you already use virtual teams?
> - Do you have the problem of multiple subordination associated with network organization under control?

(continued)

- Do you have incentive mechanisms in place to deal with the problem of "sandwich positions" in the case of multiple subordinations?
- What about the role flexibility of your managers?
- Can a manager also be "only" a network team member?
- Have you already had experience with the use of external networks?
- Where could such external networks be used to add value?

3.6.8 Instruments to Increase Communication Efficiency

Teamwork:
Coming together is a beginning.
Keeping together is progress.
Working together is success.
Henry Ford

3.6.8.1 *Sherpany*

An increasing challenge for most companies is not only to **reduce the number of meetings**, but also to **increase meeting efficiency**. An international study shows that executives and supervisory boards spend up to 70% of their time in meetings. What is particularly dramatic is that 83% of the participants are dissatisfied with the results achieved in each case. To make matters worse, meetings nowadays take up much more time—time that is lacking for dealing with other strategic tasks (cf. Sherpany, 2021). The cause of these problems can often be found in **outdated meeting processes** that do not take advantage of **digital opportunities to increase efficiency** (better time-output ratio) **and effectiveness** (answering the strategic questions).

A major hurdle to achieving these goals, in addition to convincing coordination in **setting the meeting agenda**, is often disorganized **distribution of materials** for the respective meetings. A lack of prioritization of the topics to be discussed in combination with a "bombardment with documents" ultimately leads to information overload in the most important steering groups of a company. In addition, **slow decision-making processes** are too often observed.

Finally, the **lack of efficient follow-up** of decisions taken means that meetings often do not lead to the results that were intended. Inefficiencies are further exacerbated by the fact that the people involved often use **different solutions** for preparing, conducting, documenting, and following up on meetings. The resulting **inconsistent and possibly even uncertain exchange of information** at the top of the company jeopardizes goal-oriented management in uncertain times.

Sherpany (2021), for example, offers a solution to overcome these challenges. This company has developed **governance software** for efficient meeting management for board meetings and other management bodies. The **meeting platform** developed by *Sherpany* enables **paperless meetings**. Meeting participants can access all their meetings and the necessary **documents in real time** at the click of a button. This is also possible for multiple mandates. Within the meeting platform, it is possible to create private notes—just like on paper, only online and thus always available to the respective user at the right place. This minimizes the risk of relevant notes disappearing into analogue or digital nirvana.

The **meeting platform** also enables immediate **access to the history of the respective topic** because the relevant documents are networked with each other. Finding relevant information is facilitated by a **full-text search**. Here, secure access to the respective documents and personal notes takes place through a **personal login** to the session platform.

Circular resolutions are made possible by electronic signatures—which at the same time also indicate the progress of processing by all authorized persons. Finally, the processed documents are **automatically archived** in accordance with the respective company's internal **compliance rules**. For this purpose, *Sherpany's* solution has been certified according to ISO 27001 and ISAE 3000. It also complies with the GDPR regulations (cf. Sherpany, 2021).

These functions not only facilitate and support the activities of the meeting participants themselves. The persons responsible for organizing such meetings (such as administrators, assistants, etc.) are also supported in their work. An **automatically generated digital meeting folder** contributes to this. This allows the relevant documents to be distributed securely and easily. Even short-term updates of the documents can be handled easily. All in all, such a solution is an interesting way to increase the efficiency and effectiveness of meetings—and at the same time to increase the satisfaction of all participants.

3.6.8.2 Slack and Microsoft Teams

Beyond the management level, increasingly networked companies require additional tools to increase the efficiency and effectiveness of collaboration in middle management as well as in the operational area of the company. *Slack*, for example, offers itself as a central **platform for improving collaboration in networked companies** (cf. Slack, 2021a). In 2021 *Salesforce* completed its acquisition of *Slack*. *Salesforce* paid US-$ 27.7 billion to add this solution to its suite of enterprise software. Based on this acquisition *Salesforce* will offer enterprise software to support a digital headquarters that enables organization to help customers and employees succeed from anywhere.

To support collaboration in teams, work in *Slack* takes place in **channels**. These channels represent a central place where people working on the same projects communicate with each other. In these channels, they can also share relevant documents and files and make decisions. The channels bring together people from cross-functional and cross-departmental teams. Access to shared digital documents ensures that everyone involved can access the latest status and thus immediately identify project progress as well as project delays.

If teams that previously worked in isolation need to network with other teams, they can be connected through shared channels. External partners (such as clients, agencies) can also be integrated into the project work in this way. The **creation of**

channels can therefore be geared towards teams, projects, clients, or other topics. People can join—and leave—the different channels as needed. This supports a high degree of **agility in collaboration**—without having to redefine endless e-mail distribution lists and merge previous project results from different documents.

Decentralized and digital data access helps to reduce the number of meetings necessary for project work. In addition, one can do without many e-mails with comprehensive lists of recipients and important details that only become visible on pages 7 and 15 of the e-mail. Instead, the information and work steps necessary for processing are stored in a systematic form for all to see. An intelligent search function supports the quick retrieval of relevant information.

Since the current project statuses are to be documented on the platform, **communication in real time** (via direct and group messages, file sharing, audio or video calls, with split screen if required) as well as **communication based on real time data** becomes possible. For this purpose, PDFs, images, videos, and other files can be stored directly in *Slack* via drag-and-drop. To enable mobile access as well, *Slack* offers a mobile app that includes all the functions of the desktop app. This supports location-independent collaboration, which is indispensable in times of home offices and mobile working (cf. Slack, 2021a).

The *Slack Enterprise Grid* solution can be used to manage large and complex teams (cf. Slack, 2021b). For this purpose, the necessary **workspaces** are installed. These offer the respective active teams and areas their own place to organize their work. For the administrators of this application, **centralized management functions** are offered via an interface. Here, the relevant security settings are made to map the company's **compliance rules**. These rules can apply either to the entire company or only to specific workspaces. At the same time, the application is **highly scalable**. This means that further workspaces for additional teams and/or tasks can be set up without high additional costs.

An alternative to *Slack* is *Microsoft Teams*. This solution is available to corporate customers in ***Microsoft's Office 365 package*** as a free add-on (cf. Microsoft, 2021b). This solution not only supports video conferences. Here, files can also be jointly edited in real time by distributed teams. In addition, different tasks and important business processes can be processed through embedded apps and workflows.

3.6.8.3 Tools for Video Conferencing

In addition, companies—partly in response to necessity—have now installed various concepts to replace physical meetings with virtual conferences. Frequently used **tools for video conferences** are:

- *BigBlueButton*
- *Cisco Webex Meetings*
- *GoToMeeting*
- *Jitsi*

- *Microsoft Teams*
- *Skype*
- *Zoom*

These programs have long offered important functions that make a face-to-face meeting—both internal and external—superfluous. These include the following **functions of video conferencing systems**, although not all providers cover them equally well:

- Text chat (public and private)
- Audio transmission (microphone)
- Video transmission (web cam)
- Screen sharing
- Integration of external guests
- Waiting room function (participants are admitted by the host and can also be sent back to the waiting room)
- Breakout sessions (host can form various small groups that can act autonomously and work out solutions; the host can visit these small groups and support the processing of tasks)
- Possibility to record a session

In 2020 within a few weeks, these tools have become standard equipment for many companies worldwide. In the decades before, it was common to travel for many hours or even several days even for a one-hour appointment. Often, people even regularly jetted around the world to hold face-to-face meetings. The majority considered **personal encounters with external partners** to be indispensable for introductions, product presentations, sales discussions, consultations, coaching sessions, etc. However, **personal encounters with internal partners** at team meetings, coordination discussions, creative sessions, etc. were also frequently considered indispensable. In many universities, people were also very skeptical about **online teaching**.

▶ **Storytelling** As recently as February 2020, I myself was convinced that I could only lead and inspire my audience professionally in **face-to-face lectures**. I was firmly of the opinion that I needed—analog—eye contact to convey my content in a motivating way. Far from it!

After **familiarizing myself with online teaching** through white papers and webinars from *Harvard University*, I conducted my first online lecture—after intensive *Zoom* training with a cooperation partner. The most surprising thing was that it worked perfectly if you take a few rules into account.

Firstly, individual **blocks** must not last longer than **an hour**—followed by a **15-min break**. And this grid must be strictly observed. Secondly, in live events, participants must be continuously involved in the content by asking questions—the popular **cold calls**. This not only increases attention, but also allows the content to be "digested" during the course. Questions, which are welcome from the participants at any time, also contribute to this.

In the meantime, I am an **enthusiastic online teacher**. Why? The results are very convincing—and a lot of traveling is eliminated!

By the way: even **acquisition, coaching, and consulting appointments**, for which I used to jet around the world, are now increasingly taking place online. And with discipline, this also works very well and delivers great results!

The importance of direct communication in your company before Corona can be seen in the **travel budget** and the **intensity of booking conference** rooms. Then in March 2020, many companies experienced a **leap digitization**: from one day to the next, many millions of managers and employees found themselves in the home office. This is where many IT departments did a great job getting powerful systems up and running! All of a sudden, many of us realized what was possible!

3.6.8.4 Serendipity: Collaboration Tools for Creative Meetings

When more and more employees work and stay in their home offices, when meetings and conferences are held virtually and trade fairs and exhibitions are shifted into the digital space, one thing is lost: the chance stumbling upon an idea, a product, a service, a company—as well as the unplanned meeting and exchange with people due to chance. As a result, **opportunities for personal and professional growth** and, above all, **impulses for innovation** at all levels are lost.

Such chance observations and encounters with things not originally sought, which lead to new and possibly surprising discoveries, insights, and developments, are referred to as **serendipity**. The term serendipity goes beyond a simple happy coincidence, because the actors—based on the random observations and encounters—draw their own conclusions or derive concrete measures. Consequently, the art consists in gaining and exploiting important insights from such encounters, which were discovered rather by chance while searching for other things.

The origin of the term is traced back to *Horace Walpole. Walpole* mentioned the Persian fairy tale *"The Three Princes of Serendip"* in a letter as early as 1754. **Serendip** is an old name for Ceylon—today's Sri Lanka. In this fairy tale, the three princes make unexpected discoveries. The US sociologist *Robert K. Merton* finally introduced this term to science in 1945 in his work *"The Travels and Adventures of Serendipity"* (cf. Merton & Barber, 2011; Busch, 2020).

There is no shortage of examples of the **importance of serendipity**: one can think of the discovery of America in search of a shipping route to India, which also gave the indigenous American population the name "Indians." Other examples are the discovery of X-rays, penicillin, and *Viagra*. Accidental discoveries with international repercussions were the discovery of *Teflon*, the *post-its,* and many more.

What is important in these examples is that something was made out of **chance hits** and **chance finds**. We must therefore be open and curious—and seize opportunities as they arise. Here—in addition to serendipity—the term *kairos* fits wonderfully. *Kairos* is the favorable moment for a decision or action. We say: "seize a favorable opportunity by the scruff of the neck." Why is that? In Greek mythology,

Fig. 3.101 Idea of serendipity

Kairos is described as a deity with a long curl hanging from his forehead towards the front, while the back of his head is bald and smooth. Since *Kairos* moves quickly and incessantly, we must try to grab him by his forelock just as he is passing by—like a good opportunity!

According to a study by *Naresh Agarwal*, serendipity is based primarily on two factors: **preparedness** and **noticing** (cf. Agarwal, 2015). One must be ready for the beckoning of chance and notice it at the right moment. People who are characterized by **curiosity** and **flexibility of thought and action** are more likely to "grab it." A higher **frustration tolerance** of these people helps because not every grab immediately leads to a gold bar! In addition, a high degree of **attention** is necessary because it is often the small things that—when viewed intensively—can trigger greater effects (cf. Fig. 3.101).

As *Daniel Goleman* (2015, p. 44) so aptly put it:

"An open mind creates a mental platform for creative breakthroughs and unexpected insights."

You can all now look back on such favorable opportunities that you took advantage of—or let pass by unused. But what does this have to do with our core issue?

When there is less serendipity in everyday life due to a decrease in physical encounters, a source of inspiration and entrepreneurial development dries up.

It is estimated that 17% of **global economic output** could be lost if **business trips** were permanently eliminated (cf. Bernau, 2020, p. 17). In addition, serendipity also suffers from the fact that when offices are almost empty or only half occupied, opportunities for **inspiring conversations** in the hallway, during coffee breaks or over a shared meal are lost to a large extent.

Statistics help us **prove** this. If there are **40 people** in the office, there are theoretically **780 different pairings of 1:1 dialogues**. If an office is occupied by only **20 people**, only **190 1:1 dialogues** can occur. We have to calculate "n over k" in each case, where "n" defines the number of people in a dialogue group (here 2), while "k" designates the number of employees present in the office (here 40 or 20). Consequently, halving the number of employees is accompanied by a 75% decrease in the number of possible conversations. This also significantly reduces the **probability of value creating meetings**!

Fig. 3.102 Number of possible encounters with different group sizes

Number of employees at each meeting	20 employees	40 employees
1	20	40
2	190	780
3	1.140	9.880
4	4.845	91.390
5	15.504	658.008
6	38.760	3.838.380
7	77.520	18.643.560
8	125.970	76.904.685
9	167.960	273.438.880
10	184.756	847.660.528

The differences are even more dramatic when not only 1:1 discussions are taken into account, but also discussion constellations of 3, 4, or more employees. With 20 or 40 employees, the possible constellations in Fig. 3.102 arise when several (spontaneous or planned) people get together.

Our task is to deliberately **create such moments of personal encounter** in order to **close a possible creative gap**. Be it that we arrange to meet with our employees—individually—before virtual meetings in order to exchange ideas in a small circle to the right and left of the topic of the next conference. Or we stay a little longer with individual colleagues after a meeting to talk about what we have just experienced—without a strict agenda.

We must—and I really mean must—initiate such **virtual tea-kitchen conversations**. Otherwise, important aspects of encounter and communication—also for human togetherness—will fall away. It is precisely in personal, rather non-committal conversations without a fixed agenda that managers pass on their know-how and ideas to employees. If we do not become active here, we may lose the more introverted employees who are less likely to become active on their own initiative.

To create "chance" encounters, you can also use **network triggers**. Through an algorithm—initiated by HR—two people from your company are brought together once or twice a week for a virtual exchange of about 15 min. Each person briefly reports on his or her work and what particularly moves him or her there at the moment. Does this seem strange to you? Just give it a try. After the initial fear of contact that can occur when a trainee is brought together virtually with the CEO, you will realize one thing:

This **cross-hierarchical communication**, which can connect anyone with anyone for a short exchange, not only promotes creativity, but also has an impact on the culture of your company, because many people have to leave their comfort zone (see Sect. 3.6.4).

Motto: Give chance a chance!
Or—to speak with *Seneca*:
Luck is what happens when preparation meets opportunity.

▶ **Storytelling** At a brand conference at the *Adlon* in Berlin, I approached a participant while tapping tea. Even before the conference began, I had won the lady over as an author for a book project of mine. In the refectory at my university, a colleague I had not known before joined my table. We talked briefly about our teaching focus—and by the end of lunch, I had recruited him as a lecturer for the data analytics part of my Master's program. On a trip to China in 2020—just before Corona—I met a managing director with whom I quickly bonded over many substantive issues that led to intensive collaboration.

Chance encounters that led to exciting results that moved us forward together because we made something out of the coincidences.

However, one thing also became clear to most participants after many online sessions: for larger **creative projects**, a **physical presence** of the participants is often indispensable. Only then does brainstorming work perfectly, one picks up the ideas of the other and develops them further. Only then can everyone stand together in front of a board and simply let their ideas and thoughts flow.

> **Memory Box**
> **The creative energy that can arise at physical meetings is missing at purely online events.**
>
> Nevertheless, there are tools to achieve good results in **online sessions with creative tasks**. Miro (2021), for example, provides proven tools for this. In addition to a wide range of tools for marketing use (e.g., for developing customer journeys, user story maps), various other templates are offered with which you can work very creatively and with friends on joint products. Another exciting feature is the whiteboard, which sets no limits to your creativity.
>
> You can find an example of its use in Fig. 3.103. Here the **result of a creative meeting** between two people is documented. The beauty of this tool is that you can work with similar mechanisms as in the analogue creative space (e.g., with *post-its*). This result can be shared with other people and continuously developed.
>
> Another interesting tool is the so-called *Collaboard* (cf. Collaboard, 2021). This is also an online **whiteboard solution** for real time collaboration. *Collaboard* offers a virtually infinite virtual surface on which a wide variety of objects can be worked with. These include cards, pictures, and shapes as well as videos and websites. Moderators, teachers, and professors can also control and guide larger groups of participants on the board. Special **moderator functions** allow easy handling. Due to a high degree of simplicity, the concept opens up intuitively and can be used productively after just a few minutes.
>
> To work together with *Collaboard*, the participants of a workshop, training, or meeting log on to the same board. They can then work together on the whiteboard in **real time**. Everyone can see what is being done. This can make

(continued)

3.6 Human Resources Strategies for the Digital Age

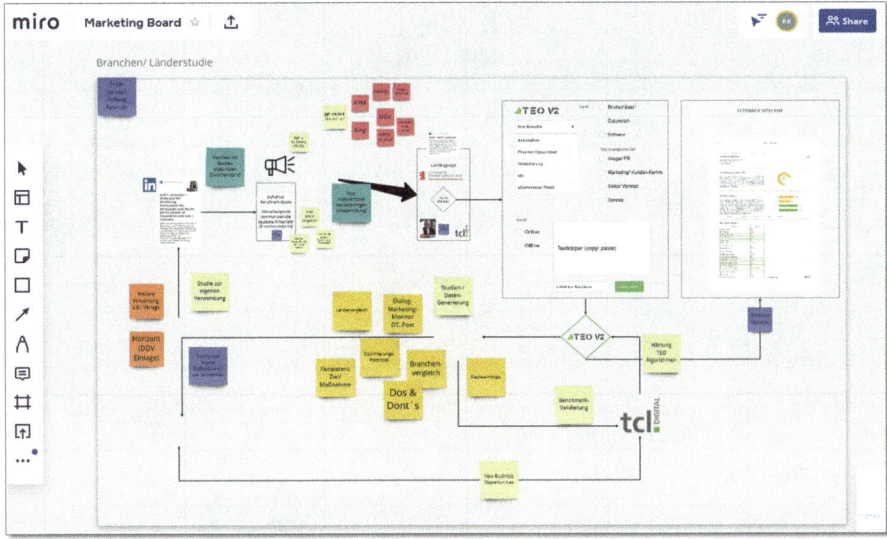

Fig. 3.103 Own marketing board for creative working

> **online events** more productive, creative, interactive, and entertaining. It is important that this software solution takes into account high standards of data security (including the GDPR). **Data hosting** can be either in Switzerland, Germany or on-premise.
>
> You should try out different tools in order to ideally acquire a set of online tools that are particularly suitable for certain tasks. To create further opportunities for—at least virtual—encounters, you can also use a tool such as TriCAT (2021). The platform offers you the possibility to build **3D learning and working worlds** and **3D classrooms**. Solutions are created here so that people can learn, train, and work together at a distance. Comparable **offers for virtual meetings** are also provided by wonder.me (2021).
>
> *TriCAT's* guiding principle is that the best solutions are always created when people can exchange ideas intensively. For this purpose, the company creates customized **learning, training, and simulation solutions**. The resulting **3D worlds** can be networked with other IT solutions via interfaces or even integrated into an existing IT landscape (cf. TriCAT, 2021).

▶ **Storytelling** Figure 3.104 shows what such a solution can look like. The employees of *NetCologne* were invited by the Zukunftsagenten (2021) to discuss the exciting topic of **Work Culture 4.0**. For this, I was invited as a **keynote speaker**—to be seen as a speaker next to the big screen in a red suit! The fact that individuals are standing during the lecture can be explained by the fact that you also first have to learn how to sit down digitally!

Fig. 3.104 Virtual meeting at *NetCologne* concerning work culture *TriCAT*—organized by *Zukunftsagenten*—presentation part

Fig. 3.105 Virtual meeting at *NetCologne* concerning work culture *TriCAT*—organized by *Zukunftsagenten*—group work

Following my presentation, individual aspects were discussed in **small groups**. For this purpose, the participants were divided into different **virtual group rooms**. There they were able to discuss various issues without being disturbed by the other groups. The solutions developed were summarized on a **common board** (cf. Fig. 3.105). After the group work, the results were presented to all participants in the **plenum**.

Afterwards, the **debriefing** with the head of the *Zukunftsagenten* and the organizer could also take place in the digital space (cf. Fig. 3.106).

I openly admit: When I was trained in *TriCAT* on Monday morning to be ready for the lecture on Wednesday, I was rather skeptical. I had to create an avatar for myself (with a red suit!) and learn how to move in this 3D world. After initial—in the truest sense of the word—teething problems (in the meantime I can also run digitally), more and more joy arose about what can be achieved with this platform.

3.6 Human Resources Strategies for the Digital Age

Fig. 3.106 Virtual meeting at *NetCologne* concerning work culture *TriCAT*—organized by *Zukunftsagenten*—debriefing

From skeptic to fan in less than 60 min—only a few solutions have managed that so far! And again, I was able to expand my comfort zone a bit! More sessions on *TriCAT* are already planned!

> **Think Box: Questions You Should Ask Yourself**
> - What measures do you use to reduce the number of meetings to the necessary level?
> - What steps can you take to (further) increase meeting efficiency?
> - What solutions do you use for efficient meeting management (e.g., for board meetings and other management bodies)?
> - Are you satisfied with these solutions or is there still a need for optimization?
> - Which platforms do you use to improve collaboration in your company (e.g., *Slack* or *Microsoft Teams*)?
> - Where is there still room for improvement?
> - What tools have worked well for video conferencing?
> - Have you provided training so that all managers and employees can move safely in these digital environments?
> - Have you ever thought about how to avoid the omission of "serendipity"?
> - How can you systematically give chance to value creating encounters even in times of home office and mobile working?
> - Which online tools do you use for creative meetings?
> - Which online tools are used for creative work (e.g., *Miro* or *Collaboard*)?
> - Have you ever used a tool like *TriCAT* for meetings?

(continued)

> - What experience have you gained with it and what potential for optimization still exists?
> - Which department and who are responsible for these questions?

3.6.9 Further Fields of Action in Human Resource Development

You can never solve problems with the same way of thinking that created them.
Albert Einstein
Therefore: Hire people who think differently!

In the following, further concrete measures of **human resource development** are presented that have already proven their worth in the digital age. Here we can partly speak of **education 4.0,** because many offers are not only networked, but also geared to individual needs and can take place independently of time and space (cf. on future trends in lifelong learning Sect. 3.6.2). In many of these offerings, the trainer is no longer a "pure lecturer," but becomes much more of a **facilitator and designer of the participants' self-learning processes**. This applies above all to digital learning offers, but can also be implemented to some extent in "analogue" events.

Gamification approaches can be used to support learning processes. These try to use incentives familiar from the gaming environment for learning tasks as well. For example, points can be awarded for the successful completion of tasks that lead to different game levels or, in this case, know-how levels. In this way, motivation should also be maintained in the long term (cf. Franke & Schönbohm, 2016; Schönbohm et al., 2017; Schönbohm 2019).

In order to support the continuous **qualification of one's own employees**, which is indispensable today, **external qualification offers** can be used. These are provided by many universities, but also by classic seminar organizers and specialized companies—sometimes in-house. In addition, innovative concepts have become established. These include internal qualification and reverse mentoring, bar camps, hackathons, MOOCs, fuckup bights, and escape rooms. The individual concepts are presented below.

- **Internal qualification – reverse mentoring**
  Many companies still neglect to systematically involve their own **managers and employees with specialized knowledge** in qualification measures as lecturers. The motto "the prophet is not valid in his own country" must be consistently overcome.

  The **internal qualification offers** therefore also include **informal events** (often lasting about an hour) in which the company's own specialists pass on their knowledge to interested colleagues. This can be done by meeting in the cafeteria or in a conference room "for a pizza"—and learning (see Sect. 3.2.9.3 for a convincing concept in the *Otto Group*).

Reverse mentoring is a particularly important instrument of this internal qualification, which also makes a cultural change in the company visible. Here, the roles of classic mentoring are reversed: no longer does an "old" or "experienced" senior take a junior under his wing to integrate him into the company and familiarize him with the vision, the values, the culture, and above all the experience gained so far. In reverse mentoring, it is the junior who coaches a senior based on his or her **specialized knowledge**.

A whole variety of topics apply, in which juniors have knowledge that is not to be found at senior level, or only selectively. These include the use of social media. But first-hand information about how members of generations Y and Z obtain information, how they shop (keyword "customer journey"), and how they organize their leisure time is also indispensable for the management of companies with these core target groups.

▶ **Food for Thought**
Why should the management in your company obtain such information via classic methods of market research or via external lectures when information from a competent source is available in your own company?

At the same time, the appreciation of the juniors and their knowledge conveyed by reverse mentoring can have a lasting effect on their motivation.

However, a few **prerequisites** must be met **for reverse mentoring**. First of all, managers must step down from their—still frequently seen—**pedestal** and be willing to learn from young people as well. This only seems to be a matter of course. In addition, the **classic competitive situations** as well as **hierarchical dependency between the participants** must be mentally overcome.

For the exchange of information based on **voluntariness** on both sides, absolute **discretion** must also be ensured. Only then can the openness and honesty necessary for this special learning process be achieved in the dialogue. The participants must also be a good human match for each other and see each other as equals in the process in order to be able to meet at eye level (cf. Schüller 2019).

- **Bar camp**
  A bar camp (also called a participatory conference) is an **open event format**. This openness means that at the beginning of the bar camp neither the content nor the concrete schedule of the event is fixed. Both the content and the schedule are determined on site by and with the participants. The focus of a bar camp is on the exchange between and the discussion with the participants.

  Usually, the participants of a bar camp introduce themselves briefly in an **opening session** at the beginning. This is often done with three self-selected keywords, the **hashtags**. Afterwards, anyone who would like to give a presentation or contribute to a discussion can introduce their topic. This does not always have to be a presentation. An open question can also be an

important contribution to a bar camp. Participants can indicate whether they are particularly interested in a suggestion by raising their hands.

The organizer of the bar camp then decides which **topics** should be discussed in depth. For this purpose, the organizer distributes the individual sessions in terms of time and space on a **grid**. This **session plan** is then hung up in a clearly visible place and/or published digitally.

At the end of a bar camp there is often a **feedback round** and/or a **summary of the day**. The individual results of the different sessions are usually not presented in detail. They can be documented by a video recording and made available to the learning community. Depending on the goal of a bar camp, concrete work results can also be presented here. This is the case, when such bar camps are held within a company.

However, more new ideas can often be gained when own employees participate in externally organized bar camps. Here there is a connection to the ideas of the open innovation concept (see Sect. 3.5.3.2).

- **Hackathon**

The term hackathon is a portmanteau of the words "hack" and "marathon." "Hack" here refers to a process of achieving a goal as quickly as possible in an unusual way. The second part of the word is derived from "marathon"—and is rather misleading here. After all, the marathon, with its 42.195 km, is the longest Olympic running discipline. On the contrary, the aim of a hackathon is to develop a working solution for a specific task within a deliberately short period of time (a few days or even just a few hours). A **hackathon** is therefore an event to **develop solutions for given problems** within a **narrowly defined time frame**.

Usually, **software development** is the focus of a hackathon. Classic software development is usually a lengthy task. The goal of a software hackathon is to come up with convincing solutions in a short time. The participants of such a hackathon usually come from different areas of the software or hardware industry (mainly software developers). The tasks at hand are to be worked on in cross-functional teams. Here, the **swarm intelligence** is to be integrated into problem solutions in a very targeted way.

For many participants, **the joint processing of demanding tasks in high-performance teams** is the most important motivator for participation. However, there is something else that can spur participants to peak performance: hackathons are often set up as a **competition between different teams**, where the winners can gain interesting prizes.

Hackathons usually focus on **a specific topic**. There are hackathons that are developer conferences focusing on specific applications. This can be the development of mobile apps or specific web applications. The focus can also be on programming an API (application programming interface). An API is a programming or application interface for specific services (e.g., *Amazon, Facebook, Google, Instagram*). Other hackathons do not have a **narrow thematic focus** in advance so as not to limit the creativity of the participants.

Even if you are not a software developer yourself, participating in hackathons can be an enlightening experience. You not only see the way proven specialists approach certain issues. You also have the opportunity to **network with developers and clients**, to **exchange knowledge** and to **explore opportunities for cooperation**.

- **MOOC**
  A MOOC (for Massive Open Online Course) is an **Internet-based course** that is aimed at the **general public** and for which **no participation fee** is payable. In addition to being free of charge, one advantage of these online courses is the wide range of topics that are also covered by recognized specialists. *Harvard University, Stanford University,* and the *Massachusetts Institute of Technology (MIT)* are among the MOOC pioneers.

  Another advantage is that employees and managers can access these **learning opportunities** whenever and from wherever they want. However, these advantages of e-learning go hand in hand with a disadvantage: only really highly motivated people stay on the ball continuously, resulting in very high dropout rates. There is also uncertainty for companies when it comes to selecting or recommending suitable courses. After all, there is a very large and sometimes confusing range of courses with a large number of certificates of different value.

- **Fuckup night**
  Fuckup colloquially stands for "mishap" or "mistake." During a so-called fuckup night, **company founders** report on their **failures**. The concept of fuckup nights is intended to contribute to making it not only visible but also acceptable to everyone that failure is always part of start-ups and innovations. Through such events, one wants to get "failed" founders out of the "dirty corner" and deliberately give them a space in which they can talk about their experiences. After all, other founders and innovators can also gain important insights from failure. This concept is used, for example, by the *Otto Group* (see Sect. 3.2.9.3).

  Many companies are already talking about the need for a **fault-tolerant corporate culture**—but without actually living it in many cases. We all know the nice sayings:

- Success is walking from failure to failure with no loss of enthusiasm.
  Winston Churchill
- Failure is the opportunity to begin again more intelligently.
  Henry Ford
- If you stop making mistakes, you stop learning.
  Theodor Fontane
- I have not failed. I've just found 10,000 ways that won't work.
  Thomas A. Edison
- It's not you who failed. It's the idea which failed.

- To motivate founders and innovators to be creative and courageous, we need a **change of perspective** on the failure of ideas and projects. Through such fuckup nights, the **emergence of a culture of failure** can be promoted—or much better: a **learning culture**. Recognizing actions that have led to failure is a valuable experience for others to learn from. A more **error-friendly culture** is essential for the courage to innovate and thus also to start-up.

- **Escape rooms for team building**
  Escape room offers represent an innovative approach to team building. In these, either the entire team or different groups are invited into an escape room, which is then locked. The challenge is to get out of such a **mystery room** together. In order to achieve this goal, a wide variety of qualities are required from the team trapped inside. These range from logic, creativity, the ability to combine and abstract to the management of the solution process.

  Due to the time pressure—such a game often lasts only 60 to 90 min—you can determine the **strengths**, but also the **weaknesses of each individual as well as the entire team** under extreme conditions. Here it also becomes visible who steps out of their **comfort zone** and how quickly and faces new challenges (see Sect. 3.6.4). Possible **communication deficits** become visible as well as different **types of escape room participants**. Here a distinction is made between scouts, managers, communicators, thinkers, and tinkerers (cf. Virtual Escape, 2021).

Memory Box
In the escape rooms, however, one thing becomes apparent again and again:

A convincing solution is only found if there is **cross-team communication** that involves all participants with their specific strengths and weaknesses.

Just like in the classic everyday working life!

Ideally, the (positive) **experiences gained in an escape room** are integrated into daily work. However, since weaknesses of individuals and/or the entire team can also become (over)evident in an escape room, an **accompanying coaching concept** is required. You must not leave supposed "losers" alone after such an event! Otherwise, trust will not be created but rather destroyed.

When choosing a suitable **escape room provider**, you can consider the following questions:
- Does the provider have its own event location?
- Are mobile concepts offered?
- Can escape games be held indoors and/or outdoors?
- Are VR escape games offered?
- How many people can participate in a game at the same time?

(continued)

- Is a provider able to adapt live escape games to specific team and/or company contexts?
- Can suitable coaching offers be booked—based on the insights gained?
- What are the conditions for a standard event and/or for a tailor-made offer?

This is where your creativity, but also your initiative, is required to create and, above all, use the method mix that is relevant for your company!

Think Box: Questions You Should Ask Yourself
- What human resource development measures are already being used in your company today?
- Do you use gamification approaches to motivate managers and employees for continuous learning?
- Have you already developed concepts of internal qualification in which your own managers and employees become active as trainers?
- Have you already established reverse mentoring?
- Have you ever organized or participated in a bar camp?
- Is a hackathon an opportunity for your company to develop quick and convincing solutions to current problems?
- Do you help your managers and employees to get an overview of MOOCs on offer to support external qualification?
- Have you or other employees and managers ever participated in a fuckup night?
- What is happening in your company to establish a more fault-tolerant corporate culture – or better: a convincing learning culture?
- Can you use escape rooms for team building?
- Where does the overall responsibility for answering these questions lie?

3.6.10 From an Enabler Culture to Holacracy

We want to learn to talk to each other. That means we don't just want to repeat our opinion, but listen to what the other person thinks. We don't just want to assert, but to reflect in context, to listen to reasons, to remain willing to come to new insights. We want to try to put ourselves in the other person's position. Yes, we want to seek out that which contradicts us. It is more important to grasp what is common in what is contradictory than to hastily fix mutually exclusive points of view with which one ends the conversation as hopeless.
Karl Jaspers

3.6.10.1 Enabler Culture

In order to be able to operate successfully in a very challenging environment, companies need **agile management** (see Sect. 3.7.1). In order to establish this successfully, however, it must first become accepted in the minds of those in positions of responsibility that the **intelligence of a community** rather than that of an individual is necessary for many tasks today. This means that **managers in established companies** in particular must redefine their own role (cf. Hofert & Thonet, 2018; Laloux, 2017; Lasnia & Nowotny, 2018; Laudon, 2017).

Today, a manager should no longer lead "par ordre de Mufti," but see himself as an **enabler of his team**. However, this reverses the **distribution of roles.** This can be seen in Fig. 3.107. The manager is no longer at the top of the pyramid—but promotes and supports the directly assigned employees and their teams.

With such an "enabler" leadership approach, the teams manage themselves to a greater extent. However, this requires that the team members also have the necessary **methodological competence** as well as a corresponding **mindset**—and that they actually want to bear the additional **responsibility**. Especially the latter is not a matter of course. After all, responsibility also means standing up for developments that do not deliver the desired results.

What is the **core idea** of the so-called **enabler culture**? The most important prerequisite is that managers do not (any longer) see themselves as commanders who define goals and tasks for their employees (keyword "transactional leadership"; see Sect. 3.6.6.1). In an enabler culture, they rather act as promoters of their employees and support them sustainably in the fulfillment of tasks as well as in their own development. This support should enable employees and the team to work on assigned tasks with a high or higher degree of autonomy and to make decisions in line with the **company's purpose**. Such a **change in leadership culture** must be integrated into the corresponding further development of the corporate culture. If this succeeds, managers become networkers, as Fig. 3.108 shows.

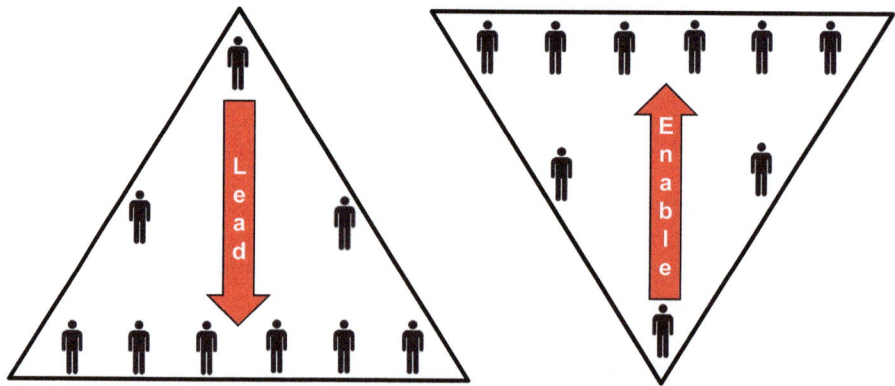

Fig. 3.107 Leadership duties—from "par ordre de Mufti" to being an enabler

Fig. 3.108 Leadership duties of networking

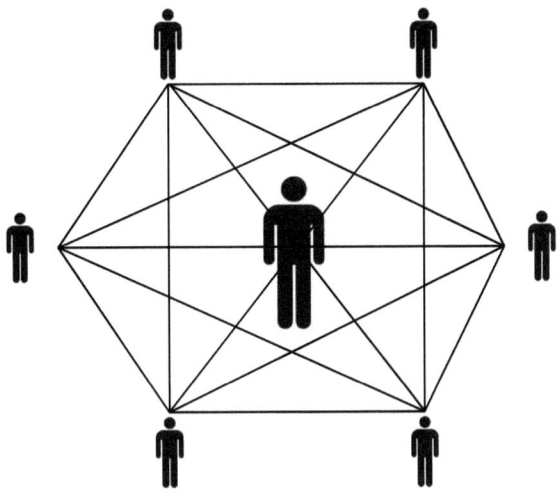

> **Memory Box**
> Self-management of employees and teams is based on an accepted purpose—which guides action here!

▶ **Personal Reading Tip**
Cal Newport: Deep Work—Rules for Focused Success in a Distracted World

3.6.10.2 The Concept of Holacracy

Figure 3.109 shows the **consequences** that can be associated with a radical **cultural change**—if one is very courageous (cf. Aghina et al., 2017, p. 5)! Organizations that were often seen as **"machines"** and managed like them are increasingly moving towards **"organisms."** This requires overcoming the top-down approach ("hierarchy"), superfluous bureaucracy, detailed instructions, and extensive silo thinking. The **leadership of an organism** is characterized by the fact that the direction in the sense of the purpose is communicated—together with the abilities to aim for it. The **purpose or meaning** of an organization serves as orientation for all those involved and is at the center as a **source of energy**. Every circle and every role has a purpose, which is derived from the overarching purpose. The purpose is inherited through the circle hierarchy.

Through this process, the classic organizational chart with "boxes and lines" loses its significance. Responsibility is delegated to a large extent to the teams themselves. They can make necessary changes in the achievement of goals themselves and use the necessary resources flexibly. In sum, strict guidelines and the completion of lists

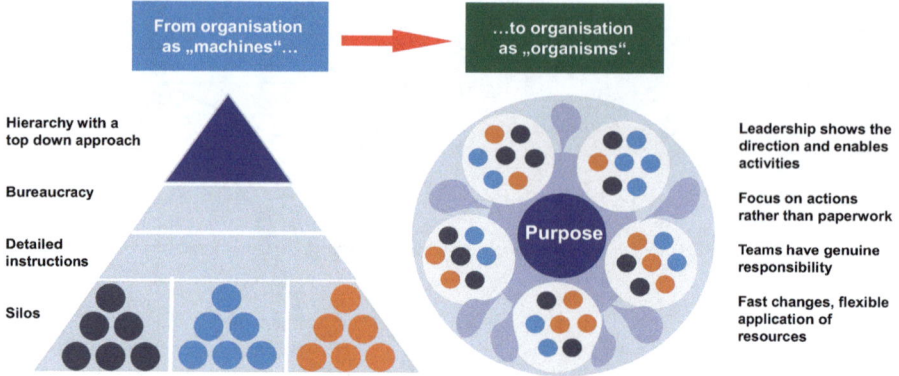

Fig. 3.109 From organization as „machine " to organization as "organism"

are less important than actions and the results achieved. Figure 3.109 already hints at a new concept described by the term **holacracy**.

A few companies today are already striving for—or have already implemented—**holacracy** as an organizational form. The term is formed from the syllables "holostic" for "whole, complete" or from holarchy, a term that stands for "self-transcendence"‟ (formation of higher units) and "self-dissolution" (disintegration into its components). The second word component comes from "cracy" for "rule." The aim of this approach is to implement decision-making in such an organization with a maximum of transparency and comprehensive participation opportunities for all employees. The basis for this is usually a specific set of rules called a **holacracy constitution**.

The following guidelines have emerged for **establishing a holacracy in the company** (cf. Bättig, 2020; Robertson, 2016; Müller & Wrobel, 2021, p. 302):

- **Circles**

  In a holacracy, the company is organized in circles that bring together different roles. The circles stand for a bundling of work. The **roles** are derived from the tasks of the enterprise and include fixed responsibilities. Different roles are grouped into sub-circles and several **sub-circles** are grouped into one **circle** (cf. Fig. 3.110). The roles that are combined in a circle organize themselves in each case. For this purpose, they can define new roles, change or abolish them—in each case depending on the tasks to be accomplished.

  An employee can take on **different roles**. If a role becomes too complex or the workload too large, a new role can be defined. In the same way, different roles can be merged if the respective workload no longer requires a separate role. Several roles together make up a **sub-circle**. These sub-circles, as well as the **top circles**, can change if the tasks require new ways of working and new roles. Both the roles and the circles are designed dynamically for this purpose. The organization can thus change in an evolutionary way, in small steps and continuously.

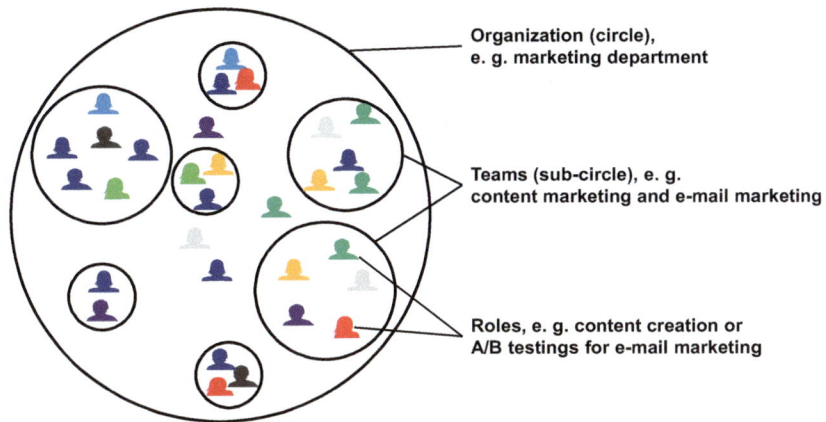

Fig. 3.110 Circles being the fundamental element of holacracy

Since the role is not a fixed position in the hierarchy, the respective employee does not have to worry about his or her future work if this role is eliminated. In the team, the task is to find a suitable role—based on the respective qualifications and expectations—within a sub-circle or in another circle. This is where **decentralized organizational development** comes in, without the pain of a classic reorganization and on a continuous basis—and in small steps.

- **Double connection**
To ensure an exchange between the circles of the different levels, a double liaison takes place. For this purpose, each circle elects one (or more) representatives to the next higher circle. These in turn send **representatives** to the general corporate circle. There, the strategic issues are discussed and the necessary overarching decisions are made.

  In addition, one (or more) **representatives are appointed for each of the external circles** with which the own circle is related. **Delegation to neighboring circles** can also be useful for cooperation. The delegates pass on information from "their" circle and represent its interests in the respective circles. Their voice must be heard here and taken into account in finding solutions.

  This structure overcomes the classic hierarchical communication structure: orders and feedback are now no longer to be passed on from the top. There is much more **network-like communication** between the roles and the different circles that work on interconnected projects.

- **Separation between control and operational work**
In the course of **steering meetings** of each circle, decisions are made on how the work in the respective circle is to be carried out. Here agreements are made on the respective tasks, responsibilities, and competences. In the course of these meetings, current problem areas of the company as well as ideas for optimization can also be discussed. The **operational meetings** deal with the day-to-day business.

- **Responsibilities and roles**
 The holacracy approach deliberately dispenses with a classic organizational chart with defined responsibilities and reporting lines—which often cannot be valid for long in a VUCA world anyway. The focus is on the roles and responsibilities already mentioned, which are important for the achievement of corporate goals.

 For smooth cooperation within an organization, it is nevertheless important that the **responsibilities and roles are clearly defined** and lived out accordingly by the respective persons. In this context, responsibilities do not represent demarcations as in classical organizational concepts. On the contrary, they describe the expectations of the roles and circles. Consequently, other tasks can be carried out that are outside the responsibility of a role, as long as it serves the purpose. The idea is to create as much **clarity** as possible so that more **self-organization** is possible.

 It is precisely the "**unspoken trust**" towards other key players in the company that is indispensable for an efficient organization. If the IT security person does not protect the company from cyberattacks, if the distribution of incoming mail does not work, or if the payment of bills and monthly salary transfers do not take place, the organization will fail.

 It is therefore important that these tasks are highlighted in the **steering meetings** in the light of options for action and provided with suggestions for implementation. This is initially done without naming specific persons. The necessary **assignment to persons** is done by the **lead link** of a circle or in the team when personnel and budget responsibilities are discussed. The lead link does not have the function of a boss, because that would be a personification of hierarchy. Rather, the lead link is a role with **responsibilities** defined from the beginning, which are also quite weighty. Responsibilities can be removed from a role. No responsibilities may be added after the constitution, so that bosses do not actually arise again.

- **Dynamic control**
 Decisions are made in the various circles. The decisions can—if necessary—be changed at any time if the intended goals are not achieved or serious changes have occurred. Here, every circle member is called upon to contribute **own proposals for solutions**—without having to pay attention to the respective "hierarchy" as in the past. The aim is to find solutions that fit the task and not the organizational form of the company or the opinion of the "higher-ups"! This is to avoid the HIPPO syndrome already mentioned (see Sect. 2.1.1).

 In dynamic control, other processes are also used for decision-making. Decisions are to be made with **consensus**. Seeking consensus means that it is not the majority that decides, but the most convincing solution or the best argument. A consensus reached in this way remains valid until a better solution or an even better argument is found. The aim of building consensus is to **minimize resistance**. It is therefore not about consensus working towards **maximizing consent**.

Several companies have already implemented holacracy. These include mymuesli (2019) in Germany, Unic (2021) in Switzerland and Zappos (2021b) in the USA.

3.6.10.3 Evaluative Analysis of the Holacracy Approach

It remains to be seen whether the concept of holacracy will catch on in very large organizations and especially in companies with a very heterogeneous skills spectrum. After all, the old insight still applies that a team only functions well when the **pecking order** has been clarified. That is why **informal hierarchies** are also forming in holacracies—after all, an alpha animal does not automatically relinquish its claim to leadership or even its leadership ability at the company door. However, such developments should be minimized through strict processes. And yes, **leadership** is also needed in a holacracy as an important ingredient of self-organization—here through the lead links.

Such aspects also play an important role in the evaluation of **career opportunities** as well as in **salary determination**. Moreover, not every employee wants to share a **high level of responsibility**—nor is everyone able to anticipate the **implications of their own actions on more complex systems**. This aspect is particularly important for listed companies, where not every employee should declare himself press spokesperson in order to report on critical company developments to the interested press.

Thus, the question arises whether holacracy could be a suitable **concept for managing (digital) challenges**. The high degree of flexibility that underlies the holacracy approach has serious advantages when a company has to prove itself in rapidly changing conditions. Combined with a high qualification level of the employees (for example, in consulting companies, in SW development, in the creative environment), holacracy can be the organizational form of the hour (keyword "innovation engine"; see Sect. 3.7.4).

However, even in the VUCA world, there are still tasks that need to be managed over a longer period of time (not only months, but also years) with the highest quality and precision without serious changes (keyword "performance engine"; see Sect. 3.7.4). Here we can think of the production of paper, detergents, automobiles, and also machines. It would be very detrimental to efficiency if too much flexibility were to be introduced, if tried and tested processes were to be permanently called into question—possibly also by people who lack the necessary expertise.

Therefore, in many companies it will come down to the **duality** already mentioned, both enabling a high degree of flexibility in sub-areas and at the same time ensuring through a distinct hierarchy that standard processes function with the highest efficiency (keyword "ambidexterity").

> **Memory Box**
> **Holacracy** is a revolutionary approach to achieving **self-organization in companies**. Today, only a few companies fulfil the prerequisites for establishing a holacracy. Also, few classically socialized leaders are willing to embark on such a challenging journey, which involves relinquishing many trappings of power. Nevertheless, these approaches offer interesting food for thought for the further development of leadership and organization in the digital age.

> **Think Box: Questions You Should Ask Yourself**
> - How do the managers in your company define themselves—as classic leaders or as enablers of their teams?
> - Do you know whether your employees—at least the majority of them—have the methodological competence and the mindset to want and be able to carry not only tasks but also the associated responsibility?
> - Which image corresponds more to your organization, that of a "machine" or that of a dynamic "organism"?
> - Have you ever considered the concept of holacracy?
> - Even if this concept may not be entirely feasible for your company, does it provide you with exciting food for thought?
> - Who is responsible in your company for answering such questions?

3.7 Organizational Concepts for the Digital Age

Hope is not a solution!

The **challenge for an organization in the digital age** is to combine the tried and tested with the new, to discard ballast and enter new territory, to retain qualified and motivated employees and managers and to attract new potential. All this is done with the aim of developing value-added services that ideally bind profitable customers to the company for a long time.

To ensure this, a **self-learning organization** is required in which all organizational units have the necessary (digital) tools, the required know-how and the indispensable mindset to develop themselves and their processes independently and to be able to react to changing market requirements at short notice. In the following, we will show through which organizational steps such a further development of the company can be achieved in order to reach the goal of digital excellence.

3.7.1 Requirements for Organizations in the Digital Age

Think big! Start small! Learn fast! Improve instantly!

When designing organizations, Chandler's (1962) legendary statement still applies: **structure follows strategy!** There is no overarching "optimal" structure for your company, but only structures that are better suited than others to successfully implement a particular strategy. It is precisely the **implementation of big ideas** that represents the **strategic bottleneck**—in both the private and professional spheres. In order to help innovations achieve a breakthrough, corresponding structures in the form of processes must be designed as the content of the so-called **operational structure**. These have already been discussed in the previous sections and will be examined in more detail here. In addition, concepts of the

3.7 Organizational Concepts for the Digital Age

organizational structure are presented here, which are to be intensively dovetailed with the various processes. Consequently, this section focuses on **org development**.

To this end, it is indispensable in established companies to break up the structures of the organizational structure that have often been firmly cemented for decades—especially in corporate groups. Only more independent units, often managed as subsidiaries and focused on a core area, can achieve the necessary **agility** today in dynamically developing markets and with a multitude of technological options. Therefore, a **trend towards splitting up** and **creating flexible organizational structures** can be seen in corporations today (e.g., at *Siemens*). The end of endless coordination processes and overlong decision-making paths must be achieved today rather than tomorrow—in order to give employees and thus also companies more breathing space!

The development towards **agility in management** was fueled by the *Agile Manifesto*. There, it was formulated in a deliberately provocative manner (cf. Beck et al., 2018):

- **Individuals** and **interactions** are more important than processes and tools.
- **Functioning software** is of greater importance than comprehensive documentation.
- **Intensive collaboration** with the client is more important than contract negotiations.
- **Responding to change** is much more important than simply following a plan once it has been developed.

In the following, particularly important **principles of the *Agile Manifesto*** are outlined (cf. Beck et al., 2018):

- Our top priority is **customer satisfaction**.
- We **welcome changing requirements**—even at late stages of development.
- We use **change to achieve competitive advantage**.
- Continuous **"testable" results** are produced.
- **Clients and developers** must **work together on a daily basis** throughout the project.
- The most efficient and effective method of communicating information to and within a development team is **face-to-face**.
- **Simplicity**—and thus the art of maximizing the amount of work that does not need to be done—is essential.
- The best architectures, requirements, and designs emerge from **self-organizing teams**.
- At regular intervals, the **team reflects** on how it can become more effective—and adjusts its behavior accordingly.

This already shows that such an approach is fundamentally different from the classical **principles of project management**. These differences are deliberately highlighted in Fig. 3.111 (cf. Preußig, 2018, p. 41f.).

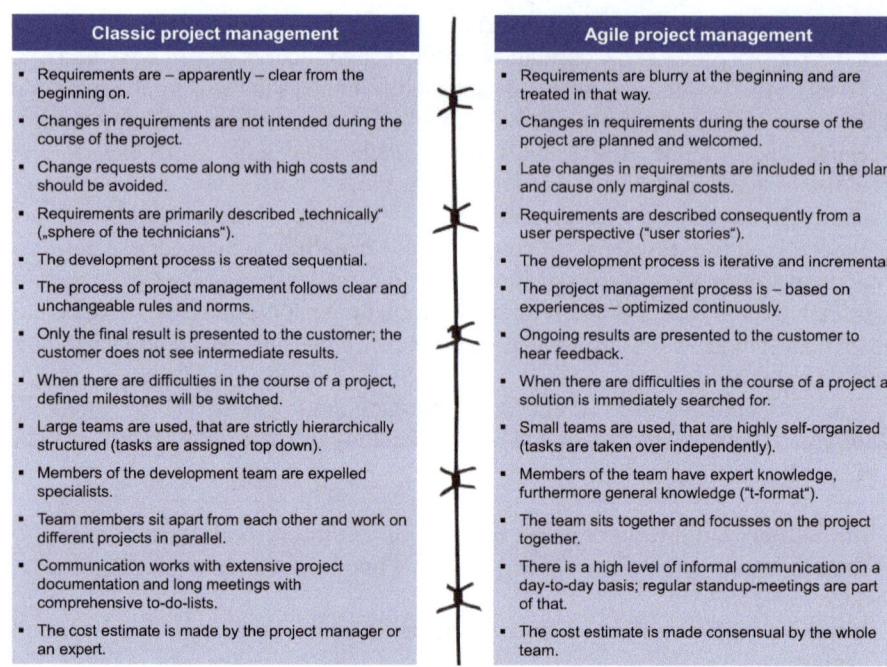

Fig. 3.111 Differences between classical and agile project management

Fig. 3.112 Visible changes in the competence map

With the principles mentioned in Fig. 3.111, the **methods of agile project management** take much greater account of the dramatically changed framework conditions than was the case with classic project management. In order to create the necessary **mindset** for this, these changes must also be reflected in the **competence map of your company**. Figure 3.112 shows which changes are to be aimed for. The "competences required today" described there form the basis for the further explanations.

In summary, the **mindset of agile management** can be depicted as in Fig. 3.113. The **linchpin** is a consistent **customer orientation**—in all areas of the company. An

3.7 Organizational Concepts for the Digital Age

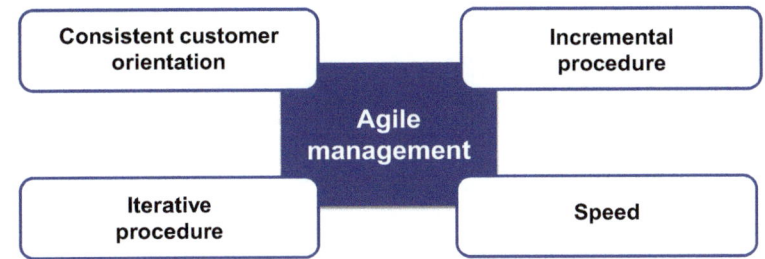

Fig. 3.113 Mindset of agile management

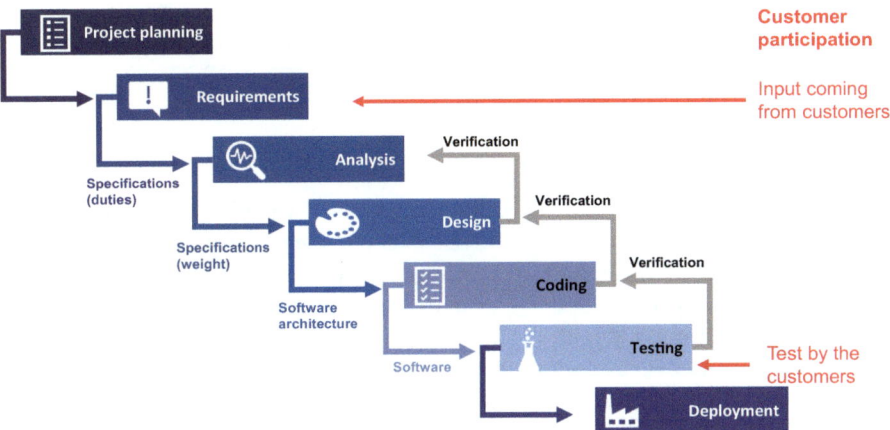

Fig. 3.114 Waterfall concept

incremental approach is chosen for innovation processes. Innovations are advanced step by step—and tested again and again in the market. Process steps are repeated in an **iterative procedure** until the desired results are achieved. The most important result is a passing grade in the eyes of the customers. All processes are trimmed for **speed**—oriented to the time-to-value approach. The time-to-value approach is, as it were, an epitome of customer orientation (see Sect. 3.2.7.3).

The goal of agile management is to replace the **waterfall concept** that still dominates in many companies (cf. Fig. 3.114). In this approach, **customer requirements** are obtained and defined—usually technically—at the start of the project. This is followed by the **creation of requirements and specifications**, the **development of the software architecture,** and the **programming of the software** itself. All these steps often take place without further customer participation. At the same time, this procedure leads to the illusion that it is possible to define at the beginning of a process what the solution should look like after 6, 12, or 24 months. Here, action is taken as if no new requirements of the customers and also no new technological possibilities or legal restrictions could arise during this time that would be worth considering.

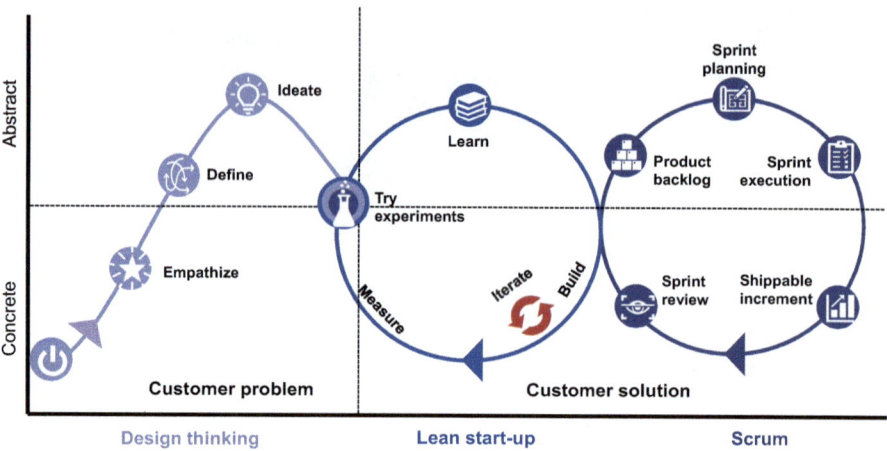

Fig. 3.115 Joining design thinking, lean start-up, and scrum

With the **waterfall concept**, the customer is only called upon again after the programming has been completed—often much too late to correct a course that was wrongly set 6, 12, or 24 months ago. This is why it is important here—but also in many other areas of the company—to think about processes that are based on the **mindset of agile management**.

In order to make the innovation process successful, the **company organization** must therefore also be further developed in the sense of a desired **agility**. To achieve customer orientation, it is indispensable to make your organization more permeable to impulses from outside. The relevance of the open innovation approach has already been pointed out in Sect. 3.5.3.2. In addition, you should bring together the central ideas of the **design thinking, lean start-up,** and **scrum** concepts as shown in Fig. 3.115 (cf. Gartner, 2016).

Figure 3.115 shows the **value adding linkage** of the different methods. **Design thinking** is used in the creative phase. The ideas found here are further developed through the **lean start-up approach** and tested with regard to their acceptance in the market. The concrete development of a product or service then takes place through the **scrum concept**.

> **Think Box: Questions You Should Ask Yourself**
> - Have you already found your "optimal" organizational form?
> - Should your company also deal with the trend towards splitting up and creating flexible organizational structures?
> - What do you think of the core ideas of the *Agile Manifesto*?
> - Are they relevant to your company?
> - Which areas could particularly benefit from an agile approach?

(continued)

- Do the principles of the *Agile Manifesto* have relevance for your company?
- Where do your company, your managers, and your employees stand in terms of project management—rather in the classic or in the agile area?
- Have you already realigned your company's competence map?
- How sustainable is the agile management mindset already anchored in your company?
- Or does the waterfall concept still dominate?
- Are the ideas of the design thinking, lean start-up, and scrum concepts consistently brought together in your company?
- Have you adopted the slogan "Think big! Start small! Learn fast! Improve instantly!"—and do you live by it?
- Who is driving the discussion process on these questions in your company?

3.7.2 Social Media Listening Center: Newsroom

The art of living is the art of leaving out the right things!
Coco Chanel

In order to anchor the openness necessary for an innovation process in the organization, companies are increasingly setting up the so-called **social media listening centers**. These are also called **social media war rooms**, **mission control rooms** or, more comprehensively, **newsrooms**. Here, communication in the social media—the so-called **social media buzz**—is constantly monitored. In addition, however, it is also important to determine other company-relevant information about the market, customers, competitors, etc. as early as possible.

American Red Cross, Dell, Gatorade, and *Marriott,* for example, have installed a newsroom. On the one hand, this is intended to **harmonize and accelerate internal and external communication processes**. On the other hand, possible reasons for complaints from customers and partners can be identified at an early stage. In addition, interesting suggestions for the further development of products, services, and business models can be gained from customers.

Due to its particular relevance, the **newsroom concept** is presented here in more detail. In a **newsroom**—analogous to the procedure in the editorial offices of newspapers, magazines, and TV/radio channels—all current news about the offer, the brand, and/or the company come together in a central place in order to be able to react quickly and consistently. In this place, the contents of the communication in the social media and from the customer service center can be brought together with the findings of the web and/or social media monitoring and analyzed in connection with the further challenges of the market. Then it is also important to proactively define central topics and coordinate the channels and concrete content relevant to their processing throughout the company. In this way, the often demanded **360° view on**

the markets can be ensured—an important prerequisite for achieving a high degree of customer centricity in entrepreneurial activities.

The **advantage of newsrooms** is to be able to react more quickly to communicative challenges of the market and to act powerfully forward. The concept of the newsroom, which brings together responsible persons from the relevant corporate divisions, avoids lengthy coordination processes, as is often still the case in large companies. In this way, a **one voice policy** can be ensured—despite the high reaction speed. This can succeed both in reacting quickly to market opportunities and in implementing actions at short notice.

▶ **Storytelling** As a social media team member of a large corporation reported in a lecture at my university: "If we start the approval process for a *St. Nicholas* promotion in June, we have no guarantee that it can be obtained by 6 December of the same year."

By **bringing together knowledge and responsibility holders** in a (virtual) team, companies can govern quickly and consistently—across all communication channels. For this purpose, incoming information is continuously analyzed and evaluated with regard to its relevance. At the same time, important clues for the further development of own offers can be gained based on the results of this screening.

For most companies, the **implementation of a newsroom concept** goes hand in hand with a change process. After all, long-established process and data silos have to be broken down and an information network established. Here, too, the greatest difficulties will lie in the **cognitive firewalls**—the firewalls in the heads of the employees and managers concerned. These can only be successfully won over to the change if the opportunities for the company associated with breaking down silos are made visible. In order to make the necessary change physically visible, the so-called **open-space offices** are often used in newsrooms. This breaks down communication barriers—also visibly for everyone.

Despite all the desired agility that such concepts strive for, newsroom concepts cannot do without structures. **Formal meeting routines** (for example, in the form of strategy conferences or meetings to discuss the morning situation) contribute to structuring the work. They also provide the communicative space to exchange ideas about larger projects. In addition, **informal arrangements** are used to deal with routine tasks.

The overall responsibility for the newsroom is often—as in traditional editorial departments—held by a **chief in charge**. His task is to responsibly develop the agenda of topics and to set communicative priorities for action. He is also the final authority for critical coordination processes. In addition, the chief of service and his team must ensure that the information generated from the markets is also forwarded to the relevant departments in the company to support the outside-in process (cf. Fig. 3.116).

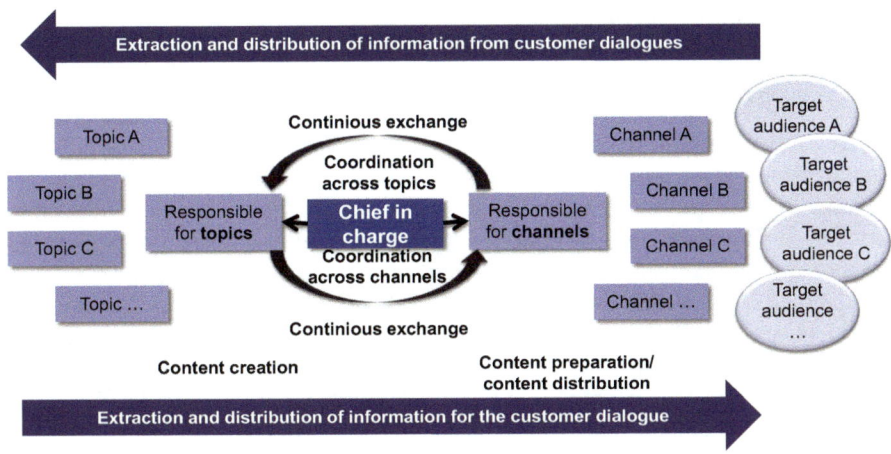

Fig. 3.116 Operating processes in a newsroom

Think Box: Questions You Should Ask Yourself
- Have you ever dealt with the concepts of social media listening centers or newsrooms?
- Is a social media listening center or newsroom installed in your company to continuously monitor social media buzz and more?
- How is important information from the market channeled to the relevant departments in your company?
- Who could test such a concept for relevance for your company?

3.7.3 Strategic Entrepreneurship

Curiosity is the fuel for innovation!

The question for you is how to anchor consistent **innovation management** in your company in order to achieve digital excellence. Here, the concept of **strategic entrepreneurship** comes to mind (cf. Lehmann & Wilhelm, 2018, pp. 259–261). You can implement this in your company in two different ways:

- Corporate entrepreneurship
- Corporate venturing

The goal of **corporate entrepreneurship** is to permanently anchor the entrepreneurial approach, the basic mindset, the methods and, above all, the dynamics that companies show in the start-up phase in established companies (cf. Engelen et al., 2015; Kuratko et al., 2014). In **corporate venturing**, mature companies use the founding, spin-off, and/or purchase of start-ups or participation in start-ups to significantly increase their own innovative clock rate.

3.7.3.1 Corporate Entrepreneurship

Corporate entrepreneurship is discussed here first. After all, an entrepreneurial person does not always have to start his own company in order to drive an innovation forward. Such a necessity would be an indictment of all established organizations! Instead, they should ensure that their employees and managers can also act as entrepreneurs within their own companies. **Entrepreneurship within the company** should be promoted. The terms **intrapreneurship, strategic entrepreneurship,** or—as a part of it—**corporate entrepreneurship** are used for this.

Corporate entrepreneurship is not about training managers and employees to implement a developed strategy or business model. Rather, the challenge is to motivate **managers and employees to become initiators and drivers of innovations in strategy and business models**—and then to let them do so (cf. Lipinski & Wilhelm, 2021).

> **Memory Box**
> **Corporate entrepreneurship is the in-sourcing of creativity and innovation management!**
>
> The goal is to permanently anchor the spirit of entrepreneurship in established companies as well. Companies should think and act like start-ups in spirit.
>
> In order to anchor corporate entrepreneurship in his company, *Jeff Bezos* has issued the slogan for *Amazon* that it is always **"day one"** at *Amazon*. With this **day-one philosophy**, *Bezos* wants to ensure that *Amazon* still behaves like a start-up. For *Bezos*, "day two" is already stagnation, followed by irrelevance and an agonizingly painful decline (cf. Hamilton, 2020). For *Bezos*, the required **start-up DNA** is concretized above all in four areas, which have already been addressed in Sect. 3.1.3.4 as part of the **leadership principles**.
>
> - **Customer obsession**
> - **Deliver results**
> - **Bias for action**
> - **Learn and be curious**
>
> Even if this approach is a **rebellion against operational blindness and organizational inertia**, I think it falls short. It ignores the fact that every start-up has to emerge from the birth pangs to become a solid, reliable, and profitable business partner. Moreover, the decline of a company does not start on day 2—maybe not even after day 100, 1000, or 10,000!

(continued)

3.7 Organizational Concepts for the Digital Age

What we can take away from the **day-one philosophy**, however, is the willingness to have **entrepreneurial people thinking and acting** at as many levels of the organization as possible—and not just at the management level. The following valuable **ingredients of a start-up mindset** should therefore also be built up and secured in your company:

- Curiosity
- Creativity
- Fun in the further development of strategies and business models
- Consistent customer orientation across all business areas
- Thinking outside the box of one's own area of responsibility
- Intensive communication—without a silo mentality
- Working in networks
- Willingness to constantly question the status quo in order to become better
- Willingness to take risks

At its core, **corporate entrepreneurship**, like the **start-up mindset**, is consequently about generating and keeping the **entrepreneurial spirit** alive throughout the organization. If we are honest, we also recognize that it is essential for healthy business development that the above ingredients are embedded in experiential knowledge. In this way, we can bring together "best of both worlds":
Start-up DNA and experience!

Memory Box
You only gain experience by making it!
   And that happens over time.
   Corporate entrepreneurship tries to avoid the often encountered **operational blindness**. Instead, the company's own business model must be consistently developed further. Here, it is also important to advance into new business areas—all driven from within the company itself. Corporate entrepreneurship thus presupposes the existence of an existing organization. If you are active in such a company, you can take the following first **steps towards corporate entrepreneurship**:

- **Implementation of innovation managers/innovation teams**
  In this approach, individuals or a group of people within the company deal specifically with innovative issues. The responsible persons are usually completely assigned to the generation of innovative ideas and the

(continued)

coordination of innovation projects. For this purpose, it is important to bring together people from different areas of the company in order to look beyond their respective horizons.

- **Internal innovation lab/innovation center**
  In order to initiate and keep the innovation process alive, one or more internal innovation labs can be established. Here, creativity and innovation methods (e.g., design thinking, lean start-up) are used to work on new business models and new offers. The people working here have their own budget responsibility and control the entire innovation process. Employees and managers from different company divisions are regularly involved in the innovation process. Workshops or longer-lasting formats for generating customer insights are used to find concrete ideas or to evaluate and further develop already generated solution proposals (see Sect. 3.5.3).

  External knowledge is made available through temporarily employed experts or through a regular exchange with start-ups, research institutions, and/or universities. Promising projects are developed as innovation projects in the existing company and, if successful, are either transferred to the company's existing portfolio or handed over to a separate company structure through a spin-off.

- **External innovation lab/external innovation center**
  Companies like *Convidera* offer corporate innovation teams the spaces necessary for concentrated and creative work, as well as an efficient infrastructure. For innovation units, the motto is (Pelser, 2021):

  "The decisive factor is the optimal distance to the core business!"

  The reason for this is the **dualism between the performance engine and the innovation engine** described in Sect. 3.7.4. This is about the clash between efficient day-to-day business and the spirit of innovation. If an innovation team is set up in the "catchment area" of the core business, this automatically narrows the creative space. Incremental improvements are often the result. Too much distance from the core business can lead to a lack of acceptance of the results and jeopardizes the transfer of new insights and methods to the head office. Moreover, too much distance cuts the innovation team off from relevant information streams from the performance engine.

  The challenge can be described as follows. On the one hand, the innovation team should remain a **part of the whole**, but at the same time have sufficient **creative freedom** to think big (cf. Pelser, 2021). To achieve this balancing act, *Convidera* provides the necessary technical infrastructure for creative work (e.g., modern IT collaboration tools).

  The members of the innovation team are given a **permanent workplace** on the *Convidera* campus. A **360° service and support approach** enables a smooth day-to-day work. Targeted **further training** is provided to team

(continued)

members depending on their individual requirements. A close exchange and a good working relationship between the members of an innovation team and the performance engine staff are ensured through regular contact.

An **innovation lab** specifically geared towards the **human resource development of tomorrow** is offered by Alternus (2021). As HR development plays a central role as a driver of the necessary cultural changes, the HR innovation lab sees itself as a culture designer to develop the organizations of the future. The HR innovation lab is an important initiator for the HR strategy. The partners involved—supported and promoted by an innovative set of methods—develop solutions for the organization of tomorrow. For this purpose, speakers are regularly invited to drive the creative process through **impulse presentations** and **workshops**.

Human resource development based on solidarity and trust should promote the **emergence of a "we" culture**. Only by promoting willingness to change, attitude, creativity, and implementation competence can the future viability of organizations be secured.

The approaches described make an important contribution to **strengthening the innovation potential of companies**. However, the **responsibility for innovation** remains limited to individuals or a group. The whole organization is then not permeated by a spirit of innovation—oriented towards the goals of corporate entrepreneurship. Think here again of *Google's Nine Principles of Innovation* (see Sect. 3.1.3.4). Here it says, among other things:
Innovation comes from everywhere.

To achieve this, **corporate entrepreneurship** deliberately supports the goal of involving all employees and managers in innovation processes. It is important here that such **innovation initiatives** are not suppressed by day-to-day business because they are important but not urgent (see the *Eisenhower* matrix in Fig. 3.13). Rather, it is important to encourage such initiatives by entrepreneurial individuals by **providing necessary resources**. In addition, the **visibility of what has been achieved and what is possible** within the company must be ensured—to make self-efficacy visible! In the case of innovations with great potential, a **spin-off of the business ideas** can take place in the course of the development process in order to further increase this visibility—and to make very transparent resource allocations.

▶ **Food for Thought**
To continuously support this **process of entrepreneurship in the company**, managers in particular, but also colleagues, can use a **go-for-it card** every now and then. This game—with a very serious and important background—is about **fostering innovation in your own teams** and **encouraging them to**

Fig. 3.117 Go-for-it card

keep going. To do this, use the go-for-it card shown in Fig. 3.117. You will see that it works wonders!

In this way, you can **strengthen the innovative power of your company** through small measures by regularly **motivating your employees and managers to keep going**.

3.7.3.2 Corporate Venturing

The second approach to strategic entrepreneurship is **corporate venturing**. "Venturing" stands for "to dare/risk." In contrast to corporate entrepreneurship, a company does not try to integrate a start-up mentality into its own organization. In corporate venturing, established companies hope to gain new impetus by founding, spinning off, and/or buying start-ups or investing in start-ups.

Large companies develop their own **accelerator programs** or **incubators** for these tasks. The investments made here usually have a strategic character. This means that the investing companies are not interested in a pure financial investment. Rather, they expect creative impulses for their own business model. Smaller companies can invest in start-ups that are interesting as strategic business and innovation partners—or they involve themselves in these concepts at least informatively.

In **corporate venturing**, companies that do not belong to the financial sector use **equity capital** (**venture capital**) to achieve strategic goals. This can serve to secure sales markets, but can also be geared towards the procurement of personnel, technologies, production facilities, and/or R&D facilities. Larger companies also set up their own **venture capital funds**. Here, however, the focus is often more on the motive of a capital investment. **Venture capital** is referred to here because these investments are associated with a particular risk. Leveraging capital for start-ups can help connect incumbents with relevant information flows. At the same time, business ideas can be tested here before they are integrated into a transformation of the entire business model. This reduces innovation risks.

> **Memory Box**
> Somewhat disparagingly, venture capital is also referred to as OFM: "other fools money."

(continued)

3.7 Organizational Concepts for the Digital Age

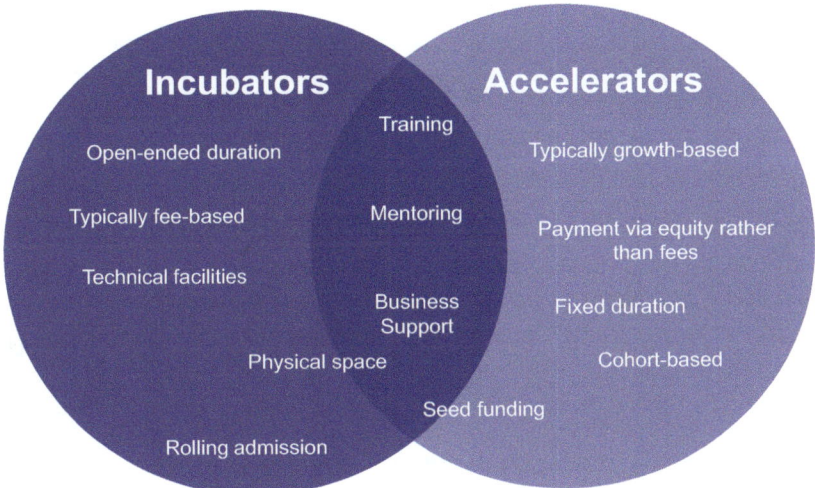

Fig. 3.118 Incubators versus accelerators

> Entrepreneurial activities in **accelerators** or **incubators** also count as **corporate venturing**. Accelerators and incubators can either be set up by a company itself—or companies can participate in them. In either case, the companies involved make a—risky—**financial investment** outside of the established business areas. The overlaps between accelerators and incubators can be seen in Fig. 3.118.
>
> An **accelerator** is an institution that helps start-ups to develop quickly within a **limited period of time** through coaching and other measures. The intended acceleration of entrepreneurial growth has led to the name "accelerator." The activities of an accelerator are similar in many respects to those of the incubator presented below; however, there are some differences. Accelerators usually support start-ups in an early **phase of development** both by **transferring know-how** and by providing **further resources**. This support is often limited to a few months in which the business idea is to be developed into a market-ready concept.
>
> In order to participate in an accelerator program, the founders usually have to apply. This often involves checking whether a start-up fits the industry focus of the accelerator. The founders have to convince the organizers of their idea in the course of a competition called **pitch**. Those who successfully pass this pitch process are often supported by the following:
>
> - provision of workspace,
> - technical support,

(continued)

- operational and strategic coaching (e.g., advice on the development of business plans and marketing campaigns),
- training on corporate and staff management (e.g., the use of methods such as scrum or design thinking),
- dealing with legal issues,
- integration into a network.

In this phase, the innovation projects remain in the start-ups, which employ their **own staff** and use their **own resources** for this purpose. There is only limited exchange with the supporting organization. Through **access to technologies** and/or through **access to the distribution channel** of the participating (established) company, an acceleration of the start-ups' corporate development is sought.

In the course of **corporate venturing**, companies can either set up their own accelerator in the form of a subsidiary, found one jointly with other companies or participate in already existing accelerators. In return for this comprehensive support, the accelerators can receive a share in the start-ups and thus in their future development.

Promising start-ups whose development has been supported in the accelerator can continue to operate as **independent companies** after the end of the phase in the accelerator. If there is interest on the part of the founding team and the investing company, the start-up can be **integrated into an already existing company** through takeover.

Here is an **overview of relevant accelerators** that can be interesting for start-ups. Payment is often made in the form of company shares (cf. T3N, 2021):

- *A2 Energy Adlershof*
  The *Adlershof Science and Technology Park* in Berlin offers start-ups the chance to benefit from coaching, free infrastructure services, and intensive networking with industrial companies for 5 months.
- *APX by Axel Springer und Porsche*
  The *Plug-and-Play Accelerator* initiated by the publishing house *Axel Springer* and *Porsche* aims to help founding teams with ambitious digital ideas and global ambitions to succeed. The program lasts 100 days. Projects are rewarded with, for example, 25,000 € for 5% of the company shares.
- *DB Start-upXpress*
  The accelerator *DB Start-upXpress* is aimed at young companies whose technologies, apps, or business models have the potential to complement *Deutsche Bahn's* service portfolio and/or support its digital transformation. The start-up financing can amount to 25,000 €, without having to cede shares in the business.

(continued)

- **Digital Hub**
  The *digitalhub.de* is a start-up network that offers an accelerator program for start-ups. Coworking workplaces are provided. The network includes interesting partners.
- **German Accelerator**
  The *German Accelerator* supports high-potential German start-ups in the field of information and communication technologies that want to conquer US and Southeast Asian markets (#GoFarGrowFast). During the program, which lasts 3–6 months, founders receive business coaching, their own mentor and contacts to potential partners and financiers in the USA and Germany. They can also work in the accelerator's offices in Palo Alto, San Francisco, or New York City.
- **Merck Accelerator**
  This accelerator supports start-ups in the fields of healthcare, life sciences, and special chemical materials. The programs, which take place in Darmstadt and Shanghai, offer start-up funding of up to 50,000 €, mentoring and coaching as well as access to the *Merck Innovation Center* and the global network of the corporate group.
- **Metro Accelerator**
  Here, mainly hospitality and retail start-ups are supported. Depending on the program chosen, access to more than 500 hotel and restaurant chains or the *Metro Group's* retail network is offered. During the 3-month program, participants are coached and have access to *Metro's* infrastructure services. The average funding amount is 120,000 €.
- **Startplatz**
  Startplatz in Cologne and Düsseldorf offers a mixture of coworking space, scene meeting place, and start-up support. It offers founders a workplace in the coworking space, mentoring and access to various workshops and numerous corporate partners.

Memory Box
Accelerators are like the pushers on a bobsleigh ride. The founders have to steer themselves—and they also have to master the handling of the higher speed themselves! To be successful, however, the founders have qualified coaches from all important disciplines at their disposal—and the bobsleigh itself is also trimmed for top performance!

Incubators are special institutions that accompany and support start-ups on the path to business creation. The term incubator comes from medicine. It names the **incubator for premature babies** who would not yet be able to survive in the "harsh reality." To enable safe growth in the first weeks, the incubator provides an optimal climate for the growth of premature babies. The incubator assumes a comparable function for new ideas. These new ideas should also be able to develop first in a **protected area** before being exposed to competition. For this purpose, incubators offer start-ups an optimal environment to let a business idea grow.

Incubators are **independent facilities** in which start-ups initially remain **without a time limit**. The incubator usually also exists spatially—for example, in the form of a **start-up center**. In these incubators, start-ups are usually supported more comprehensively and for longer periods of time than is the case in accelerators. The range of support begins with the **provision of rental space or entire offices** as well as a **comprehensive infrastructure.** In addition, comprehensive **consulting services** and **coaching for the founders** are offered. The goal here is also to sustainably increase a start-up's chances of success.

All innovation projects remain in **independent companies** that also employ their **own staff**. An exchange with established companies takes place on individual demand and on the basis of exploiting entrepreneurial synergies to accelerate the growth of the start-up. Promising companies of the incubator will continue to operate as **independent organizations** or will be **integrated into an already existing organization** through takeover. Funding can be provided through public business development measures. Companies can also participate in incubators or in the start-ups supported there in the course of corporate venturing.

Here is an overview of **interesting incubators** (cf. T3N, 2021):

- *First Mover*
  In Düsseldorf, the incubator *first Mover* supports start-up teams from the publishing, marketing, and production segments. The pre-seed and seed start-ups receive up to 100,000 € in start-up funding. In addition, advice, operational support, and a discounted infrastructure are offered.
- *Greenhouse Innovation Lab*
  The *Greenhouse Innovation Lab* for *Gruner + Jahr* and *Mediagroup RTL* promotes internal and external ideas around new media formats, e-commerce models, apps, and social media tools. Start-ups are supported with office space, coaching, a start-up budget, and access to the *Gruner + Jahr* brands.
- *Hubraum*
  The *Hubraum* incubator in Berlin, which belongs to *Deutsche Telekom*, also focuses on 5G, edge computing, Internet of Things, and artificial intelligence. Up to 300,000 € in funding is available for start-ups that have a scalable idea and can already show at least one product or at least

(continued)

one prototype. In addition, there is access to *Deutsche Telekom's* customer base and infrastructure.
- **Innowerft**
  Innowerft sees itself as the start-up center from Walldorf (where *SAP* is headquartered) for innovative B2B start-ups from all over the world. Start-ups in various stages of development are supported by a network of co-founders, coaches, investors, and potential customers. In some cases, *SAP* also invests itself. For established companies, *Innowerft* sees itself as an intermediary into the start-up world. *Innowerft* also provides support in developing profitable business models from the ideas of employees of established companies.
- **Next Big Thing**
  Under the motto "all creation is collaboration," *Next Big Thing* brings together different stakeholders as a European incubator for business models. The team actively supports with its own experts during the growth phase and can also take on the role of "first investor."
- **Rheingau Founders**
  The *Rheingau Founders* target start-ups that have the potential to sustainably disrupt existing processes and value chains. They support founding teams and solo entrepreneurs from the earliest possible stage. In addition to mentoring and infrastructure, up to 250,000 € in capital is possible, followed by a later commitment as a co-investor.
- **Team Europe Ventures**
  The Internet incubator *Team Europe Ventures* invests in promising Internet start-ups at early stages. *Team Europe Ventures* puts together founding teams and supports them in setting up the company, in marketing measures as well as in IT deployment (cf. Deutsche Start-ups, 2021a).

In addition, the **company builders** should be considered here as special forms. These include companies such as *Hitfox, Project A Ventures,* and *Rocket Internet*. These are neither incubators nor accelerators in the strict sense. At the same time, these companies are more than "mere" financiers. These companies, which can be described as company builders, usually rely on their own start-up ideas and then put together internal teams to develop successful start-ups from them. Sometimes external founders are also brought in to benefit from their know-how.

As a company builder, *HitFox* focuses on the development and acquisition of companies in the field of game distribution and user acquisition. The company works with over 100 game publishers and more than 1000 media companies (cf. Deutsche Start-ups, 2021b). *Project A Ventures* cooperates with entrepreneurs operating at the frontiers of digital innovation. Here, capital is combined with operational assistance so that founders receive the optimal

(continued)

support (cf. Project A, 2021). **Rocket Internet** incubates and invests in Internet and technology companies worldwide under the motto "We enable entrepreneurship." Start-ups are offered comprehensive operational support in building market-leading companies (cf. Rocket Internet, 2021).

In sum, it must be stated that the types presented—**accelerator, incubator,** and **company builder**—cannot be clearly distinguished from each other. The transitions between the different concepts are fluid and are flexibly adapted to market requirements. For you, the diversity presented here means that you should embark on a journey to determine which of the concepts offers the greatest innovation potential for your company.

The advantage of all these approaches is that the viability of product/service innovations and business model innovations are first determined in an area isolated from the existing organization. Only when a certain level of **maturity** has been achieved is a **transfer to the existing organization** to be considered. Business areas that do not fit the existing business model can be established in parallel to the existing business model in the course of a diversification strategy—often in organizations that remain separate (cf. Fig. 3.38).

Your company does not have the necessary **resources** to invest in accelerators or incubators or directly in start-ups itself? Then the task for you is to network with the **digital innovation hotspots** that are particularly important for your industry. A look at the accelerators and incubators presented here will give you a first impression of the direction in which you should strengthen your networks. If you are primarily active in Germany, then you should establish contacts with the **start-up strongholds** in Berlin, Bonn, Düsseldorf, Cologne, etc.

▶ **Food for Thought**
By the way: not only those managers and employees should be invited to start-up meetings who are already involved in innovation topics. If you want to create an **entrepreneurial spirit** in the entire company, top performers from controlling, customer service, purchasing, production, sales, and marketing should also take part in such visits.

After all, there is a germ cell for innovation in every employee!

In this way, the **fear of new things** is ideally displaced by a **desire for new things**. And what more do you want?

In addition, you can also get in direct **contact with universities** that actively support start-ups. In the technical field, it is primarily the *TU Munich* with the non-profit organization *Unternehmens-TUM,* which translated is a combination of the term "entrepreneurial" and the university name. The core mission of this company is to promote start-ups. *RWTH Aachen* and the *Karlsruhe Institute of Technology* are also involved in this area.

Focal points in the commercial field are offered by Leipzig's HHL (2021), which has already implemented successful corporate entrepreneurship programs with companies such as *E.ON, Porsche,* and *Postbank* (cf. HHL, 2021). The *Berlin School of Economics and Law* has set up its own start-up center, the **Start-up Incubator Berlin**. Here, start-up ideas are developed to market maturity. To achieve this goal, academic start-up teams are provided with know-how, infrastructure, and scholarships. In the form of a lean incubator, special emphasis is placed on speed in the development and testing of business models. The offer here is aimed at people who are only at the beginning of their start-up project or are already in the active start-up phase (cf. HWR, 2021).

Depending on your company's focus, you should also take a look at ***Berlin Adlershof***. This is Germany's largest science and technology park and also the largest media location in Berlin. It is home to 1203 companies and scientific institutions with about 24,000 employees. In the **science and technology park**, 556 companies and non-university research institutes concentrate on the technology fields of photonics and optics, photovoltaics and renewable energies, microsystems, information technology, and media as well as biotechnology and the environment. In addition, there are several relevant institutes of the *Humboldt University Berlin*.

189 companies are located in the **media city**. Here everything revolves around stage, screenplay, post-production, dubbing, and x-rooms. The film studios located in *Berlin Adlershof* offer good conditions and locations for shows, e-sport events, magazines, and the big cinema (cf. Berlin Adlershof, 2021).

A worthwhile place for you and your team to visit could also be the ***Swiss Smart Factory*** (cf. SSF, 2021), founded by *Switzerland Innovation* (Park Biel). This is the first open and neutral **test and demonstration platform on the topic of industry 4.0** in Switzerland. Its vision is to become Switzerland's leading and internationally recognized **center of excellence in application-oriented research and in the transfer of industry 4.0**. To this end, an **ecosystem of partners** is being established in which innovations and activities around the topic of industry 4.0 are being created.

The *SSF* was founded in May 2017 as the first **digital innovation hub** in Switzerland and acts as a regional and national multiplier for digital innovation. Here, small and medium-sized enterprises (SMEs) and start-ups are supported in the **introduction and development of product and business model innovation**. The *Swiss Smart Factory* is operated by an association model of more than 50 paying partners from industry and research. As the initiator and operator of the lighthouse project industry 4.0, a holistic production ecosystem is on display on 1000 m^2. Here, interested parties can experience within a glass factory how industry 4.0 already works today and which trends will become important in the future (cf. SSF, 2021).

Memory Box
If you do not have the resources to invest more in start-ups, accelerators, and/or incubators yourself, then it is important to network with the innovation hotspots.
The indispensable mindset for this is: to be curious, courageous and, above all, active!

Think Box: Questions You Should Ask Yourself
- How familiar are you and your company with the concepts of strategic entrepreneurship?
- Do you already promote corporate entrepreneurship?
- Where could corporate entrepreneurship be particularly exciting for your company?
- Through which concepts can corporate entrepreneurship be anchored in your company?
- What can you derive from *Amazon's* day-one philosophy for your company?
- How can you succeed in anchoring a start-up DNA in your company?
- Which ingredients of a start-up mindset are already present in your company and which need to be strengthened?
- Does your company have innovation managers or innovation teams?
- Do you have internal innovation labs and/or innovation centers?
- Are external innovation labs and/or innovation centers used?
- What do you think of the go-for-it card to promote innovation within your own teams?
- Has your company already looked into the various possibilities of corporate venturing?
- Do you use venture capital to access sources of innovation?
- Does your company engage with accelerators and/or incubators?
- Can you set up and/or participate in accelerators and incubators yourself?
- Do you have an overview of relevant accelerators that might be of interest to your company and industry?
- Do you know the incubators that are relevant for you and which business models are being worked on there?
- What is the importance of company builders for your industry?
- Where can you best network to keep your hand on the innovative pulse?
- Who is dealing with these central questions in your company?

3.7.4 Performance Engine and Innovation Engine as Concepts for Actions

*First we shape **our** buildings **and** afterwards **our** buildings shape us.*
Winston *Churchill*

The **corporate entrepreneurship** presented in Sect. 3.7.3.1 is specifically expressed in the form of a so-called **innovation engine**. This represents the epitome of the concretization of a **day-one philosophy** that is to be understood as a guiding idea. The focus here is on the **start-up DNA**.

In order to achieve radical creative (digital) innovations of products, services, and business models, not only a strategic **anchoring of these innovations in top management** and **digital knowledge in the entire organization** are required. It is also necessary to check whether the **framework conditions** exist in the company so that new business models, products, services, and processes can take hold. Govindarajan and Trimble (2010, pp. 10–14) have developed the following concept for this, which you can use as a basis for your internal company analyses and measures.

The majority of **(established) companies** today are only prepared to a very limited extent for the development of groundbreaking innovations, which may even call their own business model, products, and services into question in whole or in part (cf. also Christensen, 2016). The heart of established companies is rather a so-called **performance engine**. This corresponds to an engine whose raison d'être is to reliably produce products and services with the highest possible efficiency in the desired quality at defined costs—often in high quantities. And that is right!

Here we can think of the assembly lines at *Volkswagen* and *Audi*, but also the production lines at *BASF, Henkel*, and *Unilever* and the project work at many thousands of other companies. With the **performance engine**, stability, predictability, routine, and zero-error tolerance are the dominant success factors. However, the performance engine usually dominates the entire company. Therefore, all activities that run counter to the known pattern and that could thus cause uncertainty and (temporary) inefficiency are blocked, under-provisioned in terms of time and/or resources, or even blocked altogether. From the performance engine's point of view, the behavioral patterns aimed at continuity and stability are not unintentional misbehavior, but serve to safeguard its own success model.

The **performance engine** thus represents the opposite of an approach geared towards disruptive product, service, and/or business model innovations. Therefore, the performance engine should be contrasted with a more network-like concept that can—and is allowed to—react much more quickly to changes in the environment. The term **innovation engine** can be used for this. The innovation engine represents an additional organizational unit to be set up. It should develop innovative (digital) projects with a radical and/or disruptive character largely independently of the company's established core business. The central guiding ideas here are system openness, fault tolerance, and the search for future strategically valuable business opportunities—independent and uninfluenced by previous activities and thus independent of the company's own performance engine.

An **innovation engine** does not necessarily have to be integrated within one's own organization—in fact, it often should not be. This is because proximity to the operational business can prove counterproductive for (digital) transformation activities. In many cases, it has proven successful to establish **innovation centers** that are often spatially detached from the "heart of the company." The establishment of and/or participation in **independent digital companies** can also create the necessary **creative freedom** that is indispensable for an innovation engine.

An **innovation engine** conceived in this way is initially only relatively loosely linked to the current organization. The linkage of the corresponding investments would primarily exist at the level of company law—as well as through (top) managers who are active in the steering committees of the innovation engines. The task of these managers is to be regularly informed about exciting developments and to carry this knowledge into the established company. However, these must be managers who love to think outside the box. They must also not be afraid to cut off dearly-held braids (such as analogue products and services) if they no longer fit the times (see Sect. 4.1 on this).

Within the innovation engine, different **fields of activity** can be defined. For example, the development of a digital platform for the realization of a new business model for a new target group can be worked on here. If such a development takes place in an innovation engine, it is not necessary to check at every step whether one's own previous activities are cannibalized. In addition, "smart" and networked products with deep anchoring in digital applications can be developed. These digital versions of the previously distributed product and service offerings from the analogue sector can make them obsolete. The innovation engine is thus the instrument to drive the development of innovations and business models on horizons 2 and 3 (cf. Fig. 3.10).

The big challenge for you is to resolve the **organizational dilemma**:

On the one hand, there is the **hierarchical-mechanistic management system** of today's operational activities (in the sense of the **performance engine**). On the other hand, there is an increasing need for **evolutionary and network-like structures** to support successful innovative action (in the sense of the **innovation engine**). And both have to happen at the same time. Here we are again dealing with the issue of **ambidexterity**—specifically **structural ambidexterity**, as ambidexterity is cast in a structural form (see introductory Sect. 3.2.2).

The exciting task for your management is to build the **dual organization** necessary for this, which is to be further developed in the parts described in Fig. 3.119 (cf. Kotter, 2014).

Figure 3.120 shows an example of the tasks to be processed in the performance engine, on the one hand, and the innovation engine, on the other.

In this context, it is important to ensure that the link between the performance engine and the innovation engine is not only selective. What is required is **cooperation** between the two areas in a **spirit of partnership**. A prerequisite for the success of this cooperation is that all employees and managers of both engines recognize the relevance of the other and value it. Only then does the division of tasks between the performance and innovation engines become comprehensible in terms of their

3.7 Organizational Concepts for the Digital Age

Performance engine	**Innovation engine**
(hierarchically structured part of the organization)	(network-oriented part of the organization)
• Well-defined and proven process and organizational structure • Operational business management based on reliability, efficiency and zero errors • Small steps are needed for change	• Work in the organization is done with agility (innovation and speed) • Management of projects with a radical, disruptive, possibly cannibalizing character • Openness, fault tolerance, flexibility and speed are key requirements
Important:	**Important:**
Here money is earned <u>today</u>!	Here money will be earned <u>tomorrow</u>!

Fig. 3.119 Ensuring acceptance of a dualism during the transformation process

Performance engine	**Innovation engine**
• Introduction of a company-wide content management system for maintaining the corporate website and additional channels • Introduction of a CRM system • Step-by-step digitization of customer journeys • Partial digitization of internally and externally oriented processes • Optimization of production processes to reduce costs	• Development of a digital platform for the realization of a new business model for a new target group • Development of an "intelligent" and networked product with deep anchoring in digital applications • Development of "digital versions" of previously sold products and service offerings in the analog sector • AI-based production planning and control • Development of a smart factory

Fig. 3.120 Fields of activity of the performance or the innovation engine

importance for the long-term survival of the company. In this way, new business ideas emerge in the innovation engine that are indispensable for the sustainable development of the company. A prerequisite for this, however, is the provision of the financial resources that must first be generated by the performance engine.

Below is a list of how various companies have organized their **innovation engine** to consciously break away from the core DNA of the respective company. Some of the concepts already mentioned that were presented in the context of accelerators and incubators also appear in this list (see Sect. 3.7.3):

- *Axel Springer Verlag*: *Plug & Play Accelerator GmbH*, Berlin and Silicon Valley
- *BASF*: *BASF New Business GmbH, BASF Venture Capital GmbH*, Ludwigshafen
- *Boehringer Ingelheim: Labor BI X*
- *Deutsche Telekom*: *Hubraum*, Berlin
- *Gruner + Jahr: Greenhouse – Innovation*, Hamburg

- *Henkel: Henkel X*, Düsseldorf
- *Hyundai Motors: Cradle*, Tel Aviv
- *IKEA*: *Space 10*, Copenhagen
- *Merck*: *Innovation Center*, Darmstadt
- *Microsoft*: *Microsoft Accelerator*, San Francisco – Berlin
- *Procter & Gamble*: *Clay Street Project*, Cincinnati
- *SAP*: *SAP Innovation Center Network*, Berlin

All these **innovation engines** have one thing in common: they are mostly—also spatially—detached from the corporate headquarters and can (largely) lead a creative and cultural life of their own and develop their own DNA. In this way, new ideas can grow, even if they may threaten or destroy existing business activities in the long term (cf. Poguntke, 2019).

▶ **Food for Thought**
A particularly exciting task for the innovation engine is to develop ideas for a business model that would disrupt, i.e., destroy, the business model of its own performance engine. After all, the sentence applies:
If we don't create the thing that kills us—somebody else will!
Then it is already better if you recognize these ideas in your own company and apply them to further develop or replace the existing business model.
All these initiatives will only be successful if **full support from top management** is not only promised but, above all, lived—every day, and even when innovation projects fail. Especially then!
In addition, the incentive mechanisms must also be designed in such a way that courage is rewarded—even if courageous action does not always lead to success. Those who (unwaveringly) stick to the status quo and even—visibly or less visibly—boycott innovation processes should not be rewarded. Preventing this is also a **non-delegable top management task**.

> **Think Box: Questions You Should Ask Yourself**
> - Have you ever looked more closely at the concept of performance and innovation engines?
> - Which engine dominates your business?
> - What opportunities are there for you to build an innovation engine?
> - What resistance would you have to overcome?
> - What aspects suggest that the establishment of an innovation engine can succeed?
> - How could you manage the organizational dilemma that comes with the parallel operation of a performance engine and an innovation engine?

(continued)

- Are there promoters at the top management level to support such a step in the long run and also in case of failures?
- Have you already taken a closer look at the innovation engines of your competitors and of companies from other sectors?
- What conclusions could you draw from this analysis for your company?
- Who is driving such a topic forward in your company?

3.7.5 Installing a Chief Digital Officer

Paths are created by walking them!

In order to drive the overall process of digital transformation, **Chief Digital Officers** (CDO for short) are increasingly being hired today. The CDO is the top **digitalization officer of a company** and is responsible for the guidelines, the formulation of goals and the implementation of the digital transformation—together with the people responsible for the other company divisions. In this interaction, the CDO has the central role as an **impulse generator** to drive the transformation of traditional, analogue business models into future-oriented digital processes, offers, and business models. To give these tasks the necessary (hierarchical) weight, the CDO is part of the executive board (C-level). The CDO advises the executive board on issues of digital transformation and digitalization strategy.

Consequently, the **CDO** is the central **driver of the digital transformation**. His task is to always keep the profitability of the entire company and, above all, the customers in mind when further developing the corporate strategy. This is about creating a convincing (digital) customer experience so that customers remain loyal to the company in the long term. However, the CDO is not only the driver of the digital transformation, but also the **initiator, controller, and pilot of the transformation process**—always in close coordination and intensive cooperation with the specialist departments. In addition, the CDO takes the initiative and provides support for **internal digitalization** in order to introduce innovative technologies and methods and to promote more networked working within the company. The CDO exercises a **cross-sectional function** with all business and functional areas.

The CDO should also be a **disruptor** who acts entrepreneurially and strategically in the sense of the network organization, penetrates new sectors, and turns existing market standards upside down. The CDO is also the first point of **contact for the operational digitalization** of existing business areas. He should also be an important **facilitator of digital competencies** throughout the whole company. This role requires considerable diplomatic skill and can be a possible starting point towards a dual organizational design with a performance and an innovation engine (see Sect. 3.7.4).

The CDO acts as an **interface** between the CIO (Chief Information Officer) as well as the CMO/CSO (Chief Marketing Officer/Chief Sales Officer) and reports

Fig. 3.121 CDO as a networker

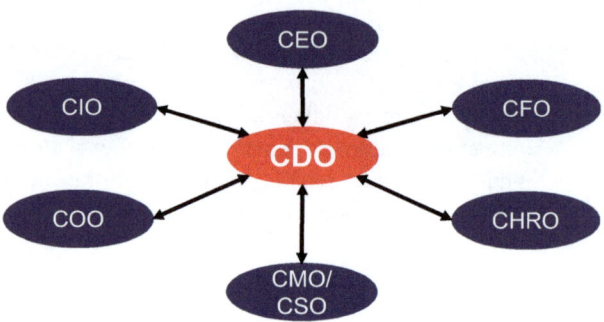

directly to the CEO. There is also close coordination between the CDO and the CHRO to prepare managers and employees for future tasks. With the COO, digitalization potentials in the company's operations are analyzed and raised. In dialogue with the CFO, all these concepts are screened for their financial implications (cf. Fig. 3.121).

What should the **qualification profile of a CDO** look like? The answers to this question were obtained from an evaluation of job advertisements for CDO positions (cf. Digital Magazin, 2021):

- Understanding of digital structures: 57%
- Strong communication skills: 54%
- Many years of management experience: 46%
- Fluent negotiation skills in English: 46%
- Assertiveness: 43%
- Strategic mindset: 43%

The same method was used to determine what the **core tasks of a CDO** are (cf. Digital Magazin, 2021):

- Digitization strategy planning: 57%
- Interface management: 54%
- (Further) development of digital business models: 43%
- Project management: 36%

Various questions arise when installing a CDO. On the one hand, a CDO seems indispensable as at least a **temporary option** in order to guide the change towards a digital organization as directly as possible from a suitable position and to be able to realize it successfully. On the other hand, with regard to future developments, it should be asked whether the CDO should or must remain **a regular member of the C-level in the long term**, because the digital transformation will never be over.

▶ **Food for Thought**
From my point of view, the question of a time limit for the tasks of a CDO does not really arise. Due to the ever-increasing digitization, the digital transformation is losing the character of a project—with a defined beginning and end.
The digital transformation is a process that begins once and will never end.

In order to fulfill the tasks described, a CDO must initiate various measures. These include the following **activities of a CDO**:

- **Establishing an innovation team**
  The CDO should bring together a **team of creative thinkers** and analysts to analyze relevant developments in their own company, in the market as well as in other sectors and evaluate them for usability for their own company. The tools necessary for this were presented in Chaps. 1, 2 and 3. A particularly important tool for the CDO is the analysis of digital business performance at the start of his activity and for the ongoing controlling of what has been achieved.

  One task of this innovation team is also **networking with start-ups, incubators, and accelerators** (see Sect. 3.7.3). In addition, **networking with innovation islands in the own company** must be ensured in order to bundle the creative processes. An **innovation engine** can also be installed for this purpose (see Sect. 3.7.4). It must be ensured that customers are involved in the creative process sufficiently early and comprehensively (see Sect. 3.5.3).

- **Agenda setting**
  Based on the insights gained, the core of the agenda setting is to set the central topics. The digital challenges and possible solutions must be communicated and discussed comprehensively and regularly within the company. The employees and managers must be prepared for the foreseeable changes through a **digital agenda**.

- **Drivers of the digital transformation—developing a road map**
  The CDO must continuously bring **energy into the transformation process** and try to win as many **like-minded people** as possible as **supporters**. A **network of transformers**—especially at the highest corporate level—is essential. Finally, enormous resistance emerges in the course of the transformation process, which must be consistently overcome (see Chap. 4).

  An important aspect here is **making new technologies available** as well as **conveying the knowledge** to make these technologies usable for one's own company. Therefore, the CDO must either be a **technology trend scout** himself—or have one in his innovation team.

  The **road map** should include, for example, the question of how **internal processes** can be made more efficient through digitalization. To this end, the prerequisites for structures or technologies that need to be created must be clarified. In **marketing and sales**, such a definition of a corresponding digital

strategy belongs right at the front of the road map. Here, it must be decided in which areas the customer journey is to be digitalized and which budgets are necessary for this. The processes of customer acquisition, customer retention, and customer recovery must also be assessed for their digitalization potential (see Sect. 3.5; cf. Kreutzer, 2021a, b).

Digitization potential must also be identified with regard to the company's own **products and services**. This includes the development of new digital products and services. These can either replace or complement existing offerings. In connection with this, **data management** must be further developed in order to provide the processes with the relevant information flows (see Sect. 3.4.2). In addition, the advantages that can be achieved by **digitizing the entire value chain** must be explored (see Sect. 3.3). This process step, too, can only be mastered through intensive cooperation with those responsible in the various areas.

A major task that can only be accomplished with the HR department is the necessary **development of know-how** and the **cultural change**. The CDO supports the development of a **digital training agenda** to provide employees and managers with the necessary know-how. An important step towards the necessary cultural change is the agenda setting described above.

To keep the process going, a **road map** with precise milestones for these tasks must be developed and continuously maintained. The board must continuously report on the completion of the defined milestones in order to permanently focus management attention on the transformation process.

Motto: The best time was 3 years ago. The second-best time is today!

- **Developing a digital, customer-centric ecosystem or a corresponding platform**
  A core task of the CDO is to explore the possibilities of building a digital, customer-centric ecosystem or platforms. This can be done either alone or in collaboration with other key service providers. A company may also have to be content with only being a service provider for the ecosystems or platforms of other operators (see Sects. 3.3.2 and 3.3.3).

- **Economic analysis of the digital transformation**
  An indispensable prerequisite for acceptance of a CDO is a consistent **analysis of the economic effects of transformation processes**—especially in the performance engine. The existing, but especially new digital business models as well as innovative products and services must be analyzed for their economic viability. In addition, the economic effects that can be achieved through the digitalization of processes and structures must be examined on an ongoing basis. This requires comprehensive cooperation with the CFO and the entire controlling department.

  With regard to the innovation engine, on the other hand, the CDO has the task of avoiding a too strong and too early **fixation on the profitability of innovation projects**, because otherwise many ideas that are only promising in the long term would be stopped too early.

3.7 Organizational Concepts for the Digital Age

To meet these challenges, a **CDO** must fulfill a very **demanding qualification profile**. These include—often after an intensive training phase in the company—above all the following skills:

- Extensive business know-how
- Solid IT knowledge and technical understanding
- Broad knowledge of the different service areas of the company
- Ability to develop and evaluate digital business models
- Comprehensive methodological know-how
- Experience in transformation processes
- Strong communication skills to communicate and work in an open, transparent, non-hierarchical, agile, and collaborative manner
- Resilience and assertiveness to be able to overcome the manifold resistances

A look at the **qualification profile of a CDO** shows what high expectations an applicant for such a position must fulfill. During an assignment as a CDO, many things can be learned anew. However, a CDO must have strong communication skills, resilience, and assertiveness right from the start in order to have a high chance of success.

Storytelling
In a company I accompanied in the process of digital transformation, a freshly installed CDO was also active. He was a **terrific thinker** and had the necessary **mental power** to drive the company forward. However, he only had a secretary and an assistant and could only have a very limited effect from a **position of lacking in-house power**.

Opponents at the top management level, some of whom had already spent many decades in the company, were always able to erect new **barriers** to **stop the transformation process**. Since those involved were simultaneously warming up for the replacement of the CEO, the imperative intensive cooperation did not take place either.

In such a constellation, important external impulses meet with a high level of understanding, but are nevertheless often not implemented—for the sake of one's own career goals!

▶ **Food for Thought**
CDOs are often particularly smart thinkers who can stringently analyze the challenges to be met and convincingly develop promising solutions. However, for a CDO to be able to put his "horsepower" on the road, he must also be equipped with budget and staff.

Since CDOs are often "bought in" externally, they usually lack the power to break up existing structures and processes. A lack of in-house power can be compensated for either by transferring responsibility for IT and/or production, or by sustained and clearly visible support from the CEO.

Without such comprehensive support, a CDO runs the risk of failing in the process of digital transformation.

> **Think Box: Questions You Should Ask Yourself**
> - Is a CDO already installed in your company?
> - What resources does he or she have (staff and budget)?
> - Does your CDO have the necessary in-house power and/or CEO support to be able to successfully act forward even in the face of resistance?
> - Have you already thought about installing a Chief Digital Officer as your company's top digitalization officer?
> - Who has been the central driver of digital transformation in your company so far?
> - Or does such a person not exist?
> - What tasks do you see for a CDO in your company?
> - What would the qualification profile of a CDO look like for your company?
> - Does a team of creative thinkers and analysts already exist in your company to manage the digital transformation?
> - Who is responsible for agenda setting at your company and what position does digital transformation occupy there?
> - Is there a road map for the transformation process?
> - Who regularly deals with profitability analysis of the digital transformation?
> - Who examines such questions in your company?

3.8 Controlling for the Digital Age

It also applies to the digital age:
You can only manage what you can also measure!

It is still the **core task of controlling** to **transform** operational and strategic **goals into key figures for control and management systems**. These systems make an indispensable contribution to ensuring that employees and managers can fulfill their tasks—in a goal-oriented manner (cf. Caviezel, 2020, p. 103). The digital age has not changed this task.

However, two questions arise for **controlling in the digital age**. On the one hand, it is about the content orientation of controlling and thus about the **transformation of the controlling self-image** in order to optimally support the process of digital transformation. On the other hand, it is about the **digitalization of the controlling activities** themselves. Both areas are examined below.

3.8.1 Controlling as an Enabler of Digital Transformation

Control is good, trust is better?

3.8.1.1 Self-Conception of Controlling in the Digital Age
In the course of **transforming the controlling self-image**, the following steps must be taken (cf. Schönbohm & Egle, 2017, pp. 224–226; Schönbohm & Dymke, 2020) to support the achievement of digital excellence:

- **Controller as "navigator of the digital transformation"**
  In this concept, the controller's understanding of his role must be adapted to the new challenges so that controllers are involved as creative and critical partners in the digital transformation. In this context, controllers should not trigger new battles over competencies, but rather contribute to the **pacification of a goal-oriented cooperation** between the Chief Marketing Officer (CMO), Chief Sales Officer (CSO), Chief Information Officer (CIO), Chief Financial Officer (CFO), Chief Digital Officer (CDO), Chief Human Resources Officer (CHRO), and the Chief Executive Officer (CEO). With a **comprehensive, silo-transcending supply of information** across departmental boundaries, the controller can make an important contribution to successful digital transformation.
- **Developing competences in strategic controlling**
  The **competence profile of the controller** must be realigned in the course of the digital transformation in many companies. **Budgeting** and **cost accounting** remain indispensable core tasks of controlling. However, it is also important to constructively accompany the **development and evaluation of new (digital) business models and new products and services**.
  For this purpose, controlling has to implement two different orientations. With regard to the **performance engine**, hard KPIs are to be continuously checked in order to support a value creating corporate management of the existing business model. At the same time, with regard to the activities of the **innovation engine**, softer criteria must be applied so that new ideas are not nipped in the bud by elaborate requirements for business plans to be submitted. These aspects must be taken into account when defining relevant key figures.
  The innovation engine is also primarily about supporting the **identification of weak signals**. These so-called weak signals indicate relevant changes and structural breaks at an early stage. The earlier **crisis symptoms** or **new business opportunities** are recognized, the more options there are for action. Recognizing and evaluating these becomes an important additional task of controlling. Then **dangers for the business model or the company** as a whole can be averted or **profitable market fields** can be developed before competitors.
- **Rounding off the key figures used**
  In controlling, a large number of strategic and operational indicators are already used today to present relevant information in a condensed form to the key players. Since the effects of digitalization are often no longer limited to individual functional areas, specific indicators need to be developed that reflect such

interrelationships and interdependencies. The management of the digital transformation requires a **multidimensional control system** that integrates qualitative and quantitative indicators simultaneously.

Which key figures should be used here depends on the business model, the size of the company, and the achieved development phase. In any case, it is important that the controllers are familiar with (future) business models, digital ecosystems, and platform concepts and develop suitable key figures for evaluation.

To what extent has such a **transformation of the controlling self-image** already taken place? In many companies there was or still is a more or less strict **separation between strategic and operational management**. In line with this, a **separation between strategic and operational controlling** is often made. This resulted—almost inevitably—in a **strict division of labor** between the processes of strategy development, its operationalization and implementation, and controlling. Accordingly, cooperation was very much focused on quarterly rhythms and on the key data of the budget and planning process (cf. KPMG, 2018, p. 7).

Such a **filleting of the tasks of planning, implementation, and controlling** no longer meets today's market requirements. Instead, the tasks associated with these activities must be interlinked in an **agile process** in order to be able to act quickly and soundly. Controlling the achievement of goals and compliance with budgets are still important. However, the speed at which these processes have to be carried out has changed. Due to the increasing dynamics in the market, corresponding analyses can no longer be carried out on a monthly or quarterly basis. More and more frequently, **project-accompanying evaluations** have to be carried out in order to be able to make necessary corrections as quickly as possible. With comprehensively digitalized processes, **results can be determined in real time** and corrections can be made in real time. Here, the controller can become an **advisor for strategic interventions**, the number of which will increase in the digital age.

In the future, the CFO and his team will be measured by how successfully the entire company supports the achievement of the following **goals in the course of a digital transformation** (cf. Deloitte, 2021, KPMG, 2018, p. 8):

- **Company-wide consolidation and evaluation of central information streams** to enable a holistic and consolidated data view of the entire company and its service areas (incl. **ensuring data integrity and compliance** in the company).
- Bringing in additional **data insights** for decision-making on strategic challenges.
- Use of **predictive analytics** based on small and big data.
- **Shortening of planning phases**, sometimes combined with a significant increase in the level of detail in planning.
- **Faster, interconnected, and pervasive responsiveness** to avert risks as well as exploit identified opportunities.
- **Management of end-to-end business processes** as well as in the **adaptation of standardized processes** to changing business requirements.

- **Increased transparency regarding important business and market developments**—also across different hierarchical levels to avoid information silos.
- **Reduction of the information gap** in order to promote motivation and creativity of all employees and managers.
- **Greater degree of visualization of information** in standard reporting and exploratory analyses to make relevant developments more easily accessible to non-data specialists (cf. Hofer et al., 2020).

In order to cope with these tasks, **lifelong learning** is also required for the controller. This primarily involves the acquisition of additional skills in statistics, artificial intelligence, visualization, modelling, and interpretation of data. In addition, the controller should increasingly see himself as a **coach for the departments,** providing important impulses for the transformation process with his expertise. Here, the controller can make an important contribution to overcoming the silo mentality that still exists.

In this context, the question also arises as to whether a **Chief Financial Officer** (CFO) should be installed to achieve the aforementioned goals. Such a C-level function takes controlling out of a "supporting function." It positions controlling as an indispensable "strategic partner" in top management. Such a central role falls to controlling especially in the course of the digital transformation of business models. If the CFO is also responsible for the **value creation of the company** and supports its creation through comprehensive operational and strategic transparency, a positioning at the C-level is appropriate (cf. Becker et al., 2020).

This raises the question of what the **competence profile of a CFO** should be. A distinction can be made between being allowed, wanting, being able, and knowing (cf. Becker et al., 2020, pp. 388–392). If controlling in the form of a CFO is located at the C-level, the **degree to which it is allowed to do** so is already defined to a large extent by the hierarchical position. To ensure a comprehensive digital transformation to achieve digital excellence, the CFO must also have the corresponding **will**. After all, there is a wide range of resistance to overcome during the transformation process. With regard to **skills**—similar to other executives—the ability to be a convincing communicator is required in addition to the indispensable **knowledge**. Such a competence profile—in combination with a corresponding mindset—predestines the CFO to be another **value creator and change agent** at the top management level (cf. Becker et al., 2020, pp. 388–392).

In the next sections it becomes clear that controlling—regardless of its hierarchical positioning—must comprehensively expand its **toolbox** in order to comprehend, plan, and control the opportunities and risks of the digital transformation at an early stage and in a holistic manner. Here, the managers responsible for controlling must learn to think and act holistically in (digital) business models and digital ecosystems. Only then can they accompany management in all phases of digitalization as a **critical and constructive pilot** at the same time (cf. Schönbohm & Egle, 2017, p. 233).

The establishment and development of a balanced scorecard is an important prerequisite for this (see Sect. 3.8.1.6). In order to be effective, the KPIs used here should be developed free of any silo mentality and continuously reviewed for their value contributions. **Controlling as a learning system then equally fertilizes the entire company as an overarching, learning system.**

In your **learning organization**, you should work towards identifying the respective causes—without ideological blinkers—in the case of both target achievement and target failure and take them into account in the subsequent planning process. Only then can you "objectively" determine whether planning premises were inaccurate, competitor activities were over- or undervalued or market potentials were wrongly assessed. You must succeed in clearly identifying and documenting the **causes of success and failure** so that these can be incorporated into future planning processes. Only then can the results achieved improve from planning round to planning round. The informational creation of **closed impact cycles** is indispensable for achieving digital excellence.

In order to achieve these closed circles of action, a **goal-oriented condensation of information** is required, for which controlling is indispensable. In detail, the following five characteristics can be distinguished with their respective core questions, which are discussed in more detail below:

- **Reporting:** What happened?
- **Analyze:** Why did it happen?
- **Monitoring:** What happens right now?
- **Prediction:** What will happen?
- **Prescription:** What should happen?

A major challenge is to make such information available—precisely and on time—for mobile access as well. So far, **mobile devices and apps** have not been widely used in controlling. However, you should sound out the corresponding needs of your target groups in order to make the relevant **key figures of the controlling and management systems** also available **on the move**. In doing so, you must take into account not only the expectations of the users but also the relevant security requirements and the IT solutions required for this. A convincing **mobile controlling solution** can only be developed in cooperation between controlling, IT, and the respective departments (cf. Nunkesser & Thorn, 2020).

3.8.1.2 Reporting

Reporting is about the question: "**What happened?**" Reporting is understood as internal, regular, and often standardized information for employees and managers. The focus of management reporting is to provide managers with success-relevant information.

With regard to the phenomena to be recognized early or—better—to be avoided, a distinction must be made between crisis stages and crisis symptoms (cf. Fig. 3.122; cf. Hohberger & Damlachi, 2019, p. 42). In the case of **crisis stages**, the readiness for fire ranges from a stakeholder crisis to a sales crisis to the threat of insolvency. Among the **crisis symptoms** that can lead to such crisis stages, attention should be

3.8 Controlling for the Digital Age

Fig. 3.122 Crisis stages and crisis symptoms

paid to blockades of important stakeholders, insufficient utilization of production capacity, and cash flow slumps. This task has always been part of the core area of controlling. However, corresponding crisis stages can occur much faster today—and as the Corona pandemic shows—also globally. In order to increase the company's reaction speed, the supply of information by controlling must be optimized in many cases!

Contents of a **reporting for marketing and sales** are the various success indicators that provide an overview of how well the various campaigns have worked. In order to **keep track of customer relevant changes**, the use of the so-called **dashboards** is useful. An example of a **marketing management dashboard** is shown in Fig. 3.123.

This **dashboard** clearly shows that region A falls well short of the target for **new customer acquisition**. The **churn rate** is also far above the target value. In contrast, the **loyalty rate** has improved significantly. The average number of **friend referrals** has also increased. Critically, the **newsletter subscribers** have not reached the target value. In contrast, the **average turnover** and **gross margin** per customer are above target. At the same time, however, there is a significantly higher **rate of bad**. If the traffic lights are on "yellow" or especially on "red," a more in-depth root cause analysis must be carried out. When the light is "green," it can be determined which measures have led to this improvement. In each individual case, it is important to learn and optimize.

Another important report can be devoted to the question of how comprehensively the **CRM database** is filled with relevant information. Here we speak of a **filling level report**. It evaluates the extent to which the characteristics defined as necessary are present in the addresses contained in the database. The basic structure is shown in Fig. 3.124. This shows how successful the company has been in **collecting data** and

Region A	Estimate	Actual	Evaluation
Customer acquisition quote (new customers in the last 3 months) – measured by the whole customer base	10 %	9 %	🟡
Churn rate (not purchased in the last 6 months) – measured by the whole customer base	7 %	12 %	🔴
Loyality quote (share of repeat customers within 3 months) – measured by the number of loyality card customers	25 %	28 %	🟢
Share of friend & family referrals per customer– measured by the whole customer base	0,5	0,7	🟢
Share of customers that signed up for the newsletter – measured by the whole customer base	22 %	19 %	🔴
Amount of an average sale – measured by the whole customer base	68 €	74 €	🟢
Gross-margin per customer	25 €	28 €	🟢
Rate of bad debts within online-shop – measured by the whole customer base	0.5 %	1 %	🔴
...			

Fig. 3.123 Management dashboard for customer reporting—region A, third quarter

Feature	Filling level (in %)
Last name	100
First name	85
Date of birth	62
Address origin	49
Creation date	100
Marital state	32
Income group	16
Car ownership	27
Living situation	34
E-mail permission	21
Telephone permission	9
Permission for push notifications	56
Permission for geo localisation	78
Permission for access to pictures	14
Permission for access to data	23
...	...

Fig. 3.124 Filling level report

obtaining permissions in the past. These permissions are of great importance for the digitalization of the customer journey (see Sect. 3.5.1).

Based on the insights gained through a filling level report, measures can be derived that aim to systematically obtain the information and permissions that are considered particularly relevant. If it is not possible to obtain the necessary **information through direct dialogue with customers** (first party data), further information can be generated by entering into partnerships or joint actions with other companies (second party data). The possibilities of **address enrichment** already mentioned can provide further important characteristics (third party data; see Sect. 3.4.2; in more detail Kreutzer, 2021a, pp. 107–112).

3.8.1.3 Analytics: Real Time Analytics

However, you cannot stop at describing the status quo, but must get to the bottom of developments. Therefore, **analyses** focus on the question "**Why did it happen?**". To find appropriate answers to this question, you can carry out **customer value analyses** as well as **penetration analyses** and **analyses of the market sales area**. You should pay special attention to **customer structure analyses** (cf. Kreutzer, 2021a, p. 133f.).

A **customer structure analysis** can be seen in Fig. 3.125. On the left side is a breakdown of corporate customers according to their number of employees. It shows that more than half of the customers have between 50 and 100 employees. This is the description of the status quo.

Much more meaningful, however, is the **analysis of the development of the customer structure** over time, which can be seen in Fig. 3.125 on the right. To determine this, a **cohort evaluation** is used. **Cohorts** (i.e., groups) are formed for this purpose. In this case, the grouping is based on the year in which the customers were newly acquired. This shows that the company under investigation has acquired

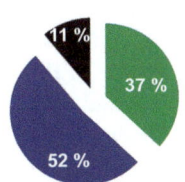

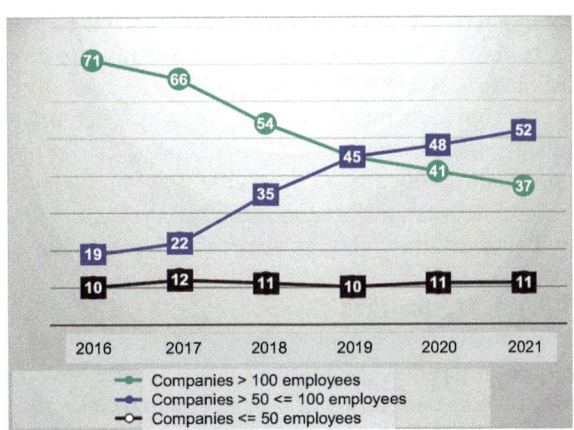

Fig. 3.125 Customer analysis results—for the entire company and on a cohort basis

fewer and fewer large customers over time and has been more successful with medium-sized companies. The results of an analysis on an annual basis are much more relevant for the orientation of the company's strategy than a purely average view at the present time. Based on the additional knowledge gained, the company can now examine whether this development was intentional or whether other factors led to the lack of acquisition success with large companies.

▶ **Storytelling** We conducted such a cohort analysis for an innovative **telecommunications service provider**. Only now did we realize that the company initially acquired mostly men as customers, but that in the meantime over 70% of new customers were women. This development was not known to the management before!

Today, **real time analytics** are of particular importance. This means the analysis of data as soon as it is available. The responsible managers receive insights into the results achieved immediately or very quickly after the data enters their system and can draw conclusions on this basis. Real time analysis makes it possible to react to ongoing developments without delay. In comparison, with the previously dominant **batch analysis**, it often takes not only hours but even days and weeks until important results are available. In this way, important findings were often only obtained after the fact. In contrast, real time analytics allow relevant findings to be obtained virtually in sync with ongoing developments and—assuming agile management—to react to them quickly.

Such **real time analyses** are relevant for **creditworthiness checks**. Here it is important to react very promptly, especially to emerging deteriorations in creditworthiness, in order not to have to write off receivables later. Current improvements in creditworthiness can be a decisive trigger to enter into a business relationship now—possibly from competitors (cf. Kreutzer, 2021a, pp. 126–128).

Due to the particular relevance of R&D activities for the digital transformation, a so-called **R&D audit** should be carried out regularly—initiated by controlling. This can provide systematic support in setting the right priorities in the R&D area—and in saying goodbye to unsuccessful activities (cf. Fig. 3.126).

In addition to the analysis of successfully and unsuccessfully completed projects, the planned **R&D activities** should also be critically examined. Perhaps this will also identify projects that should be divested. Then the measures described in Fig. 2.12 (disinvestment, shutdown or divestment) can be initiated. At the same time, new opportunities open up to invest the freed-up budgets in more promising projects.

An important task of innovative controlling is to support the various departments in their work through new analytical concepts and methods.

3.8.1.4 Monitoring

Monitoring is the process of finding answers to the question "**What is happening now?**" Monitoring stands for the direct, systematic observation, recording and thus monitoring of processes and developments. The objective of monitoring is to intervene in the ongoing process on the basis of the knowledge gained, if critical developments become apparent.

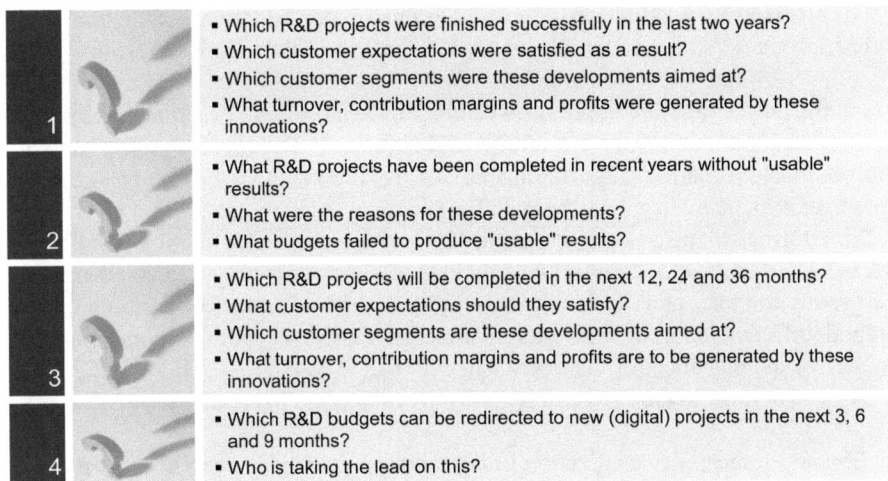

Fig. 3.126 R&D audit to identify potential for improvement in R&D spending

In the case of **online marketing measures**, it is particularly easy to observe—often in real time—how many recipients of an e-mail newsletter open it and which links are clicked on. The activities on one's own website can also be monitored continuously. Of particular interest are the activities in one's own online shop. In ongoing marketing campaigns, it can be determined which products are viewed, placed in the shopping basket and then purchased or not purchased (cf. Kreutzer, 2021b).

Social media monitoring, in which you monitor the activities in social media, is of particular importance here. This monitoring is done with regard to the publicly accessible area of social networks as well as forums, communities, and blogs. You can use a **newsroom** (see Sect. 3.7.2) to determine how intensively people are talking about topics relevant to you. This could be questions about new fashion trends or concepts of pollution avoidance. The social media monitoring should pay special attention to the posts that are placed on *Twitter* or *Facebook*. The easiest way to do this is to install a *Google Alert* for the most important terms (your own company name, your brands—and competitors' names, if applicable). You can also monitor who is currently talking about your own company, your own offers, and/or employees and where—in order to enter into a dialogue if necessary (cf. Kreutzer & Sirrenberg, 2019, pp. 161–164; Kreutzer, 2021b).

Through **customer monitoring**, critical developments can be identified at an early stage and acted upon accordingly. This could be a deterioration in the consumer's credit rating. As soon as such a signal is present, the online shop should check the open invoices and, if necessary, switch to more secure payment methods. However, changes may also become apparent that indicate additional sales potential. This can be family offspring, which can lead to a variety of additional purchases. This is where the transition to real time analytics becomes visible (see Sect. 3.8.1.3).

Monitoring in production is becoming even more important in the context of industrial automation and intelligent manufacturing of the future (keyword "smart factories"). In many cases, a **smart factory** offers an intelligent solution for monitoring the production line based on AI and IOT technologies. This makes it possible to monitor production from a central **live dashboard**. The corresponding tools for this use machine learning algorithms that can also predict machine failures (keyword "predictive maintenance," see Sect. 3.3.1.3).

Monitoring can also be used to control the **systems of value chains** described in Sect. 3.3.1 worldwide. Appropriate solutions allow manufacturers to connect multiple production lines and machines, collect data at different stages of production from several different sources, and enable functions such as remote monitoring and predictive maintenance (cf. the companies in Sect. 3.3.4).

A **production dashboard** can help drive efficiencies in production processes:

- Demand forecasts (visualization of demand—promptly or even in real time)
- Capacity planning
- Prediction of possible bottlenecks in the supply chain
- Automated product routing—based on foreseeable bottlenecks in procurement, production, storage, and/or distribution logistics
- Production-related detection of anomalies and symptoms indicating possible equipment failures
- Predictive maintenance
- Intelligent ticketing systems to track problems
- Instant notifications on mobile devices for immediate response and resolution of problems
- Automated root cause analysis for faster traceability and resolution of issues
- Remote troubleshooting
- Digital twins to optimize production
- Production monitoring with predictive analytics
- Detect suspicious events or system abuse.

The range of application areas shown in production already leads in part to the areas of prediction and prescription.

3.8.1.5 Predictions/Predictive Analytics and Prescription

Predictions about future behavior are of great importance. Today, this is referred to as **predictive analytics**. In marketing and sales, it is about **predicting the future behavior of prospects and customers**. The following questions can be at the center of this:

- Which customers should be invited to the next event because they have the highest sales or contribution margin potential?
- For which customers is it worthwhile to send a special catalogue because further online or offline purchases are expected?

- Which customers should only be sent an e-mail, which a postcard and which a (personal) letter?
- Which churned customers should be attempted to win back?
- Which members of a customer loyalty program will respond particularly well to the 10% coupons?
- With which customer segments will a cross-sell push be particularly successful?
- Which customers will be highly compliant with a friend referral request?

The knowledge gained from the described measures now leads through recommendations, specifications, and **prescriptions** to the decisive question: "**What should happen?**" In the development of such guidelines, the following contents are central:

- Customer A is offered an attractive package because there is a very high probability that this customer will cancel the contract at the end of the month.
- Customer B of a customer club receives a 20% coupon for activation (10% coupons were not successful with this customer in the past).
- Customer C is excluded from the customer dialogue because as a troubleshooter he only causes problems.
- Customer D has a high influencer potential and from now on will be especially courted through VIP support.
- Sporadic donor E receives the large acquisition package because it is highly likely that he can be developed into a permanent donor.
- Customer F receives a cross-sell push.
- Customer G is approached with a request to become active as a referrer.
- Customer H is offered an additional loan because of his good credit rating.

> **Memory Box**
> In the future, more and more data will be available, faster and cheaper. In the future, competitive advantages will be developed—even more so than before—by powerful algorithms.

3.8.1.6 Balanced Scorecard for the Digital Transformation

The proven financial indicators remain valid in the process of digital transformation. However, they must be supplemented by new KPIs (Key Performance Indicators). For this purpose, the instrument of the **balanced scorecard** must be further developed—aligned with the digital vision or mission (cf. Fig. 3.127). Accordingly, goals in the form of **key performance indicators for the digital transformation** should be defined at the company level and then broken down to the various company divisions. The following questions can help with the definition:

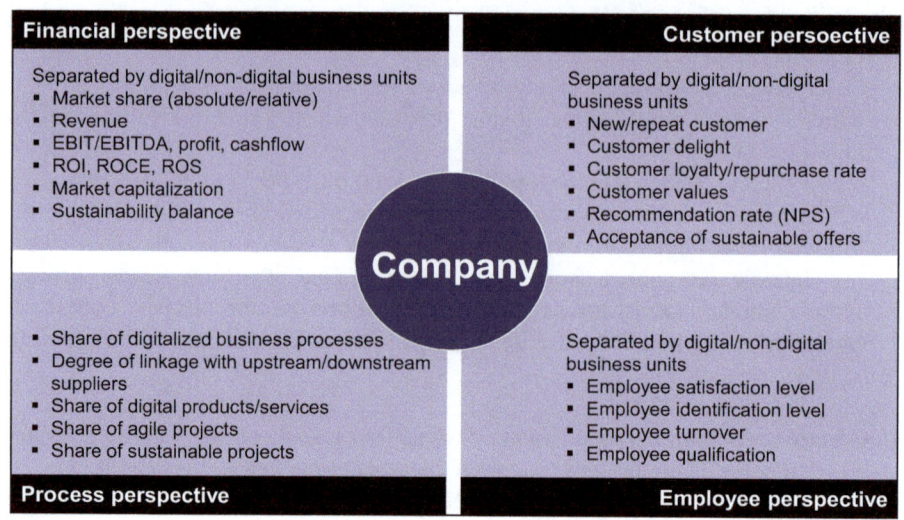

Fig. 3.127 Balanced scorecard for analyzing a company's performance

- **Financial perspective**
  How do we want to document our financial success to our shareholders? In this context—not only for digital companies—the scope of intangible investments, e.g., for software, patents, trademark rights, professional development, investments in organizational development, which are not reflected in classic KPIs, should also be reported.
- **Customer perspective**
  How do we want to measure the extent to which we convince customers with our business model, products, and services when implementing our vision?
- **Process perspective**
  How do we want to determine which processes are efficient and effective and whether they are already exploiting the potential of digitalization?
- **Employee perspective**
  How will we determine whether our employees and managers are convinced of our vision and whether they are actively involved in its implementation?

Such a **balanced scorecard** can also be used to define central corporate goals for the digital transformation. The **goal-setting process** ensures that several company-relevant perspectives are simultaneously taken into account in the transformation process at the highest company level. In this way, it can be achieved that the customer and employee perspectives are not played off against each other. Trade-offs become visible and can be dealt with in a targeted manner.

The challenges outlined in Chap. 1 have an impact not only on the processes, but also on the content of controlling activities. If the **ESG criteria** (environment, social, governance) described there are to be taken into account in corporate controlling, they must be reflected not only in the balanced scorecard, but also in a **triple bottom line**. The **triple bottom line approach** helps your company to ensure that its activities are sustainable. This is based on the following three pillars (cf. Elkington, 1999):

- Economy (the classic bottom-line)
- Ecology
- Social

If you expand the classic bottom line, which is oriented towards commercial success, to include the areas of ecology and social issues, you can orient your company—based on goals—towards **acting in a more sustainable way**. Here it is important to clarify whether the three pillars of entrepreneurial success are on an equal footing or whether there is a **superordination or a subordination**. The question has a direct impact on the **handling of conflicting goals**, which are unavoidable here.

In the **modified (economic) triple bottom line**, the economic dimension comes first. The social and ecological goals are subordinated to the economic goal. In the **classic triple bottom line**, sustainable action only results when economic, ecological, and social goals are pursued with equal priority (cf. Steinke et al., 2014).

The **triple bottom line approach** aims to ensure the **guiding principle of "sustainable entrepreneurial action"** through a corresponding orientation of controlling. **Sustainability** is to be understood here in the sense that the needs of the present generation are met in such a way that future generations can meet their own needs in a comparable manner. It is about ensuring long-term survival on earth—and not just for humans! Sustainability is about **justice between generations**. An even more far-reaching aspiration would be to "hand over" the world to the next generation in a better condition than one has "taken over" it oneself. However, we are currently far from such an ideal!

▶ **Food for Thought**
If you have developed a powerful **vision** for your company whose **purpose** also includes aspects of sustainability, you can support this focus through controlling activities. However, even an inspiring vision and a compelling purpose are no substitute for a clear **quantification of the goals to be striven for** in order to be able to systematically check their achievement. Neither an inspiring vision nor a compelling purpose is sufficient for the survival of the company if it is not managed profitably.

The entrepreneurial sub-goals identified within the balanced scorecard must be backed up with programs of measures in the **planning process** to ensure that the goals are achieved. For each sub-goal, it must be regularly checked whether the company will achieve it. If necessary, additional measures must be introduced in the current business year to ensure this. Due to the documentation of the goals within a scorecard, possible interactions with other goals can be checked at an early stage. Since the "digital clock" runs much faster than in the analogue age, these **interim checks** are particularly important. In addition, on a monthly or quarterly basis and consolidated at the end of the business year, the balanced scorecard should be used to check whether you are on track with the defined goals. The need for action becomes visible at the highest level of the company.

Think Box: Questions You Should Ask Yourself
- What is the self-image of your controlling today?
- Do your controllers see themselves as "navigators of the digital transformation"?
- Has further competence development already taken place in strategic controlling?
- Does your controlling have different evaluation grids ready for the evaluation of the performance and the innovation engine?
- Is your controlling geared towards identifying weak signals in order to recognize opportunities and risks for business models at an early stage?
- Has your company already overcome the filleting of the tasks of planning, implementation, and controlling?
- Which goals dominate the strategic controlling activities of your company today?
  - Is it about the company-wide consolidation and evaluation of central information flows?
  - Are data integrity and compliance to be ensured in the company?
  - Are predictive analytics based on small and big data expected?
  - Is end-to-end business process management envisaged?
  - Is a shortening of planning phases targeted?
  - Is the company's responsiveness to be increased?
  - Is the focus on increasing transparency with regard to important company and market developments?
  - Is the aim to reduce the information gap?
  - Is a stronger visualization of information to be achieved?
- Is a Chief Financial Officer installed in your company?
- Would such a function be appropriate because controlling sees itself as a "strategic partner" of top management and acts accordingly?
- Does controlling contribute sustainably to the value creation of the company?
- Are mobile devices and apps already used in controlling in your company?
- What are the expectations of the departments?
- How well is your controlling set up in terms of reporting?
- Are the corresponding needs of the departments regularly surveyed?
- To what extent are real time analytics or real time analyses already being carried out?
- Where do you see a need for urgent optimization?

(continued)

- Do you regularly use an R&D audit?
- How efficient is your social media monitoring?
- How successfully have you used monitoring in production, including predictive maintenance?
- How good are you at predictive analytics?
- How strongly do your controlling systems support recommendations, targets, and prescriptions?
- Do you use a balanced scorecard?
- Is your balanced scorecard aligned with digital transformation?
- Do you take ESG (environment, social, governance) criteria into account in your results reporting?
- Do you follow a triple bottom line approach?
- Who initiates such processes for you?

3.8.2 Digitalization of the Controlling Itself

Technology changes—economic laws don't!

The **basic concepts of controlling** remain valid even in a digitalized organization. Nevertheless, the question arises as to which digitalization potentials need to be raised in controlling itself. It should be noted that important "homework" must first be done before digitization can take place. This includes a **convincing, company-wide data management** in order to establish a so-called **single point of truth** (see Sect. 3.4.2). Parallel to this is the **standardization of controlling processes** themselves in order to reduce friction and information loss. Such a concern can be sustainably promoted by the **introduction of an ERP system** (ERP stands for Enterprise Resource Planning). All in all, this creates the conditions for the use of further innovative technologies in controlling (cf. Keimer & Egle, 2020, pp. 6–14).

Section 3.4.3 has already highlighted the great importance of artificial intelligence for many companies. With regard to controlling, it is necessary to examine what exciting fields of application **artificial intelligence** has in this area itself. After all, AI-supported systems can already take over controlling tasks today—24/7, without holiday entitlement and sick days!

Repetitive and time-consuming tasks offer a particularly exciting **field of application for AI applications**. For these, the so-called **robotic process automation** can be increasingly used in the future. This technology supports the entire process from data collection to data preparation and consolidation to preparation as reports and a basis for decision-making (possibly even including recommendations for action).

Through the so-called **cognitive computing**, artificial intelligence opens up further interesting fields of application in controlling in addition to the automation of processes (cf. Grund et al., 2020, p. 14f.). AI systems increasingly make it possible to evaluate data in a form that was previously reserved for human intelligence. In many cases, the applications even go beyond this. Self-learning systems can discover previously unknown patterns in the data and in this way directly promote the creation of knowledge. Such **cognitive insights** can support controllers in an increasingly comprehensive way in assessing the situation, analyzing causes, making predictions as well as making decisions themselves.

The challenge for the design of the use of **AI in controlling** is to achieve optimal cooperation between the human performers and the AI systems. In this context, the boundaries of what tasks can be shifted towards AI will increasingly shift in favor of the AI systems. The controllers themselves can concentrate more on the "human" aspects of their tasks, which primarily require empathy and thus also emotional intelligence—for example, in the communication of insights. The AI applications can take over the time- and labor-intensive processes of data preparation and data evaluation. Tools such as **predictive planning, self-service reporting,** and the use of **digital assistants** specifically geared towards controlling will take over many of these tasks.

This can free up controlling capacities that are becoming increasingly indispensable for overarching, **strategically important issues** in the digital age. In this way, controlling—oriented to a corresponding self-image—can comprehensively help in the analysis of strategic challenges and use the methods that were presented above all in Chap. 2. This makes controlling a **driver and supporter of the digital transformation**, as discussed in Sect. 3.8.1.1.

You should carefully examine which areas of controlling in your company should be supported first by digital technologies. In doing so, you can and should concentrate on the "low hanging fruits"—measures with a high level of effectiveness with a limited use of resources! In this way, you can also build up ever greater acceptance for new technologies.

> **Memory Box**
> Every controller is well advised to familiarize himself comprehensively with the **fields of application of digital technologies**. Due to the high data-heaviness of many controlling tasks, controlling represents a particularly suitable field of application for (AI-supported) digital technologies.

> **Think Box: Questions You Should Ask Yourself**
> - What importance do you attach to artificial intelligence in controlling?
> - Can you already use robotic process automation today—or do you see starting points for this in the near future?
> - What opportunities does cognitive computing offer you in controlling?
> - Where can you gain particularly valuable cognitive insights?

(continued)

- Are there interesting fields of application for predictive planning, self-service reporting, and/or digital assistants in your controlling?
- Are your controllers on the way to becoming consultants for strategic interventions?
- Are your controllers willing to invest in lifelong learning?
- Do your controllers see themselves as coaches for the departments today or tomorrow?
- Where do you see the most exciting opportunities for an interaction of controlling activities and digital technologies?
- Who is responsible for these issues?

Literature

Accenture. (2020). *Weltmarktführer von morgen, TOP500-Studie Deutschland, Neue Ökosysteme in den Industrien – Wertschöpfungsketten neu gedacht*, Kronberg.
Adobe. (2019) *Unternehmenskultur und fehlende Technologien bremsen deutsche Marken bei der Customer Experience aus.* Accessed 12.10.2020, from https://www.adobe-newsroom.de/2019/11/12/unternehmenskultur-und-fehlende-technologien-bremsen-deutsche-marken-bei-der-customerexperience-aus/
Agarwal, N. K. (2015). Towards a definition of serendipity in information behaviour. *Information Research, 20*(3), paper 675. Accessed 8.10.2020, from http://InformationR.net/ir/20-3/pape675.html
Alibaba. (2021). *Global Trade starts here.* Accessed 2.1.2021, from https://www.alibaba.com
Alsamawi, F. (2018). *Digitale Innovation bei Amazon – warum Working Backwards ein Muss ist.* Accessed 22.9.2020, from https://www.management-circle.de/blog/warum-working-backwards-ein-muss-ist/
Alter, U. (2019). *Teamidentität, Teamentwicklung und Führung, Wir-Gefühl am Arbeitsplatz ermöglichen – das Potenzial des Teams nutzen* (2nd ed.). Springer Gabler.
Alternus. (2021) *Die Denkwerkstatt der Personalentwicklung von morgen.* Accessed 2.1.2021, from https://www.alternus.de/PE-innovation-lab.170.0.html
Amazon. (2020). *Come build the future with us.* Accessed 21.9.2020, from https://www.amazon.jobs/en/working/working-amazon
Amazon. (2021a). *Amazon Halo.* Accessed 7.1.2021, from https://www.amazon.com/Amazon-Halo-Fitness-And-Health-Band/dp/B07QK955LS?th=1
Amazon. (2021b). *Amazon Braket.* Accessed 8.1.2021, from https://aws.amazon.com/de/braket/
Anderson, C. (2018). *Chris Anderson und The Long tail: Ein Internetgeschäftsmodell*, 50Minuten.de.
Andree, M., & Thomsen, T. (2020). *Atlas der digitalen Welt.* Campus Verlag.
Ankenbrand, H. (2020). Die chinesische Ameise gerät ins Visier. *Frankfurter Allgemeine Zeitung*, 17.10.2020, p. 25.
Apple, F. (2020). Im Sommer haben wir unser Leben zurück. *Frankfurter Allgemeine Sonntagszeitung*, 27.12.2020, p. 22.
Armendia, M., Ghassempouri, M., Ozturk, E., & Peysson, F. (2019). *Twin-control: A digital twin approach to improve machine tools lifecycle.* Springer.
Axel Springer. (2020a). *Chronik Axel Springer.* Accessed 9.12.2020, from https://www.axelspringer.com/de/unternehmen/geschichte-2/geschichte

Axel Springer. (2020b). *Axel-Springer-Neubau*. Accessed 9.12.2020, from https://www.axelspringer-neubau.de/
Axel Springer. (2020c). *Company presentation*. Hamburg.
Bae, H. (2015). *Bill Gates' 40th anniversary email: Goal was 'a computer on every desk'*. Accessed 21.9.2020, from https://money.cnn.com/2015/04/05/technology/bill-gates-email-microsoft-40-anniversary/index.html
Baghai, M., Coley, S., & White, D. (2000). *The alchemy of growth*. Perseus.
Bardwick, J. (1995). *Danger in the comfort zone: How to break the entitlement habit that's killing American business*. American Management Association.
Bass, B. M. (1990). From transactional to transformational leadership: Learning to share the vision. *Organization Dynamics, 18*(3/1990), 19–31.
Bättig, I. (2020). *Agiles Management – in der Praxis, Einführung einer Selbstorganisation in Form von Holacracy*. Universität Bern.
BCG. (2019a). *Why agile works*. München.
BCG. (2019b). *Decoding global trends in upskilling and reskilling*. Accessed 30.11.2020, from https://www.bcg.com/de-de/publications/2019/decoding-global-trends-upskilling-reskilling
Beck, K., Beedle, M., van Bennekum, A., Cockburn, A., Cunningham, W., Fowler, M., Grenning, J., Highsmith, J., Hunt, A., Jeffries, R., Kern, J., Marick, B., Martin, R.C., Mellor, S., Schaber, K., Sutherland, J., & Thomas, D. (2018). *Manifest für Agile Softwareentwicklung*. Accessed 6.10.2020, from http://agilemanifesto.org/iso/de/manifesto.html
Becker, W., Eierle, B., Fliaster, A., Ivens, B., Leischnig, A., Pflaum, A., & Sucky, E. (Eds.). (2019). *Geschäftsmodelle in der digitalen Welt, Strategien, Prozesse und Praxiserfahrungen*. Springer Gabler.
Becker, W., Nolte, M., & Schuhknecht, F. (2020). Die Rolle des Chief Financial Officer im Rahmen der digitalen Transformation von Geschäftsmodellen. In I. Keimer & U. Egle (Eds.), *Die Digitalisierung der Controlling-Funktion – Anwendungsbeispiele aus Theorie und Praxis* (pp. 373–399). Springer Gabler.
Berger, C., Blauth, R., Boger, D., Bolster, C., Burchill, G., DuMouchel, W., Pouliot, F., Richter, R., Rubinoff, A., Shen, D., Timko, M., & Walden, D. (1993). kano's methods of understanding customer defined quality. *Center for Quality of Management Journal, 2*(4/1993), 3–36.
Berlin Adlershof. (2021). *Berlin Adlershof: Daten und Fakten*. Accessed 4.1.2021, from https://www.adlershof.de/adlershof-in-zahlen/
Bernau, P. (2020). Wie Corona uns den Zufall raubt. *Frankfurter Allgemeine Sonntagszeitung*, 4.10.2020, p. 17.
Bertelsmann Stiftung. (2020). *Erfolgskriterien betrieblicher Digitalisierung*, Gütersloh.
Bitkom. (2020). *Digitale Plattformen*. Accessed 26.11.2020, from https://www.bitkom.org/Bitkom/Publikationen/Chartbericht-Digitale-Plattformen-2020
BKA. (2020). *Cybercrime Bundeslagebild 2019*. Accessed 8.10.2020, from https://www.bka.de/DE/AktuelleInformationen/StatistikenLagebilder/Lagebilder/Cybercrime/cybercrime_node.html
Blank, S. (2015). *Innovation at 50x*. Accessed 22.9.2020, from https://steveblank.com/2015/08/21/innovation-50x-in-companies-and-government-agencies/
BMI. (2018). *Projekt zur Gesichtserkennung erfolgreich*. Accessed 9.10.2020, from https://www.bmi.bund.de/SharedDocs/pressemitteilungen/DE/2018/10/gesichtserkennung-suedkreuz.html
BMWI. (2021). *Fragen und Antworten zum Projekt GAIA-X*. Accessed 4.1.2021, from https://www.bmwi.de/Redaktion/DE/FAQ/Dateninfrastruktur/faq-projekt-gaia-x.html
Boehme-Neßler, V. (2017). Die Macht der Algorithmen und die Ohnmacht des Rechts. *Neue Juristische Wochenschrift*, 70. Jg., pp. 3031–3038.
Bonprix. (2020). *"fashion connect" Storekonzept von bonprix gewinnt "World Retail Award"*. 11.1.2021, from https://www.bonprix.de/corporate/presse/meldung/fashion-connect-storekonzept-von-bonprix-gewinnt-world-retail-award/
Brands, R. (2017). *Google's 9 principles of innovation*. Accessed 22.9.2020, from https://innovationedge.com/2017/06/23/googles-9-principles-of-innovation/

Bruhn, M., Hepp, M., & Hadwich, K. (2015). *Vom Produkthersteller zum Serviceanbieter – Geschäftsmodelle der Servicetransformation.* In M. Bruhn & K. Hadwich (Eds.), *Interaktive Wertschöpfung durch Dienstleistungen* (pp. 132–146). Springer Gabler.

Brynjolfsson, E., & McAfee, A. (2018). *The second machine age: Wie die nächste digitale Revolution unser aller Leben verändern wird.* Plassen Verlag.

Bughin, J., Catlin, T., Hirt, M., & Willmott, P. (2018). *Why digital strategies fail.* McKinsey.

Bünte, C. (2018). *Künstliche Intelligenz – die Zukunft des Marketing: Ein praktischer Leitfaden für Marketing-Manager.* Springer Gabler.

Busch, D. (2020). *The serendipity mindset: The art and science of creating good luck.* Pinguin.

C24. (2020). *Die Open Banking Plattform: Erleben Sie 2020 eine neue Dimension des mobilen Bankings.* Accessed 29.9.2020, from https://www.c24.de/

Capgemini. (2014). *Monetizing the Internet of things: Extracting value from the connectivity opportunity.* Accessed 24.9.2020, from https://www.capgemini.com/.../wp.../iot_monetization_0.pdf

Caviezel, R. (2020). *Mit Business Intelligence die Unternehmenssteuerung digitalisieren, Das Reporting bei Ticketcorner wird neu definiert.* In I. Keimer & U. Egle (Eds.), *Die Digitalisierung der Controlling-Funktion – Anwendungsbeispiele aus Theorie und Praxis* (pp. 103–123). Springer Gabler.

Chandler, A. D. (1962). *Strategy and structure.* M.I.T.

Chang, D.-S. (2016). *Mein Hirn hat seinen eigenen Kopf: Wie wir andere und uns selbst wahrnehmen.* Rowohlt.

CheMondis. (2021). *Discover a new way to buy or sell chemical products online today.* Accessed 2.1.2021, from, https://chemondis.com

Christensen, C. M. (2016). *The innovator's dilemma: When new technologies cause great firms to fail.* Harvard Business Review Press.

Coca-Cola. (2021). *Dein Geschmack, deine Mischung: Coca-Cola freestyle.* Accessed 5.1.2021, from https://www.coca-cola-deutschland.de/verantwortung/getranke/ausgewogenes-produktportfolio/coca-cola-freestyle

Collaboard. (2021). *Die besten Ideen entstehen im Team.* Accessed 12.1.2021, from https://www.collaboard.app/de/

Collins, J. (2020a). *Hedgehog concept in the business sectors.* Accessed 30.11.2020, from https://www.jimcollins.com/article_topics/articles/hedgehog-concept-business-sectors.html#articletop

Collins, J. (2020b). *Der Weg zu den Besten: Die sieben Management-Prinzipien für dauerhaften Unternehmenserfolg.* Campus.

Cornelius, A. (2019). *Künstliche Intelligenz, Entwicklungen, Erfolgsfaktoren und Einsatzmöglichkeiten.* Haufe.

CrossEngage. (2021). *Damit Kunden kommen, um zu bleiben.* Accessed 2.1.2021, from https://www.crossengage.io/de/

Cunningham, C., Ederer, F., & Ma, S. (2020). *Killer acquisitions.* Accessed 25.11.2020, from https://ssrn.com/abstract=3241707

Dahan, E., & Hauser, J. (2002). The virtual customer. *Journal of Product Innovation Management, 5*(2002), 332–353.

DeepMind. (2017). *AlphaGo Zero: Starting from scratch.* Accessed 15.12.2020, from https://deepmind.com/blog/article/alphago-zero-starting-scratch

Deloitte. (2021). *Digitalisierung im Controlling: Mensch oder Maschine? Wie digitale Technologien die Arbeit und das Berufsbild des Controllers verändern.* Accessed 3.1.2021, from https://www2.deloitte.com/de/de/pages/finance-transformation/articles/digitalisierung-controlling.html

Deutsche Start-ups. (2021a). *Team Europe Ventures.* Accessed 6.1.2021, from https://www.deutsche-Start-ups.de/verzeichnisse/investors-a-z/team-europe-ventures/

Deutsche Start-ups. (2021b). *Hitfox.* Accessed 6.1.2021, from https://www.deutsche-Start-ups.de/verzeichnisse/Start-ups-a-z/hitfox/

Deutsche Telekom. (2021). *5G Geschwindigkeit ist Datenkommunikation in Echtzeit.* Accessed 3.1.2021, from https://www.telekom.com/de/konzern/details/5g-geschwindigkeit-ist-datenkommunikation-in-echtzeit-544496

Digital Magazin. (2021). *Aufgaben eines CDO – als Störenfried die Digitalisierung voranbringen.* Accessed 16.8.2021, from https://digital-magazin.de/aufgaben-eines-cdo/

Dillerup, R., & Stoi, R. (2016). *Unternehmensführung: Management and leadership.* Vahlen.

Direktgruppe. (2016). *Das Führen in bi-modalen IT-Landschaften.* Accessed 23.11.2020, from https://blog.direkt-gruppe.de/fuehrung-bi-modale-it/

Drath, K. (2018). *Die resiliente Organisation.* Haufe.

DUB Unternehmer. (2020). *Genie braucht Wahnsinn* (pp. 8–14).

Ebers, M., & Maurer, I. (2014). Netzwerktheorie. In A. Kieser & M. Ebers (Eds.), *Organisationstheorien* (7th ed., pp. 386–406). Schäffer Poeschel.

eCom. (2019). *Denken wir Jeff Bezos, um erfolgreich zu sein,* 2/2019, p. 20f.

Eggheads. (2021). *Keep your employees in the know. With your internal bot.* Accessed 12.1.2021, from https://eggheads.ai/#home

Elkington, J. (1999). *Cannibals with forks: Triple bottom line of 21st century business.* Wiley.

Emarsys. (2021). *Vollständig integrierte Customer Engagement Plattform.* Accessed 9.1.2021, from https://emarsys.com/de/cep/

Ematinger, R., & Schulze, S. (2020). *Spielend Ziele setzen und erreichen, objectives and key results mit LEGO SERIOUS PLAY.* Springer Gabler.

Engelen, A., Engelen, M., & Bachmann, J.-T. (2015). *Corporate entrepreneurship, Unternehmerisches Management in etablierten Unternehmen.* Gabler.

Erpenbeck, J. (2020). *Kompetenzen.* Accessed 16.10.2020, from https://www.kodekonzept.com/wissensressourcen/kompetenzen

EU. (2020a). Horizont Europa, Das nächste Investitionsprogramm der EU für Forschung und Innovation (2021-2027). Accessed 28.12.2020.

EU. (2020b). Weißbuch, Zur Künstlichen Intelligenz – ein europäisches Konzept für Exzellenz und Vertrauen. Accessed 28.12.2020.

Farsi, M., Daneshkhah, A., Hosseinian-Far, A., & Jahankhani, H. (Eds.). (2019). *Digital twin technologies and smart cities (Internet of things).* Springer.

Fasse, M. (2019). *Warum Daimler und BMW jetzt auf Kooperation setzen.* Accessed 17.9.2020, from https://www.handelsblatt.com/unternehmen/industrie/autokonzerne-warum-daimler-und-bmw-jetzt-auf-kooperation-setzen/24373450.html?ticket=ST-88171295-CBO6pJBbb6GxVXH4fhTh-ap5

Felten, C. (2018). *Im Zeitalter des Customer Experience-Wettbewerbs.* Accessed 2.4.2020, from https://www.muuuh.de/hub/consulting/im-zeitalter-des-customer experience-wettbewerbs

Fink, V. (2020). *KI-Projekte – einfach machen, Künstliche Intelligenz in Service, Marketing und Sales erfolgreich einführen.* Springer Gabler.

FitchRatings. (2020). *Loan default rate hits decade high 4%.* Accessed 27.11.2020, from https://www.fitchratings.com/research/corporate-finance/loan-default-rate-hits-decade-high-4-22-07-2020

Fitzek, F. H. P., & Boche, H. (2020). 5G – Warum der neue Mobilfunkstandard wirklich revolutionär ist. *Frankfurter Allgemeine Zeitung,* 19.10.2020, p. 20.

Franke, F., & Schönbohm, A. (2016). *Gamification in business innovation, quasi-experimental research results on gamified idea generation.* BWV.

Fuji. (2021). *History.* Accessed 8.1.2021, from https://www.fujifilm.com/products/skincare/history/

Gallup. (2019). Warum der Faktor Mensch im Zeitalter der Digitalisierung so wichtig ist. *Pressegespräch, 12*(9), 2019.

Gallup. (2020a). *What is employee engagement and how do you improve it?* Accessed 13.11.2020, from https://www.gallup.com/workplace/285674/improve-Employee Engagement-workplace.aspx?utm_source=paper&utm_medium=in_text&utm_campaign=ee_meta_analysis#ite-285701

Gallup. (2020b). *Employee engagement and performance: Latest insights from the world's largest study*, Washington.
Gartner. (2016). *Gartner IT symposium*, .
Gartner. (2020a). *Gartner magic quadrant*. Accessed 13.10.2020, from https://www.gartner.com/en/research/methodologies/magic-quadrants-research
Gartner. (2020b). *Download roadmap that's most relevant to your organization*. Accessed 15.10.2020, from https://www.gartner.com/en/confirmation/information-technology/trends/thank-you-2020-2022-emerging-technology-roadmap
Gartner. (2020c). *Hype cycle for artificial intelligence*. Accessed 21.20.2020, from https://www.gartner.com/smarterwithgartner/2-megatrends-dominate-the-gartner-hype-cycle-for-artificial-intelligence-2020/?utm_campaign=RM_GB_2020_ITCIO_C_NL11_October-15_Control_CB&utm_medium=email&utm_source=Eloqua&cm_mmc=Eloqua-_-Email-_-LM_RM_GB_2020_ITCIO_C_NL11_October-15_Control_CB-_-0000
Gassmann, O., Frankenberger, K., & Csik, M. (2017). *Geschäftsmodelle entwickeln: 55 innovative Konzepte mit dem St. Galler business model Navigator* (2nd ed.). Hansa-Verlag.
Gassner, L. (2021). *Growth Hacking - konsequent umsetzen: Prozesse, Instrumente und Mindset für ein schnelles und nachhaltiges Wachstum – mit Roadmap und Checklisten*. Springer Gabler.
Gentsch, P. (2019). *Künstliche Intelligenz für Sales, Marketing und Service: Mit AI und Bots zu einem Algorithmic Business – Konzepte und Best Practices* (2nd ed.). Springer Gabler.
Germis, C. (2020). VW-Chef bläst zur Tesla-Jagd. *Frankfurter Allgemeine Zeitung*, 17.11.2020, p. 21
Gnirke, K., Hecking, K., Mingel, G., & Müller, P. (2020). Himmel und Hölle. *Der Spiegel*, 27(2020), 68–72.
Goleman, D. (2015). *Konzentriert Euch!: Eine Anleitung zum modernen Leben*. Piper Verlag.
Govindarajan, V., & Trimble, C. (2010). *The other side of innovation – How to solve the execution challenge*. Harvard Business Review Press.
Great Place to Work. (2021). *Was steckt hinter Great Place to Work®?* Accessed 3.1.2021, from https://www.greatplacetowork.de/
Grinschuk, E. (2019). *Blockchain game changer und revolution: Blockchain Grundlagen für Anfänger*. Independently Published.
Grover. (2021). *Erlebe gemeinsam mit 700.000+ Menschen die Schwerelosigkeit des Mietens*. Accessed 3.1.2021, from https://www.grover.com/de-de/g-about/how-it-works
Grund, T., Schönbohm, A., & Tran, K. (2020). *Unternehmensplanung im Zeitalter der Digitalisierung, Ansätze und Erfolgsfaktoren in der Praxis*. Springer Gabler.
Halecker, B., & Hartmann, M. (2014). Das Geschäftsmodell als "Strategic Deployment" im strategischen Denken. In D. Schallmo (Ed.), *Kompendium der Geschäftsmodell-Innovation, Grundlagen, aktuelle Ansätze und Fallbeispiele zur erfolgreichen Geschäftsmodell-Innovation* (pp. 209–232). Springer Gabler.
Haller, S., & Wissing, C. (2018). Normstrategien für das Service Business Development zur Berücksichtigung digitaler Plattformen in der Wertschöpfung. In M. Bruhn & K. Hadwich (Eds.), *Service Business Development, Methoden – Erlösmodelle – Marketinginstrumente, Band 1* (pp. 168–189). Springer Gabler.
Hamilton, S. A. (2020). *"Amazon wird pleitegehen": Jeff Bezos erklärt, warum der Tod von Amazon unausweichlich ist*. Accessed 6.10.2020, from https://www.businessinsider.de/wirtschaft/bezos-erklaert-tod-von-amazon-ist-unausweichlich-r/
Hannig, U. (Ed.). (2017). *Marketing und Sales-Automation, Grundlagen – Tools – Umsetzung, Alles, was Sie wissen müssen*. Springer Gabler.
Hannig, U. (2020). Marketing-Automation – automatisch mehr Markterfolg. In M. Stumpf (Ed.), *Die 10 wichtigsten Zukunftsthemen im Marketing* (2nd ed., pp. 207–229). Haufe.
Harari, Y. N. (2018). *Homo Deus, Eine Geschichte von Morgen*. Beck.
Hauck, E., & Bauer, D. (2020). Am Rande der Gesellschaft. *Frankfurter Allgemeinen Sonntagszeitung*, 11.10.2020, p. 9.

Hauschildt, J., Salomo, S., Schultz, C., & Kock, A. (2016). *Innovationsmanagement* (6th ed.). Vahlen.
Heise. (2020). *Airbnb: Gewinn vor Börsengang – Profitabilität ungewiss.* https://www.heise.de/news/Airbnb-Gewinn-vor-Boersengang-Profitabilitaet-ungewiss-4962498.html. Accessed 10.12.2020.
Heller, J. (Ed.). (2019). *Resilienz für die VUCA-Welt.* Springer.
Hensel-Börner, S., Schmidt-Ross, I., & Merkle, W. (2018). Digitale transformation. *Marketing Review St. Gallen, 3*(2018), 20–26.
Hermes. (2021). *Kontaktlose Paketlieferung.* Accessed 15.1.2021, from, https://www.myhermes.de/kontaktloser-paketempfang/
Heyse, V. (2020). *Kompetenzen.* Accessed 16.10.2020, from https://www.kodekonzept.com/wissensressourcen/kompetenzen/
HHL. (2021). *Corporate entrepreneurship.* Accessed 6.1.2021, from https://www.hhl.de/entrepreneurship/corporate-entrepreneurship/
Hofer, P., Perkhofer, L., & Mayr, A. (2020). Interaktive Big Data Visualisierungen – Potenzial für das Management Reporting, Eine Zusammenfassung empirischer Untersuchungen zur Auswahl, zum Einsatz und zum Design neuartiger Visualisierungstypen. In I. Keimer & U. Egle (Eds.), *Die Digitalisierung der Controlling-Funktion – Anwendungsbeispiele aus Theorie und Praxis* (pp. 159–187). Springer Gabler.
Hofert, W., & Thonet, C. (2018). *Der agile Kulturwandel: 33 Lösungen für Veränderungen in Organisationen.* Springer Gabler.
Hoffmann, G. P. (2018). *Personalentwicklung und –controlling, Strategien für den Mittelstand.* Springer Gabler.
Hoffmeister, C. (2013). *Digitale Geschäftsmodelle richtig einschätzen.* Hanser.
Hofstadter, D. R. (2018). Das letzte Refugium menschlicher Intelligenz. *Frankfurter Allgemeine Zeitung*, 27.6.2018, p. N 4.
Hohberger, S., & Damlachi, H. (2019). Die Unternehmenskrise: Arten, Ursachen, Stadien und Analyse. In: Hohberger, S., & Damlachi, H. (Hrsg.). *Praxishandbuch Sanierung im Mittelstand* (4th Ed., pp. 33–82).
Hoong, V. (2013). *The digital transformation of customer services.* Accessed 9.12.2020, from https://www2.deloitte.com
Hubspot. (2021). *Das Kreislaufmodell.* Accessed 3.1.2021, from https://www.hubspot.de/flywheel
Hundertmark, S. (2021). *Digitale Freunde, Wie Unternehmen Chatbots erfolgreich einsetzen können.* Wiley.
Hungenberg, H. (2014). *Strategisches Management im Unternehmen: Ziele – Prozesse – Verfahren* (8th ed.). Springer Gabler.
HWR. (2021). *Co-Working im Industrieloft*, Accessed 6.1.2021, from https://www.Start-up-incubator.berlin/
IBM. (2021). *Watson anywhere.* Accessed 7.11.2021, from https://www.ibm.com/de-de/watson
Jacobs, J.C., Kagermann, H., Spath, D. (Hrsg.) (2017). *Arbeit in der digitalen Transformation, Agilität, lebenslanges Lernen und Betriebspartner im Wandel*, Bremen.
Jäger, A. (2020). *Arbeit 4.0.* Fraunhofer-Institut, Donau-Universität Krems.
Jodlbauer, H. (2018). *Digitale Transformation der Wertschöpfung.* Kohlhammer.
Johnsson, J., & Beene, R. (2020). *Designed by clowns ... supervised by monkeys.* Accessed 3.12.2020, from https://fortune.com/2020/01/10/designed-clowns-supervised-monkeys-internal-boeing-messages-slam-737-max/
Kaa. (2021). *Build your own cloud-to-edge IOT solution on a single platform.* Accessed 2.1.2021, from https://www.kaaproject.org
Kahle, T. (2020). Voice-Marketing – Produkte und Services werden dialogfähig. In M. Stumpf (Ed.), *Die 10 wichtigsten Zukunftsthemen im Marketing* (2nd ed., pp. 107–129). Haufe.
Kahle, T., & Meißner, D. (2020). *All About Voice: Konzeption, Design und Vermarktung von Anwendungen für digitale Sprachassistenten.* Haufe.

Kaplan, K. (2016). *When and how to create customer journey maps.* Accessed 12.10.2020, from https://www.nngroup.com/articles/Customer Journey Mapping/

Keimer, I., & Egle, U. (2020). Digital controlling – Grundlagen für den erfolgreichen digitalen Wandel im Controlling. In I. Keimer & U. Egle (Eds.), *Die Digitalisierung der Controlling-Funktion – Anwendungsbeispiele aus Theorie und Praxis* (pp. 1–16). Springer Gabler.

Kersten, W., & Dörries, F. (2019). *Arbeit 4.0, Kompetenzzentrum Hamburg*, Hamburg.

Kilian, K., & Kreutzer, R. (2022). *Digitale Markenführung, Digital Branding in Zeiten divergierender Märkte.* Springer Gabler.

Kim, W. C., & Mauborgne, R. (2016). *Der Blaue Ozean als Strategie: Wie man neue Märkte schafft, wo es keine Konkurrenz gibt.* Hanser.

Klimmer, M. (2016). *Unternehmensorganisation: Eine kompakte und praxisorientierte Einführung mit Online-Training.* nwb.

KODE. (2021). *Kompetenzdiagnostik und Kompetenzentwicklung mit KODE.* Accessed 6.1.2021, from https://www.kodekonzept.com/leistungen/kode/

Kofler, T. (2018). *Das digitale Unternehmen, Systematische Vorgehensweise zur zielgerichteten Digitalisierung.* Springer Gabler.

Körber. (2021a). *Maschinen effizienter einsetzen - mit künstlicher Intelligenz.* Accessed 4.1.2021, from https://www.koerber.com/digital#

Körber. (2021b). *Wenn Papier digital wird.* Accessed 4.1.2021, from https://www.koerber.com/tissue/wenn-papier-digital-wird#

Kotter, J. P. (2014). *Accelerate – building strategic agility for a faster-moving world.* Harvard Business Review Press.

KPMG. (2018). *Das controlling als Treiber der transformation.* Hohe Flexibilität und nachhaltige Ergebnisse vereinen.

Kreutzer, R. (2019). *Toolbox for marketing und management, creative concepts, forecasting methods, and analytical instruments.* Springer Gabler.

Kreutzer, R. (2020). *Die digitale Verführung, Warum wir uns auch mit den Schattenseiten moderner Entwicklungen beschäftigen sollten.* Springer Gabler.

Kreutzer, R. (2021a). *Kundendialog online und offline, Das große 1x1 der Kundengewinnung, Kundenbindung und Kundenrückgewinnung.* Springer Gabler.

Kreutzer, R. (2021b). *Praxisorientiertes Online-Marketing. Konzepte – Instrumente – Checklisten* (4th ed.). Springer Gabler.

Kreutzer, R., & Land, K.-H. (2016). *Digitaler Darwinismus – Der stille Angriff auf Ihr Geschäftsmodell und Ihre Marke* (2nd ed.). Springer Gabler.

Kreutzer, R., & Sirrenberg, M. (2019). *Künstliche Intelligenz – Grundlagen, Use-cases, Methoden für die unternehmenseigene KI-Journey.* Springer Gabler.

Kreutzer, R., & Vousoghi, D. (2020). *Voice-marketing, Der Siegeszug der digitalen Assistenten.* Springer Gabler.

Kudernatsch, D. (2019). *Personalentwicklung und -führung im digitalen Zeitalter.* Accessed 13.10.2020, from https://industrie.de/management/personalentwicklung-und-fuehrung-im-digitalen-zeitalter/

Kuratko, D. F., Covin, J. G., & Hornsby, J. S. (2014). Why implementing corporate innovation is so difficult. *Business Horizons, 57,* 647–655.

L'Oreal. (2021). *Wo Schönheit auf Technologie trifft.* Accessed 5.1.2021, from https://www.loreal.com/de-de/germany/articles/science-and-technology/digitalisierung-beauty-tech-und-innovationen/

Lackes, R. (2021). *Neuronale Netze.* Accessed 12.10.2021, from https://wirtschaftslexikon.gabler.de/definition/neuronale-netze-41065#definition

Laloux, F. (2017). *Reinventing Organizations, Ein illustrierter Leitfaden sinnstiftender Form der Zusammenarbeit.* Vahlen.

Lasnia, M., & Nowotny, V. (2018). *Agile evolution: Eine Anleitung zur agilen transformation.* Business Village.

Laudon, S. (2017). Wie die Digitalisierung die Führungskompetenz komplett neu definiert. In: Jochmann, W., Böckenholt, I., Diestel, S. (Hrsg.) *HR-Exzellenz, innovative ansätze in leadership und transformation* (pp. 65–77). Wiesbaden: Springer Gabler.

Lecinski, J. (2014). *Why it matters now more than ever.* Accessed 12.10.2020, from https://think.storage.googleapis.com/docs/zmot-why-it-matters-now-more-than-ever_articles.pdf

Lehmann, E. E., & Wilhelm, D. (2018). Digitalisierung, disruption und corporate entrepreneurship. In F. Keuper, M. Schomann, L. I. Sikora, & R. Wassef (Eds.), *Disruption und transformation management, digital leadership – digitales mindset – digitale strategie* (pp. 239–266). Springer Gabler.

Lennarz, H. (2017). *Growth Hacking mit Strategie, Wie erfolgreiche Start-ups und Unternehmen mit Growth Hacking ihr Wachstum beschleunigen.* Springer Gabler.

Liebherr. (2021). *Kühlen auf MyStyle-Art: Für mehr Farbe in Ihrem Leben.* Accessed 5.1.2021, from https://home.liebherr.com/shop/de/deu/my-style-konfigurator-gerateubersicht

Lipinski, T., & Wilhelm, D. (2021). *Corporate Entrepreneurship, Wie wir unternehmerisches Denken und Handeln in unserer Organisation fördern.* Accessed 3.1.2021, from https://www.alternus.de/Corporate-Entrepreneurship.173.0.html

Mahrenholz, P. J. (2019). Absturz Strategie. *Horizont, 47*(2019), 25.

Marketo. (2021). *Der Definitive Leitfaden zur Marketing Automation.* Accessed 2.1.2021, from https://de.marketo.com/definitive-guides/marketing-automation/

Marx, U. (2020). Künstliche Intelligenz für Klopapier. *Frankfurter Allgemeine Zeitung*, 14.12.2020, p. 23.

Maschewski, F., & Nosthoff, A.-V. (2021). Das vermessene Selbst. *Frankfurter Allgemeine Sonntagszeitung*, 3.1.2021, p. 39.

Mauritz, S. (2020). *Resilienztraining.* Accessed 14.10.2020, from https://www.resilienz-akademie.com/resilienz-staerken/

Maxwell, J. C. (2007). *21 Irrefutable laws of leadership.* American Bible Society.

Maxwell, J. C. (2013). *The 5 levels of leadership: proven steps to maximize your potential.* CenterStreet.

MCG. (2021). *Verhaltens-Präferenz-Analyse.* Accessed 6.1.2021, from http://www.mcg-fasch.de/kommunikation/vpa-verhaltens-praeferenz-analyse.html

Meinhardt, S., & Pflaum, A. (2019). *Digitale Geschäftsmodelle – Band 1, Geschäftsmodell-Innovationen, digitale Transformation, digitale Plattformen, Internet der Dinge und Industrie 4.0.* Springer Gabler.

Mercateo. (2021). *Die Beschaffungsplattform für Geschäftskunden.* Accessed 2.1.2021, from http://www.mercateo.com/

Merck. (2016). *Seien Sie neugierig, Neugier-Studie 2016*, Darmstadt.

Merck. (2018). *Seien Sie neugierig, Neugier-Studie 2018*, Darmstadt.

Merton, R. K., & Barber, E. (2011). *The travels and adventures of serendipity, a study in sociological semantics and the sociology of science.* Princeton University Press.

Mezger, F., & Bader, K. (2014). Innovationskultur als Erfolgsfaktor für Geschäftsmodellinnovationen: Eine fallstudienbasierte Übersicht. In D. Schallmo (Ed.), *Kompendium der Geschäftsmodell-Innovation, Grundlagen, aktuelle Ansätze und Fallbeispiele zur erfolgreichen Geschäftsmodell-Innovation* (pp. 233–255). Springer Gabler.

Microsoft. (2021a). *Andere befähigen, mehr zu erreichen.* Accessed 24.11.2020, from https://www.microsoft.com/de-de/about

Microsoft. (2021b). *Microsoft Teams, Erleben Sie Teamarbeit ohne Grenzen.* Accessed 21.10.2020, from https://www.microsoft.com/de-de/microsoft-365/microsoft-teams/group-chat-software#office-CustomSpacingTemplate-sybjvjm

Microsoft Azure. (2021). *Lösungen sicher programmieren, gemeinsam entwickeln und bereitstellen – praktisch von jedem Ort.* Accessed 7.1.2021, from https://azure.microsoft.com/de-de/

MindSphere. (2021). *MindSphere - Connecting the things that run the world (Siemens).* Accessed 2.1.2021, from https://siemens.mindsphere.io/de

Miro. (2021). *All boards*. Accessed 2.1.2021, from https://miro.com/app/dashboard/
monday.rocks. (2021). *Teams schneller und nachhaltiger formen*. Accessed 3.1.2021, from https://www.monday.rocks/team-analytics/
Morhart, F., Jenewein, W., & Tomczak, T. (2012). Mit transformationaler Führung das Brand Behavior stärken. In T. Tomczak, F.-R. Esch, J. Kernstock, & A. Herrmann (Eds.), *Behavioral Branding, Wie Mitarbeiterverhalten die Marke stärkt* (pp. 389–406). Springer Gabler.
Müller, R. (2021). Wer die Macht hat. *Frankfurter Allgemeine Zeitung*, 12.1.2021, p. 1.
Müller, H.-E., & Wrobel, M. (2021). *Unternehmensführung: Strategie – Management – Praxis* (4th ed.). Walter de Gryter.
MyMuesli. (2019). "Ich bin Head of HR nur für die Visitenkarte". *Interview mit Heike Ehmann*. Accessed 2.12.2020, from https://www.haufe.de/personal/hr-management/interview-heike-ehmann-ueber-selbstorganisation-bei-mymuesli_80_488790.html
Nerdinger, F., Blickle, G., & Schaper, N. (Eds.). (2014). *Arbeits- und Organisationspsychologie* (3nd ed.). Springer.
Nespresso. (2021). *Prodigio Titan, Krups*. Accessed 9.1.2021, from https://www.nespresso.com/de/de/order/machines/original/prodigio-mch-titan-c70-eu-krups-kaffeemaschine
Nike. (2021). *Nike by you*. Accessed 2.1.2021, from https://www.nike.com/de/de_de/c/nikeid
Nokia. (2020). *Nokia: 5G set to add $8trn to global GDP by 2030*. Accessed 20.10.2020, from https://www.nokia.com/about-us/news/releases/2020/10/11/nokia-5g-set-to-add-8trn-to-global-gdp-by-2030/
NTT. (2020). *2020 global customer experience benchmarking report the connected customer: delivering an effortless experience*. NTT International.
Nunkesser, R., & Thorn, J. (2020). Möglichkeiten und Einschränkungen mobiler Applikationen für das Controlling. In I. Keimer & U. Egle (Eds.), *Die Digitalisierung der Controlling-Funktion – Anwendungsbeispiele aus Theorie und Praxis* (pp. 265–286). Springer Gabler.
Oracle. (2021). *Intelligente IOT-Anwendungen*. Accessed 7.1.2021, from https://www.oracle.com/de/Internet of things/
Osterwalder, A., & Pigneur, Y. (2011). *Business model generation: Ein Handbuch für Visionäre, Spielveränderer und Herausforderer*. Campus.
Otto Group. (2017). *About You steigt ins Cloud-Geschäft ein*. Accessed 11.1.2021, from https://www.ottogroup.com/de/newsroom/meldungen/About-You-steigt-ins-Cloud-Geschaeft-ein.php
Otto Group. (2021a). *Beispiele für Transfromationscases der Otto Group seit Dezember 2015 – Start des Kulturwandelprozesses 4.0*, Hamburg.
Otto Group. (2021b). *Unser Angebot*. Accessed 11.1.2021, from https://www.agilecommunity.ottogroup.com/de/agilegroupies/Angebot-Formate
Otto Group. (2021c). *Das sind wir*. Accessed 11.1.2021, from https://developer.de/ueber-uns/
Otto Group. (2021d). *#Watnschiet – die 3. FuckUp-Night der Otto Group*. Accessed 11.1.2021, from https://www.ottogroupunterwegs.de/blog/posts/Watnschiet-Dritte-FuckUp-Night-der-Otto-Group-mit-Mut-zur-Fehlerkultur.php
Otto Group. (2021e). *OTTO investiert in Plattform, baut neue Firmenzentrale – und wächst weiter*. Accessed 11.1.2021, from https://www.otto.de/unternehmen/de/news-presse/otto-investiert-in-plattform-baut-neue-firmenzentrale-und-waechst-weiter
Otto Group. (2021f). *Otto Group launcht Startup für KI-gestütztes, automatisiertes Suchmaschinenmarketing*. Accessed 11.1.2021, from https://www.ottogroup.com/de/newsroom/meldungen/Otto-Group-launcht-Startup-fuer-KI-gestuetztes-automatisiertes-Suchmaschinenmarketing.php
Otto Group. (2021g). *AboutYou*. Accessed 11.1.2021, from https://www.ottogroup.com/de/ueber-uns/konzernfirmen/AboutYou.php
Pelser, J. (2021). *Wie man Innovationseinheiten richtig gestaltet: Der entscheidende Faktor ist die optimale Entfernung zum Kerngeschäft*. Accessed 7.1.2021, from https://blog.convidera.com
Peppers, D., & Rogers, M. (2017). *Managing customer experience and relationships: a strategic framework* (3rd ed.). Wiley.

Piller, F., Möslein, K., Ihl, C., & Reichwald, R. (2017). *Interaktive Wertschöpfung kompakt: Open innovation, Individualisierung und neue Formen der Arbeitsteilung*. Springer Gabler.
Poguntke, S. (2018). *Design thinking*. Accessed 22.10.2020, from https://wirtschaftslexikon.gabler.de/definition/DesignThinking-54120
Poguntke, S. (2019). *Corporate think tanks: Zukunftsforen, innovation center, design sprints, Kreativsessions & Co* (3rd ed.). Springer.
Porter, M. E. (2004). *Wettbewerbsvorteile*. Campus.
Predix. (2021). *Predix Platform (General Electric)*. Accessed 2.1.2021, from https://www.ge.com/digital/iiot-platform
Preußig, J. (2018). *Agiles Projektmanagement, Scrum, Use Cases, Task Boards & Co*. Haufe.
Project A. (2021). *Invest. Enable. Thrive*. Accessed 6.1.2021, from https://www.project-a.com/
Pruitt, J., & Adlin, T. (2006). *The persona lifecycle – keeping people in mind throughout product design*. Morgan Kaufmann.
PWC. (2017). *eascy – die fünf Dimensionen der Transformation der Automobilindustrie*. Accessed 10.12.2020, from www.pwc.de
Rechtien, W. (2007). *Angewandte Gruppendynamik* (4th ed.). Beltz.
Reinsclassen. (2019). Interview. In: Unckrick, B. Sprache ist das neue Wischen. In: *Horizont, 34/2019*, p. 21.
Retently. (2020). *What is a good net promoter score? (2020 NPS Benchmark)*. Accessed 12.10.2020, from https://www.retently.com/blog/good-net-promoter-score/
Ries, E. (2017). *The lean start-up: How today's entrepreneurs use continuous innovation to create radically successful businesses*. Penguin.
Rifkin, J. (2015). *Zero marginal cost society*. Palgrave Macmillan.
Robertson, B. J. (2016). *Holacracy: The revolutionary management system that abolishes hierarchy*. Henry Holt and Company.
Rocket Internet. (2021). *Rocket – We enable entrepreneurship*. Accessed 6.1.2021, from https://www.rocket-Internet.com/
Rossmann, J. (2014). *Amazon's 14 leadership-principles von Jeff Bezos*. Brilliance Publishing.
SAP. (2021). *Branchenspezifische Cloud bietet SAP-Kunden spürbare Vorteile*. Accessed 2.1.2021, from https://news.sap.com/germany/2020/08/cloud-branchen-vorteile/
Schallmo, D. (2014). Theoretische Grundlagen der Geschäftsmodell-Innovation. In: Schallmo, D. *Kompendium der Geschäftsmodell-Innovation, Grundlagen, aktuelle Ansätze und Fallbeispiele zur erfolgreichen Geschäftsmodell-Innovation* (pp. 1-30), Wiesbaden.
Schallmo, D., & Rusnjak, A. (2017). Roadmap zur Digitalen Transformation von Geschäftsmodellen. In D. Schallmo, A. Rusnjak, J. Anzengruber, T. Werani, & M. Jüner (Eds.), *Digitale Transformation von Geschäftsmodellen, Grundlagen, Instrumente und Best Practice* (pp. 1–31). Springer Gabler.
Scholz, C. (2014). *Personalmanagement: Informationsorientierte und verhaltenstheoretische Grundlagen* (6th ed.). Vahlen.
Schönbohm, A., & Dymke, T. (2020). Hack yourself: Ein Aufruf zur künstlerischen Metamorphose des Controllers in der digitalen Transformation. In I. Keimer & U. Egle (Eds.), *Die Digitalisierung der Controlling-Funktion – Anwendungsbeispiele aus Theorie und Praxis* (pp. 401–419). Springer Gabler.
Schönbohm, A., & Egle, U. (2017). Controlling der digitalen transformation. In D. Schallmo, A. Rusnjak, J. Anzengruber, T. Werani, & M. Jünger (Eds.), *Digitale Transformation von Geschäftsmodellen – Grundlagen, Instrumente und Best Practices* (pp. 231–236). Springer Gabler.
Schönbohm, A., Marwede, L., & Graffius, M. (2017). *Spielräume, Facetten von Gamification in Unternehmen und Weiterbildung*. Flying Kiwi Media.
Schütze-Kreilkamp, U. (2017). Führung in digitalen Zeiten. In W. Jochmann, I. Böckenholt, & S. Diestel (Eds.), *HR-exzellenz, innovative ansätze in leadership und transformation* (pp. 17–32). Springer Gabler.

Schwartz, S. H. (1992). Universals in the content and structure of values: Theoretical advances and empirical tests in 20 countries. In M. Zanna (Ed.), *Advances in experimental social psychology* (pp. 1–65). Academic Press.

Schwarzer, C. M. (2013). *VWs teurer Elektrospaß, VW startet ins Elektrozeitalter*. Accessed 24.9.2020, from https://www.zeit.de/mobilitaet/2013-09/elektroauto-volkswagen-up

Scrappel. (2021). *B2B-Plattform für den Handel von Schrott und Metall*, Accessed 2.1.2021, from https://scrappel.com/

Severlein, C., & Bromberger, L. (2020). *Wirtschaft Volkswagen will keine "Sammlung wertvoller Marken" mehr sein*. Accessed 8.10.2020, from https://www.automobil-industrie.vogel.de/volkswagen-will-keine-sammlung-wertvoller-marken-mehr-sein-a-967869/

Sherpany. (2021). *Sherpany board portal*. Accessed 4.1.2021, from https://www.sherpany.com/de/

Siemens. (2021). *Digitale transformation: Mit gutem Beispiel voran*. Accessed 9.1.2021, from https://new.siemens.com/global/de/unternehmen/stories/industrie/elektronik-digitalenterprise-zukunftstechnologien.html

Singleton. (2021). *Singleton change*. Accessed 2.1.2021, from https://www.singleton.life/

Skywise. (2021). *The leading data platform for the aviation industry*. Accessed 2.1.2021, from https://skywise.airbus.com/

Slack. (2021a). *Zusammenarbeit war nie einfacher*. Accessed 4.1.2021, from https://slack.com/intl/de-de/

Slack. (2021b). *Was ist Slack enterprise grid?*. Accessed 4.1.2021, from https://slack.com/intl/de-de/help/articles/360004150931-Was-ist-Slack-Enterprise-Grid

Smart Insights. (2021). *What happens online in 60 seconds?* Accessed 6.8.2021, from https://www.smartinsights.com/wp-content/uploads/2020/06/what-happens-online-in-60-seconds.png

SpaceX. (2020). *About SpaceX*. Accessed 21.9.2020, from https://www.spacex.com/about

Sprenger, R. K. (2017). Transformationale Führung – Was will sie? Wie geht sie? In W. Jochmann, I. Böckenholt, & S. Diestel (Eds.), *HR-Exzellenz, Innovative Ansätze in Leadership und Transformation* (pp. 3–16). Springer Gabler.

SSF. (2021). *Switzerland Innovation Park Biel/Bienne, Connecting Great Minds*. Accessed 3.1.2021, from https://www.sipbb.ch/

Stadelmann, M., Pufahl, M., & Laux, D. D. (2020). *CRM goes digital, Digitale Kundenschnittstellen in Marketing, Vertrieb und Service exzellent gestalten und nutzen*. Springer Gabler.

Statista. (2021). *Amazon's share of online retail sales in selected regions as of September 2020*. Accessed 3.8.2021, from https://www.statista.com/statistics/1183515/amazon-market-share-region-worldwide/

Steinke, K.-H., Schulze, M., Berlin, S., Stehle, A., & Georg, J. (2014). *Green Controlling: Leitfaden für die erfolgreiche Integration ökologischer Zielsetzungen in Unternehmensplanung und -steuerung*. Haufe.

Strack, M., Gennerich, C., & Hopf, N. (2008). Warum Werte? In E. H. Witte (Ed.), *Sozialpsychologie und Werte* (pp. 90–130). Papst Science Publisher.

Strategyzer. (2020). *Business model Portfolio Part 3: The Business Portfolio Map*. Accessed 24.9.2020, from https://www.strategyzer.com/blog/posts/2017/9/4/business-model-portfolio-part-3-the-business-portfolio-map

Sultan, F., & Banerjee, S. (2018). Enhancing customer insights with public location data. *Harvard Business Review*, July/2018, pp. 2–6.

T3N. (2021). *Die große Übersicht: Inkubatoren und Accelerator für Start-ups in Deutschland*. Accessed 6.1.2021, from https://t3n.de/news/inkubatoren-accelerator-Start-ups-deutschland-655475/2/

ThingWorx. (2021). *Den Erfolg mit der ThingWorx IIOT Lösungsplattform beschleunigen*. Accessed 1.1.2021, from https://www.ptc.com/de/products/iiot/thingworx-platform

TOII. (2021). *Produktions-Digitalisierung mit toii*. Accessed 2.1.2021, from https://www.thyssenkrupp-materials-services.com/de/dienstleistungen/industrial-Internet of things

Tontio. (2021). *Tontio*. Accessed 6.1.2021, from https://tontio.com/about-us

TriCat. (2021). *Enterprise Solutions*. Accessed 5.1.2021, from https://www.tricat.net/enterprise-solutions/
Trusple. (2020). *Trust Made Simple*. Accessed 20.10.2020, from https://www.trusple.com/
TÜV. (2020). *Künstliche Intelligenz in Unternehmen, TÜV Studienbericht 2020, Chancen nutzen — Risiken begegnen,* .
Unckrich, B. (2019). Sprache ist das neue Wischen. *Horizont, 34*(2019), 20–21.
Unic. (2021). *Digitalagentur in der Schweiz und in Deutschland. Wir machen Digitales menschlich*. Accessed 4.1.2021, from https://www.unic.com
Virtual Escape. (2021). *6 Gründe für Teambildung in einem VR Escape Room*. Accessed 4.1.2021, from https://www.virtual-escape.at/post/6-gr%C3%BCnde-f%C3%BCr-teambuilding-in-einem-vr-escape-room
von Rosenstiel, L., & Nerdinger, F. W. (2011). *Grundlagen der Organisationspsychologie, Basiswissen und Anwendungshinweise* (7th ed.). Schäffer Poeschel.
von Westphalen, F. G. (2020). Wie man sich gegen Digital-Giganten wehrt. *Frankfurter Allgemeine Zeitung*, 3.12.2020, p. 15.
Wambach, A., & Müller, H. C. (2018). *Digitaler Wohlstand für alle. Ein Update der Sozialen Marktwirtschaft ist möglich*. Campus.
Waymo. (2021). *We're building the World's Most Experienced Driver*. Accessed 6.1.2021, from https://waymo.com/
Weber, J. (2020). *Bewegende Zeiten: Mobilität der Zukunft*. Springer.
Weise, K. (2020). *Pushed by pandemic, Amazon goes on a hiring spree without equal*. Accessed 30.11.2020, from https://www.nytimes.com/2020/11/27/technology/pushed-by-pandemic-amazon-goes-on-a-hiring-spree-without-equal.html
Wikipedia. (2021). *Wikipedia: Über Wikipedia*. Accessed 6.1.2021, from https://de.wikipedia.org/wiki/Wikipedia:%C3%9Cber_Wikipedia
Wirtz, B. (2018). *business model Management, Design – Instrumente – Erfolgsfaktoren von Geschäftsmodellen* (4th ed.). Springer Gabler.
Wirtz, B. W., & Thomas, M.-J. (2014). Design und Entwicklung der business model-Innovation, in: Schallmo, D. (ed) *Kompendium der Geschäftsmodell-Innovation, Grundlagen, aktuelle Ansätze und Fallbeispiele zur erfolgreichen Geschäftsmodell-Innovation* (pp. 31-49), Wiesbaden.
Wirtz, B., & Weyerer, J. C. (2019a). Künstliche Intelligenz: Erscheinungsformen, Nutzungspotenziale und Anwendungsbereiche. *WiSt - Wirtschaftswissenschaftliches Studium, 48*. Jg., 10/2019, pp. 4–7.
Wirtz, B. & Weyerer, J. C. (2019b). Künstliche Intelligenz: Chancen, Risiken und strategische Governance. *WiSt - Wirtschaftswissenschaftliches Studium, 48*. Jg., 11/2019, pp. 4–9.
Wolfangel, E. (2018). Künstliche Dummheit. *Süddeutsche Zeitung*, 14./15.07.2018, p. 33.
Wonder.me. (2021). *Online gatherings that are fun*. Accessed 2.1.2021, from https://www.wonder.me/
Wucato. (2021). *Digitale Beschaffung, die maximal einfach ist*. Accessed 2.1.2021, from https://www.wucato.de/
Youyou, W., Kosinski, M., & Stillwell, D. (2015). Computer-based personality judgments are more accurate than those made by humans. *PNAS, 4/2015, 112*, 1036–1040.
Zalando. (2021a). *Dein Zugang zu unserer Plattform Partnerprogramm*. Accessed 8.1.2021, from https://www.zalando.de/zms/zalando-partner-program/
Zalando. (2021b). *Unsere Geschäftsfelder*. Accessed 8.1.2021, from https://corporate.zalando.com/de/unternehmen/unsere-geschaeftsfelder
Zappos. (2021a). *About us*. Accessed 6.1.2021, from https://www.zappos.com/about/?utm_campaign=zappos&utm_medium=zappos-home&utm_source=footer&utm_content=text

Zappos. (2021b). *Holacracy and Self-Organization*. Accessed 7.1.2021, from https://www.zapposinsights.com/about/holacracy

Zhai, K., Zhu, J., & Leng, C. (2020). *How billionaire Jack Ma fell to earth and took Ant's mega IPO with him*. Accessed 4.8.2021, from https://www.reuters.com/article/ant-group-ipo-suspension-regulators-idUSKBN27L2GX

Zollenkop, M. (2014). Management des Geschäftsmodell-Portfolios – Konzept, Fallstudie, Erfolgsfaktoren. In D. Schallmo (Ed.), *Kompendium der Geschäftsmodell-Innovation, Grundlagen, aktuelle Ansätze und Fallbeispiele zur erfolgreichen Geschäftsmodell-Innovation* (pp. 137–178). Springer Gabler.

Zukunftsagenten. (2021). *Zukunftsagenten*. Accessed 6.1.2021, from https://www.zukunfts-agenten.com/

Change Management: Shaping Change Processes Successfully

> *People are usually afraid of change because they fear the unknown. But the greatest constant in history is that everything changes.*
>
> Yuval Noah Harari

In this chapter, the **basics and tools of change management** are taught. The most important concepts and tools for the successful management of change processes are presented. Only those who have mastered these basics can successfully shape the process of digital transformation.

4.1 Guiding Principle of Change Management

"If you discover you are riding a dead horse, get off."
Wisdom of the Dakota Indians

We have heard this wisdom many times before. At the same time, there is talk of a **zombification of the economy**. A "**zombie company**" is a highly indebted company that, due to a non-profitable business model, is no longer able to bear the interest burden associated with the loan financing. By taking out new loans, the accruing interest payments and redemptions are financed. The low-interest rate policy facilitates such behavior—which, however, is not sustainable in the long run.

We can also speak analogously of "**zombie business units**" and "**zombie projects.**" These are activities that are only kept alive by cross-subsidization from profitable business areas. However, they do not have a profitable future either.

We should all ask ourselves whether we and our companies always take the above wisdom of the *Dakota Indians* to heart. Or do we rather resort to the strategies listed below (cf. Schäfer 2021)? You can check for yourself which of these approaches have already been used by yourself, by your colleagues, by your company, by competitors, by politicians and others. If we are completely honest, we realize self-critically that we too have tried to ride a dead horse on one or two occasions. But as the saying goes:

Self-awareness is the first step to improvement.

With this in mind, I hope you enjoy your **self-check on how to deal with dead horses!**

- We change the riders for the dead horse.
- We say: "This is how we have always ridden the dead horse."
- We visit other companies to see how they ride dead horses (looking for best practice examples).
- We form a task force to revive the dead horse.
- We change the criteria that say if a horse is dead.
- We buy in people from outside to ride the dead horse.
- We harness several dead horses together to make them faster.
- We raise extra funds to increase the dead horse's performance.
- We declare that our horse is "better, faster and cheaper" dead.
- We form a quality circle to find a use for dead horses.
- We insert a training session to learn to ride dead horses better.
- We instruct the rider to stay seated until the horse gets back up.
- We offer the successful rider the prospect of a promotion.
- We order overtime for rider and horse.
- We conclude a target agreement with the rider on riding dead horses.
- We give the rider a performance bonus to increase his motivation.
- We organize sessions with an external coach to improve communication between rider and dead horse.
- Employees who point out that the horse is dead are denounced as worrywarts and enrolled in the motivational seminar "positive thinking."
- We explain to the horse that its behavior could lead to outsourcing and/or offshoring.
- We get a bigger whip.
- We double the feed ration for the horse.
- We change the feed supplier.
- We change the horse supplier.
- We change the straw in the stable.
- We have the stable renovated.
- We appoint a circle of experts to analyze the dead horse.
- We find out that other companies are also trying to ride dead horses and declare this the normal state of affairs.
- We launch a creative competition to ride dead horses.
- We commission a consulting company to do an expert opinion on whether there are cheaper and more efficient dead horses.
- The expert opinion states that the dead horse does not need any feed and recommends to only use dead horses.
- We have the dead horse certified according to DIN EN ISO 9001.
- We make comparisons of different dead horses.

- We declare: "No horse can be so dead that it cannot be motivated after all."
- We declare: "If you can't ride the dead horse, at least it can pull a carriage."
- We revise the service instructions for riding horses.
- We develop a new product: "riding dead horses."
- We create a presentation to show what the horse could do if it was not dead.
- We exchange our dead horse for another dead horse that, according to the product description, runs faster.
- We exchange the dead horse for a dead cow.
- We strap a lighter saddle on the dead horse to give it a chance to recover on its own.
- We explain that a dead horse was our goal from the beginning.
- We claim that the dead horse was procured by the predecessors.
- We put the dead horse in someone else's stable and declare that it is his.

In many cases, however, the following maxim is applied:

"If you realize you are riding a dead horse, make sure you have a comfortable saddle. It could be a long ride!"

> **Memory Box**
> **In the world, man learns only by necessity or conviction.**
> *Johann Heinrich Pestalozzi*

> **Think Box: Questions You Should Ask Yourself**
> - In which sectors can you see a zombification of the economy?
> - Where are there zombie businesses in your industry?
> - Are there zombie business units or zombie projects in your own company?
> - Are these kept alive through cross-subsidization?
> - Which of the methods described above are used in your company to avoid having to "pull the plug?"
> - Who could prevent this?

4.2 Stakeholder Analysis as a Starting Point for Change Managements

Everyone said it couldn't be done.
   Then someone came along who didn't know that and just did it!

The **core of change management** is the goal-oriented and planned management of change processes. The aim is to transform the initial state into a more or less precisely described target state. In order to achieve this, a variety of procedural, structural and, above all, cognitive change processes must be initiated—and constructively continued even in the face of (expected) resistance. Various concepts and instruments can be used for this purpose. A major challenge of change management is to identify the stakeholders necessary for a successful change process at an early stage.

4.2.1 Stakeholder of a Change Process

Half dumplings don't roll!
Folk wisdom

Stakeholders are not "shareholders" in the legal sense, as the literal translation of "to have a stake in something" would lead one to expect. Rather, it refers figuratively to the groups of people who have an interest in the activities of your company and thus also in its change projects. Instead of stakeholders, we can also speak of **interest groups**.

The different **stakeholders** have their **own goals** and often want to influence the results in different ways (promote or slow down). Therefore, they must be taken into account at an early stage of a change process. We are called upon to recognize their different interests and demands on the company in the course of the change process in good time and to take them into account appropriately.

The most **important stakeholders in a change process** who need to be involved in terms of information and/or processes are presented below:

- **Managers and Employees**
  Initially, change processes primarily affect the company's own managers and employees. They feel the effects of the (digitally caused) changes most directly in their everyday work and often have to drive them forward in the company itself. Therefore, the entire team must be comprehensively integrated into the change process.
- **Prospective Buyers and Customers**
  The effects of many change processes are not limited to the internal relationship of the company (e.g., through the digitalization of internal processes), but also have a lasting impact on the products and services of a company. Therefore, the expectations of prospects and customers must be comprehensively considered in the course of the change process. After all, their acceptance largely determines whether a company is successful in the long term or not.
- **Suppliers and Service Partners**
  Change processes are often accompanied by a further integration of suppliers and service partners along the value chain. For example, ordering processes can be completely digitalized and, if necessary, automated. The integration of logistics service providers can also be controlled via digital platforms. Orders for the company itself can also be transmitted via various digital channels. Consequently, suppliers and service partners are another important stakeholder group.

- **Competitors**
  Competitors are also a stakeholder group, even if their wishes and expectations are usually not taken into account comprehensively in the course of a change process. Nevertheless, it is indispensable for a successful process to know their positions and to anticipate possible reactions to one's own change process. This is especially the case in oligopolistic markets dominated by a few large players. In this case, the competitors' reactions are to be expected. Considering competitors as stakeholders is good "strategic management"!
- **General Public**
  The general public is also a stakeholder. After all, a company like *Volkswagen* that is aligning its vision in the direction of mobility provider and e-mobility wants to be applauded by the public, or at least to find acceptance for it. Possible resistance must be recognized at an early stage and ideally overcome.
- **Shareholders**
  A change process will not succeed without taking into account the interests of the shareholders, be they financing institutions (e.g., banks) or shareholders or venture capitalists. After all, these shareholders provide the financial resources directly or indirectly. For this reason, the shareholders in particular must be informed early and comprehensively about the upcoming changes and in many cases also actively agree to them (in the case of public limited companies, for example, via the supervisory board or the general meeting).
- **Governments and Legislators**
  Governments and legislators may initially seem surprising as further stakeholders. However, they can significantly influence upcoming change processes through the application or development of legal framework conditions. This applies to the promotion of research and development as well as subsidies or tax benefits for industrial settlements. However, change processes can also be blocked or prevented by laws or government initiatives. Such measures are to be expected if changes trigger job losses or a relocation of research and/or production facilities abroad. The sale of companies into foreign hands can also be legally prevented.

An indispensable prerequisite for successfully shaping a change process is therefore first of all **listening** to these different stakeholders. If a company or a change manager remains stuck in broadcast mode alone, it will not be able to manage a change process successfully. Like every good conversation, every change process must begin with appreciative listening Only then can the needs, interests, and moods of the various stakeholders be identified. A special focus here must of course be on the company's own employees and managers. But the expectations of other service partners, customers, shareholders, and governments must not be neglected.

The second step of the change process is about **learning**. This is where the information gained is evaluated, and solutions for one's own approach are derived. Finally, the implementation (**act**) follows in order to implement the developed concepts step by step. For a learning organization, it is indispensable to now follow up with the **control** phase—in order to check after each step, after each measure

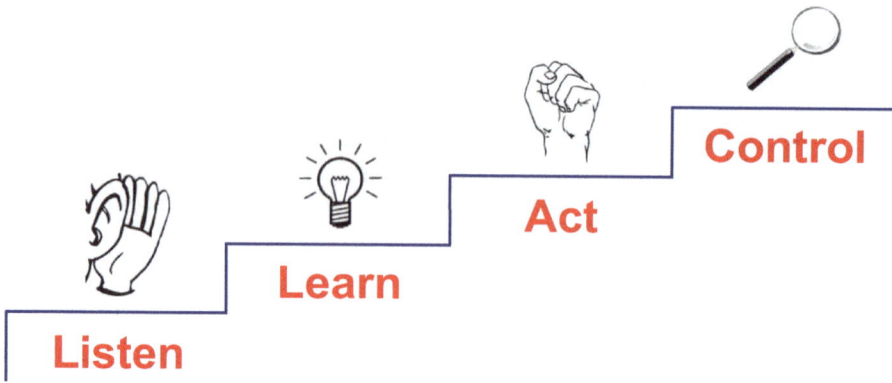

Fig. 4.1 Guiding principle for change management

introduced, after each realignment, whether the desired effects have occurred. Then the sequence **listen—learn—act—control** shown in Fig. 4.1 begins anew.

This guiding principle is not only important for change processes, but for all kinds of processes—professional and private!

> **Memory Box**
> We should never leave the place of knowledge before we have agreed on concrete action.

> **Think Box: Questions You Should Ask Yourself**
> - Which stakeholders need to be considered for the change processes in your company? Think not only about management and employees, but also about prospects and customers, suppliers and service partners, relevant competitors, the general public, shareholders, government and legislators.
> - Have you established a cycle of listen—learn—act—control to keep your finger on the pulse of relevant stakeholders?
> - Who is responsible for answering these questions?

4.2.2 Stakeholder Onion Model

The digital transformation starts in your mind!

With the **stakeholder onion model** shown in Fig. 4.2, you can visualize the relationships of stakeholders to a project goal—in this case, digital transformation. In order to achieve the **highest possible transparency**, further information can be

4.2 Stakeholder Analysis as a Starting Point for Change Managements

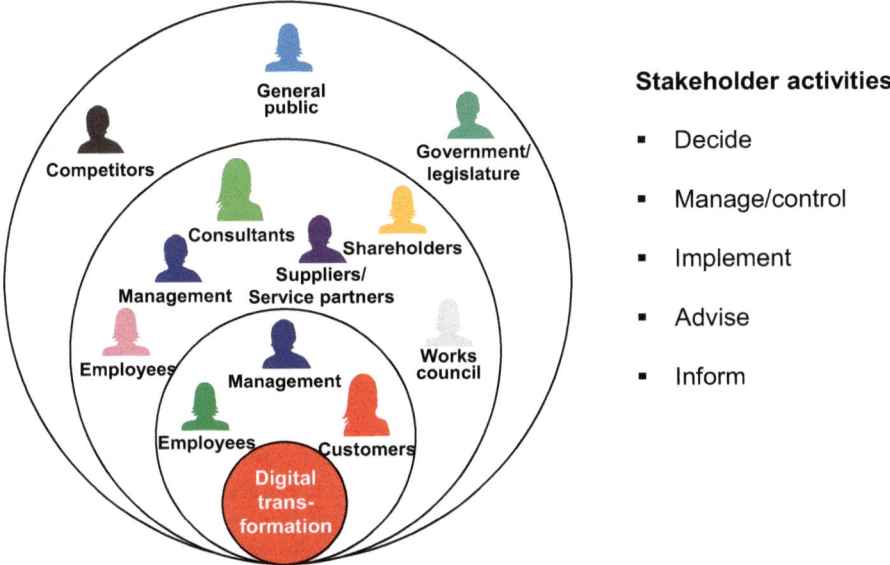

Fig. 4.2 Stakeholder onion model for identifying and supporting the relevant stakeholder

added to the description of the respective relationships in the stakeholder onion model. To do this, you analyze the different layers in the onion model from the inside out. These layers have given the model its name.

Depending on the task, four or five layers can be developed and filled with appropriate stakeholders. Here it is important that the relationship of the stakeholders to the project is not shown on the basis of power, influence, or support, but on the basis of the **intensity of their respective involvement**. After all, it is often stakeholders with little power and influence (such as employees) who are most comprehensively challenged and affected in the course of a project (especially in a change process; cf. the analysis with the tool in Fig. 4.5).

The **steps for using the onion model** are presented below:

- **First Step**
  First, a small circle is drawn at the bottom of a sheet of paper. This visualizes the product, the service or the topic that is to be developed. The focus here is on **digital transformation**.
- **Second Step**
  A second circle is placed around this first circle. This circle contains the stakeholders who are directly affected by the product, service, or topic to be developed. Either the stakeholders to be located here are directly involved in the **process of development** or in the **process of use**. In the process of digital transformation, these are first of all the **employees** and **managers** internally and above all the **interested parties and customers** externally.

- **Third Step**
  In a third circle, the stakeholders who are involved in the development or implementation are positioned. These can initially be **other employees and managers**. Although they are not directly involved in the process of digital transformation, they are nevertheless influenced by it in their daily work. In addition, there are **service partners** (e.g., consultants, IT service providers) and **suppliers** (e.g., for 3D printers, robots) whose input is indispensable for the change process. The **shareholders** are also to be found in this circle.
- **Fourth Step**
  In the fourth circle, stakeholders should be positioned who are outside the company but are still very important for the success of the process. These include **governments** and **legislators**. The **general public** and **competitors** should also be included in this circle.
- **Fifth Step**
  The onion model already contains a lot of information after these four steps. In the fifth step, **relationship arrows** can be added to this model. The direction of the arrow indicates in which direction a relationship runs or whether it is mutual, if applicable. The thickness of the arrows can represent the **intensity of the relationship** and the color the **quality of the relationship**. According to a traffic light, tense relationships can be marked with red, neutral, purely working relationships with yellow and supportive relationships with green.

  In another level of information, the different **roles of the stakeholders** can be highlighted. For example, they may actively manage or control a process. Other roles are responsible for implementation or have an advisory function. Another group of stakeholders is only to be informed about upcoming changes. Shareholders and possibly also the works council may have to approve serious measures first.

  Another interesting level of information can be added if the **stakeholders' attitude towards the project** is marked by different colors. According to the traffic light method already presented, opponents can be marked with red, neutrals with yellow and supporters with green.

  In addition, the **importance of the stakeholders** can be shown. Particularly important stakeholders are marked in bold. These additional information levels were not integrated in Fig. 4.2 in order not to overload this representation here.

The greatest **importance of this stakeholder analysis** is attached to the information gained in the course of creating the onion model. The onion model "forces" users to broaden our perspective and not only consider the "usual suspects" in the stakeholder analysis. This ensures—already at the start of a change process—that no important stakeholder perspective is neglected.

If such a comprehensive inventory of the expectations and fears of the various stakeholders is not carried out, this can "fall on the feet" of the responsible managers later on. Then the change process may be slowed down or even stopped. This must be avoided by acting with foresight.

> **Think Box: Questions You Should Ask Yourself**
> - Do you already use the stakeholder onion model to integrate stakeholder management early and comprehensively in the change process?
> - Are all departments involved in filling out the stakeholder onion model with information?
> - Do you plan sufficient time in your change management to develop the stakeholder onion model before the start of the change process?
> - Where does the expertise for the use of the stakeholder onion model lie?
> - Who gives the go-ahead for such an analysis?

4.3 Tools for Identifying and Steering Change Management

When we let go of the idea that things must always go on as before, suddenly a thousand new possibilities invite new life.

4.3.1 Information Needs to Start a Change Process

One waits for the times to change, the other grabs hold of them and takes action.
Dante Alighieri

For most managers, a merger, a takeover or a strategic reorientation (e.g., the "digital transformation" of the company) is the biggest challenge they have or had to master. At the same time, it is often the task for which they have been least prepared. The following applies here:

Within the first 6 months after a sweeping strategic change, corporate value is created—or the opportunity to do so is lost.

After 6 months, the company is either on its way to normality—or mired in chaos. This is why it is essential for successful change management to work out the **relevant information needs** of a change process. To do this, it is important to consider the different **types of change processes** that come with the challenges of the digital age:

- **Change Management on the Level of Organizational Structures**
  In this case, the organizational structure of a company is further developed, which is reflected in the organization chart. This is often referred to as reorganization. Many measures discussed in Sect. 3.7 can lead to such changes.
- **Change Management on the Level of Processes**
  At the process level are the concepts for accelerating or improving internal processes, which relate to innovative concepts of project management (e.g., through the use of agile methods), a redesign of procurement or further

developments in production and sales. Many of the developments highlighted in Chap. 3 are reflected here.

- **Change Management on the Level of Business Models**
 Change management in this area takes place at the level of horizon 2 and horizon 3 business models (see Sect. 3.2). Business model innovations fall into this category. The acquisition of new business areas or entire companies is also often accompanied by change processes on horizons 2 and 3. However, this also includes the sale of entire divisions if they no longer fit the further developed vision and thus the corporate strategy.
- **Change Management on the Level of the Whole Business**
 At this stage, the entire company is realigned, as it were. This may be necessary if the existing performance engine is to be replaced by concepts developed in the course of the innovation engine (see Sect. 3.7.4; cf. Fig. 3.37).

The more comprehensive changes are initiated, the stronger the **internal resistance** will become—especially if top management does not present the new vision powerfully and does not consistently work towards its implementation through convincing storytelling (see Sect. 3.1). Then, in the eyes of the managers and staff affected by the change, what was previously seen as the "worst organization" becomes the supposedly best form. Because to the question "do we need change?" most people will answer "yes." When asked "would you like to change?" they are usually silent.

> **Food for Thought**
>
> *Elke Weber, Princeton University* (Frey 2020, p. 60):
>
> **"On average, we estimate the costs of change to be twice as high as the expected benefits."**
>
> This is why it is so important to find out early on what makes the relevant stakeholders "tick" and what their wishes, expectations, hopes and fears are (see Sect. 4.2). Only if this information is known—especially by the company's own managers and employees—and is taken into account in the change process, can the indispensable **cultural change** in the company succeed (cf. Schönbohm 2019a, b for more details). Without cultural change, (digital) change management will not succeed. After all:
>
> **Culture eats strategy for breakfast!**
>
> *Peter Drucker*
>
> Without a thorough cultural development, the entry into horizon 2 and horizon 3 business models in particular cannot be achieved. If a cultural transformation does not succeed, the classic **rejection reactions** set in, which can also be observed in organ transplantation:
>
> **Rejection of non-genuine cells**—or of new ideas, concepts, products, services, strategies!

4.3 Tools for Identifying and Steering Change Management

Memory Box
Digitalization is not a process or technology issue, but a cultural issue!
Cultural changes must be anchored in the company through structural and process-related adjustments.

When **designing the change management process**, a distinction must be made between the following phases. These phases are also accompanied by different information needs on the part of those affected (cf. Lewin 1947; cf. in further detail Rasche and Rehder 2018; Doppler and Lauterburg 2019):

- **Phase 1: Unfreezing**
  The starting point for any kind of change process is the realization that the corporate status quo—at the various levels discussed—no longer meets the requirements of the markets and/or the corporate strategy. The need for change processes is now increasingly entering the consciousness of the people concerned—or at least it should. In order to make change possible, a **"thawing" of the existing state** must be achieved, as it were (cf. Fig. 4.3; cf. Ryerson University 2011, p. 18).

  Only in this way can the willingness to change be achieved. However, since the company is often in a **state of equilibrium** before the change process is initiated, many forces are released here to maintain the previous state. In order to overcome these inertial forces, the desired goal of the change process must be visibly worked out in this phase. It is imperative that it becomes clear why change is necessary and unavoidable. A new corporate vision is particularly important in this process (see Sect. 3.1).

- **Phase 2: Moving**
  In this second phase, the task is to initiate the necessary changes in the most diverse areas—oriented towards the change goals. Here, those affected have to say goodbye to "things they have grown fond of" and enter new territory in many areas. The often balanced initial state in the company is left behind in order to create space for new structures, processes, strategies, offers, and business areas. In this phase, a **new state of equilibrium is to be defined** and achieved step by step.

  The **task** to be accomplished here becomes clear in Fig. 4.3. In every change process, a previously largely balanced state must be left behind, e.g., in order to develop and implement new products, services and/or business models. For this, managers and employees have to leave their respective comfort zones—without already having a certainty of where the journey is to go in concrete terms (cf. Fig. 3.94). Finally, powerful visions also allow for different ways to implement them.

  In this second phase, the staff often "feels" that they are standing on **quicksand** and—again from a subjective perspective—has not yet found any **anchor points for the new direction**: the existing is melting away (phase 1), the new has not yet taken concrete shape (phase 3). In between, a large neutral zone opens up in phase 2, which must be creatively and energetically shaped if a change process is to be successful (cf. Fig. 4.3).

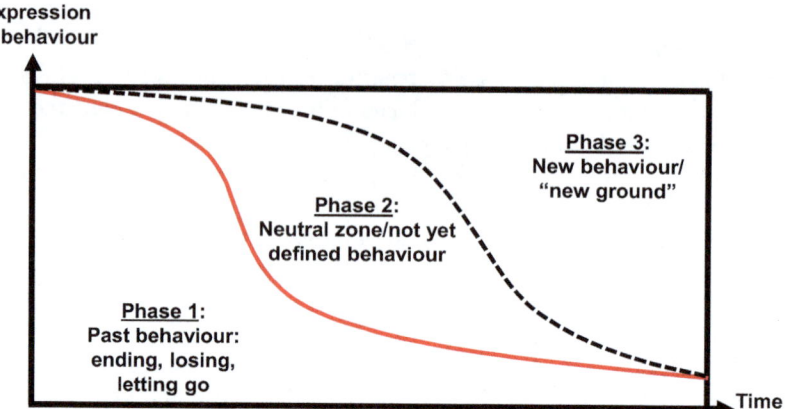

Fig. 4.3 Challenges in the change process

> **Memory Box**
> In this phase of the change process, we need **flexicurity**—flexibility and security together! On the one hand, we need to be flexible in order to enter new territory. On the other hand, we also need security for all concerned to enter this terra incognita. The necessary security for this can be provided by the still valid **corporate values**. These values can—like a concrete slab—enable steadfastness even in the change process. At the same time, the **company's vision** provides us with certainty about the **destination of the journey** through its directional function. As leaders, we have to convey both when we demand **flexibility** from our team and from ourselves.
>
> - **Phase 3: Refreezing**
>   In the third phase, an attempt is made to **anchor the new state of equilibrium**. It is crucial that processes are used to anchor this new state. These include incentive systems for managers and employees that reward the implementation of the new strategy. In addition, qualification profiles must be further developed and many internal processes adapted accordingly (see Sect. 3.6).
>   If this does not succeed, the **inertia in companies** can lead to a quick return to the "old rut" and the change process fails. The refreezing of the new target state in the company is a necessary prerequisite for the changes to become sustainable and have the desired effects.
>
> Often, however, the desired **goal of a new state of equilibrium** is not achieved, not comprehensively and/or not within the planned time corridor. What causes can be responsible for this? Experiences with change
>
> (continued)

management processes show that above all the following eight **obstacles of successful change management** have to be overcome:

- The **lack of understanding of the necessity of the change process** among managers and employees is often the biggest hurdle in the implementation of change. This need for information must be met as early as possible and as comprehensively as necessary.
- The **lack of a guiding figure for the change process at top management level** undermines acceptance of the required changes. Therefore, it must be consistently signaled through words and deeds that top management support is available—especially in challenging change situations.
- A **lack of experience with change processes** in the workforce makes successful implementation difficult. To overcome this, appropriate training programs should be set up and, if necessary, external consultants should be brought in as change managers.
- **Insufficient know-how to cope with new tasks** slows down the transformation process. Therefore, in addition to training in "change management," content-related training should also be carried out. These can cover topics such as the development of new business models, digitalization in production, the use of artificial intelligence in marketing and sales, agile management, digitalization of controlling or networking via the Internet of Things—classic contents of a (digital) training agenda (see Sect. 3.6.2).
- **Trench warfare between different people, levels, and departments** ties up important energy on side issues. Therefore, such unproductive disputes must be recognized promptly and consistently stopped. It is imperative to overcome silo and competitive thinking. Management must not allow any room for such "games"!
- The **lack of a remuneration and incentive system corresponding to the new vision**, the new goals and the new strategy can be misinterpreted as insufficient management approval of the change process. In this case, HR must ensure in good time that the vision, goals, and strategy on the one hand and the incentive system on the other are aimed in the same direction.
- If the **core business is very demanding** in terms of time and no additional staff is involved, there will not be sufficient resources left to drive the change process forward energetically and creatively—even if one wants to!
- The **inability or unwillingness** of parts of the workforce **to change** is also a major obstacle. Therefore, it is important to recognize the "resistance fighters" in one's own organization as early as possible—and to say goodbye to them if necessary.

▶ **Food for Thought**
If the **incentive system** is not aligned with the new strategic goal line, managers, and employees come into conflict. Should behavior be aligned with the new goals if at the same time the "old" behavior is rewarded? In such a situation, one should not be surprised if the majority of the workforce follows the monetary incentives. Finally, an unadjusted incentive system can also be interpreted to mean that the management itself is not yet convinced of the new strategic direction. Otherwise, they would have already adapted the incentive system accordingly.

How strongly your company's incentive system is already aligned with the new requirements—for example, in the direction of agility, innovative strength and thinking and acting in networks and new business models—can be determined yourself using the following **litmus test**. For this purpose, you could and should carry out a **self-critical analysis** of what your employees and managers are rewarded for:

- Are employees and managers rewarded for achieving precisely defined goals in their own area?
- Are they rewarded (also) for network thinking—beyond their own area of responsibility?
- Is breaking out of well-trodden paths rewarded?
- Is challenging long-established processes and structures singled out as particularly praiseworthy?
- Are those rewarded who are willing to "lend" their best employees to virtual teams?
- Are those employees and managers who come up with the boldest ideas to cannibalize the existing business incentivized?
- Or are those rewarded—as before—who continue unwaveringly along the path once taken?

The answers to the questions show you what distance you may still have to overcome.
Motto: Everything remains different!

Think Box: Questions You Should Ask Yourself
- How well prepared are your managers and employees for a digital transformation?
- What kind of change process do you have?
- Is it primarily a question of changes at the level of organizational structures?
- Do you have to develop processes comprehensively?
- Do you have change management at the level of business models?

(continued)

- Does change management cover the entire company?
- What importance is attached to cultural change in your company?
- How consistently are the unfreezing phase, the movement phase and the freezing phase developed in your company?
- Do you take sufficient account of the demand for flexicurity—flexibility and security?
- Do you have the biggest obstacles to successful change management in mind?
- Have you succeeded in gaining a comprehensive insight into the necessity of the change process?
- Do you have a leading figure for the change process at top management level?
- Can you overcome a lack of experience with change processes in the workforce through training programs?
- Do you support your managers and staff in building up the necessary know-how to cope with new tasks?
- Can you contain trench warfare between different people, levels, and departments?
- Are your remuneration and incentive systems aligned with the new vision, goals and strategy?
- Are sufficient human and financial resources available for the change process?
- If necessary, do you part with managers and staff who are neither able nor willing to support the change process?
- Where does the main responsibility of change processes lie in your company?

4.3.2 Instruments to Manage Change Processes

First the mindset—then the technique!

For the management of change processes, you need powerful tools. The **most important tools for successful change management** are presented here:

- **Involvement and communication of the CEO or members of the management board**
  The CEO and other top managers must be continuously involved in the change process. It is also their task to communicate the vision of the change process and the progress achieved to the staff.
- **Divisional/departmental meetings on the topic of change**
  Regular divisional/departmental meetings on the topic of change keep all managers and staff continuously informed about the need for change. Here,

information must also be provided on the measures that have been introduced or are still necessary. Above all, it is important to continuously inform about the successes already achieved in the change process in order to give courage for the next steps (keyword "self-efficacy;" see Sect. 3.6.4).
- **Appreciation of the contributions made**
  In addition to the still indispensable day-to-day business, a change process brings with it a multitude of other tasks and consequently a high level of additional (time) commitment. The contributions of key performers, which are needed for the change, must be recognized regularly.
- **Developing the new requirements for managers and staff**
  In order to overcome the "neutral zone" of the not yet defined area shown in Fig. 4.3 as quickly as possible, the new requirements must be specified quickly. To this end, a redefinition of tasks, responsibilities, and competencies is indispensable.
- **Conduct face-to-face meetings**
  In order to manage the emotional sensitivities of the employees concerned, it is also necessary to have regular face-to-face meetings. Managers must plan and allocate a lot of additional time for this.
- **Adjusting individual performance evaluations**
  To ensure that the incentive systems are in line with the new strategic orientation, these systems must be aligned with the new goals in a timely manner.

As a **change manager**, you need to know which managers and employees you can rely on during the change process and which ones are more likely to resist change. The **types of people to be distinguished in change processes** can be analyzed by accessing Fig. 4.4. Whether managers and employees are more likely

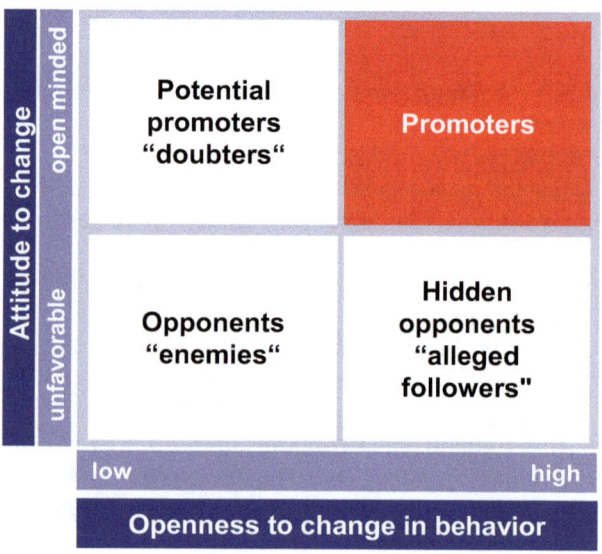

Fig. 4.4 Matrix to segment employees within change processes

4.3 Tools for Identifying and Steering Change Management

to be positive or negative about change depends on the extent of **perceived personal risks**.

When managing the change process, it can be assumed that—especially at the start—a small **team of promoters** will be confronted with a large majority of people with a negative attitude. These include **sceptics** who do not believe in the success of the process. The **resisters** and especially the **brakemen** deliberately oppose the changes. They delay decisions and consistently boycott their implementation. If people with such resistance potential are not won over to the cause in the course of the change process or leave the company, the change process will fail or be significantly delayed.

> **Memory Box**
> Therefore, one important guiding principle must be taken to heart:
> **Turn those affected into participants.**
>
> Ideally, it is even possible to turn managers and employees in the course of the change process not only into people who "fulfill tasks," but into people who are "fulfilled" by the "tasks themselves." Then these people are convinced of the direction of the change. A powerful vision can make an important contribution to this.
>
> Brakemen, resisters and sceptics must be consistently integrated into the change process with appropriate tasks. However, care must be taken that individual teams do not consist only of brakemen or sceptics. In all teams, promoters are particularly called upon. These promoters must be trained and positioned as **change managers**. They are the central resource for the successful implementation of the change process.
>
> In order to recognize why the workforce reacts so differently to the emerging changes, the extent to which they are affected by a change process must be determined. This can be done using the **matrix of concern** in Fig. 4.5. We distinguish between the two axes "extent of changes in mindset and behavior patterns" on the one hand and "extent of threat" on the other. This matrix enables a **typology of the perceived changes**. At the same time, it shows typical behavioral patterns that are to be expected as reactions to the emerging changes. The tasks for change management and the managers entrusted with it are derived from this.
>
> Based on the **matrix of concern**, the **intensity of the change** for the affected managers and employees, but also for the involved areas and departments, must be recorded. The two dimensions mentioned above must be taken into account (cf. Fig. 4.5):
> - **Extent of the threat—from the perspective of each individual employee**
>   The following applies: the greater the extent of the perceived threat, the greater the need for orientation and security. As the threat increases, resistance also tends to increase.
>
> (continued)

- **Extent of the necessary changes in thinking and behavior patterns—related to each individual employee**
  The more extensive the necessary changes in thinking and behavior, the more unwillingness and resistance are to be expected and the stronger the defensive reactions will be.

If the extent of change is considered low, but the personal threat is considered high, **fear** and a **feeling of powerlessness** are often the reaction (first field Fig. 4.5). If the extent of the changes and the personal threat are rated as low, **lack of interest** in the change process and the resulting consequences is the consequence (second field). If the extent of the changes is high but the personal threat is low, this can also result in **lack of interest** and possibly also **reactance** in the sense of a rejection of the changes (third field). If the extent of the changes and the personal threat are high, **fear** and **reactance** combine to form an explosive mixture (fourth field).

The analysis based on the **matrix of concern** is to be carried out by the managers from the **perspective of each individual employee**—a **training in empathy**! This is because the same changes can be interpreted and evaluated differently against the background of the individual experiences of each employee. Young, risk-taking employees may see such changes as a career opportunity, while established and often older employees fear for their earned vested rights (cf. also Fig. 2.1).

Figure 4.6 shows which reactions are "typically" to be expected in certain change processes. Here—in addition to the digital transformation—other change triggers are positioned depending on the changes they entail and the threat intensity. It becomes clear that the **digital transformation** is one of the change processes that are usually accompanied by **comprehensive changes in mindset and behavior patterns** on the one hand and a **high threat potential** on the other.

The assessment in Fig. 4.6 of the typical behavioral patterns can diverge significantly between the employees and managers concerned. In the majority of cases, however, the various triggers of the change processes can be located as in Fig. 4.6 with regard to the reactions to be expected. Depending on these results, the employees are to be supervised in each case—individually.

4.3 Tools for Identifying and Steering Change Management   517

Fig. 4.5 Matrix of concern-typology of perceived changes and possible reactions

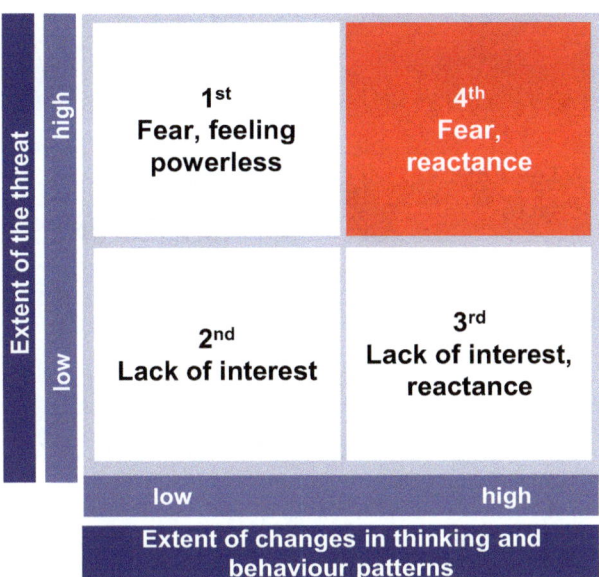

Fig. 4.6 Influencing factors in the change process

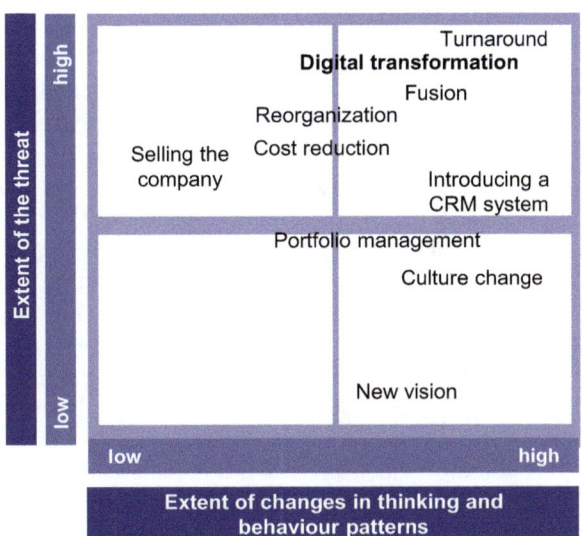

▶ **Food for Thought**
We would rather bear the evils we have than flee to the unknown.
After *William Shakespeare, Hamlet*.
It is important that you, as a change manager, are aware of which **influencing factors lead to positioning in the matrix of concern**. A look at

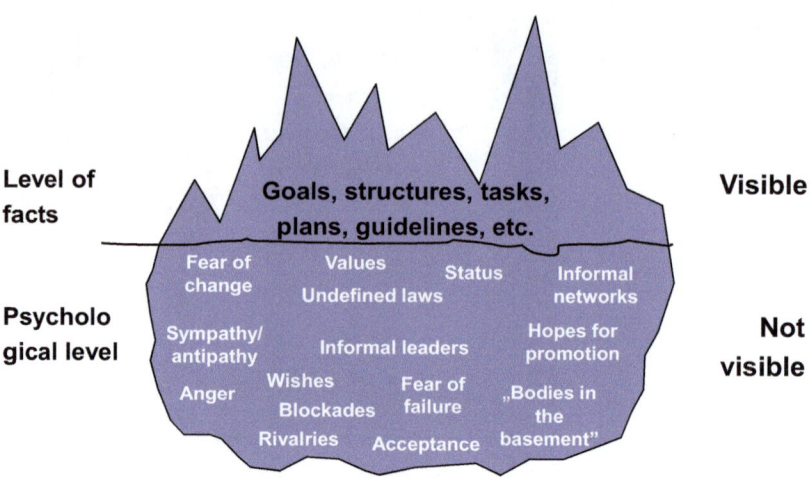

Fig. 4.7 Iceberg model: factors influencing the change process

the **iceberg model** in Fig. 4.7 will help you here (cf. Doppler and Lauterburg 2019, p. 254). In the course of a change process—but not only then—rather rationally controlled managers focus on the visible **level of "facts and figures."** However, no change process can be successfully designed on this level alone! The **invisible elements of the psychological level** are much more important. You should take these into account comprehensively in the course of the change process, because this is where acceptance or resistance to change manifests itself (cf. Schein and Schein 2018).

The aspects in the iceberg model are presented again in a different framework in Fig. 4.8. The **action matrix of the change process** shows where the areas "should," "can," "may," and "want" are located and what the contents of each are. In order to influence the **"should,"** the company's systems must be developed accordingly. The **"can"** is dominated by the—possibly newly acquired—skills. The **"may"** is dominated by the values of the company, which are part of the cultural experience of the company. The **"want"** is based on the values and beliefs of each individual member of the workforce. Every change manager is well advised to influence all these areas—a focus on "should" and "can" alone is not enough!

Figure 4.9 shows the **motivation triangle** for filling out the "shoulds" (cf. Graf 2018, p. 420). The requirements shown here are not only to be considered when **setting up change teams**, but are also important when **recruiting employees and managers** to achieve digital excellence. To analyze the profiles of individuals, you can use the concepts presented in Sect. 3.6.3.

One thing should be emphasized in addition to these factors:

The biggest obstacle to a change process is (previous) success!

4.3 Tools for Identifying and Steering Change Management

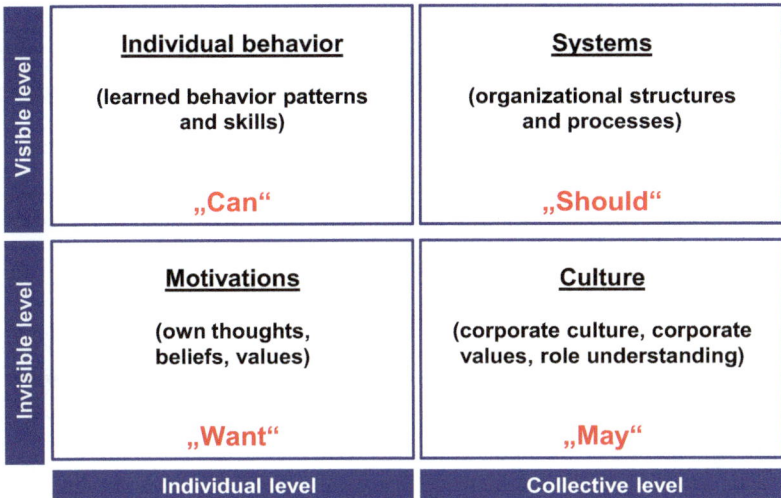

Fig. 4.8 Action matrix of the change process

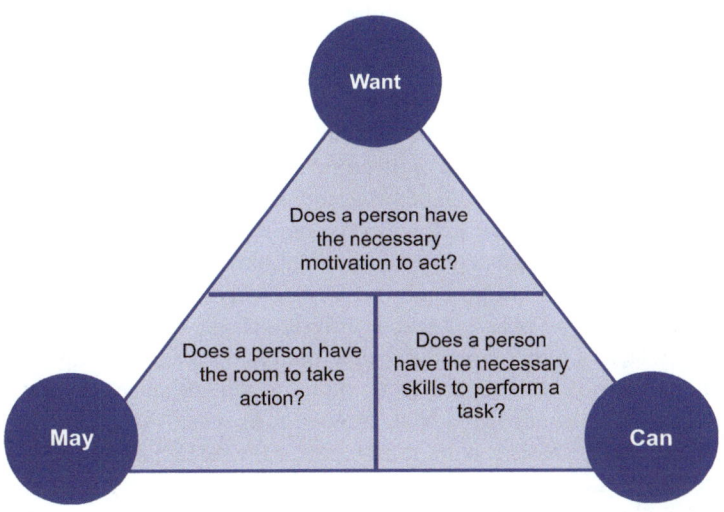

Fig. 4.9 Motivation triangle

▶ **Storytelling** At the beginning of a bank's summer university, which I was privileged to attend as a keynote speaker, the CEO stood in front of his team and said:

"Ladies and gentlemen, we have had our company's best financial year—and that is why we need to change!"

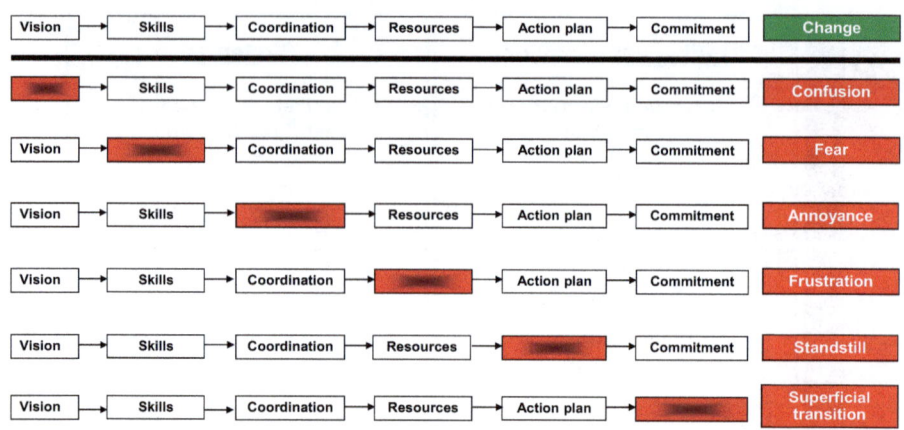

Fig. 4.10 Preconditions for successful change management

What a powerful announcement—against the forces of inertia that claim: "We are doing fine after all. Why should we change?"

In order to successfully shape a **change process** as a whole, the prerequisites shown in Fig. 4.10 must be fulfilled. First and foremost, a convincing **vision** must be communicated, and the **skills** necessary for implementation must be built up within the company. In addition, **coordination** is needed to harmonize and network the individual implementation steps. Furthermore, as already mentioned, the necessary **resources** for the change process must be made available: financially, in terms of personnel and in terms of time. To ensure coordinated and goal-oriented steps, an **action plan** with concrete milestones must be implemented. Finally, a **commitment** is needed—from top management to the "last" employee. If all elements are considered equally, the desired **change** can be achieved. Whenever even one element is not considered, failure is pre-programmed in different ways.

If there is a lack of entrepreneurial vision, **confusion** arises (cf. Fig. 4.10). All or many move—but not with regard to a common goal because this has not been communicated or does not even exist. **Fear** sets in when the managers and staff concerned lack the necessary skills to implement the realignment, and no opportunity is created to acquire them. And fear is always the worst possible advisor! **Annoyance** and also anger are the result if the individual steps are not coordinated and therefore a lot of work is done "for the waste paper basket"—for example, through unwanted parallel work on comparable tasks.

Frustration builds up when the resources for the change steps that are recognized as necessary are lacking and therefore it is not possible to take the necessary steps. If there is no **action plan**, there is a risk of stagnation because no one wants to move in the wrong direction and there is no concrete impetus for action. Finally, if there is a lack of **commitment**, only a superficial change is achieved. The company only appears to be picking up speed—under the surface, however, everything remains the same and many do not leave their comfort zone (cf. Fig. 3.94)! Once again, it

4.3 Tools for Identifying and Steering Change Management

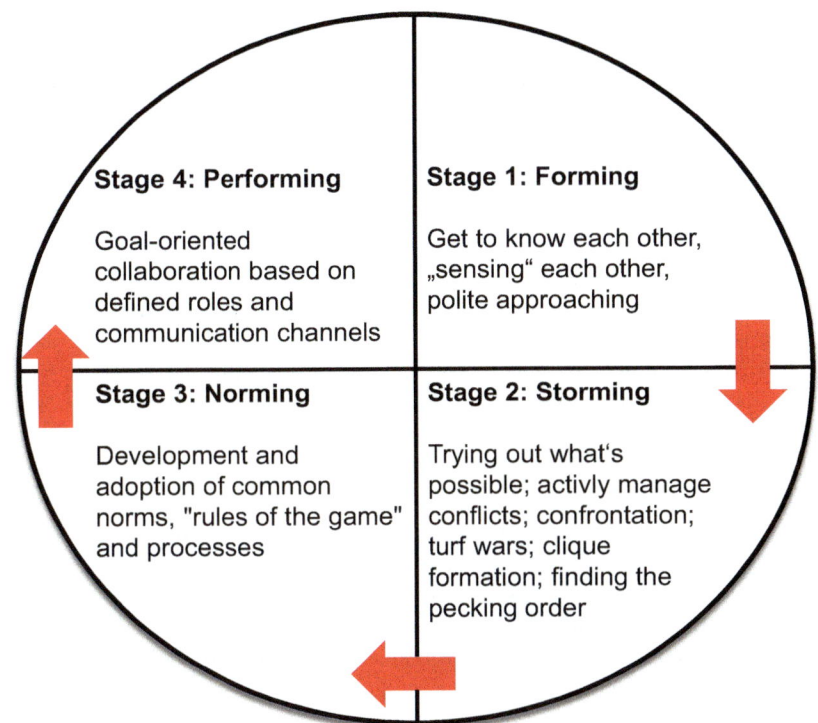

Fig. 4.11 Team development clock

becomes clear how comprehensively the task of change management must be understood.

The change processes associated with a digital transformation also affect the teams. The **team development clock** (also known as the **team clock**; cf. Tuckman, 1965) shows which tasks are associated with this. First of all, you can use the team development clock to **analyze the status quo of your team**—especially if it is not "functioning" properly (cf. Fig. 4.11).

The use of the team development clock is also indicated when there are **changes in the team composition or in the team leadership**. Here, too, the—usually balanced—system of the team is disturbed and all members have to realign themselves. This necessity also exists when **taking on innovative tasks** that force a realignment of the team. You should also use the team development clock when **forming new teams**. With all these changes, the team development clock starts running again.

The **team development clock** distinguishes between four phases (cf. Fig. 4.11). Your task is to design these phases in an active and goal-oriented way.

- **Forming Phase**

  Team building begins with the forming phase (cf. Fig. 4.11). The term "forming" can best be translated as "formation." Here the **initial getting to know** of all team members is in the foreground. They "get to know" each other and approach each other politely. At this stage, neither the goals nor the processes are known to the team as a whole. There are still uncertainties about how team meetings are conducted, how tasks are coordinated, what forms of communication are appropriate and what the incentives are—official and unofficial (e.g., image points with the boss!). The generally **"acceptable" rules of conduct in the team** are also still unclear. These team rules may include punctuality, reliability and the extent of private joint activities.

  The **performance of your team** is rather low in this phase because every person is still too preoccupied with himself. Therefore, you have the **non-delegable task** of first actively promoting the process of getting to know each other—as a host, so to speak. This can be achieved through welcome meetings, mentoring, rounds of introductions, etc. In addition, important information for further cooperation should be provided proactively. It has often been shown that a well-managed entry of team members pays off over many years through good cooperation. In the forming phase, it is your task as a leader to make **"clear announcements,"** to inform and to be available for exchange with the team members. Otherwise, missing information in this phase will be replaced by assumptions and rumors.

> **Memory Box**
> You must actively shape the forming phase and keep it as short as possible.

- **Storming Phase**

  The term "storming" already makes it clear that in this phase, the calm is over (cf. Fig. 4.11). All team members are—more or less—aware that now "the cake" is being distributed. Each team member has slowly formed a picture of the other members. **Sympathy** and **antipathy** become visible, cliques are formed. The first **conflicts** and **tensions** arise, which are also actively fought out. In a trial-and-error process, the team members try out what works and what does not in this team.

  In this phase, the so-called **pecking order** develops. This defines who is in which position in the **team hierarchy**. Who is the (perhaps only informal) leader, who belongs to the inner circle, who is more of a supporter and who is an outsider? Studies show time and again that teams are only productive when this pecking order has been found. In this finding process, there are often also intense **turf wars**, which have less factual than personal causes (cf. von Rosenstiel and Nerdinger 2011, pp. 280–356).

(continued)

In this phase, too, a lot of **energy is spent on team dynamics** that is not available for dealing with the actual tasks. Therefore, as a team leader, you are also called upon to actively shape things here and must not leave the team to its own devices. You must set limits by sanctioning certain patterns of behavior. However, you are also called upon as a **mediator, moderator** and **coach** to steer the group dynamics into a constructive path. This includes addressing conflicts openly and not escalating them. In this phase, you should help more introverted team members to be heard. Your primary task is to avoid psychological injuries during the disputes.

Memory Box
Only if you actively shape and steer this storming phase will you reach the next phase. At the same time, you demonstrate your ability as a true leader and earn respect from your team.
Because respect is not awarded, it is earned!

- **Norming Phase**
  In this phase—based on the results of the storming phase—**norms, rules, and processes for further cooperation** are defined (cf. Fig. 4.11). Without a preceding "storming," this **consolidation** will not take place. Now the team has (ideally) reached a higher level of maturity and knows how to deal with conflicts constructively and how to achieve problem solutions in an appreciative way. Rules of the game have been defined that are acceptable (to all).

  In this phase, you should work towards positioning yourself as an **emotional point of contact**. If leaders—due to inability, unwillingness and/or lack of knowledge—do not fill the role as **emotional leader**, this important role is taken over by another team member or even by a person outside the team. This person then becomes the so-called "mother of the company" and is the sought-after contact person in emotional questions—and no longer the "appointed" leader.

▶ **Food for Thought**
One thing should be given—especially to **male leaders**—on the way. Disputes (to avoid the martial term "battles") are usually not won with factual arguments (alone), even if these are often used as a pretext for decisions.

The truth is that our decisions—even in the business environment—are often more than 90% emotionally dominated! Male leaders in particular have to prove their ability as emotional people.

At the end of the norming phase, you have distributed the tasks and roles in the team. Everyone (ideally) knows what is expected of them. This clarifies the "how" of the cooperation. Now—and really only now—have the conditions been created for working together in a goal- and thus solution-oriented way.

> **Memory Box**
> In the **norming phase** you are also required to act as an **advisor** and **coach**. However, you no longer have to intervene as often and as energetically as before. Now you are more active in your role as a professional authority and as a coach who discusses the tasks at hand with the team and provides professional and personal support. Therefore, the forming phase should not last too long either.
>
> - **Performing Phase**
>   A team has reached its **highest level of productivity** only with the performing phase (cf. Fig. 4.11). The group conflicts have been resolved, so that now (ideally) full concentration on the tasks can take place. The **appreciative cooperation** necessary for this is achieved through the **common rules and norms**—and remains until the next disruptive event causes the cycle of the team development clock to start again with the forming phase.
>
> Such an ideal-typical process presupposes an appropriately trained manager who also focuses on appreciation, open and honest communication and fairness in cooperation. However, this is not always the case in everyday business life.

▶ **Storytelling** In my leadership seminars, I always inform the participants that a leader should always have **two pieces of luggage** at hand. One is a **classic toolbox** equipped with a wide variety of tools and methods for everyday business. Ideally, you have already been able to add some tools to your toolbox while working through this book.

In addition, all managers, but also all employees, partners, teachers, parents—in fact all people—need another toolbox in the shape of a **red cross kit.** The most important ingredients here are "listening" and "empathy"! After all, many of our interlocutors don't want to be presented with a solution right away, but "just" an open ear!

By the way, this is often the case in private life as well!

You should develop a **deep understanding** of the individual **phases of the team development clock** and the associated emotional and rational sensitivities in order to be able to act appropriately in the various phases. It is important to note that none of these phases can be skipped during team building—even if leaders would (sometimes) like to. However, it is also true that as a leader you have to step on the gas so that the first three phases are passed through cleanly but also quickly. Otherwise, the team will never work together productively. Therefore, you should lead the team purposefully from phase to phase.

▶ **Food for Thought**
For a change process, it is important that all managers and employees are mentally in motion. If you are moving, it is easier to move in a new direction. Those who stand still—mentally and physically—must first fight against inertia before movement becomes possible.
And: **inertia slows down the necessary dynamics in the change process.**

> **Think Box: Questions You Should Ask Yourself**
> - Are all change managers aware of the most important tools of successful change management?
> - Are these tools also used competently by the managers on a regular basis?
> - Have you identified the relevant types of people in change processes for your company?
> - Has the team of promoters for the change process been put together using this matrix to segment employees within change processes?
> - Do your managers work with the matrix of concern in order to gain an understanding of the sensitivities of the respective employees?
> - Are all your leaders aware of the influencing factors for positioning in the matrix of concern?
> - Do your managers master the action matrix of the change process?
> - Do you use the motivation triangle for setting up change teams as well as for recruiting new staff?
> - In your change process, do you have—at the same time—a focus on the vision, the necessary skills, coordination, and resources, do you have an action plan and do you strive for real commitment?
> - Are all your leaders familiar with the team development clock?
> - Can you impart this knowledge to all managers—in a timely manner?
> - Who is responsible for this knowledge transfer?

4.3.3 Flow of Change Processes

People who are crazy enough to think they can change the world are the ones who do.
Steve Jobs

If you are responsible for the successful design of a change management process, you should look at the typical **patterns of behavior within a change process.** These are illustrated in Fig. 4.12 using the **timeline** and the **perceived own competence** (cf. Streich 2016, p. 24).

Fig. 4.12 Sequences of a classic change management process

When managers and employees are presented with the prospect of a far-reaching change process (keyword "information"), this often initially triggers a **shock reaction**. The perceived own competence decreases because the person concerned does not yet know exactly how to react and master the new challenges. When body and mind have recovered from the shock ("internal processing" phase), many affected persons show **rejection** or **withdrawal**. With this behavior, the perceived competence increases again because now—but only apparently—a solution exists: to stand up to it. For managers, this behavior of employees often occurs unexpectedly and therefore also surprisingly. Every manager who is confronted with such a behavior pattern should bear in mind that this resistance corresponds to normal human behavior in the course of a change process (cf. team development clock in Fig. 4.11).

Ideally, the phase of rejection is followed by **rational acceptance** of the situation. Here the affected person rationally accepts their fate, but has not yet come to terms with it emotionally. Ideally, the affected person will then **accept the situation emotionally.** It is the task of the change manager and above all of the respective leader to ensure that this phase is actually reached.

This should be followed by **learning phases** to enable the staff to prepare for the new tasks and the new challenges ("training/coaching" phase). Appropriate offers must be made for this in the change process, because this learning does not happen by itself! After several learning phases, a **commitment**, a rational and emotional YES to change can finally be achieved. This is the prerequisite for reaching the phase of integrating the new challenges and finally the "performing" phase. Depending on the extent of the change, this process can take many months or even years!

For the **change process to be successful**, it is imperative that the following elements are in place. The **starting signal for the change process** has to be given by the CEO or the management of the company. First of all, the goals and the need for action should be formulated concisely (keyword "storytelling," see Sect. 2.1.1). In addition, it is indispensable that the contributions of top management to the change process become visible on an ongoing basis. Here it is particularly important that the "words" are followed by appropriate "deeds."

A committed **mentor in top management** accompanies the entire change process and continuously helps to overcome the obstacles that inevitably arise in the course of the change process. This mentor is highly visible in every phase and also comprehensively approachable! **Continuous communication between those responsible for change and the company management** is required in order to involve the company management in the process and to secure their support on an ongoing basis. At the same time, the defined milestones must be checked to see if they have been achieved and, if necessary, further measures must be initiated to achieve the goals.

In addition, it is necessary to act according to the **team development clock** in order to reach the performing phase as quickly as possible in all teams. Individual **performance evaluations** must be aligned with the new targets in order to reward the desired new behavioral patterns accordingly and to anchor them in the long term. Why should a person engage in a new behavior if the "old behavior" is still being rewarded?

In order to achieve sustainable changes, you should also install **change controlling** (see also Sect. 3.8)! A central prerequisite for this is the **formulation of precise change goals**. Change controlling enforces precision in implementation and makes (undesired) deviations quickly visible to everyone! Such deviations must be escalated promptly so that they are also present at the management level and countermeasures can be taken accordingly. Furthermore, the installation of change controlling underlines the seriousness and permanence of the intended changes! Throughout the company, it becomes clear that the defined change is actually being pursued in a sustainable manner.

All of the activities and processes described are necessary to successfully shape the change process associated with a digital transformation. The associated challenges are summarized in the **house of digital transformation** in Fig. 4.13.

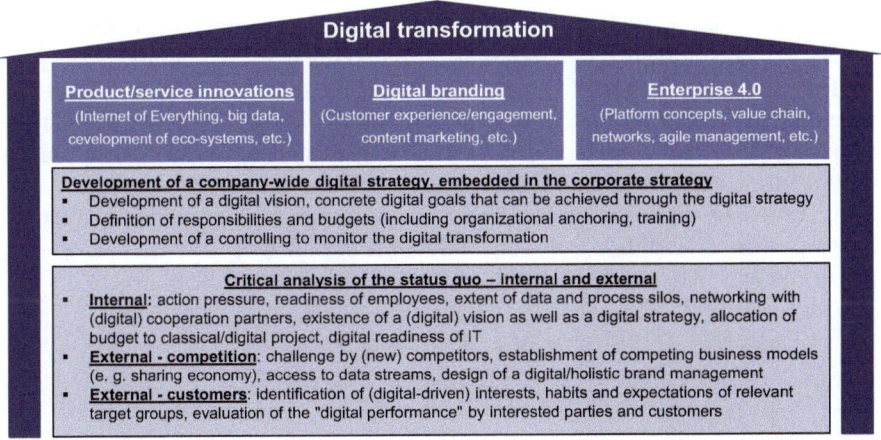

Fig. 4.13 The house of digital transformation

As with any process of strategic realignment, you should start with a critical **analysis of the status quo** in digital transformation. Consequently, this step forms the ground floor of the **house of digital transformation**. You should align the analysis equally internally and externally. On the **inside of the company**, it is about determining the experienced pressure to act and the willingness of your workforce to change. In addition, the status quo of the digital business performance should be recorded (see the analysis tools from Chaps. 2 and 3).

In the **external relationship of the company**, two directions of analysis are particularly important for you: the **competitors** and the **customers**. What challenges from (new) competitors can already be identified? Have business models already been established in your sector that have taken on the challenges better than your company? What access does your company have to relevant data streams compared to other providers? To what extent do you already implement holistic brand management—also in comparison to important competitors?

External analysis also includes the extent to which the (digitally-driven) interests, habits, and expectations of your prospects and customers have changed. How do they assess your "digital performance"—also in the light of relevant competitors? What is the need for action—from the perspective of **prospects** and **customers**—for your company (see the analytical tools in Chap. 2)?

Based on the insights gained, the **digital vision is developed**—the starting point of the goal and strategy work (see Sect. 3.1). For this purpose, you should not only develop concrete digital goals, but also define responsibilities and provide budgets. In addition, controlling should not only be geared towards monitoring the digital transformation, but also towards accompanying and supporting it constructively and in terms of content (see Sect. 3.8). Within the digital strategy, the targeted **product and service innovations** as well as the **business model innovations** must be named, which are based on the Internet of Everything and/or big data (see Sects. 3.2, 3.3 and 3.4).

Based on your strategic definitions, the implementation of **holistic brand management** is to be aimed for, which focuses, for example, on customer experience management or the implementation of an omni-channel strategy (see Sect. 3.5; Kilian and Kreutzer 2022; Esch and Kochann 2020). In order to underpin such processes organizationally, the development is moving in the direction of **enterprise 4.0**. Here, for example, the aforementioned platform concepts, value chain systems and powerful IT systems must be established as enablers. This field also includes the establishment of agile management, which uses innovative project management instruments (see Sects. 3.4, 3.6, and 3.7).

The **house of digital transformation** provides a **compass** on how to design a change process to establish your company in the digital age.

4.3 Tools for Identifying and Steering Change Management

Memory Box
It is important to emphasize once again:
  Digital transformation is not a project, but a process.
  Transformation is the new modus operandi—and it will never be over!

If you are personally responsible for the successful implementation of a change management process, you should make comprehensive use of the tools presented here. It is important that you ensure **top management support** throughout the process; otherwise, even the best instruments are of no use. At the beginning, create an understanding of the **necessity of the change process** among all managers involved. In addition, all managers should be prepared for the fact that in the course of the change process, there will be a **high degree of emotionality** on the part of the **employees concerned.** These emotional outbursts must first be accepted. Without such acceptance, the emotions cannot be managed. Only then can it be possible to direct the energy associated with the emotionality towards the common (new) goal.

Celebrate even (smaller) successfully **completed milestones** with the affected staff and managers. For the majority of your staff, the change process means one thing above all: additional work on top of the daily business that still has to be managed.

Plan enough time for the management of the change process. You will need much more time than you think at the beginning.

And do not forget the three most important **success factors of change management**:
  Communication, communication, communication.

▶ **Food for Thought**
The purest form of madness is to leave everything as it is and hope that something will change.
  Albert Einstein
  What we all need?
  A desire for the future!

Think Box: Questions You Should Ask Yourself
- Are you and your managers aware of the typical behavior patterns within a change process?
- Do your managers know that in the course of change processes, they are needed above all as managers of emotions?
- Do you already use the house of digital transformation as an orientation framework for your actions and your internal and external communication?

(continued)

- Did you carry out a comprehensive critical analysis of the status quo at the start of the digital transformation?
- Has the status quo of digital business performance been critically identified?
- Are you aware of the challenges posed by established and new competitors?
- Do you know as precisely as possible what your customers expect from you today and tomorrow?
- Do you have a convincing digital vision?
- Have you defined precise goals and strategies for the transformation?
- Is your controlling geared towards sustainable support and accompaniment of the digital transformation?
- Have you tackled product and service innovations as well as business model innovations?
- Are you already working on holistic brand management?
- Are you driving your company's development towards enterprise 4.0?
- Do you also celebrate (smaller) successfully completed milestones with managers and employees?
- Do your managers plan enough time for the management of the change process?
- Are all actors responsible in the change process aware of the three most important success factors of change management?

Literature

Doppler, K., & Lauterburg, C. (2019). *Change management: Den Unternehmenswandel gestalten* (14th ed.). Campus.

Esch, F.-R., & Kochann, D. (2020). Customer experience – auf dem Weg zum Kundenerlebnis-Champion. In M. Stumpf (Ed.), *Die 10 wichtigsten Zukunftsthemen im marketing* (2nd ed., pp. 255–279). Haufe.

Frey, A. (2020). Ich kann nicht bleiben, wie ich bin, trotz .... *Frankfurter Allgemeine Sonntagszeitung*, 27.12.2020, p. 60.

Graf, R. (2018). *Die neue Entscheidungsstruktur, Mit gemeinsam getragenen Entscheidungen zum Erfolg*. Hanser.

Kilian, K., & Kreutzer, R. (2022). *Digitale Markenführung, Digital Branding in Zeiten divergierender Märkte*. Springer Gabler.

Lewin, K. (1947). Frontiers in group dynamics, concept, method and reality in social science; social equilibria and social change. *Human Relations, 1*(1), 5–41.

Rasche, C., & Rehder, S. A. (2018). *Change management*. Kohlhammer.

Ryerson University. (2011). *Change management*. Leadership Guide.

Schäfer, R. (2021). *Fallbeispiel "Ein totes Pferd reiten", Erfolgsstrategien für die moderne Verwaltungsführung*. Accessed 2.1.2021, from http://www.roland-schaefer.de/totespferd.htm

Schein, E. H., & Schein, P. (2018). *Organisationskultur und Leadership* (5th ed.). Vahlen.

Schönbohm, A. (Ed.). (2019a). *Digitalkultur – Facetten digitaler Transformation*. Schönbohm.

Schönbohm, A. (2019b). Ludic Leadership – Spielerische Antworten auf die kulturellen Herausforderungen der Digitalisierung. In A. Schönbohm (Ed.), *Digitalkultur – Facetten digitaler Transformation* (pp. 1–19). Schönbohm.

Streich, R. K. (2016). *Fit for leadership, Führungserfolg durch Führungspersönlichkeit* (2nd ed.). Springer Gabler.

Tuckman, B. W. (1965). Developmental sequence in small groups. *Psychological Bulletin, 63(6), 384–399.*

von Rosenstiel, L., & Nerdinger, F. W. (2011). *Grundlagen der Organisationspsychologie, Basiswissen und Anwendungshinweise* (7th ed.). Schäffer Poeschel.

Glossary

3 Horizons Model The 3 horizons model expresses the fact that companies today have to be active on three levels at the same time. Level 1 is about optimizing existing business models and their design. Level 2 deals with new business model options in existing markets. Level 3 is about the development of new (disruptive) business models.

5-forces Analysis (Industry Structure Analysis) The 5-forces analysis focuses on the five drivers of industry competition. This is why it is also referred to as an industry structure analysis. It determines how the rivalry in the industry, the threat of new suppliers and substitute products, and the behavioral strength of suppliers and customers affect the dynamics in the industry.

Accelerator An accelerator is an institution that supports start-ups in the development process for a certain period of time through coaching, among other things, and thus accelerates the development of a viable business model.

Algorithm An algorithm is a work instruction in the sense of formally formulated rules for the sequence of operations or as a sequence of steps for the automatic execution of a specific task to achieve a result within a limited period of time.

Ambidexterity Ambidexterity is about both mastering day-to-day business today (horizon 1) and shaping the future on horizons 2 and 3 at the same time.

Analysis of Digital Business Performance The analysis of digital business performance is used to assess the digital maturity of a company. For this purpose, the respective maturity level is determined on the basis of the following criteria: "vision, goals and strategies for the digital age," "future viability of the business model," "digitization of the value chain," "IT infrastructure, data basis and technologies," "exploitation of digital potentials by marketing and sales," "human resources strategies," "organizational concepts," and "controlling as enabler of the digital transformation." In terms of maturity, a distinction is made between the levels "not defined," "defined but not implemented," "defined but only partially implemented," "defined, mainly implemented," and "fully transformed."

Artificial Intelligence Artificial intelligence refers to the ability of a machine to perform cognitive tasks that are usually associated with the human mind. This includes possibilities for perception as well as the abilities to reason, to learn independently and thus to find solutions to problems on its own.

Bad Profit Bad profit refers to profits made by deceiving, misleading and/or overreaching customers.

Bar Camp (Also Participatory Conference) Bar camp is an open event format in which neither the contents nor the concrete course of the event is fixed at the beginning. These are only determined on site by and with the participants. The focus of a bar camp is on exchange between and discussion with the participants.

Basic Income, Unconditional An unconditional basic income is a concept according to which every citizen, irrespective of their economic situation, receives a financial allowance from the state that is fixed by law and equal for everyone—without any consideration in return.

BAT Companies The term BAT companies covers the main Chinese companies *Baidu* (a search engine like *Google*), *Alibaba* (like *Amazon*) and *Tencent*. Today, for "B," the company most often mentioned is *ByteDance*, the owner of the social media app *TikTok*.

Benefit A benefit (also called customer advantage) arises when products and/or services help customers to satisfy existing needs. Concentrating on the provision of benefits for customers is the core of marketing. Different types of benefits can be distinguished. The functional benefit is usually the core of an offer (e.g., the cleaning function of a soap or the rain protection of an umbrella). In the case of economic benefits, the aspects of cost and time savings can be cited (e.g., in online shopping and online banking). In saturated markets, the social benefit is of particular importance; this is also referred to as additional benefit. This arises when a product or service triggers positive feelings in the user beyond the functional and/or economic benefit ("I drive a great *Audi*." "I write with a *Montblanc* pen."). A social benefit also arises, for example, in the peer group if the use of certain products or the use of certain services goes hand in hand with social recognition (in the past when driving an SUV, today more likely when buying a *Tesla*, or when doing without long-distance flights).

Big Data Big data refers to large amounts of data that originate from a wide variety of areas (including companies and private environments) and can hardly be handled with manual or classic methods of data processing. Five dimensions are used to describe it: volume (i.e., the volume of data), velocity (i.e., the speed of data generation), variety (i.e., the variety of data sources and data formats), veracity (i.e., the quality of the data and data sources) and value (i.e., the value of the data).

Bio Hacking/Body Hacking Bio hacking/body hacking is the transfer of the idea of IT hacks to biological systems and here, especially to the human body. Bio hacking aims to change the body. Here, people experiment, for example, with implants and other methods that intervene in a person's physical processes. An entry point for this can be so-called self-medical hacks, e.g., DNA tests carried out independently. Based on a multitude of data, various far-reaching forms of physical self-optimization can be carried out.

Blue Ocean Strategy A blue ocean strategy attempts to find new market segments away from highly competitive markets (so-called red oceans) that have no competition, at least for a certain period of time (so-called blue oceans).

Business Analytics Business analytics describes both the skills and technologies as well as the processes of examining corporate data in order to make business decisions on the basis of the insights gained.

Business Model A business model describes how a company creates and markets specific products and/or services for different target groups. A successful business model is characterized by the fact that it interlocks different elements of the value chain in such a way that it generates a high benefit for customers, aims for profitability and at the same time is difficult for competitors to copy.

Business Model Canvas The business model canvas is an instrument for analyzing and developing business models. Nine building blocks are distinguished for this purpose. These are: "key partners," "key activities," "key resources," "value proposition," "customer segments," "customer relationships," "sales channels," "cost structures," and "revenue structures" of the company.

Business Model Innovation A business model innovation occurs when important elements of a business model are redesigned or a completely new business model is used.

Change Management Change management encompasses the goal-oriented and planned management of change processes using various concepts and instruments.

Closed Innovation Model In the closed innovation model, companies primarily develop and market ideas that have been generated within the company itself (especially in R&D or product management).

Cloud Computing In cloud computing, formerly stationary hardware and software systems (so-called on-premise solutions) are outsourced to external service providers. The necessary connections to these are usually established via the Internet.

Comfort Zone The comfort zone describes the area determined by established habits in which a person has settled comfortably and feels at ease. Here he knows his way around and knows what is expected of him; and he also knows that he can achieve this. Learned habits and rituals contribute to this. One's comfort zone stops where the familiar area ends and overcoming or effort is required to master new challenges.

Companion Pricing With companion pricing, a product (printer, coffee machine, shaver, electric toothbrush) is offered at a relatively low price, while the necessary consumables are comparatively expensive. All in all, this results in profitable and long-lasting customer relationships for the company, because a change of supplier is associated with high switching costs for the customer.

Conversion Funnel The conversion funnel expresses the impetus through which a person can develop over various stages (conversions) from a prospective customer to a regular customer and possibly to a referrer.

Critical Success Factors Critical success factors (also strategic success factors or success determinants) are the elements of a business model (e.g., a platform concept) and/or the environment (e.g., political support) that are particularly important for the success of a business model. An analysis of critical success factors makes it possible to focus on the factors that are particularly crucial to success.

Customer Journey Map The customer journey map visualizes the process a person goes through from the first latent need to the act of purchase and the use of a product or service to a possible repurchase or feedback on corporate services. This visualization helps to identify the relevant customer needs and possible "pain points."

Customer Relationship Management (CRM) CRM refers to customer relationship management geared towards long-term value creation. This includes the conception, implementation, and controlling of all customer-oriented measures to promote the initiation and expansion of profitable customer relationships.

Data, Semi-Structured Semi-structured data have a certain basic structure.

Data, Structured Structured data have a normalized form. They can be stored directly in a row- and column-oriented database.

Data, Unstructured Unstructured data is in an unidentifiable and non-normalized data structure.

Digital Transformation Digital transformation describes a process of change—with no limit in perspective—by institutions with the aim of integrating digital technologies into their own value creation process in order to make it more efficient and/or effective. These institutions can include private households as well as companies, schools, universities, cities, communities, and entire nations. The potential opened up by digital technologies must be recognized and used in one's own area of responsibility as a manager, scientist, politician, teacher, etc. in order to optimize one's own service provision. The necessity for such optimizations often results from the changed expectations of one's own stakeholders—especially customers, but also (potential) employees and managers.

Digital Twin A digital twin is a digital representation of a tangible or intangible object. Processes can also be represented in the form of a digital twin. A digital twin consists of data and models of the represented object or process and further descriptive information. This makes the twin "computable." An object or a process does not (yet) have to exist in the analogue world in order to already create a digital twin.

Disruptive Technologies Disruptive technologies disrupt or destroy the use of previously used technologies and displace and/or replace them.

Dynamic Pricing With dynamic pricing, prices are set individually—as one-to-one pricing. The price charged in each case is based on the determined or estimated price sensitivity of the potential buyer. Different customers receive different prices for the same offer on the identical platform at the same time.

Eco System An eco system describes a complex interplay between different living beings and their environment. This results in an ecological cycle between the integrated objects. In the corporate context, the eco system describes a multitude of service fields of a company in which customers and/or suppliers are intensively integrated and which thereby achieve utilization advantages. A user does not have to leave these closed systems, which are often set up by a company, even if he wants to use completely different applications.

Empowered Team An empowered team is a relatively autonomous group of employees who work together to achieve specific goals. It has not only been given a task, but also the responsibility and competence to make independent decisions for the benefit of the company's further development.

Enabler Culture In an enabler culture, managers do not (any longer) see themselves as commanders who define goals and tasks for their employees. In this case, managers rather act as promoters of their employees and support them sustainably in the fulfilment of their tasks as well as in their own development.

FinTechs FinTechs are start-ups in the financial sector that use innovative technologies in their business models in order to develop customer benefits and/or cost advantages.

Firewall, Cognitive Cognitive firewalls are "firewalls" in the minds of the workforce that stand in the way of intensive communication and collaboration and lead to a silo mentality.

Freemium Strategy Freemium is a made-up word made up of the terms "free" for "free of charge" and "premium." With this pricing strategy, a basic service is offered free of charge. For a larger scope of services (the "premium offer"), a price has to be paid.

Frenemies Frenemies are friends and enemies alike. Such a frenemy either falsely pretends to be a friend when in fact it is an enemy. Or it is an enemy with whom you are compelled to maintain a friendly relationship because you depend on their support.

Frustration Tolerance Frustration tolerance describes the individual ability of people to deal with disappointment or frustration. People with low frustration tolerance break off very quickly when expanding their comfort zone if this is more arduous or happens less quickly than they expected or desired. People with high frustration tolerance also accept critical situations. They patiently continue on their way until they have reached their goal.

Fuckup Night Fuckup colloquially stands for "mishap" or "mistake." During a so-called fuckup night, company founders report on their failures.

GAFA Companies The term GAFA companies is used to describe the US companies *Google, Apple, Facebook,* and *Amazon*.

GAFAM Companies The term GAFAM companies is used to describe the US companies *Google, Apple, Facebook, Amazon,* and *Microsoft*.

Gap Analysis, Digital The digital gap analysis can be used to determine the threat potential in an industry. For this purpose, the potential for change due to increasing digitalization is compared with which of the available options have already been used by companies and how intensively.

GIGO Effect The GIGO effect ("garbage-in-garbage-out") describes the phenomenon that only bad insights can be gained on the basis of bad data.

Group, Strategic The strategic group is the mental grouping of those companies that use a comparable strategic concept in a particular industry.

Hackathon A hackathon is an event to develop solutions for given problems within a narrowly defined time frame.

Holacracy Holacracy is a specific form of organization. Its aim is to implement decision-making with a maximum of transparency and comprehensive participation opportunities for all employees.

Incubator An incubator is a facility that sets start-ups on the path to business creation and supports them in doing so. By creating an optimal climate for entrepreneurial growth, an incubator provides start-ups with an environment in which a business model can thrive.

Innovation An innovation describes new solutions that can relate to products, services, processes, and business models.

Innovation Engine An innovation engine represents a business unit that often develops innovative (digital) projects with a radical or/and disruptive character independently of the company's established core business. The central guiding ideas of an innovation engine are system openness, fault tolerance and the search for future strategically valuable business opportunities—independent and uninfluenced by previous activities and thus independent of the company's own performance engine.

InsurTechs InsurTechs are start-ups in the insurance industry that use innovative technologies in their business models to develop customer benefits and/or cost advantages.

Internet of Everything The Internet initially connects many things to form the Internet of Things (IOT). In addition, many processes are connected with each other, especially in the area of industry 4.0. Also, more and more data can be networked and exploited accordingly (keyword "big data"). Finally, people and other living beings can also be integrated into the network. All of this forms the Internet of Everything.

IT Hacking IT hacking is the unauthorized intrusion into a computer or a network. The persons involved in such hacking activities are called hackers. These hackers may alter system or security features to achieve a goal that deviates from the original purpose of the system.

Jobs To Be Done Concept The jobs to be done concept is about offering solutions for tasks that, from the customer's point of view, simply need to be done—without wanting or needing to put a lot of heart and soul into it. It is about completing specific tasks (a job) as simply as possible.

Killer Acquisitions In killer acquisitions, the goal is not to acquire a new technology, a product, a business idea and/or the driving force behind it. The goal is to eliminate unpopular competitors from the market before they threaten the own business.

Knowledge, Explicit Explicit knowledge can be conveyed through language. It is also called methodical knowledge or specific knowledge, mind knowledge or embrained knowledge. Words and numbers are sufficient for its transmission. Because it is formalized, explicit knowledge can be easily stored, processed in a variety of ways and passed on in a variety of media.

Knowledge, Implicit Implicit knowledge—also called tacit knowledge, experiential knowledge or embodied knowledge—arises from routines and a skill that is gained through diverse experiences. It is reflected in memories, beliefs, and values. Due to a lack of formalization, implicit knowledge cannot simply be stored, or processed in a variety of ways and passed on.

Leadership Style A leadership style encompasses all the actions and behaviors with which a superior confronts his employees and which he uses to achieve certain results.

Leadership Style, Transactional Transactional leadership focuses on the exchange process between managers and employees. Here the focus is on individual transactions. The manager defines expectations and goals, while employees receive a reward in return if they achieve them. Here, the focus is on target agreements against which the performance of employees is measured at regular intervals.

Leadership Style, Transformational The transformational leadership style focuses on transformation. Leadership focuses on the "soft" factors. This approach is based on the realization that employees can also be motivated by the prospect of self-fulfillment. The approach aims to transform employees' needs and goals so that they put their own interests behind the company's goals. Consequently, managers and employees do not confront each other as opponents, but as supporters in the pursuit of the common goal, which is derived from the overarching corporate vision.

Lead Nurturing Lead nurturing describes the nurturing of prospective buyers (leads), because not every prospect immediately becomes a buyer. In the course of this process, different impulses can take place to drive the conversion from a prospect to a buyer.

Lean Start-up Method In the lean start-up method, a business model or a product or service is developed very close to the market by continuously gathering feedback from potential customers already in the course of the development process. This results in a build-measure-learn cycle that is run through repeatedly (iteration) in order to improve innovations step by step (incremental approach).

Legacy Systems Legacy systems is a term for IT applications that have been in use in a company for many years or decades. "Legacy" also stands for inheritance and legacy.

LegalTechs LegalTechs are start-ups in the legal sector that use innovative technologies in their business models in order to develop customer benefits and/or cost advantages.

Lock-in Effect (also razor blade concept) In the case of the lock-in effect, the offering company tries to bring a customer into an (artificially created) dependency relationship. Such a dependency is achieved, for example, when the transition of a customer to another provider is uneconomical due to high switching costs.

Machine Tax The machinery tax is another tax base for social security. This is intended to compensate for the tax losses caused by a reduction in the "payroll" tax base when jobs disappear as a result of rationalization.

MarTec's Law MarTec's law describes the connection between the speed of technological change and the willingness of companies to change. Here "MarTec" stands for "marketing technology."

Matrix of Concern The matrix of concern is formed by the axes "extent of changes in mindset and behavior patterns" on the one hand and "extent of threat" on the other. This matrix enables a typology of the perceived changes. At the same time, typical behavioral patterns can be identified that are to be expected as a reaction to emerging changes. From this, the tasks for change management are derived for the managers entrusted with it.

Media Competence Media competence refers to the ability to use the various media channels and their contents competently and, above all, critically, as well as to act with and in them and also to reflect self-critically on one's own media behavior.

Minimum Viable Product A minimum viable product is a product or service that fulfils the minimum requirements to be used or deployed by customers (often on a trial basis).

MOOC A MOOC (for massive open online course) is an Internet-based course that is aimed at a broad public and for which no participation fee is payable.

Moore's Law Moore's law describes the effect of exponentiality in the IT industry. According to this "law," digital computing power doubles approximately every 2 years. This development is gradually reaching its limits.

Net Promotor Score (NPS) The net promotor score is a concept to measure the extent of customers' emotional attachment and trust in a company. For this purpose, the probability is asked with which one's own customers would recommend one's own company or its offers.

Network Effect The network effect describes the process of how the benefit for a person develops when the number of people accessing the same service changes. The benefit is therefore dependent on the total number of these people. Positive network effects occur when the benefit increases with the number of people (e.g., on social networks such as *Facebook, Instagram,* or *LinkedIn* and on platforms such as *Airbnb, Amazon, or Uber*). Negative network effects occur when the benefit decreases as the number of people increases, e.g., on motorways or when a website is accessed extensively, which leads to its crash.

Newsroom In a newsroom—analogous to the procedure in the editorial offices of newspapers and TV/radio channels—all current news about the offer, the brand and/or the company as a whole come together in a central place in order to be able to react to them quickly and consistently. In this place, the contents of the communication in the social media, from the customer service center together with the findings of the web and/or social media monitoring can be brought together and analyzed in connection with the other challenges of the market.

Open Innovation Model In addition to internally generated impulses for innovations, the open innovation model also takes up innovations from third parties and intensively integrates external development partners (customers, but also suppliers, competitors, start-ups, or universities) into innovation processes in order to expand the company's own innovation potential in this way.

Organizational Model An organizational model represents the structures of a company in an abstract way (in the sense of a company architecture). This is usually done in the form of an organizational chart.

Organizational Structure The organizational structure describes the hierarchical plan of a company and is visualized by an organizational chart.

Pain Point A pain point is an occurrence that customers typically want to avoid and/or overcome. Pain points can be rooted in the customer's everyday life. For example, it can be a specific customer problem that the customer would like to solve or avoid completely. Pain points can also occur during the customer journey and should be consistently avoided here.

Pareto Principle (Also 80:20 Rule) The pareto principle describes that many phenomena lead to concentration effects. For example, 20% of one issue (e.g., 20% of customers) leads to 80% of another issue (e.g., turnover, but also complaints).

Performance Engine The performance engine is the heart of a company. Here, products and services are to be produced—ideally with the highest possible efficiency—in a desired quality at defined costs, often in high quantities. Central guiding ideas for the performance engine are stability, predictability, routine and zero-defect tolerance.

Persona A persona is a fictitious archetype that represents a target group and gives it—literally—"a face." A persona is described like a real person. Personas have a life story, hobbies, a philosophy of life as well as a name and a photo.

PEST Analysis/PESTEL Analysis The PEST or PESTEL analysis is a tool for analyzing the macro-environment of a company. The PEST analysis looks at political factors, economic factors, social factors and technological factors. In the PESTEL analysis, ecological factors and legal factors are also examined with regard to their relevance for a company.

Platform Concept Platform concept represents an amalgamation of two-sided markets by a platform provider. On one side, there are (ideally) many suppliers, on the other side (ideally) many demanders.

Predictive Maintenance Predictive maintenance involves the proactive recognition of the need for action to maintain, repair, etc. machines and systems—even before faults occur. For this purpose, relevant data are evaluated in real time to determine the optimal time for "intervention" and to avoid breakdowns of machines and plants.

Predictive Servicing Predictive servicing is the implementation of predictive maintenance in the consumer market. Services are proactively provided for consumers. The prerequisites for this are the Internet of Things and the ability of everyday objects to receive and send information online.

Process and System Model Process and system models are used to document, analyze, and design business processes in information technology.

Process Organization The process organization describes the company's internal processes. These can relate, for example, to planning, purchasing, production, logistics, controlling or the development of innovations.

Relevant Set The relevant set comprises the offer alternatives that a customer considers to be of equal value and between which he decides in the purchase situation.

Resilience Resilience refers to people's ability to cope with stress and their inner strength. People with resilience are able to react flexibly and appropriately to changing situations in life and to different demands in changing situations. People with resilience can also cope with stressful, frustrating, difficult and stressful situations without suffering psychological consequences.

Retail Media Retail Media refers to the possibility of placing advertisements within online shops and on marketplaces.

Reverse Mentoring In reverse mentoring, the roles of classic mentoring are reversed: it is no longer an "old" or "experienced" senior who coaches a junior, but a junior who coaches a senior.

Robot Tax Robot tax is a specific form of machine tax. It is a value added tax.

Scalability Scalability describes the property of a business model to be able to significantly increase turnover without having to continuously invest to the same extent in production, marketing, sales, personnel and/or infrastructure, etc. If scalability exists, the fixed costs and also the variable costs increase much more slowly than the turnover.

Seamless Integration Seamless integration describes the simple merging of different applications from one provider, the joint use of which by the customer could previously only be achieved by overcoming interfaces of varying complexity.

Self-Efficacy Self-efficacy describes the expectation of a person to be able to successfully carry out desired actions themselves on the basis of their own abilities and competencies. People who believe that they can make a difference and achieve ambitious goals have a high self-efficacy expectation.

Serendipity Serendipity describes the possibility of arriving at new and possibly surprising discoveries, insights and/or developments through chance observations and encounters with things not originally sought. In order to achieve serendipity, the actors—based on the chance observations and encounters—derive their own conclusions or concrete measures.

Servitisation Servitisation refers to the process when manufacturing companies shift their portfolio away from physical products towards services and/or a combination of physical goods and services.

Silo Mentality Silo mentality describes the phenomenon that employees and managers deliberately withhold information in order to "secure" their own position of power.

Small Data Small data includes the data that already exists in a company due to its own business operations.

Stakeholder Onion Model The stakeholder onion model visualizes the relationships of stakeholders to a project goal. In the onion model, different layers are analyzed from the inside out, which gave the model its name. In order to achieve the highest possible transparency, further information can be added to describe the respective relationships. Here it is important that the relationship of the stakeholders to the project is not shown on the basis of power, influence, or support, but on the basis of the intensity of their respective involvement.

Stakeholders Stakeholders are not "shareholders" in the legal sense, as the literal translation of "to have a stake in something" would lead one to expect. Stakeholders designate the people who have an interest in the activities of a company. A company's key stakeholders include employees, managers, prospects and customers, suppliers and service partners, competitors, the general public, shareholders, and government and legislators.

Storytelling Storytelling means telling stories. It involves conveying explicit and implicit knowledge through narratives by means of certain motifs, symbols, metaphors, etc.

Strategic Business Model The core of a strategic business model is the holistic description of the entrepreneurial activity in aggregated form.

Strategic Window of Opportunity The strategic window of opportunity refers to a certain period of time (a window of opportunity) in which certain actions are possible (e.g., the development of a new business model). Once the window is closed, this is no longer possible.

Team Development Clock (Also Team Clock) The team development clock shows which phases each team goes through when more or less serious changes have to be processed by the team. This makes visible which tasks have to be mastered by the respective team leadership.

Technology Impact Analysis The technology impact analysis tries to determine how big the impact of different technologies will be on a company.

Time-to-Market Time-to-market is measured in days, weeks, months and/or years and characterizes the lead time between a product/service innovation and/or business model innovation and its introduction to the market.

Time-to-Value The time-to-value is measured in days, weeks, months and/or years and characterizes the lead time between a product/service and/or business model innovation and its first benefit for customers. Here, we do not wait until a perfect solution is available to introduce it to the market. A market launch takes place at the time when the first relevant benefits can be created.

Townhall Meeting In a townhall meeting, the top management of a company addresses all employees and managers in one speech. The aim is to establish a direct relationship between top management and the workforce through first-hand information.

Walled Garden The walled garden is a closed (data) platform of a company. Other companies have no or only limited access to the data available there (hence "walled"). Examples of walled gardens are *Facebook* and *Google*.

Index

A
Ability to act, 386
AboutYou, 221
Acceleration of trends, 35
Accelerators, 450–452, 533
Accompanying processes, 228
Achievement, 138
Action matrix of the change process, 518, 519
Activities of a CDO, 465
Adaptation strategy, 174
Additional benefit, 534
Address publishers, 284
Adlershof, 457
Advantage of artificial intelligence, 289
Advantages of ecosystems, 244
Advantages of established companies, 132
Advantages of platform concepts, 254
Advantages of start-ups, 131
Advertising-based model, 189
After-tax return on sales, 99
Age-appropriate living, 249
Agenda setting, 465
Age of digital by default, 42
Agile Groupies Community, 221
Agile human resources development, 371
Agile IT, 267
Agile Manifesto, 439
Agility in management, 439
Aging of society, 19
AI-driven manufacturing, 265
AI in controlling, 484
AI Journey, 301–304
Airbnb, 254
Airline-industry, 95
Alexa, 214
Algorithm, 236, 533
Alibaba, 224
Alipay, 225
Alphabet, 237

AlphaGo-computer, 144
AlphaGo Zero, 293
Alternatives for assigning responsibilities, 268
Alternus, 449
Always-on-generation, 30
Amazon, 239
   Basics, 215
   Braket, 214
   Essentials, 215
   Go, 214
   Halo, 214
   Pharmacy, 214
   Prime, 213, 239
   Robotics, 213
Amazon's 14 Leadership Principles, 140
Amazon's business development, 212
Amazon's success story, 215
Amazon Web services, 214
Ambidexterity, 156, 167, 209, 533
Ambient computing, 242
Ambiguity, 3
Analogue vision, 128
Analysis grid for digital business performance, 114
Analysis of customer experience management, 322
Analysis of digital business performance, 107, 533
Analysis of opportunities and risks, 82
Analysis of personal competences, 381–391
Analysis of the digital business performance, 109
Analysis of the effects of ecosystems, 244–251
Analytical grid for business model innovations, 199, 200
Anecdote, 67
Ant Financial Service Group, 224–227
Anticipatory maintenance, 232
Anticipatory shipping, 216, 235

APX, 452
Areas of business model innovations, 176
Artificial general intelligence, 290
Artificial intelligence, 288–90, 483, 533
Asian decade, 14
Aspects of resilience, 96
Asymmetrical power relations, 261
Attention economy, 26, 316
A2 Energy Adlershof, 452
Augmented reality, 319
Automotive industry, 249
Axel Springer, 217–220

B

Bad profit, 325, 534
Balanced scorecard, 479, 480
Banana principle, 48
Bandwidth of the depth of value added, 97
Banks, 249
Bank stress test, 90
Bar camps, 221, 427, 534
Bargaining power, 85
Bargaining power of buyers, 86
Bargaining power of suppliers, 85
Basic competencies, 386
Basic competencies and their dimensions, 387
Basic concept of a customer journey map, 340
Basic concept of the NPS, 346
Basic income, unconditional, 534
Basic logic of a company, 148
Basic requirements, 343
Basic types of digital business models, 186
BAT, 534
Batch analysis, 476
BAT companies, 534
B2B platforms, 257
Beacon technology, 327
BeautyTech, 318
Behavioral preference analysis (BPA), 381
Beiersdorf, 319
Belief in self-efficacy, 67
Be lunch or have lunch, 176
Benchmark, 30, 114
Benefit, 534
Benefit enhancer, 192
Benefit hypothesis, 191
Berlin Adlershof, 457
Berlin School of Economics and Law, 457
Big data, 41, 281, 534
Bimodal IT, 267
Bio hacking, 534

Black box artificial intelligence, 298, 299
Blind spot, 389, 390
Blue oceans, 196, 535
Blue ocean strategy, 196, 535
Blue one, 382
Blueprint for an optimal team composition, 390
Body hacking, 534
Boeing, 160, 161
Boeing 737 Max, 160
Bonprix "fashion connect" store, 223
Book publishers, 149
Brakemen, 515
Branch-method, 104
Brand language, 331
Breathing IT, 270
Building blocks, 181
Building blocks of the business model canvas, 181
Building digital resilience, 105
Build-measure-learn cycle, 201
Bulimic learning, 23
Burnout of managers and employees, 102
Burnout of the entire company, 102
Business analytics, 286, 535
Business impact analysis, 100
Business model, 121, 148, 150, 535
Business model canvas, 96, 180–185, 535
Business model innovation, 150, 535
Business model logic, 149
Business model patterns, 149
Business models of the digital age, 189

C

Calculation formula of the NPS, 346
Canvas concepts, 180
Capitalism, 17
Cascading business models, 148
Cash burner, 175
Cash burn rate (CBR), 212
Caterpillar, 319
Causes of unsuccessful market launches, 351
Challenge China, 12–16
Challenge for established companies, 152
Challenge matrix, 169
Challenge of storytelling, 65
Challenges for HR management, 367
Challenges in the change process, 510
Chance finds, 419
Chance hits, 419
Change controlling, 527
Change in values, 52

Index 547

Change management, 501, 535
Change management on the level of business models, 508
Change management on the level of organizational structures, 507
Change management on the level of processes, 507
Change management on the level of the whole business, 508
Change of perspective, 396
Characteristics and principles of design thinking, 355
Characteristics of 5G, 273
Characteristics of the best CX-oriented companies, 323
Characteristics of the business models, 178
Characterization of platform concepts, 253–254
Check 24, 255
Chief Digital Officers (CDO), 463
Chief Financial Officer (CFO), 471
Chief Human Resources Officer (CHRO), 371
Chief in charge, 444
Chief Learning Officer, 374
Chief Operating Officer/Chief Operation Officer (COO), 235, 264
Chinese master plan, 13
Circle of values, 138
Citizen developer, 279
Citizen integrator, 279
Citizen integrator tools, 279
Classic CRM, 326
Classic food retailers, 80
Classic triple bottom line, 481
Classification of people into color types, 383
Closed information loop, 317
Closed innovation model, 351, 352, 535
Closed loop analytics, 263
Closed-loop approach, 320
Closed loop of data acquisition and use, 320
Cloud computing, 165, 270, 535
Cloud solutions, 270
CO2 neutrality, 51
Coca-Cola Freestyle, 318
Cognitive computing, 483
Cognitive firewalls, 444
Cognitive insights, 484
Cohort evaluation, 475
Cohorts, 475
Collaboard, 422
Collaboration tools, 318, 319
Collaborative digital platform, 221
Color sectors, 381
Color type, 382

Colortype "blue", 383
Colortype "green", 383
Colortype "red", 383
Combinatorics, 37
Comfort zone, 391, 535
Commercial IOT-applications, 42
Common EU values, 56, 57
Common values, 56
Communication platforms, 252
Companion pricing, 194, 535
Company builders, 455
Comparison portals, 255
Compatibility of business models, 209
Competence development, 371
Competence map, 387, 440
Competence profile, 387
Competence profile of a CFO, 471
Competence profiles of employees and managers, 371
Competences, 386, 387
Competitive forces, 83
Competitive position, 84
Complexity, 2
Comprehensive Knowledge Building, 20–28
Computerization of manufacturing technologies, 229
Computer vision, 295
Concentration effects, 246
Concentration of online traffic, 246
Concentration on the core business, 174
Concepts for allocation of responsibilities, 269
Concepts for increasing benefit delivery and growth, 193–198
Configurators, 39
Conformity, 139
Connection of supply and demand, 198
Consensus, 436
Consumer IOT, 42
Containers, 278
Content payment model, 189
Content proximity to the purchase, 328
Content shock, 315
Context marketing, 329
Contractual freedom, 261
Controlling as an enabler of digital transformation, 113
Convergence of markets and offerings, 257
Conversational AI platforms, 331
Conversational microlearning, 380
Conversion funnel, 336, 535
Conversion paths, 337
Conversion rate, 307
Convidera, 448

Convincing narrative, 199
Cooperative competition, 259
Coopetition, 259
Copy, buy, kill, 176
Copycats, 174
Copy strategy, 174
Core competences, 224
Core idea of the lean start-up method, 201
Core processes, 228
Core questions of a strategic business model, 151
Core tasks of a CDO, 464
Corporate competence goals, 371
Corporate culture, 113, 122
Corporate entrepreneurship, 445–447, 449
Corporate financing, 213
Corporate language, 331
Corporate profitability in Germany, 99
Corporate resilience, 92
Corporate venturing, 445, 450, 452
Costs for the exchange of information, 316
Cost structure, 183
Courage festivals, 222
CPU accelerators, 303
Creative destruction, 5
Creative freedom, 460
Creative gap, 421
Creditworthiness checks, 476
Crime as a service, 272
CrimeTechs, 272
Crisis management, 105
Crisis stages, 472, 473
Crisis symptoms, 472, 473
Criteria of a convincing company vision, 136
Critical success factors, 80, 536
CRM database, 337
Cross-divisional cooperation, 411
Cross-hierarchical communication, 421
Cross-hierarchical cooperation, 411
Csh burner strategy, 175
Cultural acceptance factors, 210
Cultural capital, 24
Cultural change, 217, 508
Cultural change 4.0, 221
Culture, 139
Culture change progam, 221
Culture journey, 221
Culture of curiosity, 376
Culture of error, 366
Culture of experimentation, 221
Culture of learning, 366
Culture of mistakes, 222
Curiosity, 376

Customer-centric design, 354
Customer centricity, 349, 350
Customer experience, 322
Customer experience management (CXM), 311, 322–326
Customer integration, 353
Customer journey, 304, 313
Customer journey map, 306, 338, 339, 341, 536
Customer monitoring, 477
Customer-oriented approach, 79
Customer-oriented innovation management, 350
Customer-oriented test approach, 201
Customer perspective, 480
Customer relationship, 183
Customer relationship management (CRM), 326, 536
Customer segmentation, 337
Customer segments, 182
Customer structure analysis, 475
Customer touch point management, 320
Customer value models, 337
Cyberattacks, 271
Cybernetic organisms, 41
Cyborgs, 41

D

Dark side of *Amazon's* success, 215
Darwinism, 4
Dashboards, 473
Data aggregators, 284
Data-based model, 190
Data driven agriculture, 162
Data poisoning attacks, 300
Data protection specialist, 283
Data providers, 284
Data, semi-structured, 536
Data service providers, 284
Data, structured, 536
Data-sucking platforms, 11
Data, unstructured, 536
Day-one philosophy, 446
DB Start-upXpress, 452
DDOS attacks, 272
Decarbonization, 51
Decision-makers in cities and municipalities, 52
Decline in customer loyalty, 317
Deconstruction of civilization, 26
Deep fakes, 300
Deep learning, 290
Define phase, 358
De-globalization, 16, 93

Index
549

Degree of maturity, 108
Delisting, 262
Dematerialization of processes, 43
Dematerialization of products and services, 43
Dematerialization of services, 165
Democratization of sales, 197
Democratization of task processing, 279
Democratization of the means of production, 197
Demotivation seminar, 395
Deng Xiaoping, 13
Denial of service (DOS), 272
Deployment risk, 278
Depth of value added, 97
Description of a business model innovation, 206, 207
Descriptive analyses, 286
Designing customer relationships, 194
Designing the change management process, 509
Design of the customer experience, 324
Design thinking, 354, 442
Destruction of the established customer supplier relationships, 256
Determination of opportunities and risks, 82
Determining the external image, 75
Determining the self-image, 75
Detractors, 346
Develop:her, 222
Developing a (digital) vision, 128–145
Development of cyberattacks, 272
Development of digital resilience, 105
Development of the industry, 33
Diagnostic analyses, 286
Dichotomy of product and service, 187
Digital assistants, 45, 330
Digital base model, 121, 123
Digital blackmail, 271
Digital burglars, 272
Digital business performance of an organization, 107
Digital censor, 238
Digital customer journey, 306
Digital Darwinism, 4, 5
Digital development of an existing business model, 152
Digital DNA, 113, 218
Digital ecosystem, 265
Digital enterprise, 263
Digital European ecosystem, 265
Digital experts, 222
Digital extortion, 271
Digital farming, 40

Digital gap analysis, 69, 73
Digital gap analysis for the retail sector, 71
Digital Hub, 453
Digital innovation hotspots, 456
Digitalization of a company, 263–266
Digitalization of established companies, 166
Digitalization of the controlling activities, 468
Digitalization roadmap, 147
Digital learning agenda, 374
Digital natives, 20
Digital organizational development, 122
Digital overlay, 319
Digital perpetual motion machine, 240
Digital sales channels, 317
Digital training agenda, 377
Digital transformation, 7, 33, 536
Digital transformation of their own business model, 152
Digital transformation stories, 68
Digital twin, 264, 536
Digital twins of humans, 264
Digital value chain, 231, 232
Digital vision, 128
Digital voice, 332
Digitization of manufacturing, 264
Digitization of the customer journey, 304–333
Digitization of the value chain, 110
Digitizing one's own value chain, 227
Dimensions of big data, 281
Dimensions of leadership competence, 387
Dimming, 262
Direct activities, 228
Disciplinary subordination, 413
Discounters, 80
Disinvestment, 102
Disruption, 6
Disruptive, 123
Disruptive and radical innovations, 180
Disruptive business models, 74
Disruptive power, 42
Disruptive technologies, 70, 74, 536
Distributed denial of service (DDOS), 272
Distribution channels, 183
Distribution of roles, 432
Divided responsibility between the different business units, 268
Documentation of business model innovations, 205
Donation model, 190
Double economic cycle, 15
Double transformation, 5
Do ut des, 405
Downstream, 38

Drivers of user acceptance, 331
D-tasks, 159
Duality of digital challenges, 167
Dual organization, 460
Dunning–Kruger effect, 24, 25
Dynamic pricing, 324, 536
Dynamics of change, 37
Dynamics of competence development, 372

E
Earth Overshoot Day, 50
Echo chambers, 11
Ecological factors, 9
Ecological footprint, 51
E-commerce model, 190
Economic balance of power, 12
Economic benefits, 534
Economic factors, 8
Economics of digitalization, 164
Economies of scale through cooperation, 250
Economy 4.0, 35
Ecosystem, 165, 179, 236, 248, 251, 317, 536
Ecosystem of *Alphabet*, 236
Ecosystem of *Amazon*, 239
Ecosystem of *Apple*, 242, 243
Ecosystem of *Facebook*, 240, 241
Ecosystems of GAFA companies, 248
Edge computing, 263, 278
Education, 24
Education 4.0, 426
Educational platforms, 252
Effects of exponential growth, 35
Efficiency and effectiveness spiral, 236
Eight dimensions of the analysis of digital business performance, 110
80:20 rule, 198, 541
Eisenhower matrix, 158, 160
Eisenhower principle, 158
Eisenhower prioritization, 159
Elimination of unloved competitors, 176
Elon Musk's DNA for innovation management, 363–365
Elo rating, 294
Embodied knowledge, 65
Embrained knowledge, 539
Emerging Technology Roadmap 2020 to 2022, 278
Emerging Technology Roadmap for large companies, 279
Emerging Technology Roadmap for mid-sized companies, 278
Emotional leader, 523

Empathize phase, 357
Empathy, 342, 357
Empathy map, 342, 343
Employability, 374
Employee engagement, 398, 399
Employee engagement in Germany, 400
Employee Engagement Inventory, 400
Employee perspective, 480
Empowered team, 537
Empowering staff, 403
Enabler, 432
Enabler culture, 432–433, 537
Engaged employees, 397
Enterprise value, 278
Entertainment providers, 188
Enthusiasm requirements, 344
Entrepreneurial playing field, 117
Entrepreneurial spirit, 447, 456
Entrepreneurial view, 155
Entrepreneurial vision, 132
Entrepreneurship, 446
Equity capital, 450
Escape room provider, 430
Escape rooms, 430
ESG criteria, 52, 480
Establishment of network structures, 411–415
Ethical marketing, 19
European champions, 13
Evaluation matrix for business model innovations, 205, 207
Evaluation of existing platform concepts, 258
Evaluation of platforms, 260
Everyday heroes, 222
Expectations of AI, 302
Experience is the new product, 322
Experiential knowledge, 65, 539
Expert systems, 296
Explainable artificial intelligence (XAI), 298, 300
Explicit knowledge, 64
Exploitation digital potential through marketing and sales, 112
Extent of information overload, 316
External cycle, 16
External innovation center, 448
External innovation lab, 448
External networks, 414
Extrinsic motivation, 405

F
Facebook study, 241
Facial recognition, 291

Failure culture, 359
Fake-news propagators, 11
Fake-news worlds, 11
Fault-tolerant corporate culture, 429
Fear zone, 392
Fictitious press-release, 142
Field of tension, 6
Fields of action for building digital excellence, 121–485
Fields of action for business field innovations, 177
Fields of application for artificial intelligence, 294–297
Filling level report, 473
Filter bubbles, 11
Financial perspective, 480
FinTechs, 73, 226, 537
Firewall, cognitive, 537
First-copy-cost effect, 164
First industrial revolution, 33
First moment of truth (FMOT), 313
First Mover, 454
First party data, 283–285
5-forces analysis, 83, 84, 533
5G, 273
5G Business Readiness Report, 275
5G-enabled industries, 275
5G readiness, 275
Five *vs.* of big data, 283
Five-step concept of strategy development, 146
Flexible learning, 379
Flexicurity, 510
Florian's Principle, 54
Flow of change processes, 525–530
Flynn effect, 26
Flywheel of human resources, 369
Focal points for ecosystems, 249
FOMO effect, 28
Forming phase, 522
Forms of cyberattacks, 271
Fortune 500, 6
Founding myth, 63
14th Five-Year Plan of the Chinese communist party, 15
Fourth industrial revolution, 34
Framework for action, 341
Freemium strategy, 193, 537
Frenemies, 247, 537
Friction factor, 309
Friede Springer, 220
From product to service, 186
From service to service, 186
Frustration tolerance, 393, 537

Fuckup night, 429, 537
Fuck Up Nights, 222
Fuji, 224
Functional benefit, 534
Functions of video conferencing systems, 418
Future distribution of work and income, 31–33
Future trends towards lifelong learning, 379
Future viability of a business model, 199

G

GAFA companies, 537
GAFA/GAFAM, 175, 537
GAFAM companies, 248, 537
GAIA-X, 285
Gallup, 398
Gamification, 426
Gap analysis, digital, 537
Garbage-in-garbage-out, 538
Gartner, 278, 301
Gartner Magic Quadrant, 74
Gatebouncers, 248
Gatekeepers, 248
Gedgehog concept, 134
General Data Protection Regulation (GDPR), 57
Generali, 40
Generation Greta, 54
Generation Y, 53
Generics suppliers, 80
Geo-fencing, 327
German Accelerator, 453
GIGO effect, 282, 538
Global financial crisis, 90
Globalization, 16, 93
Global sourcing, 97
Glocalization, 17
Goal of profit-making, 99
Goals of the European Union, 56
Go-for-it card, 449
Google Ads, 237
Google Alert, 477
Google prison, 262
Google's 9 Principles of Innovation, 143
Gratitude journal, 395
Great Place to Work concept, 402
Greenhouse Innovation Lab, 454
Green one, 381
Greenwashing, 52
Grey box "artificial intelligence," 298, 299
Groups of business models, 149
Group, strategic, 538
Growing pains, 392

Growth hypothesis, 192, 359
Growth zone, 393
Guidelines for anchoring values in vision work, 140–145
Guidelines for leadership at a distance, 409
Guiding ideas for innovation, 144
Guiding ideas of design thinking, 360
Guiding principle of change management, 499–501

H
Hackathon, 428, 538
Hackers, 538
Halo app, 214
Hardware premium, 179
Headline-hunters, 25
Health managers, 188
Hedgehog, 136
Hedgehog concept, 135, 136
Hedonism, 138
Helicopter boss, 409
HIPPO syndrome, 61
Hitfox, 455
Holacracy, 433–436, 538
Holacracy constitution, 434
Holistic data view, 326
Home office, 410
Home office infrastructure, 273
Horizontal diversification, 175
Horizon 1 business models, 154
Horizon 2 business models, 154
Horizon 3 business models, 155
Hour of truth, 287
House of digital transformation, 527, 528
House of Freedom, 220
HR innovation lab, 449
Huabei, 225
Hubraum, 454
Humanoid robots, 297
Human resource development, 426
Human resource development and planning, 371
Human resources, 366–370
Human resources strategies for the digital age, 112, 365–438
Humboldt University Berlin, 457
Humility slide, 316
Hybrid business models, 155
Hybrid strategy, 171
Hype Cycle for Artificial Intelligence, 301

I
Iceberg model, 518
Ideate phase, 358
Identification function of a vision, 125
Identification of relevant competitors, 79
Identity abuse, 271
Identity function of a vision, 125
Identity theft, 271
"I-don't-pay" mentality, 165
Illustration of information overload, 316
Image processing, 295
Image recognition, 295
Implications of combinatorics, 43
Implicit knowledge, 65
Importance of services, 186
Important partners, 181
Impulse generator, 463
Inconsistency of human behavior, 53
Incremental approach, 204, 441
Incremental improvements, 154
Incremental innovations, 180
Incubators, 450, 451, 453, 454, 538
Indicator of personal resilience, 387
Indifferents, 346
Indirect activities, 228
Individual comfort zone, 392
Individualization of service provision, 317–322
Individualization potential, 319
Individual qualification measures, 372
Industrial IOT (IIOT), 43
Industry 1.0, 34
Industry 4.0, 33–35, 230
Industry logic, 149, 150
Industry platforms, 252
Industry structure analysis, 83, 533
Inertia, 510
Infinite customer journey, 306, 307
Inflation of expectations, 28
Informal events, 426
Informal hierarchies, 437
Informational integration of suppliers and customers, 230
Information-based competitive advantage, 254
Information monopoly, 247
Information overload, 66, 315
Information silos, 268
Information tsunami, 315
Infrastructure IOT, 43
Inner resilience, 395
Inner strength, 91
Innovation, 538

centers, 413, 448, 460
engine, 459–461, 538
hub, 265
managers, 447
of the offers, 176
platforms, 252
teams, 447
trigger, 302
Innowerft, 455
Inside-out process, 351
Insight engines, 303
Inspection, 286
Instant society, 30, 45, 118
In-store navigation, 327
Instruments for exploiting digitalization potentials, 333–349
Instruments to manage change processes, 513–525
Insular talent, 290
Insurance industry, 248
InsurTechs, 73, 538
Integration of business model innovations, 209
Intelligence of a community, 432
Intensity of use of platforms, 260
Interest groups, 502
Interim checks, 481
Internal communication, 112
Internal cycle, 15
Internal innovation lab, 448
Internal resistance, 508
International benchmarks, 348
Internet of everything (IOE), 37, 538
Internet of everything in real time, 273
Internet of Military Things (IOMT), 43
Internet of Things (IOT), 42
Interplay of online configurations, 317
Intrapreneurship, 446
Intrinsic reward, 376
IQ development of humankind, 26
Iterations, 357
Iterative loops, 356
Iterative procedure, 204, 441
IT hacking, 538
IT infrastructure, 266–304
IT infrastructure, technologies and data basis, 111

J
Jeff Bezos, 215
Jobs to be done concept, 195, 538
Johari window, 389
John Deere, 162

Joint responsibility right at the top, 268
JOMO effect, 28
"Just-do-it" personality, 105

K
Kairos, 419
Kano concept, 343–345
Kano model of customer satisfaction, 344
Karlsruhe Institute of Technology, 456
Key activities, 182
Key dimensions of competence, 386
Key performance indicators for the digital transformation, 479
Key questions during business model development, 151
Key resources, 182
Killer acquisitions, 176, 538
Kindle E-reader, 213
Kiva, 213
Knowledge, explicit, 539
Knowledge, implicit, 539
Knowledge society, 21
KODE *concept,* 385–390
Körber, 264–266
Körber Lab, 265

L
Labelling, 291
Lack of efficient follow-up, 415
Latency times, 273
Law of disproportionate information, 58
Leadership at a distance, 409–411
Leadership by physical presence and supervision, 410
Leadership by results, 410
Leadership competencies, 386
Leadership culture, 403
Leadership principles, 140
Leadership style, 404, 539
Leadership style, transactional, 539
Lead generation, 336
Lead nurturing, 337, 539
Lead scoring, 337
Lead segmentation, 337
Lean start-up, 442
Lean start-up method, 201, 539
Lean start-up model, 202
Leapfrog digitization, 91
Learning advisors, 372
Learning by reward, 293
Learning coaches, 372

Learning culture, 359
Learning in networks, 379
Learning methods of artificial intelligence, 290
Learning relationship, 193
Learning zone, 393
Legacy systems, 70, 266, 539
Legal factors, 9
LegalTechs, 73, 539
Lego Serious Play, 361
Leipzig's HHL, 457
Levels of leadership, 407
Levels of maturity, 108
Lifelong learning, 373, 374
Linguistic intelligence, 294
Linguistic positioning, 332
Litmus test, 512
Location-based services, 327
Lock-in concepts, 193
Lock-in effects, 194, 253, 540
Longevity of *S&P-500*-companies, 5
Long tail concept, 196
L'Oreal, 318
L'Oréal Perso, 318
Low-code tools, 279
Low-cost carriers, 80
Lteral diversification, 175

M
Machine learning, 290
Machine tax, 32, 540
Machine vision, 295
Macro-environment, 9
Macro-initiatives, 110
Macro strategy, 160–162
Macro stress tests, 90
Made in China 2025, 13, 14
Magnitude of cybercrime, 272
Malicious functions, 271
Malicious programs, 271
Malware, 271
Management by exception, 404
Management by objectives, 404
Managerial view, 154
Marketing and sales workflows, 336
Marketing automation, 338
Marketing automation software, 336
Marketing flywheel, 310–311
Marketing management dashboard, 473
Marketing platforms, 255
Market innovations, 176
Market-oriented process model, 201
Market-oriented testing, 359

Marketplace-like concept, 253
MarTec's law, 71, 540
Mass customization, 318
Massive open online course (MOOC), 429, 540
Mathias Döpfner, 218
Matrix of concern, 515, 517, 540
Matrix of strategic thrusts, 156
Matrix to segment employees within change processes, 514
Mature business models, 154
Maturity levels, 110
Mechanisms of the long tail concept, 197
Media city, 457
Media competence, 540
Meeting efficiency, 415
Meeting platform, 415
"Me, everything, immediately and everywhere," 29
Membership model, 189
Mental agility, 402
Mental flexibility, 388
Merck Accelerator, 453
Meta-analysis of one's own business model, 173
Meta-level, 66
Methodical knowledge, 539
Methods for developing business model innovations, 172–189
Methods for evaluating business models, 191–208
Methods of agile project management, 440
Metro Accelerator, 453
Micro initiatives, 110, 160–162
Microloans, 225
Micro-management, 406
Microsoft Teams, 417
Micro stress tests, 90
Middle management, 62
Mindful@OTTO, 222
Mind knowledge, 539
Mindset of agile management, 440, 441
Minimum viable product (MVP), 202, 203, 540
Miro, 422
Misjudging the impact of new technologies, 3
Mission control rooms, 443
Mobile controlling solution, 472
Mobile edge cloud solutions, 274
Mobile first, 331
Mobile robots, 297
Mobility ecosystem, 249
Mobility service provider, 129, 187
Mobilization function of a vision, 125
Model of the world, 296

Model of values, 138
Modiface, 318
Modified (economic) triple bottom line, 481
Moment of truth, 313
Monetization models, 179
Monitoring, 476
Monitoring in production, 478
Monitoring radar, 257
Monitoring technologies, 279
Moore's Law, 35, 540
Motivation triangle, 518, 519
Moving, 509
Muddling through, 174
Muddling through technique, 105
Multidimensional control system, 470
Multi-line system, 413
Multiple sourcing, 97
Multiple subordination, 413
Music industry, 150
Mystery room, 430

N
Narrative, 63, 64
Natural image processing, 295
Natural language processing (NLP), 294
Needs pyramid, 399
Negative Flynn effect, 26
Negative network effects, 253, 540
Net promoter score (NPS), 346, 348, 540
Network effect, 540
Network organization, 413
Network triggers, 421
Neural networks, 289
New growth strategies, 174
New normal, 94
Newsrooms, 443, 444, 540
Next Big Thing, 455
Nike, 319
Nimby principle, 54
No-code tools, 279
Noline, 305
NOMS method, 61
Non-normalized data, 282
Normalized data structure, 282
Norming phase, 523
Norm strategies for the integration of business model innovations in established companies, 210
Noticing, 420
Not-to-do list, 101, 102, 220

O
Obstacles of successful change management, 511
Obstacles to the introduction of 5G technologies, 275
OB-tasks, 159
One-man show, 405
One-minute meditation, 395
One-to-one pricing, 325
One voice policy, 444
Online configurator, 317
Online editor, 319
On-premise solutions, 270, 535
Open innovation model, 351, 352, 541
Open-space offices, 444
Operational blindness, 446
Operational structure, 122, 438
Opportunistic behavior, 174
Optimization of established business processes, 268
Options for integrating new business models, 211
Options to develop a digital business performance for digital excellence, 116–118
Organizational concepts for the digital age, 113
Organizational dilemma, 160, 460
Organizational inertia, 446
Organizational integration, 211
Organizational models, 148
Organizational structure, 122, 439, 541
Org development, 439
Otto Group, 221–224
Otto Group Agile Center, 222
Outside-in process, 352
Overall equipment efficiency (OEE), 264
Overarching network structure, 412
Own competences, 215

P
Pain point, 338, 339, 541
Pain point analysis, 339
Paradigm shift in human resource management, 398
Paradigms of the pre-VUCA world, 3
Paradigms of the VUCA world, 3
Pareto principle, 198, 541
Par ordre de Mufti, 432
Participative learning, 379
Participatory Conference, 534

Pattern recognition, 290
Patterns of behavior within a change process, 525
Pay-per-lux, 187
Pay-per-month, 187
Pay-per-part, 187
Pay-per-use, 187
Paywalls, 189
Peak of inflated expectations, 302
Pecking order, 437, 522
People with high frustration tolerance, 393
People with low frustration tolerance, 393
Performance engine, 459, 541
Performance insight app, 263
Performance requirements, 343
Performing phase, 524
Peripheral competence, 213
Perpetual motion machine, 368
Persona, 334, 541
Persona concept, 333–336
Personal competences, 381
Personal development, 393
Personal persuasion, 65
Personal qualification passport, 378
Personnel development officers, 372
PEST analysis, 8, 541
PESTEL analysis, 8, 541
Phase 1: building, 202
Phase 2: measuring, 203
Phase 3: learning, 204
Phases of convergence, 356
Phases of divergence, 356
Phases of the build-measure-learn cycle, 201
Phishing, 271
Phishing e-mails, 271
Physical value chain, 232
PillPack, 213
Pitch, 451
Pitfalls of a successful (digital) transformation, 163
Pizza rule, 414
Plateau of productivity, 303
Platform canvas, 185–186
Platform concepts, 185, 195, 251–263, 541
Platform economy, 257, 258
Platform models, 253, 317
Platforms, 165, 179, 251
Platforms for accommodation, 252
Platforms for energy, telephone, and insurance contracts, 252
Platforms for mobility, 252
Platforms for shopping, 252
Plug-and-Play Accelerator, 452

Political factors, 8
Portal provider, 243
Porter's 5-forces analysis, 83
Positioning and sources of ZMOT, 313
Positive network effects, 253, 540
Power, 138
Power-by-the-hour, 187
Power struggle, 259
Pre-Corona-normality, 94
Prediction, 287, 478
Predictive analyses, 287
Predictive analytics, 478
Predictive maintenance, 232, 263, 541
Predictive maintenance model, 233
Predictive servicing, 234, 235, 542
Pre-launch, 47
Premium carriers, 80
Preparedness, 420
Prerequisites for a successful digital transformation, 366
Prescriptions, 287, 479
Prescriptive analyses, 287
Price differentiation, 324
Price elasticity of demand, 324
Price transparency, 164, 165
Principle of solidarity, 40
Principles of project management, 439
Principles of the *Agile Manifesto,* 439
Print DNA, 218
Priorities for qualification, 377
Private person, 389
Privatization of law, 261
Process and system models, 148, 542
Process for developing business model innovations, 172
Process for integrating new business models, 208–212
Process innovations, 176
Process of design thinking, 355
Process of developing and integrating new business 208models
Process of muddling through, 104
Process of reinforcement learning, 293
Process of supervised learning, 291
Process of unsupervised learning, 292
Process organization, 542
Process perspective, 480
Proclaimers, 103
Pro-domo, 282
Pro-domo sources, 282
Product-accompanying services, 178
Product-centric design, 354
Product configurator, 320

Production dashboard, 478
Product-oriented business model, 178
Product pioneers, 222
Professional challenge, 135
Profit-oriented corporate management, 99
Project-accompanying evaluations, 470
Project A Ventures, 455
Project-related reporting lines, 413
Promoters, 346, 515
Prosociality, 139
Prototype phase, 359
Proximity, 329
Pseudo-empiricism, 61
Public person, 389
Publishing industry, 150
Purpose, 125
Push notifications, 328

Q

Qualification campaign, 366–377
Qualification passport, 378
Qualification profile of a CDO, 464
Qualification profiles, 381
Quality assurance, 228
Quantified self, 40
Quantum computing service, 214
Questionnaire to determine values, 138

R

Ransomware, 271
Rapid prototyping, 203, 359
Rating platforms, 252
Razor blade concept, 194, 540
R&D activities, 476
R&D audit, 476
Real estate sector, 249
Real time analyses, 476
Real time analytics, 476
Real time context marketing, 329
Real time human-to-machine communication, 274
Real time machine-to-machine communication, 274
Real time (informational) marketing, 329
Recipient orientation, 385
Redistribution of power, 5
Red oceans, 196, 535
Red one, 381
Reframing, 396
Refreezing, 510
Reifenhäuser, 94
Reinforcement learning, 293
Rejection reactions, 211, 508

Relevance of information, 327
Relevant market, 79
Relevant set, 79, 542
Relocation of production facilities, 16
Reporting, 286, 472
Requirements for a vision in the digital age, 124–128
Requirements for human resource management, 370
Researching pharmaceutical companies, 80
Re-settlement of economically, politically and/or socially relevant industries, 17
Reshoring, 276
Resilience, 91, 105, 394, 542
 analysis, 90–107
 analysis of the business model, 94
 of business model, 91, 199
 coaches, 395
 of companies, 91
 training, 395
Resisters, 515
Responses to the advance of platform concepts, 258–263
Responsibility focus of a two-speed IT, 268
Responsibility for digital platforms, 260
Responsibility for further qualification, 374
Retail media, 216, 240, 328, 542
Rethinking of the innovation process, 48
Revenue mechanics, 152
Revenue streams, 183
Reverse mentoring, 427, 542
Reverse product development, 143
Rheingau Founders, 455
Rivalry of the companies, 83
Road map, 465, 466
Robo-advisors, 296
Robotic process automation, 483
Robots, 297
Robot tax, 32, 542
Rocket Internet, 455, 456
Role flexibility of managers, 413
Root-method, 104
Rotational speed factor, 309
Rounding of an existing strategy, 175
Rule-based systems, 289
Rules of the game of the platform operators, 262
Rumor mill, 408
Rumors, 408
RWTH Aachen, 456

S

Sandwich position, 260, 414
SB-tasks, 159

Scalability, 194, 254, 255, 257, 542
Scalability of the business model, 194
Sceptics, 515
Schwartz's value circle, 137, 139
Scoring concepts, 337
Scrum, 442
Seamless integration, 236, 242, 542
Secondary organization, 413
Second half of the digital chessboard, 36
Second industrial revolution, 34
Second moment of truth (SMOT), 313
Second party data, 284, 285
Sector logics, 150
Security, 139
Selective perception, 315
Self-check on how to deal with dead horses, 500
Self-determination, 138
Self-determined learning, 378
Self-driving cars, 274
Self-effective action, 378
Self-efficacy, 64, 378, 542
Self-efficacy expectation, 64
Self-learning organization, 438
Self-overestimation, 25
Self-sufficiency, 17
Semi-structured data, 282
Sensor economy, 43
Separation of the different business models, 211
Sequences of a classic change management process, 526
Serendipity, 419, 420, 542
Service fees, 179
Service-oriented business model, 178
Service provider for competence development, 372
Service robots, 297
Service transformation, 177
Servitization, 186–189, 542
Set of hypotheses, 358
Share Now, 130
Share of lifestyle for customers, 329
Shares of online traffic, 245
Sherpany, 415
Shift of industry boundaries, 244
Shift to the service sector, 19
Shutdown, 102
Siemens electronics plant, 263–264
Silent geniuses, 386
Silk road project, 15
Silo mentality, 543
Silo solution, 268
Single point of truth, 283
Single source of truth, 283

Singleton app, 394
Situational leadership, 406
Situational leadership style, 406
Size factor, 309
SkinCeuticals, 318
Slack, 416
Slack Enterprise Grid, 417
Slope of enlightenment, 302
Slowbalisation, 17
Small data, 283, 543
Smart factory, 230, 265, 478
Smart farming, 40
Smart fitting rooms, 319
Smart grids, 39
Smart homes, 39, 249
Smart service terminals, 43
Smart user interfaces, 45
Social benefit, 534
Social factors, 8
Social innovations, 176
Social media burn-out, 315
Social media buzz, 443
Social media listening centers, 443
Social media monitoring, 477
Social media war rooms, 443
Social platforms, 252
Social shopping, 319
Softwarization, 274
Solution with a steering committee, 269
Sound branding, 332
Source of competitive advantage, 42
S&P 500, 6
S&P-500-companies, 5
Spatial proximity to the purchase, 327
Specialist idiot, 290
Specific knowledge, 539
Specific values, 138
Speech processing, 294
Speech-to-speech (STS), 295
Speech-to-text (STT), 295
Speed of 5G, 273
Spread of fake-news, 11
Spreadshirt, 318
Stages of the design thinking process, 355
Stakeholder analysis, 506
Stakeholder of a change process, 502–504
Stakeholder onion model, 504–507, 543
Stakeholders, 502, 543
Stakeholders in a change process, 502
Standards for business models, 262
Startplatz, 453
Start-up center, 454
Start-up DNA, 446

Index

Start-up Incubator Berlin, 457
Start-up mindset, 447
Start-up strongholds, 456
Static CRM systems, 328
Status of AI use in Germany, 297–298
Status quo analysis on innovation management, 350
Stavanger Declaration, 24
Step-by-step integration, 211
Steps of predictive maintenance, 232
Steps towards corporate entrepreneurship, 447
Stimulation, 138
Stock market value, 157
Storming phase, 522
Story about exponentiality, 36
Storytelling, 63, 64, 543
Strategic business model, 148, 543
Strategic clay layer, 62
Strategic entrepreneurship, 445
Strategic game board, 116
Strategic group, 79, 80
Strategic paralysis layer, 62
Strategic qualification gap, 372
Strategic window of opportunity, 543
Strategy and business model matrix, 173, 174
Strategy of muddling through, 104
Stream of personal data, 41
Strength of capitalism, 17
Strength of the market economy, 17
Strengths and weaknesses analysis, 80
Stress tests, 90
Structural agility, 402
Structured data, 282
Subscription model, 179, 187, 189
Substitute products, 86
Success factors of design thinking, 360
Success factors of the digital transformation, 366
Success strategies for innovation management, 363
Superordinate values, 138
Supervised learning, 290
Supplier-oriented approach, 79
Supply-demand fit, 201
Sustainability, 481
Sustainability of the business model, 110
Swarm intelligence, 428
Swiss Smart Factory, 457
Switching costs, 193, 194
Switzerland Innovation, 457
SWOT analysis, 77, 78
Synthesis of external and internal perspectives, 78
Synthesis of internal and external perspectives, 88
System of value chains, 229
System solution-oriented business model, 178

T

Tacit knowledge, 539
Tasks of voice marketing, 331
Taxi companies, 150
Taxi industry, 151
Team analytics concept, 390
Team clock, 521, 543
Team development clock, 521, 543
Team Europe Ventures, 455
Team hierarchy, 522
Team of experts, 385
Team of integrators, 385
Team of playmakers, 385
Team values map, 390
Technological factors, 8
Technology impact analysis, 76, 543
Technology trend scout, 465
TechUcation, 223
Template for a persona development, 334
Temporal proximity to the purchase, 328
TensorFlow, 293
10 x 10 x 10 rule, 67
Tenth meta-analysis of employee engagement, 401
Terra incognita, 390
Terror of diversity, 316
Terror of options, 316
Test phase, 359
Text comprehensibility, 331
Text-to-speech (TTS), 295
Text-to-Text (TTT), 295
Theft of digital identities (ID theft), 271
Think Big, 129
Thinking and acting in network structures, 412
Third industrial revolution, 34
Third party data, 284, 285
Thomas Cook Group, 165
Threat from new entrants, 85
3D classrooms, 423
Three-dimensional CRM, 326, 328
3D learning and working worlds, 423
3D planning tool, 319
3D worlds, 423
360° customer profiles, 330
360° view on the markets, 443–444
3 Horizons model, 153–158, 533
3 Horizons model for strategic analysis, 154

3-1-0, 225
Time for curiosity, 376
Time-to-market, 45, 46, 543
Time-to-value, 46–48, 201, 543
TINA principle, 18, 261
Too big to care, 248
Too big to fail, 90
Tool for self-analysis and team analysis, 385
Tools for successful change management, 513
Tools for video conferencing, 417–419
Too small to succeed, 6
Top management, 62
Townhall meetings, 65, 543
Trade-offs, 101
Tradition, 139
Traditional IT, 267
Training and development culture, 378
Training data, 291
Training dataset, 290
Training portfolio, 377
Transactional leadership, 404, 539
Transactional leadership style, 404
Transactional platforms, 256
Transaction-based model, 190
Transaction platforms, 252
Transfer task, 132
Transformational leadership, 404, 405
Transformation of the controlling self-image, 468
Transformation process, 221
Transforming the controlling self-image, 469
Transparency of algorithms, 300
Transparency of data, 299
Transparency of offers, 164
Transparency of the delivery of data, 300
Trend scouts, 170
Triad of living, working, and shopping, 52
TriCAT, 423
Trickle-up effect, 150
Trigger chains, 337
Triple bottom line, 480
Triple bottom line approach, 481
Trough of disillusionment, 302
Trusple, 226
Trust, 244
T-shape personalities, 355
T-tasks, 158
TU Munich, 456
2-1-2, 225
Two-sided markets, 253
Two-speed IT, 266, 267
Types of business model innovations, 176, 180
Types of business models, 148

Types of change processes, 507
Types of innovation, 155
Types of platform concepts, 251–253
Typology of the perceived changes, 515

U
Uber, 254
Unbundling of offers, 165
Uncertainty, 2
Unconditional basic income, 31
Unfreezing, 509
Unicorn, 117
Universalism, 139
Unknown unknowns, 390
Unstructured data, 282
Unsupervised learning, 292
Unternehmens-TUM, 456
Upstream, 38
Urban water supply systems, 39
Use of sensors, 43
User identification, 245

V
Value, 283
  added business model, 178
  adding cooperation with competitors, 259
  chain, 151, 227
  chain analysis, 227, 230–232
  circle, 137, 140
  creating triad, 312
  network, 138, 229
  proposition, 151, 182, 191, 192
  proposition of CX, 323
  structure of your company, 139
van Laack, 95
Variety, 282
Variety seekers, 317
Velocity, 282
Venture capital, 450
Venture capital funds, 450
Venturing, 450
Veracity, 282
Verivox, 255
Vertical integration, 97
Vertical range of manufacture, 97
Vesta, 214
Vigilance, 105
Virtual computing cloud, 270
Virtual conferences, 417
Virtual group rooms, 424
Virtual tea-kitchen conversations, 421

Virtual teams, 412
Visionary view, 155
Vision, goals and strategies for the digital age, 110
Vision of an industry 4.0, 265
Vision work, 136
Visual map, 181
Vitality programs, 40
VoC integration, 323
Voice commerce, 332
Voice distribution, 332
Voice first, 330
Voice integration, 332
Voice marketing, 332
Voice marketing tasks, 331
Voice of the customer (VoC), 323
Voice only, 330
Voice search, 332
Voice search engine optimization, 333
Voice SEO, 333
Volatility, 1
Volume, 281
Vrtical diversification, 175
VUCA world, 1, 2

W
Walk the talk, 414
Walled garden, 247, 544
Waterfall concept, 441
Ways to develop a (digital) vision, 128–129
Wearable technologies, 41
WeChat, 305
We-qualities, 379
Whole Foods, 213
Wimbu, 174
The-winner-takes-it-all, 248
The-winner-takes-it-all situations, 253
Workforce platforms, 252
Workhacks, 221
Working backwards, 143
Working backwards from the customer, 142
Working world 4.0, 371
Workplace analytics, 279
Workplace culture, 402
World Trade Organization (WTO), 56

X
Xianghu Bao, 225

Y
Yue Bao, 225

Z
Zalando, 174, 255
Zender, 95
Zeppelin, 319
Zero marginal costs, 164
Zero measurement, 347
Zero moment of truth (ZMOT), 314
Zero-sum game, 387
Zombie business units, 499
Zombie company, 499
Zombie projects, 499
Zombification of the economy, 499
Zoom, 194